TECHNOLOGY, THE GLOBAL ECONOMY
AND OTHER NEW CHALLENGES FOR CIVIL JUSTICE

TECHNOLOGY, THE GLOBAL ECONOMY AND OTHER NEW CHALLENGES FOR CIVIL JUSTICE

Edited by
Koichi Miki

Cambridge – Antwerp – Chicago

Intersentia Ltd
8 Wellington Mews
Wellington Street | Cambridge
CB1 1HW | United Kingdom
Tel: +44 1223 736 170
Email: mail@intersentia.co.uk
www.intersentia.com | www.intersentia.co.uk

Distribution for the UK and
Rest of the World (incl. Eastern Europe)
NBN International
1 Deltic Avenue, Rooksley
Milton Keynes MK13 8LD
United Kingdom
Tel: +44 1752 202 301 | Fax: +44 1752 202 331
Email: orders@nbninternational.com

Distribution for Europe
Lefebvre Sarrut Belgium NV
Hoogstraat 139/6
1000 Brussels
Belgium
Tel: +32 (0)800 39 067
Email: mail@intersentia.be

Distribution for the USA and Canada
Independent Publishers Group
Order Department
814 North Franklin Street
Chicago, IL 60610
USA
Tel: +1 800 888 4741 (toll free) | Fax: +1 312 337 5985
Email: orders@ipgbook.com

Technology, the Global Economy and Other New Challenges for Civil Justice
© The editor and contributors severally 2021

The editor and contributors have asserted the right under the Copyright, Designs and Patents
Act 1988, to be identified as authors of this work.

No part of this book may be reproduced, stored in a retrieval system, or transmitted, in any form, or
by any means, without prior written permission from Intersentia, or as expressly permitted by law or
under the terms agreed with the appropriate reprographic rights organisation. Enquiries concerning
reproduction which may not be covered by the above should be addressed to Intersentia at the
address above.

Artwork on cover: Olesya Karakotsya / 123RF

ISBN 978-1-78068-971-5
D/2021/7849/118
NUR 820

British Library Cataloguing in Publication Data. A catalogue record for this book is available from
the British Library.

PREFACE

In recent decades, the world has been rocked by the huge storms of dramatic social and economic change. Amongst these seismic shifts, of particular note has been the continuous expansion of globalization over the course of the last century and the advancement in computer-related technologies, which is progressing at a parabolic rate. The direct impact of such storms is inevitable even in the realm of civil justice. The judiciaries of the world today are equally faced with the challenges presented by globalization, technology, and other factors that transcend the differences between those legal systems. In the face of these, we have been sought for wisdom and ingenuity to cope with a variety of problems.

In response to such problems, the 16th World Congress of the International Association of Procedural Law, held from November 2nd to 5th, 2019 in Kobe, Japan, took "Challenges for Civil Justice as We Move Beyond Globalization and Technological Change" as its overall topic. This volume presents the papers presented at the Congress. The structure of this book is divided into two parts. Part 1 contains three keynote speeches and Part 2 contains a total of 13 General Reports, respectively, grouped as per the 6 session topics to which they correspond. In order to prepare these contributions for publication, each paper has been updated and rearranged from the original.

I would like to thank all the community members of the International Association of Procedural Law. I would also like to thank the members of the Organizing Committee of the IAPL 16th World Congress. I am particularly thankful to Professor Shusuke Kakiuchi for his devoted assistance in assisting me in editing this book.

Professor Koichi Miki
President, Japan Association of the Law of Civil Procedure
President, Organizing Committee of the IAPL 16th World Congress
Vice President, International Association of Procedural Law
July 2021

CONTENTS

Preface v

List of Contributors xiii

PART I. OVERVIEW OF THE FUTURE OF CIVIL JUSTICE AND THE
NEW CHALLENGES FACING IT

**Modern Computer-Related Technology and Judicial Procedure:
Welcome Friend or Uninvited Troublemaker?**

     Koichi MIKI 3

1. Introduction 4
2. Electronic Filing 4
3. Electronic Service 6
4. Videoconferencing for Examination 8
5. Problems with Electronic Evidence 9
6. Information on the Internet 12
7. Machine Expert Opinions 13
8. Records of Trials 15
9. Conclusion.. 16

On the Future of Civil Procedure: Should One Adapt or Resist?

     Frédérique FERRAND 17

1. Introduction 17
2. The Injunction: To Adapt and Transform 18
3. The Directions Taken or to be Taken: The Course of Reforms........ 22
4. The Alternative: Adapt or Resist? 42

Technology, the Global Economy and New Concepts in Civil Procedure

     Margaret WOO.. 45

1. From Consent to Click.. 46
2. From Service of Process to Electronic Notice..................... 50
3. From Physical Presence to Virtual Presence...................... 52

Intersentia   vii

PART II. NEW CHALLENGES AND THEIR VARIOUS ASPECTS: MULTINATIONAL RULES AND SYSTEMS OF DISPUTE RESOLUTION

Multinational Rules and Systems of Dispute Resolution in an Era of the Global Economy
Christoph A. KERN 61

1. Introduction 62
2. The Topic 64
3. The Current State of Affairs. 69
4. Perspectives 85
5. Conclusion. 96

Awards Set Aside in their Country of Origin: Two Incompatible Schools of Thought
Athanassios KAISSIS 99

1. Introduction 99
2. Recognition and Enforcement of Arbitral Awards under the New York Convention 100

Rethinking Multinational Procedure
Linda SILBERMAN 121

1. The Concept of a Multinational Rule. 121
2. Procedure is Outside of Most Multinational Rules 123
3. Lessons from the United States. 124
4. Lessons from the ALI/UNIDROIT Experience: Principles or Rules?. 126
5. Competing Developments. 128
6. Conclusion. 129

PART II. NEW CHALLENGES AND THEIR VARIOUS ASPECTS: ACCOUNTABILITY AND TRANSPARENCY

Accountability and Transparency of Civil Justice
Yulin FU 133

1. Introduction 134
2. Judicial Independence as the Premise for Judicial Accountability and Transparency 136
3. Judicial Transparency as a Principle Guaranteed by Constitutions and the Legal Devices of All States. 143
4. Judicial Accountability with Diverse Concepts and its Overlapping Relation with Transparency. 154
5. Conclusion. 163

Accountability and Transparency of Civil Justice: A Comparative
Perspective
     Daniel MITIDIERO. 165

1.   Introduction 165
2.   The Emergence of the Question from a Modern Perspective:
     Legislator-Judges? Irresponsible Judges?. 167
3.   External and Internal Judicial Independence, Impartiality
     and Objectivity of Law. 168
4.   The Interpretation and Application of Law (Legal Reasoning):
     The Duty to Give Reasons in Judicial Decisions. 174
5.   Publicity of Proceedings and Decisions. 178
6.   Civil Justice Transparency: From Traditional Communication
     and Information to New Technologies 180
7.   Who Watches the Watchmen? Third-Party Evaluation
     and Ranking of Civil Justice 182
8.   Final Considerations 183

PART II. NEW CHALLENGES AND THEIR VARIOUS ASPECTS: TRANSNATIONAL COOPERATION IN CROSS-BORDER INSOLVENCY

Transnational Cooperation and Coordination in Cross-Border Insolvency:
China, South Korea and Japan
     Junichi MATSUSHITA 187

1.   Introduction 187
2.   Reciprocity. 188
3.   Cooperation between Courts 190
4.   The Meaning and Effects of Recognition. 191

Transnational Cooperation in Cross-Border Insolvency
     Georg KODEK. 193

1.   Introduction 195
2.   Sources and Methodology. 198
3.   The Legal Basis for Cooperation. 199
4.   Recognition of Foreign Decisions 211
5.   Enforcement of Foreign Decisions. 249
6.   Coordination of Proceedings 251
7.   Other Forms of Cooperation. 260
8.   Conclusion. 261

Intersentia   ix

PART II. NEW CHALLENGES AND THEIR VARIOUS ASPECTS:
RECOGNITION AND ENFORCEMENT OF FOREIGN TITLES

**Regionalism in the Process of Recognition and Enforcement
of Foreign Titles**
Ronald A. BRAND 265

1. Introduction 266
2. The Function of Public Policy as a Ground for the Refusal
   of Recognition and Enforcement of Foreign Judgments 267
3. The Function of Public Policy as a Ground for the Refusal
   of Recognition and Enforcement of Foreign Arbitral Awards 280
4. Jurisdiction in Actions to Recognize and Enforce Foreign Decisions 287
5. Enforcement Following Recognition 308
6. Injunctive Relief 309
7. Searching and Seizing Foreign Assets 313
8. Conclusions 316

**Regionalism in the Process of Recognition and Enforcement
of Foreign Titles: Civil Law Jurisdictions**
Tanja DOMEJ 319

1. Introduction 320
2. National and Regional Approaches to Public Policy 322
3. Europe as a Breeding Ground for a Regionalized Concept
   of Public Policy? 331
4. Intensity of Review 350
5. Public Policy and Specific Grounds for Refusal of Recognition
   and Enforcement 355
6. Jurisdiction and Public Policy 356
7. The Double Function of Public Policy 357
8. Arbitral Awards 358
9. Implementing Regional Public Policy: Possible Ways Forward 363
10. Enforcement 366

PART II. NEW CHALLENGES AND THEIR VARIOUS ASPECTS:
ELECTRONIC TECHNOLOGIES IN JUDICIAL PROCEEDINGS

Application of New Technologies in Judicial Proceedings
Francisco VERBIC 381

1. Introduction 381
2. The First Dimension: Electronic Proceedings and the Tendency
   to Abandon Paper as Communication Support 382

3. The Second Dimension: Online Dispute Resolution 385
4. The Third Dimension: Artificial Intelligence in Case Management 387
5. The Fourth Dimension: New Technologies and Citizens' Access
to Public Information 390
6. Advantages, Risks, and Challenges Created by the Use of New
Technologies in Judicial Proceedings 392
7. Overall Assessment and a Look into the Future 393

The Application of Electronic Technologies in Judicial Proceedings
Ho Moon-hyuck 395

1. Introduction 396
2. Recording as a Means of Ensuring Transparency of Proceedings 400
3. The Handling of Electronic Documents 405
4. The Process of Using Video Devices 415
5. Online Dispute Resolution 417
6. The Future of the Judiciary 423
7. Conclusion 426

PART II. NEW CHALLENGES AND THEIR VARIOUS ASPECTS:
NEW TYPES OF EVIDENCE

Present and Future Issues Regarding New Types of Evidence:
Electronic and Digital Evidence in Particular
Etsuko Sugiyama 429

1. Introduction 431
2. The General Rule on Evidence in Civil Procedure 435
3. New Types of Evidence 447
4. Gathering and Preserving New Types of Evidence 462
5. Future Challenges Created by New Technology 470

The New Challenges of Evidence Law in the Fourth Industrial Revolution
Joan Picó 477

1. Neuroscience and Evidence 479
2. Facial Micro-Expression Algorithms for Lie Detection:
True or False? 485
3. Possible Problems Caused by the Increasing Prevalence of New
Technologies and Especially the "Internet of Things" in Civil
Procedure 489
4. The Scientific Knowledge of the Expert and its Inspection
in the Civil Process 494
5. Private Communications between Lawyers as Evidence 510

Intersentia

LIST OF CONTRIBUTORS

Ronald A. Brand
Chancellor Mark A. Nordenberg University Professor, Director, Center for International Legal Education, University of Pittsburgh, United States

Tanja Domej
Professor of Civil Procedure, Private Law, Private International Law and Comparative Law at the University of Zurich, Switzerland

Frédérique Ferrand
Director of the Équipe de droit international, européen et comparé (EDIEC), Director of the Institut de droit comparé Édouard Lambert (IDCEL), Honorary member of the Institut Universitaire de France, Professeure agrégée in private law, France

Yulin Fu
Professor at Peking University Law School, China

Athanassios Kaissis
Corresponding Fellow of the Institute for Foreign and International Private and Economic Law, University of Heidelberg; Faculty of Law, Aristoteles University Thessaloniki; Prof. (em.) Dr. (Heidelberg), President of International Hellenic University, Germany

Christoph A. Kern
Professor and director of the Institute for Comparative Law, Conflict of Laws and International Business Law, Ruprecht-Karls-Universität Heidelberg, Germany, and professeur remplaçant, Chaire de droit allemand, Université de Lausanne, Switzerland

Georg Kodek
Judge at the Austrian Supreme Court (Oberster Gerichtshof) in Vienna and Professor of Civil and Commercial law at the Vienna University of Business and Economics (Wirtschaftsuniversität Wien (WU)), Austria

Junichi Matsushita
Professor of Law, Graduate Schools for Law and Politics, the University of Tokyo, Japan

List of Contributors

Koichi Miki
Professor of Law, Graduate School of Law, Keio University; President of the Japan Association of the Law of Civil Procedure, Japan

Daniel Mitidiero
Associación Argentina de Derecho Procesal (AADP), Associazione Italiana fra gli Studiosi del Processo Civile (AISPC), Instituto Brasileiro de Direito Processual (IBDP), Instituto Iberoamericano de Derecho Procesal (IIDP) and Member of the International Association of Civil Procedure (IAPL), Brazil; Tenured Civil Procedure Professor at Federal University of Rio Grande do Sul (UFRGS), Porto Alegre, Brazil

Ho Moon-hyuck
Professor Emeritus, Seoul National University School of Law, South Korea

Joan Picó
Full Professor of Procedural Law, Pompeu Fabra University, Barcelona, Spain

Linda Silberman
Clarence D. Ashley Professor of Law, New York University School of Law, United States

Etsuko Sugiyama
Professor, Graduate School of Law, Hitotsubashi University, Japan

Francisco Verbic
Lawyer (UNLP), LL.M. in International Legal Studies (NYU), Adjunct Professor of Civil Procedure (UNLP). Academic Secretary of the LL.M. in Procedural Law (UNLP), United States

Margaret Woo
Professor of Law and Dean of Research and Interdisciplinary Education, Northeastern University School of Law, Boston, M.A., United States

PART I

OVERVIEW OF THE FUTURE OF CIVIL JUSTICE AND THE NEW CHALLENGES FACING IT

MODERN COMPUTER-RELATED TECHNOLOGY AND JUDICIAL PROCEDURE

Welcome Friend or Uninvited Troublemaker?

Koichi MIKI*

1.	Introduction	4
2.	Electronic Filing	4
	2.1. The Current Status of Electronic Filing	4
	2.2. The Advantages of Electronic Filing	5
	2.3. Issues in Electronic Filing	5
3.	Electronic Service	6
	3.1. Issues in Electronic Service	6
	3.2. Service upon a Person Who Exists Only on the Internet	7
	3.3. Service by Publication and the Internet	7
4.	Videoconferencing for Examination	8
	4.1. Issues in Videoconferencing for Examination	8
	4.2. How to Deal with the Issues	8
5.	Problems with Electronic Evidence	9
	5.1. The Enormous Amount of Information	9
	5.2. Easy to Modify or Erase	10
	5.3. Difficult to Search and Discover	11
	5.4. Information Unique to Electronic Data	11
6.	Information on the Internet	12
	6.1. Issues with Information on the Internet	12
	6.2. The Doctrine of Judicial Notice	12
	6.3. How to Deal with the Issues	12

---

* Professor of Civil Procedure Law at the Law School of Keio University, Tokyo, and President of the Japan Association of the Law of Civil Procedure.

7. Machine Expert Opinions 13
    7.1. The Current Status of AI in Court Proceedings 13
    7.2. Issues in Machine Expert Opinions 14
    7.3. How to Deal with the Issues 14
8. Records of Trials 15
    8.1. Issues in Electronic Recording 15
    8.2. How to Deal with the Issues 15
9. Conclusion 16

1. INTRODUCTION

As history has shown, every technological advance is always accompanied by both new de facto and legal issues.[1] Moreover, there is no doubt that the modern technology we are currently facing is mostly computer-related in some way. In the realm of procedure in civil litigation, there has already been a surge of new technology as a global trend, regardless of whether people like it or not. In any country, those who view such developments positively are trying to accelerate the trend and expand it into many aspects of the judicial process. On the other hand, more than a few scholars have identified potential problems associated with the rapid introduction of such technology. Should one view modern computer-related technology positively as a useful tool or even a welcome friend of judicial procedure? Or is it an uninvited nuisance, even if it is more or less innocent in its intentions? The purpose of this chapter is to conduct a rough examination of this theme at each stage of civil proceedings.

2. ELECTRONIC FILING

2.1. THE CURRENT STATUS OF ELECTRONIC FILING

One of the fields in which computer-related technology has made widespread inroads in a significant number of countries is in the electronic filing of various judicial documents, including complaints and answers that were previously filed as hardcopies.[2] As a technical matter, various countries have adopted different implementations to make electronic filing a real and viable system that can be used effectively. Consequently, while some countries have adopted the ordinary

---

[1] See E. KATSH, *The Electronic Media and the Transformation of Law*, Oxford University Press, Oxford 1989, p. 1.

[2] F. GASCÓN INCHAUSTI, "Electronic Service of Documents National and International Aspects" in M. KENGYEL and Z. NEMESSÁNYI (eds.), *Electronic Technology and Civil Procedure: New Paths to Justice from around the World*, Springer, Berlin 2012, p. 140.

internet as a platform, there are also countries that have built different networks separated from the internet. Here, I illustrate one representative example of electronic filing using a website on the internet,[3] a type of system that has recently been increasing in many countries.

In this system, attorneys representing parties are assigned an ID and password for logging into the electronic filing system. The attorneys use the electronic filing system to make submissions of documents electronically by uploading them to the website. When payments of fees are necessary, such payments are processed by credit card, debit card or bank transfer. Self-represented litigants are usually not allowed to access the electronic filing system and therefore must still submit paper documents. When that happens, court officials scan the paper documents and upload the data to the electronic filing system.

2.2. THE ADVANTAGES OF ELECTRONIC FILING

The main advantages of this type of electronic filing system over a traditional paper-based filling system can be summarized as follows.[4] First, it relieves the burden of keeping and maintaining paper records in storage for a long time. Second, it contributes to speeding up proceedings. Third, it leads to cost reductions such as postage costs and the cost of court officials accepting and managing paper documents. Fourth, it facilitates access to and searches of documents filed in court. Fifth, it allows attorneys to receive notices, orders, and decisions from the court electronically.

2.3. ISSUES IN ELECTRONIC FILING

On the other hand, such an electronic filing system inevitably raises issues of security and personal information protection.[5]

With regard to security, countermeasures against cyberattacks and computer viruses have been major concerns in electronic filing systems, and judicial administrations of all countries have taken several measures to combat such threats, including the installation of surveillance software. There are also countries in which private cybersecurity companies have been entrusted to perform

---

[3]   J.M. GREENWOOD and G. BOCKWEG, "Insights to Building a Successful E-Filing Case Management Service: U.S. Federal Court Experience" [2012] 4 *International Journal For Court Administration* 2; W. FENWICK and R. BROWNSTONE, "Electronic Filing: What is it – What are its Implications?" [2003] *Santa Clara High Technology Law Journal* 181, https://pdfs.semanticscholar.org/5150/df04d1bcfe6ab085f37809eacfc9bc4d8ca7.pdf.

[4]   See "The Pros & Cons of E-Filing Legal Documents" [2014], https://directlegal.com/pros-cons-e-filing-legal-documents.

[5]   F. GASCÓN INCHAUSTI, above n. 2, 165.

routine checks for security deficiencies. However, it should be remembered that security enhancement and system convenience are in a trade-off relationship. In other words, the more security you get, the harder it is to use the system. Therefore, once a certain level of security measures has been established, it may be a most balanced approach to focus in turn on training and raising awareness of staff and users.

Regarding personal information protection, measures such as the following are often observed. Whenever an attorney uploads a document to the electronic filing system, a screen is displayed to check that the document does not contain important personal information. Unless the confirmation button on the screen is clicked, the program does not permit moving to the next step. However, even when such a procedure is incorporated, it is not uncommon that a document in which important personal information is contained is uploaded due to the carelessness of an attorney.

After all, when it comes to security or personal information protection, the human factor remains a key vulnerability.

3. ELECTRONIC SERVICE

3.1. ISSUES IN ELECTRONIC SERVICE

Electronic service has many issues in common with electronic filing and it also has an essential difference. Because service of process constitutes the exercise of state power and has significant legal effects, it must withstand the scrutiny of the doctrine of due process.[6]

In particular, service on the defendant of a complaint, summons or any similar documents having the legal effect to initiate proceedings must be especially concerned with the validity of using electronic means for service. The service of these documents on the defendant is a core basis for the defendant's ability to assert its right of defense. Since electronic service does not necessarily guarantee appropriate recognition by a defendant compared to traditional vehicles of service, no country has accepted it as a primary avenue of service without the consent of the defendant.[7]

From this perspective, one prerequisite to realizing electronic service as a compulsory means of service might be establishing a duty on all citizens to be in possession of an electronic domicile to which official notices can be electronically served,[8] or perhaps achieving such de facto penetration that such a method can

---

[6] See J. BROWNING, "Your Facebook Status – Served: Service of Process Using Social Networking Sites" (2012) 2 *Reynolds Courts and Media Law Journal* 159, 161.

[7] F. GASCÓN INCHAUSTI, above n. 2, 169.

[8] Ibid., 170.

be viable or natural. However, it is hard to imagine such a day coming in the near future.[9] Thus far, electronic service is only permitted in some countries under the condition that both parties have previously agreed to it.[10]

3.2. SERVICE UPON A PERSON WHO EXISTS ONLY ON THE INTERNET

However, what has just been described is the story under ordinary circumstances. Under extraordinary circumstances, the story should naturally be different. For example, assume that a plaintiff suffered from trademark infringement by a defendant doing business on the internet, but the defendant is nowhere to be found, except on the internet. Should the plaintiff not be allowed to resort to electronic service using the defendant's contact information on the internet in order to bring an action, particularly when this is the primary or even the only method of reaching the defendant?[11]

As another example, imagine that a plaintiff has attempted personal service on a defendant at multiple of his/her last known physical addresses and all of these efforts have been unsuccessful. Under such circumstances, if it turned out that the defendant was reachable through active Twitter and Facebook accounts, should it not be allowed to use these social networking services as platforms of service?[12]

The answer is "Yes" in some countries. Some courts in some common law countries permit electronic service as a form of substituted service, provided that all other traditional means of service have been exhausted.[13] Under the common law, case law is the primary source of law, and the rules of service can be interpreted on a case-by-case basis. Unfortunately, such a flexible approach could not easily be realized in civil law countries including Japan, where the strict application of law is required.

3.3. SERVICE BY PUBLICATION AND THE INTERNET

In the case where constructive service by publication is needed, yet another story should be considered. For example, take a plaintiff who has lost contact with the defendant, and the defendant has no address where he/she can be served. In such a case, constructive service by publication is traditionally often selected.

---

[9]   See J. CABRAL ET AL., "Using Technology to Enhance Access to Justice" [2012] 26 *Harvard Journal of Law & Technology* 241, 288.
[10]   F. GASCÓN INCHAUSTI, above n. 2, 169.
[11]   See, e.g., *Rio Properties, Inc. v. Rio International Interlink*, 284 F.3d 1007 [9th Cir. 2002].
[12]   See, e.g., *Citigroup Pty. Ltd. v. Weerakoon* [2008] QDC 174, 1 (Austl.).
[13]   J. BROWNING, above n. 6, 159.

However, in reality, few people regularly examine legal newspapers or court notice boards carefully.

Compared to such means, constructive service on the internet could be a much more reasonable way of providing alternative service. It does not seem to be difficult in terms of both cost and technology to use the internet for constructive service independently or in combination with traditional service by publication.[14]

4. VIDEOCONFERENCING FOR EXAMINATION

4.1. ISSUES IN VIDEOCONFERENCING FOR EXAMINATION

In many countries, including Japan, videoconferences have been used for a number of years as a means to examine witnesses. This method offers obvious advantages to enable examination of a witness who has difficulty appearing in court, such as those living in remote areas or having been criminally injured by one of the parties. At the same time, it is also obvious that there are inevitable limitations and sometimes significant deficiencies with such a method of examination.[15] In particular, a videoconference may not be an effective means of transmitting details and nuances in relation to non-testimonial conduct of a witness, including body language and facial expressions. Non-verbal information can sometimes be more eloquent than words. It is also difficult to obtain information on anything that that occurred before or after the witness gives testimony.[16] For example, consider a witness who testifies that he ran down the stairs to get to the scene of an accident, but who can only walk with a slow shuffle in the courtroom.[17] This may be important information in terms of judging the credibility of his testimony; however, it cannot be viewed through a video camera aimed only at the witness stand. Furthermore, when a plaintiff or a defendant is examined by way of a videoconference, he/she may want to know the non-verbal information relating to the judge or the other parties.

4.2. HOW TO DEAL WITH THE ISSUES

Technically, the limitations and problems described above could be solved to a considerable extent by making full use of more elaborate modern technologies.

---

[14] Ibid. 177.

[15] See N. GERTNER, "Videoconferencing: Learning through Screens" [2004] 12 *Willian & Mary Bill of Rights Journal* 769, 783–84.

[16] See M. ROSE and S. DIAMOND, "Offstage Behavior: Real Jurors' Scrutiny of Non-testimonial Conduct" [2009] 58 *DePaul Law Review* 311, 319–20.

[17] N. GERTNER, above n. 15, 783.

For example, non-testimonial information could be received more thoroughly by using multiple video cameras with various angles and zooming ratios, and by keeping the cameras rolling for a period before and after witness testimony. Such video could be viewed as a synchronized split image in the courtroom. In addition, if a video camera aimed at the judge's bench is installed, plaintiffs or defendants who are away from the courtroom can see the reaction of the judge.

However, it would involve considerable cost to actually implement such technologies, and their cost-effectiveness is also questionable. In general, non-testimonial information may only rarely affect the outcome of litigation, so from a cost-benefit perspective, there could be little to lose by omitting it. At the end of the day, evaluation of the limitations and solutions to address such limitations in the videoconferencing of witness examinations necessarily involves a careful evaluation of trade-offs between perfect information and the cost of such information. One could imagine in the future that the cost-effective implementation of virtual reality or other new technologies could perhaps revolutionize this area.

5. PROBLEMS WITH ELECTRONIC EVIDENCE

There is no doubt as to the importance of electronically stored information as evidence in modern civil litigation. Especially, when one or both of the parties are business enterprises, it is not uncommon for electronic evidence to play an essential role in determining the outcome of the case. However, electronically stored information has many troubling aspects that are not usually found in traditional evidence.

5.1. THE ENORMOUS AMOUNT OF INFORMATION

The first issue is the overwhelming amount of electronic data that exists in our modern computerized society.[18] The development of technology has made it possible for us to generate much more information than in the paper-based society of only half a century ago. The amount of electronic data that individuals, businesses and other entities continue to create, transmit, and store every day without a break is increasing with seemingly infinite speed.[19] In addition, the

---

[18] See R. HARDAWAY, D. BERGER and A. DEFIELD, "E-Discovery's Threat to Civil Litigation: Reevaluating Rule 26 for the Digital Age" [2011] 63 *Rutgers Law Review*, 521, 546.

[19] G. PAUL and J. BARON, "Information Inflation: Can the Legal System Adapt?" [2007] 13 *Richmond Journal of Law & Technology*, 10, 12–20.

difficulty of searching, accessing, and producing the necessary information from the digital ocean has also been increasing dramatically.

Therefore, once the stage of collecting evidence is reached in civil litigation, the huge amount of electronic information bares its fangs to litigants as a heavy burden both in terms of time and cost. While this problem is particularly pronounced in the United States and other common law countries with discovery systems that allow for a wide range of searches,[20] the severity of the problem is more or less widely shared in other jurisdictions, including civil law countries such as Japan.

5.2. EASY TO MODIFY OR ERASE

The second issue is that electronic information is relatively easy to alter or delete, sometimes in untraceable ways. In fact, in the daily work of many companies or government offices, electronic documents are continually being overwritten and deleted, sometimes by the same person and sometimes by several others one after another, particularly with the introduction of cloud-based collaboration technologies that allow multiple users to have simultaneous access. Such alternations and deletions can be difficult or sometimes impossible to detect later.

In addition, computers may automatically alter or delete records as part of their normal operation.[21] Recording devices having such functions as dynamic databases constantly change in terms of both structure and content in synchronization with human activities. Programs built into them automatically discard or overwrite data, and often create information without the operator directing or being aware of this. The behavior of such programs is sometimes unpredictable and even ordinary operation, including the simple act of turning a computer on or off or accessing a particular file, can alter or destroy electronically stored information.

Such characteristics can cause serious disputes over originality and authenticity as evidence when electronic information appears in court. In particular, with regard to the authenticity of the electronic evidence, the finding of the authenticity in court procedures can sometimes be very complicated because it might be difficult or impossible to identify the author or trace the process of creation.

---

[20] See R. MARCUS, "The Impact of Digital Information on American Evidence-Gathering and Trial: The Straw That Breaks the Camel's Back?" in M. KENGYEL and Z. NEMESSÁNYI, above n. 2, pp. 29, 30–39.

[21] Ibid., pp. 40, 170.

5.3. DIFFICULT TO SEARCH AND DISCOVER

The third problem is that electronic information is often extremely difficult or impossible to search through.[22] Keyword search, the common method of searching, is often too blunt and prone to error for a variety of reasons. For example, since it can be difficult to set an appropriate keyword, keyword searches tend to be both over-inclusive and under-inclusive. This leads to extensive negotiation between parties or government authorities in countries like the United States regarding search terms. Also, it is common for search problems to stem from words that have multiple meanings, the use of unanticipated words and abbreviations, and typographical errors within the set of documents to be searched. Further, a wide variety of non-textual data, including documents recognized by search protocols as images and voicemail messages, has been increasing in recent years, which cannot be subjected to simple keyword searches.

5.4. INFORMATION UNIQUE TO ELECTRONIC DATA

As a fourth issue, there are problems inherent to backup data, metadata, and deleted data as characteristics unique to electronic data that are not included in paper-based media.[23]

With regard to backup information, it can be expensive and time-consuming to search, since typically information that has been archived is not immediately accessible for searching. Because the purpose of the archives of backup data is to make it possible to restore the original data in the event of loss, the archives contain much redundant information and duplicates of the same files. Even more troublesome is that backups may also contain many different versions of files.

Another possible source of problems is metadata. Metadata generally refer to the unique information stored in a file separate from the main portion of the file, including the last modified date, the creation date, and the last accessed date. Metadata can be a difficult challenge, since a producer must justify why the metadata are needed as evidence and may need to employ a technical expert who can provide a protocol for search and production.

Deleted data can also constitute problematic evidence. The process of search and restoration of deleted data involves many technical challenges. Therefore, it is sometimes necessary to obtain the assistance of an expert, just as in the case of metadata. And, due to these technical difficulties, naturally the cost often rises. In addition, the producer must make a convincing case that the requested data cannot be found elsewhere.

---

[22]   R. Hardaway, D. Berger and A. Defield, above n. 18, 548.

[23]   Ibid., 554.

6. INFORMATION ON THE INTERNET

6.1. ISSUES WITH INFORMATION ON THE INTERNET

Among the various issues that computer-related technology raises in the field of evidence law, the question of whether and to what extent judges are allowed to use the internet as a source of information is quite crucial. In countries that adopt an adversarial judicial system in some way, judges are in principle required to decide cases based on the evidence presented in court by the parties. If judges apply their own knowledge or do their own research, they may deprive the parties of the chance to attack that information with evidence and the chance to submit counter-evidence.[24] In addition, if judges use their personal knowledge to find facts, this could appear to demonstrate a lack of neutrality and fairness, which could lead to serious consequences, including undermining people's trust in the judiciary.

6.2. THE DOCTRINE OF JUDICIAL NOTICE

There is, however, an exception to the rule prohibiting judges from using personal knowledge. This is called the doctrine of "judicial notice" in common law countries.[25] Judges are allowed to consider certain facts that have not been proven when they are deemed uncontroversial, either because they are publicly known or because they can be confirmed accurately and easily on solid ground. Very similar procedural rules also apply in many countries with civil law systems. For example, in Japan, facts that are publicly known or can be easily confirmed are called "kencho-na-jijitsu" and parties are not required to prove them by supplying evidence. The common ground between the doctrine of *kencho-na-jijitsu* and the doctrine of judicial notice is that the truth is objectively ensured without being proven by evidence.

6.3. HOW TO DEAL WITH THE ISSUES

Traditionally, facts published in major newspapers or reported on radio and television have been regarded as common knowledge and have been treated as fulfilling the requirements for judicial notice. It has also been accepted as judicial notice for judges to read standard textbooks to obtain basic medical

---

[24] See "Can Judges Use Their Personal Knowledge When Deciding Cases?," February 16, 2016, http://www.provincialcourt.bc.ca/enews/enews-16-02-2016.

[25] See C. MANCHESTER, "Judicial Notice and Personal Knowledge" (1979) 42 *Modern Law Review* 22.

knowledge and use this in proceedings and decisions in cases involving medical malpractice. What if the source of information is the internet? Can we consider facts spread widely through social media such as YouTube, Twitter, Facebook, or Instagram as being publicly known? If a judge's Google searches are used, is it acceptable to omit verification by an expert? When the evidence produced by each party is conflicting, is it acceptable for judges to determine what is correct based on information found on the internet?

Unfortunately, it is difficult to answer these questions simply with a "yes" or a "no."[26] The variety of information overflowing in cyberspace has a vastly broad spectrum in terms of reliability and acceptance. On the one hand, there are articles written by journalists or scholars with levels of professional responsibility or that have been officially or peer-reviewed. On the other hand, there are also anonymous articles that cannot be verified as true or false, or tweets that are clearly biased. There is also "fake news" and other false information disseminated by actors with various motivations deliberately masquerading as fact, which is often difficult to discern from reality at first glance. In essence, with respect to the concept of judicial notice itself, it is not easy to draw a distinction between common and personal knowledge.[27] And this is exactly the same for information on the internet, as described above. As it turns out, we cannot draw a clear line for this problem with a standard ruler.

7. MACHINE EXPERT OPINIONS

7.1. THE CURRENT STATUS OF AI IN COURT PROCEEDINGS

One of the most remarkable developments among the many advanced technologies in this modern age, which is attracting attention and capturing the emotions of so many people, is artificial intelligence (AI). The flow of this massive tide cannot be neglected in relation to court proceedings. Although the day when AI completely takes the place of human judges may be in the distant future, it has already become a reality that computer programs trained through deep learning can competently provide expert opinions in the court.

In order to avoid any misunderstandings, I should clarify that, technically, the expert witness can only be a human and AI can only provide expert knowledge to him/her. However, since the dramatic progress of AI is shifting the specific gravity of the actual judgment from the human to the machine, I would like to refer to the expert knowledge provided by AI as a "machine expert opinion" with

---

[26] G. Kodek, "Modern Communications and Information Technology and the Taking of Evidence" in M. Kengyel and Z. Nemessányi, above n. 2, p. 271.

[27] C. Manchester, above n. 25, 27.

Intersentia

symbolic meaning. According to such terminology, the fields in which AI may perform as an expert in a trial can be varied, including handwriting analysis, facial recognition, skid mark analysis, and interpretation of medical images like X-rays, CT scans, MRIs, and so on. AI has the ability to analyze with a level of precision that far surpasses humans in certain areas, such as image recognition.

7.2. ISSUES IN MACHINE EXPERT OPINIONS

The critical problem of machine expert opinions is that AI or even its human developers cannot be cross-examined to confirm expertise and reliability, or the underlying methodologies and reasons for conclusions. AI trained by deep learning does not require human intervention for its own growth. The programs are exposed to unlabeled data from the real world. The systems use statistics and algorithms derived from probability theory to navigate ambiguous data in order to generate results. Then, the programs teach themselves to revise their own algorithms so as to increase accuracy. As no human is virtually involved in the process, humans, including developers, can explain nothing about how and why AI has reached the decision that it has made. And the same is true of AI itself. Most recently, although attempts have been made to develop technologies of explainable artificial intelligence (XAI) in order to enable humans to understand the thinking process of AI, the level of its technical goal is far from realizing something equivalent to cross-examination against AI.[28]

7.3. HOW TO DEAL WITH THE ISSUES

Cross-examination is the classic test to verify the expertise and reliability of an expert in a trial. However, cross-examination is just a means, and expertise and reliability themselves are the goal. One means that could be provided to verify the expertise and reliability of AI would be to make the AI available to the opposing party to test the program with new data.

For example, in the case of facial recognition systems, the lawyers of the opposing party could examine the decision of the programs on new data, such as photographs taken under a variety of light conditions and showing various angles of the face. Similarly, with handwriting analysis, validation data may include a variety of scrawls, initials, and grouping of letters. Parties can then spot-check the final result and score its accuracy. The degree to which testing is successful depends on a selection of a new population of items used for validation.

---

[28] See "Study to Advance to Explainable AI" [2019] *Asahi Shimbun* (Japanese), May 6, 2019, 2.

However, whether such a method is used or not, there are problems that are inherently difficult to solve in the verification of the AI program itself. Since any AI by its nature evolves over time as it is exposed to new data, complex issues arise as to how to "freeze" the AI in time in order to evaluate its judgment at the specific moment of the expert opinion and to prove that the AI being tested is in the exact same state as the AI when it provided the expert opinion.

8. RECORDS OF TRIALS

8.1. ISSUES IN ELECTRONIC RECORDING

It has already become common to utilize computer-assisted transcription to record proceedings in many countries, although unfortunately this has not yet been realized in Japan. Equally, several countries have used voice recording equipment in various aspects of civil procedure in court. Moreover, audio-video recording has been employed in some courts in some countries as the ultimate means to record a trial.[29] Audio recording, on the one hand, has the obvious advantage of precisely preserving information, but on the other hand, it also involves some disadvantages. Specifically, it is not possible to write a memo freely as in paper-based recording or it can be time-consuming to retrieve the particular part of the record.

8.2. HOW TO DEAL WITH THE ISSUES

However, these problems have already addressed to a considerable extent by the progress of technology. One of these technologies is a system that enables the combination of a full text transcript with synchronized digital audio recordings.[30] The other is a system that allows attorneys and judges to capture the text transcript onto their own computers and make private annotations on it.[31] Yet another is a system that allows the exclusion of unnecessary scenes from court records such as a voice-activated recorder.[32] For now, these do not provide a complete solution. However, further technological development will eventually lead to the full computerization of records.

---

[29] F. LEDERER, "Wired: What We Have Learned about Courtroom Technology" [2010] 24 *ABA Criminal Justice* 18, 23.

[30] See G. KODEK, above n. 26, p. 269.

[31] See F. LEDERER, above n. 29, 23.

[32] See G. KODEK, above n. 26, p. 269.

9. CONCLUSION

The overview of the current status and problems that arise in terms of computer-related technology, as considered above, thus reveals that they can be divided into two groups. The first is issues relating to procedural administration, including electronic filing, electronic service, and videoconferencing for examination and the recording of trials. The second is issues relating to judicial decision-making, including problems involving electronic evidence, information on the internet and machine expert opinions. The nature and possible solution of the issues in these two groups are different.

The former is derived from a scenario in which active attempts are made to introduce computer-related technology into the world of court proceedings with the aim of promoting the efficiency and propriety of judicial process, just as other government agencies and companies are introducing information technology into their operations. What we should watch for in this field is the correct recognition and proper response to various problems hidden behind the convenience brought about by computer-related technology. As shown above, many of the issues in this field can be technically overcome, and many practical ideas and responses to them have already been made. Considered in this way, modern computer-related technology can be seen as a useful and convenient tool, although it is somewhat cumbersome to work with. In other words, in this context, it has the face of a welcome friend for judicial procedure.

The latter, on the other hand, derives from the scenario in which judicial proceedings are passively affected by the advance of computer-related technology. The inevitable impacts of these new technologies sometimes force us to change traditional practices and legal common sense. Some of these impacts include those that place a heavy burden and those that cause confusion for both litigants and courts, but where there is no way of avoiding them. In addition, no effective silver bullets have yet been found for many of these new issues, and the future prospects are also unclear at this point. Therefore, in this context, computer-related technology cannot be considered inherently harmful, but it can be said to have the face of an uninvited troublemaker. We must learn to properly recognize the nature of each problem and find a way to reconcile with it.

ON THE FUTURE OF CIVIL PROCEDURE

Should One Adapt or Resist?

Frédérique FERRAND*

1. Introduction 17
2. The Injunction: To Adapt and Transform 18
3. The Directions Taken or to be Taken: The Course of Reforms. 22
    3.1. The First Direction: Reinforcing Confidence 23
        3.1.1. Allocation of Sufficient Resources to the Judicial Institution
            and/or Establishment of Satisfactory Management 23
        3.1.2. Reinforcement of Confidence through Greater
            Transparency 25
        3.1.3. Reinforcement of Confidence through Increased
            Specialization 28
    3.2. The Second Direction: The Technification of Civil Proceedings –
       Justice and Digital Tools 31
    3.3. The Third Direction: Flexibilization 36
4. The Alternative: Adapt or Resist? 42

1. INTRODUCTION

A strong trend is emerging in our postmodern, neoliberal world in the context of the globalized and digitalized society, which extends its tentacles further each day: namely, the firm belief in the necessity to adapt and an increasingly more forceful injunction to do so.

A number of the subjects selected for the Kobe Conference of the International Association of Procedural Law (IAPL) echo this evolution and injunction: multinational rules and systems of dispute resolution in the era of

---

*   Honorary member of the Institut Universitaire de France, Professeure agrégée in private law, Director of the Institut de droit comparé Édouard Lambert (IDCEL), Director of the Équipe de droit international, européen et comparé (EDIEC).

Intersentia   17

global economy; accountability and transparency in the course of civil justice; application of electronic technologies in judicial proceedings; and current situations and problems regarding new types of evidence.

Is it because of this necessity of adaptation that a movement of rapprochement of national civil procedures started over 20 or so years ago throughout the world, under the effect of a degree of elimination of borders, and state financial preoccupations that ineluctably have consequences for the structure of justice and the running – when required – of civil actions?

In section 2 of this chapter, we shall first examine what kind of injunction may be involved: why adapt and transform? In section 3, we shall then examine the directions to be taken or that tend to be taken where legislators and other legal protagonists follow through on the injunction to adapt. Finally, in section 4, the question is raised as to whether the purportedly required adaptation is indispensable or whether a certain resistance should not be instigated in order to safeguard certain values that are precious to the democratic processualist with a concern for fundamental rights.

2. THE INJUNCTION: TO ADAPT AND TRANSFORM

"Il faut s'adapter" – one must adapt.[1] This is the formula that has flourished not only in political and economic domains, but also in the field of law. There is allegedly an ineluctable and imperious necessity for transformation and adaptation in a globalized and increasingly digitalized society. One should not be overtaken in the fierce competition, or in world or European rankings. Justice systems are in fact increasingly compared competitively[2] and directly,[3] for example, in the EU Justice Scoreboard created by the European Union (EU);

---

[1]   See B. STIEGLER, "Il faut s'adapter," Sur un nouvel impératif politique ["One Must Adapt," On a New Political Imperative], Gallimard, 2019.

[2]   See the comments of the Commissioner for Justice of the time, V. REDING ("The attractiveness of a country as a place to invest and do business is undoubtedly boosted by having an independent and efficient judicial system"), "EU Justice Scoreboard: European Commission Broadens the Scope of its Analysis of Member States' Justice Systems", press release, March 27, 2013, IP/13/285). The Scoreboard, with its significant subtitle ("A tool to promote effective justice and growth"), published in the form of a report (Communication from the Commission, The EU Justice Scoreboard. A tool to promote effective justice and growth, COM(2013) 160 final), contains quantified data on the functioning of the judicial systems of the Member States, obtained with the assistance of the Commission européenne pour l'efficacité de le justice (CEPEJ), drawn up within the Council of Europe.

[3]   On the other hand, for a confidential comparison between German courts concerning the duration of proceedings and transaction rates, enabling a ranking of justice in the 16 Länder, see J. WAGNER, "Von Spitzenreitern und Schlusslichtern" ["Front runners and stragglers"], NJW-aktuell 24/2017.18.

each year since 2013, this tool performs a freeze frame on the efficiency and quality of justice in EU Member States, on the grounds that "the effectiveness of justice systems is essential for increased confidence in an environment that is favorable to investments and to businesses in the single market."[4] This Scoreboard, which is described as "non-binding, tool" established in the context of an "open dialogue with the Member States",[5] is not only intended, as set out by the Commission, to assist Member States and the EU institutions in formulating better justice policies, but also to invite Member States (or at least some of them) more or less firmly to "engage the reforms imposed on them."[6]

As highlighted by the philosopher Barbara Stiegler: "Evolution, as they say, demands 'mutations' enabling 'survival' and 'adaptation' to a new 'environment' henceforth described as unstable, complex, and uncertain, and in relation to which our societies are constantly of 'falling behind.'"[7] This "neoliberalism," one of whose essential differences from traditional liberalism is the reinforcement of the role of the state and its action in many spheres, has been assimilated into analysis to Darwinian evolution.[8]

The question was already addressed by the American journalist Walter Lippmann in 1937[9] with regard to the Industrial Revolution imposing new demands to which it is suggested human beings are not "adapted,". It re-emerges nowadays: how to rethink political (and legal) action through the prism of notions of backwardness, evolution and the need to re-adjust to a new environment? Lippmann defended a regulation of society by experts and by the law (in other words, a vertical vision of power and of an expert state). For him, only a representative democracy, governed by experts, could rise to the challenge of the necessary adaptation on the part of the human race, constantly backward in respect of the flow of events. The state must thus impose on society a constraining agenda enabling the course to be maintained[10] for the

---

[4]   Declaration by Věra Jourová, European Commissioner with responsibility for justice, consumers, and gender equality, April 10, 2017, available at https://ec.europa.eu.

[5]   COM(2013) 160 final, p. 3.

[6]   See also the impressive number of Member States that have implemented, or that are in the process of implementing reforms in their justice systems in The 2019 EU Justice Scoreboard, COM(2019) 198/2, pp. 5 f.

[7]   "L'évolution, dit-on, réclame des 'mutations' permettant de 'survivre' et de 's'adapter' à un nouvel 'environnement' désormais décrit comme instable, complexe et incertain, et par rapport auquel nos sociétés sont constamment accusées de 'prendre du retard.'" B. Stiegler, above n. 1, p. 11.

[8]   Ibid., p. 13.

[9]   W. Lippmann, *The Good Society*, Little, Brown and Company, Boston 1937.

[10]   The course set by neoliberalism is the broad overall environment of fair competition, with the conception that the end goal of evolution could be known in advance, which was refuted by Darwin, for whom the evolution of life took place in many different and unforeseeable directions.

necessary reforms.[11] On the contrary, the pragmatist American philosopher John Dewey recommended the involvement of citizens and experimentation through the collective intelligence of everyone – in other words, what would now be referred to as participative and horizontal democracy.[12]

This question of adaptation and evolution may be linked to the analyses of the Anglo-Polish sociologist and philosopher Zygmunt Bauman concerning society: a "liquid" modernity[13] or at least a society "in a process of advanced liquefaction" where human relations become flexible rather than durable, both at the personal level and collectively. In modern and, above all, postmodern society, the balanced relationship between security and freedom would no longer be respected. The state would be endowed with all the organizational and regulatory tools for the organizations of social life, then, with the onset of the consumer age, postmodern societies would have allegedly favored liberty to the detriment of security. Deregulation and privatization adversely impact the instruments of common security. Society would purportedly require its members to adapt to the world, but without providing them with the means for security. The state would then play the role of "gamekeeper" and no longer that of "gardener" in ensuring social order in a world in which each individual is left to their own devices – a "liquid" society rather than a "solid" society, in which the structures of common organization are created collectively. In a "liquid society," the only reference is the individual whose involvement is their act of consumption. Fluctuations and flexibilities would be in play.[14]

---

11   On the need to stay on course while teaching reform, see B. STIEGLER, "Le cap et la pédagogie – à propos du néolibéralisme et de la démocratie" ["Direction and Pedagogy – On Neoliberalism and Democracy"], https://aoc.media/analyse/2019/01/24/cap-pedagogie-a-propos-neoliberalisme-de-democratie.

12   See J. DEWEY, *The Public and its Problems*, 1927, new ed. Pennsylvania State University Press 2012.

13   See Z. BAUMAN, *Liquid Modernity*, Polity Press, Cambridge 2000; "The Role of the Intellectual in Liquid Modernity" (2011) XXVIII(3) *Theory, Culture & Society*. See also S. TABET, *Le Projet Sociologique de Zygmunt Bauman. Vers une approche critique de la postmodernité* [*Zygmunt Bauman's Sociological Project. Towards a Critical Approach to Postmodernity*], L'Harmattan, Paris 2014. As identified by Z. Bauman: "Contrairement aux corps solides, les liquides ne peuvent pas conserver leur forme lorsqu'ils sont pressés ou poussés par une force extérieure, aussi mineure soit-elle. Les liens entre leurs particules sont trop faibles pour résister … Et ceci est précisément le trait le plus frappant du type de cohabitation humaine caractéristique de la 'modernité liquide'" ["Unlike solid bodies, liquids cannot conserve their form when pressed or pushed by an external force, however slight. The links between their particles are too weak to resist … And this is precisely the most striking trait of the type of human cohabitation that is typical of 'liquid modernity'"]; see http://sspsd.u-strasbg.fr/IMG/pdf/Vivre_dans_la_modernite_liquide._Entretien_avec_Zygmunt_Bauman.pdf. See also Z. BAUMAN, *Liquid Modernity*, Polity Press, Cambridge 2000.

14   For Z. BAUMAN, the tendency in our postmodern "liquid" societies to replace the notion of "structure" by that of a "network" in the context of human interactions is topical for evolution: while "structures" sought to create solid nodes and links, networks are used to for both connecting and disconnecting.

Many thinkers[15] since the end of the twentieth century have identified a social and ideological deliquescence attached to the extension of neoliberalism in the fields of politics and economics.

The older analyses of Lippmann, in emphasizing the need for adaptation of societies and citizens – promote a neoliberalism aimed at "liquefying all stasis in the name of flux"[16] (stases of habit are opposed to the flow of innovation),[17] thus embodying a discourse of permanent reform at all costs. For him, it was a matter of integrating society into the rapid and brutal acceleration of the expansion[18] of the environment of the human race and attaining the "Good society." This reform, guided by experts, is currently operating in many countries. Evolution would demand "'mutations' enabling 'survival' and 'adaptation' to our new environment, that of an accrued 'competition' in a context of 'scarce resources.'"[19] These are the key words of the underlying trend.

In France, for example, it was possible to state that "'modernization' and the neo-managerial turning point of the state are uttered as watchwords that sound so much like injunctions to efficiency, transparency, and simplification."[20] The two categories of courts of first instance are merged with a view to pooling resources,[21] full digitization is planned to induce financial savings. This entails "rethinking the role of the courts,"[22] "redefining the role of those involved in the process,"[23] and "simplifying in order to judge better."[24]

---

[15] As well as Z. BAUMAN, see also G. LIPOVETSKY, *L'ère du vide, Essai sur l'individualisme contemporain* [*The Era of the Void: An Essay on Contemporary Individualism*], Gallimard, coll. Les Essais, Paris 1983; J.-F. Lyotard, *La condition postmoderne, Rapport sur le savoir* [*The Postmodern Condition: A Report on Knowledge*], Coll. Critique, Paris 1979, which raises the question of knowledge in postmodern societies (does digitalization lead to a reconsideration of certain aspects of the transformation of knowledge, and what are the political consequences for society and for the state?).

[16] "Liquéfier toutes les stases au nom du flux." B. STIEGLER, above n. 1, p. 18.

[17] See ibid., p. 250.

[18] At the time of Lippmann, this acceleration was due to the industrial revolution. Currently, globalization and the technological revolution constitute considerable factors of acceleration.

[19] "'Mutations' permettant de 'survivre' et de 's'adapter' à notre nouvel environnement, celui d'une 'compétition' accrue dans un contexte de 'ressources rares.'" B. STIEGLER, above n. 1, p. 274.

[20] "La 'modernisation' et le tournant néo-managérial de l'État se disent d'abord dans des mots d'ordre qui sonnent comme autant d'injonctions à l'efficacité, la transparence et à la simplification." "Éditorial" (2014) 124 *Politix* 3, no. 1. The State thus becomes the "Strategist State" (ibid., no. 5).

[21] The merger also signifies distance and remoteness; see D. SALAS, "La justice doit garder sa dimension démocratique" ["Justice Must retain its Democratic Dimensions"], *Le Monde*, January 15, 2019, p. 23. See also L. CADIET, "La réforme Belloubet ou le jeu de dés" ["The Belloubet Reform, or the Throw of the Dice"], *Procédures* 2019, Repère 6.

[22] Title of section 3 of Chapter I of Heading II of French Law No. 2019-222 dated March 23, 2019 concerning the 2018–2022 programme and judicial reform.

[23] Ibid., title of Chapter I of Heading II.

[24] Ibid., title of section I of Chapter II of Heading II.

In many states, in a wide range of territories, strands of reforms involving the modernization of the state and its justice are in play, "ranging from organizational mergers to the increasing in power of the assessment imperative, via the division of reforming words."[25] Giving rise to a normative densification,[26] the reforming injunctions of public action are many.[27] These are often accompanied by the liberation of private initiatives for the resolution of disputes outside the courts – in other words, without any state control embodied by the figure of the judge. There is intense competition between actors; this presupposes and necessitates clear, firm rules of the game that will not leave the door open to any unfair or unacceptable practices in respect of the protection of the rights of the citizen seeking justice. A sense of cohesiveness must preserve the multiple provisions of solutions both within and outside the court.

3. THE DIRECTIONS TAKEN OR TO BE TAKEN: THE COURSE OF REFORMS

In the face of the accelerations of flows described above, the law and reform are called upon. Shall the law be seen as a "highway code," intended not to stabilize the status quo, but to facilitate the liberation of new forces?[28] Does this therefore entail endlessly adapting the social order (and thus the judicial order) to scientific discoveries, technical progress, and structural changes in society? Should the law work as an instrument of adaptation to the environment and to its mutations?

It seems that the evolution at work in the domain of the organization of the courts and of civil procedure law translates into three main trends that somewhat coincide with those found in the economic world: this involves reinforcing

---

25 "Allant des fusions organisationnelles à la montée en puissance de l'impératif évaluateur, en passant par la déclinaison de mots d'ordre réformateurs." "Éditorial," above n. 24, p. 3, no. 6.

26 C. THIBIERGE et al., *La densification normative* [*Normative Densification*], Mare & Marin, Paris 2014.

27 See, for example, the decision of November 15, 2018 at the conference of German ministers of justice: "Zivilprozess durch Reformen stärken" ("Reinforcing Civil Proceedings through Reforms"). See also the German Law Act of December 12, 2019, Gesetz zur Regelung der Wertgrenze für die Nichtzulassungsbeschwerde in Zivilsachen, zum Ausbau der Spezialisierung bei den Gerichten sowie zur Änderung weiterer zivilprozessrechtlicher Vorschriften [Law Act for the regulation of the threshold value for inadmissibility of civil complaints, for the expansion of specialization in the courts and the further amendment of civil procedural regulations], *BGBl.* 2019. I. 2633, which aims to "increase the efficiency of civil proceedings" ["soll die Effizienz im Zivilprozess gesteigert werden"].

28 See B. STIEGLER, above n. 1, pp. 193 ff., which emphasizes, that, for neoliberals, and in particular Lippmann, the rule of law "doit être au fond remise au service de ce qu'il s'agissait de libérer au départ: au service de la libération des flux dans un monde ouvert et sans clôture" ["must be fundamentally submitted to the service of that which was involved initially with liberation: at the service of the liberation of flows in an open world, without containment"].

confidence (section 3.1), incorporating technology into civil justice, which translates as processes and procedures becoming more technical (section 3.2), and, finally, encouraging a measure of flexibility (section 3.3).

3.1. THE FIRST DIRECTION: REINFORCING CONFIDENCE

The reinforcement of confidence in justice may appear in many guises. This may involve the allocation of sufficient resources to the judicial institution and the putting in place of sufficient management. It may also involve increased transparency or increased specialization by judges and courts. The European Union – a model for ordoliberalism – places particular emphasis on this need to "strengthen trust".'"[29]

3.1.1. Allocation of Sufficient Resources to the Judicial Institution and/or Establishment of Satisfactory Management

This involves improving provisions – where possible – and creating satisfactory management tools enabling the government to benefit from precise information on the status of the courts and their needs in terms of personnel and budget.[30] As the 2019 Justice Scoreboard sets out, in the EU Member States, this involves developing "monitoring and evaluation of court activities."[31]

In France, for example, the Cour des comptes (Court of Auditors) recently published a report[32] in which it found that the performance of the French courts had not improved, although the implementation of Law No. 2016-1547 dated November 18, 2016 for the modernization of justice in the twenty-first century was starting to bring about a reduction in the number of new cases (*déjudiciatisation*/dejuridification).[33] The proportion of high courts in

---

[29] See, for example, the comments of commissioner V. JOUROVÁ in Vienna on November 30, 2018: "We are working on increasing the trust in justice. Providing sufficient financial resources to the justice system is not a cost, [it] is an investment ... The country with a well functioning justice is more likely to attract investors," cited in the introduction to The 2019 EU Justice Scoreboard, above n. 7.

[30] See, for example, R. CAPONI, "The Performance of the Italian Civil Justice System: An Empirical Assessment," (2016) 2(1) *Italian Law Journal* 15 and more specifically 17 ff. on the use of indicators to evaluate the performance of civil justice and the causes of its shortcomings.

[31] The 2019 EU Justice Scoreboard, above n. 7, pp. 36 ff.

[32] Cour des comptes [Court of Auditors], "Approche méthodologique des coûts de la justice, Enquête sur la mesure de l'activité et l'allocation des moyens des juridictions judiciaires" ["A methodological approach to the costs of justice, an investigation into the measurement of activity and the allocation of court resources"], December 2018, available at dalloz-actualite. fr/flash/cour-des-comptes-souhaite-une-justice-plus-manageriale#.YH1qSD8697M.

[33] See also the report by the Inspection générale de la justice [General Inspectorate of Justice], *Bilan des réformes de la procédure d'appel en matière civile, commerciale et sociale*

difficulties (marked by increases in lead times to judgment on civil matters) increased considerably in 2017. Despite an increase of nearly 9% in the justice budget since 2013 (which remains lower than that of comparable countries such as Germany, Belgium, Spain, Italy, and the Netherlands, and is also the case in terms of the numbers of magistrates and legal personnel) and slightly less activity in the courts,[34] the backlog of cases pending is increasing.[35] The Ministry of Justice's tools for analysis and monitoring of activity are insufficient. There is a lack of a common framework of workload benchmarks for all the courts. The Cour des comptes report uses a number of foreign systems of court case weightings as models for comparison and recommends the creation within three years of "a weighting system based on a typology of legal cases and on current and future management tools in order the ensure an efficient allocation of court resources and a precise knowledge of court activity" (recommendation 9).[36] The German, Norwegian, and Israeli systems are cited.[37]

---

et perspectives [*Report on the Reforms of the Appeal Procedure in Civil, Commercial, and Social Cases, and Perspectives*], July 2019, n°049/19, available at http://www.justice.gouv.fr/ le-ministere-de-la-justice-10017/remise-du-rapport-sur-la-procedure-dappel-32797.html. See also on this report F. Ferrand, "Bilan des réformes de la procédure d'appel en matière civile et perspectives – A propos du rapport de l'Inspection générale de la Justice" ["Report on Reforms of the Appeal Procedure in Civil Cases, and Perspectives – On the Report of the General Inspection of the Justice System"], JCP G 2020, n° 3. This report finds that the fall in new, completed, and backlog civil cases did not translate into a reduction in the time taken for the processing of cases (Report. p. 42 et s. and Sheet 2, p. 39). The number of new cases in 2018 is equivalent to that of 2009 (251,000 cases in 2016, 230,000 in 2018). Also, since 2016, the number of civil appeal cases has fallen by 8.5% (Sheet 2, p. 46), the processing times have steadily increased since 2011 and it is regrettable that the existing statistical tools do not enable the quantification of the processing times according to the phases in proceedings, notably between the end of the rigid deadlines established and the scheduling of case hearings. The period for processing cases has increased by 2.1 months between 2009 and 2018, from 11.4 months to 13.5 months; employment disputes (20.4 months on average) and social protection cases (17.5 months) have been affected the most: the increase in the duration of processing for an appeal is mainly due to the increase in the average time of processing of these two types of dispute.

[34]   The report of the Cour des comptes in 2018 (p. 34 seq.) shows that the courts of appeal and regional courts (of first instance) [TGI] experienced a reduction in civil disputes of, respectively, −1.75% and −6.40% between 2013 and 2017. During this period, the average lead time for processing increased from 10.5 months, to 11.8 for the regional courts [TGI] and from 11.7 months to 14.7 months for the courts of appeal.

[35]   See report by the Inspection générale de la justice, above n. 34, p. 34.

[36]   "Un système de pondération se fondant sur une typologie des affaires judiciaires et sur les actuels et futurs outils de gestion afin de garantir une allocation efficiente des moyens des juridictions et une connaissance précise de l'activité judiciaire."

[37]   In Germany, the PEBBSY system (*Personalbedarfsberechnungssystem*) ["individual requirements calculation system"] has been in place since 2005 and was revised in 2014; this is based on an initial assessment by magistrates and public prosecutors (by record-keeping over six months) of the working time by activity. The system is used to allocate human resources in the courts. In Norway, the LOVISA system – which has been in operation since 2010 – does not classify cases by type of dispute, but within each category of dispute, the average time for a case according to criteria of complexity (for example, the appointment of an expert, examination of witnesses, etc.). The court resources allocated by an independent agency are only partly dependent upon

On the Future of Civil Procedure

An evolution is emerging – or has already been engaged – that encourages a finely tuned management[38] and allocation of resources as closely matched as possible to the requirements through the establishment of weighting systems for activities, although none of which is without its problems.

In Germany, where the attractiveness of a career as a judge[39] is falling, as is the number of civil cases,[40] measures are under consideration to make justice more attractive and to reinforce litigants' levels of confidence. As well as the increasing specialization of the chambers, a return to a collegiate structure was envisaged where, in 2002, the practice of a judge sitting alone had been introduced. Some of the Länder (Hamburg and North Rhine-Westphalia) sought to have economic cases, where the stakes were particularly high, focused in proven, reputable central courts, which would thus attract professionals voluntarily fleeing into arbitration. The operation of the commercial chambers also needs improvement in the regional courts, which had lost half of their cases in between 2002 and 2016.[41]

3.1.2. Reinforcement of Confidence through Greater Transparency

Transparency of justice in play?

While total transparency tends more toward the totalitarian than the democratic, a certain level of publicity is still considered appropriate for reinforcing the

---

the results of the LOVISA system. Other countries are based on a similar system (Estonia, some courts in the Netherlands). In Croatia and in Slovakia too, systems for the analysis of cases have been established, and are now used to measure the productivity of magistrates and legal staff, which raises questions concerning the independence of magistrates. The German PEBBSY system – which also inspired Austria – cannot be used as an individual management tool for each magistrate, since it could violate the principle of independence enshrined in Article 97 of the Fundamental Law (fortunately so).

[38] Concerning the possible role of artificial intelligence in the running of judicial systems, see CEPEJ, Appendix 2 of the European Ethical Charter on the Use of Artificial Intelligence in Judicial Systems and Their Environment;, December 3, 2018, CEPEJ(2018)14, p. 50. This could enable the implementation of quantitative and qualitative evaluations, and the construction of projections (anticipation of human and budgetary resources). Key performance indicators could be constructed.

[39] See S. Rebehn, "Attraktivität schwindet" ["Waning Appeal"] (2019) 3 *NJW* 17.

[40] In 2017, 936,979 new cases were brought before the district courts (Amtsgerichte), or 50,000 fewer than in 2016. In 2018, there were still fewer: 923,933. Between 2017 and 2007, the reduction was 330,000 (a fall of 25% over ten years). With the regional courts (Landgerichte), the fall was 18% over ten years (373,331 civil cases in 2007 to nearly 66,000 fewer in 2007: 307,718). In 2018, there was an increase (338,021), see S. Rebehn, "Rechtsschutzpaket, zweiter Anlauf" ["Legal Protection Package, Second Approach"] [2018] *DRiZ* 371.

[41] R. Podszun and T. Rohner, "Die Zukunft der Kammern für Handelssachen" ["The Future of Commercial Chambers"] [2019] *NJW* 131. In 2002, 54,697 cases were given a ruling; in 2016, this fell to only 27,607. It seems that elected tradespeople assessors have become the "weak link" for these chambers; the parties can, by common accord, renounce having the presence of two elected tradespeople assessors in favor of a decision by a judge sitting alone, as a professional magistrate, and this they do in approximately 90% of cases.

Intersentia

25

confidence of litigants in justice. Germany, a country that is nonetheless very well ranked in the 2019 Justice Scoreboard in terms of user confidence concerning access to justice, has engaged in this direction, thereby hoping to reinforce the rule of law and the population's attachment to it. While the principle is that the recording of court proceedings for retransmission or public broadcast is forbidden[42] with limited derogations relating to the Federal Constitutional Court (Bundesverfassungsgericht), the government wanted to extend sound and image recording during the pronouncement of decisions by the German courts of cassation (Revision).[43] This would involve adapting broadcast to modern flow and thus "reinforcing confidence in justice, in this way."[44] The (natural) reserve of magistrates is opposed to the demands of the press to the effect that justice necessitates "acceptability and transparency" (Akzeptanz und Transparenz). The Law of October 8, 2017[45] now permits the public broadcast of the decisions of the Federal Court of Justice. But it will be for the Court to decide, at its discretion, if it will make use of this option or not (this will probably be very unusual, given the strength of the reservations of the Bundesgerichtshof[46] magistrates expressed against the "mediatization" of their persona). This is the point at which the "*will* of the *flows*" encounters the "stases" of professional reserve.

In Brazil, a large number of court trials are already broadcast live on television. Will justice succumb to the "dictatorship of transparency?"[47]

Transparency for experts and mediators

Certain actors in justice within and external to the courts play an essential role. The same is true of experts. A German law of October 11, 2016[48] reinforced

---

42   §169, paragraph 1 of the Law on Court Organization (Gerichtsverfassungsgesetz, GVG).

43   In Germany, there are five review courts: the Federal Court of Justice (Bundesgerichtshof), the Federal Employment Court (Bundesarbeitsgericht), the Federal Administrative Court (Bundesverwaltungsgericht), the Federal Social Disputes Court (Bundessozialgericht), and the Federal Finance Court (Bundesfinanzhof).

44   Comments by the Secretary of State of the Ministry of Justice Christiane WIRTZ; see A. KAUFMANN, W. TAPPERT, and J. VETTER, "Kameras im Gericht: Mehr Transparenz oder Voyeurismus?" ["Cameras in Court: More Transparency, or Voyeurism?"] (2017) 5 *DRiZ* 157.

45   Gesetz zur Erweiterung der Medienöffentlichkeit in Gerichtsverfahren und zur Verbesserung der Kommunikationshilfen für Menschen mit Sprach- und Hörbehinderungen (EMöGG) [Law on the expansion of media access in legal proceedings and for the improvement of communication aids for people with speech and hearing impairments], *BGBl.* 2017. I. 3546.

46   And primarily its president, Bettina LIMPERG.

47   F. LEMARCHAND, "Vers une dictature de la transparence : secret et démocratie" ["Towards a Dictatorship of Transparency: Secrecy and Democracy"] (2014) 16(1) *Éthique publique*, which finds that "resituée dans le contexte politique, la transparence peut ainsi apparaître comme la meilleure alliée des sociétés de contrôle et le pire ennemi de la démocratie" ["restored to the political context, transparency may thus appear as the best ally for supervisory companies and the worst enemy of democracy"] (no. 12).

48   Law modifying the law governing expert assessment, and modifying the law on proceedings in family matters and in non-contentious proceedings of October 11, 2016, *BGBl.* 2016. I. 2222. See E. STÖßER, "Änderungen im Sachverständigenrecht" ["Changes in Law Pertaining to Experts"] (2016) 22 *FamRZ* 1902.

the obligations of the expert (*Sachverständiger*), particularly with a view to increased transparency. Before the appointment of the expert, the parties could be heard by the civil judge, and give their opinion on the choice of the expert.[49] The expert appointed by the judge must "without delay" examine whether there are grounds for any doubts as to their impartiality. The expert must then immediately communicate these grounds to the court.[50] Transparency is indeed also involved, which is comparable to the obligation of disclosure incumbent upon the arbitrator, in particular in French law. The same trend also emerges in respect of mediators: in France, the consumer mediator must make available to the public and communicate certain information and their annual activity report[51] The same is the case in Brazil, where a national register and a local register of conciliators and mediators is held; all information relating to these professionals' results is recorded (number of cases conducted, the outcome in each case, the subject matter of the cases, etc.) and these data are regularly published for statistical purposes and to enable the external monitoring of a mediator's activity by making it "transparent."[52]

Transparency and financing of the process by a third party

A range of companies or platforms now offer to take charge of the costs of proceedings for a percentage of the savings achieved.[53] In Switzerland in 2015, the Federal Court confirmed its initial decision of 2004 declaring the financing of a court trial by a third party to be legal, which it found to be "widespread in practice."[54] The proposed Directive contained in a resolution of 2017 by the European Parliament on minimum standards of civil procedure[55] envisages the financing of court trials by a third party.[56] Certain obligations of disclosure may be established. In the United States, where the question of third-party funding is

---

[49]   §404, para. 2 ZPO.

[50]   On the sanction of an abstention, see ibid., §407a, para 2.

[51]   See (Arts. L. 613-1 and L. 614-4 C. consommation [consumer affairs]).

[52]   H. DALLA BERNARDINA DE PINHO and M. PEDROSA PAUMGARTEN, "The Challenges of Court Mediation from the Brazilian Perspective" (2015) 2 *Rev. int. dr. processuel* 315.

[53]   A total of 35% for example, on the site MyRight.de in the context of the polluting emissions scandal (*Abgasskandal*) concerning German vehicle manufacture.

[54]   "In der Praxis verbreitet," T. fédéral suisse, January 22, 2015, 2C_814/2014, available at www.bger.ch/ext/eurospider/live/fr/php/aza/http/index.php?lang=fr&type=show_document&highlight_docid=aza://22-01-2015-2C_814-2014&print=yes. However, the Federal Court considers that financing should be provided by a third party that is not involved in the management of the proceedings.

[55]   See resolution of the European Parliament of July 4, 2017 containing recommendations to the Commission on common minimum standards of civil procedure in the European Union, 2015/2084(INL).

[56]   Art. 16: "Member States shall ensure that in cases where a legal action is funded by a private third party, the private third party shall not: (a) seek to influence procedural decisions of the claimant party, including on settlements; (b) provide financing for an action against a defendant who is a competitor of the fund provider or against a defendant on whom the fund provider is dependant; (c) charge excessive interest on the funds provided."

assuming increasing practical importance, companies require the establishment of an obligation of disclosure of any agreement involving financing by a third party. In Wisconsin, for example, following a reform of April 3, 2018,[57] all financing agreements for the court trial must be disclosed at the start of the proceedings. A Litigation Funding Transparency Act is pending before Congress.[58] The court trials financing sector in the United States is considered to be worth approximately 10billion dollars.

3.1.3. Reinforcement of Confidence through Increased Specialization

Increased numbers of courts of specialist chambers

Many states are establishing specialist chambers for certain fields of civil disputes. For example, Germany, in a law of April 28, 2017,[59] which came into force on January 1, 2018, imposes the creation of specialist chambers in regional courts[60] (Landgerichte, equivalent to the French tribunaux de grande instance (TGI)/courts of first instance) and in the higher regional court[61] (Oberlandesgerichte, comparable to the French courts of appeal) in four domains of litigation: banking and finance contract matters; construction law (construction, architecture, and engineering contracts); clinical negligence applications; and insurance contracts. A recent Law Act of 12 December 2019 imposes additional specializations; similarly, the Länder may decide to extend the jurisdiction of certain courts beyond the boundaries of a given Land in order to ensure for certain special domains a sufficient flow of cases with the appointed courts[62]

The response to complexity is thus the specialization of one or more specialist chambers per court. The ministers of justice of the German Länder wished to

---

[57] Wisconsin Act 235, available at docs.legis.wisconsin.gov/2017/related/acts/235 "Third party agreements. Except as otherwise stipulated or ordered by the court, a party shall, without awaiting a discovery request, provide to the other parties any agreement under which any person, other than an attorney permitted to charge a contingent fee representing a party, has a right to receive compensation that is contingent on and sourced from any proceeds of the civil action, by settlement, judgment, or otherwise."

[58] See R. MARCUS, "Multiple Sources of Procedural Change in America" (2017) 22 *ZZPInt* 22 269 f. and more specifically 281.

[59] Gesetz zur Reform des Bauvertragsrechts, zur Änderung der kaufrechtlichen Mängelhaftung, zur Stärkung des zivilprozessualen Rechtsschutzes [Law on the reform of the construction of contact law, on the changing of liability under the law on liability for defects, for the strengthening of legal protection in civil proceedings], *BGBl*. 2017. I. 969. See P. FÖLSCH, "Mehr Spezialisierung in der Ziviljustiz" ["Greater Specialization in Civil Justice"] [2017] *DRiZ* 166.

[60] §72a GVG.

[61] Ibid., §119a.

[62] See Law Act of 12 Dec. 2019 (n. 28): concerning disputes relating to the law of successions, disputes relating to a situation of insolvency, and to publications via any media (press, television, radio, etc.). See also N. STACKMANN, "Zivilprozess – Effizienz, Utopie und Stückwert" ["Civil Litigation – Efficiency, Utopia, and Unitary Value] [2019] *ZRP* 193.

be authorized by the Federation to focus certain special disputes on certain courts, while at the same time being in favor of maintaining a proximity legal protection, which feels somewhat like a squaring of the circle.[63] These trends have also been noticeable in France for several years, especially with the recent Law No. 2019-222 dated March 23, 2019, on the 2018–2022 program, and reform of justice[64] which, for example, establishes a single national, 'virtual' court, with jurisdiction over the issue of a national or European order for payment.[65] Similarly, where there are several courts in a given French department, some of these can become specialist courts.[66]

With specialization, there also appears a tendency for geographic concentration of certain material competencies within a limited number of courts in order to reinforce the principle of specialization.[67]

Also in England, a new formation for complex disputes in financial markets has been in existence since October 1, 2015, and is referred to as the *Financial List*; this has jurisdiction for particularly complex and very high value (at least £50 million) cases concerning financial markets.[68] A specialist judge (a Financial List judge) from the Chancery Division or the Commercial Court rules in these cases.[69]

---

[63]   See N. STACKMANN, "Zivilprozess – Effizienz, Utopie und Stückwert" [2019] *ZRP* 193. This is now possible (see the recent Law Act of 12 Dec. 2019, n. 28, and the new drafting of §§13a, 60, 72a, and 119a GVG.

[64]   *JORF*, March 24, 2019.

[65]   Art. 27 of the law, which, however, excludes injunctions to pay falling within the jurisdiction of the tribunal de commerce [commercial court]. Article 27 adds, within the Code de l'organisation judiciaire (COJ) [Judicial Organization Code], Arts. L. 211-17 and L. 211-18. Applications for an order for payment are, in principle, submitted virtually (electronically); however, they can be submitted to the court office in paper format if they are issued by natural persons not acting in a professional capacity and who are not represented by an appointed agent.

[66]   See Art. L. 211-9-3, I COJ. Specialization will take place upon the proposal of heads of the court, following an opinion from the heads of the jurisdiction. See L. RASCHEL, "Loi de programmation 2018–2022 et de réforme pour la justice: aspect d'organisation judiciaire" ["Law on the 2018–2022 Program, and on Judicial Reform: An Aspect of Judicial Organisation"], *Procédures* 2019, Étude 11.

[67]   Thus, for example, in Germany, European injunctions to pay can only be sought from the District Court of Berlin-Wedding. Similarly, in respect of maintenance obligations in the context of a cross-border, intra-EU dispute, one single court per Land has jurisdiction. Regarding the European Insolvency Regulation of May 20, 2015 for France, see the modification of Art. L. 721-8, 20 C. com.

[68]   See N. ANDREWS, "Improving Justice Despite Austerity: Making Do or Making Better?" (2015) 20 *ZZPInt* 6. According to Part 63A.1 CPR: "'Financial List claim' means any claim which: (a) principally relates to loans, project finance, banking transactions, derivatives and complex financial products, financial benchmark, capital or currency controls, bank guarantees, bonds, debt securities, private equity deals, hedge fund disputes, sovereign debt, or clearing and settlement, and is for more than £50 million or equivalent; (b) requires particular expertise in the financial markets; or (c) raises issues of general importance to the financial markets."

[69]   Part 63A.4, (2) and (3) CPR.

Intersentia

Specialist chambers in international commercial disputes

The creation of specialist chambers in international commercial disputes has been revived in several European countries, with the announcement of Brexit, an event that has been a catalyst for change. Given that in 80% of the cases brought before the Commercial Court of the High Court of London, at least one of the parties is foreign or lives abroad,[70] the legal systems of other Member States are endeavoring to attract at least a part of this dispute into their national jurisdiction; this is indeed a question of "attractiveness,"[71] as a high-value dispute can bring substantial amounts into the state coffers. This is justice as a market:[72] something that should come as no surprise for anyone in our neoliberal societies.

The regional court (Landgericht) of Frankfurt am Main thus opened a commercial chamber in January 2018, where the language of proceedings can be English.[73] Upon the application of one of the parties, the case is allocated to this chamber.[74] Upon the joint application of both parties, the language of proceedings will be English. This initiative follows one that was initiated in 2010 in the higher regional court (Oberlandesgericht) of Cologne in the form of a pilot project. Hamburg set up a similar model in May 2018. In the spring of 2019, the ministers of justice of the Länder launched a new "Commercial Courts" initiative for very high-value commercial disputes.[75]

---

[70]   R. POSECK, "Brexit und Justizstandort Deutschland" ["Brexit, and Germany as a Location for Justice"] [2017] *DRiZ* 165.

[71]   See, for example, the German draft law Entwurf eines Gesetzes zur Regelung der Wertgrenze für die Nichtzulassungsbeschwerde in Zivilsachen, zum Ausbau der Spezialisierung bei den Gerichten sowie zur Änderung weiterer zivilprozessrechtlicher Vorschriften [Draft law for the regulation of the threshold value for inadmissibility of civil complaints, for the expansion of specialization in the courts and the further amendment of civil procedural regulations], which refers to the need for "die Attraktivität des Justizstandort Deutschland zu erhöhen und die Gerichte in Wirtschaftsstreitigkeiten zu stärken" ["increasing the attractiveness of German as a location for justice and reinforcing the courts for economic disputes"].

[72]   The higher regional court (Oberlandesgericht, OLG) of Frankfurt-am-Main (Germany) in 2015 had a level of civil proceedings cost coverage of 200% (which means that for every €100 of court operating costs, €200 was added to its coffers); see R. POSECK, above n. 71.

[73]   *NJW-aktuell* 47/2017. 36 and 46/2017. 7. See also the website of the Hesse General Court of Justice: ordentliche-gerichtsbarkeit.hessen.de.

[74]   The chamber consists of a professional magistrate (chair) with extensive experience of business law and a good knowledge of English, and two non-professional assessors (an "alderman"-type system) appointed for five years upon the recommendation of the Chamber of Commerce and Industry.

[75]   See R. PODSZUN and T. ROHNER, "Initiative der Landesjustizminister für "Commercial Court" ["Land Justice Ministers' 'Commercial Court' Initiative" [2019] *ZRP* 190, which refers to a minimum value of €1 million for commercial disputes. See also M. STÜRNER, "Deustche Commercial Courts?" ["German Commercial Courts?"] [2019] *JZ* 1122.

There is very lively competition[76] between Germany, France, and the Netherlands in this area.[77] In the Netherlands, on January 1, 2019 a Netherlands Commercial Court (NCC)[78] was set up with the Amsterdam Rechtbank (and, for appeals, with the Amsterdam Gerechtshof).[79]

In France, following the creation of an international chamber in the Paris tribunal de commerce in 2010,[80] a similar chamber was established with the Paris[81] Court of Appeal These two chambers are covered by a bilingual descriptive brochure; they hear commercial cases with an international dimension and are composed of English-speaking judges. A proceedings schedule is drawn up by common accord at the pre-trial stage, with an indication of the date of the judgment. The decision is delivered in French and English.

While the reinforcement of confidence is intended to "secure" the justice market, a second direction of evolution is more disruptive and concerning for certain litigants: the technification of civil proceedings.

3.2. THE SECOND DIRECTION: THE TECHNIFICATION OF CIVIL PROCEEDINGS – JUSTICE AND DIGITAL TOOLS

"Technology, as was the case for each industrial revolution, is a moment of rupture."[82] One should avoid the injunction to adapt civil proceedings to new

---

[76] On competition between legal systems and distortions of competition, see C.A. KERN, "Wettbewerbsverzerrungen im Wettbewerb der Rechtsordnungen – Die vergessene Seite der Medaille" ["Distortion Effect of Competition between Legal Systems – The Forgotten Side of the Coin"] (2014) 18 *GreifRecht* 114.

[77] G. DALITZ, "Justizinitiative Frankfurt – Too Little Too Late?" ["The Frankfurt Justice Initiative – Too Little Too Late?"] (2017) 8 *ZRP* 248. See also S. KRUISINGA, "Commercial Courts in the Netherlands, Belgium, France and Germany – Salient Features and Challenges," [2019] *IPRax* 277.

[78] See also C.A. KERN and G. DALITZ, "Netherlands Commercial Court and Maritime Kamer – Englisch als Verfahrenssprache in den Niederlanden" ["The Netherlands Commercial Court and Maritime Kamer [Chamber] – English as the Language of Proceedings in the Netherlands"] (2016) 21 *ZZPInt* 119.

[79] See the website of the new court, which forms part of the Dutch legal system "ranked number 1 worldwide": www.rechtspraak.nl/English/NCC/Pages/default.aspx. The entire proceedings take place in English (conclusions, report, and decisions), which is not the case for the German model in Frankfurt, which is operated under the law as it stands. Application may be made to the NCC on four conditions: (1) the court, or the Amsterdam Court of Appeal has jurisdiction; (2) the parties have expressly agreed to proceedings being conducted in English before the NCC; (3) this is a civil or commercial dispute relating to freely available rights; and (4) it is an international dispute. Collective actions can also be brought before it. Specific proceedings rules have been drawn up in English.

[80] The proceedings documents are accepted in a foreign language (German, English, or Spanish) and the hearing can also be conducted in a language other than French.

[81] See the Paris Court of Appeal website: www.cours-appel.justice.fr/paris/presentation-des-chambres-commerciales-internationales-de-paris-ccip.

[82] "La technologie, comme ce fut le cas lors de chaque révolution industrielle, est un moment de rupture." Jean-Hervé LORENZI, Chairman of the Cercle des économistes (a French think-tank

technologies (digitization) leading to disruptions that leave the litigant by the roadside, disoriented and powerless.

Many aspects of the incursion of digital technology into civil justice can be seen.[83] Not all of these present the same level of danger. Certain modern technologies enable an improvement in the operation of justice, even though they need to be handled with care so as to avoid cutting the litigant off from their judge (or from another human being involved in contributing to the resolution of their dispute). This involves mastering the technology, rather than a headlong rush, where the human being will be dependent or powerless in the process.

Electronic communication in civil justice

Electronic communication between courts, lawyers, and/or litigants is a useful evolution that has been engaged in many states.[84] In others, such as Germany, the obligation to communicate by electronic means with the court will be imposed incrementally (in 2022 in the case of Germany). Federalism does not always favor rapidity and, above all, uniformity.[85]

The 2017 European Commission Justice Scoreboard revealed the "still limited use of ICT [Information and communications technologies] in certain countries"[86] and particularly a very low level of use of electronic communication between lawyers and courts in Germany, Cyprus, Greece, Luxembourg, and Ireland. The European Commission intends to apply strong pressure on Member

---

founded in 1992, which includes economists and academics and whose mission is to organize and promote an economic debate that is open and accessible to all), in *Le Monde*, March 12 2019, supplément Cercle des économistes, p. 1.

[83] See, for example, *Digitalisierung der gerichtlichen Verfahren und das Prozessrecht* [*The Digitization of Judicial Procedures and Procedural Law*], Duncker & Humblot., Berlin, 2018.

[84] For example Estonia, France, the United Kingdom, and Chile. For Estonia, see https://e-estonia.com/solutions/security-and-safety/e-justice. Chile has extended digitized proceedings to the whole justice system (A. Pérez Ragone (2016) 2 *Rev. int. dr. processuel* 36); an electronic platform has been created for civil, family, criminal, and employment justice, which can be used in all court proceedings.

[85] Thus, at §130a, para. 2 of the German ZPO (Code of Civil Procedure), it is provided that the Federal government and the governments of the Länder shall decide by decree (*Rechtsverordnung*) for their field of jurisdiction, the date from which electronic documents can be sent to the courts, as well as the form required so that these documents can be processed.

[86] "Une utilisation toujours limitée des TIC dans certains pays." The 2017 Justice Scoreboard indicated: "bien qu'elles soient largement utilisées pour les communications entre les juridictions et les avocats dans la moitié des États membres, les TIC ne sont utilisées que de manière très limitée dans plus de la moitié de ceux-ci pour la signature de documents. De nouvelles données sur la façon dont les avocats utilisent les TIC pour communiquer avec les juridictions soulignent une fois encore l'importance des communications électroniques pour le bon fonctionnement des systèmes de justice" ["Although widely used for communications between courts and lawyers in half of the member states, ICT is only used to a very limited extent in over half of these for the signature of documents. New data on the way in which lawyers use ICT for communicating with litigants emphasizes once again the importance of electronic communications for the proper functioning of justice systems."].

On the Future of Civil Procedure

States to use modern techniques in courts and also to promote electronic access to court decisions.[87] Things are evolving quite rapidly in this field.

Videoconferencing (remote attendance)

This is also proving to be a tool that can be used to facilitate the running of civil proceedings by eliminating the problem of distance, even though not all courts have the necessary equipment yet. The EU, in its various regulations on judicial cooperation in civil matters, also promotes this tool.[88] The Resolution of the European Parliament of July 4, 2017 referred to above[89] also provides, in Article 5 §1 of its draft Directive, that: "Where it is not possible for the parties to be physically present or where the parties have agreed, with the approval of the court, to employ expedited means of communication, Member States shall ensure that oral hearings can be held by making use of any appropriate distance communication technology, such as videoconference or teleconference, available to the court or tribunal."[90] But can we compare the physical presence of one party or of a witness, who, at the time of their attendance, looks the judge in the eye with a transmission where the camera and screen present an obstacle to a subtle perception of the attitude of the interested party? Although videoconferencing may be a useful compensatory measure where physical attendance is impossible, should it be presented as a panacea for avoiding costs and travel?[91] Once again, this is an urgent question to be addressed.

The electronic trial

French Law 2019-222 dated March 23, 2019 on the 2018–2022 program and reform of justice creates a national virtual court for the order for payment at

---

[87] See The 2017 EU Justice Scoreboard, p. 23.
[88] See, for example, Art. 9 of Regulation (EC) No. 861/2007 of July 11, 2007, establishing a small claims procedure, amended by Regulation (EU) No. 2015/2421 of December 16, 2015. See Council Regulation (EC) No. 1206/2001 of May 28, 2001 on cooperation between the courts of the Member States in the taking of evidence in civil or commercial matters, which also provides for videoconferencing in its Art. 17.
[89] Resolution 2015/2084(INL).
[90] The same applies for other individuals who need to be heard and whose domicile or habitual place of residence is in a Member State other than that of the court to which application has been made (Art. 5, §2). See also the recommendation 2015/C 250/01 of the Councilm "Promoting the use of and sharing of best practices on cross-border videoconferencing in the area of justice in the Member States and at EU level" (OJEU C 250, July 31, 2015, p. 1). This technology is also favored concerning evidential matters by the Resolution of the European Parliament of 2017 (Art. 10).
[91] See D. Salas, "La justice doit garder sa dimension démocratique" ["Justice Must Retain its Democratic Dimension"], *Le Monde*, January 15, 2019, p. 23, which asks: "Un droit hors sol et formaté par des barèmes techniques ou des algorithmes a peu de chances d'être juste. Une justice qui parle à travers des plates-formes numériques ou par visioconférence, qui n'est plus construite par des silences, des paroles et des visages, est-elle digne de ce nom ?" ["A virtual law, formatted by technical scales or algorithms, has little chance of being accurate. A justice that speaks via digital platforms or videoconferencing, which is no longer constructed by silences, words, and faces, can this be worthy of its name?"].

Intersentia

both the national and European levels; this also exists in other countries. Other European states have also introduced online procedures (online dispute resolution (ODR) in England,[92] the Netherlands, and Latvia, for example). While the online services were initially limited to out-of-courts alternative dispute resolution measures for disputes, they are increasingly assuming their place in the legal proceedings context, sometimes in the form of an "electronic court," and are not limited to low value disputes. They are also used for divorce proceedings in certain states in the United States, for example.[93] In England, an online procedure has been established for "small" debt claims (Money Claim Online (MCOL))[94] not exceeding £100,000 and where there is a maximum of one single applicant and two defendants, all of which must be domiciled in England or Wales.[95] The proceedings are very clearly formulaic and lead times are short.[96]

In Canada in 2015, British Columbia created the Canadian Civil Resolution Tribunal (CRT),[97] which is an alternative route to the traditional courts for small disputes with a value of less than CA\$5,000 concerning debts, as well as disputes involving co-ownership (condominiums), which can be for any amount.[98] The court favors a "collaborative approach" for the resolution of disputes.[99]

---

[92] See, for example, the option of filing for divorce online – *digital divorce*: https://www.gov.uk/apply-for-divorce. The same website contains the standard form for completion in order to register an application.

[93] Notably Washington, California, Florida, and New York.

[94] See www.moneyclaim.gov.uk/web/mcol/welcome. The explanatory notice runs to no fewer than 25 pages!

[95] The defendant cannot be a public law legal entity.

[96] See already the recommendations of the report *Online Dispute Resolution for Low Value Civil Claims*, February 2015, available at https://www.judiciary.uk/wp-content/uploads/2015/02/Online-Dispute-Resolution-Final-Web-Version1.pdf. This report proposes three stages: (1) *Online Evaluation*, enabling the litigant to set out and categorize their problem, to be aware of their rights, and to understand the options available to them (a free-of-charge phase provided by associations or law practices working pro bono). Reference is sometimes made to a "chatbox" or "guided pathway" for this phase; (2) *Online Facilitation*: non-judge facilitators read through the declarations of the parties and help them to find an amicable solution through negotiation and mediation (as appropriate, with conference calls, but above all "automated negotiation" conducted without human intervention. The model is that of the *adjudicators* who work in the Financial Ombudsman Service and resolve 90% of cases upstream; this phase is technically paid for, but the costs are theoretically significantly lower than those in phase 3); 3. *Online Judges*: these rule via electronic means on the basis of the documents submitted by the parties with, as appropriate, a conference call (the costs are still lower than in traditional proceedings). The objective is a "court service that is intelligible, accessible, speedy, and proportionate in cost. This, in turn, calls for rules that are simple, clear, and compact."

[97] See www.civilresolutionbc.ca.

[98] From April 2019, it has also had jurisdiction for land-based motor vehicle accidents with a value of less than CA\$50,000.

[99] See https://civilresolutionbc.ca, where the different stages are explained: diagnosis by the "solution explorer"; application by form completed; negotiation platform; in the case of the failure of negotiations, having recourse to a "facilitator"; and, as a final resort, decision by a single judge.

Other models could be cited,[100] such as the Cybersettle website,[101] whose head office is in the United States: each party submits (without the other being informed of their submission: *double blind technology*) the minimum and maximum amount that they would be ready to accept and a transaction is proposed; the procedure is rapid and has a high success rate (over 65%).

These technologies are developing.[102] They require prudence and transparency to avoid the litigant being led astray. The Council of Europe European Commission for the Efficiency of Justice (CEPEJ) also highlights that the use of the term "court" excludes the involvement of private justice.[103] The use of information technologies for the resolution of disputes using alternative methods must not lead to a violation of Article 6, 8, or 13 of the European Convention on Human Rights (ECHR). When the litigant goes to an online dispute resolution platform, they need to be able to understand whether the processing of their dispute is entirely automated, or includes the involvement of a mediator, arbitrator, or judge. In the alternative, their choice is not an informed one. In France on January 17, 2019,[104] the human rights defender, an independent public authority, in their annual report,[105] raised the issue of territorial or social divides, revealing that 19% of French people do not have a computer at home and 27% do not have a smartphone.[106]

Big data, artificial intelligence and predictive justice

This is the biggest challenge for civil justice (and even more so for criminal justice). A considerable number of court decisions will be made available

---

[100]   See, for example, Art. 26 of French Law No. 2019-222 dated March 23, 2019 on the 2018–2022 program, and reform of justice, which provides for an entirely virtual procedure in both cases (new Art. L. 212-5-2, COJ): (1) for oppositions to the injunction order to pay if the initial application does not exceed an amount fixed by decree; (2) for applications made to the tribunal de grande instance (TGI) [court of first instance] (the future "tribunal judiciaire" [civil court]) concerning payment of a sum not exceeding this amount. This presupposes an application of this kind by the parties, who must agree.

[101]   www.cybersettle.com.

[102]   See N. FRICERO, "Nouvelles technologies: procès civil et numérique" ["New Technologies: Civil and Digital Proceedings"], Hors série *Banque & Droit* Oct. 2019, pp. 45 f.

[103]   Charte éthique [Ethical Charter], Appendix 1, n° 111. The denomination "tribunal en ligne" ["online court"] is often use for the platforms, whereas technically they aim to provide alternative dispute resolution services.

[104]   See *Le Monde*, January 18, 2019, p. 9.

[105]   *Rapport annuel d'activité 2018* [*Annual Activity Report 2018*], https://defenseurdesdroits.fr/ fr/rapports-annuels/2019/03/rapport-annuel-dactivite-2018.

[106]   The Human rights defender thus recommends "redéployer une partie des économies procurées par la dématérialisation des services publics vers la mise en place de dispositif pérennes d'accompagnement des usagers" ["redeploying some of the savings made by the digitizing of public services, for the establishment of a mechanism for supporting users"] in order to "faire en sorte que ce processus inéluctable et fondamentalement positif pour la qualité du service public respecte les objectifs des services publics sans laisser personne de côté" ["ensure that this inevitable and fundamentally positive process for the quality of the public service adheres to the objectives of the public services, without leaving anyone out"].

(in France[107] following pseudonymization of the parties' names, but in principle excluding the names of judges,[108] which will de facto enable a profiling of the latter, even though this is prohibited and penalized by the law).[109] It will be possible to foresee the outcome of the case and that risks having a performative effect for the judge risking the obligation of justifying themselves for having not followed the prevailing tendencies of his/her colleagues, these are the perspectives involved. The European ethical charter on the use of artificial intelligence (AI) in judicial systems, which was adopted by the CEPEJ in December 2018,[110] seeks to contain the problem by regulating it and formulates five principles: the principle of respect for fundamental rights; the principle of non-discrimination; the principle of quality and security; the principle of transparency, neutrality and intellectual integrity; and finally the principle of control by the user. Will this be enough? Does technology not risk challenging human ethics and their principles? In other words, how will the tensions between the logic of *big data* and that of the protection of human rights be resolved?

Here too, as in the case of economics, the direction has been set out: ever greater commitment to globalization and competition without losing ground in relation to other competitors.

3.3. THE THIRD DIRECTION: FLEXIBILIZATION

Flexibilization at work in civil justice today takes many forms: the creation of specialized chambers, notably for international commercial disputes, with English as the language of proceedings, optional[111] or compulsory concentrations

---

[107] See L. CADIET, "Concilier la publicité des décisions de justice et le droit au respect de la vie privée" ["Reconciling the Publication of Court Decisions with Respect for Privacy"], *Procédures* 2019, Étude 21.

[108] By virtue of Art. L. 111-13 COJ, "lorsque sa divulgation est de nature à porter atteinte à la sécurité ou au respect de la vie privée de ces personnes ou de leur entourage, est également occulté tout élément permettant d'identifier les parties, les tiers, les magistrats et les membres du greffe" ["where their disclosure is liable to present a risk to the safety or privacy of these individuals or their entourage, any element enabling the identification of the parties, third parties, magistrates and members of the court office, shall be removed"]. According to the draft implementing decree, the decision to remove any element enabling the identification of judges and court office members, by application of the second paragraph of Art. L. 111-13 COJ, shall be taken by the chair of the court prior to the decision in question.

[109] See French Law No. 2019-222 dated March 23, 2019 on the 2018–2022 program and the reform of justice, Art. 33.

[110] See https://rm.coe.int/charte-ethique-fr-pour-publication-4-decembre-2018/16808f699b.

[111] See, for example, the German Law Act of December 12, 2019, Gesetz zur Regelung der Wertgrenze für die Nichtzulassungsbeschwerde in Zivilsachen, zum Ausbau der Spezialisierung bei den Gerichten sowie zur Änderung weiterer zivilprozessrechtlicher Vorschriften [Law Act for the regulation of the threshold value for inadmissibility of civil complaints, for the expansion of specialization in the courts and the further amendment of civil procedural regulations], which enables the federal states (Länder) to focus certain disputes on courts beyond the level of a given Land (§13a GVG).

of certain disputes before a limited number of courts, proceedings, conventions, a multiplicity of modes of dispute resolution, and above all an increasing role for these, some being sometimes imposed on the parties. Flexibility is also derived from the concept of proportionality in the running of civil proceedings, particularly in respect of the extent of *discovery* in American law.

Flexibilization in respect of modes of dispute resolution: A pluralist provision

Such a pluralist provision is often presented as facilitating access to justice[112] and as a response to the excessive length of court proceedings[113] The postmodern tendency to see horizontal relations substitute the vertical model[114] notably embodied by state justice, leads toa (partial) transition from an imposed legal system to a negotiated one. But amicable settlement modes are at the core of economic issues:[115] increased growth due to the consumer and business confidence in the internal market[116] and in the resources available in the case of a dispute, but also the state's financial objectives (amicable modes of resolution,

---

[112] S. BARONA VILAR, "Die Mediation und das neue Konzept des *Access to Justice*: Vor- und Nachteile" ["Mediation and the New Concept of Access to Justice: Advantages and Disadvantages"] (2013) 18 *ZZPInt* 141 f.; C. ESPLUGUES MOTA, "Enforcement of Foreign Mediation Settlements in the European Union," (2013) 18 *ZZPInt* 223 f.

[113] For a sociological approach to the time taken for judicial proceedings, see B. BASTARD, D. DELVAUX, C. MOUHANNA, and F. SCHOENAERS, *Justice ou précipitation, L'accélération du temps dans les tribunaux* [*Justice or Precipitation: The Acceleration of Time in Courts*], PUR, Rennes 2016, p. 11. For a critical approach to amicable settlement modes, see Y. STRICKLER and L. WEILLER, "Développer la culture du règlement alternatif des différends" ["Developing the Culture of Alternative Dispute Resolution"], *Procédures* 2019, Étude 10, no 10 "les aspects positifs des modes amiables ne doivent pas gommer les excès qu'ils renferment et qui, déjà, se perçoivent en pratique"; "une justice qui n'est plus sereinement accessible aux personnes qui ne sont pas accoutumées à son vocabulaire technique ne mérite plus son nom" ["the positive aspects of amicable dispute resolution modes should not overshadow the excesses they encompass, and which can already be perceived in practice"; "justice that can no longer calmly be accessed by individuals who are not accustomed to its technical vocabulary is no longer worthy of the name"].

[114] M. MAFFESOLI, *Le temps des tribus* [*Tribal Times*], La table ronde, Paris 1988; M. MAFFESOLI, *Le réenchantement du monde, Une éthique pour notre temps* [*The Restoration of Enthusiasm in the World: An Ethic for Our Time*], Perrin., Paris 2009; M. MAFFESOLI, *Le temps revient, Formes élémentaires de la post-modernité* [*Time Returns: Elementary Forms of Post-modernity*], Descler de Brouwer, Paris 2010.

[115] See J. NIEVA-FENOLL, "Mediation and Arbitration: A Disappointing Hope" (2016) 2 *Rev. int. dr. processuel* 350 f.

[116] See also Art. 12 of the draft directive contained in the resolution of the European Parliament, July 4, 2017: "1. Member States shall ensure that at any stage of the proceedings and having regard to all the circumstances of the case, if the court is of the opinion that the dispute is suitable for a settlement, it may propose that the parties make use of mediation in order to settle or to explore a settlement of the dispute. 2. Paragraph 1 is without prejudice to the right of the parties who choose mediation to initiate judicial proceedings or arbitration in relation to that dispute before the expiry of limitation or prescription periods during the mediation process."

save "judge time").[117] However, some states do resist the facility succumbing to an angelic (or cynical!) vision of amicable resolution modes[118] and do not impose them as a preliminary stage.

Notably promoted by the EU, amicable resolution modes have seen an almost worldwide rise in popularity The new Quebec Code de procédure civile (Code of Civil Procedure), which came into force on January 1, 2016, sets out in its introductory notes that it "seeks to enable, in the public interest, the prevention and resolution of differences and disputes, by means of appropriate procedures, adopted in the spirit of justice and favoring the participation of individuals."[119] The Quebec Code devotes its Book VII to "private modes of prevention and settlement of differences",[120] but other provisions also place the amicable route at the heart of the dispute: the defendant may "propose mediation or an amicable settlement conference",[121] the purpose of which is "to assist the parties in communicating, with a view to understanding and assessing their needs, interests, and positions, and to explore solutions that may lead to a mutually satisfactory understanding in order to settle the dispute."[122] Articles 605–619 of Book VII deal with mediation. The new technology resources also tend to apply to mediation: thus, the family mediator may "with the agreement of the parties, make use of technology resources if the circumstances dictate and the resource is appropriate and readily available."[123] Online mediation or the use of other modern technologies certainly has a future. In EU law, the directive and regulation of May 21, 2013 on (online) alternative dispute resolution for consumer disputes and their transposition into national law are already testimony to this evolution.

---

[117] For Brazil and a comparative approach, see H. DALLA BERNARDINA DE PINHO and M. Pedrosa PAUMGARTEN, "The Challenges of Court Mediation from the Brazilian Perspective" (2015) 2 *Rev. int. dr. processuel* 301 and specifically 308: "Mediation has been captured in this scenario as the cure for the inefficiency of the systems of justice."

[118] See J. NIEVA-FENOLL, above n. 160, 360: "the final result can only be understood in black and white, viewing the judicial process as an institution of the dark ages, while mediation is seen as the path to illumination." See also R. CAPONI, "The Performance of the Italian Civil Justice System: An Empirical Assessment" (2016) 2(1) *Italian Law Journal* 30 ("ADR methods should not be seen as a remedy for the inefficiencies of the machinery of justice. The promotion of mediation should always be accompanied by efforts to improve the efficiency of public civil justice and not by attempts at limiting access to courts").

[119] "Vise à permettre, dans l'intérêt public, la prévention et le règlement des différends et des litiges, par des procédés adéquats, efficients, empreints d'esprit de justice et favorisant la participation des personnes."

[120] "Modes privés de prévention et de règlement des différends." The first heading deals with mediation and the second deals with arbitration.

[121] "Proposer une médiation ou une conférence de règlement à l'amiable." Art. 147 CPC québécois [Quebec].

[122] "D'aider les parties à communiquer en vue de mieux comprendre et évaluer leurs besoins, intérêts et positions et à explorer des solutions pouvant conduire à une entente mutuellement satisfaisante pour régler le litige." Ibid., Art. 162.

[123] "Avec l'accord des parties, recourir à l'utilization d'un moyen technologique si les circonstances le commandent et que le moyen est approprié et aisément disponible." Ibid., Art. 617, para. 2.

A certain appeal for compulsory mediation

French Law No. 2016-1547 dated November 18, 2016, referred to as J 21, provides in Article 4 that "on pain of inadmissibility, upon which the judge can rule as a matter of course, the application to the regional court by declaration to the court office must be preceded by an attempt at conciliation carried out by a judicial conciliator" except in three hypothetical cases.[124] Law No. 2019-223 dated March 23, 2019 on the 2018–2022 program and reform of justice[125] further reinforced this trend and imposes a preliminary conciliation, or mediation for disputes with a value of under €5,000, and also for neighborhood disputes,[126] subject to certain exceptions. Italy has also moved in this direction.[127]

Numerous examples can be given of obligations to attempt amicable resolution: in Russia[128] since 2017 for commercial cases without exception;[129] mediation in England, if both parties consider this acceptable, in the "small claim track" which applies in principle for disputes not exceeding £10,000 in value –. And in Belgium, a law of June 18, 2018,[130] which came into force

---

[124] "À peine d'irrecevabilité que le juge peut prononcer d'office, la saisine du tribunal d'instance par déclaration au greffe doit être précédée d'une tentative de conciliation menée par un conciliateur de justice." Loi de modernisation de la Justice du XXIème siècle/Law for the Modernization of Justice in the 21st Century, Art. 4.

[125] This law modifies Art. 4 of Law No. 2016-1547 dated November 18, 2016, as referred to above, which henceforth provides that "lorsque la demande tend au paiement d'une somme n'excédant pas un certain montant ou est relative à un conflit de voisinage, la saisine du tribunal de grande instance doit, à peine d'irrecevabilité que le juge peut prononcer d'office, être précédée, au choix des parties, d'une tentative de conciliation menée par un conciliateur de justice, d'une tentative de médiation ... ou d'une tentative de procédure participative" ["where the application involves payment of a sum not exceeding a certain amount, or relating to a neighborhood dispute, the application to a court of first instance must, on pain of inadmissibility, upon which the judge can rule as a matter of course, be preceded, at the choice of the parties, by a an attempt at conciliation carried out by a judicial conciliator, an attempt at mediation ... or an attempted participatory procedure"]. There are dispensations, particularly in the case of the non-availability of judicial conciliators within a reasonable time.

[126] Decree No. 2018-1333 dated December 11, 2019 reforming civil proceedings, and CPC [Code of Civil Procedure], new Art. 750-1.

[127] See M.A. Lupoi, "Facing the Crisis: New Italian Provisions to Keep Disputes out of the Courtroom (or Take Them out of it)" (2014) 19 *ZZPInt.* 95.

[128] See E. Fedorova (2017) 1 *Rev. int. dr. processuel* 196.

[129] Article 4 of the Russian Code of Commercial Proceedings. The applicant cannot bring proceedings before the commercial court until they have undertaken an attempt at amicable resolution – in other words, only 30 days after having submitted their application to their adversary and having sought to negotiate an amicable solution. If the applicant applies to the court, in violation of this prior obligation, the judge will reject the application. However, various exceptions are provided by law (insolvency, company law disputes, contestation of domestic arbitration decisions).

[130] The Law of June 18, 2018 introducing various provisions concerning civil law and provisions for the promotion of forms of alternative dispute resolution, available at etaamb.be/fr/loi-du-18-juin-2018_n2018012858.html.

on January 1, 2019, requires the following:[131] (1) that the lawyer informs the litigant of the option of mediation, conciliation, or any other mode of ADR – if they consider that an amicable resolution might be envisaged, they must seek as far as possible to encourage this;[132] and (2) the introduction of legal proceedings[133] should be preceded by an attempt to resolve the dispute by means of mediation or collaborative law, which is now regulated in the Belgian Judicial Code.[134] Various countries, such as Switzerland[135] and Japan,[136] have a long and continuous tradition of conciliation.

While some[137] maintain that compulsory prior mediation lacks legality, in that it undermines the right of access to justice and an effective judicial protection, the Court of Justice of the European Union[138] has found in relation

---

[131] For reasons of structural economic necessity and thus with the aim to reduce the number of cases brought before court.

[132] Art. 205 of June 18, 2018 "tendant à promouvoir les formes alternatives de résolution des litiges" (to promote alternative forms of dispute resolution) and thenceforth Art. 444 of the Code judiciaire [Judicial Code].

[133] See Art. 1724 of the Code judiciaire. The new rules apply to any dispute liable to be settled by a transaction, including those involving a public law legal entity.

[134] Ibid., Art. 1738. In addition, except in interim proceedings, the judge can ask the parties how they have tried to resolve the dispute on an amicable basis before bringing the case and inform them of further options remaining for the amicable resolution of the dispute. For this purpose, the judge can order the parties to appear in person (ibid., Art. 730/1).

[135] See U. HAAS and Z. BOZIC, "Das Schlichtungsverfahren nach der Schweizer ZPO im Spiegel der aktuellen Rechtsprechung" ["The Arbitration Procedure According to the Swiss ZPO (Code of Civil Procedure) as Reflected in Current Case Law"] (2015) 20 ZZPInt 249. See also Arts. 197 f. of the Code fédéral de procédure civile [Federal Civil Proceedings Code], which came into force on January 1, 2011. Many routes are available: (1) if an agreement is found, the conciliation authority records this in a report, which is then signed by the parties; the transaction, assent, or withdrawal of the action thus determined has the effect of a decision that has come into effect under Art. 208 of the Swiss CPC [Code of Public Proceedings]; (2) if no amicable agreement is found, the conciliation authority issues the authorization to proceed (in other words, to apply to the court) – the applicant must then bring their action within a period of three months, with effect from the issue of the authorization to proceed; (3) the conciliation authority may also subject the parties to a draft ruling (in certain specific fields or in all other property disputes whose property value does not exceed 5,000 Swiss francs – this draft ruling may contain a "brief exposition of grounds"; the draft ruling is considered to have been accepted and to have the effects of an enforceable decision if none of the parties opposes it within a period of 20 days with effect from the date when it was communicated in writing to the parties (Art. 211 Swiss CPC); and finally (4) if the dispute relates to property and does not exceed 2,000 Swiss francs, the conciliation authority may, upon application by the applicant, rule on the basis of a substantive examination (Art. 212 Swiss CPC). This rich palette makes the Swiss prior obligation of conciliation an extremely effective and practical tool, as it is both flexible and reliable (an absence of forms, its verbal emphasis, and confidentiality).

[136] See D. LEIPOLD and K. TANAKA, "Das japanische Zivilschlichtungsgesetz" ["The Japanese Civil Arbitration Act"] (2013) 18 ZZPInt 319.

[137] H. ROTH, "Gewissheitsverluste in der Lehre vom Prozesszweck?" ["A Loss of Certainty in the Teaching of the Purpose of Legal Process?"] [2017] ZfPW 142.

[138] Case C-75/16, Livio Menini and M.A. Rampanelli v. Banco Popolare, CJEU, June 14, 2017. See also Case C-317/08, Rosalba Alassini v. Telecom Italia, CJEU, March 18, 2010. On the same subject, see Momcilovic v. Croatia, req. n°11239/11, ECtHR, March 26, 2015.

to the Italian provisions that EU law is not opposed to the use of a mediation procedure as a condition of admissibility of the legal claim relating to consumer disputes, so long as the right of access to the judicial system is preserved; however, Directive 2013/11/EU does oppose national legislation requiring consumers to be assisted by a lawyer during mediation and which does not permit them to withdraw from a mediation procedure unless they can demonstrate a reasonable ground for doing so.

Amicable resolution modes are promoted in order to enable the dispute resolution system to be competitive and not too onerous for states, which thus regulate how to resolve a dispute at a proportionate cost.

Flexibility through proportionality

The key words of neoliberal policy in economics and justice are flexibility, adaptation, and reform. Thus, on October 1, 2015 a chamber was created in England with jurisdiction to hear particularly complex, high-value cases (at least £50 million) concerning financial markets. Two pilot procedural routes have also been tested, which are aimed at making disclosure, production of evidence, and other elements proportionate to the complexity of the case: (1) the Shorter Trials Scheme for cases where the hearing will probably last no more than four days (no pre-action protocol, reduced conclusions, concentration on the main questions, attestations of witnesses, written expert assessment, hearing from the expert being limited to only a few questions, disclosure and cross-examination strictly controlled, etc.), the central concept being to devote only such time and cost as is proportional to the size of the case; and (2) the Flexible Trials Scheme, a procedure that presupposes an agreement by the parties: in order for the judgment to be delivered as quickly as possible and at the lowest cost, the parties agree not to have the pre-trial hearings, to restrict the disclosure (production and communication) and written evidence, to avoid evidence being presented verbally, and to limit the scope of the final hearing.[139]

A similar trend can be found in the United States with a view to limiting the scope of the "discovery" in certain civil cases.[140] Three years ago, Rule 26 of the Federal Rules of Civil Procedure (FRCP) was modified, including part b), which is devoted to the scope and limitations of discovery. As an American author revealed,[141] recent reforms tend to "move proportionality to a more prominent position by making a feature of the basic scope of discovery." Thus, concerning the field of discovery, Rule 26(b)(1) sets out that:

> Parties may obtain discovery regarding any non-privileged matter that is relevant to any party's claim or defense and proportional to the needs of the case, considering the

---

[139]   N. ANDREWS, above n. 69.
[140]   R. MARCUS, "Procedural Polarization in America?" (2013) 18 *ZZPInt* 303 f.
[141]   R. MARCUS, "Modest Procedural Reform Advances in the U.S." (2015) 20 *ZZPInt* 291 and especially 293.

importance of the issues at stake in the action, the amount in controversy, the parties' relative access to relevant information, the parties' resources, the importance of the discovery in resolving the issues, and whether the burden or expense of the proposed discovery outweighs its likely benefit. Information within this scope of discovery need not be admissible in evidence to be discoverable.

Increasingly, parties need to convince the judge that a greater degree of discovery really will provide additional relevant information that will contribute to a solution to the proceedings.[142] This entails focusing discovery on that which is really necessary for resolving the dispute. The change in judicial culture has not been without its adverse effects; lawyers are reluctant to abandon their habits.[143] The reform will probably not stop there in the United States, where pilot projects have been proposed for civil actions: one of these (lasting three years)[144] called the Mandatory Initial Discovery Pilot Project began in May 2017 in a number of districts; the second, called the Expedited Procedures Pilot, seeks to encourage the rapid completion of cases preceded by an abbreviated discovery.[145] For the courts taking part in the project, the objective is to guarantee a maximum hearing lead time of 14 months in 90% of civil cases. The American judicial culture[146] is in the process of evolving toward greater proportionality.

4. THE ALTERNATIVE: ADAPT OR RESIST?

We find ourselves in a state of tension between two worlds, at a crossroads, and at the dawn of a new world. Such tensions are inevitable when paradigms change and when innovative technology opens up realms of the possible that had hitherto been unimaginable and hence often overlooked.

Following the end of the First World War, the French writer Paul Valéry wrote: "We civilizations now know that we are mortal."[147] To this disquieting assertion, Arnold Toynbee would have replied: "the end of a world is not the end of the world." This is true.

---

[142] Ibid.,p. 294.

[143] Ibid.,p. 298 f.

[144] In Arizona, involving a party from Illinois and one from Texas; see https://www.fjc.gov/content/321837/mandatory-initial-discovery-pilot-project-overview.

[145] For details, see R. MARCUS, above n. 142, 301. See also https://www.fjc.gov/content/320247/expedited-procedures-pilot-project-overview. The slogan here is "just speedy and inexpensive."

[146] On this subject, see R. MARCUS, "Misgivings about American Exceptionalism: Court Access as a Zero-Sum Game," University of California, Hastings College of Law, *Legal Studies Research Paper Series*, Research Paper No. 248, also published in A. UZELAC and C.H. VAN RHEE (eds.), *Revisiting Procedural Human Rights: Fundamentals of Civil Procedure and the Changing Face of Civil Justice*, Intersentia, Cambridge 2017.

[147] "Nous autres, civilisations, nous savons maintenant que nous sommes mortelles." P. VALÉRY, *La crise de l'esprit* [*The Crisis of the Spirit*] Manucius, Paris 1919, reprinted 2016.

However, in an article recently published in the French newspaper *Le Monde*, the historian Pierre Nora raised the following question:

> All digital technologies bring not only a new capitalist economy, reconfigured by a globalized context, but also a revolution which is this time more revolutionary than all those that have gone before, and leading to a different type of civilization.
>
> Does this involve simple tools at the service of human intelligence? Or do these technologies manufacture for us another way of living and even a different kind of human, a transhumanist universe?[148]

Are we also entering the age of surveillance capitalism?[149] Progress has never been so ambivalent in terms of its effects on human beings and on society; this is no longer in effect the progress in which Kant[150] incited us to believe. And at the same time, the fear of being "in a perpetual state of backwardness compared to the advance of the world in permanent evolution"[151] prevents any vague impulse to disconnect from the movement of eternal and endless adaptation. It seems that one should not depart from the "direction" – the course that has been set.

We know very well that new AI and digital technologies tend to move away from the rules of "fair competition," which seeks to put in place a neoliberal society, and give way to a "ultraliberal project of predatory capitalism."[152] The rules of the game need to be constantly adapted to the inventiveness of technology, which cares little for the human element, or major, fundamental

---

[148]   "Toutes les technologies numériques sont porteuses non seulement d'une économie capitaliste nouvelle, reconfigurée par un contexte mondialisé, mais d'une révolution cette fois plus révolutionnaire que toutes les précédentes et débouchant sur un autre type de civilisation. S'agit-il de simples outils au service de l'intelligence humaine ? Ou nous fabriquent-elles, ces technologies, une autre manière de vivre et même un autre homme, un univers transhumaniste?" Article published in *Le Monde*, March 11, 2019; see www.lemonde.fr/economie/article/2019/03/11/pierre-nora-la-fin-d-un-monde-n-est-pas-la-fin-du-monde_5434275_3234.html.

[149]   See S. Zuboff, *The Age of Capitalism Surveillance*, Public Affairs, New York 2019.

[150]   See I. Kant, "Über den Gemeinspruch: 'Das mag in der Theorie richtig sein, taugt aber nicht für die Praxis'" ["On the Common Saying: 'That May Be True in Theory, But it is of No Use in Practice'"] in H. Reiss (ed.) and H. Nisbet (trans.), *Kant: Political Writings*, Cambridge University Press, Cambridge 1989, p. 89: "Besides, various evidence suggests that, in our age, as compared with all previous age, the human race has made considerable moral progress, and short-lived hindrances prove nothing to the contrary. Moreover, it can be shown that the outcry about man's continually increasing decadence arises for the very reason that we can see further ahead, because we have reached a higher level of morality. We thus pass more severe judgements on what we are, comparing it with what we ought to be, so that our self-reproach increases in proportion to the number of stages of morality we have advanced through during the whole of known history." See also A. Philonenko, "L'idée de progrès chez Kant" ["The Idea of Progress in Kant"] (1974) 79(4) *Revue de Métaphysique et de Morale* 433 f.

[151]   "En perpétuel retard sur une marche du monde en permanente evolution." B. Stiegler, above n. 12.

[152]   "Projet ultralibéral de capitalisme prédateur." Ibid.

principles and ethics. Transhumanism raises the same questions: following an initial phase where technology takes possession of society – thus removing policy in favor of scientific management, it may, in a subsequent phase, take possession of the human being, who will no longer be a social being, but a human enclosed in and by technology.

"To avoid sleepwalking, let us be vigilant."[153] This means that we must be mindful to ensure that the technical breakthrough taking place includes individuals and litigants in the pursuit of justice, in the same way that populations should also be included in globalization. Technical advances should not be at the cost of the right of access to a judge, to fundamental rights within a procedure, to equity, and, quite simply, to justice.

As one must strive against "democracy fatigue"[154] by ideologically and politically rearming the individual citizen, it is now essential that we should combat the threat to major, fundamental principles of procedure, and that we ensure that technological advancement is not a moment of irremediable rupture. The individual seeking justice, the human must remain at the heart of the justice system – or be put back there once more in their rightful place.

---

[153] "Pour ne pas être des somnambules, soyons des sentinelles." Jean-Hervé LORENZI, Chairman of the Cercle des économistes.

[154] "Fatigue des démocraties." P. ROSENVALLON, cited by F. FRESSOZ, *Le Monde*, March 12, 2019, supplément Cercle des économistes, p. 3.

TECHNOLOGY, THE GLOBAL ECONOMY AND NEW CONCEPTS IN CIVIL PROCEDURE

Margaret Woo*

1. From Consent to Click 46
2. From Service of Process to Electronic Notice 50
3. From Physical Presence to Virtual Presence 52

More than ten years ago, at the 2010 International Association of Procedural Law (IAPL) conference, the focus was on technology and adapting systems of civil procedure to electronic technology (hereinafter "e-technology"). The most recent IAPL Congress, the 16th World Congress for the IAPL, held in Kobe, Japan, asks us to think about "Challenges for Civil Justice as We Move Beyond Globalization and Technological Changes." I posit here that "moving beyond" would require us to focus on the fundamental ways in which globalization and technology have changed civil justice. Perhaps unsurprisingly, globalization and technology have impacted civil procedure in invidious and fundamental ways.

The global economy produces disputes spanning national borders, and e-technology spurs such transactions. We are now seeing technology not only in ways that shape how litigation is conducted, but also in how civil justice is delivered. Ten years ago, the issue was electronic filings, e-discovery, video-conferencing and proceedings on the Web.[1] The concern was on how technology can aid procedure, increase access to courts, and the development of "social electronic justice" rules. Today, the issues are perhaps more fundamental.

What I would like to focus on here is the more invasive effects of e-technology on civil procedure. Not only is technology changing *how* we process disputes, but

---

*   Professor of Law & Dean of Research and Interdisciplinary Education, Northeastern University School of Law, Boston, M.A., United States. The author would like to thank Professors Rick Marcus, Oscar Chase, and Lucy Williams for their thoughtful reading of and comments on this chapter.

[1]   See, for example, R. MARCUS, "Only Yesterday: Rulemaking Responses to E-Discovery or "Looking Backward to 1938" (2014) 162 *University of Pennsylvania Law Review* 1671.

Intersentia

it has also changed our views of *what* process is due. I argue that technology has also changed some fundamental legal concepts in civil procedure, specifically, American civil procedure. Through the technology lens and the global economy filter, we see how the notion of "consent" has been stretched; "notice" and ideas of "presence" have been modified, and judgments have been replaced by algorithms. If due process is fundamentally notice and the opportunity to be heard, with a decision rendered by an impartial decision maker, then notions of due process itself may have been altered. Lessons drawn from the U.S. context will have resonance in other countries too.

Moving away from the concept of physicality, electronic presence and digital consent have shifted our barometers of notice and opportunity to be heard. And human decision makers may be replaced by artificial intelligence. Protection of the due process rights of the individual may be taking a second seat to sovereignty. Private "agreements" have taken over the public function of adjudication. At the time of writing, the COVID-19 pandemic has rendered courts physically inaccessible and has pushed many hearings online.[2] Spurred by this global emergency, e-technology offers tempting options more than ever, but we need to cognizant of its pervasive effects even as we grasp at its potential.

1. FROM CONSENT TO CLICK

Dispute resolution has both a private and a public function. It settles disagreements between private individuals, but it also represents public authority and power when the dispute is brought to the attention of governmental judicial systems. As such, consent in civil procedure has always carried within it the potential for the private usurpation of the public regime. Individual consent challenges the "publicness" of adjudication by dissolving the dispute to its private nature. Resolution is taken out of the public eye as private agreements decide when, where, and how the dispute is to be resolved. In recent years, what constitutes consent has expanded exponentially with technology and the click consent, and, in the process, has subverted the "publicness" of adjudication.

---

[2] For example, for the first time, the highest court in the United States will open a live audio feed as it hears arguments in ten sets of cases. A. LIPTAK, "The Supreme Court Will Hear Oral Arguments on Line, the Public Can Listen in" *New York Times*, April 13, 2020, https://www.nytimes.com/2020/04/13/us/politics/supreme-court-phone-arguments-virus.html; J. FORTIN, "When Courts Move Online, Does Dress Code Still Matter?" *New York Times*, April 15, 2020, https://www.nytimes.com/2020/04/15/us/coronavirus-lawyers-court-telecommute-dress-code.html.

Generally speaking, consent means "to give assent or approval" or "to agree."[3] Consent is not only the cornerstone of contract law, but in the American democratic context, it also forms the basis of our governance as "the social contract" between individuals and the government. As such, consent can be the justification for the waiving of fundamental individual rights. In the context of U.S. civil procedure, where "consent" is found, courts have not hesitated to uphold arbitration clauses, waiver of collective actions, agreement to jurisdiction, forum selection clauses, and choice of law. These contract clauses are often boilerplate terms, but nevertheless are consistently upheld in written contracts so long as there is some kind of "consent" identified on the part of the consumer. Today, these terms may not only be found in written contracts, but are also widespread in any number of global commercial websites and in any one of the numerous digitally mediated businesses. The pervasiveness of these terms as enabled by the internet, the impossibility of negotiating with a computer, and the ease with which one can quickly "click" without knowledge work together to result in these consents failing to provide "due notice."[4]

Today's consent is often invoked by a single click, but does the act of clicking really count as consent? Should one affirmative push of the finger eliminate an individual's rights altogether – to jurisdiction, to choice of law, to having a case heard by a judicial court, and to bring collective action? Do we really actually read our "consent"? Studies have shown that consumers largely do not read boilerplate contracts.[5] Worse still, many non-legal consumers may not even truly know or understand the waiver of such rights as fundamental as the right to forum selection, choice of law, or trial. And in the online context, these "clicks" are also often the precursor to our entry to a number of services over which we have no meaningful choice or ability to exit.

American courts have distinguished between two primary types of internet contracts – browsewrap and clickwrap – but come out almost unanimously in favor of upholding both when they can find notice or constructive notice.[6]

---

[3]   "Consent," *Merriam Webster Dictionary*, https://www.merriam-webster.com/dictionary/consent. Indeed, the often litigated contractual defenses of fraud, misrepresentation, duress, undue influence, and lack of capacity are all premised on invalid consent, but consent itself lacks a solid definition. See O. GAN, "The Many Faces of Contractual Consent" (2017) 65 *Drake Law Review* 619. "Consent is the moral component that distinguishes valid from invalid transfers of alienable rights." R. BARNETT, "A Consent Theory of Contract" (1986) 86 *Columbia Law Review* 269.

[4]   Y. BAKOS, F. MAROTTA-WURGLER, and D. TROSSEN, "Does Anyone Read the Fine Print? Consumer Attention to Standard-Form Contracts" (2014) 43 *Journal of Legal Studies* 1.

[5]   See ibid. (noting that only one or two out of every 1,000 retail software shoppers access the license agreement, and most who do access it do not actually read it).

[6]   "Even when there is no signature, such as when we click 'I agree' online, courts are likely to find that a contract has been formed unless there is some other reason for invalidating the terms." M.J. RADIN, "Reconsidering Boilerplate: Confronting Normative and Democratic Degradation" (2012) 40(3) *Capital University Law Review* 617, 620.

The more pervasive clickwrap contracts require website users to click an "I agree" box after "being presented with the terms and conditions."[7] In a clickwrap situation, no signature is required, just a single click. Clickwrap agreements have routinely been upheld, without much backlash, by U.S. courts over the last 15 years.[8]

A common example of a court upholding a clickwrap agreement occurred in *Novak v. Overture Services, Inc.* In this case, an individual challenged a forum selection clause contained in the terms and conditions of a website.[9] Prior to completing the registration process, the individual was required to click a button indicating acceptance of the terms and conditions. The court found that by clicking the "I accept" icon, the plaintiff agreed to be bound by the forum selection clause contained therein.[10] To stretch the notion of clickwrap consent a bit further, one Californian court found the existence of consent even where a website's End User License Agreement and Terms of Sale were presented during the summary page of the checkout process and in a hyperlink, and even where agreement to the End User License was blended with agreement to the purchase. The court found that the plaintiff had affirmatively agreed to the arbitration clause in question by clicking a button stating both "Agree and Place the Order."[11]

In browsewrap contracts, the terms are located on an interior webpage and the user does not affirmatively click a link to accept the terms. There is no outward manifestation of assent to the terms; rather, a user "consents" simply by using the website.[12] Even then, up to this point, U.S. courts have held that a browsewrap agreement is valid if the user has actual or constructive knowledge of the applicable terms.[13] Constructive notice is defined as when the recipient

---

[7]   Ibid. "A click-wrap license presents the user with a message on his or her computer screen, requiring that the user manifest his or her assent to the terms of the license agreement by clicking on an icon." *Specht v. Netscape Communications Corp.*, 150 F. Supp. 2d 585, 593–94 (S.D.N.Y. 2001).

[8]   See *Burcham v. Expedia, Inc.*, 2009 WL 586513, at *2–3; *Register.com, Inc. v. Verio, Inc.*, 356 F.3d 393, 401–04 (2d Cir. 2004).

[9]   *Novak v. Overture Servs., Inc.*, 309 F. Supp. 2d 446, 451 (E.D.N.Y. 2014).

[10]   Ibid.; see also *Forrest v. Verizon Communications. Inc.*, 805 A.2d 1007 (D.C. App. Ct. 2002) (finding that the plaintiff entered into a binding contract with Verizon by clicking an "Accept" icon indicating his assent, where the plaintiff "presumably" read the agreement in the scroll box, since the "Accept" button was located below the scroll box).

[11]   *Nathan v. Symantec Corp.*, 2018 WL 7201833 (Cal. Sup. Ct. May 11, 2018). This court coined the terms of sale at issue in this case as "sign-in wrap agreements," whereby a user signs up to use an internet service and it is at the sign up screen – before the user is able to use the product – that the user accepts the separate agreement. Ibid. at 2.

[12]   *Nguyen v. Barnes & Noble, Inc.*, 763 F.3d 1171, 1175–76 (9th Cir. 2014). In other words, a "browsewrap agreement usually involves a disclaimer that by visiting the website – something that the user has already done – the user agrees to the Terms of Use not listed on the site itself but available only by clicking a hyperlink." *Fteja v. Facebook, Inc.*, 841 F. Supp. 2d 829, 837 (S.D.N.Y. 2012).

[13]   *U.S. v. Drew*, 259 F.R.D. 449, 462 n. 22 (C.D Cal. 2009).

was "not aware that there were terms and did not see them, but somehow could have or should have done so."[14] This is a fact-specific inquiry of the particular website – for example, was the term of use hidden in a hyperlink or was it more visibly displayed on the sign-up screen?[15] While courts have been reluctant to enforce browsewrap agreements against individual consumers,[16] they have nevertheless found *constructive* assent in cases involving commercial users and where the browsewrap agreements resemble clickwrap agreements.[17]

But the question of course is whether an individual can "validly be said to agree to have his or her freedom of choice engaged by the mere fact that a list of terms exists somewhere in his or her physical vicinity."[18] The basis of contract law is the idea of free exchanges between willing parties.[19] The gold standard for consent is one between parties of equal bargaining power, and one that is given voluntarily and knowingly. Almost all countries, including the European Union, use an analogous standard to require consent that is "freely given, specific, informed," and voluntary. Scholars such as Neil Richards and Woodrow Hartzog have argued that this ideal can only exist under certain circumstances – that is, consent is or should be valid only when "we are asked to choose *infrequently*, when the potential harms that result from the consent are *easy to imagine*, and when we have the correct *incentives to consent* consciously and seriously."[20] This version of consent is sorely lacking in many of the "click" consent webpages.

The courts have also essentially been chipping away at the notions of "exchange" and "willing parties" over the years. The sheer prevalence of boilerplate electronic contracts in our modern-day economy has set a precedent in which consent itself has been replaced by a take-it-or-leave-it regime. Where parties once bargained for and were, at a minimum, knowledgeable of such exchanges, today's technological advancements have made it such that parties

---

[14] M.J. Radin, "The Deformation of Contract in the Information Society" (2017) 37(3) *Oxford Journal of Legal Studies*, 505, 522.

[15] See, e.g., *In re Zappos.com*, 893 F. Supp. 2d 1058, 1064 (D. Nev. 2012) (finding that where the terms of use are buried in the middle to bottom of every webpage among other links, the user did not consent to terms of use).

[16] Ibid. (holding that where "a website makes its terms of use available via a hyperlink on every page of the website but otherwise provides no notice to users nor prompts them to take any affirmative action to demonstrate assent, even close proximity of the hyperlink to relevant buttons users must click on – without more – is insufficient to give rise to constructive notice").

[17] *Nguyen*, above n. 12, at 1176.

[18] M.J. Radin, "From Baby-Selling to Boilerplate: Reflections on the Limits of the Infrastructure of the Market" (2017) 54 *Osgood Hall Law Journal* 339.

[19] See *Restatement (Second) of Contracts* §18 (1981) ("Manifestation of mutual assent to an exchange requires that each party either make a promise or begin or render a performance").

[20] N. Richards and W. Hartzog, "The Pathologies of Digital Consent" (2019) 96 *Washington University Law Review* 1461, 1465, https://papers.ssrn.com/sol3/papers.cfm?abstract_id= 3370433.

may not even be aware when they give their "consent" and thus enter into a contract. It is precisely this notion of constructive notice which devolves to "as-if" or "hypothetical" consent.[21] Arguably, the danger, if we are not there already, is that of eliminating the notion of consent entirely. "Both in the world of paper contracts and in the world where contracts are only 'virtual,' contract law is seemingly moving inexorably toward a state in which neither the presence nor the absence of actual consent has any real significance."[22] This in turn has ramifications in the context of civil procedure rules.

In sum, the days of bargained-for exchanges and mutual assent are long gone, with the very values defining the parameters of contract law being stretched in ways that twentieth-century scholars could not have imagined. The objective theory of consent is no longer what it once was. It has been distorted and stretched. It includes a "click," which somehow amounts to acceptance in the digital age. No longer is a meeting of the minds required; rather, autonomous consent is measured by a click of the mouse. Through a simple click, we can waive our right to a day in court, consent to a foreign forum, and agree to private dispute resolution rather than conflict resolution through the judicial system.

2. FROM SERVICE OF PROCESS TO ELECTRONIC NOTICE

In the "notice" area, there has also been a slow shift from actual notice provided by the physical service of process to mail service to constructive notice through publication. In *Mullane v. Hanover Bank & Trust Co.*, the U.S. Supreme Court defined constitutionally sufficient notice as "reasonably calculated under all the circumstances, to apprise interested parties of the action and give them an opportunity to object."[23] In most instances, the "means reasonably calculated" would entail a marshal, a professional process server or any person at least 18 years of age and who is not a party walking up to the defendant – or up to the defendant's house or into a corporate defendant's registered address – and handing him/her/it an envelope of documents. But "reasonably calculated" under *Mullane* can also include serving someone by mail or by publication and, in more recent years, by email as a last resort.

While American courts remain reluctant to adopt electronic service of process and complaint as a general matter for civil cases,[24] inroads have been

---

[21]   M.J. RADIN, above n. 6, at 627.
[22]   C. KNAPP, "Contract Walks the Plank: *Carnival Cruise Lines, Inc. v. Shute*" (2012) 12 *Nevada Law Journal* 553, 562.
[23]   *Mullane v. Hanover Bank & Trust Co.*, 339 U.S. 305 (1950).
[24]   Federal Civil Procedure Rule 4 provides for a written waiver of in-hand service of process and acceptance of mail service, but makes no mention of electronic service.

made. Electronic service has been allowed if no other means were possible. Thus, in *Rio Props., Inc. v. Rio International Interlink*, the 9th Circuit Court of Appeals authorized the use of email to serve an international online company that listed only an email address on its website.[25] Following this decision, other courts have set the general standard that service via email could be authorized if other methods of service had proven unsuccessful. New technology – especially the internet – has indeed reshaped the legal system's view of what constitutes best practicable notice and "reasonably calculated."

E-notice has also been proposed in specified circumstances. For example, recent proposals to amend Federal Civil Procedure Supplemental Rule 3, which deals with social security appeals to the federal courts, proposed allowing a notice of electronic filing rather than a service and complaint: "The court must notify the Commissioner of the commencement of the action by transmitting a Notice of Electronic Filing to the appropriate office within the Social Security district."[26] This proposal reflects the fact that social security appeals are more akin to appeals, which are decided on a review of the administrative record, as distinct from ordinary civil actions. If adopted, this amendment would have made inroads for electronic notice as social security appeals average between 17,000 and 18,000 annually, accounting for 7–8 percent of the federal civil docket.

The class action, due perhaps to its size, provides the other special case to a more receptive view of electronic methods.[27] American courts in class actions have found e-technology to be a reliable substitute[28] for notice to potential class plaintiffs, and some scholars urge the use of electronic notice in these circumstances.[29] And so, some courts have embraced technological advances

---

[25]   *Rio Props., Inc. v. Rio International Interlink*, 284 F.3d 1007, 1018 (9th Cir. 2002).

[26]   Advisory Committee of the Civil Rules, *Civil Rules Agenda Book April 2020*, https://www.uscourts.gov/sites/default/files/04-2020_civil_rules_agenda_book.pdf.

[27]   December 1, 2018 amendments to the FRCP (Rules 23, 5, 62, 65.1). Rule 23(c)(2)(B) expands notice of a proposed settlement to include electronic or "other appropriate" means. The Advisory Committee Note recognizes that "first class mail may often be the preferred primary method of giving notice," but acknowledges the reality that the courts and practitioners have already started to use new technologies to make notice more effective.

[28]   P. FLING, "Civil Procedure: Notifying Justice: 'Reasonable Actual Notice' in Service of Process – *DeCook v. Olmsted Medical Center, Inc.*" [2017] *Mitchell Hamline Law Review* 181; *Anthony v. Small Tube Mfg. Corp.*, 484 Fed. Appx. 704 (3d Cir. 2012) (attorney who registers through ECF (electronic case filing system) in the federal district court of Pennsylvania consents to be served court documents via ECF); *McMillian v. District of Columbia*, 233 F.R.D. 179, 181, fn. 4 (D.D.C. 2005) (local rules mandate that parties consent to electronic service when they sign up for the electronic case filing system); *DeCook v. Olmsted Medical Ctr., Inc.*, 875 N.W. 2d 263 (Minn. 2016) (the court held that alternative methods of service through an agent (i.e. email) are sufficient if consented to by the defendant (at 271–72)).

[29]   C. BARTHOMEW, "E-Notice" (2018) 68 *Duke Law Journal* 217, https://scholarship.law.duke.edu/dlj/vol68/iss2/1.

such as email notice and settlement website notice,[30] while other courts still treat physical mail notice as essential to class certification.[31] Within e-notice, different courts have approved/disapproved the use of text messages for class action notice,[32] and the use of social media such as Twitter, but not Facebook, as a basis for notification of potential class members' right to opt into the litigation when such members' mail or email addresses were unknown.[33]

Finally, while reluctant to move to electronic service of the summons and complaint to a defendant as a general matter, some movement has been made to recognize electronic service of other documents after the commencement of the lawsuit. The most recent amendment to Federal Rule 5 deletes even the requirement of written consent if service is made on a registered user through the court's electronic filing system. However, written consent is still required when service is made by electronic means outside the court's system.

3. FROM PHYSICAL PRESENCE TO VIRTUAL PRESENCE

Personal jurisdiction relies on the "twin pillars of state sovereignty and due process."[34] The underlying ideology of personal jurisdiction is that a state has the right to exercise its sovereign power only over a defendant and property within the forum's borders.[35] But such assertions are limited by the Due Process clause of the U.S. Constitution, which confines a state's adjudicative authority to non-residents whose affiliation and contacts with the state suggests their implicit agreement to the state's exercise of jurisdiction over them.[36]

---

[30] See, e.g., *In re LinkedIn User Privacy Litig.*, 309 F.R.D. 573, 586 (N.D. Cal. 2015) (using email and settlement website notice); *Chimeno-Buzzi v. Hollister, Co.*, No. 14-23120-CV, 2015 WL 9269266, at * 3 (S.D. Fla. December 18, 2015) (approving a plan that would include "an E-mail Notice, a Double Post Card Notice, a Publication Notice, and Banner Advertisements"); *In re HP Inkjet Printer Litig.*, No. C05-3580 JF, 2010 WL 11488941, at * 3 (N.D. Cal. October 1, 2010) (approving notice through email, publication, and a settlement website).

[31] See, e.g., *Marcus v. BMW of North America, LLC*, 687 F.3d 583, 592–93 (3d Cir. 2012) (denying certification in part because of obstacles to individualized notice).

[32] See *Jermyn v. Best Buy Stores, L.P.*, No. 08 Civ. 00214 (CM), 2010 WL 5187746 (S.D.N.Y. December 6, 2010) (denying notice plan that included Twitter, text messages, and email alerts); *In re AT&T Mobility Wireless Data Services Sales Tax Litig.*, 789 F. Supp. 2d 935 (N.D. Ill. 2011) (finding notice adequate where the defendant sent notice by text message, along with other methods).

[33] *Mark et al. v. Gawker Media LLC et al.*, (S.D.N.Y 2015). In a class action in New York brought by former interns of Conde Nast Publications, the judge allowed the claims administrator to contact possible class members with "InMail" message on LinkedIn.

[34] D. CITRON, "Minimum Contacts in a Borderless World: Voice Over Internet Protocol and the Coming Implosion of Personal Jurisdiction Theory" (2006) 39 *University of California Davis Law Review* 1481.

[35] See ibid. at 1504.

[36] L. BRILMAYER, "Consent, Contract, and Territory" (1989) 74 *Minnesota Law Review* 1, 27.

Geographic borders historically mark the boundaries of a state's assertion of jurisdiction. Traditionally, jurisdiction was based on a defendant's physical presence within a state. Later on, it was extended to a defendant's "minimum contacts with the state where the lawsuit is brought such that notions of fair play and substantial justice is not offended."[37] Previously, physical presence was required for a state to exercise its sovereign power over a non-resident, but this requirement has largely been supplanted by an inquiry into a non-resident defendant's contacts with the forum.

The stated purposes of the U.S. *minimum contacts* requirement is twofold: to "insulat[e] the defendant from the burden of litigating in an inconvenient forum *and* provid[e] a check on state power by ensuring that the State does not reach beyond the limits imposed on it by a federal system of government."[38] And so, the standard inquiry for the past 50 or so years in case-specific assertions of personal jurisdiction has been to focus on the defendant's contacts with the forum state *and* to ask whether the assertion of specific jurisdiction is fair in these instances (which includes considerations of the forum state's interest and interstate efficiency).[39]

But the inquiry of "minimum contacts" seems to fall flat in the digital age where technological advances render "virtual presence" essentially global. Indeed, global economy and technology challenge prior conceptions of territoriality and accompanying jurisdictional rules. The law of personal jurisdiction defined by the internet may run the risk of either an overly expansive state sovereignty in finding jurisdiction everywhere or minimal sovereignty in failing to capture a non-resident's virtual presence within the state's borders, or, alternatively, reduce personal jurisdiction jurisprudence to simply a matter of virtual consents.[40]

Today's interstate communication lacks "geographic markers,"[41] raising significant personal jurisdiction challenges where commerce is governed by

---

[37]   Under *International Shoe* and its progeny, personal jurisdiction only exists if the defendant has "certain minimum contacts" with the forum state such that "maintenance of the suit does not offend traditional notions of fair play and substantial justice." *International Shoe v. State of Washington*, 326 U.S. 310, 316 (1945). The courts continued to expand the notion of minimum contacts to include products placed in the stream of commerce (*Asahi Metal Indus. Co. v. Superior Court*, 480 U.S. 102, 104 (1987)) as well as acts "expressly aimed" at certain states, among others (*Calder v. Jones*, 465 U.S. 783, 789–90 (1984)).

[38]   P. MEHROTA, "Back to the Basics: Why Traditional Principles of Personal Jurisdiction are Effective Today and Why Zippo Needs to Go" [2010] *University of North Carolina Journal of Law and Technology*, 229, 232.

[39]   Case-specific personal jurisdiction is distinct from general jurisdiction under which a state can assert power over out-of-state persons and things on any claims (whether such claims are related to in-state contacts) solely because such persons have such substantial contacts with the state as to essentially render such a person to be "at home" within the state. *Goodyear Dunlop Tires Operations, S.A. v. Brown*, 565 U.S. 915 (2011).

[40]   D. CITRON, above n. 34, at 1486.

[41]   Ibid. at 1481.

technology without boundaries. Courts have agreed that minimum contacts can arise out of internet use directed at a particular forum, but what happens when a defendant does not know that his/her internet activity has even reached the foreign forum, or when a defendant knows but that his/her internet activity has reached every forum, as is sometimes the case with technology?

These questions continue to arise in the current digital age, forcing the courts to resolve this tension and redefine the already-expanded concept of personal jurisdiction. The U.S. Supreme Court was presented with an opportunity to rule on the issue of "virtual presence" and internet use in *Walden v. Fiore*, but specifically declined to do so.[42] Instead, the Court noted that "this case does not present the very different questions whether and how a defendant's virtual 'presence' and conduct translate into 'contacts' within a particular State ... We leave questions about virtual contacts for another day."[43]

In a first attempt to bring uniformity to internet commercial cases, the lower court in *Zippo Manufacturing Co. v. Zippo Dot Com, Inc.* instituted a "sliding scale" test for jurisdiction based on internet activity, and a distinction was made over an active/interactive website versus a passive website, where the former activity would give rise to jurisdiction in the forum, while the latter would not.[44] Meanwhile, other courts have struggled with this question, often ending up with a preference for a focus on the defendant's intent in targeting the forum state rather than the "fortuity" of a plaintiff's action in accessing the website or opening his/her email in the forum state.

In *Advanced Tactical Ordnance Systems LLC v. Real Action Paintball, Inc.*,[45] Advanced Tactical sought to bring Real Action within the state of Indiana's jurisdiction based solely on internet activity.[46] The Seventh Circuit held that the following individual acts – sales of product to purchasers in Indiana, Real Action's knowledge that Advanced Tactical was an Indiana company, and Real Action's sending of two emails to a list of subscribers that included Indiana residents – did not establish minimum contacts.[47] According to the court, "the connection between the place where an email is opened and a lawsuit

---

[42] *Walden v. Fiore*, 134 S. Ct. 1115, 1119 (2014).
[43] Ibid. at 1125.
[44] The first court to apply the minimum contacts test to internet usage occurred in *Zippo Manufacturing Co. v. Zippo Dot Com, Inc.*, which involved trademark infringement claims brought by a lighter manufacturer located in Pennsylvania and derived from the registration of various websites by a California website publisher. *Zippo Manufacturing Co. v. Zippo Dot Com, Inc.*, 952 F. Supp. 1119, 1121 (W.D. Pa. 1997).
[45] *Advanced Tactical Ordnance Systems, LLC v. Real Action Paintball, Inc.*, 751 F.3d 796 (7th Cir. 2014).
[46] Ibid. at 799.
[47] Ibid. at 803: "The connection between the place where an email is opened and a lawsuit is entirely fortuitous ... It may be different if there were evidence that a defendant in some way targeted residents of a specified state, perhaps through geographically-restricted online ads."

is entirely fortuitous ... It may be different if there were evidence that a defendant in some way targeted residents of a specific state, perhaps through geographically-restricted online ads."[48]

In many ways, then, the jurisprudence relating to personal jurisdiction based on internet activities mirrors the intentional torts requirement that a defendant's conduct be "expressly aimed" at the forum state before personal jurisdiction is found. But the "express aiming" requirement for an intentional tort is ineffectual in an internet context and potentially renders a defendant immune to specific jurisdiction when that defendant engages in conduct broadly via today's borderless communications. In other words, how does the concept of "minimum contacts" apply to the sending and receiving of emails, online business transactions, and even internet posts when, often, internet users do not even know how far their usage reaches?

Indeed, personal jurisdiction and the theory of minimum contacts have been complicated by the fact that transactions conducted over the internet do not always have clear boundaries. This has left American courts having to attempt to fit a square peg into a round hole. And so, the more global and diffuse a defendant's internet activity is, the more the defendant may be immune from specific jurisdiction. However, some scholars have suggested, if a defendant is technologically sophisticated and such internet activity is continuous in reaching the forum state, then such pervasive internet activities (even if diffuse and without expressly aiming to do so) should nevertheless subject the defendant to suits in the forum state.[49]

Given the existing ambiguity, companies have sought control and clarity by incorporating a clickwrap agreement into a website,[50] and thereby substituting the so-called private consent for the public factors traditionally considered by the court in deciding whether jurisdiction exists.[51] As pointed out above, these click consents are arguably entered into with full information and freely given. Furthermore, consent is about making choices, but "the fairness of holding an individual to a choice made, however, depends on the legitimacy of limiting him or her to particular set of choices."[52] Yet, given the uncertainty of "minimum contacts" in the context of internet activities, courts have privileged consent and implied contract over sovereignty and fairness concerns.[53]

---

[48]   Ibid. at 803.

[49]   A. KREVEN, "Minimum Virtual Contacts: A Framework for Specific Jurisdiction in Cyperspace" (2018) 118 *Michigan Law Review* 782.

[50]   S. BREIDENBACH, "Click Here to Limit Personal Jurisdiction," (2019) 44 (2) *Litigation News, ABA Section of Litigation*, 2.

[51]   See *Brown v. Web.com Group Inc.*, 57 F. Supp. 3d 345 (S.D.N.Y. 2014), in which the New York court found personal jurisdiction based on the fact that Florida defendant had transacted business exclusiveness through its website and 7.5% of its customers resided in New York, but nevertheless dismissed on improper venue due to the validity of the defendant's clickwrap agreement.

[52]   L. BRILMAYER, above n. 36, at 3.

[53]   D. CITRON, above n. 34, at 1486.

Tracing the trajectory of personal jurisdiction in the United States, it is possible to see just how far things have progressed from *Pennoyer v. Neff*, one of the earliest cases holding that a defendant's physical presence in the forum was required before jurisdiction was found, to *International Shoe v. State of Washington*, with the more flexible standard of "minimum contacts," and finally, to *Calder v. Jones*, where jurisdiction was found if the defendant's actions were expressly aimed at a forum, even if the defendant was physically outside the state. Today's question, of course, is whether a defendant's substantial virtual internet presence everywhere without the element of intent is sufficient for case-specific jurisdiction.

The very requirements of personal jurisdiction are meant to protect a non-resident defendant from being haled into a foreign court. Physical presence has been replaced by intended presence, directing communications at a particular forum.[54] But even the intent behind one's actions is no longer readily apparent in the digital age, for through emails, online shopping, and the like, non-residents no longer have any control over their contacts with a foreign state. Further, technology advances such as VOIP calls removes geographic markets from all of our communications, and defendants can no longer be said to direct their communications at a particular fora.

And so, we are left with a Hobbesian choice. If this intended presence concept continues to be diluted – stretched further and further by each and every technological advancement – then the very due process concerns that gave rise to *Pennoyer*'s physical presence requirement in the first place will be thrown out the window. The state could either have expansive sovereign power over the defendant based on the defendant's internet presence everywhere, (limited only by the public considerations in the "fairness" factors of the minimum contacts test)[55] or, the state must revert back to the limited tradition where the defendant is "physically present" or the internet conduct is "aiming" at the forum state.

---

[54] There is at present a deep conflict between federal and state courts over what connection due process requires between a plaintiff's claims and a non-resident defendant's forum contacts before a court would exercise case-specific personal jurisdiction. Some courts have held that a plaintiff's suit "does not arise out of or relate to" a defendant's forum state contacts, unless those contacts in some way caused the plaintiff's injury. This would render a defendant not subject to a state's jurisdiction if plaintiff's injury did not arise out of defendant's in-state contacts, even if the injury occurred in the forum state. Two cases are before the U.S. Supreme Court awaiting oral arguments. See *Ford Motor Company v. Montana Eighth Judicial District Court*, docket no. 19-368, consolidated with *Ford Motor Company v. Bandemer*, docket no. 19-369. See https://www.scotusblog.com/case-files/cases/ford-motor-company-v-bandemer.

[55] Indeed, one scholar has suggested that the only requirement of a directed online connection is that the defendant has conducted internet activity that could reach the forum under operating procedures established by the defendant. Essentially, internet-based activities that do not limit geographic scope should serve as the notice that the defendant could be hauled into distant forum arising out of activities in that forum,. In that scenario, personal jurisdiction is limited only by the "fairness" factors of the minimum contacts test.

Further, if courts seek to avoid this Hobbesian choice and continue to uphold the clicked consent, then the sovereignty considerations of interstate efficiency and the forum state's interests (the "fairness" factors of minimum contacts) would be usurped, only to be replaced by the parties' private agreement to litigate in the defendant's home state. These digital consent agreements will not have "public considerations" in mind, leaving these considerations unaddressed and substituting them with private terms. As pointed out by Danielle Citron, in light of today's borderless communication, the U.S. Supreme Court will have to decide which value is paramount: state sovereignty or the implied contract approach in due process.[56] In either event, the meaning of due process has been considerably altered.

In sum, this chapter has tried to point out the undeniable ways in which e-technology has infiltrated fundamental concepts of American civil procedure. In the same way that the automobile and the expansion of national commerce deeply changed the way we think about notice and physical presence, e-technology has worked to challenge and stretch our way of thinking about due process rights. And this shift in American civil procedure may prove predictive of other countries as well. It is up to us, international scholars of civil procedure, to be cognizant of this movement and caution against its possible erosion of fundamental rights. It is up to us to protect the meaning of justice in the changing landscape of technology and globalization.

See Z. NIELSEL, "#PersonalJurisdiction: A New Age of Internet Contacts" 94(1) *Indiana Law Journal* 103, available at https://www.repository.law.indiana.ed/ilj/vol94/iss1/3. Others have argued for finding "minimum contacts," if defendant is technologically sophisticated and the tortious conduct is substantial. See A. KLEVIN, "Minimum Virtual Contacts: A Framework for Specific Jurisdiction in Cyberspace" (2018) 116(5) *Michigan Law Review* 785, available at https://repository.law.umich.edu/mlr/vol116/iss5/4/.

[56] D. CITRON, above no. 34, at 1543.

PART II

NEW CHALLENGES AND THEIR VARIOUS ASPECTS

Multinational Rules and Systems of Dispute Resolution

MULTINATIONAL RULES AND SYSTEMS OF DISPUTE RESOLUTION IN AN ERA OF THE GLOBAL ECONOMY

Christoph A. KERN*

1. Introduction 62
2. The Topic 64
   2.1. "Dispute Resolution" 64
   2.2. "Rules and Systems" 66
   2.3. "Multinational" 67
   2.4. The Era of the Global Economy 68
3. The Current State of Affairs 69
   3.1. Multinational Rules 69
      3.1.1. Multinational Character by Virtue of "Nationality" 69
      3.1.2. Multinational Character by Virtue of "Contents" 75
   3.2. Multinational Systems 79
      3.2.1. Multinational Character by Virtue of "Nationality" 79
      3.2.2. Multinational Character by Virtue of "Contents" 82
   3.3. Observations 85
4. Perspectives 85
   4.1. Chances 86
      4.1.1. Economic Advantages 86
      4.1.2. Quality 86
      4.1.3. Integrity 87
   4.2. Difficulties 87
      4.2.1. Quality 87
      4.2.2. Budget 88
      4.2.3. The Legal Profession 89
      4.2.4. Traditions 90

---

* Professor and director of the Institute for Comparative Law, Conflict of Laws and International Business Law, Ruprecht-Karls-Universität Heidelberg, Germany, and professeur remplaçant, Chaire de droit allemand, Université de Lausanne, Switzerland.

4.2.5.	Constitutionalization	91
4.2.6.	Petrification	92
4.3.	Consequences	93
4.3.1.	Quality	94
4.3.2.	Budget	94
4.3.3.	The Legal Profession	94
4.3.4.	Tradition	95
4.3.5.	Constitutionalization	95
4.3.6.	Petrification	95
5.	Conclusion	96

1. INTRODUCTION

"Multinational Rules and Systems of Dispute Resolution in an Era of Global Economy" – the title of this chapter, based on the general report to the first session of the International Association of Procedural Law's 2019 World Conference, could be one of the objectives of the Association: Dispute Resolution is the object and one of the aims of procedural law;[1] procedural law is not only a set of principles and rules which could already be called a system, but often comes along with a supporting infrastructure, for example – and the term is telling – a court system; and the focus on multinational rules and systems is perfectly in line with the international character of our Association.[2]

"Multinational Rules and Systems of Dispute Resolution in an Era of Global Economy" – the title of this general report is also a perfect topic with which to start an international conference. It promises that every proceduralist, regardless of which part of the world and which legal background he or she is from, finds something he or she is familiar with and, in the best-case scenario, is interested in. "Dispute resolution" can be achieved in the traditional way, through decisions of public courts, or in a number of alternative ways, and both areas have their devotees. "Rules and systems" cover everything which can possibly be called procedural law, from access to the means of dispute resolution over the organization of the proceedings to the outcome, including its recognition and

---

[1] It should be noted that for a long time, the decision on the dispute by the court according to legal rules was seen as more valuable than the mere "resolution" of the dispute. Interestingly, in Germany, it was during the First World War when academics first noted that "not the decision of the matter, but the resolution of the dispute" could be the "highest aim" and that this was considered as a consequence of the general desire for peace. See W. SILBERSCHMIDT, "Deutscher Rechtsfriede" (also reviewing the homonymous collection of essays edited by R. DEINHARDT) (1917) 10 *Archiv für Rechts- und Wirtschaftsphilosophie* 377, 378.

[2] Cf. Arts. 2 and 3 of the By-Laws of the International Association of Procedural Law as amended July 25, 2011, www.iaplaw.org/index.php/en/the-association/by-laws-and-house-rules/by-laws.

enforcement. And the focus on multinational rules and systems ensures that more than one legal order is covered.

"Multinational Rules and Systems of Dispute Resolution in an Era of Global Economy" – the title of this general report is also perfect for the impressive venue in which the 2019 World Conference took place, Kōbe. Thanks to its geographic situation, Kōbe has always been a port town, and in the second half of the nineteenth century, it became one of the places in Japan where international commerce started early on.[3] Until the devastating earthquake in 1995, Kōbe was the largest port in Asia and the second-largest port in the world. As is well known, international commerce has always been an important driving force behind the development of means of dispute resolution,[4] and international commerce has always asked for, and sought to develop, solutions which transgress national boundaries.[5]

---

[3]   For an early account in the English language, see R. KIPLING, "1889. Letter Two" in H. CORTAZZI and G. WEBB (eds.), *Kipling's Japan. Collected Writings*, Bloomsbury Academic, London 2012, pp. 52 ff.; see also P. ENNALS, *Opening a Window to the West: The Foreign Concession at Kōbe, Japan, 1868–1899*, University of Toronto Press, Toronto 2014, *passim*.

[4]   See, e.g., W. MITCHELL, *An Essay on the Early History of the Law Merchant*, Cambridge University Press, Cambridge 1904, pp. 12 ff., 39 ff.; F.K. JUENGER, *Choice of Law and Multistate Justice*, Martinus Nijhoff, Dordrecht 1993, pp. 23 f. (on the English maritime and commercial courts); J. HILAIRE, "La résolution des conflits en matière de commerce à travers les archives du Parlement au XIIIe siècle" in A. CORDES and S. DAUCHY (eds.), *Eine Grenze in Bewegung: Private und öffentliche Konfliktlösung im Handels- und Seerecht / Une frontière mouvante: Justice privée et justice publique en matières commerciales et maritimes*, R. Oldenbourg, Munich 2013, pp. 1, 3 ff.; A. CORDES, "Die Erwartungen mittelalterlicher Kaufleute an Gerichtsverfahren: Hansische Privilegien als Indikator" in A. CORDES and S. DAUCHY (eds.), *Eine Grenze in Bewegung: Private und öffentliche Konfliktlösung im Handels- und Seerecht / Une frontière mouvante: Justice privée et justice publique en matières commerciales et maritimes*, R. Oldenbourg, Munich 2013, pp. 39 ff.; G.B. BORN, *International Arbitration: Law and Practice*, 2nd ed., Kluwer Law International, Alphen aan den Rijn 2016, pp. 10 f.

[5]   See J. HONNOLD, "Uniform Sales Law for International Sales" (1959) 107 *U. Pa. L. Rev.* 299, 301 (noting that by using arbitration, "businessmen seek to escape from conflicting and antiquated national laws"); A. ROSETT, "Unification, Harmonization, Restatement, Codification, and Reform in International Commercial Law" (1992) 40 *Am. J. Comp. L.* 683, 685; F.K. JUENGER, above n. 4, p. 16; U. BLAUROCK, "The Law of Transnational Commerce" in F. FERRARI (ed.), *The Unification of International Commercial Law. Tilburg Lectures*, Nomos, Baden-Baden 1998, pp. 9, 10 ff. Of course, in practice, there were many variations. However, the pure fact that there was something like a law merchant is significant. Cf. W. MITCHELL, above n. 4, pp. 7 ff. and *passim*; M.L. MOSES, *The Principles and Practice of International Commercial Arbitration*, 2nd ed., Cambridge University Press, Cambridge 2012, p. 3; G.B. BORN, *International Commercial Arbitration*, vol. I, 2nd ed., Kluwer Law International, Alphen aan den Rijn 2014, pp. 24 ff.; N. BLACKABY and C. PARTASIDES, *Redfern and Hunter on International Arbitration*, 6th ed., Oxford University Press, Oxford 2015, pp. 5 f. For the modern discussion about the *lex mercatoria*, see E. GAILLARD, "Thirty Years of *Lex Mercatoria*: Towards the Selective Application of Transnational Rules" (1995) 10 *ICSID Review* 208; N.E. HATZIMIHAIL, "The Many Lives – and Faces – of *Lex Mercatoria*: History as Genealogy in International Business Law" (2008) 71 *L. & Contemp. Probs.* 169, 180 ff.; G. CUNIBERTI, "La Lex Mercatoria au XXIe siècle. Une analyse empirique et économique" (2016) 143(3) *Journal du droit international (Clunet)* 1 ff.

The organizers of the 2019 World Conference therefore could hardly have done better than choose such a topic for the opening session of the conference, and the author wishes that the present general report in its written form meets their expectations and the expectations of the readers. This chapter will be organized as follows. First, the scope of the topic will be discussed more thoroughly. Then an overview will be provided on where we stand. On this basis, the outlook for multinational rules and systems will be discussed, assuming that the era of the global economy will continue. The final section offers a conclusion.

2. THE TOPIC

"Multinational Rules and Systems of Dispute Resolution in an Era of Global Economy" – this title comprises 13 words. If you are asked to give a presentation on a topic whose definition comprises 13 words, the first thing you have to do is to determine what exactly the audience – and the organizers – expect you to deal with. This can best be done by dissecting the title and analyzing it word per word, respecting the hierarchical order.

2.1. "DISPUTE RESOLUTION"

As a matter of grammatical-linguistic hierarchy, it is the words "dispute resolution" which form the top of the title. The term "dispute resolution" has its origins in social science, not in legal scholarship. Its approach is functional in that it asks how society deals with the social phenomenon of a dispute.[6] Thus, as already indicated before, it covers both the traditional decision of disputes in public courts and the various forms of alternative dispute resolution (ADR),[7] mainly arbitration and mediation. Legal scholars first used the term

---

[6]   R.M. COVER, "Dispute Resolution: A Foreword" (1979) 88 *Yale L.J.* 910.

[7]   This chapter sticks with the traditional interpretation of ADR as *alternative* dispute resolution. Note, however, that some authors now want to see ADR translated into *appropriate* dispute resolution; see, e.g., C. MENKEL-MEADOW, "Is ODR ADR? Reflections of an ADR Founder from the 15th IDR Conference, The Hague, Netherlands, 22–23 May 2016" (2016) 3 *IJODR* 4; also proposing, but not defending this translation and others (like "avoid disastrous results"): J. MÜNCH, "Die Privatisierung der Ziviljustiz – Von der Schiedsgerichtsbarkeit zur Mediation' in *50. Bitburger Gespräche 2008*, vol. I, C.H. Beck, Munich 2009, pp. 179, 183. For the discussion of the French term "modes alternatifs de règlement de conflits" (MARC), see L. CADIET and T. CLAY, *Les modes alternatifs de règlement des conflits*, 3rd ed., Dalloz, Paris 2019, pp. 17–30; L. CADIET, "Panorama des modes alternatifs de règlement des conflits en droit français" (2011) 28 *Ritsumeikan L. Rev.* 147, 147–150.

"dispute resolution" in the 1960s;[8] it became known to a general legal audience in the 1970s,[9] then quickly spread in the 1980s[10] and has become ubiquitous since the 1990s.[11] But the words "dispute resolution" are broad enough to cover the resolution of disputes without any involvement of third-party neutrals like judges, arbitrators, or mediators. Disputes can also be resolved by way of negotiation or consultation, perhaps on the basis of dispute escalation clauses. And, at least in theory, disputes can also be resolved online[12] and maybe even automatically[13] – this is, in any case, the promise made by some of the self-proclaimed "disruptors" from computer science who are particularly confident that artificial intelligence will be able to replace judges in the future.[14] Our analysis will try to cover all these aspects.

Of course, the resolution of a dispute is, first and foremost, concerned with the situations of the parties involved – the "outcome" of the dispute

---

[8] To our knowledge, the term "dispute resolution" was first used in the title of a U.S. law review article in 1967: S. LUBMAN, "Mao and Mediation: Politics and Dispute Resolution in Communist China" (1967) 55 *Calif. L. Rev.* 1284.

[9] As of April 23, 2019, the Law Journal Library of heinonline.org lists 25 articles containing "dispute resolution" in the title for the years of 1970–1979.

[10] As of April 23, 2019, the Law Journal Library of heinonline.org lists 322 articles containing "dispute resolution" in the title for the years of 1980–1989.

[11] As of April 23, 2019, the Law Journal Library of heinonline.org lists 710 articles containing "dispute resolution" in the title for the years of 1990–1999, 530 for 2000–2005, 540 for 2005–2010, 581 for 2010 to 2015, and 334 for 2016 to date. For the history of the French expression "modes alternatifs de règlement des conflits," see L. CADIET and T. CLAY, above n. 7, pp. 31–32.

[12] See, e.g., the UNCITRAL Technical Notes on Online Dispute Resolution 2016, http://www.uncitral.org/uncitral/en/uncitral_texts/odr/2016Technical_notes.html. On ODR generally, see, inter alia, O. RABINOVICH-EINY and E. KATSH, "Digital Justice. Reshaping Boundaries in an Online Dispute Resolution Environment" (2014) 1 *IJODR* 5; H. HABUKA and C. RULE, "The Promise and Potential of Online Dispute Resolution in Japan" (2017) 4 *IJODR* 74; C. RULE, "Designing a Global Online Dispute Resolution System: Lessons Learned from eBay" (2017) 13 *U. St. Thomas L.J.* 354, 368 f.; M. PHILIPPE, "We Walked on the Moon But Justice is Not Yet Online! Technology Revolution and Online Dispute Resolution (ODR)" Revue pratique de la prospective et de l'innovation n 1, Mars 2017, dossier 8; J. ZHANG, "On China Online Dispute Resolution Mechanism: Following the UNCITRAL TNODR and Alibaba Experience" (2017) 4 *IJODR* 14. For critical remarks, see C. MENKEL-MEADOW, above n. 7.

[13] O. RABINOVICH-EINY and E. KATSH, above n. 12, p. 23; on "legal robots," see also J. WAGNER, "Legal Tech und Legal Robots in Unternehmen und den diese beratenden Kanzleien" (2017) *BB* 898, 902 f. For a more modest approach, see, e.g., D. THOMPSON, "Creating New Pathways to Justice Using Simple Artificial Intelligence and Online Dispute Resolution" (2015) 2 *IJODR* 4, 12 ff. For an early overview, see A. KAISSIS, "Herausforderung Informationsgesellschaft: Die Anwendung moderner Technologien im Zivilprozess und anderen Verfahren" (1999) 52 *Revue Hellenique de Droit International* 503.

[14] Cf. E. KATSH and O. RABINOVICH-EINY, *Digital Justice: Technology and the Internet of Disputes*, Oxford University Press, New York 2017. Rejecting this idea for the British Columbia Civil Resolution Tribunal, see S. SALTER and D. THOMPSON, "Public-Centered Civil Justice Redesign: A Case Study of the British Columbia Civil Resolution Tribunal" (2016–2017) 3 *McGill J. Disp. Resol.* 113, 134.

resolution process. This outcome can be the result of an authoritative decision, be it by a public court or an arbitral tribunal; it can be the result of a negotiation "in the shadow of the law"[15] (i.e. a negotiation for which the potential outcome of proceedings in public courts or before an arbitral tribunal played a background role) or it can be a solution based only on the parties' interests.[16] However, for us, the "outcome" of the dispute resolution process does not matter. The "rules and systems of dispute resolution" in which we are interested are the rules governing and the systems enclosing the process of dispute resolution – not the rules and systems *for*, but the rules and systems *of* dispute resolution.

2.2. "RULES AND SYSTEMS"

The topic speaks of "rules and systems of dispute resolution." There must, then, be a distinction between rules and systems. A first, simple approach would be to distinguish between an individual rule and a coherent set of rules which would then be a system. An example for an individual rule would be Rule 3 of the U.S. Federal Rules of Civil Procedure, pursuant to which "[a] civil action is commenced by filing a complaint with the court," and a system would be the Federal Rules taken as a whole.

But as "rules" in the plural form already covers sets of rules, the word "systems" could also require that there be something added to mere sets of rules. What could this "something" be? It could be the infrastructure for the resolution of disputes – in other words, the necessary human and material resources like judges, jurors, arbitrators and mediators, secretaries and administrative staff, and court buildings, information and communication technology, and the like.[17] Indeed, such "systems" exist not only in the form of the traditional, publicly administered justice, but also in the private and the international sphere – suffice

---

[15]   A term first coined by R.H. Mnookin and L. Kornhauser, "Bargaining in the Shadow of the Law: The Case of Divorce" (1979) 88 *Yale L.J.* 950, 959 ff. The extensive literature includes, inter alia, R. Cooter, S. Marks and R. Mnookin, "Bargaining in the Shadow of the Law: A Testable Model of Strategic Behavior" (1982) 11 *J. Legal Stud.* 225; H. Jacob, "The Elusive Shadow of the Law" (1992) 26 *L. & Soc'y Rev.* 565; R.D. Madoff, "Lurking in the Shadow: The Unseen Hand of Doctrine in Dispute Resolution" (2002) 76 *S. Cal. L. Rev.* 161, 165 ff. On the role of the law in mediations, see also D. Leipold, "Schlichtung, Mediation und Zivilprozess' (2013) 30 *Ritsumeikan L. Rev.* 135, 160 ff.

[16]   For the focus on interests (but not explicitly excluding a rights orientation), see R. Fisher, W. Ury and B. Patton, *Getting to Yes*, 3rd ed., Random House, London 2012, pp. 42 ff.; from the abundant literature, see also J. Kurtzberg and J. Henikoff, "Freeing the Parties from the Law: Designing an Interest and Rights Focused Model of Landlord/Tenant Mediation" (1997) *J. Disp. Resol.* 53; D. Golann, "Beyond Brainstorming: The Special Barriers to Interest-Based Mediation, and Techniques to Overcome Them" (2011) 18 *Disp. Resol. Mag.* 22.

[17]   For a similar understanding, see, e.g., C. Leathley, "The Mercosur Dispute Resolution System" (2003) 4 *J. World Investment* 787, 787–788.

it to mention here the so-called "institutional" commercial arbitration and international centers like the International Center for Settlement of Investment Disputes (ICSID). Moreover, if we include automatic dispute resolution, a "system" is then the platform and code running the program.[18]

2.3. "MULTINATIONAL"

"Multinational" as an adjective means, according to the dictionaries, "relating to more than two *nationalities* or involving more than two *nations*."[19] The "nationality" of rules can be determined with respect to the law maker by which they have been enacted or with respect to their contents.[20] In the first case, we must first determine when rules stem from a law maker of two or more nations. Without going into the details on who is competent to decide on the conclusion of international treaties pursuant to the rules of internal law – parliament or government – multinational treaties would meet these requirements, as they presuppose the consent of all States Parties to the treaty.[21] It is therefore not important whether the text of the treaty was drafted by one or more of the States or by an international organization – or, in theory, even by a private organization. Moreover, rules adopted or systems created by international organizations which themselves are based on a multilateral treaty also fall within the category of rules or systems which have a multinational character by "nationality." Eventually, it also seems possible to include within this category of "multinationality" texts drafted by representatives of more than two States which have not been ratified at all or only by one or two nations, as the law-making process was multinational. If multinationality was defined in this rather strict and formal way, all purely national law would be excluded from the scope of the present chapter, and only truly international sources, in particular rules or systems of dispute resolution based on multilateral treaties, could be dealt with.

In the latter case, in which "multinational" is determined with respect to the contents of the "rules and systems of dispute resolution", national law is covered insofar as it is uniform or at least harmonized across more than two countries. This determination of "multinational" with respect to "nationality" is also in

---

[18] Cf. C. RULE, above n. 12, pp. 357 ff.

[19] Cf. *Merriam-Webster*, https://www.merriam-webster.com/dictionary/multinational; *Oxford Dictionaries*, https://en.oxforddictionaries.com/definition/multinational; *Collins Dictionary*, https://www.collinsdictionary.com/dictionary/English/multinational.

[20] The approach used here has some similarities with the concept of "intégration normative" used in M. DELMAS-MARTY (ed.), *Critique de l'intégration normative*, Presses Universitaires de France, Paris 2004; for criticism of this approach, see the review of J.S. BERGÉ (2005) 57 *R.I.D.C.* 541, 543 f.

[21] Cf. Arts. 9 ff. of the Vienna Convention on the Law of Treaties, concluded at Vienna on May 23, 1969, 1155 U.N.T.S. 331, 332–495 (1980).

Intersentia

line with the second possibility of interpreting the meaning of the word, namely "involving more than two *nations*." The word "involved" is very generic; it can require an action, but also describe the passive role from he who is involved. In this context, an active role can be found as soon as rules or systems have been drafted by the representatives of more than two nations, regardless of whether any of these nations finally adopted the rules. A passive role can certainly be affirmed if more than two nations are bound to apply the same rules or to adhere to a system, whether by way of a multilateral treaty or supranational law. Somewhere in between these two extremes is the situation that a national law maker decides to adopt draft rules developed by an independent institution and aimed at being adopted by more than two nations. And of course, a multinational character of rules and systems due to their contents can be affirmed for rules developed and systems created by private institutions with the aim of being applied in disputes regardless of where and between whom such disputes have arisen and where the dispute resolution proceedings are conducted.[22]

To sum up, rules and systems can have a multinational character either by their "nationality" in the strict sense (i.e., because the law makers of two or more nations were involved) or by their "contents" (i.e., the uniform or harmonized contents of rules or the multinational scope of disputes that a system wants to deal with).

2.4. THE ERA OF THE GLOBAL ECONOMY

Finally, the topic contains a temporal limitation: it wants us to focus on the multinational rules and systems of dispute resolution in the era of the global economy. This era certainly is our era, the present. It may also cover the more recent past, say, the last 70 years and maybe also the "golden" times of the 1920s. And it seems to comprise the future as well, as everybody nowadays expects that we will continue to have a "global economy." This justifies why in the following sections, we not only provide an account of the current state, but also discuss the perspectives.

The focus on the "era of the global economy" not only has a temporal aspect, but also an aspect with respect to contents: it hints at the kind of disputes we should concentrate on – disputes relating to the global economy. The global economy brings about transnational civil and commercial disputes in a very significant sense. From a proceduralist perspective, these are disputes between parties which, at least with respect to the dispute resolution proceedings, are

---

[22]   On the importance of law which does not emanate from the power of a sovereign state for (international) commerce, see F.K. JUENGER, "American Conflicts Scholarship and the New Law Merchant" (1995) 28 *Vand. J. Transnat'l L.* 487, 490 ff.

on an equal footing, which allows us to include the resolution of trade disputes between states or the resolution of investment disputes between a private investor and a state, with the state being a "normal" party to the proceedings.

3. THE CURRENT STATE OF AFFAIRS

With this more precise ascertainment of the topic in mind, let us now have a look at the current state of affairs. Where do we find multinational rules and systems of dispute resolution, and do they share characteristics? It is, of course, as impossible as it would be boring to provide a comprehensive answer. Instead, we will give a few representative examples. In doing so, we will use the distinction between multinational rules and multinational systems in the larger sense presented above, i.e., with "system" being not only a set of rules, but also encompassing human and material resources, and we will distinguish between a strict multinational character based on nationality, referring to the nationality of the law maker, and a broader multinational character derived from the contents of the rules and systems, referring to uniform or harmonized rules or to systems designed for disputes involving parties or facts from more than one nation.

3.1. MULTINATIONAL RULES

3.1.1. *Multinational Character by Virtue of "Nationality"*

Multinational rules in the strict sense of the word "multinational" are rules enacted by law makers from more than two nations, the most obvious example being multilateral treaties. Indeed, there are some multinational treaties containing dispute resolution rules. However, the scope of issues that these treaties cover is remarkably small. A perfect example is, of course, the New York Convention of 1958 on the recognition and enforcement of foreign arbitral awards.[23] This Convention has almost 160 contracting states. As its title suggests, it is concerned with (and only with) the recognition and enforcement of foreign arbitral awards.[24] Thus, it does not cover decisions from public courts,[25] nor does it contain rules on the arbitral proceedings as such; it does not even govern the

---

[23] Convention on the Recognition and Enforcement of Foreign Arbitral Awards, done at New York on June 10, 1958, entered into force on June 7, 1959, 330 U.N.T.S. 3, 38–82, available at https://treaties.un.org/Pages/showDetails.aspx?objid=080000028002a36b and https://www.uncitral.org/pdf/english/texts/arbitration/NY-conv/New-York-Convention-E.pdf.

[24] In this context, it also covers the recognition of arbitration agreements; see Art. II.

[25] Except for decisions denying jurisdiction and referring the parties to arbitration pursuant to Art. II(3) and decisions on recognition and enforcement pursuant to Art. III.

Intersentia

grounds for setting aside an award[26] or the proceedings leading to recognition and enforcement,[27] but only the circumstances under which a contracting state may refuse to recognize and enforce a foreign award.[28] However, in an indirect way, it does have repercussions on the arbitral proceedings: certain procedural errors are grounds for denying recognition and enforcement,[29] and many countries have adopted more or less the same grounds for setting aside an award.[30] Thus, arbitrators and parties to arbitration have a strong incentive to avoid procedural errors which would frustrate the result of the proceedings. Therefore, regardless of the place of arbitration, arbitrators and parties across the whole world organize the proceedings accordingly. At a regional level, the 1961 Geneva Convention on International Commercial Arbitration[31] does slightly better, as it contains at least a few rules on the arbitral tribunal and the proceedings before it.[32]

With respect to decisions of public courts, the Judgments Project of the Hague Conference marked its first success: the text of a Convention on the Recognition and Enforcement of Foreign Judgments in Civil or Commercial Matters was adopted by the Hague Conference's 22nd Diplomatic Session on July 2, 2019.[33] However, it will take a while to see a considerable number of ratifications or accessions; so far, only Uruguay has signed the text.[34] Moreover, some observers consider the benefit of the Convention to be marginal due to the limitations regarding its scope of application.[35] The idea to create uniform rules on direct

---

[26]   On this limitation, see, e.g., L. SILBERMAN, "The New York Convention after Fifty Years: Some Reflections on the Role of National Law" (2009) 38 *Ga. J. Int'l & Comp. L.* 25, 27 ff.

[27]   Except for Art. III sentence 2, pursuant to which recognition and enforcement of the awards covered by the Convention may not be subject to "substantially more onerous conditions or higher fees or charges" than recognition and enforcement of domestic awards.

[28]   Art. V.

[29]   Cf., e.g., Art. V(1) lit. b, (2) lit. b.

[30]   Cf. Art. 34(2) of the UNCITRAL Model Law on International Commercial Arbitration (1985), https://uncitral.un.org/sites/uncitral.un.org/files/media-documents/uncitral/en/06-54671_ebook. pdf; see, e.g., §1059(2) of the German Code of Civil Procedure. On the significance of the UNCITRAL Model Law, see the text accompanying note 77.

[31]   European Convention on International Commercial Arbitration, Geneva, April 21, 1961 https://treaties.un.org/doc/Treaties/1964/01/19640107%2002-01%20AM/Ch_XXII_02p.pdf.

[32]   In particular, Art. III (Right of foreign nationals to be designated as arbitrators), Art. IV (Organization of the arbitration), Art. V (Plea as to arbitral jurisdiction), and Art. VIII (Reasons for the award).

[33]   Convention on the Recognition and Enforcement of Foreign Judgments in Civil or Commercial Matters, The Hague, July 2, 2019, https://www.hcch.net/en/instruments/conventions/full-text/?cid=137.

[34]   For an updated list of Contracting Parties, see https://www.hcch.net/en/instruments/conventions/status-table/?cid=137.

[35]   H. SCHACK, "Das neue Haager Anerkennungs- und Vollstreckungsübereinkommen" (2020) *IPRax* 1.

jurisdiction is still present,[36] but the fate of this project is hard to predict. As we all know, the Hague Conference's previous attempt[37] to create uniform rules on international jurisdiction, the recognition and enforcement of judgments in civil and commercial matters only brought about the 2005 Choice of Court Agreements Convention,[38] a convention which currently has, in addition to the EU Member States, only four more contracting states, now including the United Kingdom.[39] More recently, a successful project of the Hague Conference was the 2007 Convention on the International Recovery of Child Support and Other Forms of Family Maintenance,[40] an instrument aiming at international cooperation, facilitating applications, and recognition and enforcement of maintenance decisions.[41] What is particularly remarkable is its ratification by the United States.[42] When speaking of the Hague Conference, we should also mention the various conventions in the field of international cooperation, in particular on letters rogatory, dating back as far as 1905.[43]

At a regional level, we have to mention EU law – enacted by the European legislature and applicable in all EU Member States which are, as Brexit has

---

[36] See, e.g., D.P. STEWART, "The Hague Conference Adopts a New Convention on the Recognition and Enforcement of Foreign Judgments in Civil or Commercial Matters" (2019) 113 *Am. J. Int'l L.* 772.

[37] See, e.g., H. SCHACK, "Perspektiven eines weltweiten Anerkennungs- und Vollstreckungsübereinkommens" (1993) *ZEuP* 306 ff.; A. BORRÁS, "The 1999 Preliminary Draft Hague Convention on Jurisdiction, Recognition and Enforcement of Judgments: Agreements and Disagreements" (2004) *Rivista di Diritto Internazionale Privato e Processuale (RDIPP)* 5, 10 ff.; R.A. BRAND, "The 1999 Hague Preliminary Draft Convention Text on Jurisdiction and Judgments: A View from the United States" (2004) *RDIPP* 31, 32 ff.; and the essays in J.J. BARCELÓ III and K.M. CLERMONT (eds.), *A Global Law of Jurisdiction and Judgments: Lessons from The Hague*, Kluwer Law International, The Hague 2002. On the difficulties in the negotiation and the reasons for its failure, see, e.g., B. HESS, "Steht das geplante weltweite Zuständigkeits- und Vollstreckungsübereinkommen vor dem Aus?" (2000) *IPRax* 342 f.; L. SILBERMAN, "Comparative Jurisdiction in the International Context: Will the Proposed Hague Judgements Convention Be Stalled?" (2002) 52 *DePaul L. Rev.* 319, 328 ff.

[38] Hague Convention on Choice of Courts Agreements, ILM Vol. 44, No. 6, November 2005, pp. 1294–1303.

[39] Hague Convention on Choice of Courts Agreements, Status table, https://www.hcch.net/en/instruments/conventions/status-table/?cid=98.

[40] Convention on the International Recovery of Child Support and Other Forms of Family Maintenance, ILM Vol. 47, No. 2, March 2008, pp. 257–277.

[41] For its context and history, see, e.g., C.A. KERN, in T. RAUSCHER (ed.), *EuZPR / EuIPR*, 4th ed., Otto Schmidt, Cologne 2015, Einl HUntVerfÜbk mn. 9 ff., 21 ff.

[42] Convention on the International Recovery of Child Support and Other Forms of Family Maintenance, Status table, https://www.hcch.net/en/instruments/conventions/status-table/?cid=131.

[43] 1905: Convention du 17.07.1905 relative à la procédure civile; 1954: Convention of March 1, 1954 on civil procedure; 1965: Convention of November 15, 1965 on the Service Abroad of Judicial and Extrajudicial Documents in Civil or Commercial Matters; 1970: Convention of March 18, 1970 on the Taking of Evidence Abroad in Civil or Commercial Matters.

shown us, still nation states rather not merely parts of a true federation. The instruments that are of relevance for our discussion here are, first of all, the Brussels I *bis* Regulation on the jurisdiction, recognition, and enforcement of court decisions in EU Member States,[44] an instrument whose predecessor was a Convention of 1968,[45] which has been supplemented by the Lugano Convention,[46] which contains similar rules for Denmark,[47] Switzerland, Norway and Iceland. In certain matters like divorce, child custody, and maintenance obligations, EU regulations with a sectoral approach also contain rules on recognition and enforcement.[48] Drawing on the respective Hague Conventions, EU regulations also cover the service of judicial and extrajudicial documents,[49] and the taking of evidence in other Member States.[50] Moreover, the Regulation creating a European Enforcement Order for uncontested claims[51] establishes minimum requirements for the proceedings which may benefit from such an order.[52] Nevertheless, once again, these texts do not contain rules which directly govern the proceedings as such, but limit their objective to recognition and enforcement, with the important add-on of (direct) international jurisdiction. So far, the only instrument which also addresses the court proceedings as such

---

[44] Regulation (EU) No 1215/2012, OJ L 351 of December 20, 2012, pp. 1–32.

[45] Convention on Jurisdiction and Enforcement of Judgements in Civil and Commercial Matters 1968, ILM Vol. 8, No. 2, pp. 229–244, March 1969 / OJ L 299 of December 31, 1972, pp. 32–42.

[46] Convention on Jurisdiction and Enforcement of Judgements in Civil and Commercial Matters 1988, ILM Vol. 29, No. 6, pp. 1413–1446, November 1990 / OJ L 319, November 25, 1988, pp. 9–48; replaced by Convention on Jurisdiction and the Recognition and Enforcement of Judgments in Civil and Commercial Matters, Lugano, October 30, 2007, entered into force on November 1, 2010, 2658 U.N.T.S. 197-406 / OJ L 339 of December 21, 2007, pp. 3–41.

[47] A curiosity: Denmark is an EU Member State, but does not automatically participate in judicial cooperation; see Protocol on the Position of Denmark annexed to the Lisbon Treaty, OJ C 83 of March 30, 2010, pp. 299–303; P.A. NIELSEN, "Denmark and EU Civil Cooperation" (2016) *ZEuP* 300 ff.; H.P. MANSEL, K. THORN and R. WAGNER, "Europäisches Kollisionsrecht 2015: Neubesinnung" (2016) *IPRax* 1, 3; H.P. MANSEL, K. THORN and R. WAGNER, "Europäisches Kollisionsrecht 2016: Brexit ante portas!" (2017) *IPRax* 1, 2.

[48] Chapter III of Regulation (EC) No 2201/2003 of the Council concerning jurisdiction and the enforcement of judgments in matrimonial matters and the matters of parental responsibility, OJ L 338 of December 23, 2003, pp. 1–29; Chapter IV of Regulation (EC) No 4/2009 of the Council on jurisdiction, applicable law, recognition and enforcement of decisions and cooperation in matters relating to maintenance obligations, OJ L 7 of January 10, 2009, pp. 1–79.

[49] Regulation (EC) No 2393/2007 of the European Parliament and of the Council of November 13, 2007 on the service in the Member States of judicial and extrajudicial documents in civil or commercial matters (service of documents), and repealing Council Regulation (EC) No 1348/2000, OJ L 324 of December 10, 2007, pp. 79–120.

[50] Council Regulation (EC) No 1206/2001 of May 28, 2001 on cooperation between the courts of the Member States in the taking of evidence in civil or commercial matters, OJ L 174 of June 27, 2001, pp. 1–24.

[51] Regulation (EC) No 805/2004 of the European Parliament and of the Council of April 21, 2004 creating a European Enforcement Order for uncontested claims, OJ L 143 of April 30, 2004, pp. 15–39.

[52] Ibid., Arts. 12–19.

is the Small Claims Regulation.[53] However, its procedural rules are rather basic and in terms of quantity as well as quality are far from being a procedural code.[54] To make a last point concerning proceedings in public courts, it must be mentioned that certain particular questions, mainly concerning access to evidence, are covered by sectoral EU directives – i.e., instruments which must be transposed by the national legislatures[55] – namely the so-called Enforcement Directive[56] and the so-called Directive on Antitrust Damages Actions.[57] In the field of ADR, the EU has enacted a Directive on Mediation,[58] but here again, the instrument deals with rather peripheral aspects like the enforceability of agreements resulting from mediation and the confidentiality of information arising out of or in connection to mediation in later court proceedings.[59]

It has already become clear from the above that even within the EU, there is no complete set of multinational procedural rules. In this context, it must be stressed that in the EU, unlike in federal states like the United States or Brazil, there is no system of European courts that would mirror the system of state courts.[60] The only common courts are the European Court of Justice (ECJ)[61] and the General Court (GC).[62] And, indeed, the rules concerning the jurisdiction of and procedure before the ECJ[63] and the GC[64] are multinational by virtue of the

---

[53]   Regulation (EC) No 861/2007 of the European Parliament and of the Council of July 11, 2007 establishing a European Small Claims Procedure, OJ L 199 of July 31, 2007, pp. 1–22, as amended.

[54]   For a criticism, see C.A. KERN, "Das europäische Verfahren für geringfügige Forderungen und die gemeineuropäischen Verfahrensgrundsätze" (2012) JZ 389–398.

[55]   Art. 228(3) of the Treaty on the Functioning of the European Union (TFEU).

[56]   Arts. 6 ff. of Directive 2004/48/EC of the European Parliament and of the Council of April 29, 2004 on the enforcement of intellectual property rights, OJ L 157 of April 30, 2004, pp. 45–86 as corrected.

[57]   Arts. 5 ff. of Directive 2014/104/EU of the European Parliament and of the Council of November 26, 2014 on certain rules governing actions for damages under national law for infringements of the competition law provisions of the Member States and of the European Union, OJ L 349 of December 5, 2014, pp. 1–19.

[58]   Directive 2008/52/EC of the European Parliament and of the Council of May 21, 2008 on certain aspects of mediation in civil and commercial matters, OJ L 136 of May 24, 2008, pp. 3–8.

[59]   Ibid., Arts. 6 and 7.

[60]   For an academic discussion, see R. STÜRNER, "Europäische Justiz und Demokratie" in C.E. EBERLE, M. IBLER and D. LORENZ (eds.), Der Wandel des Staates vor den Herausforderungen der Gegenwart. Festschrift für Winfried Brohm, C.H. Beck, Munich 2002, pp. 153, 163 ff.; M. WEBER, Europäisches Zivilprozessrecht und Demokratieprinzip, Mohr Siebeck, Tübingen 2009, pp. 133 ff.

[61]   Arts. 13(1) and 19 of the Treaty on European Union (TEU); Arts. 251 ff. of the Treaty on the Functioning of the European Union (TFEU), OJ C 202 of June 7, 2016.

[62]   Arts. 13 and 19 TEU; Arts. 254 ff. TFEU.

[63]   Jurisdiction: Arts. 259, 261, 262, 267, 269, 271, and 275(2); procedure: Title III of the Statute of the Court of Justice of the European Union, Protocol No 3 annexed to the Treaties as amended, available at https://curia.europa.eu/jcms/jcms/Jo2_7031/en; Rules of Procedure of the Court of Justice of September 25, 2012, as amended, available at https://curia.europa.eu/jcms/upload/docs/application/pdf/2012-10/rp_en.pdf.

[64]   Jurisdiction: Art. 256 TFEU, referring to Arts. 263, 265, 268, 270, and 272; procedure: Title III of the Statute of the Court of Justice of the European Union, Protocol No 3 annexed to the

"nationality" of the law maker. However, access to the European courts is very limited. Leaving aside the limited areas in which the ECJ or the GC have first instance jurisdiction in civil and commercial matters, citizens do not have direct access to the European courts – not even at the appeals level.[65] Only national courts can, on the suggestion of the parties or on their own initiative, refer a question concerning the interpretation of EU law to the ECJ[66] – the proceedings for a preliminary ruling.[67] Thus, the ECJ does not even resolve a concrete dispute, but only provides an answer on a question of interpretation. In most cases, the European courts therefore cannot be understood as a full dispute resolution system, and the multinational rules governing proceedings for a preliminary ruling of the ECJ again relate to a rather peripheral situation.

Finally, an interesting example of multinational character by virtue of the "nationality" of the law maker are the UNCITRAL Arbitration Rules,[68] which are widely used not only in ad hoc arbitrations, but also in arbitrations administered by private arbitration institutions so that, in the latter case, they are a link to dispute resolution systems. These rules can be applied in any arbitration, regardless of where the parties are from, where the facts have taken place, or where the proceedings will be conducted. They are listed here under the headline "multinational character by virtue of nationality" because they have been adopted by Resolutions of the United Nations (UN) General Assembly.[69] The UN, in turn, is an international organization which can be understood as a multinational law maker. As the UNCITRAL Arbitration Rules directly address the proceedings before the arbitral tribunal, but do not come with a full dispute resolution system in the sense described above, they are one of the few examples of procedural rules whose multinational character is based on the rules' "nationality."

Treaties as amended, available at https://curia.europa.eu/jcms/jcms/Jo2_7031/en; Rules of Procedure of the General Court as amended, available at https://curia.europa.eu/jcms/upload/docs/application/pdf/2018-11/tra-doc-en-div-t-0000-2018-201810296-05_01.pdf.

[65] For a reform proposal, see A. Bruns, "Die Revision zum Europäischen Gerichtshof in Zivilsachen – akademische Zukunftsvision oder Gebot europäischer Justizgewährleistung?" [2011] *JZ* 325.

[66] Or under the conditions of Art. 256(3) of the GC. So far, the "specific areas" in which the GC shall have jurisdiction have still not been defined in the Statute, and commentators do not expect this to happen in the near future; see U. Karpenstein in E. Grabitz, M. Hilf, and M. Nettesheim (eds.), *Das Recht der Europäischen Union*, C.H. Beck, Munich, looseleaf, 66th delivery, February 2019, Art. 256 mn. 68; B.W. Wegener, in C. Calliess and M. Ruffert (eds.), *EUV/AEUV*, 5th ed., C.H. Beck, Munich 2016, Art. 256 AEUV mn. 29.

[67] Art. 267 TFEU.

[68] UNCITRAL Arbitration Rules (2010), ILM Vol. 49, No. 6, pp. 1640–1658, December 2010 / UNCITRAL Arbitration Rules (2013), https://uncitral.un.org/sites/uncitral.un.org/files/media-documents/uncitral/en/uncitral-arbitration-rules-2013-e.pdf.

[69] For the 2013 Arbitration Rules, see Resolution adopted by the General Assembly on December 16, 2013, Sixty-Eighth Session, Agenda item 79, A/RES/68/109, available at https://undocs.org/en/A/RES/68/109.

3.1.2. Multinational Character by Virtue of "Contents"

Turning now to rules which cannot claim to be multinational by virtue of their "nationality," but by virtue of their multinational contents, it is worthwhile mentioning first the various projects aiming at a harmonization of procedural law. The first projects were the Código Procesal Civil Modelo para Iberoamérica[70] and Marcel Storme's idea of a European Civil Code,[71] followed by Geoffrey C. Hazard, Jr. and Michele Taruffo's project of transnational rules,[72] which brought about the American Law Institute (ALI) and UNIDROIT's Principles of Transnational Civil Procedure, accompanied by a proposal of rules.[73] Currently, the European Law Institute (ELI) and UNIDROIT are working on European Rules of Civil Procedure.[74] All these projects are very ambitious, in that they aim at influencing or at least inspiring national legislatures,[75] but to date, none

---

[70] On this project, see, e.g., J.C. BARBOSA MOREIRA, "Le code-modèle de procédure civile pour l'Amérique latine de l'Institut Ibéro-Américain de Droit Processuel" (1998) 3 *ZZPInt* 437; C. LIMA MARQUES, "Procédure Civile Internationale et MERCOSUR: Pour in Dialogue des Règles Universelles et Régionales" (2003) 8 *Unif. L. Rev.* 465, 467, 481 f.; N.J. BETTINGER, *Prozessmodelle im Zivilverfahrensrecht*, Mohr Siebeck, Tübingen 2016, pp. 139 ff.; E. OTEIZA, "Latin America as a Cultural Space: Trends and Tensions among Nation-States and the International Community as Regards Reforms" in H. PEKANITEZ, N. BOLAYIR, and C. SIMIL (eds.), *XVth International Association of Procedural Law World Congress, May 25th–28th 2015, İstanbul*, On İki Levha, İstanbul 2016, pp. 445, 469.

[71] M. STORME, *Rapprochement du Droit Judiciaire de l'Union Européenne/Approximation of Judiciary Law in the European Union*, Nijhoff, Dordrecht 1994; for a discussion, see, e.g., C. GIOVANNUCCI ORLANDI, "Le rapprochement des procédures civiles internationales" in F. FERRARI (ed.), *The Unification of International Commercial Law. Tilburg Lectures*, Nomos, Baden-Baden 1998, pp. 173, 176–180.

[72] G.C. HAZARD JR. and M. TARUFFO, "Transnational Rules of Civil Procedure Rules and Commentary" (1997) 30 *Cornell Int'l L.J.* 493, 495 ff.; see also G.C. HAZARD JR. and M. TARUFFO, "Transnational Rules of Civil Procedure, Preliminary Draft No. 1" (1998) 33 *Tex. Int'l L.J.* 499 ff. For a discussion, see G.B. BORN, "Critical Observations on the Draft Transnational Rules of Civil Procedure" (1998) 33 *Tex. Int'l L.J.* 387; R.J. WEINTRAUB, "Critique of the Hazard-Taruffo Transnational Rules of Civil Procedure" (1998) 33 *Tex. Int'l L.J.* 413; G. WALTER and S.P. BAUMGARTNER, "Utility and Feasibility of Transnational Rules of Civil Procedure: Some German and Swiss Reactions to the Hazard-Taruffo Project" (1998) 33 *Tex. Int'l L.J.* 463; C. KESSEDJIAN, "First Impressions of the Transnational Rules of Civil Procedure" (1998) 33 *Tex. Int'l L.J.* 477; C. GIOVANNUCCI ORLANDI, above n. 71, at 181–184; for the history of the project, see G.C. HAZARD, "Developing Civil Procedure Rules for European Courts" (2010) 100 *Judicature* 58, 59.

[73] ALI/UNIDROIT, *Principles of Transnational Civil Procedure, as Adopted and Promulgated by the American Law Institute at Washington, May 2004 and by UNIDROIT at Rome, April 2004*, Cambridge University Press, Cambridge 2006, also available at https://www.unidroit.org/english/principles/civilprocedure/ali-unidroitprinciples-e.pdf.

[74] ELI/UNIDROIT *Transnational Civil Procedure – Formulation of Regional Rules*, https://www.unidroit.org/work-in-progress/transnational-civil-procedure.

[75] For a discussion on the possible implementation of the ALI/UNIDROIT Principles, see, e.g., H.P. GLENN, "The ALI/UNIDROIT Principles of Transnational Civil Procedure as Global Standards for Adjudication" (2004) 9 *Unif. L. Rev.* 829, 839 ff.; R. STÜRNER, "The Principles of Transnational Civil Procedure: An Introduction to Their Basic Conceptions" (2005) 69

of these projects has been enacted by a national legislature word for word.[76] It is, again, a text in the field of arbitration which can claim to be most successful in terms of "harmonizing" procedural law: the 1985 UNCITRAL Model Law on International Commercial Arbitration.[77] A considerable number of national legislatures, including Australia,[78] Japan,[79] and Germany,[80] were not only motivated by this instrument, but also reformed their existing law accordingly. The 2006 Amendment[81] has been less influential thus far,[82] but nevertheless is another example of an important set of rules which are "multinational" with respect to their contents.

Apart from cases in which the national legislature has taken over a model text or was invited to do so, procedural rules which are "multinational" in terms of their contents can also be found in purely private agreements. It might be doubtful whether individual procedural agreements like arbitration clauses[83] are already a multinational "rule" if concluded by parties from different nations. In our eyes, at least those procedural agreements which are used frequently do

---

RabelsZ 201, 209 ff.; M. Taruffo, "Harmonisation in a Global Context: The ALI/UNIDROIT Principles" in X.E. Kramer and C.H. van Rhee (eds.), *Civil Litigation in a Globalising World*, Springer, The Hague 2012, pp. 207 ff.

[76] But note that Uruguay's Code of Civil Procedure of 1989 was strongly influenced by the Código Procesal Civil Modelo para Iberoamérica; see J.C. Barbosa Moreira, above n. 70, p. 443; J.A. Jolowicz, "On the Comparison of Procedures" in J.A.R. Nafziger and S. Symeonides (eds.), *Law and Justice in a Multistate World – Essays in Honor of Arthur T. von Mehren*, Transnational Publishers, Ardsley, N.Y. 2002, pp. 721, 727; E. Oteiza, above n. 70, pp. 475 f.

[77] UNCITRAL Model Law, above n. 30.

[78] Amendments to the Arbitration (Foreign Awards and Agreements) Act 1974 by the International Arbitration Amendment Act 1989 No. 25 (1989), https://www.legislation.gov.au/Details/C2004A03773.

[79] Law No. 138 of 2003, entered into force on March 1, 2004, English translation available at http://japan.kantei.go.jp/policy/sihou/arbitrationlaw.pdf. On arbitration in Japan and the reform, see, e.g., S. Nakano, "International Commercial Arbitration under the New Arbitration Law of Japan" (2004) 47 *Japanese Ann. Int'l L.* 96, 97 ff.; F. Kun, "Salient Features of International Commercial Arbitration in East Asia: A Comparative Study of China and Japan" (2016) 5 *Am. U. Bus. L. Rev.* 447, 457–462.

[80] Gesetz zur Neuregelung des Schiedsverfahrensrechts (Schiedsverfahrens-Neuregelungsgesetz – SchiedsVG) of December 22, 1997, BGBl. I, p. 3224.

[81] UNCITRAL Model Law on International Commercial Arbitration 1985 with amendments as adopted in 2006, http://www.uncitral.org/pdf/english/texts/arbitration/ml-arb/07-86998_Ebook.pdf.

[82] Cf. J. Münch, in *Münchener Kommentar zur ZPO*, vol. 3, 5th ed., C.H. Beck, Munich 2017, Vorbemerkung zu §1025 mn. 185 (calling the 2006 UNCITRAL Amendments concerning interim measures and preliminary orders in Art. 17–17j "almost hypertrophic").

[83] Cf. A. do Passo Cabral, *Convenções Processuais*, JusPODIVM, Salvador 2016, p. 76; C.A. Kern, in Stein/Jonas, ZPO, vol. 2, 23rd ed., Mohr Siebeck, Tübingen 2016, Vor §128 mn. 250; C.A. Kern, "Procedural Contracts in Germany" in A. do Passo Cabral and P.H. Nogueira (eds.), *Negócios Processuais*, 3rd ed., JusPODIVM, Salvador 2017, pp. 213 ff. For an account of the scholarly discussion about the "nature" (procedural or substantive) of the arbitration agreement, see G. Wagner, *Prozeßverträge*, Mohr Siebeck, Tübingen 1998, pp. 578 ff.

have, in practice, the character of multinational rules. Admittedly, in the field of procedure, there are no model clauses which have attained the same level of influence as, for example, the Incoterms or the International Chamber of Commerce (ICC)'s Uniform Customs and Practice for Documentary Credits (UCP) in the field of substantive (more particularly, transportation and documentary credit) law.[84] However, over the last few years, model clauses dealing with aspects of dispute resolution procedure have become increasingly important. This is particularly true for so-called "escalation clauses," i.e., clauses that determine which steps the parties to a contract must undertake before they are allowed to resort to arbitration or the public courts.[85] Prominent examples of this are the dispute resolution clauses in the forms of contracts proposed by the International Federation of Consulting Engineers (FIDIC). These forms of contracts provide that once negotiation has failed, disputes must be referred to a Dispute Avoidance/Adjudication Board or a Dispute (Adjudication) Board as a condition preceding arbitration.[86] A party that is not willing to accept the Board's decision must issue a notice of dissatisfaction within a certain period of time. This opens the door for arbitration, but the commencement of arbitration proceedings may be postponed until the project is complete. It is the aim of such clauses to maintain communication between the parties and enable the project to proceed.[87] Under our broad understanding of dispute resolution, rules that deal with the pre-arbitration phase are clearly "rules of dispute resolution," particularly as they should be given effect by arbitral tribunals and public courts when determining the admissibility of the complaint, provided the clause is formulated as a condition to subsequent arbitral or court proceedings.[88]

While such contract clauses somehow mirror the recognition and enforcement rules, in that they deal with a peripheral issue, at least from the perspective of the core arbitration or court proceedings, with the former dealing with a pre- and the letter with a post-core aspect, there are also purely private rules

---

[84]   On their character as law, see, e.g., F.K. JUENGER, above n. 22, pp. 494 f.; A. ROSETT, above n. 5, p. 685.

[85]   See, e.g., K.P. BERGER, "Law and Practice of Escalation Clauses" (2006) 22 *Arbitr. Int'l* 1; O. KRAUSS, "The Enforceability of Escalation Clauses Providing for Negotiations in Good Faith under English Law" (2015–2016) 2 *McGill J. Disp. Resol.* 142, 144 ff.

[86]   See, e.g., A.J. ROQUETTE, "Am Ende des Regenbogens – Die neuen FIDIC Dispute Adjudication/Avoidance Boards" [2018] *SchiedsVZ* 233; R. TSCHERNING, *Construction Disputes in International Energy and Natural Resources Infrastructure Project Delivery: Re-stating the Dispute Avoidance Objective of the FIDIC Dispute Adjudication Board Mechanism*, Dr. Kovač, Hamburg 2020, pp. 52 ff. On the introduction of the board, replacing the engineer, see C.R. SEPPALA, "The New FIDIC Provision for a Dispute Adjudication Board" (1997) 1997 *Int'l Bus. L.J.* 967; C.R. SEPPALA, "FIDIC's New Standard Forms of Contract: Claims, Resolution of Disputes and the Dispute Adjudication Board" (2001) 2001 *Int'l Bus. L.J.* 3.

[87]   K.P. BERGER, above n. 85, p. 2.

[88]   Cf. E. KAJKOWSKA, *Enforceability of Multi-tiered Dispute Resolution Clauses*, Hart Publishing, Oxford 2017, *passim*; K.P. BERGER, above n. 85, pp. 4 ff.; O. KRAUSS, above n. 85, pp. 147 ff.

which deal directly with the proceedings as such. In most legal systems, there is only very limited room for such private rules in proceedings before courts.[89] But there is ample room for such private rules in arbitration. And, indeed, the International Bar Association has succeeded in codifying guidelines and rules which have found widespread acceptance in the community.[90] Note, once again, that multinational rules are most important in arbitration – and with this observation in mind, let us now turn to multinational systems.

In a sense, purely national procedural law could also be listed here insofar as it applies to disputes which are, in one sense or another, international in nature. A good example here is the Swiss Private International Law Act, which contains rules for international arbitration,[91] while the rules for purely national arbitration are contained in the Civil Procedure Code.[92] However, such national law lacks the multinational character due to the lack of harmonization or uniformity. Insofar as the general rules of national procedural law for public courts or arbitration apply to international disputes,[93] there might be parallels for historical reasons.[94] However, there is mostly no particular interest in maintaining these parallels, and these rules have not been designed particularly for international disputes. Therefore, we do not consider purely national law as "multinational" for our purposes here.

---

[89]   C.A. Kern, in A. do Passo Cabral and P.H. Nogueira, above n. 83, p. 217.

[90]   Guidelines on Conflicts of Interests in International Arbitration (2014); Guidelines on Party Representation in International Arbitration (2013); Rules on Taking of Evidence in International Arbitration (2010), available at https://www.ibanet.org/publications/ publications_IBA_guides_and_free_materials.aspx#Practice%20Rules%20and%20 Guidelines.

[91]   Chapter 12 of the Private International Law Act 1987 (PIL Act), available at https://www. swissarbitration.org/files/34/Swiss%20International%20Arbitration%20Law/IPRG_english.pdf.

[92]   Part 3 of the Swiss Civil Procedure Code (CPC) of December 19, 2008, available at https://www.admin.ch/opc/en/classified-compilation/20061121/201801010000/272.pdf.

[93]   For a discussion of the *lex fori* principle, see H. Kronke, "Das Lex-fori-"Prinzip" im internationalen Zivilprozessrecht" (2016) 20 *ZZPInt* 399.

[94]   Parallels in the area of procedure can be the result of colonialization (for a short overview of the reception of English civil procedure in the American colonies, see L.M. Friedman, *A History of American Law*, Simon & Schuster, New York 1973, pp. 49 ff.; R.W. Millar, *Civil Procedure of the Trial Court in Historical Perspective*, Law Center of New York University for the National Conference of Judicial Councils, New York 1952, pp. 39 ff. For law and colonialism, see generally H.P. Glenn, *Legal Traditions of the World. Sustainable Diversity in Law*, 4th ed., Oxford University Press, Oxford 2010, pp. 273 ff.; M. Siems, *Comparative Law*, Cambridge University Press, Cambridge 2014, pp. 205 ff.) or of a voluntary adoption for reasons of quality (on the influence of German law, mainly in the end of the nineteenth century, see, inter alia, H. Matsumoto, "Die Rezeption des deutschen Zivilprozessrechts in der Meiji-Zeit und die weitere Entwicklung des japanischen Zivilprozessrechts bis zum Zweiten Weltkrieg" (2007) 120 *ZZP* 3 ff.; M. Deguchi, "Das Spannungsverhältnis im Zivilprozessrecht" in P. Gottwald (ed.), *Recht und Gesellschaft in Deutschland und Japan*, Carl Heymanns, Cologne 2009, pp. 125–127; and the essays in W.J. Habscheid (ed.), *Das deutsche Zivilprozeßrecht und seine Ausstrahlung auf andere Rechtsordnungen*, Gieseking, Bielefeld 1991).

3.2. MULTINATIONAL SYSTEMS

3.2.1. *Multinational Character by Virtue of "Nationality"*

If multinational systems are understood as sets of rules together with an infrastructure for their administration, and if we start with systems created by the law makers of more than two nations or a multinational law maker, we find some very prominent examples.

A first and perhaps unexpected example is the World Trade Organization (WTO) Dispute Settlement. Indeed, the WTO itself calls its dispute settlement a "system."[95] Broadly speaking, in this system of dispute resolution, WTO Member States try to settle their trade disputes.[96] The system consists of sets of detailed procedural rules – the Dispute Settlement Understanding[97] and the Working Procedures for Panels[98] and for Appellate Review[99] – and the dispute resolution infrastructure. This infrastructure comprises an indicative list of experts[100] who can be nominated to the three- or five-member panels,[101] the WTO Director-General's power to appoint the panelists failing an agreement by the countries in dispute on the panelists,[102] a permanent seven-member Standing Appellate Body out of whom three members hear an appeal[103] and, something that is very important in practice, a secretariat responsible for assisting

---

[95]   *A Handbook on the WTO Dispute Settlement System, Prepared by the Legal Affairs Division and the Rules Division of the WTO Secretariat, and the Appellate Body Secretariat*, 2nd ed., Cambridge University Press, Cambridge 2017.

[96]   See E.U. PETERSMANN, *The GATT/WTO Dispute Settlement System*, Kluwer Law International, The Hague 1998, p. 67 and *passim*; WTO, "A Unique Contribution, Principles: Equitable, Fast, Effective, Mutually Acceptable," https://www.wto.org/english/thewto_e/whatis_e/tif_e/disp1_e.htm.

[97]   Understanding on Rules and Procedures Governing the Settlement of Disputes (DSU), Annex 2 of the WTO Agreement, ILM Vol. 33, No. 1, pp. 112–135, January 1994; on the reform discussion, see WTO, "Negotiations to Improve Dispute Settlement Procedures," https://www.wto.org/English/tratop_e/dispu_e/dispu_negs_e.htm; J. LEE, "A More Widely Available Public Good: Proposed DSU Reform and its Implication for Developing Members" (2017) 51 *J. of World Trade* 987.

[98]   Art. 12.1 DSU and Appendix 3 to the DSU.

[99]   Art. 17.9 DSU; Working Procedures for Appellate Review, ILM Vol. 35, No. 2, pp. 495–519, March 1996, as amended, current version available at https://www.wto.org/english/tratop_e/dispu_e/ab_e.htm.

[100]   Art. 8.4 DSU. For the indicative list, see https://docs.wto.org/dol2fe/Pages/FE_Search/FE_S_S006.aspx?Query=(@Symbol=%20wt/dsb/44%20or%20wt/dsb/44/*)&Language=ENGLISH&Context=FomerScriptedSearch&languageUIChanged=true#. Also, an expert who is not included in the indicative list may be considered; see WTO, "A Unique Contribution – How are Disputes Settled?", https://www.wto.org/english/thewto_e/whatis_e/tif_e/disp1_e.htm.

[101]   Art. 8.5 DSU.

[102]   Ibid., Art. 8.7. See WTO, "A Unique Contribution – Appeals," https://www.wto.org/english/thewto_e/whatis_e/tif_e/disp1_e.htm.

[103]   Art. 17 DSU.

the panels.[104] As is well known, respect for the rulings is based on the possibility of countermeasures if the losing party does not comply with a ruling.[105] WTO Dispute Settlement is the successor to the General Agreement on Tariffs and Trade (GATT) settlement procedure which was based on less detailed rules and was much less effective.[106] It is important to note that WTO Member States can neither block the proceedings nor the adoption of a ruling, as a ruling can only be rejected if there is a consensus among WTO Member States, including the adversary in the case.

A second example is ICSID, with its rules for arbitration and conciliation. The Center, comprising an Administrative Council with rule-making power and a Secretariat, was created by the 1966 ICSID Convention,[107] a multilateral treaty today ratified by 154 Contracting States.[108] ICSID arbitration presupposes a written arbitration agreement – which, however, is typically established once there is an arbitration clause in an investment treaty or investment law, interpreted as standing offer, and the written request for arbitration by the investor.[109] Regardless of the discussions about a legitimacy crisis of investment arbitration,[110] it is beyond any doubt that since the last two decades ICSID arbitration has become a very important multinational dispute resolution system.[111] For the purposes of the discussion here, it is interesting to note that commentators observe a convergence between international trade and investment dispute resolution.[112]

---

[104]   Ibid., Art 27.

[105]   Ibid., arts. 3.7, 22; see also WTO, "The Process – Stages in a Typical WTO Dispute Settlement Case. 6.10 Countermeasures by the Prevailing Member (Suspension of Obligations)," https://www.wto.org/English/tratop_e/dispu_e/disp_settlement_cbt_e/c6s10p1_e.htm.

[106]   E.U. Petersmann, above n. 96, pp. 66 ff., 92 ff.

[107]   Convention on the settlement of investment disputes between States and nationals of other States. Opened for signature at Washington, D.C. on March 18, 1965, 575 U.N.T.S. 159.

[108]   Status table by UNTC, https://treaties.un.org/pages/showDetails.aspx?objid=080000028012a925.

[109]   See G. Bastid-Burdeau, "Nouvelles perspectives pour l'arbitrage dans le contentieux économique intéressant les États" (1995) 3 Rev. de l'arb. 15; T.W. Wälde, "Investment Arbitration under the Energy Charter Treaty" (1996) 12 Arb. Int'l 429, 435; UNCTAD, "Denunciation of the ICSID Convention and BITs: Impact on Investor-State Claims" IIA Issues Note No. 2, December 2010, p. 2.

[110]   See, e.g., S.D. Franck, "The Legitimacy Crisis in Investment Treaty Arbitration: Privatizing Public International Law through Inconsistent Decisions" (2005) 73 Fordham L. Rev. 1521, 1582 ff.; C.N. Brower and S.W. Schill, "Is Arbitration a Threat or a Boon to the Legitimacy of International Investment Law?" (2009) 9 Chi. J. Int'l L. 471.

[111]   For numbers, see ICSID, "The ICSID Caseload – Statistics," https://icsid.worldbank.org/en/Pages/resources/ICSID-Caseload-Statistics.aspx.

[112]   See, e.g., R.P. Alford, "The Convergence of International Trade and Investment Arbitration" (2013) 12 Santa Clara J. Int'l L. 35; F. Li, "The Driving Forces of the Convergence of WTO Dispute Settlement Mechanism and International Investment Arbitration" (2018) 52 J. of World Trade 479, 491 ("homogeneity of trade and investment dispute resolution"); and the essays in J.A. Huerta-Goldman, A. Romanetti, and F.X. Stirnimann (eds.), WTO Litigation, Investment Arbitration, and Commercial Arbitration, Kluwer Law International, Alphen aan den Rijn 2013.

A regional system of dispute resolution created by the law makers of more than two nations is the European court system insofar as it is not limited to the preliminary ruling discussed above but directly decides the dispute. This is the case where the European courts have exclusive jurisdiction. Exclusive jurisdiction of European courts is a matter of course for disputes among EU institutions and Member States. More relevant with respect to the global economy are disputes for which "specialized courts" have been created[113] – which currently do not exist – and which fall within the jurisdiction of the GC, such as actions against acts of the institutions, bodies, offices, or agencies of the EU (in particular, the EU Commission), actions seeking compensation for damage caused by the institutions, etc. of the EU, and actions relating to intellectual property brought against the EU Intellectual Property Office and the Community Plant Variety Office. Decisions of the GC may be appealed before the ECJ, but will be limited to points of law.[114] In all these cases, both the applicable procedural rules and the court infrastructure have been created by the EU Member States – a multinational system of dispute resolution with a regional scope.

A quite different example from the three which have been presented so far is the World Intellectual Property Organization (WIPO) Arbitration and Mediation Center. Nevertheless, it deserves to be mentioned here as it has been created by WIPO, an international organization and therefore a multinational law maker, and as its caseload has been growing considerably over the last decade.[115] The WIPO Arbitration and Mediation Center offers dispute resolution in the forms of mediation, arbitration, expedited arbitration and expert determination in intellectual property and domain name disputes. For each of these forms, there is a detailed set of rules.[116] Moreover, administrative support is provided by "the Center," which is de facto a secretariat,[117] and an online electronic case facility (eADR).[118] Although sponsored by an international organization, these dispute resolution services are offered to private parties like normal ADR. They presuppose consent which can be expressed before or after the dispute has arisen.

---

[113] Art. 257 TFEU. So far, the only "specialized court" was the Civil Service Tribunal, which was created in 2005 but was dissolved in 2016.

[114] Art. 256(1) TFEU.

[115] WIPO Caseload Summary, https://www.wipo.int/amc/en/center/caseload.html; see also J. SCHALLNAU and J. FELDGES, "WIPO Mediation und Schiedsgerichtsbarkeit für den Grünen Bereich" [2017] GRUR Int. 21.

[116] WIPO Mediation Rules, https://www.wipo.int/amc/en/mediation/rules; WIPO Arbitration Rules, https://www.wipo.int/amc/en/arbitration/rules; WIPO Expedited Arbitration Rules https://www.wipo.int/amc/en/arbitration/expedited-rules; WIPO Expert Determination Rules https://www.wipo.int/amc/en/expert-determination/rules/ (all accessed 29.04.2019).

[117] Cf. WIPO, "Role of the Center," https://www.wipo.int/amc/en/center/role.html.

[118] WIPO, "WIPO Online Case Administration Tools," https://www.wipo.int/amc/en/eadr/index.html.

Intersentia

For this purpose, WIPO recommends certain contract clauses and submission agreements.[119]

3.2.2. *Multinational Character by Virtue of "Contents"*

From WIPO ADR it is not far to examples of systems of dispute resolution whose multinational character does not follow from the "nationality" of the law maker, but from the availability of the system for the global economy. In the first place, we have to name here the so-called "institutional" arbitration provided by (mostly) privately organized arbitration institutions. Most of these systems offer their services for international commercial disputes, with a broad definition of what is commercial in this sense. The classic example is arbitration under the auspices of the ICC, but other examples would make up a long list, ranging from the Japan Commercial Arbitration Association (JCAA) to the Hong Kong International Arbitration Centre (HKIAC) and the Arbitration Institute of the Stockholm Chamber of Commerce (SCC) to the American Arbitration Association (AAA).[120] All these private arbitration institutions offer ADR services, arbitration being only one of them, based on sets of rules enacted by the respective institution[121] or borrowed from an international standard-setting

---

[119] WIPO, "Recommended WIPO Contract Clauses and Submission Agreements," https://www.wipo.int/amc/en/clauses; see J. Schallnau and J. Feldges, above n. 115, pp. 23 f.

[120] For disputes relating to China, parties favor the China International Economic and Trade Arbitration Commission (CIETAC) in Beijing, the Shanghai International Economic and Trade Arbitration Commission (SHIAC) in Shanghai, and the Shenzhen Court of International Arbitration (SCIA) (a merger, on December 25, 2017, of the South China International Economic and Trade Arbitration Commission with the Shenzhen Arbitration Commission) in Shenzhen; see L. Pan, "A Guide to Commercial Contracts under Chinese Law" [2017] *IHR* 102, 105; C.K. Tahbaz and J.R. Rassi, "The Development of Arbitral Institutions in Asia" (2018) 13 *U. Pa. Asian L. Rev.* 102, 111–115 (reporting the recent split of what later became SHIAC and SCIA from CIETAC).

[121] For the ICC, see, e.g., the ICC Rules of Arbitration, the ICC Mediation Rules, the ICC Expert Rules, the ICC Dispute Board Rules, and the ICC Rules for a Pre-arbitral Referee Procedure, all available at https://iccwbo.org/dispute-resolution-services; for the JCAA, see the JCAA Arbitration Rules, available at http://www.jcaa.or.jp/e/arbitration/rules.html, and the JCAA International Commercial Mediation Rules, available at http://www.jcaa.or.jp/e/mediation/docs/rules.pdf; for the HKIAC, see the Administered Arbitration Rules, available at http://www.hkiac.org/arbitration/rules-practice-notes/hkiac-administered-2018, the Mediation Rules, available at http://www.hkiac.org/mediation/rules/hkiac-mediation-rules, the Adjudication Rules, available at http://www.hkiac.org/adjudication/adjudication-rules, and various additional rules for domain name dispute resolution, available at http://www.hkiac.org/arbitration/rules-practice-notes/hkiac-administered-2018; for the SCC, see the Arbitration Rules, the Expedited Arbitration Rules, and the Mediation Rules, all available at https://sccinstitute.com/dispute-resolution/rules; for the AAA, see the various arbitration, mediation, and other dispute settlement rules, available at https://www.adr.org/active-rules. On the increasing number of rules and regulations, see M. Chen, "Emerging Internal Control in Institutional Arbitration" (2018) 18 *Cardozo J. Conflict Resol.* 295, 297 ff.

organization – mainly the UNCITRAL Arbitration Rules mentioned above.[122] In addition to the rules, these institutions provide for an infrastructure relating to, *inter alia*, the appointment of arbitrators, the control of deadlines, translation services, the review of awards, travel assistance, hearing rooms, and, last but not least, fee collection.

Another area of truly multinational arbitration should not go unmentioned here: sports arbitration by the Court of Arbitration for Sports (CAS) in Lausanne, Switzerland. The CAS was originally created by the International Olympic Committee in the 1980s, but in 1994 became a formally independent institution, controlled by the International Council of Arbitration for Sport (ICAS).[123] Despite doubts as to its actual independence which have not been completely wiped away by a number of reforms,[124] the Swiss Federal Court has, in two famous decisions, considered the CAS to be a true arbitral tribunal whose awards may be challenged like other international arbitration awards.[125] The CAS arbitration system is based on Statutes and Procedural Rules codified in the so-called Code of Sports-Related Arbitration.[126] The CAS administers justice through the Ordinary Arbitration Division, the Appeals Arbitration Division, which reviews decisions of federations, associations, or other sports-related bodies, and a new permanent Anti-doping Division established in January 2019 to resolve disputes relating to anti-doping matters.[127] Moreover, since the 1996 Olympic Games in Atlanta, the CAS has regularly provided on-site Ad Hoc Divisions for major events such as the Olympic, Asian or Commonwealth Games.[128] In addition to arbitration, the CAS also offers sports-related mediation services, based on its

---

[122]   For the JCAA, see, e.g., the Administrative Rules for UNCITRAL Arbitration as amended and effective on January 1, 2019, http://www.jcaa.or.jp/e/arbitration/docs/UNCITRAL_Arbitration_Rules.pdf; for the SCC, see "UNCITRAL at SCC," https://sccinstitute.com/dispute-resolution/uncitral-at-scc; G.B. BORN, above n. 4, pp. 29, 32; N. BLACKABY and C. PARTASIDES, above n. 5, p. 47.

[123]   See, e.g., CAS, "History of the CAS," https://www.tas-cas.org/en/general-information/history-of-the-cas.html; M. REEB, "Le Tribunal Arbitral du Sport: son histoire et son fonctionnement" in M. REEB (ed.), *Recueil des sentences du TAS – Digest of CAS Awards III (2001–2003)*, Kluwer Law International, The Hague 2004, pp. XVII ff.

[124]   See, e.g., A. BRUNK, *Der Sportler und die institutionelle Sportschiedsgerichtsbarkeit*, Nomos, Baden-Baden 2016, *passim*; K. THORN and C. LASTHAUS, "Das Pechstein-Urteil des BGH – ein Freibrief für die Sportschiedsgerichtsbarkeit?" [2016] *IPRax* 426, 429 ff.; T. SUMMERER, "Die Zukunft der Schiedsgerichtsbarkeit im Sport – Reformvorschläge für den CAS" [2018] *SpuRt* 197.

[125]   BGE 119 II 271 E.3.b – *"Gundel"*; on this decision, see, inter alia, A. RIGOZZI, *L'arbitrage international en matière de sport*, Helbing Lichtenhahn, Basel 2005, mn. 521 ff. See also BGE 129 III 445 E.3.3.4 – *"Lazutina/Danilova"*; on this decision, see, inter alia, M. BADDELEY, "Thoughts on Swiss Federal Tribunal Decision 129 III 445" [2004] *Causa Sport (CaS)* 91 ff.

[126]   The current version of this Code has been in force since January 1, 2019; see https://www.tas-cas.org/fileadmin/user_upload/Code_2019__en_.pdf.

[127]   Art. S 20 of the Code of Sports-Related Arbitration.

[128]   For more details, see R.H. MCLAREN, "CAS Ad Hoc Division: An Olympic Experience!" [2004] *SchiedsVZ* 187 ff.

own Mediation Rules.[129] These sets of procedural rules, together with lists of arbitrators and mediators specializing in sports law,[130] as well as a secretariat known as the Court Office, facilities in Lausanne, and decentralized offices in Sydney and New York,[131] make the CAS system one of the most comprehensive multinational ADR systems in the world. The fact that not only its decisions on the merits but also its procedural rules have become the object of serious academic research,[132] and the increasing number of cases[133] are proof of the significance of the CAS.

Examples which at first sight do not seem to have much in common with the foregoing are optional resolution mechanisms offered by certain industries to their customers. These dispute resolution mechanisms can take various forms, ranging from internal "complaint management centers" over privately organized ADR institutions to ADR entities established or run by public authorities. These centers, institutions, or other entities are equipped with the necessary administrative and case management staff. They operate according to a set of relatively simple – and, from the point of view of a proceduralist, sometimes simplistic – procedural rules. Proceedings are conducted in writing or online, with increasing levels of IT support. These dispute resolution mechanisms normally do not block access to the public court system and do not end in a binding decision, but rather a proposal to settle the dispute.[134] In the beginning,

---

[129] CAS Mediation Rules, available at https://www.tas-cas.org/en/mediation/rules.html. For details, see D. MAVROMATI, "Mediation of Sports-Related Disputes: Facts, Statistics and Prospects for CAS Mediation Procedures" (2015) 2 *CAS-Bulletin* 24 ff.

[130] For more details, see https://www.tas-cas.org/en/arbitration/list-of-arbitrators-general-list. html; https://www.tas-cas.org/en/arbitration/list-of-arbitrators-football-list.html; https:// www.tas-cas.org/en/mediation/list-of-mediators.html.

[131] For more details, see https://www.tas-cas.org/en/general-information/addresses-and-contacts.html. Also, Alternative Hearing Centres in Shanghai (China), Abu Dhabi (UAE), Kuala Lumpur (Malaysia) and Cairo (Egypt) have been established.

[132] See, e.g., A. DUTTIG, *Comfortably Satisfied?*, Nomos, Baden-Baden 2019, *passim*; F. OSCHÜTZ, *Sportschiedsgerichtsbarkeit – Die Schiedsverfahren des Tribunal Arbitral du Sport vor dem Hintergrund des schweizerischen und deutschen Schiedsverfahrensrechts*, Duncker & Humblot, Berlin 2005, *passim*; M. VIRET, *Evidence in Anti-doping at the Intersection of Science and Law*, Asser Press, Springer, The Hague 2016, *passim*.

[133] In 2016, 599 procedures began. Cf. https://www.tas-cas.org/fileadmin/user_upload/CAS_statistics_2016_.pdf.

[134] But see Art. 10(2) of Directive 2013/11/EU of the European Parliament and of the Council of May 21, 2013 on alternative dispute resolution for consumer disputes and amending Regulation (EC) No 2006/2004 and Directive 2009/22/EC (Directive on consumer ADR), OJ L 165 of June 18, 2013, pp. 63–79. See also PayPal Buyer Protection Policy, https://www.paypal.com/ de/webapps/mpp/ua/buyerprotection-full?locale.x=en_DE, Rule 4.5: "The decision about the Claim under PayPal Buyer Protection is final and any legal actions against PayPal with respect to this decision are excluded; your statutory rights remain without limitation apart from the provisions of this PayPal Buyer Protection policy." The German Federal Supreme Court held, in two landmark decisions, that the seller's claim for payment of the purchase price is "revived" if PayPal refunds the buyer and claims the "payout amount" from the seller: BGH 22.11.2017 – VIII ZR 83/16, ZIP 2017, 93; 22.11.2017 – VIII ZR 213/16, ZIP 2018, 226.

some industries have created such mechanisms by self-interest.[135] During the last decade, a number of legislatures like the EU have mandated that such dispute resolution mechanisms be available for disputes arising out of certain consumer contracts.[136] To date, most of these mechanisms are not completely multinational; in other words, they are not completely identical throughout the whole world, but are somehow adapted to the countries in which they are employed. However, these adaptations are mostly a consequence of language and culture. With respect to procedure, the differences are rather small, as legislatures see no need to regulate these dispute resolution mechanisms in detail due to their optional character.

3.3. OBSERVATIONS

Coming back to the question asked above, what is the current state of affairs? First, we have seen that there are various kinds of multinational rules and systems of dispute resolution. Some of these are multinational due to the law makers that created them; some of them are multinational with respect to their scope. Second, multinational rules and systems are very important in the area of ADR, i.e., in situations in which the parties, by consent, opt out of the public court system.[137] Third, outside ADR, multinational rules cover rather peripheral aspects of dispute resolution. To this category belong, inter alia, the rules on recognition and enforcement, the mostly regional rules on "direct" jurisdiction, the rules on letters rogatory, and the similarly regional procedural rules on the proceedings for a preliminary ruling of the ECJ. This means, fourth, that for the core procedural issues of the proceedings before public courts, there are still no multinational rules or systems. This leads us readily to the question of whether this will change in the future – the question of perspectives.

4. PERSPECTIVES

Isn't it astonishing that in an era of global economy, multinational rules and systems of dispute resolution are, generally speaking, limited to ADR and peripheral aspects of dispute resolution by the courts? And if the era of the

---

[135] See, e.g., C. RULE, above n. 12, pp. 355 ff. (describing the introduction of eBay's dispute resolution system).

[136] See Directive 2013/11/EU, above n. 134; and Regulation (EU) No 524/2013 of the European Parliament and of the Council of May 21, 2013 on online dispute resolution for consumer disputes and amending Regulation (EC) No 2006/2004 and Directive 2009/22/EC (Regulation on consumer ODR), OJ L 165 of June 18, 2013, pp. 1–12.

[137] For a similar observation, see U. BLAUROCK, above n. 5, pp. 16 f., 25.

Intersentia

global economy with transnational litigation[138] continues – which seems probable despite the developments since 2017 – shouldn't we expect to find, or maybe even promote to create, multinational rules and systems of dispute resolution also concerning the core procedural issues of the proceedings before public courts?

4.1. CHANCES

4.1.1. Economic Advantages

Underlying these questions is the idea that the global economy should push for multinational rules and systems.[139] And, indeed, multinational rules and systems could secure equal treatment, prevent divergent decisions, enhance legal certainty and reduce the costs for parties and the justice system as a whole.[140] It is true that until now, parties, and in particular businesses, face different rules and systems of dispute resolution in every country in which they are involved in a dispute before the public courts. Multinational rules and systems would make it possible to use the same strategy everywhere, would eventually make it possible to have one lawyer deal with all cases of a certain type, regardless of where they were tried, and would perhaps even bring about decisions that have a global *res judicata* and persuasive authority effect.

4.1.2. Quality

Moreover, for a number of countries, multinational rules would bring about an important improvement if they were a codification of best practices, and a multinational system could even do away with the deficient infrastructure that affects many court systems. Therefore, multinational rules and systems seem

---

[138] On this term, see, e.g., L. SILBERMAN, Transnational Litigation: Is There a "Field"? – A Tribute to Hal Maier" (2006) 39 *Vand. J. Transnat'l L.* 1427.

[139] In this sense, see M. TARUFFO, "A Project of Rules for Transnational Litigation" in F. FERRARI (ed.), *The Unification of International Commercial Law*, Nomos, Baden-Baden 1998, pp. 189 f.; C. KESSEDJIAN, above n. 72, p. 480; G.C. HAZARD JR. and M. TARUFFO, "Discussion Draft N° 01: Transnational Rules of Civil Procedure" (1998–1999) 52 *Derecho PUCP* 621 (claiming that uniform rules "reduce the uncertainty and anxiety that particularly attend parties obliged to litigate in unfamiliar surroundings"); G.C. HAZARD, JR., M. TARUFFO, R. STÜRNER, and A. GIDI, "Introduction to the Principles and Rules of Transnational Civil Procedure" (2001) 33 *N.Y.U. J. Int'l L. & Pol.* 769; C. GIOVANNUCCI ORLANDI, "Procedural Law Issues and Uniform Law Conventions" (2000) 5 *Unif. L. Rev.* 23, 40 f.; however, see also G.B. BORN, above n. 72, pp. 402, 410 f.

[140] For a thorough analysis of the deficiencies of transnational civil proceedings in the absence of harmonized rules, see S. HUBER, *Entwicklung transnationaler Modellregeln für Zivilverfahren*, Mohr Siebeck, Tübingen 2008, pp. 11 ff.

desirable at least with respect to those countries where the public court system is hampered by procedural rules which are not state of the art as well as inadequate equipment and staffing of the judiciary.

4.1.3. Integrity

Last but not least, multinational rules and systems could, for a number of countries, enhance the independence of the judiciary, reduce corruption, and foster confidence in the legal system and the state as a whole. Indeed, multinational rules could make it more difficult for the current parliamentary majority or autocratic governments to exert pressure on judges by modifying their legal and institutional environment. This would not only improve the situation for parties to litigation in the respective countries, but would also stimulate business and attract foreign investors.

All of these are good arguments which would make us expect, or even push for, more multinational rules and systems.

4.2. DIFFICULTIES

Nevertheless, the fact that multinational rules and systems of dispute resolution to date have avoided the core procedural issues of the proceedings before public courts is not without reason.

4.2.1. Quality

First, those countries which enjoy a well-functioning judiciary are afraid of importing problems if the national procedural rules or even the system as a whole were to be changed. Actually, a number of successful law reforms[141] suggest that procedural law is at least one factor influencing the performance of a country's court system. And the huge differences in the performance of

---

[141]   For the 1976 reform in Germany, see Gesetz zur Vereinfachung und Beschleunigung gerichtlicher Verfahren (Vereinfachungsnovelle) of December 3, 1976, BGBl. I, p. 3281; for a first presentation, see H. Putzo, "Die Vereinfachungsnovelle" [1977] *NJW* 1, 1–10; H. Franzki, "Die Vereinfachungsnovelle und ihre bisherige Bewährung in der Verfahrenswirklichkeit" [1979] *NJW* 9, 9–14. The reform was inspired by a speech delivered by F. Baur in 1965 (F. Baur, *Wege zu einer Konzentration der mündlichen Verhandlung im Prozeß*, Walter de Gruyter, Berlin 1966) and was first realized in the form of the so-called Stuttgart model; see R. Bender, "The Stuttgart Model" in M. Cappelletti and J. Weisner (eds.), *Access to Justice, Vol. II, Promising Institutions*, Giuffrè, Milan 1979, pp. 431–475; R. Bender, "Die 'Hauptverhandlung' in Zivilsachen" [1968] *DRiZ* 163–167; see also "Erfolg im System" (1968) 34 *Der Spiegel* 27 ff.; Interview with R. Bender (1970) 8 *Der Spiegel* 36 ff.; N.J. Bettinger, above n. 70, pp. 61 ff.

national court systems shows that there is a real risk of decay for those who believe that their system is, all in all, working satisfactorily or even well.[142] This risk is particularly high with respect to the proceedings in public courts as in this area, multinational rules or systems can only by introduced by the law makers of the countries involved. Law makers typically try to strike a compromise. A compromise is often somewhere in between the existing solutions, sometimes the smallest common denominator, but rarely the most ambitious solution.[143] Of course, measuring the performance of a court system is intricate.[144] However, a positive overall perception is something no politician and no proceduralist would like to put at risk.

4.2.2. Budget

Second, changes in procedural rules, and even more so introducing a completely new procedural system, affect the caseload of the courts at the different levels and thereby, ultimately, the state budget.[145] Take as an illustration the rules on appeals, in particular appeals to the Supreme Court of a country. These rules are important for a number or reasons: the role of the Supreme Court between private and public interest,[146] the law-making function of the court,[147] and – last, but not least – the costs for the justice system and therefore the state budget. If the parties have an unrestricted right to appeal to the Supreme Court, it is clear that the number of appeals, and therefore also the need for judges in the Supreme

---

[142] This aspect which is not limited to procedural law is often completely ignored by those who deplore the state's resistance to harmonizing or unifying law; cf., e.g., J.P. TERHECHTE, "Die Europäische Union als Innovationsverbund – Innovationsverfassung und rechtliche Innovationen in der EU" [2017] *EuR* 3, 11 f., 21 ff.

[143] On the difficulties of drafting and the problem of "diplomatic" solutions, see A. ROSETT, above n. 5, p. 688.

[144] See C.A. KERN, "Perception, Performance and Politics: Recent Approaches to the Qualitative Comparison of Civil Justice Systems" (2009) 14 *ZZPInt* 445–496 = "Percepção, Performance e Política: recentes formas de abordagem da comparação qualitativa dos sistemas de justiça civil" *RePro* 198, ano 36, agosto 2011, 321–385 (translation into Portuguese by Alessandra Will and Teresa Arruda Alvim Wambier).

[145] See, e.g., L. CADIET, Pour une 'théorie générale du procès'" (2011) 28 *Ritsumeikan L. Rev.* 127, 143 f.

[146] See M. BOBEK, "Quantity or Quality? Reassessing the Role of Supreme Jurisdictions in Central Europe" (2009) 57 *Am. J. Comp. L.* 33, 40 f.; C.A. KERN, "The Role of the Supreme Court" *RePro* 228, ano 39, fevereiro 2014, 15–36 = "O papel das Cortes Supremas, in: Clèmerson Merlin Clève (org)" *Doutrinas Essencias Direito Constitucional, Volume X, Tomo I, Processo Constitucional, São Paulo: Revista dos Tribunais* 2015, pp. 115–144 (translation into Portuguese by Maria Angélica Feijó and Ronaldo Kochem) = "El rol de la Corte Suprema" in M. TARUFFO, L.G. MARINONI and D. MITIDIERO (coords), *La misión de los tribunales supremos, Colección Proceso y Derecho*, Marcial Pons, Madrid/Barcelona/Buenos Aires/São Paulo 2016, pp. 53–76 (translation into Spanish by Álvaro Pérez Ragone).

[147] See F. MAULTZSCH, *Streitentscheidung und Normbildung durch den Zivilprozess*, Mohr Siebeck, Tübingen 2010, pp. 334 ff.

Court, is much higher than in a system in which such appeals are restricted.[148] And where there is such a restriction, the caseload of the Supreme Court depends on the criteria and on the question of which court decides whether the criteria are met. If the restrictions are easy to apply, like a defined number of the minimum amount in dispute, the caseload depends on how high or low this number is set; the Supreme Court has almost no influence on its caseload, and a certain number and type of cases like consumer cases might never be decided by the Supreme Court. If the criteria are more open to interpretation, like the need to secure the uniformity of the jurisprudence or the significance of the question, the court which decides on the admissibility of the appeal has a certain amount of leeway – although no outright discretion – to influence the caseload for better or worse. If, finally, the Supreme Court itself has discretion to decide which appeals to take, it can take its caseload into account. It is quite obvious that countries in which restrictions exist are not willing to abandon them as long as there is not a high level of dissatisfaction with this system among the country's population. Therefore, it does not come as a surprise that only a few proposals to harmonize procedural law include the appeals level and that court organization is still considered a possible impediment to the harmonization of procedural law.[149]

4.2.3. The Legal Profession

Third, the legal profession in most countries has an interest in preserving the system as it is. Without reforms, lawyers as well as judges can continue their work as they are used to doing, and sometimes can benefit from inefficiencies to the detriment of the parties or the state budget. In the field of procedural law as well as in other fields, any reform (and in particular harmonization or uniformization) can have the effect of a redistribution, thus provoking the resistance of stakeholders.[150] Therefore, only rarely have reforms in the area of procedural law been welcomed with enthusiasm by the legal profession. Even academia is often rather skeptical when it comes to big reforms.

---

[148]   See M. BOBEK, above n. 146, p. 33 f.

[149]   For a more optimistic view, see F. FERRAND, "La procédure civile internationale et la procédure civile transnationale: l'incidence de l'intégration économique régionale" (2003) 8 *Unif. L. Rev.* 397, 400 (noting that the strong link between procedural law and court organization had been used as an argument against harmonization, but that these times are over); with respect not to international harmonization, but to the situation within the U.S., see also L. SILBERMAN, "Judicial Adjuncts Revisited: The Proliferation of Ad Hoc Procedure" (1989) 137 *U. Pa. L. Rev.* 2131, 2176 (noting that "institutional and organizational reform is always easier than specific and particularized rules").

[150]   H. KRONKE, "Ziele – Methoden, Kosten – Nutzen: Perspektiven der Privatrechtsharmonisierung nach 75 Jahren UNIDROIT" [2001] *JZ* 1149, 1150.

4.2.4. Traditions

Fourth, legal traditions in the field of procedural law are still more important than one might imagine, and these traditions do not necessarily have something to do with the "legal origins" which a group of economists,[151] using a debatable econometric approach,[152] wanted to make responsible for actual or alleged differences in the performance of court systems. It is worth giving short anecdotes from the current ELI/UNIDROIT Project "European Rules of Civil Procedure" in which I am involved as a co-reporter of two Working Groups: the "Judgments" Working Group and the "Appeals" Working Group. In the "Judgments" Working Group, one member argued that her country's legal profession would never accept "default judgments" in the event of non-appearance at a later hearing, as lawyers would often not attend a hearing in order to save time. In the "Appeals" Working Group, a draft rule containing restrictions to appeal was sent back with a comment saying: "Red line for [name of the country]." By no means do I want to blame those who highlighted the "red lines"; they were probably right. However, it is interesting to note that a rule which has been applied for more than a century in some countries and is perfectly acceptable for other countries may be completely unthinkable – behind the "red line" – for another country. Note that these differences in tradition exist within Europe, for which ELI and UNIDROIT believed that a harmonization of rules would be feasible with more ease than on a global scale,[153] taking into account the fact that the project's predecessor, the joint ALI/UNIDROIT project, in the end limited itself to principles and added rules only as a suggestion of the drafters ("Reporters' Study").[154]

---

[151] S. Djankov, R. La Porta, F. Lopez-de-Silanes, and A. Shleifer, "Courts" (2003) 118 Q. J. Econ. 453.

[152] See C.A. Kern, *Justice between Simplification and Formalism: A Discussion and Critique of the World Bank Sponsored Lex Mundi Project on Efficiency of Civil Procedure*, Mohr Siebeck, Tübingen 2007, *passim*; C.A. Kern, "Statistical Methods in Comparative Civil Procedure: Chances and Risks" in L. Cadiet, B. Hess, and M. Requejo Isidro (eds.), *Approaches to Procedural Law: The Pluralism of Methods*, Nomos, Baden-Baden 2017, pp. 121 ff.

[153] Cf. D. Wallis, "Introductory Remarks on the ELI-UNIDROIT Project" (2014) 19 *Unif. L. Rev.* 173; L. Cadiet, "The ALI-UNIDROIT Project: From Transnational Principles to European Rules of Civil Procedure" (2014) 19 *Unif. L. Rev.* 292, 293; R. Stürner, "Principles of European Civil Procedure or a European Model Code: Some Considerations on the Joint ELI-UNIDROIT Project" (2014) 19 *Unif. L. Rev.* 322, 323; J. Sorabji, "The ELI-UNIDROIT Project. An Introduction and an English Perspective" in A. Nylund and M. Strandberg (eds.), *Civil Procedure and Harmonisation of Law*, Intersentia, Cambridge 2019, pp. 35, 39–41.

[154] ALI/UNIDROIT, above n. 73; R. Stürner, above n. 75, p. 209. On the advantages and disadvantages or principles, rules, and their combination, see T. Pfeiffer, "The ALI/UNIDROIT Project: Are Principles Sufficient, without the Rules?" (2001) 6 *Unif. L. Rev.* 1015.

4.2.5. Constitutionalization

Fifth, but closely connected to the fourth point, the "constitutionalization" of procedural law has erected important obstacles to harmonization, let alone uniformization.

Many constitutions contain articles concerning procedural law. While most of these articles embrace general procedural principles like judicial independence, the right to be heard, or the right to the "lawful" or "natural" judge,[155] some of them go into detail in the form of explicit and unequivocal prescriptions, thereby limiting the possibility of multinational harmonization. A notable example of this can be found in countries like Italy, whose Constitution guarantees every party a right to appeal to the Supreme Court.[156] Not only is amending the Constitution difficult because of the special majority requirements for amendments, but abolishing a right to appeal is also politically unthinkable, as the normal citizen would only see that he/she might no longer be allowed to challenge an unfavorable decision, without taking into account that he/she would also benefit from the improvement that a reasonable restriction would bring about in the system as a whole.

Apart from such clear cases, it has been the jurisprudence of constitutional courts, mainly over the last few decades, which has ennobled a number of – until then – purely procedural solutions into constitutional rules. As is well known, this is the case for the U.S. Supreme Court's interpretation of the due process clause[157] and, more specifically, the interpretation of the "minimum contacts" term,[158] which makes it difficult to create multilateral rules on jurisdiction.[159] This is also the case for the German Federal Constitutional Court's strict

---

[155]   See, e.g., Arts. 97, 101 and 103(2) of the German Constitution.

[156]   Art. 111(7) of the Italian Constitution; for critical remarks, see R. CAPONI, "The Performance of the Italian Civil Justice System: An Empirical Assessment" (2016) 2 *Italian L.J.* 15, 21 ff.

[157]   US Constitution, Amendment XIV, §1 cl. 3; on its significance for personal jurisdiction, see the fundamental decision in *Pennoyer v. Neff*, 95 U.S. 714 (1877).

[158]   See generally for *in personam* jurisdiction *International Shoe v. State of Washington*, 326 U.S. 310 (1945); on this case, see, e.g., L. SILBERMAN, "Two Cheers for *International Shoe* (and None for *Asahi*): An Essay on the Fiftieth Anniversary of *International Shoe*" (1995) 28 *U.C. Davis L. Rev.* 755, 762 (noting that "[i]n the United States, the issue is a legal constitutional one"); extended to quasi-in rem jurisdiction in *Shaffer v. Heitner*, 433 U.S. 186 (1977); on this case, see, e.g., L. SILBERMAN, "*Shaffer v. Heitner*: The End of an Era" (1978) 53 *N.Y.U. L. Rev.* 33.

[159]   See, e.g., R.A. BRAND, above n. 37, pp. 42 ff.; B. HESS, above n. 37, p. 343; F.K. JUENGER, "Judicial Jurisdiction in the United States and in the European Communities: A Comparison" (1984) 82 *Mich. L. Rev.* 1195, 1207; J. REGAN, "Recognition and Enforcement of Foreign Judgments: A Second Attempt in the Hague" (2015) 14 *Rich. J. Global L. & Bus.* 63, 69 f.; C.A. KERN, above n. 41, mn. 16.

interpretation of the constitutional guarantee of the natural judge, requiring courts to enact detailed court rules assigning each case to an individual judge via abstract rules.[160] As important as these interpretations are, and as much good as they have brought about, they make it very difficult to draft harmonized or even uniform rules.[161]

4.2.6. *Petrification*

Sixth, multinational rules are difficult to modify. This clearly entails one intrinsic risk of uniform law: the risk of petrification.[162] Developing the law on a multinational scale is much more difficult than in a nation state, at least if there is no common Supreme Court. It is important to note that in the field of ADR – where multinational rules and systems of dispute resolution play a much more important role than with respect to traditional public court proceedings – there is a lot of competition, competition among sets of rules, and competition among dispute settlement systems – and there is a freedom to choose. All this cannot easily be copied over to proceedings in public courts.

It would be possible to list a number of other difficulties here. However, the difficulties identified should be sufficient to illustrate the challenges that projects drafting uniform procedural rules face and to cast doubt on the idea of multinational dispute resolution systems outside the field of ADR.

---

[160]   Cf. C.A. KERN, "Der gesetzliche Richter – Verfassungsprinzip oder Ermessensfrage? Teil I" (2017) 130 *ZZP*, 91, 100 f.

[161]   Again, for a more optimistic view, see F. FERRAND, above n. 149, p. 400 (noting that national constitutions had been used as an argument against harmonization, but that these times are over).

[162]   See, e.g., P. BEHRENS, "Voraussetzungen und Grenzen der Rechtsfortbildung durch Rechtsvereinheitlichung" (1986) 50 *RabelsZ* 19, 26 f.; S. GOPALAN, "The Creation of International Commercial Law: Sovereignty Felled" (2004) 5 *San Diego Int'l L.J.* 267, 295; U.P. GRUBER, *Methoden des internationalen Einheitsrechts*, Mohr Siebeck, Tübingen 2004, pp. 106 f.; J. KROPHOLLER, *Internationales Einheitsrecht: Allgemeine Lehren*, J.C.B. Mohr, Tübingen 1975, p. 281; K. LINHART, *Internationales Einheitsrecht und einheitliche Auslegung*, Mohr Siebeck, Tübingen 2005, p. 40; G. RÜHL, *Statut und Effizienz*, Mohr Siebeck, Tübingen 2011, pp. 66 f.; T. KONO and K. KAGAMI, "Is a Uniform Law Always Preferable to Private International Law: A Critical Review of the Conventional Debate on Uniform Law and Private International Law from the Viewpoint of Economic Analysis" (2013) 56 *Japanese Y.B. Int'l L.* 314, 326; cf. also S.C. SYMEONIDES, "A New Conflicts Restatement: Why Not?" (2009) 5 *J. Priv. Int'l L.* 383, 419 f.; P. WIDMER, "The International Institute for the Unification of Private Law: Shipyard for Worldwide Unification of Private Law" (1999) 1 *Eur. J.L. Reform* 181, 185 (describing the discussion about unification and petrification "the present-day version of the struggle of Savigny versus Thibault [*sic*]"). A related problem is that uniform law precludes the innovative effects of a competition of legal systems; see, e.g., R. STÜRNER, "Some European Remarks on a New Joint Project of the American Law Institute and UNIDROIT" (2000) 34 *Int'l L.* 1071, 1075; G. RÜHL, cit., at 65 f. However, whether there is such competition in the field of civil procedure is questionable, see S. HUBER, above n. 140, pp. 43–46.

4.3. CONSEQUENCES

What does all this mean for the perspectives of multinational rules and systems of dispute resolution in the era of the global economy? In short, the perspectives continue to be good insofar as rules and systems of dispute resolution outside public courts are concerned, which is certainly a positive finding, and the perspectives are less good insofar as rules and systems of dispute resolution by the public court system are concerned – a finding which must attract our attention. Of course, the chances and difficulties of multinational law making generally and in the field of procedural law more specifically are nothing new. However, the comprehensive approach of our study shows that outside the public court system, everything seems to be easier. This is confirmed if we go through our six-point list of difficulties point by point. First, with respect to quality, as all forms of dispute resolution which take place outside the public court system are additional options, well-functioning systems, be they public or private, have nothing to fear. Second, with respect to budget, as almost all forms of dispute resolution which take place outside the public court system must be completely funded by the parties, there is no immediate concern for the state budget. Third, the legal profession is typically positive in relation to mediation and arbitration, as it offers possibilities to act as counsel and arbitrator. Fourth, this may also be a reason for why, quite surprisingly, traditions defended by the legal profession and academia with respect to procedural rules in public courts are not even mentioned by the same individuals once they are in an arbitration – for example, default judgments in arbitration are very rare[163] as parties and counsel rarely fail to attend a hearing or to comply with deadlines, and the absence of review is even accepted as an advantage of this dispute resolution mechanism.[164] Fifth, "constitutionalization" only has a very limited, filtered impact: it may only play a role for the *ordre public* argument in annulment proceedings and attacks on the recognition and enforcement of awards. However, not every departure even from a constitutional principle by an arbitral tribunal is necessarily a violation of the *ordre public* in this sense.[165] Sixth, the petrification risk is very limited, as there are many competing rules and systems of dispute resolution outside the public courts.

---

[163] Note that the UNCITRAL Model Law (Art. 25 lit. c) and national arbitration laws (e.g., §1048(2) of the German Code of Civil Procedure) do not provide for a default judgment in such a situation; however, if the parties agreed on the possibility of a default judgment, the arbitral tribunal may enter such a judgment; see, e.g., OLG Rostock, decision of January 30, 2003, 1 Sch 01/02, sub 3; J. MÜNCH, above n. 82, §1048 mn. 28.

[164] H. KRONKE, "Introduction. The New York Convention Fifty Years on: Overview and Assessment" in H. KRONKE, P. NACIMIENTO, D. OTTO, and N.C. PORT (eds.), *Recognition and Enforcement of Foreign Arbitral Awards: A Global Commentary on the New York Convention*, Kluwer Law International, Alphen aan den Rijn 2010, p. 8; G.B. BORN, above n. 4, p. 10; N. BLACKABY and C. PARTASIDES, above n. 5, p. 29; M.L. MOSES, above n. 5, pp. 2 f.

[165] Cf. A. DUTTIG, above n. 132, pp. 229–232.

This comparison may seem trivial. However, we can derive from it some ideas on how creating multinational rules (or even systems) for *public* courts – that is, the fallback dispute resolution mechanism[166] – can be facilitated. Whether we like these ideas is another question; as sober researchers, we have to spell them out. What, then, are these ideas, point by point?

4.3.1. Quality

First, with respect to quality, the drafters of multinational rules should take inspiration from those legal systems whose courts work efficiently. This sounds easy, but it is not. It means that those legal systems whose courts do *not* bring about satisfactory results will be confronted with new rules – or even a new system – which is very different from what they are used to. It also means that the representatives of those legal systems should not be given too much credit in the drafting process when they want to promote the solution of their own system. This, of course, will inevitably strain the atmosphere within the drafting committee if the representatives of those countries cannot cope with the situation but think that it is their role to defend as much as possible of their national law.

4.3.2. Budget

Second, with respect to budget, multilateral rules and systems may only be possible if the participating countries are willing to adapt their spending on the judiciary to the model chosen in return for a well-functioning system. For a number of countries, this could mean that more funds must be made available for the judiciary.[167] As businesses in particular have an interest in well-functioning multinational rules and systems, one might think about increasing court fees for these players who will benefit the most – a politically sensitive concept, but one which should be discussed.

4.3.3. The Legal Profession

Third, it is clear that any reform needs the support of the legal profession. Therefore, drafters should not only come from bureaucracy and academia, but

---

[166] Cf. L.B. Solum, "Alternative Court Structure in the Future of the California Judiciary: 2020 Vision" (1993) 66 *S. Cal. L. Rev.* 2121, 2145 (noting that from the perspective of economic theory, "[i]t is not clear that a private judicial system can work without the coordinating fallback mechanism provided by the public court system").

[167] On the need to invest in public justice, cf. R. Stürner, "The Role of Civil Procedure in Modern Societies" (2016) 33 *Ritsumeikan L. Rev.* 73, 77; see also R. Stürner and Peter L. Murray, *German Civil Justice*, Carolina Academic Press, Durham, N.C. 2004, p. 20 (noting that "Germany is more generous with the provision of judicial resources than any ohter modern state").

also from legal practice. This means that lawyers' and judges' representative bodies should be involved from the very start.

4.3.4. Tradition

Fourth, in relation to tradition, drafters should take a fresh look at other systems and refrain from setting red lines where these lines are only national ones. It is helpful to keep in mind that what is a red line for a proceduralist in one country is not necessarily a red line for a citizen of this very country, particularly if the citizen, in return for giving up the red line position, is promised that the whole system will be improved.

4.3.5. Constitutionalization

Fifth, almost the same can be said with respect to constitutionalization. It is important that drafters, before playing the unconstitutionality card when discussing individual rules, have a look at the new draft as a whole, as constitutional judges would do in most countries. If there is no other way, amendments to the constitution should at least be discussed. If, in the end, a country decides that the price of participating in certain multinational rules or systems is too high, this should not block the whole project for those countries for which harmonization and uniformization actually brings an advantage,[168] and the door should always remain open to join later – something which cannot be stressed enough following Brexit.

4.3.6. Petrification

Sixth, the petrification risk must be reduced by providing for means to reform the new system quickly if this becomes necessary. This can be done, for example, by establishing a standing committee with the task of monitoring the application of the rules and proposing reforms, or even the power to itself reform less important rules without the need to renegotiate with all the countries involved, combined with the possibility of having such reforms abolished only after a certain period of time in which they may prove their adequacy.[169] This is an approach which, to a certain degree, has nowadays been taken by a number of law makers all around the world in many areas of regulation, such as with respect to technical aspects

---

[168] Cf. H. KRONKE, above n. 150, p. 1155.

[169] For the U.S. Federal Rules of Civil Procedure, cf. 28 U.S. §2073; on C.E. CLARK's interest in installing a permanent Advisory Committee for the Federal Rules of Civil Procedure, see D. MARCUS, "The Federal Rules of Civil Procedure and Legal Realism as a Jurisprudence of Law Reform" (2010) 44 *Ga. L. Rev.* 433, 504; for U.S. state civil procedure, see Z.D. CLOPTON, "Making State Civil Procedure" (2018) 104 *Cornell L. Rev.* 1.

in capital markets law.[170] Such an approach has been discussed for multinational texts as well.[171] It might also work in civil procedure.

In our eyes, these ideas deserve to be discussed if we want to see more multinational rules and systems at the heart of dispute resolution, which is in the public courts. And the present conference would be the most perfect moment to start such a discussion.

5. CONCLUSION

"Multinational Rules and Systems of Dispute Resolution in an Era of the Global Economy" – this title first needed some interpretational effort. For the purposes of this chapter, we conceived *dispute resolution* very broadly, encompassing all forms of ADR. We then distinguished between mere sets of *rules* and complete *systems*, which, in addition to rules, comprise the necessary infrastructure. According to our understanding, rules and systems are *multinational* if they either come from a law maker who derives its power from more than two nations or if they have a multinational aim. Finally, we derived from the focus on the *era of global economy* the task of dealing with the present state of affairs and of discussing perspectives.

The current state of affairs is characterized by a number of multinational rules and systems in the area of ADR, i.e., dispute resolution outside public courts. Yet, regarding public courts, multinational rules mostly relate to the periphery, and multinational systems are scarce.

The outlook for the existing multinational rules and systems in the area of ADR is, from today's point of view, good: these rules and systems will most probably continue to thrive, to compete with each other, and to react to the needs – or trends – of the time rather quickly.[172] The outlook for multinational rules and systems concerning the fallback dispute resolution system – public courts – is, in our eyes, less good, for despite the chances of multinational uniformity or at least harmonization, there are considerable difficulties terms of in reaching them. We have listed six such difficulties. A comparison of these six difficulties present in the dispute resolution world of public courts with the dispute resolution world of ADR has allowed us to identify six ideas which could

---

[170] For delegated law-making power of the EU Commission, see Art. 290 TFEU.

[171] H. KRONKE, above n. 150, p. 1155; cf. also K.P. BERGER, *The Creeping Codification of the New* Lex Mercatoria, 2nd ed., Kluwer Law International, Alphen aan den Rijn 2010, pp. 254 ff.; P. BEHRENS, above n. 162, pp. 28 ff.; K. LINHART, above n. 162, pp. 241 f.

[172] But see D.R. HENSLER and D. KHATAM, "Re-inventing Arbitration: How Expanding the Scope of Arbitration is Re-shaping its Form and Blurring the Line between Private and Public Adjudication" (2018) 18 *Nev. L.J.* 381, 393 ff. (seeing a risk for arbitration in the current pressure to incorporate due process protections, public appointment or arbitrations, and process and outcome transparency).

pave the way for more multinational rules and systems in the world of public courts. These are: to use efficient systems as a model for the draft and try to overcome diplomatic sensitivities; to make available the necessary funds from governments, but also from parties, in return for a well-functioning system; to integrate the legal profession from the very beginning; to not stick with traditions where there are sensible alternative solutions; to look at the system as a whole before arguing for the unconstitutionality of individual rules; and to provide for mechanisms to avoid petrification.

It is now up to the esteemed reader to discuss whether these are good ideas – and, of course, to discuss the basic question, i.e., whether more multinational rules and systems are desirable at all, and whether we ought to make an effort to achieve them. The basic question, however, could be the topic of another world conference of our Association …

AWARDS SET ASIDE IN THEIR COUNTRY OF ORIGIN

Two Incompatible Schools of Thought

Athanassios KAISSIS[*]

1. Introduction 99
2. Recognition and Enforcement of Arbitral Awards under the New York Convention 100

1. INTRODUCTION

I am deeply obliged to the organizers of this World Congress for giving me the opportunity to be co-speaker together with the eminent colleagues Prof Dr Christoph Kern and Prof Dr Linda Silberman.

I would like to thank profoundly the organizers because they have chosen Japan to be the venue for the Congress: As the great Frenchman, Professor for Social Anthropology, Claude Levi-Strauss wrote in his famous book The Other Side of the Moon, writings about Japan, Japan was able to "… modernize itself while at the same time retaining a close connection to its spiritual roots."

---

[*] Prof. (em.) Dr. (Heidelberg), President of International Hellenic University; Faculty of Law, Aristoteles University Thessaloniki; Corresponding Fellow of the Institute for Foreign and International Private and Economic Law, University of Heidelberg. I dedicate this chapter to my dear friend Professor Dr. Dres. h. c. Herbert Kronke, an influential and eminent researcher and author, a charismatic teacher, a leading authority on the New York Convention, and one of the world's most prestigious arbitrators with my deepest thanks for all he has done for me personally, for helping establish the LL.M. program at the International Hellenic University in Thessaloniki, and for teaching many grateful students. I am also grateful to Professor Dr. Chris Thomale, Vienna, for his linguistic review of this contribution. Any inaccuracies remain my own. The present chapter has already been published in BENICKE & HUBER (Hrsg.), National, International, Transnational: Harmonischer Dreiklang im Recht, Festschrift für Herbert Kronke zum 70. Geburtstag, Gieseking Verlag, 2020, p. 1433 et seq. (KAISSIS, Awards Set Aside in Their Country of Origin – Two Incompatible Schools of Thought). Gieseking Verlag gave the permission for the reprint and retains the copyright for the chapter at hand.

May the Japanese people, as he continues, maintain for a long time "… this precious balance between the traditions of the past and the innovations of the present …; not only for its own good, as it can be for all mankind an example of reflection.".

Prof Kern rightly pointed out the importance of NYC. With my following remarks, I would like to show the functional interdependence between NYC and Convention States.

2. RECOGNITION AND ENFORCEMENT OF ARBITRAL AWARDS UNDER THE NEW YORK CONVENTION

The successful challenge of a commercial award at the seat of the arbitral tribunal does not necessarily signify the end of the dispute.[1] The award debtor fears that, despite the final setting aside of the award at the seat, the henceforth annulled award still will be enforced in one of the New York Convention on the Recognition and Enforcement of Arbitral Awards (NYC) contracting states.[2] Conversely, the arbitral creditor, who has been defeated in the setting aside proceedings, is hoping for recognition and enforcement of the annulled award in a country where enforcement of annulled awards can be granted.[3] This constellation generates great legal uncertainty.[4]

The NYC is an instrument of transnational commercial law, arguably the most successful United Nations (UN) Convention, which celebrated its 60th anniversary in 2018. The importance of the NYC[5] is justifiably emphasized, inter alia, because it offers legal certainty to the effect that the national courts of currently almost 167 contracting states[6] will recognize and enforce a

---

[1]   See PETIT/GRANT, Awards set aside or annulled at the seat, in Norton Rose Fulbright, International arbitration report 2018, Issue 10, 20.

[2]   United Nations Convention on the Recognition and Enforcement of Foreign Arbitral Awards (New York Convention, June 10 1958) (hereinafter "NYC").

[3]   DE COSSÍO, Arb. Intl. 32 (2016), 17, 18, classifies the cases enforcing set aside awards in three groups: "(i) those enforcing in accordance with domestic law, (ii) those ignoring the annulment decision, and (iii) those which assess the annulment decision in order to determine if it deserves deference."

[4]   See Luxembourg Pemex decision (fn. 71) and USA Pemex decision (fn. 122, 123).

[5]   LIEBSCHER, in WOLFF (ed.), New York Convention on the Recognition and Enforcement of Foreign Arbitral Awards – Commentary (2012), prelim. 3, paras. 18–20.

[6]   The importance of legal certainty is emphasized in particular by KRONKE, Introduction, in KRONKE/NACIMIENTO/OTTO/PORT (eds.), Recognition and Enforcement of Foreign Arbitral Awards: A Global Commentary on the New York Convention (2010), pp. 4 ("a predictable outcome") and pp. 3: "Generally speaking, the single most important advantage of arbitration over litigation as a means of resolving transborder business disputes is the degree of certainty a party can have that an award will be recognized and enforced almost anywhere in the world." BORN, International Commercial Arbitration, 2nd ed. (2014), Vol. III, para. 22.04 [A] [1], p. 2989; SOLOMON, Die Verbindlichkeit von Schiedssprüchen in der internationalen privaten

Awards Set Aside in their Country of Origin

foreign award[7] rendered in a country other than that in which recognition[8] or enforcement is sought.[9] For this purpose, the formal requirements of Article IV NYC must be met and none of the grounds exhaustively[10] provided for in Article V NYC based upon which recognition and enforcement may be refused, must be justified. The purpose of the recognition-friendly NYC is to reduce complexities, uncertainties, and delays in enforcement proceedings.[11] Therefore, the NYC abolishes the double exequatur provided for in the Geneva Convention[12] and limits the grounds for refusal of recognition to only the reasons listed in Article V (1) and (2) NYC.[13] Legal certainty is a strong incentive for international companies to choose arbitration over ordinary courts. Since a corresponding transnational instrument for recognition and enforcement of ordinary court judgements does not exist,[14] foreign arbitral awards can be enforced more easily than foreign court judgments.[15]

Schiedsgerichtsbarkeit (2007), pp. 550 et seq.; LIEBSCHER above n. 5, para. 18; JUNITA, Indonesia Law Review (2015), Issue 2, 140 et seq.

[7] For the term, see EHLE, in WOLFF (ed.), above n. 5, Art. I, paras. 12 et seq. the recognition of arbitration agreements is also regulated and standardized by the NYC. See ADOLPHSEN, in MüKoZPO, Vol. 3, 5th ed. (2017), annex 1 to sec. 1061, paras. 1 et seq.

[8] For the dogmatic difference between recognition and enforcement, see BLACKABY/PARTASIDES/REDFERN (eds.), Redfern and Hunter on International Arbitration, 6th ed. (2015), para. 11.19; BLACKABY/PARTASIDES/REDFERN (eds.), REDFERN and HUNTER on International Arbitration, 5th ed. (2009), para. 1. 20; KRÖLL, in BÖCKSTIEGEL/NACIMIENTO/KRÖLL (eds.), Arbitration in Germany (2015), pp. 421 et seq.; KRONKE, above n. 6, pp. 1, 7: "The enforcement is governed by the national enforcement law of the state of recognition"; SPOHNHEIMER, Materiellrechtliche Einwendungen bei der Vollstreckung auf Grundlage eines Schiedsspruchs, in FS SIMOTTA (2012), pp. 559, 562 et seq.

[9] MUSTILL, Arbitration: History and Background (1989), 6 JIntlArb, 43, 49 et seq.; SCHWEBEL, A celebration of the United Nations' New York Convention (1996), 12 Arb. Intl., 823; Wetter, the present status of the International Court of Arbitration of the ICC: An Appraisal, ARIA 1 (1990), 91; But see also the critical considerations by PAULSSON, M., The New York Convention in Action (2016), XXII: "Here and there, for all its remarkable success the Convention has proven itself to be (i) unreliable, (ii) unpredictable, and (iii) inconsistent." See also OTTO, Die Auslegung von Art. IV Abs. 1 des New Yorker Schiedsgerichtsübereinkommens im Lichte der Rechtsprechung des OGH, in FS Simotta (2012), p. 417: "however, these provisions are not interpreted uniformly in all contracting states."

[10] VAN DEN BERG, The New York Convention of 1958: Towards a Uniform Interpretation (1981), p. 265: "the grounds mentioned in Art. V are exhaustive"; BORRIS/HENNECKE, in WOLFF, above n. 5, Art. V, paras. 1 et seq. (this also refers to the exceptions in the United States and Australia); GOODE/KRONKE/MCKENDRICK, Transnational Commercial Law, Texts, Cases and Materials, 2nd ed. (2015), para. 19.135.

[11] GOODE/KRONKE/MCKENDRICK/WOOL (eds.), Transnational Commercial Law, International Instruments and Commentary, 2nd ed. (2012), p. 969; LIEBSCHER, above n. 5, para. 17.

[12] BORRIS/HENNECKE, above n. 10, Art. V, para. 15; LIEBSCHER, in WOLFF above n. 5, para. 355; SCHLOSSER, in STEIN/JONAS, Kommentar zur ZPO, 23rd ed. (2014), Vol. 10, annex to sec. 1061, para. 1.

[13] VAN DEN BERG, above n. 10, p. 337: "The intent of the drafters to eliminate the so-called 'double exequatur' by using the term 'binding' in Art. V (1) (e) has been almost unanimously affirmed by the courts"; BORN, above n. 6, para. 22.04 [A] [1], p. 2989; BORRIS/HENNECKE, above n. 10, Art. V, para. 14; DARWAZEH, in KRONKE/NACIMIENTO/OTTO/PORT, above n. 6, pp. 301, 305–308; LIEBSCHER, in WOLFF, above n. 5, Art. V, paras. 353, 355, 357.

In this chapter, I will limit myself to presenting two schools of thought, which depict two different answers regarding the most relevant[16] ground provided in Article V(1)(e). This states that an arbitral award which has been set aside "by a competent authority of the country in which, or under the law of which that award was made" can be recognized and enforced in contracting states of the NYC. This must happen in accordance with the minimum requirements for recognition and enforcement of foreign awards set out by the NYC.

This question is hotly debated among opposing scholars and practitioners of different jurisdictions.[17] Domestic courts of some of the most relevant countries for international arbitration have also given different answers to this question.

---

[14]   The Hague Convention on Choice of Court Agreement has been ratified by only a few states. On July 2, 2019, the EU adopted the Hague Convention on Recognition and Enforcement of Foreign Judgments in Civil or Commercial Matters by signing the Final Act. the Convention has not yet been ratified. For the European Union (EU), see Brussels I *bis* Regulation 1215/2012 and MAGNUS/MANKOWSKI (ed.), ECPIL Commentary – Brussels Ibis Regulation (2016); RAUSCHER (ed.), Europäisches Zivilprozess-und Kollisionsrecht EuZPR/ EuIPR, Kommentar, Bd. I, Brüssel Ia-VO. 4.Aufl. (2016); WIECZOREK/SCHÜTZE, Zivilprozessordnung und Nebengesetze – Großkommentar, 4th ed. (2019), Vol. 13/2, Brüssel Ia-VO.

[15]   CUNIBERTI, Rethinking International Commercial Arbitration towards Default Arbitration (2017), p. 180, para. 66. Within the EU, as is generally known, court judgments are governed by Regulation 1215/12, which excludes arbitration from its scope of application in accordance with Art. 1(2)(d) thereof. the arbitration agreements are also excluded from the scope of application of the Rome I Regulation pursuant to Art. 1(2) lit. e.

[16]   SOLOMON, in BALTHASAR (ed.), International Commercial Arbitration: A Handbook (2016), §2, para. 276: "For all practical purposes, the relevant case is the setting aside (annulment, vacatur) of the award in its country of origin, as a court-ordered suspension of the award rarely occurs."

[17]   For detailed discussion with further references to case law of different contracting states to the NYC and commentaries, see in particular the following: ADOLPHSEN, above n. 7, paras. 60 et seq.; ALFONS, Recognition and Enforcement (2010); BABINIOTIS, in FS NIKAS (2018), pp. 861 et seq. (in Greek); BADAH, 41 N.C.J. Int'l L. (2015), 59; BAJONS, Croat. Arb. Y. B. 7 (2002), 55 et seq.; BĚLOHLÁVEK, 31 ASA Bulletin 2/2013, pp. 262 et seq.; VAN DEN BERG, above n. 10; VAN DEN BERG, JIntlArb 27, (2010), Issue 2, 179 et seq.; VAN DEN BERG, ICC-Bull 9 (1998), No. 2, 15 et seq.; VAN DEN BERG, ICSID Review 29 (Spring 2014), Issue 2, 263; BERMANN (ed.), Recognition and Enforcement (2017); BESSON, in VAN DEN BERG (ed.), ICCA Congress Series, No. 17 (2013), pp. 378 et seq.; BIRD, 37 N.C. J. Int'l L.& Com. Reg. (2011–2012), 1013 et seq.; BOOR, Der aufgehobene ausländische Schiedsspruch (2016); BORN, above n. 6, pp. 3621–3646; BREKOULAKIS, Am. Rev. Int'l Arb 19 (2008), 515 et seq.; RADICATI DI BROZOLO, Les Cahiers de l'arbitrage 2013, 1027 et seq.; RADICATI DI BROZOLO, ARIA 25 (2014), Issue 1, 47 et seq.; RADICATI DI BROZOLO, Les Cahiers de l'arbitrage 2011–3, 663 et seq.; RADICATI DI BROZOLO, in VAN DEN BERG (ed.), Arbitration: ICCA Congress Series, No. 16 (2012), pp. 74 et seq.; CABRERA/FIGUEROA/Wöss, Arb. Intl. 2015, 1 et seq.; CHAN, B. U. Int'l. L. J. 17 (1999), 141 et seq.; DAVIS, TILJ 37 (2002), 43 et seq.; DE COSSÍO, above n. 3, 17 et seq.; DELAUME, JIntlArb 12 (1995), Issue 1, 5 et seq.; DEL DUCA/WELSH, in BERMANN (ed.), Recognition and Enforcement (2017), pp. 995 et seq., 1026–1029; DERAINS/KIFFER, National Report, in BOSMAN (ed.), ICCA (Suppl. No. 99, June 2018), pp. 1 et seq.; DONOVAN, in BREKOULAKIS/LEW et al. (eds.), The Evolution and Future of International Arbitration (2016), pp. 231 et seq.; DRAHOZAL, Am. Rev. Int'l Arb. 11 (2000), 451 et seq.; DUNMORE, in KLAUSEGGER/KLEIN/KREMSLEHNER, et al. (eds.), Austrian Yearbook on International Arbitration (2014), pp. 285 et seq.; FERRARI/ROSENFELD, IPRax 2016, 478 et seq.; FREYER, in GAILLARD/DI PIETRO (ed.), Enforcement of Arbitration Agreements and International

The different treatment of awards set aside in the country of the seat of arbitration by the enforcement states under the NYC is primarily due to the differing legal understanding of international commercial arbitration in these states, which leads to different interpretations of Article V(1)(e).

Arbitral Awards: The New York Convention in Practice (2008), 757 et seq.; FREYER, JIntlArb (2000), Issue 2, 1 et seq.; GAILLARD, Legal Theory of International Arbitration (2010); GAILLARD, The Enforcement, ICSID Review 14 (1999), 16 et seq.; GAILLARD, The Present-Commercial Arbitration, in VAN DEN BERG, (ed.), ICCA Congress Series, No. 16 (2012), pp. 66 et seq.; GAILLARD, N. Y. Law J. 28 (2007), No. 67; GAILLARD, Transcending, in VAN DEN BERG (ed.), ICCA Congress Series, Volume 17 (2013), pp. 371 et seq.; GEIMER, in ZÖLLER, ZPO, 32nd ed. (2018), sec. 1061 ZPO, paras. 25–29; GEIMER, IZPR, 7th ed. (2015), paras. 3944 et seq.; GHARAVI, The International Effectiveness (2002); GIARDINA, in FS BÖCKSTIEGEL (2001), pp. 205 et seq.; GIRSBERGER/VOSER, International Arbitration, 3rd ed., (2016), pp. 443 et seq.; GOLDSTEIN, ARIA 25 (2014), 19 et seq.; GRAIG, 4 Arb. Intl. (1988), 174; HANSON, Geo. J. Int'l L. 45 (2013–2014), Issue 3, 825 et seq.; HENDEL/PEREZ NOGALES, in GOMEZ/LOPEZ-ROTRIGUES (ed.), 60 Years of the New York Convention (2019), 187 et seq.; HOLMES, Enforcement, Arb. 79 (2013), 244 et seq.; HORVATH, JIntlArb 26 (2009), 249 et seq.; KAISSIS, in FS PRÜTTING, pp. 843 et seq.; KAISSIS., in KRONKE/MANSEL/ WELLER (eds.), Liber amicorum Giuseppe B. Portale (2019), 87 ff.; KAUFMANN-KOHLER/RIGOZZI, International Arbitration (2015), paras. 8.268 et seq.; KENDRA, IBLJ 35 (2012); KIM/MINKKINEN, in MENAKER (ed.), ICCA Congress Series, No. 19 (2017), pp. 382–421; KONTOGIANNIS, Kluwer Arbitration Blog, May 15, 2019; KOCH, JIntlArb 26 (2009), 267 et seq.; KRÖLL, SchiedsVZ 2009, 40; LASTENOUSE, JIntlArb 16 (1999), 25 et seq.; LEE, The Applicable Law in International Arbitration (1978); LEE/SIPPEL, CYIL 8 (2018), 135 et seq.; LEVENTHAL, Les Cahiers de l' arbitrage 2018-1, 273 et seq.; Lew, Arb. Intl. 22 (2006), 179 et seq.; LIEBSCHER, in WOLFF (ed.), above n. 5, paras. 351 et seq.; MAKRIDOU, in BERMANN (ed.), Recognition and Enforcement (2017), pp. 379 et seq., 391; MANN, ICLQ 33 (1984), 193 et seq.; MAYER, ULR 3 (1998), Issues 2–3, 583 et seq.; MAYER, The Trend, in HUNTER/MARRIOTT/VAN VECHTEN VEEDER (eds.), Internationalization of International Arbitration (1995), pp. 37 et seq.; Chief Justice Sundaresh MENON, http://www. ciarb.org.sg/wp-content/uploads/2015/09/Keynote-Speech-Standards-in-need-of-Bearers-Encouraging-Reform-from-.pdf; MISTELIS, in BACHAND/GELINAS (ed.), The UNCITRAL Model Law (2013), pp. 167 et seq.; MISTELIS, in BERGER/BORGES/HERRMANN/SCHLÜTER-WACKERBARTH (eds.), Zivil-und Wirtschatsrecht (2006), pp. 1005 et. seq; MISTELIS/DI PIETRO, in MISTELIS (ed.), Concise International Arbitration, 2nd ed. (2015), pp. 1 et seq.; MOSES, The Principles and Practice, 2nd ed. (2012), pp. 223 et seq.; MOSK/NELSON, JIntlArb 18 (2001), 463; NACIMIENTO/DROP, SchiedsVZ 2009, 272 et seq.; NAGEL/GOTTWALD, Internationales ZPR, 7th ed. (2013), pp 904–905; NIENABER, Die Anerkennung und Vollstreckung im Sitzstaat aufgehobener Schiedssprüche (2002); OBERHAMMER, in FS KERAMEUS, 2009, pp. 969 et seq.; PAMBOUKIS, YPIL 17 (2015/2016), 83 et seq.; PARK, Arbitration, 2nd ed. (2012), pp. 351–355; PARK, ICLQ 32 (1983), 21 et seq.; PAULSSON, J., Arbitration Unbound, ICLQ 30 (1981), 358 et seq.; PAULSSON, J., Delocalisation, ICLQ 32 (1983), 53 et seq.; PAULSSON, J., Enforcing Arbitral Awards, APLR 6 (1998), Issue 2, 1 et seq.; PAULSSON, J., May or Must, Arb. Intl. 14 (1998), 227 et seq.; PAULSSON, J., The Case for Disregarding LSAS, ARIA 7 (1996), Issue 2, 99; PAULSSON, J., The Idea of Arbitration (2013), pp. 32 et seq.; PAULSSON, J. Towards Minimum Standards, in VAN DEN BERG (ed.), ICCA – Improving the Efficiency of Arbitration Agreements and Awards: 40 Years of Application of the New York Convention (1999), pp. 574 et seq.; PAULSSON, M., above n. 9, pp. 157 et seq.; PAULSSON, M./SURESH, in GÓMEZ/LÓPEZ-RODRÍGUEZ (ed.), 60 Years of the New York Convention (2019), 269 et seq.; PETROCHILOS, ICLQ 48 (1999), 856 et seq.; PETROCHILOS, Procedural Law, (2004), paras. 7.50–7.67, 7.86–7.88; PINSOLLE, Arb. Intl. 24 (2008), 277 et seq.; POLKINGHORNE, ICLR 25 2008, No. 1, 48 et seq.; POUDRET/BESSON, Comparative Law, 2nd ed. (2007); RAESCHKE-KESSLER, in

The wording of Article V(1)(e)[18] NYC ("Recognition and enforcement of the award may ... be refused ... only if ...")[19] leaves room for the enforcement court to exercise discretion. According to this wording, a court could either recognize or refuse to recognize or enforce an award which has been set aside, or the effect of which has been suspended by a competent authority of the country in which or under the law of which that award was made.[20] However, the NYC

PRÜTTING/GEHRLEIN, ZPO Kommentar, 11 Aufl. (2019), sec. 1061, para. 33; RAU, ARIA 21 (2010), No. 1–4, 47 et seq.; REID/RIVKIN, GAR, 2015, sec. 2; REINER, IPRax 2000, 323 et seq.; REISMAN/RICHARDSON, in VAN DEN BERG (ed.), ICCA Congress Series, No. 16 (2012), pp. 17, 25 et seq.; RIVKIN, in VAN DEN BERG (ed.), VAN DEN BERG (ed.), ICCA – Improving the Efficiency of Arbitration Agreements and Awards: 40 Years of Application of the New York Convention (1999), pp. 528 et seq.; RUBINO-SAMMARTANO, 3rd ed. (2014), pp. 1446 et seq.; SAENGER, in SAENGER/EBERL, Schiedsverfahren: Kommentierung der §§1025–1066 ZPO (2019), sec. 1061, para. K13; id., ZPO, 8th ed. (2019), sec. 1061, para. 13; SANDERS, ICCA's Guide to the Interpretation of the 1958 New York Convention: A Handbook for Judges (2011), pp. 102–103; SASSON, ADR 18 (2014), Issue 1, 10 et seq.; SCHACK, Internationales ZVR, 7th ed. (2017), paras. 1474–1478; SCHERER, Effects of International Judgments, PLR 43 (2016), 637 et seq.; SCHERER, in MENAKER (ed.), ICCA Congress Series – No. 19 (2017), pp. 691 et seq.; SCHÜTZE, Die Bedeutung, JPS 3 (1989), 118 et seq.; SCHÜTZE, in WIECZOREK/SCHÜTZE, ZPO, Vol. 11, 4th ed. (2014), sec. 1061, paras. 125 et seq.; SCHÜTZE, Schiedsgericht und Schiedsverfahren, 6th ed. (2016), paras. 708–713; SCHWARTZ, JIntlArb 14 (1997), Issue 2, 125 et seq.; SIEHR, ZZP 115 (2002), 143 et seq.; SILBERMAN, GA. J. INT'L & COMP. L. 38 (2009), 25, 32 et seq.; SILBERMAN/SCHERER, Forum Shopping, Peking University Transnational Law Review 2 (2014), Issue 1, 115 et seq.; SILBERMAN/SCHERER, in FERRARI (ed.), Forum Shopping (2013), pp. 313 et seq.; SLATER, Arb. Intl. 25 (2009), 271 et seq.; SLEIMAN, Int. Lit. Quarterly 30, (2013), 14 et seq.; SMIT, in NEWMAN/HILL (eds.), The Leading Arbitrators' Guide to International Arbitration, 3rd ed. (2014), pp. 909 et seq.; SÖDERLUND, JIntlArb 22 (2005), 301 et seq.; SOLOMON, above n. 16, §2, paras. 260, 276–289; SOLOMON, in BERMANN (ed.), above n. 17, pp. 329–364; STEINBRÜCK, IHR 8 (2008), Issue 4, 152 et seq.; SCHLOSSER, above n. 12; THADIKKARAN, JIntlArb 31 (2014), 575 et seq.; THÖNE, SchiedsVZ 2016, 257 et seq.; TRAIN, in BERMANN (ed.), above n. 17, pp. 281, 304–306; YEO/LIN, Disp. Resol. Int'l 10 (2016), 91 et seq.; VARGIU/AHMED, in BERMANN (ed.), above n. 17, pp. 977 et seq., 988; VOIT, in MUSIELAK/VOIT, ZPO, 16th ed. (2019), sec. 1061, paras. 18 et seq.; WAHL, JIntlArb 16 (1999), 131; WEBSTER, JIntlArb 23 (2006), 201 et seq.; WEINACHT, ZVglRWiss 98 (1999), 139 et seq.; WEINACHT, JIntlArb 19 (2002), 313 et seq.; WILSKE/MARKERT, in VORWERK/WOLF, BeckOK ZPO, 33rd ed. (July 2019), sec. 1061, paras. 40 et sec.; WOLFF (ed.), New York Convention – Commentary (2012).

[18] Art. V(1)(e) represents "a compromise between conflicting interests of different states," according to SMIT, above n. 17, p. 913. This provision raises some difficult and complex questions of interpretation. See Kronke, above n. 6, p. 10: "That is a difficult and complex question"; LERCH, Recognition/Enforcement of Annulled Awards under special Consideration of the Amsterdam Court of Appeals' Decision of 28 April 2009, in Selected Papers on International Arbitration (2011), Swiss Arbitration Academy, Vol. 1, pp. 101, 107: "Unsurprisingly, the recognition/enforcement of vacated arbitral awards is a perennial issue in international arbitration."

[19] The English version of Art. V, expresses the judicial discretion more strongly than the German "darf." See RAESCHKE-KESSLER, above n. 17, sec. 1061, para. 33; See GOODE, Arb. Intl. 17 (2001), 19 et seq., 22; the French version is interpreted differently, see BORN, above n. 6, para. 26.03[B], p. 3428 et seq., with further references.

[20] For the required binding character of the award see ADOLPHSEN, above n. 7, para. 56; VAN DEN BERG, above n. 10, pp. 336, 338–339: "In finding the answer to the question at which

does not specify the criteria based upon which this judicial discretion should be exercised.[21] By doing so, the NYC does not completely detach "the fate of the award in the enforcement State from its fate of the seat of arbitration."[22] As a result, different domestic solutions to solve the dilemma have emerged.[23] The defense[24] in Article V(1)(e) NYC makes no sense in relation to domestic awards.[25] The possibility of refusing recognition and enforcement of an award set aside afforded by Article V(1)(e)[26] does not constitute a mandatory rule for the enforcing court to recognize the annulment decision and to refuse to enforce the annulled award.[27]

---

moment the award can be considered binding, the prevailing judicial interpretation seems to be that this question is to be determined under the law applicable to the award"; BERGER, Private Dispute Resolution in International Business: Negotiation, Mediation, Arbitration, 3rd ed. (2015), p. 453, paras. 21–32; BORN, above n. 6, §26.05 [C] [e], pp. 3610–3621; DARWAZEH, above n. 13, pp. 301, 311 et seq., with an overview of national regulations (pp. 314–319); GEIMER, in ZÖLLER, above n. 17, para. 24; KREINDLER/WOLF/RIEDER, Com. Arb. in Germ., 2016, §2, para. 6.313; LIEBSCHER, above n. 5, para. 357; MISTELIS/DI PIETRO, above n. 17, Art. V, para. 13; NAGEL/GOTTWALD, above n. 17, §18, para. 215: "es sei denn, dass das ausländische Recht etwas anderes bestimmt"; SANDROCK, Wann wird ein ausländischer Schiedsspruch im Sinne des Art. V (1) (e) der New Yorker Konvention und des §1044 ZPO verbindlich, in FS TRINKER, (1995), pp. 669 et seq.; SCHACK, above n. 17, paras. 1477; SCHWAB/WALTER, Schiedsgerichtsbarkeit, Kommentar, 7. Aufl., Chap. 30, p. 262, para. 16. On the final validity of the annulment decision, see OBERHAMMER, FS KERAMEUS, 2009, pp. 969 et seq. Especially for the case law in Germany, see RAESCHKE-KESSLER, above n. 17, §1061, para. 32; SOLOMON, above n. 6, pp. 89 et seq., 364 et seq.; SOLOMON, above n. 16, §2, paras. 261 et seq.; SOLOMON., The Recognition and Enforcement of Foreign Arbitral Awards, in SCHMIDT-KESSEL (ed.), German National Reports on the 19th International Congress of Comparative Law, (2014), pp. 55 et seq., 101–102. An interim award (provisional award) is generally considered unenforceable; see HOPE, in ROWLEY/GAILLARD/KAISER (eds.), The Guide to Challenging and Enforcing Arbitration Awards (2019), p. 13; LIEBSCHER, above n. 5, paras. 369–370; OLG Rostock, October 28, 1999 YCA XXV (2000), 717 et seq., 719, para. 4. For "The award has not yet become binding on the parties ..." see LIEBSCHER, above n. 5, par. 351. For the jurisdictions of Austria, England, France, Germany and Switzerland jurisdictions see LIEBSCHER, above n. 5, paras. 385 et seq.

[21] BORN, above n. 6, pp. 3623–3624: "nor articulates standards for when non-recognition of such an award is appropriate and when it is not"; LIEBSCHER, above n. 5, para. 391: "The NYC is silent on the criteria to be followed by the enforcing court in exercising its discretion"; OSTROVE/CARTER/SANDERSON, in ROWLEY/GAILLARD/KAISER, above n. 20, pp. 22, 23.

[22] LIEBSCHER, above n. 5, para. 354.

[23] Id.

[24] Art. V(1)(e) represents a compromise between conflicting interests of different states, according to SMIT, above n. 17, p. 913, fn. 16. This provision raises some difficult and complex questions of interpretation. See KRONKE, above n. 6, p. 10: "That is a difficult and complex question"; LERCH, Recognition/Enforcement of Annulled Awards under special Consideration of the Amsterdam Court of Appeals' Decision of 28 April 2009, in Selected Papers on International Arbitration (2011), Swiss Arbitration Academy, Vol. 1, pp. 101, 107: "Unsurprisingly, the recognition/enforcement of vacated arbitral awards is a perennial issue in international arbitration."

[25] KRÖLL, above n. 8, p. 521.

[26] Art. 36 (1) (a) (v) UNCITRAL Model Law.

[27] VAN DEN BERG, above n. 10, p. 265; PAULSSON, J., May or Must, above n. 17, pp. 227 et seq.; BORN, above n. 6, p. 3623: "Textually, the language of Art. V and VI strongly suggest

However, the mere possibility of submitting an application for the setting aside of the award or for the suspension of its enforcement to a competent authority, as referred to in Article V(1)(e), does not prevent an award from being binding on the parties,[28] nor does it stop it from being enforced in the enforcement state.[29] The ground for refusal is the actual setting aside of the award in the country of the seat of arbitration.[30]

The court before which a set-aside action has been brought forward has the discretion to adjourn the decision on the enforcement of the award, with or without ordering a payment of suitable security, if it deems it fit to do so.[31] If the filing of the application for setting aside were to automatically entail the suspension of the enforceability of the award, it would amount to an *ex lege* suspension, which would not be sufficient to prevent enforcement. This is because under Article V(1)(e) NYC, the suspension of effects has to be pronounced by a court or by a competent authority at the seat of arbitration.[32] Concurring jurisdiction to set aside the award should be granted to the court at the place of arbitration, i.e., the court at the seat of the arbitral tribunal[33] or, alternatively, the courts of the state under whose procedural law[34] the award was made.[35] Both these states may be primary jurisdictions[36] under the NYC. The setting aside of

---

that an annulled or suspended award may – but need not – be denied recognition in other Contracting States"; ANDREWS, in GOTTWALD/HESS (eds.), Procedural Justice, XIV. IAPL World Congress, Heidelberg 2011, p. 602: "Moreover, it should be noted that the New York Convention (1958) states, Art. V(10(e), [sic], that an enforcing court can choose not to recognise or enforce a foreign award if it has been annulled in the courts of the relevant seat. But this is not regarded as a mandatory ground for refusing to recognise or enforce such an award"; PARK, 93 Am. J. Int'l L. (1999), 805; DARWAZEH, above n. 13, pp. 308 et seq.

[28] SOLOMON, above n. 16, §2, para. 277; SOLOMON, in BERMANN, above n. 17, pp. 329, 362; KRÖLL, above n. 8, p. 484; NAGEL/GOTTWALD, above n. 17, §18, para. 215: "Die Möglichkeit einer Aufhebungsklage nimmt dem Schiedsspruch noch nicht seine Verbindlichkeit, aber auch insoweit entscheidet das ausländische Verfahrensrecht"; OBERHAMMER, in FS KERAMEUS, (2009), pp. 969 et seq.

[29] LIEBSCHER, above n. 5, para. 380; SCHACK, above n. 17, para. 1450.

[30] SOLOMON, above n. 16, §2, para. 277.

[31] Art. VI, par. 1. PORT/SIMONOFF/BOWERS, in KRONKE, above n. 6, Art. VI, III A, pp. 415, 419 et seq.; LIEBSCHER, above n. 5, Art. VI paras. 6, 18; SOLOMON, in BERMANN, above n. 17, pp. 363–364.

[32] VAN DEN BERG, above n. 10, p. 352; POUDRET/BESSON, above n. 17, para. 923.

[33] VAN DEN BERG, above n. 10, p. 350: "The 'competent authority' as mentioned in Art. V(1),(e) for entertaining the action of setting aside the award is virtually always the court of the country in which the award was made"; SOLOMON, above n. 6, p. 143; SOLOMON., above n. 16, §2, paras. 28, 282.

[34] VAN DEN BERG, above n. 10, p. 350; SOLOMON, above n. 16, §2, para. 282: "procedural law."

[35] In practice, it is rare for the award to have been made under a law other than that of the state in which the Arbitral Tribunal is seated. See NIENABER, above n. 17, p. 245, fn. 956. See also generally BERGER, Internationale Wirtschaftsschiedsgerichtsbarkeit (1992), p. 507.

[36] PIZZURO/GARCIA/PERLA, in ROWLEY/GAILLARD/KAISER, above n. 20, pp. 74 et seq., 79. In the literature, the term "supervisory jurisdiction" is also in use. See NAZZINI, American Journal of Comparative Law 66 (2018), 603 et seq., 606: "This supervision jurisdiction concerns, in particular, the remedies against the award available under national arbitration legislation."

the award by a court other than the courts designated in Article V(1)(e) does not affect the enforceability of the award in an NYC contracting state.[37]

As mentioned above, the provision of Article V(1)(e) gives room to national courts to exercise a certain amount of discretion[38] and to rely on their own judgments regarding the recognition and enforcement of awards that have been set aside. The question of whether the enforcement court is able to exercise its discretion to recognize and enforce an arbitral award set aside by a foreign court decision – thus ignoring that the foreign setting-aside decision is an expression of the judicial function of a sovereign state – or whether it can refuse recognition and enforcement without taking into account the ground on which the award has been set aside is of great practical importance and, accordingly, is controversially discussed at an international level.

An award may be set aside at the seat of arbitration, in accordance with the provisions of the applicable national law.[39] The NYC "establishes neither a minimum nor a maximum standard of review in the country of origin."[40] Despite the NYC serving as a model for national regulations regarding the grounds for setting aside an arbitral award, it effectively defers the question entirely to national legislation.[41] Therefore, the arbitral award may also be set aside in the state of the seat for parochial reasons. However, this is usually not the case, because in reality "national laws tend to provide for similar grounds," which in general are substantially the same as those provided in Article V NYC[42]

---

[37] Van den Berg, above n. 10, p. 350; Born, above n. 6, §22.04 [A] [1], p. 2989; Liebscher, above n. 5, para. 403; Solomon, above n. 16, §2, para. 28; For the U.S. case law, see *Juan Jose Castillo Bozo v. Leopoldo Casillo Bozo and Gabriel Castillo Bozo* in the U.S.D.C. for the Southern District of Florida, May 23, 2013; *Karaha Bodas Co., L.L.C. v. Perusahaan Pertambangan Minyak Dan Gas Bumi Negara et al.*, U.S.C.A, Fifth Circuit, March 23, 2004, YCA XXIX (2004), 1262.

[38] In German law interprets Adolphsen, in MüKoZPO, above n. 7), UNÜ Art. V, para. 60 the wording "darf versagt werden" from the perspective of International law and asserts that the competent authority is not granted any discretion in this respect. So already earlier: Kröll, above n. 8, sec. 1061, para. 45, regards the theory of the lack of discretion as the prevailing opinion in the German courts: "'May' is interpreted as 'shall'"; Schwab/Walter, Schiedsgerichtsbarkeit, Chap. 56, p. 456, para. 3. Judicial discretion must be exercised with caution, see Kronke, above n. 6, p. 12: "a discretion which itself should be exercised with caution."

[39] See Liebscher, above n. 5, para. 379.

[40] See Blackaby/Partasides/Redfern, above n. 8, para. 11.90; Solomon, above n. 16, §2, para. 280: "It neither establishes nor limits the grounds on which other countries may base the jurisdiction of their courts to set aside the award. Furthermore, as a matter of principle, the NYC establishes neither a minimum nor a maximum standard of review in the country of origin."

[41] Liebscher, above n. 5, para. 379; Solomon, above n. 16, §2, para. 280.

[42] See Ostrove/Carter/Sanderson, above n. 21, pp. 22 et seq., 23. See also Art. 36 1 a v UNCITRAL Model Law, which replicates Art. V 1 e of the NYC. For grounds for challenge in Austria, England, France, Germany, and Switzerland, see Liebscher, above n. 5, pp. 147 et seq.

and Article 34 of the United Nations Commission on International Trade Law (UNCITRAL) Model Law.[43]

Different theoretical approaches[44] seek to provide a well-founded dogmatic answer to the question asked above. Two of them are predominant: the territorial or jurisdictional-procedural approach[45] and the internationalist or delocalized approach.[46] Both approaches differ in their treatment of the setting aside of arbitral awards in the state of their execution.[47] Nevertheless, neither of these approaches has reached unanimous prevalence across all contracting states to the NYC.[48]

The classical theoretical approach, namely the territorial approach,[49] considers arbitration anchored in the legal system of the seat of the arbitral tribunal.[50] The seat of the arbitral tribunal – i.e., the seat of arbitration – is usually the result of a contractual agreement between the parties and is thus an expression of their autonomy.[51] The arbitral tribunal has a forum, namely the seat of the arbitral tribunal. This is entirely independent from the place where any part of the arbitration actually takes place.[52] The award is a product of the legal system of the state in which the arbitral tribunal has its seat. In choosing the seat deliberately, the parties[53] implicitly adopt the laws and legal system of the country in which this seat is located. The award draws its validity and legal

---

[43] PIZZURO/GARCIA/PERLA, in ROWLEY/GAILLARD/KAISER, above n. 20, pp. 74 et seq., 79. For the Application for Setting Aside Pursuant to Article 34 of the UNCITRAL Model Law, see BINDER (ed.), International Commercial Arbitration and Mediation in UNCITRAL Model Law Jurisdictions, 4th ed. (2019).

[44] See in detail BOOR, above n. 17, pp. 26 et seq.; see also the approach taken by BOOR in Chapters 3 and 4 of his work, where constitutional and international law criteria are used for the exercise of the judicial discretion. See also PAMBOUKIS, YPIL 17 (2015/2016), 83 et seq., who argumentatively underpins the principle of internationality. See also SILBERMAN/SCHERER, Peking University Transnational Law Review 2 (2014), Issue 1, 115 et seq.; SILBERMAN/SCHERER, in FERRARI, above n. 17, pp. 313 et seq. However, the adoption of a Protocol to the UN Convention is not an easy undertaking as it involves 167 contracting states.

[45] BOOR, above n. 17, p. 43; LEE/SIPPEL, above n. 17, pp. 137–139.

[46] LEE/SIPPEL, above n. 17, pp. 139–142; PAULSSON, J., ICLQ 30 (1981), 358 et seq.; PAULSSON, J., ICLQ 32 (1983), 53 et seq.; PAULSSON, J., The Idea of Arbitration, above n. 17, pp. 32 et seq.

[47] See GAILLARD, The Enforcement, above n. 17, 16, 17–18.

[48] DUNMORE, above n. 17, p. 285.

[49] DARWAZEH, above n. 13, pp. 301, 326 et seq. The term "territoriality principle" is also commonly used.

[50] MANN, in SANDERS (ed.), International Arbitration: Liber Amicorum for Martin Domke (1967), pp. 157 et seq.; See also BESSON, above n. 17, p. 379, under III. 1; GAILLARD, The Enforcement, above n. 17, pp. 16–45; GAILLARD, Transcending, above n. 17, pp. 371–377.

[51] See PRÜTTING, in PRÜTTING/GEHRLEIN, above n. 17, sec. 1043, para. 1; SCHÜTZE, Schiedsgericht above n. 17, §8, pp. 103 et seq.; SOLOMON, above n. 16, §2, para. 28. BĚLOHLÁVEK, above n.17, p. 273.

[52] VON SCHLABRENDORFF, in SALGER/TRITTMANN (eds.), Internationales Schiedsverfahren (2018), §2, para. 2.137; SOLOMON, above n. 6, p. 143; SOLOMON, above n. 16, §2, para. 28.

[53] See MENON, above n. 17, No. 33 b.

effect from the domestic procedural law[54] of the seat state.[55] It should be noted that this state provides a neutral forum,[56] as it is often sought instead of the state of origin of the parties. The setting-aside proceedings, the grounds for setting aside an award, the stages of eventual appeal, and the time and costs of the arbitral proceedings and for the court proceedings up to the final confirmation or setting aside of the award all play an important role in the parties' choice of the seat of arbitration.[57] The parties are after all the ones that will have to live with the consequences of their choice.[58]

The seat of arbitration is of fundamental importance.[59] The courts of the seat supervise the proper conduct of the arbitral proceedings and confirm or set aside the award. The law of the seat of arbitration may even permit the conduct of new arbitration proceedings[60] in the event that the award is set aside.

According to the territorial or jurisdictional-procedural approach, an award that is set aside by a court at the seat of the arbitral tribunal or under its law loses its legal validity. This means that the decision of the court of primary jurisdiction prevents any other court of the contracting states to NYC from hearing enforcement applications of the same award.[61] As the set-aside award no longer exists,[62] recognition in the enforcement state must therefore be refused[63] in accordance with the "ex nihilo nil fit" principle.[64] It is not possible[65] for an annulled arbitral award to be revived[66] in the enforcement state.

---

[54] See Liebscher, above n. 5, Art. V, para. 382. In any case, parties may choose a procedural law that is different from the law of the arbitral seat; see Mayer, above n. 17, pp. 285 et seq.

[55] Dunmore, above n. 17, pp. 285 et seq.

[56] Cuniberti, above n. 15, p. 227: "the seat of arbitration should be in a third State"; Kronke, above n. 6, pp. 1, 7.

[57] Silberman/Scherer, Forum Shopping, above n. 17, 115 et seq.; Silberman/Scherer, in Ferrari (ed.), above n. 17, p. 315: "therefore understand possible exposure to set aside."

[58] Menon, above n. 17, No. 27.

[59] Goode, above n. 19, p. 29; Caron/Caplan, The UNCITRAL Arbitration Rules, A Commentary, 2nd ed. (2012), pp. 86/87; Prütting, in Prütting/Gehrlein, above n. 17, sec. 1043, para. 1; Schütze, Schiedsgericht, above n. 17, paras. 397, 402, 708–713; Underhill/Cardenas, Awards: Early Stage Consideration of Enforcement Issues, in Rowley/Gaillard/Kaiser, above n. 20, p. 5.

[60] For the revival of the arbitration agreement, see Schütze, in Wieczorek/Schütze, above n. 17, sec. 1059, paras. 2, 91 et seq.

[61] See Nolan/Aitelaj, in Rowley/Gaillard/Kaiser, above n. 20, p. 48.

[62] van den Berg, ICC-Bull 9 (1998), above n. 17, 16: "after annulment, an arbitral award no longer exists under the applicable arbitration law (which is mostly the arbitration law of the place of arbitration)."

[63] Id.; van den Berg, JIntlArb 27, (2010), above n. 17, 179, 187; Paulsson, M., above n. 9, p. 202 (fn. 186) and p. 211; Rau, above n. 17, pp. 47 et seq.

[64] Especially Menon, above n. 17, No. 33c. For the nullity approach, see Liebscher, The Healthy Award, Challenge in International Arbitration (2003), p. 384.

[65] Sanders, NILR 43 (1959), 55.

[66] Van den Berg, JIntlArb 27 (2010), above n. 17, 179 et seq. (notably 187).

Intersentia

The territorial approach is based on the understanding that the decision setting aside an award has an international *erga omnes* effect.[67] The adoption of the territorial approach could reduce forum shopping.[68] Regarding the question of which court has the last word with respect to the validity of an arbitral award at an international level, the territorial approach[69] answers in favor of the state of the seat of arbitration, since it is the state of primary or supervising jurisdiction.[70]

The courts of most contracting states to the NYC[71] follow this view[72] and principally they deny granting enforcement to awards that have been annulled in their country of origin.

---

[67] See Court of Appeal – Civil Appeals, Nos. 150 and 151 of 2012, October 31, 2013, *PT First Media TBK (formerly known as PT Broadband Multimedia TBK) v. Astro Nusantara International BV and others*, and another appeal [2013] SGCA 57, Singapore Law Reports [2014] 1 SLR, 372 et seq., 401, no. 77; VAN DEN BERG, JIntlArb 27 (2010), above n. 17, 179 et seq., 182: "In contrast, the setting aside or an arbitral award has an erga omnes effect." But see also PAMBOUKIS, above n. 17, pp. 100 et seq.; SCHACK, above n. 17, para. 1475; SIEHR, above n. 17, 143, 154 et seq.; SMIT, above n. 17, 917: "binding force only in the country of its rendition."

[68] MENON, above n. 17, No. 29. See also SILBERMAN/SCHERER, Forum Shopping, in FERRARI (ed.), above n. 17, pp. 313 et seq.

[69] See in particular VAN DEN BERG, ICSID Review 29 (Spring 2014), Issue 2, above n. 17, 24: "That the courts in the country of origin should have the last word is the prevailing view in practice."

[70] REISMAN/RICHARDSON, above n. 17, pp. 17, 25.

[71] For Argentina, see DE HOZ/AMALLO, in ROWLEY/GAILLARD/KAISER, above n. 20, pp. 155 et seq., p. 164. For Austria, see KONRAD/PETERS, in ROWLEY/GAILLARD/KAISER, above n. 20, pp. 170 et seq., p. 178. For Belgium, see BOULARBAH/VAN DER HAEGEN/RAYEE, in ROWLEY/GAILLARD/KAISER, above n. 20, pp. 187 et seq., p. 196. For Canada, see KAISER, in ROWLEY/GAILLARD/KAISER, above n. 20, pp. 204 et seq., p. 217. For Colombia, see QUIJANO/FONSECA, in ROWLEY/GAILLARD/KAISER, above n. 20, pp. 225 et seq., p. 232. For the Czech Republic, see SNABLOVA/MIKOLANDOVA, in ROWLEY/GAILLARD/KAISER, above n. 20, pp. 237 et seq., p. 245. For Greece, see BABINIOTIS, above n. 17, pp. 861, 879–881; MAKRIDOU, above n. 17, p. 391: "Greek case law invariably adopts the 'territoriality' approach." For Italy, see BENEDETTELLI/TORSELLO, in ROWLEY/GAILLARD/KAISER, above n. 20, pp. 345 et seq., p. 353: "As a general rule, awards set aside by the courts at the seat cannot be enforced in Italy.". For Kazakhstan, see TLEULINA/IDAYATOVA, in ROWLEY/GAILLARD/KAISER, above n. 20, pp. 376 et seq., p. 383. For Korea, see KIM/WHITE, in ROWLEY/GAILLARD/KAISER, above n. 20, pp. 389 et seq., p. 395. For Luxembourg, see Court of Justice of Appeal, Decision of April 27, 2017, No. 59/17, *Pemex-Exploration y Produccion (Mexico) v. Corporation Mexicana de Mantenimiento Integral, S. de R.L. de C.V. (Mexico)*, YCA XLII (2017), 433 et seq. See also in GAR 5.5.2017, Annulled Pemex award can't be enforced in Luxembourg. For Malaysia, see ABRAHAM/AMIRUDIN/SYAFIQ, in ROWLEY/GAILLARD/KAISER, above n. 20, pp. 403 et seq., p. 410. For Nigeria, see AJIBADE/MAYOMI, in ROWLEY/GAILLARD/KAISER, above n. 20, pp. 442 et seq., p. 449. For Portugal, see PEREIRA et al., in ROWLEY/GAILLARD/KAISER, above n. 20, pp. 454 et seq., p. 461: "Portuguese courts will in principle reject the recognition.". For Qatar, see WALKER/WITKAMP/HAGE, in ROWLEY/GAILLARD/KAISER, above n. 20, pp. 468 et seq., p. 475. For Romania, see VASILE, in ROWLEY/GAILLARD/KAISER, above n. 20, pp. 481 et seq., p. 486. For Russia, see DYAKIN/RASCHEVSKY/KAYSIN/BEZRUCHENKOV/LAKHNO, in ROWLEY/GAILLARD/KAISER, above n. 20, pp. 493 et seq., p. 499. For Singapore, see Court of Appeal-Civil Appeals, Nos. 150 and 151 of 2012, October 31, 2013, *PT First Media TBK (formerly known as PT Broadband Multimedia TBK) v. Astro Nusantara International BV and others*, and another appeal [2013] SGCA 57, Singapore Law Reports (2014) 1 SLR, 372 et seq.,

Awards Set Aside in their Country of Origin

According to §1061(1), para. 1 of the German Code of Civil Procedure (ZPO), the recognition and enforcement of foreign arbitral awards in Germany is governed by the NYC.[73] The prevailing view in German case law is that courts ought to refuse the recognition of arbitral awards set aside at the seat.[74] Conversely, the views expressed in German legal literature vary.[75] The prevailing view is that an annulled award at the seat cannot be recognized and enforced in Germany. However, a gradual shift from dogmatism to an internationalist approach has been discernible in recent years.[76]

In England and Wales,[77] foreign arbitral awards from contracting states to the NYC are generally recognized and declared enforceable based on

---

401, No. 77; LEE/SIPPEL, above n. 17, para. 7.31; HASAN/LAHIRI, in ROWLEY/GAILLARD/KAISER, above n. 20, pp. 505 et seq., p. 514; LIEBSCHER, above n. 5, paras. 369–370. For Spain, see REMON et al., in ROWLEY/GAILLARD/KAISER, above n. 20, pp. 521 et seq., p. 545. For Switzerland, see FUNTES/MARQUERAT/BLAKEMORE/REAZDON, in ROWLEY/GAILLARD/KAISER, above n. 20, pp. 551 et seq., p. 560.

[72]   See GREENBERG/KEE/WEERAMANTRY, International Commercial Arbitration: An Asia-Pacific Perspective (2011), para. 9.172; NOLAN/AITELAJ, in ROWLEY/GAILLARD/KAISER, above n. 20, p. 48: "This position or variations thereof, is the most widely adopted."

[73]   KREINDLER/WOLF/RIEDER, Commercial Arbitration in Germany, (2016), para. 1.76; SCHÜTZE, Schiedsgericht, above n. 17, para. 694.

[74]   BGH, 23.04.2013 – III ZB 59/12, SchiedsVZ 2013, 229, para. 9; BGH Beschluss vom 17.4.2008-III ZB 97/06, SchiedsVZ 2018, 196 et. seq., 198 paras. 15, 16; OLG München, Beschluss vom 30.7.2012-34 Sch 18-10, SchiedsVZ 2012, 338 et. seq., 341, para. 3 a); OLG Dresden, 31.01.2007–11 Sch 18/05, SchiedsVZ 2007, 327 (329), Nr. 4, obiter dictum; WOLFF, LMK 2008, 265473. See further BOOR, above n. 17, p. 22: "Obwohl das UN-Übereinkommen dem Vollstreckungsstaat ein Ermessen einräumt, gehen die Deutschen Gerichte aus dogmatischen Gründen davon aus, das ein aufgehobener Schiedsspruch aufgrund der Verwurzelung in der Rechtsordnung des Ursprungsstaates ein 'legal nullum' darstellt, sodass eine Anerkennung und Vollstreckung auf deutschem Boden nicht mehr möglich ist," and further p. 26 (fn. 31) and pp. 37–43 with an analysis of the case law of the German Higher Regional Courts. See also KREINDLER/WOLFF/RIEDER, above n. 20, para. 6.314; KASOLOWSKY/WENDLER, Germany in ROWLEY/GAILLARD/KAISER (ed.), the Guide, above n. 20, p. 300 et seq., p. 307.

[75]   See BOOR, above n. 17, pp. 43–46; DARWAZEH, above n. 13, pp. 301, 329 et seq.; GEIMER, in ZÖLLER, above n. 17, para. 61; GEIMER, IZPR, above n. 17, para. 3944; MÜNCH, in MüKoZPO, above n. 7, sec. 1061, para. 28; POSEK, in SALGER/TRITTMANN, Internationales Schiedsverfahren (2019), §23.5, para. 20; RAESCHKE-KESSLER, above n. 17, sec. 1061, para. 33; SCHLOSSER, above n. 12, para. 311: "nur möglich, wenn ein ausländisches Urteil, das einen Schiedsspruch aufhebt, nach §328 Nr. 2 oder 4 anerkennungsfähig ist." In the view of SCHÜTZE, Schiedsgericht, above n. 17, para. 712, the annulled arbitral award at the seat of the Arbitral Tribunal cannot be recognized and enforced if the annulment decision is capable of recognition in Germany; SCHÜTZE. in WIECZOREK/SCHÜTZE, above n. 17, sec. 1061, para. 131; SCHWAB/WALTER, Schiedsgerichtsbarkeit, above n. 20, Chap. 30, p. 261, para. 14; SOLOMON, in BERMANN, above n. 17, pp. 363 et seq. with further references. See also Stürner's view reported by ANDREWS, above n. 27, p. 603, fn. 253.

[76]   See, e.g., SIEHR, above n. 17, 154 et seq. See also GEIMER, IZPR, above n. 17, para. 3944c; ROSENBERG/SCHWAB/GOTTWALD, Zivilprozessrecht, 18th ed. (2018), §183, para. 25; SCHACK, above n. 17, para. 1477: "Der Schiedsspruch ist und bleibt eine privatautonome Gestaltung, die nicht am Gängelband des Ursprungsstaates hängt, sondern von jedem Staat der Welt (nach Maßgabe der Staatsverträge) autonom zu beurteilt wird."

[77]   Sec. 100–104 Arb. Act. 1966: Art. V (1) (e) NYC is incorporated in sec. 103(2) (f) Arb. Act. 1966.

Intersentia

111

the NYC.[78] The courts there traditionally follow the territorial approach without excluding *ab initio* that the award may be enforced.[79] The internationalist concept of "floating arbitration" is not recognized by these courts.[80] Accordingly, the arbitral awards set aside at the seat are generally neither recognized nor enforced.[81] However, an arbitral award set aside at the seat may be recognized and enforced in England and Wales if the national setting-aside decision of a foreign court violates the "basic principles of honesty, natural justice and domestic concepts of public policy."[82] On July 27, 2017, the English High Court in *Maximov*[83] refused to enforce an arbitral award set aside by a Russian court (the Moscow Arbitrazh Court). The High Court was not convinced that the setting-aside decisions[84] were products of actual judicial bias. A different outcome was reached in *Yucos Capital SARL v. OJSC Rosneft Oil Company*. Several awards set aside in Russia were recognized and enforced because, according to the Court, the setting-aside decision was a result of a partial and dependent judicial system.

The counterpart to the territorial approach outlined above is the internationalist approach[85] of arbitration. According to this approach, local law and local courts "have no control or regulatory competence over international arbitral proceedings held on their territory."[86] The setting aside of the award at the seat of the arbitration is irrelevant for the enforcement of the award in the enforcement state.

The perception of arbitration as an independent legal order, free from the *lex arbitri*,[87] is largely a result of the French school of thought.[88] A central concern

---

[78] See VARGIU/AHMED, in BERMANN, above n. 17, p. 988, para. 3.2.5: "The setting aside ... of an arbitral award by a judgment ... does not necessarily preclude its enforcement in [the] UK."

[79] HENDEL/PEREZ above n. 17, p. 197; MARSDEN/DAVIES, in ROWLEY/GAILLARD/KAISER, above n. 20, p. 268 et seq., 278.

[80] LEE/SIPPEL, above n. 17, pp. 142–143, para. 7.25: "In particular, English jurisprudence recognizes no concept of 'arbitral procedures floating in the transnational firmament, unconnected with any municipal system of law." See also DARWAZEH, above n. 13, pp. 340 et seq.

[81] *Malicorp v. Government of Egypt* [2015] EWHC 361, refused to enforce an award set aside by the Cairo Court of Appeal.

[82] See *Yukos Capital SARL v. OJSC Oil Co. Rosneft* [2014] EWHC 2188.

[83] EWHC (Comm.), *Maximov v. NMLK Open Joint Stock Comp.* [2017] EWHC 191.

[84] CORBY/KO/MATHESON/OAKLEY/LEVITT/BROWN, in The Baker McKenzie IAY (2017–2018), pp. 369 et seq. (notably p. 373).

[85] Others adopt the delocalized approach or the universalistic conception of arbitration; see BOOR, above n. 17, pp. 50 et seq.; DARWAZEH, above n. 13, pp. 301, 331 et seq.; GIRSBERGER/VOSER, above n. 17, pp. 445 et seq. See also the *Born v. Menon* dispute in Singapore, in ROSS, https://globalarbitrationreview.com/article/1034834/clash-of-the-singapore-titans.

[86] MISTELIS, in BACHAND/GELINAS (eds.), The UNCITRAL Model Law (2013), pp. 168, 171.

[87] For the *termini internal lex arbitri* and *external lex arbitri*, see MISTELIS, in BERGER/BORGES/HERRMANN/SCHLÜTER-WACKERBARTH (eds.), Zivil-und Wirtschatsrecht (2006), pp. 1010–1011.

[88] See CUNIBERTI, above n. 15, p. 180: "the seat of the arbitration is an intellectual concept which is hardly physical, and arbitral hearings do not take place in locations which are related

of this school of thought to this day remains the importance of negating the role of the seat in modern international arbitration law.[89] In his 2010 treatise *Legal Theory of International Arbitration*, Gaillard put forward the thesis that the NYC has clearly moved away from the old classical concept, stating that the "juridicity" of arbitration was rooted exclusively in the legal order of the seat of the arbitral tribunal.[90] Arbitration is based on a "distinct transnational legal order,"[91] which is not founded on a national legal system, neither that of the country of the seat of the arbitral tribunal nor that of the place or places of enforcement.[92] Arbitrators "do not derive their powers from the State in which they have their seat, but rather from the sum of all legal orders that recognize … the validity of the arbitration agreement and the award."[93] In a more recent essay, Gaillard attempts to give tangible shape to this transnational vision. He proposes "an arbitral legal order that is founded on national legal systems, while at the same time transcending any individual national legal order."[94] However, as Schlosser[95] correctly pointed out, it remains unclear which substantive-legal substrate should underpin this legal order.

According to the internationalist school of thought,[96] the arbitral award draws its legitimacy not only from the seat of the arbitral tribunal but also from various other sources. Arbitration is a "sui juris or autonomous dispute resolution process."[97] Since international disputes are not governed by the law of a specific legal system, they are deemed "to belong to a supranational plane, given their subsection to international instruments such as the

---

    to the dispute, but rather in locations which are convenient … places which are precisely wholly unconnected with the dispute"; FOUCHARD, Revue de l'Arbitrage (1965), 99 et seq.; GOLDMAN, in Collected Courses of the Hague Academy of International Law, Vol. 109 (1963), pp. 347 et seq.; LALIVE, GIUFFRÉ (ed.), Liber Fausto Pocar – New Instruments of Private International Law (2009), Vol. II, pp. 599 et seq.; MAYER, The Trend, above n. 17, p. 37 et seq.; PAMBOUKIS, above n. 17, pp. 83 et seq.

89   MISTELIS, Reality Test, above n. 17; THÖNE, above n. 17, 257 et seq.

90   GAILLARD, Legal Theory, above n. 17, p. 31: "the New York Convention has clearly broken away from the ancient conception which considers the juridicity of International arbitration to be exclusively rooted in the legal order of the seat."

91   GAILLARD, Legal Theory, above n. 17, p. 35: "the juridicity of arbitration is rooted in a distinct, transnational legal order, that could be labeled as the arbitral legal order, and not in a national legal system, be it that of the country of the seat or that of the place or places of enforcement."

92   GAILLARD, Transcending, above n. 17, pp. 371 et seq.; however, see PAULSSON, J., The Idea of Arbitration, above n. 17, pp. 39 et seq.

93   GAILLARD, ICSID Review 14 (1999), above n. 17, 16, 18.

94   GAILLARD, Transcending, above n. 17, p. 373.

95   SCHLOSSER, above n. 12, before sec. 1025, paras. 6, 8. See also MISTELIS, in BERGER/BORGES/HERRMANN/SCHLÜTER-WACKERBARTH (eds.), Zivil-und Wirtschatsrecht (2006), p. 1740: "The main argument against delocalized arbitration is that arbitration cannot operate in a legal vacuum."

96   On the "delocalization" debate, see GOODE/KRONKE/MCKENDRICK, above n. 10, paras. 19.78 et seq.; MISTELIS, in BACHAND/GELINAS (eds.), The UNCITRAL Model Law (2013), pp. 169 et seq.

97   LEW, Arb. Intl. 22 (2006), 179, 181.

New York Convention."[98] Arbitral awards are therefore anational.[99] Their annulment in the place of arbitration is irrelevant in relation to its treatment in other legal systems. Even after its annulment in the state of origin, the arbitral award "does not become a zero, but remains a fact in the world."[100]

To confirm the delocalized approach, various arguments have been put forward, but an in-depth discussion would go beyond the scope of this chapter.[101] A first stage win of the delocalized school can be observed in the ongoing emancipation of international arbitration from national procedural law and the limitation of mandatory provisions relating to the arbitral procedure.[102] Instances of delocalized arbitration (at least regarding the fictionality of the arbitral seat) can also be found in sports arbitration and in e-arbitration.[103]

The delocalized approach is consistently applied by the French courts in particular.[104] Article VII(1) alt. 2 NYC introduces the more-favorable-right

---

[98] See NOLAN/AITELAJ, in ROWLEY/GAILLARD/KAISER, above n. 20, p. 49. On the concept of *lex mercatoria*, see BASEDOW, UnifLRev 4 (2014), 697 et seq.; BERGER, The Creeping Codification of the New *Lex Mercatoria*, 2nd ed. (2010); BERGER, The Practice of Transnational Law (2001); LANDO, ICLQ 34 (1985), 747 et seq.; GAILLARD, Arb. Intl. 2001, 59 et seq.; Rt. Hon. Lord Justice Mustill, in BOS/BROWNLIE (eds.), Liber Amicorum for Lord Wilberforce (1987), pp. 158 et seq.; PAMBOUKIS, La Lex Mercatoria reconsidérée in Melanges en l'honneur de Paul Lagarde (2005), pp. 635 et seq. See also CALLIESS (ed.), Transnationales Recht, Stand und Perspektiven (2014), which contains many interesting contributions.

[99] On the question of whether the NYC also applies to anational or transnational arbitral awards, see in particular VAN DEN BERG, above n. 10, pp. 34–40; GRAIG, above n. 17, p. 201; SOLOMON, above n. 16, §2, paras. 2, 35 et seq.; BERGER, above n. 35, p. 506.

[100] SCHACK, above n. 17, para. 1475. See the original German wording: "wird der Schiedsspruch nicht etwa zu einem Nullum, sondern er bleibt als Faktum in der Welt."

[101] See the overview in DUNMORE, above n. 17, p. 287; MISTELIS, in BACHAND/GELINAS (eds.), The UNCITRAL Model Law (2013), p. 170; MISTELIS, Setting Aide of Arbitral Awards and Forum Shopping in International Arbitration, in FERRARI (ed.), Forum Shopping in the International Commercial Arbitration Context (2013), pp. 277 et seq., 281. See also the critique of THÖNE, SchiedsVZ 2016, 257 et seq. (notably p. 261): "Moreover, the idea of delocalization leads to arbitrary results, uncertainty jeopardises the rights of the parties and carries the risk of multiplication of proceedings; it thus leads to results international arbitration actually aims to avoid." See also RADICATI DI BROZOLO, Les Cahiers de l'arbitrage 2011–3, above n. 17, 663 et seq.

[102] See in this direction: MISTELIS, in BACHAND/GELINAS (eds.), The UNCITRAL Model Law (2013), p. 174.

[103] See MISTELIS, in BACHAND/GELINAS (eds.), The UNCITRAL Model Law (2013), p. 171; MISTELIS, Setting Aide of Arbitral Awards and Forum Shopping in International Arbitration, in FERRARI (ed.), Forum Shopping in the International Commercial Arbitration Context (2013), pp. 283–284. For ICSID, see KONTOGIANNIS, above n. 17. For dispute resolution in international sports law, see HESS, The Private-Public Divide in International Dispute Resolution (2018), pp. 154 et seq.; HEERMANN, Bindung von Vereinsmitgliedern und Nichtmitgliedern an die Sanktionsvorschriften übergeordneter (Sport-)Verbände; HEERMANN, Die Sportsschiedsgerichtsbarkeit nach dem Pechstein-Urteil des BGH, NJW 2916, 2224 et seq.; HEERMANN, Sportsschiedsgerichtsbarkeit 2019 – Eine Standortsbestimmung, NJW 2019, 1560 et seq. See also BGHZ 212, 70 (79).

[104] DARWAZEH, above n. 13, p. 301, 334 et seq.; HENDEL/PEREZ NOGALES, above n. 17, p. 194 ("established practice") with the relevant case law of the French courts; LEVENTHAL, above n. 17, 279 et seq.; PINSOLLE, above n. 17, 277 et seq.

provision[105] and, by doing so, opens the door to more arbitration-friendly treatment of the party seeking enforcement.[106] The main purpose of Article VII NYC is to allow the party seeking enforcement[107] to have recourse to national rules (i.e., more favorable domestic law) or to rules of international agreements which are "more favorable" toward recognition and enforcement.[108] In the latter case, the court has no discretion as to whether the more favorable provision should be applied or not.[109] It is crystal clear that Article VII NYC "is here a stumbling block in that it encourages states to bypass Article V and invoice their own laws."[110] According to the prevailing opinion, the court must apply Article VII(1) alt. 2 NYC *ex officio*.[111] Contracting states are not permitted to impose more onerous conditions than those laid down in the NYC.[112] Taking into account the principle of maximum effectiveness, it follows that arbitral awards which have been set aside at the seat may still be recognized and enforced in the contracting states to the NYC,[113] "even if a ground under Article V is established, provided that national law allows the court to do so."[114]

French jurisprudence recognizes and enforces annulled foreign arbitral awards based on the more favorable national enforcement law in the application of Article VII(1) NYC[115] and to the exclusion of Article V(1)(e) NYC.[116]

---

[105] QUINKE, in WOLFF, above n. 5, Art. VII, paras. 37–39. For Austria, England, France, Germany, and Switzerland, see LIEBSCHER, above, n. 64, pp. 385 et seq.

[106] So MISTELIS: MISTELIS/DI PIETRO, in MISTELIS (ed.), Concise International Arbitration, 2nd ed. (2015), p. 28, who characteristically uses the expression "'pro' enforcement bias" of the NYC.

[107] QUINKE, in WOLFF, above n. 5, Art. VII, para. 3.

[108] CZERNICH, New Yorker Schiedsübereinkommen – Kurzkommentar (2008), Art. VII, para. 1, p. 69. For the principle of most favorable law, see POUDRET/BESSON, above n. 17, paras. 926 et seq., p. 847; SCHLOSSER, in STEIN/JONAS, above n. 12, Annex to §1061, para. 378. For the relation between Art. V (1) and Art. VII NYC, see in particular PETROCHILOS, above n. 17, 856, 874. For the cases in which Art. IX(1) of the European Convention and the NYC simultaneously govern the enforcement of an award, see LIEBSCHER, above n. 5, Art. V, para. 392; QUINKE, in WOLFF, above n. 5, Art. VII, paras. 88 et seq.; SOLOMON, in BERMANN (ed.), above n. 17, p. 363.

[109] MISTELIS/DI PIETRO, above n. 17, Art. VII, para. 2.

[110] GOODE, above n. 19, 39: "Article VII of the New York Convention is here a stumbling block in that it encourages states to bypass Article V and invoke their own laws."

[111] QUINKE, in WOLFF, above n. 5, Art. VII, paras. 40–41.

[112] Art. III NYC. See GAILLARD/SIINO, in ROWLEY/GAILLARD/KAISER, above n. 20, pp. 86, 97.

[113] For Germany, see ROSENBERG/SCHWAB/GOTTWALD, above n. 76, §185, para. 42; SCHACK, above n. 17, para. 1477.

[114] NAZZINI, above n. 36, p. 603, 608.

[115] LEVENTHAL, above n. 17, 279–281; POINTON, in LÉVY/DERAINS (eds.), Liber Amicorum en l'honneur de Serge Lazareff, (2011), pp. 499, 501; HENDEL/PEREZ NOGALES, above n. 17, p. 196: "French courts do not find any provision precluding the enforcement of an annulled award. Article 1520 (former 1502) of the French Code of Civil Procedure does not include among the grounds for refusal the fact that the award has been previously annulled by another court"; RUBINS/RIVOIRE, in ROWLEY/GAILLARD/KAISER, above n. 20, pp. 285 et seq., p. 292. See also ANDREWS, above n. 27, p. 602 (fn. 230), who cites Lord Collins: "They rest rather on the power of the enforcing court under the New York Convention, Art. VII (1), to apply laws

The ground on which the award was set aside is not decisive. France ignores setting-aside decisions at the seat regardless of whether the seat is located in England, Switzerland,[117] or Canada.[118] Dutch case law[119] follows a similar path. An award annulled at the seat may be enforced in the Netherlands in exceptional circumstances.[120]

The general rule in the United States is to respect foreign setting-aside decisions.[121] However, the U.S. courts have[122] set limits to the comity doctrine

---

which are more generous to enforcement than the rules in the New York Convention," with further references.

[116] For the *Norsorol* (1984), *Hilmarton* (1994), and *Putrabali* (2007) decisions, see BLACKABY/ PARTASIDES/REDFERN, above n. 8, paras. 11.94–11.97; BOOR, above n. 17, pp. 55–62; DE Cossío, above n. 3, p. 17, 18–20; GIRSBERGER/VOSER, above n. 17, pp. 444–445; LEVENTHAL, Les Cahiers de l'arbitrage, 2013–4, 279 et seq.; KOCH, above n. 17, pp. 269 et seq. See among the many comments on the *Norsorol* decision DUTOIT, Rev. Crit DIP 1985, 551; GOLDMAN, Rev. Arb. 1985, 430; KAHN, J. du Droit International 1985, 679; THOMSON, JIntlArb 1 (1985), 67. On the *Chromalloy* and *Yukos* decisions, see BLACKABY/PARTASIDES/REDFERN, above n. 8, paras. 11.95, 11.97; LEE/SIPPEL, above n. 17, p. 147; LIEBSCHER, above n. 64, p. 387: "Under French law this question is irrelevant as French courts do not apply art.V (1), (e)"; PAULSSON, M./SURESH, above n. 17, §17.03: "The French do not apply the New York Convention. They don't apply Article V(1) (e)"; SAMPLINER, Mealey's International Arbitration Report 11 (1996), 22 et seq.; LAZIĆ-SMOLJANIĆ, Enforcing Annulled Arbitral Awards: A Comparison Of Approaches In the United States And In the Netherlands, in Zbornik Pravnog fakulteta case Sveucilista u Rijeci, vol. 39 (2018), no. 1, 215 et seq., 219–221 (*Chromalloy*), 225–233 (*Yucos*).

[117] This was the case in Hilmarton Ltd v. Omnium de traitement et de valorisation-OTV, CourCass, 23.3.1994, YCA XX (1995), 663.

[118] VAN DEN BERG, ICSID Review 29 (2014), Issue 2, above n. 17, 24.

[119] See DARWAZEH, above n. 13, pp. 301, 330 et seq.

[120] LEIJTEN/CRONJE/ZIRAR, in ROWLEY/GAILLARD/KAISER, above n. 20, pp. 428 et seq., 436: "A special circumstance exists if the award was set aside in foreign proceedings on grounds that do not match with those in Article V, (1)(a) to (1)(d) of the New York Convention, and grounds that are not generally accepted according to international standards." See also Gerechtshof (Court of Appeal of Amsterdam), September 18, 2012 – Case No. 200.100.508/01, *Nikolai Viktorovich Maximov v. OJSC Novolipetsky Metallurgichesky Kombinat*, in YCA XXXVIII (2013), 427; Gerechtshof (Court of Appeal of Amsterdam), April 28, 2009 – Case No. 200, 005, 269, *Yukos Capital v. Rosneft*; VAN DEN BERG, JIntlArb 27, (2010), above n. 17, 179 et seq.; BONDAR/GERMINY, *Tomskneft v. Societe Yukos Capital* French Court of Cassation, November 5, 2014, EIAR 3 (2015), Issue 2, 167 et seq.; BOOR, AVR 2016, 297 et seq.; FERRARI/ROSENFELD, above n. 17, 478 et seq.; GUNTHER/GUNTHER, Disp. Res. J. 70 (2015), Issue 1, 41 et seq.; SCHRAMM, SchiedsVZ 2016, 314 et seq.; SEHAN, Tex. L. Rev. 95 (2016), 101 et seq.; STRUYCKEN, in HESS/JAYME/MANSEL (eds.), Europa als Rechts- und Lebensraum, Liber Amicorum für Christian Kohler zum 75. Geburtstag am 18. Juni 2018 (2018), pp. 489 et seq.; WELLS, International Energy Law Review (2016), 101 et seq.

[121] AMIRFAR/REID/POPOVA, in BOSMAN, above n. 17, pp. 84–86; LAHLOU/POPTINGER/WALTERS, in FRISCHKNECHT/LAHLOU et al., Enforcement of Foreign Awards and Judgments in New York (2018), pp. 115 et seq. (notably under [D]); DEL DUCA/WELSH, above n. 17, p. 1029: "courts in the U.S. will defer to a judgment of annulment made by a court in the originating country. Indeed this is the norm."

[122] BASTIAN, Does the Enforcement Of Annulled Foreign Arbitral Awards In the United States Come Down to Normative Judgments?, Kluwer Arbitration Blog, 13.12.2017,

with the *Pemex* ruling. As a result, the court of recognition has the discretion to ignore a foreign decision if it is based on local annulment standards.[123] Enforcement of the annulled award is granted if the annulment decision violates the most basic notions of morality and justice in the United States.[124]

If the opposing basic positions were to be compared, they would end up moving between two poles. According to the classic territorial approach, the annulled award is deemed unenforceable in any jurisdiction. The enforcing court has no room for the discretion granted in Article V(1)(e) NYC, because the arbitral award ceased to exist with the annulment decision. Obviously, this is in direct opposition to the wording of Article V(1)(e), which gives to national courts the discretion to enforce the set-aside award.[125]

According to the modern internationalist approach, the arbitral award, once set, enjoys eternal life "because international awards are deemed to belong to a supranational plane, given their subjection to international instruments such as the New York Convention."[126] The setting-aside decision is, according to the internationalist theory, irrelevant for the enforcement court. At this point, the ambivalence of the internationalist approach becomes apparent. On the one hand, the internationalist approach ignores the setting-aside decision of the state of origin and, by doing so, undermines its sovereignty, which is one of the

---

     http://arbitrationblog.kluwerarbitration.com/2017/12/13/18965/; LEE/SIPPEL, above n. 17, pp. 144–145; SILBERMAN/YAFFE, Fordham Int'l L.J. 40 (2017), 799, 812.

[123]   On the situation in the United States, see DARWAZEH, above n. 13, pp. 301, 337 et seq.; FELLAS, N. Y. Law J. 2016, 256; FERRITO, DRJ (2013), 33 et seq.; LEE/SIPPEL, above n. 17, 144–5; FRIEDMAN/LIVSHIZ/LEITNER, in ROWLEY/GAILLARD/KAISER, above n. 20, pp. 567 et seq., 574. On the *Chromalloy* (1996), *Baker Marine* (1999), *Karaha Bodas* (2004), *Termo-Rio* (2007), *Castillo Bozo* (2013), and *Commisa* (2013) decisions, see DE COSSÍO, above n. 3, pp. 17 et seq.; GOLDSTEIN, above n. 17, pp. 19 et seq. On *Commisa* see notably, see RADICATI DI BROZOLO, above n. 17, Les Cahiers de l'arbitrage, 2013–4, 1027 et seq. For the *Termo-Rio* and *Pemex* decisions, see CABRERA/FIGUEROA/WÖSS, above n. 17; PAULSSON, M., above n. 9, pp. 205–209; LAZIC-SMOLJANIC, above n. 116, pp. 215 et seq., 219–221. See also U.S.D.C., Southern District of New York, February 6, 2014 – Case No. 10-CV-5256 (KMW), *Thai-Lao Lignite Co., Ltd. & Hongsa Lignite Co., Ltd. v. Government of the Lao People's Democratic Republic*, http://www.kluwerarbitration.com/CommonUI/document.aspx?id=KLI-KA-1411004; *Pemex – Exploration y Produccion (Mexico) Corporation Mexicana de Mantenimiento Integral, S. de R.L. de C.V. (Mexico), v. Pemex- Exploration y Produccion (Mexico)*, YCA XLII (2017), 763 et seq.; BRENNAN, http://kluwerarbitrationblog.com/blog/2014/10/15/the-pemex-case-the-ghost-of-chromalloy-past/#fn-11067-1; RADICATI DI BROZOLO, http://blogs.law.nyu.edu/transnational/2014/03/the-fate-of-awards-annulled-at-the-seat-in-light-of-thai-lao-lignite; PAULSSON, M., Kluwer Arbitration Blog, August 24, 2017, http://arbitrationblog.kluwerarbitration.com/2017/08/24/1958-new-york-convention-turning-battle-judgments-latest-us-attitude-towards-enforcement-annulled-awards; SALOMON/VAZOVA, https://www.lw.com/thoughtLeadership/LW-commissa-arbitral-award-Mexico.

[124]   PAULSSON, M./SURESH, above n. 17, §17.05, p. 286.

[125]   See PAULSSON, J., APLR 6 (1998), Issue 2, above n. 17, 1, 6, et seq., 10.

[126]   NOLAN/AITELAJ, in ROWLEY/GAILLARD/KAISER, above n. 20, p. 49.

pillars of the NYC.[127] On the other hand, it relies on the enforcement state[128] for the enforcement of the award. The NYC allows the contracting states to maintain control over arbitration by granting them certain discretion to allow or to deny the enforcement of the annulled award. This leads to an inconsistent interpretation and application of the provisions of the NYC. Without the assistance of state courts,[129] it is impossible for international arbitration, which is a private dispute resolution mechanism,[130] to manage several important practical problems. One of these problems is the enforcement of the award, which, if not done voluntarily, must take place *manu militari*, i.e., with the assistance of the state of enforcement.[131]

Self-regulation instruments and commercial diplomacy in international arbitration become more necessary and desirable every day. The legal uncertainty regarding the enforcement of annulled awards for the users of international arbitration turns self-regulation instruments into an *ultimum refugium*.

In 2008, Albert Jan van den Berg suggested a new NYC text.[132] His suggestions included the proposal to refuse enforcement if the party asserts and proves that "(g) the award has been set aside by the court in the country where the award was made on grounds equivalent to grounds (a) to (e)" of Article V of his hypothetical draft convention. However, it was not successful.[133] It remains to be seen whether the recent clarifications regarding the burden of proof,[134] the suggestions to give priority to constitutional norms over local standards or

---

[127] PAULSSON, M., above n. 9, p. 72.

[128] SANDERS, in UN (ed.), Enforcing Arbitration Awards under the New York Convention – Experience and Prospects, Papers presented at "The New York Convention Day," 10 June 1998, United Nations Publication (1999), pp. 3, 4, compared international commercial arbitration "with a young bird. It rises in the air, but from time to time it falls back on its nest." See also RAAPE, Internationales Privatrecht, 5th ed. (1961), p. 557: "Das Schiedsgericht thront nicht über der Erde, es schwebt nicht in der Luft, es muß irgendwo landen, irgendwo 'erden.'"

[129] See KAUFMANN-KOHLER, Arb. Intl., 29 (2013), Issue 2, 153 et seq., 173: "the current design of international commercial arbitration is still characterized by the important role played by national law and domestic courts."

[130] SCHROEDER, in BÖCKSTIEGEL/NACIMIENTO/KRÖLL, above n. 8, p. 575.

[131] PFEIFFER, in Bitburger Gespräche Jahrbuch (2016), pp. 13 et seq., 29: "„Die Schiedsgerichtsbarkeit geht nun in einem entscheidenden Punkt über die bloße vertragliche Bindung hinaus, weil wir Schiedssprüche mit den Mitteln des staatlichen Vollstreckungsrechts durchsetzen."

[132] UN Secretariat, New York Convention 1958 Guide, http://newyorkconvention1958.org/index.php?lvl=cmspage&pageid=10&menu=625&opac_view=-1.

[133] See TIRADO/ACEVEDO/COSIO, in GÓMEZ/LÓPEZ-RODRÍGUEZ (eds.), 60 Years of the New York Convention: Key Issues and Future Challenges (2019), pp. 295 et seq., 309–310.

[134] PAULSSON, M./SURESH, above n. 17, §17.07, p. 287: "a very heavy onus rests on the party resisting enforcement."

public policy,[135] and the creation of a "Supplementary Commentary"[136] will be helpful in this regard.

It is too early to state whether the internationalist approach will prevail at a global level.[137] Annulled awards, which have been enforced in an NYC contracting state, are rather exceptional. The internationalist approach is arbitration-friendly and decisively promotes international arbitration,[138] hence its continued existence as an invaluable, indispensable mechanism for alternative dispute resolution in international trade.[139]

According to the mediating view of the international arbitration community[140] followed here, foreign setting-aside decisions are to be respected in the state of recognition as long as the arbitral award has not been set aside at the seat of arbitration on the basis of "local standards,"[141] for "political reasons,"[142] by fraud discovered only after the judgment has been reached,[143] being contrary to natural justice, or on the basis of "unobjective considerations."[144] A set-aside court decision of a sovereign state cannot be reasonably disregarded without important reasons. Such reasons are, only primarily, those which protect the interest of the enforcement state[145] or such which protect both the interests of

---

[135] Id., §17.07, p. 289: "Matters engraved in constitutional norms could form exceptions to the rule of thumb (ex nihilo nil fit) and lead to an enforcement of an award that has been set aside."

[136] Supplementary Commentary which at least has the power of soft law; see PAULSSON, M./SURESH, above n. 17, §17.07, pp. 289–290.

[137] See ANDREWS, above n. 27, p. 602: "it is too early to decide that this is likely to become the predominant possibility among leading trading nations."

[138] This aspect is discussed in Germany among others by GEIMER, IZPR, above n. 17, para. 3944c; SCHACK, above n. 17, para. 1477; SIEHR, above n. 17, 154 et seq.

[139] See PFEIFFER, above n. 131, pp. 13 et seq., 15–16.

[140] PAULSSON, M. /SURESH, above n. 17, §17.06, p. 286.

[141] For the term "local standard annulment," see in particular PAULSSON, J., Enforcing, above n. 17; PAULSSON, M., Resisting, above n. 17, p. 212; But see also VAN DEN BERG, JIntlArb 27 (2010), above n. 17, 179 et seq. (notably pp. 188 et seq.); PAULSSON, M./SURESH, above n. 17, §17.06, pp. 286–287: "Local standards for annulment should not be transported internationally and find legitimacy under the Convention. It is an expression of Article IX of the 1961 European Convention that provides for the applicability of Article V with the small and improved alteration that an award may only be refused if an award had been annulled on grounds similar to those under Article V (1) (a)–(d)." LIEBSCHER, above n. 64, p. 384 state that an international standard annulment is "based on the grounds mentioned in art. IX European Convention." It can be assumed that all states that have adopted the UNCITRAL Model Law or that have comparable standards are states within the meaning of the International Standard Annulment. See VON SCHLABRENDORFF, above n. 52, §2, para. 143.

[142] ROSENBERG/SCHWAB/GOTTWALD, above n. 76, §183, para. 25.

[143] GOODE, above n. 19, p. 39. Regarding the issues of corruption which are resolved by Arbitral Tribunals with rules of transnational public policy, see GAILLARD, Arb. Intl. 35 (2019), 1, 13–14.

[144] SCHÜTZE, in WIECZOREK/SCHÜTZE, above n. 17, sec. 1061, para. 131 ("aus unursachlichen Erwägungen"); SCHÜTZE, Schiedsgericht, above n. 17, paras. 708–713.

[145] See LIEBSCHER, above n. 5, prelim. 2, para. 17: "and at the same time ensuring that the various fundamental legal principles of different States are observed."

Intersentia

the enforcement state and of the award debtor. Sovereign states, according to Articles V and VII NYC, are qualified to exercise control over foreign awards within their territories. In Articles V(1)(e) and VII, the NYC leaves the right to have the last word with the enforcement courts.[146] These Articles[147] protect not just the interests of the award debtor, but even more so the fundamental legal principles and interests of the enforcement countries.

Much work must be done in the contracting states in order to persuade the local courts that the discretionary power given to them by the NYC must be exercised restrictively and with caution.[148]

The increasing reliance by national courts on the more favorable right provision of Article VII(1) is to be expected.[149] Nothing can prohibit the contracting states from introducing into their legislation a more favorable right provision.[150] This will damage the "process of internationalization which the Convention itself has done so much to foster."[151] The well-known UNCITRAL Guide to New York Convention[152] and the International Council for Commercial Arbitration Guide for judges constitute very helpful instruments in the hands of national courts.[153]

---

[146] PETROCHILOS, Procedural Law in International Arbitration (2004), para. 7.87: "The best option would be that under the Convention this is a question left open to be decided by the courts, which must deal with it by regarding the Convention as made of a single texture and 'not alter the material of which it is woven, but ... iron out the creases.'"

[147] And more intensively Art. V(2)(b) NYC.

[148] See KRONKE, above n. 6.

[149] GAILLARD/SIINO, in ROWLEY/GAILLARD/KAISER, above n. 20, pp. 86 et seq., 99.

[150] SANDERS, above n. 17, pp. 102–103.

[151] GOODE, above n. 19, p. 39.

[152] UN SECRETARIAT, New York Convention 1958 Guide, http://newyorkconvention1958.org/index.php?lvl=cmspage&pageid=10&menu=625&opac_view=-1.

[153] SANDERS, above n. 17.

RETHINKING MULTINATIONAL PROCEDURE

Linda SILBERMAN[*]

1. The Concept of a Multinational Rule............................... 121
2. Procedure is Outside of Most Multinational Rules 123
3. Lessons from the United States.................................... 124
4. Lessons from the ALI/UNIDROIT Experience: Principles or Rules?..... 126
5. Competing Developments... 128
6. Conclusion.. 129

1. THE CONCEPT OF A MULTINATIONAL RULE

I am delighted to comment upon Professor Christoph Kern's extensive and thoughtful report on "Multinational Rules and Systems of Dispute Resolution in an Era of Global Economy."[1] In his discussion of "multinational rules," Professor Kern notes that the most obvious example of a "multinational rule" – which he defines as rules enacted by law makers of more than two nations – is the multilateral treaty. Indeed, if the concept is to embrace a formal rule that multiple nations accept as binding, it will usually be a treaty implemented in multiple jurisdictions that has that effect. Of course, in the absence of a supranational institution for interpretation of a particular treaty, non-uniformity in the interpretation of treaty provisions is not only possible but also likely.[2]

A model law, if enacted in multiple countries, is another example of a "multinational rule" (per Kern's definition), but, unlike with a treaty, each country is free to vary its enactment as well as to offer its own interpretation

---

[*] Professor, New York University School of Law, Clarence D. Ashley Professor of Law.

[1] C.A. KERN, "Multinational Rules and Systems of Dispute Resolution in an Era of Global Economy", in this volume.

[2] See F. DIEDRICH, "Maintaining Uniformity in International Uniform Law via Autonomous Interpretation: Software Contracts and the CISG" (1996) 8 *Pace International Law Review* 303 (describing the trend among international lawyers in interpreting the language of international uniform laws consistent with their home fora, creating issues of uniformity).

Intersentia

of the provisions of such a law. That is indeed the experience under the United Nations Commission on International Trade Law (UNCITRAL) Model Law on International Commercial Arbitration that Professor Kern highlights in his contribution to this volume.[3] The UNCITRAL Model Law provides a structure for the relationship between courts and arbitral tribunals, but it is often implemented with variations in a number of jurisdictions.[4] In addition, it should be noted that the most significant seats for international arbitration – New York, France, England, and Switzerland – do not have the Model Law and indeed depart from it dramatically.

In the United States, there is a Uniform Law Commission, made up of commissioners who come from every state in the United States,[5] and that body promulgates uniform and "model laws" on various subjects for potential enactment in every state.[6] But even in a federal system like the United States, there has been only limited success in achieving pervasive enactments of such Uniform Acts,[7] and even when they do, there is not necessarily uniform adoption or interpretation.[8] Moreover, most of these Acts do not address issues of procedure and the few that do have not had broad adoptions.[9]

---

[3]   UNCITRAL Model Law on International Commercial Arbitration (1985), https://uncitral.un.org/sites/uncitral.un.org/files/media-documents/uncitral/en/19-09955_e_ebook.pdf,.

[4]   Among the differences are the approach to the procedures for challenging arbitrators (Art. 13), the choice of law approach for determining the applicable law (Art. 28(2)), and the grounds for setting aside an award (Art. 34). For a more extensive discussion of the adoption of the Model Law regime into national arbitration legislation in different countries, see P. SANDERS, "Unity and Diversity in the Adoption of the Model Law" (1995) 11 *Arbitration International* 1.

[5]   The Uniform Law Commission (ULC) was established in 1892 to "provide states with non-partisan, well-conceived and well-drafted legislation that brings clarity and stability to critical areas of state statutory law." It does this by reviewing the law of each state to determine legal areas that might benefit from uniformity, and then drafting proposed statutes for state legislatures to consider and adopt. See Uniform Law Commission, "About Us," https://www.uniformlaws.org/aboutulc/overview.

[6]   The most well-known example is the Uniform Commercial Code. Others include the Uniform Trade Secrets Act, the Uniform Interstate Family Support Act, the Uniform Child Custody Jurisdiction and Enforcement Act, and the Uniform Electronic Transactions Act.

[7]   While the uniform laws mentioned in note 6 above have been adopted by nearly all states, many others have met with more limited success – for example, the ULC's Business Organizations Code (2011) (adopted by two states), the Management of Public Employee Retirement Systems Act (1997) (adopted by two states), and the Statute and Rule Construction Act (1995) (adopted by one state).

[8]   For example, there are two Uniform Acts addressing the recognition and enforcement of foreign money judgments: the 1962 Uniform Foreign Money-Judgments Recognition Act and the updated 2005 Uniform Foreign-Country Money Judgments Recognition Act. Thirty-four states have adopted one of the two Uniform Acts. Neither of the Acts has a requirement of reciprocity for recognition/enforcement, but several states have included such a provision in their adoption of the Act.

[9]   Such acts are often drafted in the form of "model" laws. As opposed to "uniform" acts, which promote interstate uniformity and contemplate uniform enactment, "model" acts are

2. PROCEDURE IS OUTSIDE OF MOST MULTINATIONAL RULES

More critically, the subject of procedure has not been the object of any these more traditional "multinational rules." Multinational *treaties* have generally not addressed procedural rules applicable in national courts. Professor Kern references the New York Convention on the Recognition and Enforcement of Arbitral Awards,[10] but he correctly notes that the coverage is limited to the narrow issue of recognition/enforcement and the New York Convention itself does not speak to procedural rules more generally. Indeed, Article III of the Convention states that such awards shall be recognized and enforced "in accordance with the rules of procedure of the territory where the award is relied upon."[11]

Similar limitations are found when one looks at other treaties that, like the New York Convention, have a broad multinational level of acceptance. For example, treaties negotiated under the auspices of the Hague Conference on Private International Law cover a wide range of areas and have broad state ratifications, but they too have stayed away from addressing specific procedural rules for national courts. Instead, these Conventions provide frameworks for judicial cooperation in cross-border cases, but leave the details of procedure to national law. For example, the Hague Convention on Service Abroad of Judicial and Extrajudicial Documents in Civil and Commercial Matters (hereinafter "the Hague Service Convention")[12] introduced the mechanism of a Central Authority in each receiving state to serve process pursuant to its own internal law of service of documents in domestic actions upon persons in its territory.[13] Other methods of service under national law are authorized if they are consistent with the standards set out in the Convention.[14] Thus, the treaty architecture suggests normative standards for national laws by imposing something like "minimum standards."

---

   promulgated with the understanding that the main purposes of the act may be substantially achieved even when only partially adopted by each state. See Uniform Commercial Code, "Acts Overview," https://www.uniformlaws.org/acts/overview. ULC Model Laws addressing procedure have had very few adoptions. Examples include the ULC's Model Class Actions Act (1976) (adopted by two states), the Model Rules of Evidence (1999) (adopted by one state), and the Model Rules Relating to the Discovery of Electronically Stored Information (2007) (adopted by three states).

[10] Convention on the Recognition and Enforcement of Foreign Arbitral Awards, done at New York, on June 10, 1958, entered into force on June 7, 1959, 330 U.N.T.S. 3, 38–82, available at https://www.uncitral.org/pdf/english/texts/arbitration/NY-conv/New-York-Convention-E.pdf.

[11] Ibid.

[12] The Hague Convention on Service Abroad of Judicial and Extrajudicial Documents in Civil and Commercial Matters, https://assets.hcch.net/docs/f4520725-8cbd-4c71-b402-5aae1994d14c.pdf.

[13] Ibid. at Art. 2.

[14] Ibid. at Arts. 11 and 19.

It is noteworthy that many of these treaties and model laws relate to cross-border cases, and it is the cross-border transaction that is often the catalyst for a treaty that looks to achieve a uniform approach that will be acceptable to the relevant countries. That was certainly true of the Hague Choice of Court Convention and the recently negotiated Hague Judgments Convention. But both of these treaties also deal only with the rules for the recognition and enforcement of judgments, and, in the case of the Choice of Court Convention, provides for rules and criteria to give effect to the choice of court agreement itself.

These examples provide empirical evidence for my thesis in this contribution – that the best one can do at the global procedural level is to articulate "principles" of procedure and not detailed rules. As Professor Michele Taruffo has written, "a procedural code is not a mere set of more or less complex rules of thumb but above all is a 'cultural product,' the form, structure and contents of which are the product of historical, political, institutional, ethical and economic developments."[15]

3. LESSONS FROM THE UNITED STATES

Rules of procedure are developed and molded by various forces that do not lend themselves to harmonization. For example, the requirements of a written constitution (as in the United States), the structure and organization of the court systems, the role of lawyers, along with the structure and ethics of the legal profession, the appointment of judges and their training, and the principles for financing of litigation have all shaped national procedural regimes.[16]

Of course, the more common and aligned these elements are in different jurisdictions, the more likely it is that a uniform set of procedural rules would be possible. Let me illustrate some of the difficulties by using an example from the United States, which experienced the development of a uniform set of procedural rules for the *federal courts* in 1938.[17] Prior to that time, not only did each state system of courts in the United States have its own set of procedural rules, but a federal statute (the Conformity Act) also required federal courts in each state to follow the state's rules of procedure. Thus, a lawyer from a particular state would know the procedural rules that applied in a state or federal court in that state. However, various forces pushed for the creation of a single system of rules for

---

15 M. Taruffo, "Harmonisation in a Global Context: The ALI/UNIDROIT Principles' in X.E. Kramer and C.H. van Rhee (eds.), *Civil Litigation in a Globalising World*, Springer, Dordrecht 2012, pp. 207, 209.

16 See generally R.L. Marcus, "Putting American Procedural Exceptionalism into a Globalized Context" (2005) 53 *American Journal of Comparative Law* 709.

17 See generally S.N. Subrin, "How Equity Conquered Common Law: The Federal Rules of Civil Procedure in Historical Perspective" (1987) 135 *University of Pennsylvania Law Review* 909.

the federal courts. First, criticisms of some of the more technical and formalistic aspects of the existing procedure were a catalyst for reform, generally as a means to "secure the just, speedy, and inexpensive determination" of proceedings.[18] Second, the expansion of commercial and financial businesses and the growing number of interstate transactions meant that jurisdiction was often possible in different fora, and thus the differences in the procedural systems of different states invited forum shopping even among the federal courts. Curiously, during that period, the applicable substantive law would have been the same in the state and federal courts – the result of clear, predictable and uniform choice of law rules. However, cases could turn out substantially differently in the federal courts in different states due to differences in state procedures, and this result was considered undesirable. Third, the interstate nature of business led to the growth of national law firms that began to establish offices in different states, and there was a desire for a uniform set of procedures such that law firms and lawyers could develop and conduct a national federal practice.

Because the U.S. Congress could enact (or, to be precise, delegate to the Supreme Court) a set of procedural rules for the federal courts, a uniform system was indeed possible. Interpretation of the rules would be subject to precedent, and the U.S. Supreme Court would have ultimate authority to ensure the uniform interpretation of those rules in the event of conflicting interpretations.

Notwithstanding this single set of procedural rules for the federal courts promulgated by a group of experts that formed the Advisory Committee on Federal Rules, state systems did not move in the same direction. The states are, of course, autonomous, and thus the federal Congress could not impose procedural rules on the state judicial systems. A few states did adopt the package of Federal Rules as a matter of choice for their own state,[19] but by and large, the important states, such as New York, Illinois, California, and Texas, retained their own set of procedural rules. Thus, even in a system that appears on the surface to have constituents (i.e. the states) that are historically and culturally very similar, this uniform system of federal procedure did not extend to the states.

Nonetheless, a more subtle effect did initially occur. The reforms undertaken in the Federal Rules had an impact on the states and influenced reforms in state procedure. Even when the details of the rules were different, broad principles reflected in the Federal Rules affected state procedural codes.[20] And various amendments to the Federal Rules over the years often had resonance for

---

[18] Federal Rules of Civil Procedure, Rule 1.

[19] For example, by 1977, just over 30 states, including Alabama, Arizona, Colorado, Georgia, Maine, Massachusetts, New Jersey, Washington, and Wisconsin, as well as the District of Columbia and Puerto Rico, had modeled their procedural rules on the Federal Rules of Civil Procedure. See J.B. OAKLEY AND A.F. COON, "The Federal Rules in State Courts: A Survey of State Court Systems of Civil Procedure" (1986) 61 *Washington Law Review* 1367, 1371 fn. 27.

[20] See ibid., at 1367.

procedural rule changes in some state systems. However, as Professor Steve Burbank has so eloquently written in several articles, procedural rules are also a reflection of power and ideology, and have broad repercussions on substantive outcomes.[21] And to the extent that there was disagreement over the ideology as reflected by the federal rule makers in their subsequent amendments, particularly as regards discovery and class actions, states adopted procedural rules that moved in the opposite direction to provide alternative models and, in some instances, to encourage that litigation be brought in the state system.[22]

A few years ago, a proposal was put forward in the United States that the states should band together to address procedural reform for the state systems and provide a uniform model for the states.[23] Professor Richard Marcus, who has served as Associate Reporter on the Advisory Committee on Civil Rules, which considers amendments to the Federal Rules, questioned the value of uniformity and whether uniformity was even possible in today's more complex litigation environment.[24] He pointed out that the different needs in the federal courts in different districts had led to an expansion of numerous detailed "local" rules, undermining even federal procedural uniformity in the modern era. He pointed out that state judicial dockets and needs of the individual states were even more disparate, indicating that the variety of settings in which different state courts operate may call for something other than uniform solutions.

I offer these examples to Europeans who advocate for a European Code of Civil Procedure. If deep-seated concerns about state sovereignty in their judicial systems have led states in the United States to maintain their own codes of civil procedure, it would seem to be an *a fortiori* proposition for countries in the European Union.

4. LESSONS FROM THE ALI/UNIDROIT EXPERIENCE: PRINCIPLES OR RULES?

Are there other options that might be more feasible for Europe? A more attractive prospect might be to identify "principles" rather than "rules," such as those in the ALI/UNIDROIT Principles of Transnational Civil Procedure.[25]

---

[21]   See, e.g., S.B. BURBANK, "Procedure, Politics, and Power: The Role of Congress" (2004) 79 *Notre Dame Law Review* 1677.

[22]   See G.S. KOPPEL, "Toward a New Federalism in State Civil Justice: Developing a Uniform Cod of State Civil Procedure through a Collaborative Rule-Making Process" (2005) 58 *Vanderbilt Law Review* 1167.

[23]   Ibid.

[24]   R. MARCUS, "Confessions of a Federal "Bureaucrat": The Possibilities of Perfecting Procedural Reform" (2007) 35 *Western State University Law Review* 103.

[25]   The American Law Institute (ALI) and the International Institute for the Unification of Private Law (UNIDROIT) embarked on a joint project to develop principles of procedure for

As procedural scholars know, the ALI-UNIDROIT project was intended to help reduce the impact of differences between legal systems in lawsuits involving transnational commercial disputes. The initial object of the Project was to design of set of "procedural rules," but those "rules" gave way to "principles," which were drafted at a more general and abstract level.[26] (Rules were also promulgated but not adopted by either the ALI or UNIDROIT.) As for the Principles, they have not elicited much debate in general and it is difficult to quarrel with many of them. For example, there is a broad consensus for requirements such as the "independence, impartiality, and qualifications of the Court and its judges," "procedural equality of the parties," "obligations of the parties and lawyers to conduct themselves in good faith," and ensuring "procedures for the speedy and effective enforcement of judgments." The approach taken by the Principles was particularly well suited to the ALI/UNIDROIT Project, the scope of which was worldwide and faced the difficulty of harmonizing not only the divide between common law and civil law systems, but also significant differences in procedures among the countries within those two basic regimes.

Given the Amsterdam Treaty providing for European competence for instruments on judicial cooperation, the present European project (ELI-UNIDROIT) with its regional focus does not face the same hurdles. Nonetheless, even within Europe, the organization and structure of courts in different countries that hear transnational commercial cases is quite different, as is the professional training and experience of their judges.[27] The role of lawyers and methods of financing litigation also affect issues of procedure and there is no unanimity of approach there either. The adoption of "principles" rather than specific or detailed rules might alleviate some of the tensions resulting from engrained traditions that Professor Kern identified in offering several anecdotes with respect to his work on the European Rules project.

The difficulty with a "principles" approach, as illustrated by the ALI/UNIDROIT project, is that it may be so basic as to offer no impactful harmonization at all. Alternatively, a "rules" approach is more likely to invade areas of long-standing practice and tradition in some jurisdictions and be unacceptable for that reason. Moreover, there is still much to be said for experimentation in certain areas, such as pre-trial procedure, multiparty litigation, collective actions, and appellate practice. In the context of Europe, perhaps something that approximates a treaty model of "minimum standards" would be desirable.

---

commercial disputes to be applied by different legal systems. For background on the project, see O. CHASE et al., *Civil Litigation in Comparative Context*, 2nd ed., West Academic Press, St. Paul 2017, pp. 718–719.

26   For a critique of the attempt at "Rules," see G. WALTER AND S.P. BAUMGARTNER, "Utilizing and Feasibility of Transnational Rules of Civil Procedure: Some German and Swiss Reactions to the Hazard-Taruffo Project" (1998) 33 *Texas International Law Journal* 463.

27   A. UZELAC, "Harmonised Civil Procedure in a World of Structural Divergences? Lessons Learned from the CEPEJ Evaluations' in X.E. KRAMER and C.H. VAN RHEE, above n. 15.

5. COMPETING DEVELOPMENTS

A more recent development suggests a phenomenon that is antithetical to a proposal for a uniform procedural code for commercial disputes. Various countries have established their own specialized commercial courts in order to compete for international commercial cases.[28] Of course, one might view this development as consistent with the desire for a uniform or harmonized regime of procedure, since it was inspired in part as an alternative to arbitration for commercial cases, which Professor Kern has identified as a prototypical system with multinational rules. To some extent, all of these new commercial courts tend to offer rules that embrace many of the attractions of the procedure identified with arbitration: limited discovery, expert decision makers, expeditious proceedings, and the use of the English language. However, what is also being featured in many of these courts is not so much a set of procedural rules, but rather a body of expert adjudicators. And each of these commercial courts appears to be less interested in "harmonization" than in "differentiation" as a means of attracting litigation business, much like what has occurred in the market for arbitration.

The English Commercial Court in London has traditionally been a center for international commercial litigation. A well-developed and understood body of English law along with England's receptivity to choice of forum and choice of law clauses made the English Commercial Court an attractive litigation destiny for sophisticated commercial parties in cross-border disputes. Moreover, the English judges sitting in the Commercial Court are persons regarded as sophisticated in business, independent, and having respect for the rule of law.

For some European countries, the possibility that the English Commercial Court is a less attractive option in the face of Brexit may have been an impetus to offer their owned specialized commercial courts as alternatives. Other countries in Asia and the mid-East may have looked to create their own specialized geographic markets, and the English experience may have served as a model.

For example, in 2015, Singapore opened the Singapore International Commercial Court as a division of the Singapore High Court. Potential judges to hear cases in the Commercial Court, at both first instance and on appeal, include not only Singaporean judges but also "International Judges" who are eminent jurists from other jurisdictions.[29] In addition, foreign lawyers are permitted to handle cases in the court.

---

[28] International commercial courts, which have been "considered or established" in countries such as China, Singapore, Qatar, Dubai, the Netherlands, France, and elsewhere. See P.K. BOOKMAN, "Is Private International Law International Law?" (2019) 99 *Boston University Law Review Online* *9, *12.

[29] See A. GODWIN, I. RAMSAY AND M. WEBSTER, "International Commercial Courts: The Singapore Experience" (2017) 18 *Melbourne Journal of International Law* 2.

Several judicial systems in Europe have opened a new court or division of their courts devoted exclusively to international commercial disputes. On January 1, 2019, the Netherlands Commercial Court was launched.[30] It includes a trial court (the Netherlands Commercial Court) and an appellate court (the Commercial Court of Appeal). Unlike the Singapore approach, the judges are all selected from the Dutch judiciary based on their experience in commercial disputes. Although the procedure is Dutch procedure, the proceedings and judgments are in English. Appeals first go to the Commercial Appeals Court and then to the Dutch Supreme Court, at which point proceedings will take place in Dutch.

Other models have been developed in Paris, Frankfurt, Dubai, Abu Dhabi, and China.[31] This chapter is not the place to review the specific structures of these courts and their various differences, but what these developments suggest is that parties may want "choice" about procedure and that uniform rules are not necessarily optimal. One common feature of these courts is that they appear open to permitting the parties to "customize" their own procedures, similar to arbitration.

6. CONCLUSION

In our comparative procedure casebook *Civil Litigation in Comparative Context*,[32] which is now in its second edition, we discuss the structure of legal education, the legal profession, and the judicial profession in different countries, and the effects these matters have on civil procedure. We also consider how the organization of a country's courts has a bearing on procedure. It is perhaps because our book emphasizes civil procedure as peculiarly tied to these issues and to local culture and traditions that I remain a skeptic about multinational rules.[33] At the same time, I am a strong advocate for the study of comparative procedure. There is a role for transplants in specific areas as long as they are sensitive to context and conscious of the interconnectivity to other features in the system. Japan is an example of a system with a unique tradition of borrowing and overlay. Civil law influences have led to a more managerial role for the judge in the United States in the context of its own system. U.S. class actions have inspired different models of collective actions elsewhere, although resisting specific aspects of the U.S. model. Such is the regime of multinational procedure that I envision.

---

[30] See Netherlands Commercial Court (NCC), "Who We are," https://www.rechtspraak.nl/English/NCC/Pages/default.aspx.

[31] See P.K. BOOKMAN, "The Adjudication Business" (2020) 45 *Yale Journal of International Law* 227.

[32] O. CHASE ET AL., above n. 25.

[33] For additional arguments against harmonization, see G.P. MILLER, "The Legal-Economic Analysis of Comparative Civil Procedure" (1997) 45 *American Journal of Comparative Law* 905, 917–918.

PART II

NEW CHALLENGES AND THEIR VARIOUS ASPECTS

Accountability and Transparency

ACCOUNTABILITY AND TRANSPARENCY OF CIVIL JUSTICE

Yulin Fu*

1.	Introduction	134
2.	Judicial Independence as the Premise for Judicial Accountability and Transparency	136
	2.1. The Concept and Definition of Judicial Independence	137
	2.2. Institutional or External Judicial Independence	137
	2.3. The Internal or Personal Independence of a Judge	139
3.	Judicial Transparency as a Principle Guaranteed by Constitutions and the Legal Devices of All States	143
	3.1. Judicial Publication Generally Guaranteed by the Constitutions with Some Exceptions	144
	3.2. The Role of Publication of Judgments and Reasoning from Diverse Perspectives	145
	3.3. The Scope and Objects of Publication of Trials/Hearings	148
	3.4. Exposure of Invisible and Unfair Influence	149
	3.5. Remedies for Breach of Publication of Judgments and Trials	150
	3.6. The Role of New Technology in the Publication of Judgments and Trials for Judicial Transparency	151
4.	Judicial Accountability with Diverse Concepts and its Overlapping Relation with Transparency	154
	4.1. The General Concepts and Experiences of Judicial Accountability	154
	4.2. The Disciplinary and Criminal Accountability of an Individual Judge	159
	4.3. Remedies for Sanctioned Judges	162
5.	Conclusion	163

---

* Professor at Peking University Law School, China.

Intersentia

1. INTRODUCTION

This chapter is a comparative view of four samples from Asia and another four from Europe. These samples neither compose a complete picture of "Eastern countries", nor are they limited within "Eastern". Actually, the concept of "Eastern" or "Western," if defined from the perspective of comparative law, is related much less to the location of a state than to its constitution, institutions, legal culture, and politics. For instance, this chapter supports an understanding that Japan is more "Western" than "Eastern," though it is located in Asia; while "Eastern" China shares fewer problems with Singapore and South Korea in Asia than it does with Croatia in Europe.

The basic contents of accountability and transparency of civil justice focus on such issues as the external and internal independence of judges, regulations and forms of the reasoning of judgments and decisions, the transparency of civil justice through the use of information and communications technology (ICT), the publication of judicial proceedings and decisions, and the evaluation and ranking of civil justice by outsiders. To clearly get hold of such information from the sample countries, I issued a questionnaire to the national reporters to discover the concept, definition, doctrine of and relationship among judicial accountability, transparency, and independence that are embodied in the Constitution, court institutions, procedural laws, and other regulations.[1] When the academic peers filled in the questionnaire, they provided their own analysis of the background and practical situations combined with their answers to the questionnaire. Based on the academic peers' contributions, I will try to give the general view as an introduction as follows.

First, in all the sample countries (which are Japan, Korea, Germany, Netherland, Croatia and China), judicial independence is generally taken as a premise of judicial transparency and accountability, and is clearly provided in the constitutions. However, in some countries such as the Netherlands, judicial transparency and accountability are regarded as a guarantee of judicial independence. Similarly, in Japan, Singapore, and Germany, judicial independence of the judges is also highly respected, while in some other countries such as China, judicial independence is defined in a limited way in the Constitution and now is strengthened by promoting judicial transparency and accountability, in contrast to Croatia, where judicial independence is deemed to have gone too far to be afforded by the judicial level. Combining with the judicial

---

[1] The national reporters, four from Asia and four from Europe, are: Professor Shusuke Kakiuchi of the University of Tokyo (Japan), Professor Hanki Sohn of Yonsei University Law School (Korea), Assistant Professor Zhixun Cao of Peking University Law School (China), and Shaun Wong of RHT Law Taylor Wessing LLP (Singapore); and Professor C.H. van Rhee of Comparative Civil Procedure in Maastricht & E.A. Maan (the Netherlands), Professor Alan Uzelac of the University of Zagreb (Croatia), Professor Marco de Benito of IE University (Spain), and Professor Michael Stürner of the University of Konstanz (Germany).

background of each country, it seems that the better the judicial situation in a country is, the more judicial independence and less accountability there will be.

Second, judicial transparency is generally emphasized and is guaranteed by the Constitution and laws. All the above countries place emphasis on the concept and system of transparency of the judicial process, and all the procedural laws provide plenty of detailed rules to put this into practice, with some exceptions only in extreme situations. But the scope, means, and goals of transparency are defined in various ways. Japanese and Korean academic peers introduced judicial transparency in two levels: transparency to the litigants and openness to the public. China shares the same definition, but stresses more on transparency to the litigants "inside" the proceedings so as to decrease the powerful judges' operation under the table. In contrast, the Netherlands and Singapore regard judicial transparency to the public as part of judicial accountability, while transparency to the parties seems to be left unstated or implied. In Croatia, where judicial independence is deemed to have gone too far, and strong arguments propose that public judges should be a part of judicial transparency. In Spain, judicial transparency seems to be no more than the publication of government data and there is no other mention of the special institution of judicial transparency in the report from the Spanish academic peers.

Thirdly, judicial accountability generally consists of the judge's individual accountability for disciplinary matters, the judge's criminal accountability for his/her judicial misconduct, and civil accountability of the state. In all the above countries except Spain, a judge cannot be charged for civil liability. However, the above countries vary dramatically in terms of defining the concept, scope, and test of judicial accountability. In Netherlands, Japan and Singapore, the issue of judicial accountability is too infrequent to attract the notice of researchers because the problem has never or rarely occurred. While Spain provides a very clear definition and rules on the dimensions of state accountability and the individual accountability of judges, and has a unique civil compensation system for the responsible judge's individual accountability, German law provides civil and criminal accountability for damage caused by public officials, including judges, but it is the state that undertakes civil liability. Croatia shares a similar definition, though the issue of judicial accountability is much more visible. In China, it is the state that is accountable for judicial damages made by the judges under a separate system as "state compensation"; the concept "judicial accountability" is only used to mention a judge's individual accountability for discipline and crimes committed, and more basically, used to divide the boundary of the responsibility between the judge/tribunal and the various "supervisors" over the judge or tribunal after the judicial reforms since 2013.

Finally, the procedural rules, mechanisms, and techniques in civil justice are generally sound in the sample countries, and new technology like artificial intelligence (AI) is used more frequently to promote judicial transparency to some extent. Comparatively, China as a "newcomer" that strongly desires judicial transparency and has fewer obstacles in terms of traditional norms is going much faster in this respect than the other sample countries mentioned in this chapter through the mandatory publication of judgments and rulings, access to tracing processes of litigation and enforcement, and live webcasts of trials on the official website of the court; as a result, the internet is creating judicial transparency breakthroughs and revolutionary innovation in China. In contrast, Germany seems to be quite cautious concerning judicial independence, and worry about over-exposure of judicial process though internet may cause improper invasion of individual privacy. The Netherlands, Korea and Japan have quite effective judicial transparency systems in a traditional sense, but also appear to be more open to new technology. Croatia and Singapore have paid little attention to new technology in the judicial system.

In sum, the definition, doctrine, or idea of accountability and transparency varies from jurisdiction to jurisdiction, and is based on the diverse politics, constitution, and institutional technique, as well as social background, depending on the value orientations that are chosen in the actual problems to be solved in specific jurisdiction. However, all the above national reports underline judicial independence as a premise of judicial accountability, though the concept of judicial independence itself is not universal.

2. JUDICIAL INDEPENDENCE AS THE PREMISE FOR JUDICIAL ACCOUNTABILITY AND TRANSPARENCY

All the academic peers completing the questionnaire mentioned above stressed the premise role and fundamental importance of judicial independence to judicial accountability and transparency. When answering the questions of "what's dominating doctrine or theoretical consensus about judicial 'accountability' in your country?" and "what is the (most) valuable concept that should be specially stressed on while accountability and transparency is studied?" The South Korean academic peer stressed, under the title "Judicial Independence as a Prerequisite of Judicial Accountability," that: "Judicial independence is a necessary requirement for judicial accountability. Judicial independence and accountability cannot be thought of separately because judicial accountability cannot be imposed without judicial independence. Judicial independence is a prerequisite of judicial accountability, while transparency of processes and decisions of justice are components of judicial accountability." The German academic peer said: "Both accountability and transparency are limited as the idea of judicial independence is considered to be a more important goal to be achieved." And the other national reporters provided similar answers. Nevertheless, there are numerous expressions or definitions of judicial independence and specific institutions to guarantee a judge's independence.

2.1. THE CONCEPT AND DEFINITION OF JUDICIAL INDEPENDENCE

"Judicial independence" is referred to as the independence of a judge in all jurisdictions except China and includes both external and internal independence. Under external independence or "institutional independence," as the German academic peer noted, a judge will only be subject to the law and nobody may give a judge any direction either from inside the judiciary (e.g., the president of the chamber or of the court) or from outside (e.g., government officials). Internal independence or "personal independence" means that a judge will be provided with a sufficient level of material and mental safety to carry out his/her judicial duties. By contrast, the disparity mainly exists in internal independence among the countries who share the same definition of "judicial independence", while material guarantee, life tenure, and accountability appear to be core factors.

China is the only exception in terms of defining "judicial independence." The Chinese Constitution provides that: "The people's courts exercise judicial power independently, in accordance with the provisions of the law, and are not subject to interference by any administrative organ, public organization or individual."[2] Based on this article, judicial independence is defined in a narrow way: (1) "judicial independence" is independence of the court rather than of a judge; and (2) judicial independence does not mean that "a judge shall be subject only to the law," but that a judge is independent only from administrative organs, public organizations or individuals. On the contrary, judicial power is vested in "judicial supervisors," including institutional supervisors from inside the court (e.g., by the judicial committee) and outside (e.g., by the procuratorates and the congress). Accordingly, the concept and mechanism of "judicial supervision" plays a very important role in judicial independence in both the institutional and personal dimensions, though the revision of the Court Organic Law in 2018 and Judges Law in 2019 shows a strong tendency to promote a judge's external and internal independence and to prohibit non-institutional interference into judicial processes both inside and outside of court.

2.2. INSTITUTIONAL OR EXTERNAL JUDICIAL INDEPENDENCE

Under the constitutional framework, each state organizes its judiciary system as a separate and specialized organization and the courts composed of judges exercise judicial power independently. The main differences exist in terms of the internal structure of a court and judicial management that dramatically

---

[2]   Article 126 of the Constitution. The Court Organization Law (COL) and procedure laws all copy this content.

influence the level of judicial independence of a judge. Among the factors that influence judicial independence, judicial accountability can be considered as a passive factor. However, while most governments are founded on the principle of the separation of powers of the legislative, executive and judicial functions as a fundamental basis and context for institutional judicial independence, China is exceptional in that the term "separation of powers" is a "sensitive word" and is replaced by "division of labor" of the governmental branches under the unified leadership of the Communist Party of China (CPC).

In Korea, for example, judges should be shut off from the external influence exercised by interest groups and the general public while conducting trials. To this end, petitions to interfere with trials or that are otherwise related to cases being tried are not accepted (Article 5(1) of the Petition Act) and outdoor assemblies and protests are prohibited within 100 meters of the boundaries of courts of all levels (Article 11(1) of the Assembly and Demonstration Act). Judges who judge according to their consciences pursuant to the Constitution and the law should not bear any accountability to the legislature or the executive for the outcome of the trial. In order to guarantee such independence, important issues, including the scope of the court's organization and authority, and judges' qualifications and status guarantees, are explicitly stipulated in Chapter 5 of the Constitution and are further elaborated upon in the Court Organization Act. Articles 101 and 102 of the Constitution and the Court Organization Act stipulate that the court organizations are to be free from the intervention of the executive or legislative branches. Article 76(3) of the Constitution provides: "All judges shall be independent in the exercise of their conscience and shall be bound only by this Constitution and the laws." This means that judges should not yield to any physical or non-physical external pressure or to any temptation. Thus, the Constitution guarantees not only the independence of the judiciary, but also that of each judge in charge of making his/her judicial decisions. Accordingly, judges' decision making will not be interfered with by the government or the parliament on the one hand, nor will it be controlled by the leading executives of the judiciary itself on the other hand. In order to ensure this independence, the status of judge is strongly protected.

In Spain, the entire legal status of judges is built on the independence of the power of the judiciary and of each individual judge. Jurisdictional authority in the hands of each individual judge "emanates from the people" and is "administered in the name of the King," "subject only to the rule of law" (Article 117.1 of the Constitution). In order to guarantee independence, the Constitution removed the main administrative aspects of the judiciary from the Ministry of Justice and vested them in the General Council of the Judiciary, the constitutional body where the judiciary self-governs. Also, in order to ensure compliance with the "obligation placed on all public authorities and individuals to respect the independence of the judiciary and the total shielding of the legal status for judges against any possible interference from other state powers," judges are irremovable: they "may only be dismissed, suspended, transferred or retired on the grounds, and subject to the guarantees provided by law" – by an organ which requires a qualified majority in Parliament. With the same goal of avoiding indirect pressures from the executive, the economic retribution of judges is regulated by law, e.g., the parties may challenge judges on the ground of lack of independence or impartiality if the judge himself/herself did not abstain in the first place.

In China as a counterpart, "supervision" seems to be more important than "independence." Under the Constitution and the Organic Law of the Courts, judicial organs are created by the congresses to which they are responsible and by which they are supervised. The Supreme Court supervises the administration of justice by the courts at various local levels and by the special courts. Courts at higher levels supervise the administration of justice by those at lower levels. Besides, "the procuratorates are state organs for legal supervision" supervise the administration of justice under legal regulations. Accordingly, the Judicial Committees in each court play their supervision role through "discussing important or difficult cases"; the Civil Procedure Law (CPL) provides extra approaches to attack "grievous judicial errors" in effective judgments under "Procedure of Judicial Supervision," which are moved by the proposal of the president of the courts and are decided by the Judicial Committees, or by protest of the procuratorates, or/and by petitions of the litigants. In practice, frequent judicial interventions in the name of "judicial supervision" from outside are operated through the Judicial Committee and the president of the court who has the power to trigger the supervisory procedure. In this way, judicial independence is not only weakened by definition but also institutionally threatened by judicial supervision. Since the 1990s and especially since 2013, judicial reforms have been aimed at promoting trial judges' independence from their "leaders" of the court and the courts' independence from local governments.

2.3. THE INTERNAL OR PERSONAL INDEPENDENCE OF A JUDGE

Most of the academic peers helping to file the questionnaire for the comparative study of this chapter agree that internal independence is guaranteed by some material factors (such as life tenure and fair salary), whether or not this is the actual case in their country, and mental factors (such as no fear of being accountable).

In Germany, the legal institutions, which are concerned with a judge's role, selection, evaluation, protection, petition, disciplinary and even judicial publication, are to protect judicial independence as enshrined in Article 97 of the Constitution, which has two dimensions: material and personal. The material independence of a judge entails complete freedom from all influence from inside or outside the judiciary – a judge shall be independent and subject only to the law, and nobody may give a judge's directions, either from inside the judiciary (e.g., the president of the chamber or of the court) or from outside (e.g., government officials). A judge's personal independence is guaranteed by life tenure and a fair salary. As section 97(2) of the Constitution states:

> Judges appointed permanently to full-time positions may be involuntarily dismissed, permanently or temporarily suspended, transferred or retired before the expiration of their term of office only by virtue of judicial decision and only for the reasons and in the manner specified by the laws. The legislature may set age limits for the retirement of judges appointed for life. In the event of changes in the structure of courts or in their districts, judges may be transferred to another court or removed from office, provided they retain their full salary.

It is obvious that in Germany, the system of judicial liability is primarily undertaken by the state (*Amtshaftung*) and not by the individual judge, so the office of judge is exercised without potential pressure, with exceptions when a judge deliberately decides wrongly and is charged for criminal liability.

In Korea, judicial independence is guaranteed by the court's organization and authority, judges' qualifications and status guarantees, which are explicitly stipulated in Chapter 5 of the Constitution and are further elaborated upon in the Court Organization Act. The judges can conduct trials free from interference, either from within or outside the judiciary. Professor Hanki Sohn, the Korean academic peer who helped filling in the questionnaire for this research, further argued that judges should be completely free from political responsibility and although they are accountable to the general public, they cannot be held accountable to a third party other than the parties to a lawsuit. Judges in Korea have no fear of being held directly accountable by the general public. However, judges do not have lifetime tenure and so are subject to a term limit. Accordingly, they are held accountable in the sense that they are subject to a re-appointment process after a given term (Article 105(3) of the Constitution) and in special cases may be dismissed following impeachment or a sentence of imprisonment or more severe punishment (Article 106(1)). It should be understood that such a strong guarantee of a judge's status is not to serve the interests of judges, but rather to ensure that they can perform their judicial responsibilities to the people at large. Moreover, the independence of the courts' budgets is guaranteed by the Court Organization Act and the National Finance Act: "Expenses of courts shall be appropriated independently in the national budget; and the autonomy and independence of the Judiciary Branch shall be respected in formulating the budget of the courts."[3] If the executive intends to give the judiciary smaller

---

[3]   Korea: Article 82 of the Court Organization Act; Article 40 of the National Finance Act.

expenditure budgets than requested, it must seek the opinions of the Chief Justice of the Supreme Court, and if such smaller amounts are allocated, the executive must submit to the National Assembly the size and reason for the reduction and the Chief Justice's opinion on the reduction.

In China, greater emphasis is placed on strengthening the professional protection of judges as a result of the judicial reforms after 2013. The revision of the Court Organic Law (COL) in 2018 and the Judges Law in 2019 added some provisions to guarantee the independence, dignity, and safety of judges. The new COL added a special chapter "guaranteeing judges' rights and the courts' financial, personnel and information resources," and the appointment, evaluation, promotion and legal function of a judge is much more clear and independent from the local government. Moreover, in order to guarantee internal independence of the judges, the "post-judges" who have been newly picked out from the judges of the old system by an independent institute have seen their salary increased dramatically after 2017. Now a post-judge's salary is at least 50 percent more than the public servants of the districts where the court located and will increase steadily if he/she survives routine judicial evaluation. Yet, the achievement of this reform is surprising and depressing people are leaving judicial posts in greater numbers than the reform before even if the salary has been increased. The most important reasons for this are that: (1) judicial independence is still unclear, while the individual's risk of liability for his/her judicial decisions after reform is quite clear; (2) the increased and increasing salary cannot compensate for the increasing work burden and the hurt caused to judges' professional dignity by the never-ending process of judicial evaluation. Therefore, the judicial profession fails to attract many promising candidates, largely because the greater independence of a judge results in greater pressure, accountability, and risk to himself/herself.

In contrast, Croatia provides a paradoxical phenomenon: instead of the development of independent high-quality judiciary, the institutional independence and self-management of judicial power led to the freezing of a situation in which judicial office-holders who were appointed in the 1990s continued to discharge judicial functions, even though their quality and the motives for their appointment were often below the desired standards. The low level of trust in the judiciary led to ever-louder demands from the public for more accountability and more transparency in respect of courts and judges. As a result, from a critical view on the current situation in the national judiciary, the notion of judicial accountability together with the overlapping notion of transparency are used as the antithesis to an overly broad notion of judicial independence. The Chinese case is the opposite of that in Croatia. The concepts of "accountability" and "transparency" were both becoming popular due to the development of the separation of powers and judicial reforms aimed at strengthening judicial independence, with guarantees that the judiciary should not be interfered with from outside and inside the courts on one hand, and that the judge should be liable for grave disciplinary offenses on the other hand.

Professor de Benito presented the idea in a different way by arguing that: "Judicial accountability is a natural consequence of judicial independence – judges are independent, hence accountable." Judicial independence in Spain enjoys full, strong constitutional and legal protection, from the method of recruiting judges to the self-governing General Council of the Judiciary; while judicial accountability is a natural consequence of judicial independence, judges are independent and hence accountable, in a delicate equilibrium to prevent any of the two terms from stifling the other. This close interconnection already manifests itself in the Constitution. Accountability is the necessary counterpart to the great power that is placed in the hands of each judge. Unsurprisingly, the majority of disciplinary infractions for which a judge can be held accountable relate to his/her independence; Article 417 of Organic Law of the Judiciary classifies "affiliation to political parties or trade unions, or performing duties or services for them," "unwarranted interference by means of orders or pressure in any sense in the exercise of the judicial functions of any other judge," or the lack of his/her own abstention "in spite of being aware that he is under any of the legal circumstances" that may hinder his/her independence or impartiality as serious infractions. Similarly, the most common crimes for which a judge can be convicted are those relating to acts of corruption or perverting the course of justice (Articles 419 and 446 of the Spanish Criminal Code), both of which punish a lack of independence. Finally, each individual judge remains personally liable toward the state for errors stemming from willful misconduct or gross negligence.

In contrast to Spain, Professor van Rhee from the Netherlands repeatedly stated that: "Judges are accountable through their well-reasoned judgments to the parties and society at large; individual accountability of judges for 'wrong' decisions is considered to be an undesirable solution since it will interfere with the independence of the judiciary; therefore it is the state to shoulder the primary duty for judicial errors." From a Japanese perspective, "the major factor affecting the accountability or transparency is the persuasive power of judgment reasons," for which "the independence, neutrality and quality of judges are essential." The Singapore academic peer filling in the questionnaire for this research understood judicial independence as the basis of judicial accountability, since the concept of judicial accountability and judicial independence are intertwined, and both are connected to the rule of law.

In sum, judicial independence is a written legal principle in all the above institutions, but the actual level of independence differs according to the specific measures relating to material support and mental freedom for individual accountability. In countries such as Croatia and China, which share a socialist legal heritage and a shorter history of a separation of powers, the situation is more complicated and the concept is less distinct. Instead of the sole emphasis on judicial independence as the premise of accountability or transparency, Croatia also takes the negative effect of judicial independence into consideration, while China is seeking a balance between judicial independence against individual corruption and judicial interference against institutional corruption. In Croatia, the concepts of "accountability" and "transparency," which have more political meaning than legal meaning, both became popular with the public due to two parallel developments: the international pressure relating to the judiciary and human rights during the accession process to becoming a member of the European Union;[4] and the national development of judicial reforms that play a central role in this process. The separation of powers led the main direction of judicial reforms toward strengthening judicial independence, with judicial immunity from prosecution only if they have been finally convicted of crimes or if they have been found to be liable for grave disciplinary offenses by the State Judicial Council, whose basic function is to guarantee judicial independence.

3. JUDICIAL TRANSPARENCY AS A PRINCIPLE GUARANTEED BY CONSTITUTIONS AND THE LEGAL DEVICES OF ALL STATES

Judicial transparency is so important that the introduction of the rules governing it was particularly stressed by Professor Kakiuchi. In the Netherlands, transparency acts as a core issue of judicial accountability and an important instrument in enhancing confidence in the administration of justice and the accountability of judges. Moreover, Professor van Rhee commented: "Obviously, Publication is not only a fundamental right according to the Constitution of the Netherlands, but also part of many national constitutions in Europe and it is also expressed in Article 6 of the European Convention of Human Rights to which all the 47 members states of the Council of Europe are bound. It is part of the Charter of the EU too." In the same way, the Spanish academic peer participating in this research said that judicial transparency in Spain is a part of the reform of accessing public information which aims at promoting good governance, as Article 11(2) of the Treaty on European Union foresees that "the institutions shall maintain an open, transparent and regular dialogue with representative associations and civil society". In China, the reforms to promote judicial transparency have always been the most important and least controversial reforms in the past 30 years.

---

[4] Professor Uzelac stated in his national report: "As Croatia was preparing for the membership in the European Union, it had to comply with a series of criteria in the context of the European accession process … The EU negotiators noted the problematic state of Croatian judiciary and requested a significant improvement as a condition for the closure of the negotiations. As a part of the measures that were agreed in order to complete the process of accession, some had direct reference to accountability and transparency."

Though the notion of "transparency" is quite fuzzy and its role and emphasis differs from country to country, the academic peers collectively introduce judicial transparency in three dimensions: (1) what information should be put in public, i.e., the information on trials/hearings, recorders, (reasoned) judgments, case law, statistical data, and even judge's asset status; (2) to whom the information should be publicly disclosed, i.e., the transparency to the litigants, the openness to the third party who have private interests, and the publication to the public; (3) how should the information be put in public, i.e., how new technologies such as internet and AI supplement or challenge the traditional means to guarantee judicial transparency.

3.1. JUDICIAL PUBLICATION GENERALLY GUARANTEED BY THE CONSTITUTIONS WITH SOME EXCEPTIONS

In all the countries studied in this chapter, publication is provided under the respective Constitutions. Publication of judicial process is a universal principle, and some of the provisions are even written in a similar way, but variation in terms of details may make things quite different in practice.

In Japan, for example, publication includes the visibility of judicial process, the visibility of judicial decisions, and publication relating to unfair influence in the judicial process and decision making. The publication of trial and the rendering of judgment is guaranteed by the Constitution, leaving some exceptional situations governed by very strict conditions.[5] The trial process can avoid publication where public order or good morals will be menaced if it can be accessed by public, while the trial result, i.e., the judgment declaration, allows no exception for publication. However, in cases where political offenses involving the press or the protection of fundamental rights guaranteed by the Constitution are in question, trials will always be conducted publicly with no exceptions. A judgment must be always rendered in a courtroom that is open to the public and the content of any judgment will be made available to the public, though in practice it is rare that someone other than the parties attends the rendering of judgment.

In contrast, in China, the Constitution provides that "all cases in the courts are heard in public, except in special circumstances as specified by law," and the COL and the CPL specify the special circumstances as "those involving state secrets, private affairs of individuals and the commission of crimes by minors."

---

[5]   The exception should satisfy the legal conditions, for instance, the trial can avoid publicity if it concerns with the examination of a party or a witness about a grave secret regarding her private life (See Article 22 (1) of the Personal Status Litigation Act), or with the examination for a patent litigation about trade secret (See Article 105-7(1) of the Patent Act). Moreover, it is quite common for Japanese judges to operate conciliation by hearing the parties separately outside the "oral argument"; thus, such proceedings are not open to the public.

A court will pronounce its judgment publicly without exception, whether a case is tried openly or in camera. It appears that the principles, general provisions, and exceptional situations on judicial publication in China are almost the same as in Japan; moreover, China's publication of judgments online make it easier than in Japan to access all judgments.[6] In addition, China's live streaming of trials in some cases[7] also makes it easier for the public to view ordinary cases than in Japan. However, in those "sensitive" cases in which there is a high level of public interest, there is little opportunity to access the trial, neither by viewing it online nor by sitting in court. It is the court that defines which cases are "sensitive," i.e., which may impact social order or/and political evaluation of the local government against some political background, so the definition of "sensitive cases" and the judicial transparency of specific cases largely rely on the political climate and vary from time to time, from district to district, and from court to court.

Another comparable example is the different operations towards deciding not to go public in exceptional circumstances. In answer to the question "What are the remedies for the parties when the transparency rules are broken?", German Professor Stunner said: "It is difficult to conceive how a judge would be in a position to violate rules on transparency. All proceedings must be held in public. Hearing before the adjudicating court, including the pronouncement of judgments and rulings, shall be public. As the rules on transparency were designed against the historical experience in Germany where secret proceedings were normal, any violation of the duty to render a written decision (sec. 313 Zivilprozessordnung) would amount to a violation of a basic procedural principle and may trigger a civil appeal (provided that this violation has any impact on the outcome as such). But a judge may exclude the public without reason; the valuable concept is that both accountability and transparency are limited as judicial independence is considered to be a more important goal to be achieved." In contrast, Korean Professor Hanki Sohn stated that: "Trials and decisions of the courts shall be open to the public; but trials may be closed to the public if opening them might endanger national security, public peace and order, or public morality. Decisions to make trials closed must be announced with the reasons for the decision; violation of the disclosure obligation is absolute grounds for appeal to the Supreme Court."

3.2. THE ROLE OF PUBLICATION OF JUDGMENTS AND REASONING FROM DIVERSE PERSPECTIVES

Publication of judgments is a general requirement as noted by all the academic peers participating in the research of this chapter. In the Netherlands, where

---

[6]   http://wenshu.court.gov.cn.
[7]   http://tingshen.court.gov.cn. See also the websites of local courts.

transparency or publication is a core feature of judicial accountability and an important instrument in enhancing confidence in the administration of justice and the accountability of judges, the most important device for judicial accountability and transparency is well-reasoned judgments that are made public. The duty to provide reasons is required by Article 121 of the Dutch Constitution, according to which judges make themselves accountable for their decisions and that can be checked on appeal and later in cassation proceedings by other judges. Article 121 also requires the publication of the hearing and the judgment in order to make judges accountable for their decisions and how they reached their decisions, and to provide access to the way in which the law is administered by the courts for the public at large. So, one transparency test is the availability of means of recourse allowing the higher courts to evaluate the reasoning of the lower courts (evaluation by the judiciary). Another test is publication, making the judgment available to the scrutiny of society at large (evaluation by the public, including legal scholars). The publication of case law makes the reasoning of the judges available for scrutiny by other people than judges, e.g., legal scholars or interest groups who may criticize the judgments and the reasons behind them. The Dutch's emphasis on the perspectives of reasoning for "evaluation by the judiciary" and for justification as core accountability is especially impressive.

In comparison, other sample countries mentioned in this chapter place more emphasis on the publication of judgments for public evaluation. In Korea, Japan, and Germany, though with the same requirements for reasoned judgments under their procedural laws (instead of the Constitution), they put more emphasis on "transparency to the litigants" as an implementation of the rights of participating in the proceedings and with regard to appeals as relief if the transparency requirement is violated. In Japan, as the original judgment is included in the case records, anyone may check the content of judgment that was rendered in a specific case; any person may view case records in ordinary civil litigation; and a third party having shown a legitimate interest in the case may also have access to a copy of the case record, including settlement records, even if the negotiation process for the settlement is not open to the public, unless the party shows that an important secret regarding a party's private life is recorded and that inspection would be substantially detrimental to his/her social life, or if a trade secret of a party is recorded. In Korea, procedural law provides the principle of the judges' free evaluation of evidence. But judges must disclose the evidence used to confirm a certain alleged fact by a party. However, there are conflicting theories and judicial precedents as to whether judges must explain why they thought the evidence to be persuasive, and majority theories claim that judges should offer such explanations to make Supreme Court trials more convictive and to better protect litigants' right to information, while the precedents do not support the disclosure of such explanations.

In Singapore, judicial transparency is ensured by a set of systematic rules and approaches. Except for some exceptions – for example, considering the need to protect the confidentiality of the parties – trials are to be conducted in open court. The judge is required to give reasons for his/her decision. However, the court may choose not to deliver a written ground for the decision. Moreover, as a common feature of the common law tradition, judges are bound to follow the doctrine of *stare decisis*. *Stare decisis* implicates the principle of "treating like cases alike" in order to achieve fairness and justice. It aims to remove human arbitrariness from the processes of law and government, and serves the interest of legal certainty for litigants and lawyers. Most of the written decisions are published online with free access to the general public. Selected cases are reported and published in the Singapore Law Reports. It is submitted that the minimum threshold for legal transparency should include: letting the parties knew why they had won or lost; letting the legal profession and the community know the reasons of reaching a decision; and enabling the appellate court to understand and correct the decisions taken in the first instance.

The Spanish experience in relation to judicial transparency is unique. Professor de Benito reported general manner on the transparency rules in Spain, but legislation on transparency in the context of civil justice has not been specifically enacted. The Constitution provides that all persons have the right to access public information in the terms provided for in Article 105.b. The efforts to ensure transparency have focused more on the development of judicial statistics, which has grown in recent years to provide an increasingly detailed and comprehensive picture of the functioning of civil justice. As part of this effort to achieve greater transparency, the General Council of the Judiciary (GCJ) has run the "José Luis Terrero Chacón Transparency Portal" since 2015, which aims to provide citizens with access to information on the GCJ, including its activities, use of public funds, the criteria and motives for its decisions, and other matters of public interest; information in this webpage includes a directory of judicial organs.[8] Every year, the GCJ also publishes a comprehensive Annual Report and a useful summary entitled "Justice to Date."[9] But there are no specific rules regarding transparency in the judicial system; only sectorial rules contain specific obligations of transparency in terms of contracts, subsidies, budgets, or activities of senior officials so that in the judicial accountability regime, transparency in judicial procedures is absent from the list of infractions giving rise to disciplinary responsibility.

---

[8]   http://www.poderjudicial.es/portal/site/cgpj/menuitem.e3861fbe34a12841eabae273c684caa
0/?vgnextoid=be82be46c7416410VgnVCM1000006f48ac0aRCRD&vgnextlocale=en&vgnex
tfmt=default&lang_choosen=en.

[9]   A brief summary of the available data on the status of the judicial system in the year, including organization and means, workload and resolution, and quality of justice, adding as an appendix the key indicators of the year.

3.3. THE SCOPE AND OBJECTS OF PUBLICATION OF TRIALS/HEARINGS

From three perspectives of publication of trials – transparency to the litigants, publication to the third party with private interests, or/and publication to the public – it is generally accepted that judicial decisions must be based on open trials/hearings which are accessible to the public; yet, the specific scope, objects, and means of publication vary from country to country.

Some academic peers helping the research in this chapter only mentioned the judicial transparency of their countries as the publication to the public including third party. This may be because the publication to the litigants in their countries is self-evident without any problems. However, they classified publication of trials into the transparency in relation to the litigants and the transparency to the public, and especially emphasized the transparency to the litigants, as it concerns with the litigants' right to know about judicial process. Therefore, whether a case is tried openly or in camera, the litigants shall be kept informed of the adjudication. As clearly provided in Article 68 of the Chinese CPL, all proofs shall be presented in court and cross-examined by the parties, even though it is evidence fallen into the exceptional situations which shall not be presented in an "open" court that is available to the public. Otherwise, the judgment shall be attacked and the case shall be reopened for retrial through the Judicial Supervision Procedure (Article 200(4)). Korea has the same provision, providing that all the evidence as base of fact-finding should be presented and cross-examined in hearings open to the litigants.

By comparison, Japan and Korea provide special accesses to the "third party" who expresses a particular interest. In Japan, hearings or "oral arguments" in ordinary civil litigation should be conducted publicly, though the "litigation" here only means those where substantial right is claimed and the court decision should be rendered in a form of judgment with *res judicata* effect. The publication of adjudication even includes case records. In Japan, not only litigants but also third parties with sufficiently compelling interests may file a request with an administrative officer of a court to view and copy litigation records, to be given authentic, certified, or abridged copies of judicial documents or protocols, or to be given a certificate of matters relating to particular cases. But the court may limit the scope of disclosure of records to third parties upon the request of the litigants when grave secrets concerning a litigant's private life or business secrets are contained in the records. The situation in Korea is similar to that in Japan, where the availability of litigation records to be viewed by litigants or third parties with sufficiently compelling interests to do so is prescribed by the opinion of the Supreme Court. Furthermore, anyone may apply to view the records of final and conclusive judgments for protection of their own rights, for academic research, or for the sake of the public interest, but such requests made by third parties must receive the consent of the litigants and, when important secrets concerning a litigant's private life are contained in the records and disclosure of such information would significantly deteriorate the litigant's social life, or when the record contains a litigant's business secrets, the court may limit the scope of disclosure of the records to third parties upon the request of the litigants.

3.4. EXPOSURE OF INVISIBLE AND UNFAIR INFLUENCE

The exposure of invisible and unfair influence is a part of judicial transparency and also of judicial independence. Professor Kakiuchi states that in order to exclude any invisible and unfair influence from outside, there are various concepts and rules that serve this purpose, such as the independence of judicial power, the neutrality or impartiality of judges, and the secrecy of deliberations and rules concerning the nomination of judges. Thus, in Japan, there are many regulations to secure transparency of the judicial process. Some rules, such as those relating to the disqualification of and challenges brought against judges to avoid any prejudice due to the relationship between judges and the parties involved are also found in the other countries that are the subject of this chapter.

Meanwhile, in Croatia and China, some special exposure mechanisms aim to tackle judicial corruption. Professor Uzelac from Croatia emphasized judicial asset declarations in a particular way. As another device for ensuring the transparency of judicial office and the accountability of judges, judges' obligations to report on their assets should show that they live on their legitimate judicial income, thus preventing any illicit enrichment stemming from corruption or activities incompatible with their judicial functions. This submission obligation of asset declaration which was introduced by the Act on State Judicial Council in 2010 is relatively comprehensive and requires the annual submission of information on real estate, movables, business shares, savings, and other assets of higher value for judges, their spouses, and their minor children. Due to a silent boycott of a number of judges, the Act on State Judicial Council inserted a separate disciplinary offense of failure to submit the judicial asset declaration to the list of offenses, and about 20 judges were censured for this reason in 2015 and 2016. Since then, all judges regularly report their assets. Professor Uzelac commented that it is too early to give a full assessment of whether and to what extent this obligation successfully contributes to the fight against corruption in the judiciary and to the accountability of judicial power in general. The asset declarations for state officials were from the beginning a part of the public register, which has been publicly accessible on the internet since 2013, while the information on the asset declarations of individual judges were only given following a request. Still, since September 2018, in order to take another step toward transparency and to equalize the position of judges and state officials, the asset declarations of judges will also be publicly accessible on the website of the State Judicial Council in a form that excludes sensitive data protected by the rules on private data protection. As of July 2019, however, this public register had not been established.

In contrast to Croatia, where the judiciary might have been released from political influence and is launching an attack on judges' individual corruption, China is still struggling between the exclusion of political influence from outside court, the limitation of interference of the "leaders" inside court for political causes or private sake as corruption, and the attack of corruption of the individual judges who are gaining more power from the judicial reforms in the 2010s. On one hand, the reforms in China aimed at dramatically promoting the judicial independence by excluding the disturbance from outside and the interference from the judges' "leaders" inside. On the other hand, they have to remain certain degrees of political interference as justified external "supervisions" for court. As a balance, China has launched a new device called "leaving trails in the whole processes," which requires the presiding judges to note or "record" any of the disturbance occurring during adjudication, with details such as the time, the leaders' name, a precise record of their words, and the witness (if any). But since such a record is enclosed in the "auxiliary volume" of a case file, which is not made public and can only be reviewed by the superior courts, procurators, or other systematic supervisors from the authorized organs of the CCP, this device may be functional in terms of tackling individual corruption and avoiding interference for private sake. However, it will not be helpful when it comes to political interference. Nevertheless, as a more important reform, a "judicial committee" that has been criticized for operating in black box as a systematic "judicial supervisor" in court must show its component (members) and concise decisions in the judgment. This means that publication of the reasoned decisions of the judicial committee of "supervision" will be supervised by the litigants and the public in the same way as the judges do.

3.5. REMEDIES FOR BREACH OF PUBLICATION OF JUDGMENTS AND TRIALS

The breach of publication of judgments and trials can be remedied through appeals. Besides this, there are no other approaches of relief that are universally applied in all countries studied in this chapter. As stated by German academic peers, it is difficult to conceive how a judge would be in a position to violate rules on transparency. A judge may exclude the general public without reason and thereby violate Article 169 of the Courts Constitution Act. This would amount to a violation of a basic procedural principle and may trigger a civil appeal (assuming that this violation has any impact on the outcome as such). However, the judge will not be held liable for this mistake under civil or criminal law. If transparency is to be understood as a duty to render a written decision, any violation would have an impact on the proceedings. For instance, the time limit to lodge an appeal would not start to run (starting from the time when a written judgment has been received). But again, there would be no liability for the violation. Similarly, in Japan, a violation of the principle of publication is also considered as a ground for final appeal against a second instance court judgment. In addition, if a judge who is not permitted by law to participate in the judgment has participated in the judgment, there is a ground for a final appeal.

The Spanish experience shows an administrative way to secure transparency. Only the competent authority has the power to monitor compliance with the state's transparency obligations. Thus, if an individual pursues a remedy in a case of non-compliance, he/she must register the claim with the Council of Transparency and Good Governance. The purpose of this public body is to promote the transparency of public activity, ensure compliance with publication obligations, safeguard the exercise of the right of access to public information, and ensure compliance with good governance provisions (Article 34).

3.6. THE ROLE OF NEW TECHNOLOGY IN THE PUBLICATION OF JUDGMENTS AND TRIALS FOR JUDICIAL TRANSPARENCY

For all the countries mentioned in this chapter, it seems that using new technology to achieve publication of judgments is much more acceptable than making the trial accessible to the public, though the extent of this development varies from countries. In the Netherlands, the judgments are available to interested parties, which used to be done via the publication of case law in legal journals from the early 1900s and currently is also done by publication online. The designated address for the publication of case law is www.rechtspraak.nl, on a wealth of statistical data on functioning of the courts can be found, even including the annual reports of the various courts. These data obviously also serve accountability. In Korea, since 2011, anyone may view or duplicate the written judgments of finalized cases from the internet and other electronic systems, except for those made in proceedings that were not publicly disclosed. In some cases, court officials are required to apply an anonymity process to ensure that personal information remains confidential before the case is made available to the public. Japan tends to rely on the traditional approaches of publication, such as law journals and law reports, though some decisions, including those from lower courts, are also available on the Supreme Court website. Nowadays, many court decisions are made available through electronic commercial databases such as Westlaw and LexisNexis, and there is a discussion about the possibility of making all the court decisions available online, for example, applying AI and deep learning technology to analyze and predict court decisions.

Intersentia

In China, the Supreme Court issued "The Regulations of the People's Courts Publishing Judgments and Rulings on Internet" in 2013 (revised in 2016), providing that all judgments, rulings, and decisions in effect (hereinafter "judgments") shall be made public online, except in special circumstances as specified by law. According to this regulation, "China Judgments Online"[10] was established in 2014 to publish all the effective judgments universally entered and transmitted by the national courts level after level in the judicial hierarchy. Anyone can easily find a specific judgment on the "map" of China or through an advanced search using the key information of the case. As of 9 May 2021, there were 120,126,816 judicial documents on this website (including 74,133,507 civil documents, 10,295,779 criminal documents, 3,222,502 administrative documents, 147,115 state compensation documents, 31,644,988 enforcement documents, and 682,925 other documents), and the site had received 61,354,073,410 visits in total. Judgments publishing online being a mandatary accountability of the courts, the status of judgments published on the internet is a part of judicial evaluation operated by the higher courts. It is also evaluated separately by an independent institution that is funded by certain academic programs. The SPC entrust this independent institution to carry out independent investigations and research and offer data for the SPC's annual report. At the same time, the local courts have their own website on which they publish their judgments and other judicial documents and data, as well as providing the litigants and their lawyers with access to the details of their cases.

As part of the "wise court" reform for the transparency of trials, the public may also watch a live stream of trials of most cases heard by the SPC and some cases heard by the local courts on the SPC website.[11] And ordinary cases heard in the local courts can be generally watched online on the official website of this local court. Since the 1990s, when live broadcast of the hearings began, there has been a concern that over-exposure of the trial might be harmful to judicial independence, which is especially weak in the context of China; this issue has been aggravated by live streaming online and become more serious since the three internet courts were established after 2015. These internet courts all operate their trials online, with publication to anybody, even including those who entered in fictitious names. However, the worries on over-exposure are submersed under the overwhelming pursue of judicial transparency to compensate the long time problem of judicial secrecy. The online technology can help broaden judgement publication to an extent which is unavailable by the traditional approaches, thus making greater progress in fighting against common judicial corruption and gaining public's trust. To achieve this, China is willing to sustain more tolerance of over exposure of the trial. After all, of all the goals of judicial reforms that began in the 1990s, judicial transparency is the

---

[10]   http://wenshu.court.gov.cn.
[11]   http://tingshen.court.gov.cn.

most important and the least controversial project, and the internet provides a visual approach for "supervisors" to monitor the lower courts in terms of performing their publication responsibilities under the law. After several years' of development of judicial online publication, there seems to be no arguments on the over-exposure of the court. On the contrary, criticisms still focus on the lack of transparency in those "sensitive" cases which normally draw the public's attention but are hard to get access to. The public will even face difficulty in viewing the trial by sitting in court as an audience.

Professor Stunner provided his answer to this issue in the context of Germany. In Germany, the legislator is taking cautious steps toward permitting live broadcasting in the courtroom. The reasons for this lie in the desire to protect judicial independence, as both judges and parties may act differently in the presence of microphones and TV cameras, not to mention an online presence. Professor Stunner justified his comment by recalling the pertinent provision in section 169 of the Courts Constitution Act:

(1) The hearing before the adjudicating court, including the pronouncement of judgments and rulings, shall be public. Audio and television or radio recordings as well as audio and film recordings intended for public presentation or for publication of their content shall be inadmissible. Audio transmission to a workroom for persons reporting for the press, radio, television or for other media may be permitted by the court. Audio transmission may be partially prohibited in order to safeguard interests meriting protection on the part of the participants or of third parties or to safeguard the proper course of proceedings. In all other respects, the second sentence above shall apply to the audio transmitted to the workroom, mutatis mutandis.

(2) Audio recordings of the hearing, including of the pronouncement of judgments and rulings, may be permitted by the court for academic and historical purposes if the proceedings are of outstanding historical significance for the Federal Republic of Germany. Audio recordings may be partially prohibited in order to safeguard interests meriting protection on the part of the participants or of third parties or to safeguard the proper course of proceedings. The recordings shall not be put on file and may neither be issued nor used or exploited for purposes of the recorded proceedings or of other proceedings. Upon conclusion of the proceedings, they shall be offered by the court to the competent Federal or Land archive which, under the Federal Archive Act or a Land Archive Act, is required to ascertain whether the recordings are of lasting value. If the Federal Archive or the respective Land archive does not accept the recordings, they shall be deleted by the court.

(3) Notwithstanding paragraph (1), second sentence, the court may in special cases permit audio and television or radio recordings as well as audio and film recordings intended for public presentation or for publication of their content of the pronouncement of judgments of the Federal Court of Justice. Recordings or their transmission may be partially prohibited or subjected to compliance with conditions in order to safeguard interests of the participants or of third parties meriting protection and to safeguard the proper course of proceedings.

4. JUDICIAL ACCOUNTABILITY WITH DIVERSE CONCEPTS AND ITS OVERLAPPING RELATION WITH TRANSPARENCY

Judicial accountability may be understood in different ways. It could mean publication during the civil proceedings, the well-prepared reasoning of the operative parts of any judicial decisions, the availability of enough appealing or even all necessary demands for good judicial administration. The notion of accountability and transparency are usually parallel stated and correlated strongly: on the one hand, the two concepts could serve together for a higher value such as rule of law; on the other hand, concept "transparency" can be included by "accountability" as either a component or a precondition. Normally, judicial accountability may be defined from two perspectives, one is the responsibility of the state and the individual accountability of judges, the other is the accountable means including civil, criminal, and disciplinary ones. Furthermore, the following principles should be kept in mind: (1) civil judicial "accountability" is (mainly) the state's accountability to the parties and the public in the event of judicial errors, while direct civil action against judges is excluded; (2) the individual judge could be accountable to the state only for his/her gross misconduct; (3) the committed judge's individual accountability could also be disciplinary and/or criminal accountability; and (4) remedies for both the injured party and the sanctioned judges should be developed.

4.1. THE GENERAL CONCEPTS AND EXPERIENCES OF JUDICIAL ACCOUNTABILITY

Looking at the practice of different countries, it seems that the judicial accountability as discipline over individual judges is more emphasized in countries where the judicial administration operates in bad (or more difficult) conditions. In contrast, the countries with more satisfying justice status will stress more on judicial independence rather than judge's discipline and will especially protect the judges' internal independence through high living security and professional dignity. Professor Uzelac argued that the accountability and transparency of the judiciary are usually more important if the public is not satisfied with the judiciary.

In Netherlands, Japan and Singapore, for instance, judicial accountability has never become a subject of academic debate. Professor Remco van Rhee from Netherlands stated that accountability presupposes transparency: "Say what you do; do what you say; show that you do what you say." Issues relating to accountability are presented in legal writing, including: (1) the publication of the hearing and the judgment; (2) the requirement of a reasoned judgment on the basis of which the decision of the judge can be understood and reconstructed; (3) means of recourse such as appeal and/or cassation; and (4) disciplinary proceedings in cases of gross judicial misconduct. However, judicial accountability is not widely discussed (apart from perhaps in criminal matters). Judicial accountability is first and foremost related to the fact that judgments need to contain adequate reasons, and publication of the hearing and the judgment are instruments to make judges accountable for their decisions and the manner in which these decisions are reached. The goal of providing reasons, publication, and the means of recourse against judgments is that the judges decide cases in the correct manner according to the law.

In Japan, as Professor Kakiuchi stated, the idea of accountability is normally not mentioned at all in the Constitution or procedural law, whereas it is quite common to mention the publication of the trial or the independence of the judiciary. However, a vague common idea seems to exist that a judicial decision and its reasoning should be comprehensible to the parties and the general public, and the idea that the judiciary should be responsive to the general public's expectations is reflected in the constitutional right of the people to review the appointment of the SPC Justices and to dismiss them if this is demanded by the majority of voters. In Professor Kakiuchi's view, it is argued that the concept of accountability implies a positive action of explaining and justifying the activities of the judiciary, whereas that of transparency refers to a rather passive aspect of not hiding what is going on. In Singapore, no clear concept of judicial accountability has been explicitly discussed, but transparency is regarded as one of the measures to limit arbitrariness and to warrant natural justice, which is another aspect of the rule of law. Hence, accountability and transparencies are both means to achieve the rule of law. The Lawyer Shaun Wong provided numerous comments that judicial accountability is closely associated with judicial independence and judicial impartiality, and a judge is accountable from the perspectives of judicial impartiality and natural justice, which contain two procedural sub-rules in fair hearing and anti-bias.

When discussing why judicial transparency is regarded as an indispensable component of judicial accountability, German scholar Professor Stunner stated: "As judges in Germany are not being elected by the public, there is no public reporting on the judicial activity. To the contrary, the judges remain largely anonymous; the published decisions at least in the lower courts do not state the name(s) of the judges on the bench." Moreover, the parties have a right to receive a reasoned decision and to be informed about the legal position of the judge before the decision is sent out, and the general public has a right to be present during the hearings. Korean Professor Hanki Sohn argued: "Trials must be credible to both the litigants and the general public." In order to build such credibility, judges must be independent of internal and external influence as stated above and the process of the trial must be transparent.

Therefore, judicial accountability, judicial independence, and transparency of judicial procedures cannot be thought of separately. Judicial independence is a prerequisite of judicial accountability, while the transparency of judicial procedures and the justice of judicial decisions are components of judicial accountability.

In Croatia, the notions of "accountability" and "transparency" are not clearly defined by the law. However, Professor Uzelac commented that accountability and transparency have different focuses and scope. Transparency is a part of the ideal of the good administration of justice, which means that tasks and responsibilities in the civil justice system are clearly and logically distributed; that court decisions are consistent and understandable; that everyone can swiftly and inexpensively find relevant information on pending cases; that the outcomes and the length of judicial proceedings are foreseeable, both generally and in concrete cases; that the judiciary is as a whole competent and free, open to the needs of society, receptive of criticisms, and free from bias and undue influence; and that the public can see it, feel it and therefore have trust in the judicial system. While the notion of judicial accountability deals with the individual and collective responsibility of courts and judges to discharge their functions in an honest and competent way without improper influences, free from corruption and in line with the applicable provisions of the law, interpreted scrupulously, consciously, and according to personal conviction and the best judgment of each member of the tribunal to which the case has been entrusted. This notion also denotes the desire to ensure that judges are loyal to their social goals and functions, and that they need to put the public good and the interests of the parties before their own private interests and agendas.

In China, the concept of "judicial accountability" is explicitly used to cover the individual (or collective) accountability of the judges – mainly disciplinary and also criminal accountability. It is the state that is liable for damages made by the judges' judicial errors, but under a separate system named "state compensation." The notion of "judicial accountability" always synchronizes with the judicial reforms aimed to judicial independence and transparency, and the developments intensified around 2015, when the CCP drew its attention to judicial impartiality, and the SPC accordingly launched the reforms of judicial administration to solve the bureaucratic problems causing lack of independence, transparency and efficiency, and resulting in loss of trust from litigants and satisfaction from society. However, as a key to the whole comprehensive judicial reform, establishing "the system of judicial accountability" means: (1) to define/clarify the boundary of power between the trial judges and the judicial supervisors, and to enhance the judges' independent power in judicial decisions; (2) to unify power and responsibility, and to ensure the person who exercises power is the same person who undertakes the corresponding responsibility; (3) to confine judicial power within a legitimate scope and to call for accountability of judicial rascality fallen in the laws and the regulations issued by the Supreme Court. This is a compromise between the needs of judges' independence as a judgment maker, the needs of necessary supervision against judicial corruption, and the needs of political control against the judiciary under "important" circumstances.

In Spain, where "judicial transparency" is not clearly defined in the law, the notion and system of "judicial accountability" is defined and clarified in a very clear way. As a general notion and under the Constitution, anyone who has violated a duty of conduct that exists in relation to another person/party is obliged to repair the damaged caused and thus is to be held accountable; public authorities are accountable for any arbitrary actions that cause damage to citizens; and accountability of public authorities in the realm of judicial power because "damages caused by judicial errors, as well as those arising from irregularities in the administration of justice, shall be subject to compensation by the State." At the same time, the Constitution also provides rules on the disciplinary consequences of any such conduct: judges "are independent, have fixity of tenure, are accountable, and are subject only to the rule of law," and these provisions are developed in Articles 292, 405–410, and 414 ff. of the Organic Law of the Judiciary, which address accountability from two perspectives: the individual accountability of judges and the responsibility of the state for judicial errors or the abnormal functioning of the administration of justice. In particular, in 2015, Spanish law eliminated the direct civil liability of judges, which was traditionally bought against individual judges; however, now the state can file an action for reimbursement against the judge who caused the harm where willful misconduct or gross negligence on his/her part has been established.

German law takes a similar approach, in that generally speaking, there are two types of judicial accountability, criminal liability and civil liability for a judge's harmful judicial activity, which is regulated by Article 839 of the German Civil Code. But the German Basic Law confirms that it is the Federal State, instead of the judge personally, that should be liable for the damage. Among the detailed regulations on the civil responsibility of the state, the relationship between this civil responsibility and the normal appeals system is worth noting. Judges' liability, as a part of officials' liability for damage caused by a culpable breach of their official duties, is restricted to those cases in which the breach amounts to a criminal offense.

In the Netherlands, as reported by Professor van Rhee, the personal accountability of judges in the sense of judges being financially liable in the event of "wrong" decisions is considered to be an undesirable solution, since it will interfere with the independence of the judiciary. Judges should not be liable for the way they establish the facts of the case or the way they interpret the law. The latter is even true if their interpretation is inconsistent with established case law. It should be recalled that continental legal systems do not follow the principle of binding precedent. Judges are therefore free to disagree with existing case law, since this may stimulate a legal debate between the courts and help the development of the law. However, there are mechanisms available in cases of gross judicial misconduct, which may give rise to criminal liability, and related matters which would make a judge incompetent in the exercise of his/her office. Such measures[12] can be requested against individual judges by the Procurator General at the Supreme Court of the Netherlands. The procedure and the grounds[13] for this are provided by the Law on the Legal Position of Judicial Civil Servants (1996). In most cases, the SPC or another authority from within the judiciary decides on the matter. It is also possible to submit a complaint against a judge with the president of his/her court. The president will hear the judge and the complainant and will reach an adequate decision if required to do so; however, this is extremely rare. The president has also such powers when a judge is accused of malpractice.

Compared with the abovementioned foreseeable liabilities, some discussion on judicial immunity and its exceptions in the common law tradition is also useful. In Singapore, for instance, all judicial officers of the State Courts and registrars of the Supreme Court enjoy judicial immunity from suit for acts performed in the discharge of their judicial duties, whether within or outside the limits of their jurisdiction, as long as the judicial officer in question at all times believed in good faith that he/she had jurisdiction to perform or order the act complained of. Supreme Court Judges and Judicial Commissioners enjoy the same immunity from suit at common law. Nevertheless, it is still possible for the state to ensure judicial officers behave responsibly in the exercise of their duties.

---

[12] The following disciplinary measures can be taken by the judiciary in such situations (Article 46ca):

1. a written reprimand;
2. reduction of the judge's salary of at most half a month;
3. suspension of the judge for a maximum period of three months;
4. dismissal of the judge from his office.

If the judge by his/her behavior seriously harms the administration of justice or the public trust in it.

[13] Disciplinary measures can be taken in the following situations (Article 46c):

1. if the judge acts in contravention to the dignity of his/her office, or if he/she neglects his/her obligations;
2. if the judge acts in contravention to provisions prohibiting him/her from exercising a specific occupation, where he/she ignores the rules that lay down that he/she should have a fixed and permanent abode, that prohibit him/her from taking part in a private conversation with a party of his/her lawyer or to accept a written document from them, that prescribe that he/she should keep a certain matter confidential, or inform the authorities of occupations exercised by him/her outside his office.
3. if the judge by his/her behavior seriously harms the administration of justice or the public trust in it.

4.2. THE DISCIPLINARY AND CRIMINAL ACCOUNTABILITY OF AN INDIVIDUAL JUDGE

Even in countries where the judicial systems are deemed to be operating very well, disciplinary accountability is still accepted to some extent. In Singapore, for instance, the Supreme Court Judges (including judicial commissioners, senior judges and international judges) may only be removed based on the procedure prescribed in the Singapore Constitution. First, the Prime Minister (or the Chief Justice after consulting the Prime Minister) must make a representation to the President that a Supreme Court Judge ought to be removed on the ground of misbehavior or inability, due to infirmity of body or mind or any other cause, to properly discharge the functions of his/her office. Second, the President must appoint a tribunal which consists of at least five persons who are Supreme Court Judges or any persons who hold or have held equivalent office in any part of the Commonwealth, and must refer the representation to the tribunal. Meanwhile, the President may suspend the judge from exercising his/her judicial functions. Third, if the tribunal produces a report and recommends that the judge in question should be removed, the President may then remove him/her from office. Alternatively, other judicial officers who are Legal Service Officers are subject to the discipline jurisdiction of the Legal Service Commission.

In Germany, apart from the aforementioned civil liability, the criminal liability of a judge whose conduct or decision in a legal matter perverts the course of justice for the benefit or to the detriment of one party is also covered by Article 339 of the German Criminal Code. The potential punishment for this offense varies from one to five years' imprisonment. In addition, there is a Disciplinary Court, a special division of the Federal Court of Justice, which is competent to decide on all disciplinary issues relating to Federal Judges. Each Federal State has its own Disciplinary Court for state judges. Proceedings before such Disciplinary Courts will be instituted *ex officio* by the President of each ordinary court in the case of disciplinary offenses. However, as judicial independence may be affected by such proceedings, Article 26 of the German Judiciary Act plays a central role in deciding the proper approach in order to strike a balance between the operation of the proceedings and the judicial independence. The law explicitly states that a "judge shall be subject to supervision only in so far as there is no detraction from his independence," while "supervision shall also include the power to censure an improper mode of executing an official duty and to urge proper and prompt attention to official duties." Therefore, "where a judge contends that a supervisory measure detracts from his independence a court shall, on application being made by the judge, give a ruling in compliance with this Act." Moreover, it should be noted that there are very few complaints against judges and disciplinary proceedings, because the Federal States usually chooses among the best candidates of the cohort when they hire judges, forming a high-quality judicial team. Legal education is quite demanding in Germany – while exams are centralized only at the level of Federal States, this leads to a very strict selection process and a high-quality of the results achieved.

In Korea, judges are given a guarantee of status that is much stronger than that of ordinary civil servants. No judge shall be expelled for reasons other than impeachment or a sentence of imprisonment or more severe punishment, nor shall any judge be subject to suspension, wage reduction, or any other unfavorable treatment for reasons other than disciplinary action (Article 106(1) of the Korean Constitution). Disciplinary actions are taken by the Judicial Disciplinary Committee of the Supreme Court. The reasons why judges may be subject to disciplinary actions include breaches or negligence of an official duty, or defaming their dignity or the prestige of the court. Judges can be subject to three types of disciplinary actions: suspensions, wage reductions, and reprimands (Articles 2 and 3 of the Korean Discipline of Judges Act). Disciplinary actions are imposed against judges as the result of a single trial by the Supreme Court.

The Croatian constitutional provisions on the disciplinary liability of judges have been further elaborated in the Act on State Judicial Council, Article 62(2) of which lists offenses by judges that are subject to disciplinary action. The list of disciplinary offenses was initially shorter, but in light of experience, it has expanded to cover nine categories. Most of these relate to judicial accountability. This list indicates a number of situations identified in practice as problematic. Still, in spite of the long list of offenses, in practice there are relatively few disciplinary sanctions against judges. They are also not reported regularly and it seems that their frequency changes according to the composition of the State Judicial Council (a new Council is elected every four years) and the political situation (there were many more sanctions in the period prior to EU accession than afterwards). Obviously, in the past, some councils were more proactive and some were less so in disciplinary proceedings.[14] This indicates that disciplinary proceedings may need to be redefined and reshaped in the future. The problematic issues that can be noted are multiple. First, it seems that (some) State Judicial Councils were relatively lenient, where it appeared that the members were reluctant to sanction their peers. Second, there is a lack of capacity to conduct disciplinary proceedings effectively; 11 members of the Council only work part time in the Council, along their other duties, and there are no standing professional tribunals for disciplinary cases. Therefore, in various

---

[14] For instance, in 2016 and 2017 there were altogether 26 disciplinary proceedings. In the same period, only nine disciplinary decisions were made. Five cases were discontinued, in three cases judges were sentenced on monetary sanctions (withdrawal of a part of their salary), and only in one case a judge was dismissed from judicial office. In comparison, in 2011 and 2012 there were 76 proceedings and 43 decisions, out of which 3 dismissals, 7 monetary sanctions, 1 conditional dismissal, 23 admonitions, 6 discontinued cases, and 3 cases where no liability was found.

cases, where indicted judges used delaying tactics and procedural maneuvers, this led to lengthy proceedings or even to proceedings being discontinued. Even very clear cases sometimes lasted an unreasonably long time.

The Spanish rules on disciplinary responsibility and criminal responsibility are clarified by Professor de Benito. The basis for criminal responsibility of judges "on felonies against the judicial power" (Articles 446–449 of the Spanish Criminal Code) codify the crimes or delicts committed by judges in the exercise of their functions. Meanwhile, disciplinary sanctions are imposed by the only competent authority, the General Council of the Judiciary. The Organic Law of the Judiciary distinguishes very serious, major, and minor offenses, and regulates the sanctions that may be imposed: a warning, a fine, a forced transfer to a specific court or tribunal, suspension for up to three years, and, most serious of all, removal from the judicial post. Accordingly, the disciplinary sanctioning procedure is regulated in Articles 423 ff. of the Organic Law of the Judiciary. As a general rule, the proceeding may not last more than a year. It is initiated *ex officio*, at the request of the injured party or the public prosecutor. Once initiated, the parties involved are notified and the proceeding will move forward *ex officio*.

In China, the management, evaluation, and discipline of judges are based on a system that specifies the number of different categories of personnel, and now discipline of judges is overseen by the Commission for the Examination and Assessment of Judges in the court concerned following the amendment of the Judge Law (2019). The Commission will consist of five to nine members and will be chaired by the president of the court. The norms of sanctions of the judges are strictly limited within the behaviors of willful breaches of law and the behaviors of gross mistakes with serious result. In another word, the judges can only be sanctioned by the behaviors fallen in one of the seven behaviors listed by the "Regulation of Judicial Accountability of the SPC" (No. 13 Fa-fa (2015)). However, evaluation is carried out regularly, with emphasis placed on a judge's achievements in judiciary work, professional morality and manner, competence, mastery of legal theories, and work attitude and style. Following their annual appraisal, judges are evaluated in terms of demonstrating excellence, competence, basic incompetence, or incompetence, which then constitutes the basis of re-adjusting his/her rank and salary, punishment, and/or removal/dismissal. As remedy, the judge in question shall receive a written copy of his/her evaluation result and be given an opportunity to apply for a reconsideration if he/she disagrees with the result. In practice, it is rare for a judge to be removed from his/her judicial post or even from the court based on routine evaluation, but the results of routine evaluation can be an important basis for a judge's status and/or removal or promotion. Judges should also receive regular salary increases based on a system of routine evaluation rather than a system of rivalry for promotion to the next administrative rank.

4.3. REMEDIES FOR SANCTIONED JUDGES

When a judge is threatened with disciplinary sanctions, he/she is supposed to be able to ask for due process and some suitable remedies. In Spain, according to Articles 423 ff. of the Organic Law of the Judiciary, both the indicted party and the public prosecutor are notified of the resolution of the disciplinary sanctioning procedure. The indicted judge may then only appeal to the contentious-administrative courts, while the public prosecutor may file either an administrative appeal or an appeal directly before the contentious-administrative jurisdiction. The sanction ruling will be enforceable when all administrative channels have been exhausted, despite the fact that a contentious-administrative appeal may have been lodged, unless the court orders its suspension.

Also, for Croatia, in cases where judges were found accountable for disciplinary offenses, they were entitled to a full-fledged appeal to the Constitutional Court. The Constitutional Court, which is also poorly equipped in terms of conducting concrete disciplinary proceedings – sometimes issued decisions which sent mixed messages, striking down several infrequent decisions that handed down punishments to judges for the disorderly discharge of their functions. This is one of the reasons why the disciplinary proceedings ought to be reshaped.

On the contrary, Professor van Rhee looks at sanctions on judges in a different way. In a democratic society based on the separation of powers and the rule of law, such as in the Netherlands, judges should not experience any adverse consequences of their judgments being reversed on appeal, apart from in cases of gross judicial misconduct. Even in the case of a miscarriage of justice, as mentioned before, in principle it should not be the judge who is personally liable, but the state that has appointed him/her; personal liability is only allowed in cases of gross judicial misconduct (e.g., in cases of criminal liability). Other forms of accountability and transparency are undesirable in the administration of justice through independent judges. When they exist, they are often proof of a justice system that does not work well – e.g., a system where legal training is inadequate, where the courts do not function well, and where there is a high level of bureaucracy and/or corruption. It is said that the more additional measures of accountability are needed, the more problematic the functioning of the justice system in the jurisdiction at hand may be. It is also worth noting that the usual approach in the Dutch judiciary is: judges are well-selected, trained, and organized; and if a judge is not properly motivated to do his/her job anymore, sanctions will not work. One has to look for other solutions and in daily practice these solutions are almost always found. For instance, thanks to the work of the autonomous institution inside each court, the judge struggling in his/her role may get the chance to undertake additional and focused training and education or to transfer to a different section of the same court. This approach prevents the need to impose any sort of sanction against judges. Only once in the history of the Dutch judiciary has a judge been dismissed against his/her will. As a result, it may be concluded that there are nearly no genuine issues on sanctions in respect of judicial accountability, and therefore neither will there be any genuine remedies that are need for the (if any) sanctioned judges.

5. CONCLUSION

Judicial independence and transparency as well as accountability together serve for judicial impartiality and a higher value such as rule of law, and there is a tense and accordingly complicated relationship among them. Judicial independence is generally regarded and practically act as a premise of judicial transparency and judicial accountability, because only an independent judge may dispose a case in a neutral and impartial way on his/her own direct judgment based on hearings of statements and proofs of the disputing parties. This proposition is right but should rely on a precondition that the judge is competent enough to deserve independence, as we learned from Croatia, which can be considered as an opposite example of Japan and the Netherlands. However, China (and perhaps Spain) provides proof that, given a lack of sufficient level of independence, judicial accountability will make the judicial situation even worse because of improper pressure and loss of attraction to legal elites.

The relationship between accountability and transparency, as stated by a Compendium adopted by the Committee of Experts on Public Administration to be basic terminology in governance and public administration in 2006 as follows. Transparency and accountability are interrelated and mutually reinforcing concepts. Without transparency – that is, unfettered access to timely and reliable information on decisions and performance – it would be difficult to call public sector entities to account. Unless there is accountability – that is, mechanisms to report on the usage of public resources and consequences for failing to meet the stated performance objectives – transparency would be of little value. The existence of both conditions is a prerequisite to effective, efficient, and equitable management in public institutions.[15] Therefore, transparency is universally regarded as a component of judicial accountability; Japan and Korea pay more attention to sufficient publication to the litigants and related third parties, while the Netherlands places stress on reasoned judgment to be checked by legal experts. As to the exposure of the trials to the public, the scope and approaches must be within control, doing no harm to judicial independence. This is why Germany and Japan keep prudent about live cast of hearings. China, on the other hand, care less about over-exposure due to its eager to overcome the defects of operation under the table.

---

[15] In its Fifth Session on March 27–31, 2006, the Committee of Experts on Public Administration, set up by the United Nations Economic and Social Council, adopted a Compendium of basic terminology in governance and public administration (E/C.16/2006/4).

ACCOUNTABILITY AND TRANSPARENCY OF CIVIL JUSTICE

A Comparative Perspective

Daniel MITIDIERO*

1. Introduction 165
2. The Emergence of the Question from a Modern Perspective:
   Legislator-Judges? Irresponsible Judges? 167
3. External and Internal Judicial Independence, Impartiality and
   Objectivity of Law 168
4. The Interpretation and Application of Law (Legal Reasoning):
   The Duty to Give Reasons in Judicial Decisions 174
5. Publicity of Proceedings and Decisions 178
6. Civil Justice Transparency: From Traditional Communication and
   Information to New Technologies 180
7. Who Watches the Watchmen? Third-Party Evaluation and Ranking
   of Civil Justice 182
8. Final Considerations 183

1. INTRODUCTION

The International Association of Procedural Law, chaired by Professor Loïc Cadiet, will host the XVI World Congress in Kobe, Japan. This year the general topic of the event is "Challenges for Civil Justice as We Move Beyond Globalization and

---

*   Tenured Civil Procedure Professor at Federal University of Rio Grande do Sul (UFRGS), Porto Alegre, Brazil; Member of the International Association of Civil Procedure (IAPL), Instituto Iberoamericano de Derecho Procesal (IIDP), Associazione Italiana fra gli Studiosi del Processo Civile (AISPC), Associación Argentina de Derecho Procesal (AADP) and Instituto Brasileiro de Direito Processual (IBDP). This English version of the contribution has been provided by Regina Caballero Fleck, whom I wish to thank. I would also like to thank Ahmed Hegazi (Intersentia) and Victória Franco Pasqualotto (UFRGS) for the accurate review.

Technological Change." The local organization will be led by Professor Koichi Miki. Among the many interesting subjects that will be addressed, we will, along with Professor Yulin Fu (who will deal with the problem from the perspective of Eastern countries), address the issue of accountability and transparency of civil justice in Western countries.

In order to do so, our study included national reports from Germany (written by Christoph Kern, Johannes Kist, and David Carnal), Argentina (Maria Victoria Mosmann), Brazil (Luiz Guilherme Marinoni and Sérgio Cruz Arenhart), Canada (Gerard Kennedy), Scandinavia (Anna Nylund), Spain (Enrique Vallines-García), the United States (Scott Dodson), France (Soraya Amrani Mekki), England (John Sorabji), Italy (Luca Passanante), and Portugal (Paula Costa e Silva). We thank in advance for the fundamental collaboration and partnership of all colleagues and in this endeavor.

The professors who accepted our invitation wrote essays addressing the following issues – all of which proposed by our Association: i) external and internal judicial independence; ii) form of judgments and legal reasoning of judicial decisions; iii) transparency of civil justice in relation to the use of new technologies procedural information and communication; iv) third-party evaluation and ranking of civil justice. As we can see, all these matters refer, in different ways, to the way in which civil justice reflects and concretizes the basic foundations of the democratic rule of law: without independence, impartiality and legal reasoning, there is no way to promote and assess the relationship between judges and the law, whereas without transparency and publicity, the control over judicial acts by the participants to the proceedings and by society in general would be impossible to obtain.[1] Lastly, the evaluation of civil justice by its consumers represents the public perception of its results, which is important for the creation of an environment of institutional improvement, mutual trust and social development.

The basic idea behind this chapter is that the evolution of the relationship between the different functions of the state – notably the relations established between the legislative and executive powers over the judiciary – and society in general creates the need to think about and evaluate civil justice from a new perspective. Therefore, we try to identify what is at the root of this change and how it points out different indicators for institutional design and for a behavioral model that is compatible with reality.

---

[1]   For an account on the link between democratic ideology and civil justice administration from the perspective of the right to be heard, of the duty to give reasons, and of publicity, see V. DENTI, *La Giustizia Civile – Lezioni Introduttive*, 2nd ed., Il Mulino, Bologna 2004, p. 104; M. TARUFFO, *La Motivazione della Sentenza Civile*. Cedam, Padua 1975, p. 407 (it was translated into Portuguese as *A Motivação da Sentença Civil* by D. MITIDIERO, R. ABREU and V.P. RAMO, Marcial Pons, São Paulo 2015).

2. THE EMERGENCE OF THE QUESTION FROM A MODERN PERSPECTIVE: LEGISLATOR-JUDGES? IRRESPONSIBLE JUDGES?

In 1983, at the Congress of Würzburg, Germany, the International Institute of Civil Procedural Law – whose work began in 1950 in Florence, Italy – agreed to leave behind the term "Institute" and the qualifier "Civil" in its name, and decided to adopt a new name – one which emphasized the aggregative character and the broader thematic scope of the group. The International Association of Procedural Law was then consolidated and Mauro Cappelletti was elected as its President.

This memory is not a mere digression. On the contrary, it aims to highlight the close connection of the Association and the transformation of the way in which the relations among civil justice, the other powers of the state, civil society and the people who consume it can be understood. In 1984, Mauro Cappelletti asked: "Legislator-Judges?"[2] Soon after, in 1988, he completed his own question: "Irresponsible Judges?"[3]

These questions point to a significant transformation in the mode of production of law and, consequently, in the way in which the reliability of the actors involved in the proceedings is promoted and assessed. Moreover, they point to the need for seeking an institutional design capable of properly holding these actors to account.

This chapter aims to analyze the consequences of the first question: what is required of the civil justice in terms of accountability and transparency, due to the advent of the transformations of the relations between the powers of the state and civil justice and its consumers? Also, what is the impact produced by new technologies on the administration of civil justice?

For the present purposes, we will explore the idea that there is a generalized perception, which emerges from the culture of the twentieth century, that judicial decisions are not merely declarations of norms with univocal and totally pre-existing meanings, obtained by a simple logical syllogism.[4] Indeed, there is some consensus that judicial decisions represent a collaborative effort between legislative and judiciary powers, with judges being called upon to give meaning to the text of the constitution and of legislation. They do so not only by using logic, but also argumentation concerning the different possible meanings

---

[2]   M. CAPPELLETTI, *Giudici Legislatori?*, Giuffrè, Milan 1984 (it was translated into Portuguese as *Juízes Legisladores?* by C.A.A. OLIVEIRA, SAFE, Porto Alegre 1993).

[3]   M. CAPPELLETTI, *Giudici Irresponsabili?*, Giuffrè, Milan 1988 (it was translated into Portuguese as *Juízes Irresponsáveis?* by C.A.A. OLIVEIRA, SAFE, Porto Alegre 1989).

[4]   Highlighting the porousness of legal texts as a source of uncertainty of law in the civil law tradition, see e.g., H. KELSEN, *Reine Rechtslehre*, Verlag Österreich, Vienna 2000, p. 348; in the common law tradition, see e.g., H.L.A. HART, *The Concept of Law*, 3rd ed., Oxford University Press, Oxford 2012, pp. 127–128.

that these texts can present.[5] If this is true, then it is necessary to revisit some essential themes around which civil justice is placed in a democratic rule of law.

First, it is necessary to examine the relationship between the executive, the judiciary and society from the perspective of the independence of judges, without which it is not possible to speak of impartiality and objectivity of law. Second, it is necessary to examine the relationship between the legislature and the judiciary with regard to the interpretation and application of law, without which one cannot understand the radical importance of the legal reasoning behind judicial decisions. Without examining these two issues, the rule of law risks becoming an illusory promise.

Third, it is important to examine the transparency of civil justice, especially regarding the use of new technologies, without which the ideal of access to justice and its control by the parties and by society at large can be unduly restricted. Fourth, it is important to analyze the publicity of proceedings and decisions, without which control of judicial work by the parties and society at large can be easily eclipsed. Without analyzing these two issues, the democratic state runs the risk of having the participation of the consumer of justice in the management of public affairs unduly obstructed.

Furthermore, in order for there to be a broader framework for analysis, it is essential to examine such issues not only in abstract terms, but also from the rich experience provided by comparative law. It is with the aid of comparative law that one can think of scales of greater or lesser compliance with the requirements imposed by the need for an accountable and transparent civil justice.

3. EXTERNAL AND INTERNAL JUDICIAL INDEPENDENCE, IMPARTIALITY AND OBJECTIVITY OF LAW

Judicial independence is a "statut" that makes the "vertu" of impartiality possible.[6] Independence is therefore the basic assumption of impartiality: without certain guarantees, it is difficult to safeguard the position of third parties which characterizes the functions of the judge in proceedings (the

---

[5]   This is the reason why it is not a coincidence that the twentieth century witnessed the advent of a number of argumentation theories: for the civil law tradition, see R. ALEXY, *Theorie der juristische Argumentation*, Suhrkamp, Frankfurt am Main 1983; for the common law tradition, see N. MACCORMICK, *Legal Reasoning and Legal Theory*, Oxford University Press, Oxford 2003; N. MACCORMICK, *Rhetoric and the Rule of Law*, Oxford University Press, Oxford 2005.

[6]   S. GUINCHARD, *Droit Processuel – Droit Commun et Droit Comparé du Procès Équitable*, 4th ed., Dalloz, Paris 2007, pp. 669 and 704. See further J.N. FENOLL and E. OTEIZA (eds.), *La Independencia Judicial: un Constante Asedio*, Marcial Pons, Madrid 2019.

"Unparteilichkeit" in German doctrine[7] and the "impartialité objective," also known as "impartialité fonctionnelle," of the French doctrine)[8] and the necessary absence of personal interest of the judge in the result ("Unbefangenheit," and the "impartialité subjective").[9]

As can be seen, independence and impartiality are necessary but not sufficient conditions for promoting the objectivity of law, i.e., its intersubjective control in its interpretation and application, avoiding institutional and personal interference in judicial decisions. Without independence and impartiality, a "congruence between official action and declared rule"[10] can hardly be verified. Hence the frequent link between independence, impartiality and the "Bindung an Recht und Gesetz"[11] that is expected from judges, i.e., between independence, impartiality, and the "rule of law."[12]

The problem of judicial independence can be resolved in two distinct directions: external and internal. Externally, it is important to analyze the relations between civil justice, other powers, and civil society. Internally, the importance lies in the relationships established within civil justice itself. The problem of impartiality, in its turn, is basically solved by analyzing cognitive biases, which may concern the person of the judge and his/her family and social circle or his/her prejudices.

The challenges faced and the solutions adopted by the different legal systems in relation to these problems differ in certain respects. However, there is no doubt that all countries studied converge around the need to promote the independence of civil justice and judicial impartiality as indispensable means for the organization of a fair trial[13] and accountable civil justice. It is no accident that independence and impartiality are two of the first principles listed by the American Law Institute and the International Institute for the Unification

---

7   L. ROSENBERG, K.H. SCHWAB, and P. GOTTWALD, *Zivilprozessrecht*, 17th ed., C.H. Beck, Munich 2010, p. 127.

8   L. CADIET, J. NORMAND, and S.A. MEKKI, *Théorie Générale du Procès*, PUF, Paris 2010, p. 598.

9   Ibid.

10   L. FULLER, *The Morality of Law*, 2nd ed., Yale University Press, New Haven 1969, p. 81.

11   O. JAUERNIG and B. HESS, *Zivilprozessrecht*, C.H. Beck, Munich 2011, p. 44.

12   S. BURBANK, B. FRIEDMAN, and D. GOLDBERG, "Introduction" in S. BURBANK and B. FRIEDMAN (eds.), *Judicial Independence at the Crossroads – An Interdisciplinary Approach*, Sage, Thousand Oaks 2002, p. 3. It is a common association as it can be seen in SORABJI ("Accountability and Transparency in the Course of Civil Justice in England and Wales", in MITIDIERO (ed.), Accountability *e Transparência da Justiça Civil – Uma Perspectiva Comparada*. São Paulo: Revista dos Tribunais, 2019, pp. 97 ff.) and KERN, KIST, and CARNAL ("Accountability and Transparency in the Course of Civil Justice in Germany", in MITIDIERO (ed.), Accountability *e Transparência da Justiça Civil – Uma Perspectiva Comparada*. São Paulo: Revista dos Tribunais, 2019, pp. 185 ff.).

13   V. DENTI, *La Giustizia Civile – Lezioni Introduttive*, 2nd ed., Il Mulino, Bologna 2004, pp. 91 ff. and 95 ff. Establishing a link between the right to a fair procedure, democracy, and judicial independence, see E. OTEIZA, *El Debido Proceso y su Proyección sobre el Proceso Civil en América Latina*, Revista dos Tribunais, São Paulo 2009, p. 181, n. 173.

of Private Law (UNIDROIT) as essential to the proper administration of civil justice.[14]

From the point of view of independence, the different jurisdictions seek to surround civil justice with guarantees aimed at preventing undue interference by other powers and society in general. Thus, it is common to find the existence of lifelong guarantees, usually acquired after a probationary phase and generally requiring due process for removal of the judge. Also, it is common to find the existence of guarantees of irremovability and the existence of a compatible remuneration, generally kept at the same level in case of retirement.[15]

However, the institutional design of each country, which sometimes seeks to promote the greater democratization of civil justice by means of political and social participation in its management, ends up also putting certain challenges

---

[14] ALI – UNIDROIT, *Principles and Rules of Transnational Civil Procedure*, ALI – UNIDROIT, Philadelphia and Rome 2004, Principle 1; N. Andrews, "Fundamental Principles of Civil Procedure: Order out of Chaos" in X.E. Kramer and C.H. van Rhee (eds.), *Civil Litigation in Globalising World*, Springer, Dordrecht 2012, p. 23.

[15] As registered in the cases of Germany (Kern, Kist, and Carnal, Op. cit., pp. 185 ff.), Argentina (Mosmann, "Accountability *y Transparencia en el Curso de la Justicia Civil en Argentina*", in Mitidiero (ed.), Accountability *e Transparência da Justiça Civil – Uma Perspectiva Comparada*. São Paulo: Revista dos Tribunais, 2019, pp. 51 ff.), Brazil (Marinoni and Arenhart, "Accountability *e Transparência da Justiça Civil no Brasil*", in Mitidiero (ed.), Accountability *e Transparência da Justiça Civil – Uma Perspectiva Comparada*. São Paulo: Revista dos Tribunais, 2019, pp. 65 ff.), Canada (Kennedy, *"Accountability and Transparency in Canadian Civil Justice"*, in "Accountability *e Transparência da Justiça Civil no Brasil*", in Mitidiero (ed.), Accountability *e Transparência da Justiça Civil – Uma Perspectiva Comparada*. São Paulo: Revista dos Tribunais, 2019, pp. 84 ff.), Scandinavia (Nylund, "Accountability and Transparency in the Course of Civil Justice in the Nordic Countries", in "Accountability *e Transparência da Justiça Civil no Brasil*", in Mitidiero (ed.), Accountability *e Transparência da Justiça Civil – Uma Perspectiva Comparada*. São Paulo: Revista dos Tribunais, 2019, pp. 253 ff.), Spain (Vallines-García, *"Responsabilidad y Transparencia en el Curso de la Justicia Civil en España"*, in "Accountability *e Transparência da Justiça Civil no Brasil*", in Mitidiero (ed.), Accountability *e Transparência da Justiça Civil – Uma Perspectiva Comparada*. São Paulo: Revista dos Tribunais, 2019, pp. 122 ff.), the United States (except for the state judges, who are periodically elected, according to Dodson, "Accountability and Transparency in U.S. Courts", in "Accountability *e Transparência da Justiça Civil no Brasil*", in Mitidiero (ed.), Accountability *e Transparência da Justiça Civil – Uma Perspectiva Comparada*. São Paulo: Revista dos Tribunais, 2019, pp. 282 ff.), France (Mekki, *"Responsabilité et Transparence de la Justice Civile"*, in "Accountability *e Transparência da Justiça Civil no Brasil*", in Mitidiero (ed.), Accountability *e Transparência da Justiça Civil – Uma Perspectiva Comparada*. São Paulo: Revista dos Tribunais, 2019, pp. 159 ff.), England (Sorabji, Op. Cit., pp. 97 ff.), Italy (Passanante, "Accountability and Transparency in the Course of Civil Justice in Italy", in "Accountability *e Transparência da Justiça Civil no Brasil*", in Mitidiero (ed.), Accountability *e Transparência da Justiça Civil – Uma Perspectiva Comparada*. São Paulo: Revista dos Tribunais, 2019, pp. 236 ff), and Portugal (Costa e Silva, "Accountability and Transparency in the Course of Civil Justice in Portugal", in "Accountability *e Transparência da Justiça Civil no Brasil*", in Mitidiero (ed.), Accountability *e Transparência da Justiça Civil – Uma Perspectiva Comparada*. São Paulo: Revista dos Tribunais, 2019, pp. 269 ff.).

on the table of discussions regarding judicial independence. Thus, issues relating to the administrative and budgetary autonomy of the judiciary and the selection of judges usually play a sensitive role in this respect.

In general, there is concern about the need of granting civil justice administrative and financial autonomy: even in countries where, for example, the judicial budget is in the hands of the executive, notably in the hands of the Ministry of Justice, such a solution tends to entail a lower degree of judicial independence.[16] In light of this, Western jurisdictions seek to ensure the administrative and financial autonomy of civil justice by entrusting their government to the judiciary itself,[17] to agencies,[18] or to councils that are independent of other powers.[19]

In Spain, there is also a specific concern related to the administrative autonomy of civil justice because the "oficinas judiciales" or "judicial offices" – the organs that provide administrative support to the judiciary – are practically in the hands of the executive, which can lead to an undue level of management by the executive in judicial matters.[20] For this reason, this dependence is viewed with great reserve by legal doctrine, which strives for the autonomization of the administrative apparatus linked to the functioning of civil justice.[21]

---

[16] As recorded in France, for example, where the need for budgetary autonomy is highlighted by MEKKI (Op. cit., pp. 159 ff.), given that the judicial budget is currently subject to political decisions. In Germany, however, there is relative administrative and budgetary autonomy: apart from the Constitutional Courts, which have full administrative and budgetary autonomy, the organs of the judiciary enjoy relative administrative and budgetary autonomy insofar as questions concerning the budget, education, training, and judicial management are defined by the executive. According to KERN, KIST, and CARNAL (Op. cit., pp. 190 ff.), this relative autonomy aims to promote a democratic balance between judicial independence and political representation stemming from the administrative management of the judiciary entrusted to the executive, rather than being viewed as something that tends to be bad from the point of view of judicial independence.

[17] As is the case in England (where, since 2005, the Lord Chief Justice has been responsible for administrative and financial autonomy, notably by defining the appropriated budget of the judiciary, according to SORABJI, Op. cit., pp. 97 ff.), Canada (according to KENNEDY, Op. cit., pp. 84 ff.), and Brazil (according to MARINONI and ARENHART, Op. cit., pp. 65 ff.).

[18] As is the case in the Scandinavian countries, which seek to ensure the administrative and financial autonomy of the courts through the so-called National Courts Administration Agencies (according to NYLUND, Op. cit., pp. 252 ff.).

[19] As is the case in Italy, which seeks to ensure administrative and financial autonomy of the judiciary by handing over its management to the Consiglio Superiore della Magistratura (according to PASSANANTE, Op. cit., pp. 243 ff.).

[20] The judicial offices are headed by the Letrado de la Administración de Justicia, which is appointed by the executive. Judicial offices are responsible for the management of the administrative staff and resources of the judiciary (according to VALLINES-GARCÍA, Op. cit., pp. 123 ff.).

[21] See VALLINES-GARCÍA (Op. cit., pp. 123 ff.).

In general, judges are chosen by public tender, which usually means they will serve for life.[22] The exception here is the United States, where federal judges are politically selected – they are appointed to a lifelong position by the President, with the advice and consent of the Senate, under Article III of the Constitution. State judges, in turn, are elected. This contingency leads to a concern about the independence of state judges regarding public opinion in the United States.[23] Although this model ends up promoting greater accountability to the people, which raises the democratic index of judicial activity, it also tends to entail a lower level of judicial independence.[24]

These guarantees aim at underlining the need for submitting civil justice to law and to law only: judges who do not feel threatened by external and internal pressures have no reason to bow to attempts to interfere with their functioning. Faced with transformations in the sources of law and the gradual convergence of legal traditions,[25] countries that do not normally recognize judicial precedent as the primary source of law – such as Italy – question whether attachment to precedents could in any way violate the need for independence.[26]

This issue is obviously difficult and depends on other questions concerning the meaning given to the interpretation of law and the way in which the different legal systems seek to organize the role of the Supreme Courts and to promote

---

[22] In Argentina, according to MOSMANN (Op. cit., pp. 53 ff.), there was a practice of admitting the appointment of judges without a public tender to fill vacant positions during the period in which public tenders are held (the so-called *jueces subrogantes*). However, the Supreme Court of the Argentine Nation understood that this possibility harms judicial independence, declaring the unconstitutionality of its legal provision in the *Uriarte Case* judged in 2015. Nevertheless, in other countries, the appointment of temporary judges, which usually takes place to meet the needs arising as a result of professional or medical leave taken by permanent judges, is not necessarily seen as a bad thing. The same applies to the appointment of deputy judges, who act by assisting the permanent judges for a certain period of time. This is exactly the case in the Scandinavian countries (according to NYLUND, Op. cit., pp. 254 ff.).

[23] See DODSON (Op. cit., pp. 285 ff.).

[24] See ibid.

[25] The literature on the subject is immense and space constraints mean it is not possible to give an account of the state of the art here. Nevertheless, such convergence is usually signalled by specialized doctrine: see, for example, J. WALKER and O. CHASE (eds.), *Common Law, Civil Law and the Future of Categories*, LexisNexis, Toronto 2010; A. DONDI, V. ANSANELLI, and P. COMOGLIO, *Processi Civili in Evoluzione – Una Prospettiva Comparata*, Giuffrè, Milan 2015.

[26] It is the inquiry launched by PASSANANTE (Op. cit., pp. 241 ff.). For an account on the subject from the Italian perspective, see L. PASSANANTE, *Il Precedente Impossibile*, Giappichelli, Turin 2018. For a comparative approach, see M. TARUFFO, "Precedente e Giurisprudenza" in *Rivista Trimestrale di Diritto e Procedura Civile*, Giuffrè, Milan 2007; L.G. MARINONI, *Precedentes Obrigatórios*, 5th ed., Revista dos Tribunais, São Paulo 2016; D. MITIDIERO, *Precedentes – da Persuasão à Vinculação*, 3rd ed., Revista dos Tribunais, São Paulo 2018; H. ZANETI JR., *O Valor Vinculante dos Precedentes*, 4th ed., JusPodium, Salvador 2019; T. ARRUDA ALVIM, "*Estabilidade e Adaptabilidade como Objetivos do Direito: Civil Law e Common Law*", Revista de Processo. Revista dos Tribunais, São Paulo 2009, n. 172. For an analysis of Latin American law, see E. OTEIZA, "*El Problema de la Uniformidad de la Jurisprudencia en América Latina*", Revista de Processo. Revista dos Tribunais, São Paulo 2006, n. 136.

the binding nature of judicial precedents.[27] In general, however, a realistic perspective tends to consider the need to promote, by force of judicial action, the principles of legal security, freedom and equality of all citizens before the law by granting binding force or – at least – persuasive force to the precedent.[28]

From the perspective of impartiality, the main concern stems from the need to avoid biases in decision making. Therefore, one must seek to prohibit the jurisdictional activity in situations where the judge may have a conflict of interests or in situations that may bring his/her deep-rooted prejudices to surface.

In the English experience, for example, such situations were appreciated in *Locabail (UK) v. Bayfield Properties Ltd.*, which was tried in 2000, and later collected by the Lord Chief of Justice in the "Guide to Judicial Conduct." In summary, judicial activity is prohibited when there is a bias against or in favor of a certain party, when the judge has patrimonial or other direct interest in the case, or when a reasonable and fair third party, after evaluating all the facts of the case, arrives at the conclusion that the decision is biased.[29]

Prohibitions which are normally identical usually take place in different Western countries, which is proving to be a general trend. Judges, for instance, are often barred from participating in any partisan party-political activities or performing their functions in relation to issues in which involves their own interests or those of people from their social and family circle (*nemo iudex in re propria*). These prohibitions clearly seek to safeguard the judicial function of a possible conflict of interest. Less common, however, is the possibility of denouncing a deep-rooted prejudice of the judge as a factor of judicial partiality. The English formula, which consists of the possibility of submitting suspect cases to a "reasonable" and "fair-minded" third party, seems to be an interesting solution.

An independent, impartial judge enables law to be carried out in an objective manner, i.e., free from subjectivity However, in order for the decision to be effectively bound to law and thus understood by the consumers of justice, it

---

[27] The literature on the subject is immense and space constraints mean it is not possible to give an account of the state of the art here. Nonetheless, it is possible to get a good picture on the subject by consulting R. SUMMERS and N. MACCORMICK (eds.), *Interpreting Statutes – A Comparative Study*, Ashgate, Dartmouth 1991; R. SUMMERS and N. MACCORMICK (eds.), *Interpreting Precedents – A Comparative Study*, Ashgate, Dartmouth: 1997; M. TARUFFO, L.G. MARINONI, and D. MITIDIERO (eds.), *La Misión de los Tribunales Supremos*, Marcial Pons, Madrid 2016.

[28] See D. MITIDIERO, *"The Ideal Court of Last Resort: a Court of Interpretation and Precedent"*, *International Journal of Procedural Law*, Intersentia, Cambridge 2015; D. MITIDIERO, *Cortes Superiores e Cortes Supremas – do Controle à Interpretação, da Jurisprudência ao Precedente*, 3rd ed., Revista dos Tribunais, São Paulo 2017; D. MITIDIERO, *Precedentes – da Persuasão à Vinculação*, 3rd ed., Revista dos Tribunais, São Paulo 2018.

[29] See SORABJI (Op. cit., pp. 105 ff.).

must be formulated in a legally justified manner, stating the reasons why certain interpretations of facts, evidence and law were preferred to the detriment of others, the reasons why certain forms of evidence was given more weight to the detriment of other forms, and the reasons why certain norms were applied in preference to others.

4. THE INTERPRETATION AND APPLICATION OF LAW (LEGAL REASONING): THE DUTY TO GIVE REASONS IN JUDICIAL DECISIONS

The duty of justifying judicial decisions is inherent to the constitutional state[30] and is a true benchmark of the right to a fair hearing of the parties.[31] Without legal reasoning, without being accountable to the parties and to society as to the reasons why the decision was guided in a particular direction,[32] the jurisdictional function becomes a simple exercise of power and may possibly be the result of influences extraneous to law and dictated under the sign of partiality.

If law works with at least four variables of indeterminacy (the existence the non-existence, and the meaning of facts; the existence, the non-existence, and the meaning and weight of proof; the meaning of texts; and the scope of norms), the act of interpreting and applying laws must account for these different dimensions in the most objective way, that is, enabling an intersubjective control of reasons based on the judicial decision. It is no coincidence that the existence of "reasoned explanation" about its "essential factual, legal, and evidentiary basis" is one of the basic principles of transnational civil proceeding listed by the American Law Institute and UNIDROIT.[33]

---

[30] M. TARUFFO, *La Motivazione della Sentenza Civile*, CEDAM, Padua 1975, p. 412; J.C. BARBOSA MOREIRA, *"A Motivação das Decisões Judiciais como Garantia Inerente ao Estado de Direito"* (1978), Temas de Direito Processual (1980), 2nd ed., Saraiva, São Paulo 1988, pp. 83–95, Segunda Série.

[31] Hence the reason why specialized doctrine emphasizes the connection between *richterliche Begründungspflicht* and *Anspruch auf rechtliches Gehör* (Jürgen Brüggemann, *Die richterliche Begründungspflicht – Verfassungsrechtliche Mindestanforderungen an die Begründung gerichtlicher Etnscheidungen*, Duncker & Humblot, Berlin 1971, pp. 152–161), between the right to effective judicial protection, the right to defense and motivation, and between the *derecho a la tutela judicial efectiva, derecho a la defensa*, and *motivación judicial* (T.J. ALISTE SANTOS, *La Motivación de las Resoluciones Judiciales*, Marcial Pons, Madrid 2011, pp. 145–148).

[32] By demonstrating the existence of an endoprocedural function (justified by procedural reasons – for the parties and the other judges of the appeals chain) and an extraprocedural function (justified by social reasons – for society), see M. TARUFFO, *La Motivazione della Sentenza Civile*, CEDAM, Padua 1975, p. 416, which even lends relevance to this dichotomy as a key to reading the history of motivation. In fact, this dual function is expressly invoked in English law in the case of *English v. Emery*, j. 2002, according to SORABJI (Op. cit., pp. 107 e ff.); still, see PASSANANTE (Op. cit., pp. 249 ff.);

[33] ALI – UNIDROIT, above n. 14, Principle 23.

174

Intersentia

In general, the different Western legal systems converge in terms of holding that there is a need for a reasoned decision. What changes is the greater or lesser level of detail of these requirements for the characterization of a duly reasoned decision. At times, different functions that can be attributed to the reasons invoked in judicial decisions are also highlighted.

Procedural systems converge in relation to the necessity of a decision that deals with fact issues, demonstration issues and law issues.[34] What varies is the degree of detail of this requirement. In Spain, for example, decisions must not only contemplate facts, evidence and legality, as is generally required, but must also consider the different elements of fact and law, individually and jointly, in the light of the rules of logic and reason (Article 218.2 of the Ley de Enjuiciamiento Civil).[35] In Portugal, it is the duty of the judge to specifically state the facts he/she has considered to be proven and not proven and the pertinent reasons for this (Article 607 of the Código de Processo Civil.[36]

In Argentina, judges are required to issue decisions considered "razonablemente fundadas" (Article 3 of the Código Civil y Comercial Argentino de 2015), even mentioning doctrine according to which, based on the jurisprudence of the Corte Suprema de Justicia de la Nación, decisions that neglect their precedents cannot be considered "razonablemente fundadas," thus being qualified as arbitrary.[37] In Germany, even though judicial precedent does not have a binding value ("established legal doctrine"), its persuasive value requires judges to explain in precise detail the reasons why they did not follow the precedent in the event that they did not do so.[38] In Italy, legislators even allow legal reasoning to be based exclusively on precedents.[39]

Of all the countries considered, Brazil may be the one which provides more details regarding law issues. This is because Brazilian law seeks to go beyond a positive prescription regarding the content of legal reasoning (Article 489,

---

[34] Theoretical discussions on the possibility of separation between fact and law will not be dealt with here, since our interest at this moment is predominantly comparative. Thus, we limit ourselves to alluding to the classic distinction between fact, evidence, and law. For this reason, it suffices to mention that we understand that there is an ontological unity between fact and law, although a functional separation is possible: there is an ontological indivisibility, because every narrative in fact already enters the process from a certain normative framework (that is, the norm functions here as a "scheme of interpretation" of facts – "Norm als Deutungsschema"; see H. KELSEN, above n. 4, p. 3). However, it is possible to separate fact and law in the process – once the cause has been established in all its factual-juridical contours – for certain functions (for example, for individualization of the object of proof and for comparison between cases in their factual aspects). Hence the reason why one can affirm in these limits the possibility of functional right to partition of the cause.

[35] See VALLINES-GARCÍA (Op. cit., pp. 143 ff.).

[36] See COSTA E SILVA (Op. Cit., pp. 270 ff.).

[37] According to MOSMANN (Op. cit., pp. 58 ff.). However, she makes a critical observation when she says that even the Supreme Court is, at times, incoherent when applying this rule.

[38] See KERN, KIST, and CARNAL (Op. cit., pp. 215 ff.).

[39] See PASSANANTE (Op. cit., pp. 249 ff.).

paragraph II and §2 CPC). There is also a negative prescription (Article 489, §1 CPC) in which the legislator expressly outlines what he/she means by a decision without justification: (i) one that limits itself to indicating, reproducing, or paraphrasing its legal basis, without explaining its relation to the cause or the matter decided; (ii) one that uses indeterminate legal concepts, without explaining the concrete reason for its incidence; (iii) one invoking grounds that would justify any other decision; (iv) one that does not face all the arguments deduced in the proceeding that are capable, in theory, to rebut the conclusion adopted by the judge; (v) one that limits the invocation of precedent or summary, and neither identifies determinant foundations nor demonstrates that the case in question fits those grounds; (vi) one that no longer follows a precedent, case law, or precedent statement invoked by the party, without showing the existence of a distinction in the case in question or the overruling of the precedent. When considering the cases in which the deficient reasoning is considered, Brazilian legislation requires a concrete and complete legal reasoning: one that effectively addresses the concrete case, and enables and effective dialogue among the participants in the proceedings.[40]

In some countries, there is still some flexibility regarding the content of legal reasoning. This is the case, for example, in Canada and Italy. Canadian law stands out because it expressly emphasizes the flexibility of the requirement of legal reasoning: it is expected that a decision on a less complex case will have a less detailed legal reasoning than a decision on a relevant constitutional issue.[41] Italian law also stands out for the same reason by allowing a more concise legal reasoning for the solution of simpler cases.[42]

Viewed from the perspective of the right to a fair hearing, the duty of legal reasoning has two possible solutions. On the one hand, in England, for example, according to the common law principle concerning open justice and in regard to Article 6 of the European Convention on Human Rights, judges are required to indicate how they arrived to their conclusions,[43] but it is not necessary to examine all the arguments put forward by the parties; it suffices to show that the decision is not arbitrary.[44] On the other hand, in Brazil, for example, it is required that judges talk to the parties about all the relevant grounds they are

---

[40] See MARINONI and ARENHART (Op. cit., pp. 70 ff.). See also D. MITIDIERO, *Colaboração no Processo Civil – do Modelo ao Princípio*, 4th ed., Revista dos Tribunais, São Paulo 2019, pp. 149–168; L.G. MARINONI, S.C. ARENHART, and D. MITIDIERO, *Curso de Processo Civil*, 5th ed., Revista dos Tribunais, São Paulo 2019, vol. II; L.G. MARINONI, S.C. ARENHART, and D. MITIDIERO, *Código de Processo Civil Comentado*, 5th ed., Revista dos Tribunais, São Paulo 2019.

[41] See KENNEDY (Op. cit., pp. 86 ff.).

[42] See PASSANANTE (Op. cit., pp. 249 ff.).

[43] See SORABJI (Op. cit., pp. 107 ff., alluding to the *English v. Emery* case (2002) and the European cases *Ruiz Torija v. Spain* (1994) and *Van de Hurk v. The Netherlands* (1994).

[44] *English v. Emery* (2002).

accused of and that this requirement is understood as a basic consequence of the right to a fair hearing (Articles 9, 10 and 489, §1, item IV and 1.022, item II CPC), which in turn results from the need to ensure the democratic participation of the parties in the construction of judicial decisions.[45]

In relation to the function that reasoning plays, it is usually linked to the need for accountability of civil justice and control by the parties and public opinion regarding the reasons underlying judicial decisions, which can be well demonstrated in English law.[46] This requirement is associated with the growing desire to make decisions – especially Supreme Court decisions – accessible to the public. For this reason, in France, the doctrine points to the need to promote the use of clearer language in decisions (without prejudice to the inevitable use of technical and legal terms), noting that the brief and outdated style of the Cour de Cassation necessitates the supplying of "understanding supports" in relation to the decisions, which testifies to the difficulty of interpreting the decisions and the need to adopt a more direct and modern style in their writing.[47] Similarly, in Scandinavia, there is a desire to make the courts more reliable, so that judges strive to make their decisions understandable to the public, thus ensuring they enjoy greater social acceptance.[48]

This connection between the performance of Supreme Courts and the understanding of their decisions by the general public is linked to the subject of judicial precedent. And this is the case for a very simple reason: it is precisely for the reasons given by the judges in the justification of their decisions that the precedent is capable of gaining life and enriching the legal system.[49]

Finally, an unexplored but very important perspective concerns the way in which decisions are made: how are reasons for decisions created? The case of the United States is very interesting in this regard, especially because it seeks to emphasize – realistically – that the decision is the result of a proceeding marked by a mixture of transparency and privacy.

As legal reasons are made public, one can understand that there is transparency of the content of the decision. However, this does not mean that the whole process of decision making is guided by transparency. As the doctrine shows, the judge must first decide in order to be able to decide. To reach a judicial decision, the court usually shares duties with its law clerks, ordering investigations and discussing with them the arguments raised by the parties to

---

[45] For an account on the relationship between civil procedure and democracy in Brazilian doctrine, see O. BAPTISTA DA SILVA, *Processo e Ideologia – O Paradigma Racionalista*, Forense, Rio de Janeiro 2004. See also P. CALAMANDREI, "Processo e Democrazia" in M. CAPPELLETTI (ed.), *Opere Giuridiche*, Morano Editore, Naples 1965, vol. I, pp. 618 ff.

[46] *English v. Emery* (2002).

[47] MEKKI (Op. cit., pp. 166 ff.).

[48] See NYLUND (Op. cit., pp. 257 ff.).

[49] See MARINONI and ARENHART (Op. cit., pp. 70 ff.). See also L.G. MARINONI, above n. 26; D. MITIDIERO, above n. 26.

resolve the case. This proceeding is not public, being carried out under the guise of judicial *privacy* (i.e., it is carried out in chambers).[50]

This angle of analysis allows us to perceive a fundamental aspect of proceedings and judicial decisions: their relationship with publicity and transparency. An accountable form of proceeding is one permeated by public scrutiny and access to information, two elements without which one can hardly think of an effectively democratic proceeding.

5. PUBLICITY OF PROCEEDINGS AND DECISIONS

Publicity is essential to the democratic principle and to the principle of the rule of law (*auf dem Demokratie- und dem Rechtsstaatsprinzip*).[51] For this reason, it is an essential element for the construction of a fair trial and an accountable civil justice, constituting a necessary consequence of the democratic character of the administration of justice.[52] It is not by chance that this is one of the fundamental principles of civil procedure listed by the ALI and UNIDROIT.[53]

However, the advantages of a public proceeding can be well summarized from the reasons enumerated by the English doctrine. In addition to the link between the democratic rule of law and publicity, the right of the public and the media to monitor procedural acts aims at ensuring judicial accountability, facilitating freedom of expression, enhancing social debate and collaborating with the public on an adequate understanding of the law. In a way, the permanent public scrutiny of procedural acts makes "every judge sitting in judgment on trial." Moreover, the right to know who the parties to a dispute are discourages judicial adventures, promotes the honesty of the parties and their witnesses, and enables proceedings to be seen as a community-shared enterprise aimed at promoting the rule of law.[54]

Based on the scheme established by legal doctrine, it is possible to outline the publicity in the proceedings as general publicity and restricted publicity, immediate publicity and mediated publicity.[55] General publicity is a situation in which everyone has access to the contents of the case. Restricted publicity is one

---

50   According to DODSON (Op. cit., pp. 287 ff.).
51   L. ROSENBERG, K.H. SCHWAB, and P. GOTTWALD, above n. 7, p. 113. In the same vein, see KERN, KIST, and CARNAL (Op. cit., pp. 208 ff.).
52   V. DENTI, *La Giustizia Civile*, 2nd ed., Il Mulino, Bologna 2004, p. 104. On linking equally publicity, democracy, and control of state activity by the society in general, see M. TARUFFO, *La Motivazione della Sentenzo Civile*, CEDAM, Padua 1975, p. 407; E. COUTURE, "Las Garantías Constitucionales del Proceso Civil" in *Estudios de Derecho Procesal Civil*, Ediar Editores, Buenos Aires 1948, vol. I. pp. 20–21.
53   ALI – UNIDROIT, above n. 14, Principle 20.
54   All according to SORABJI (Op. cit., pp. 114 ff.), based on the reasons given in several cases appreciated by English Civil Justice.
55   R.W. MILLAR, *The Formative Principles of Civil Procedure* (1923), in A. ENGELMANN, *A History of Continental Civil Procedure*, Little, Brown, and Company, Boston 1927, pp. 69–70.

in which only the parties or their attorneys have access to the records. Immediate publicity is one in which the public at large, the parties, and their lawyers are allowed to be present at the time of the performance of the procedural acts. Mediated publicity, in turn, is one in which only the result of the practice of the procedural act is accessible to the public, the parties, and their lawyers.

The experience of different Western countries can be well understood from this well-known classification. In civil proceedings, the rule is general and immediate publicity.[56] Third parties may have access to procedural acts, provided that they can demonstrate a legitimate interest. Specifically in the case of journalists, this interest is presumed and is especially supported by the freedom of the press. Exceptionally, publicity may be restricted, which is usually associated with cases in which public access may violate the right to privacy of parties, frustrate the public interest, or threaten national security. Media publicity is also an exception and is normally associated with urgent acts in which the presence of the parties is incompatible with the urgency or the purpose of the ordered measure.[57]

Publicity of decisions is also the rule in civil proceedings. Besides the aforementioned reasons for this, it is an important factor in the development of case law and the promotion of the unity of law by means of precedents. Most Western countries maintain websites where decisions can be accessed not only by the parties and their lawyers, but also by the general public. In cases in which publicity is restricted, decisions are made under fictitious names or simply by mentioning the initials of the names of the parties involved.[58]

Moreover, demands linked to the need for a more direct understanding of the everyday life of civil justice make the publicity of the proceedings and decisions only a step in the approximation of the judiciary power with civil society. In order to make this approximation even more effective, transparency in the functioning and conduct of judicial affairs is required.

---

[56]　According to KERN, KIST, and CARNAL (Op. cit., pp. 208 ff.); MOSMANN (Op. cit., pp. 59 ff.); MARINONI and ARENHART (Op. cit., pp. 78 ff.); KENNEDY (Op. cit., pp. 87 ff.); NYLUND (Op. cit., pp. 257 ff.); VALLINES-GARCÍA (Op. cit., pp. 148 ff.); DODSON (Op. cit., pp. 287 ff.); MEKKI (Op. cit., pp. 173 ff.); SORABJI (Op. cit., pp. 114 ff.); PASSANANTE (Op. cit., pp. 248 ff.); COSTA E SILVA (Op. cit., pp. 271 ff.).

[57]　According to, for German law, KERN, KIST, and CARNAL (Op. cit., pp. 208 ff.); for Argentinian law, MOSMANN (Op. cit., pp. 59 ff.); for Brazilian law, MARINONI and ARENHART (Op. cit., pp. 78 ff.); for Canadian law, KENNEDY (Op. cit., pp. 87 ff.); for Scandinavian law, NYLUND (Op. cit., pp. 257 ff.); for Spanish law, VALLINES-GARCÍA (Op. cit., pp. 148 ff.); for American law, DODSON (Op. cit., pp. 287 ff.); for French law, MEKKI (Op. cit., pp. 173 ff.); for English law, SORABJI (Op. cit., pp. 114 ff.); for Italian law, PASSANANTE (Op. cit., pp. 248 ff.); and for Portuguese law, COSTA E SILVA (Op. cit., pp. 271 ff.).

[58]　According to, for German law, KERN, KIST, and CARNAL (Op. cit., pp. 208 ff.); for Argentinian law, MOSMANN (Op. cit., pp. 59 ff.); for Brazilian law, MARINONI and ARENHART (Op. cit., pp. 78 ff.); for Canadian law, KENNEDY (Op. cit., pp. 87 ff.); for Scandinavian law, NYLUND (Op. cit., pp. 257 ff.); for Spanish law, VALLINES-GARCÍA (Op. cit., pp. 148 ff.); for American law, DODSON (Op. cit., pp. 287 ff.); for French law, MEKKI (Op. cit., pp. 173 ff.); for English law, SORABJI (Op. cit., pp. 114 ff.); for Italian law, PASSANANTE (Op. cit., pp. 248 ff.); and for Portuguese law, COSTA E SILVA (Op. cit., pp. 271 ff.).

6. CIVIL JUSTICE TRANSPARENCY: FROM TRADITIONAL COMMUNICATION AND INFORMATION TO NEW TECHNOLOGIES

Apart from publicity, it is also essential for a democratic rule of law to enable effective access to information. This is an important condition for the promotion of an increasingly transparent and comprehensible civil justice for the parties and the general public. Since transparency in relation to judicial information is a fundamental requirement for the construction of an accountable civil justice, the legal doctrine increasingly emphasizes its importance in the construction of fair proceedings, especially from the angle of the promotion of the right to participate in proceedings and notably the right to a fair hearing.[59]

The need for transparency in civil justice is a subject that has had a significant impact with the advent of new technologies. If, on the one hand, these new technologies increase judicial transparency, on the other hand, they challenge civil justice to solve certain emerging problems. The comparison of different Western legal systems is illustrative in this field too.

In general, several legal systems rely on courts that use websites to provide information on their precedents, to inform the parties about the progress of their cases and the general public in relation to the news concerning cases faced by civil justice.[60] To illustrate this, we can mention expressions such as "open-court principle,"[61] "open data,"[62] and "Gobierno Abierto Judicial"[63] at judicial facilities.

As a rule, access to this information is public and free. However, the question concerning the economic value – so to speak – of this information was not set aside by legal doctrine.[64] In France, for example, there is a necessity to preserve judicial production as a public good[65] and therefore it is a widespread, free service. The discussion is far from innocuous: in Norway, for example, it is necessary to pay private companies in order to gain access to the case law produced by the

---

[59] Particularly in connection with the right to due notice and the right to be heard, including the adoption of new technologies to facilitate access to judicial information and dialogue, according to ALI – UNIDROIT, above n. 14, Principle 5, especially regarding the adoption of new technologies, such as telecommunications (Principle 5.7).

[60] For example, Germany (according to KERN, KIST and CARNAL, Op. cit., pp. 219 ff.), Argentina (according to MOSMANN, Op. cit., pp. 59 ff.), Brazil (according to MARINONI and ARENHART, Op. cit., pp. 76 ff.), Spain (VALLINES-GARCÍA, Op. cit., pp. 150 ff.), Italy (according to PASSANANTE, Op. cit., pp. 249 ff.), Finland (NYLUND, Op. cit., pp. 263 ff.), and France (according to MEKKI, Op. cit., pp. 169 ff.).

[61] See KENNEDY (Op. cit., pp. 87 e ff.).

[62] See MEKKI Op. cit., pp. 169 ff.).

[63] See MOSMANN Op. cit., pp. 59 ff.).

[64] As observed by L. CADIET, quoted by MEKKI (Op. cit., pp. 169 ff.).

[65] According to L. CADIET, quoted by MEKKI, (Op. cit., pp. 169 ff.).

courts. As can be seen, this commodification of judicial information reduces judicial transparency.

The use of mass media for the establishment of a direct channel between civil justice and society has also been a constant. Even in countries where televising, filming, sound recording, or even photographing procedural acts is forbidden, such as England, it is common practice make exceptions in order to allow the televising of hearings at the United Kingdom Supreme Court and, with the express permission of the Lord Chancellor, the recording and televising of certain procedural acts in general.[66] At times, the interest in judicial matters is so great that the express prohibition on televising, recording, or photographing judicial proceedings is exceptionally left aside. This happened in Norway, which, in light of the trial of Anders Breivik, accused of the terrorist attacks of 2011, made an exception to this rule in this case.[67]

Moreover, courts in several countries, notably the respective Supreme Courts, have their judgments televised, in some cases even on their own channels.[68] In Brazil, for instance, there is not only a TV channel but also a radio station that broadcasts judgments.[69] The new possibilities of communication with the public also extend to new social media: for example, the use of Twitter for this end is quite common in Canada.[70] This opening promotes greater transparency for civil justice.

New technologies also impact on how proceedings are conducted, stored, and managed. In Brazil, for example, there is a very significant contingent of totally electronic proceedings.[71] In Spain, there is also an electronic judicial management system (Lexnet), as well as the requirement of making both audio and video recordings of court hearings to provide electronic support.[72] By preserving the personal data of the parties, and the publicity to legally interested third parties and journalists, electronic proceedings and electronic judicial management tend to increase the transparency of civil justice. They even allow more reliable access to the material used for the composition of judicial statistics.[73] In Norway, it is quite common to hold preliminary hearings and even some less complex hearings in the form of teleconferences and telephone calls. If it is true that such an expedient is more efficient to all parties, it is also true

---

[66]   See SORABJI (Op. cit., pp. 163 ff.).
[67]   See NYLUND (Op. cit., pp. 257 ff.).
[68]   This is the case, for instance, in Argentina (according to MOSMANN, Op. cit., pp. 59 ff.), Brazil (according to MARINONI and ARENHART, Op. cit., pp. 76 ff.), Canada (according to KENNEDY, Op. cit., pp. 87 ff.), and England (according to SORABJI, Op. cit., pp. 113 ff.).
[69]   See MARINONI and ARENHART (Op. cit., pp. 76 ff.).
[70]   See KENNEDY (Op. cit, pp. 87 ff.).
[71]   See MARINONI and ARENHART (Op. cit., pp. 76 ff.).
[72]   See VALLINES-GARCÍA (Op. cit., pp. 150 ff.).
[73]   See MARINONI and ARENHART (Op. cit., pp. 76 ff.).

Intersentia

that this practice is potentially contrary to the publicity of the proceedings, since judges usually conduct hearings by teleconference and direct telephone calls from their offices, which reduces the transparency of procedural acts.[74]

Finally, it is important not to overlook the problems that may arise from the use of new technologies in the proceedings. They bring about two major problems.[75] The first concerns the publicity or anonymity of the judges' names in their decisions that are published online: if, on the one hand, it increases the social responsibility of magistrates, on the other hand, it exposes the judges to social pressure, which may put their independence at risk. The second concerns the possibility of solidifying certain jurisprudential lines by mapping them electronically, which may lead, on the one hand, to an increase in legal certainty due to the greater predictability of decisions, but, on the other hand, to a trend toward an automatic, convenient reproduction of decisions.

In any case, the use of new information and communication technologies tends to bring civil justice closer to justice consumers, thus increasing its transparency and level of accountability. And this is fundamental in order to be able to evaluate the quality of civil justice from an external perspective.

7. WHO WATCHES THE WATCHMEN? THIRD-PARTY EVALUATION AND RANKING OF CIVIL JUSTICE

Naturally, the adequate functioning of civil justice is essential for the promotion of the basic purposes of civil procedure in a democratic rule of law, especially the protection of rights in an environment guided by the principles of legal security, freedom, and equality. Equally important, however, is the existence of a public perception about the proper functioning of civil justice – hence the growing concern about evaluation and the establishment of a ranking of civil justice by its consumers.

Several are the indexes that seek to value and establish a ranking of civil justice. Evidently, the assumption of any evaluation lies in the criteria that should guide the evaluation, which obviously must be relevant to the indicated purposes.[76] This means that it is necessary to take into account the intended purposes in order to know whether the selected criteria are capable of reflecting them or not.

---

[74] See Nylund (Op. cit., pp. 257 ff.).

[75] According to L. Cadiet, quoted by Mekki (Op. cit., pp. 169 ff.).

[76] For a broad discussion on the ends of civil justice, see A. Uzelac, "Goals of Civil Justice and Civil Procedure in the Contemporary World" in A. Uzelac (ed.), *Goals of Civil Justice and Civil Procedure in Contemporary Judicial Systems*, Springer, Dordrecht 2014, pp. 3–31 (a work derived from the 2012 Moscow Conference).

It is precisely in this choice of ends that the critical point of the indexes that seek to parameterize the performance of civil justice lies.[77] Studies such as "Doing Business" (promoted by the World Bank), the "EU Justice Scoreboard" (promoted by the European Union), the one promoted by the European Commission for the Efficiency of Justice (CEPEJ), and the "Rule of Law Index" end up carrying out an eminently numerical in detriment of the quality of decisions. This means that even the goal of systems harmonization – which encourages many of these studies – must take into account not only the results, but also the different structures and different functions that civil justice can be called upon to perform in the various systems. This explains the certain level of mistrust with which they are perceived by many authors.

Finally, in addition to these studies, an important aspect of civil justice is its direct evaluation by the public. Even considering the limitations of sample studies, it is significant that European countries have a much higher approval rate than Latin American countries in relation to the perception of civil justice by its consumers.[78]

8. FINAL CONSIDERATIONS

Independence, legal reasoning, publicity, and transparency are essential elements for the construction of an accountable civil justice system. More than a comparison between the results obtained by its functioning, however, it should be borne in mind that it is difficult to legitimize it from a purely quantitative perspective, without taking into account the fundamental rights of the parties involved in the proceedings – especially the right to a fair hearing – and the quality of the decisions.[79]

---

[77]   As observed by C. KERN, *Justice between Simplification and Formalism – A Discussion and Critique of the World Bank Sponsored Lex Mundi Project on Efficiency of Civil Procedure*, Mohr Siebeck, Tübingen 2007; and MEKKI (Op. Cit., pp. 180 ff.). For a broad discussion on this topic, see also L. CADIET, *"La Justice Civile Française entre Efficacité et Garanties"*, *passim* (it was translated into Portuguese as *Perspectivas sobre o Sistema da Justiça Civil Francesa – Seis Lições Brasileiras*, by D. MITIDIERO, B.G.T. OLIVEIRA, L.R. ALMEIDA, and R. LOMANDO, Revista dos Tribunais, São Paulo, 2017).

[78]   According to KERN, KIST, and CARNAL (Op. cit., pp. 220 ff.); MOSMANN (Op. cit., pp. 60 ff.); MARINONI and ARENHART (Op. cit., pp. 79 ff.); KENNEDY (Op. cit., pp. 90 ff.). For Scandinavian law, see NYLUND (Op. cit., pp. 266 ff.); for Spanish law, VALLINES-GARCÍA (Op. cit., pp. 156 ff.); for American law, DODSON (Op. cit., pp. 287 ff.); for French law, MEKKI (Op. cit., pp. 180 ff.); for English law, SORABJI (Op. cit., pp. 117 ff.); for Italian law, PASSANANTE (Op. cit., pp. 248 ff.); and for Portuguese law, COSTA E SILVA (Op. cit., pp. 271 ff.).

[79]   Highlighting the necessity of thinking more about the quality of decisions than the performance of civil justice, see C.A.A. OLIVEIRA, *Do Formalismo no Processo Civil – Proposta de um Formalismo-Valorativo*, 4th ed., Saraiva, São Paulo 2010.

Daniel Mitidiero

In summary, it is necessary to combine results with the means used to obtain them and, fundamentally, the content of the judicial action, without which civil justice loses not only in terms of accountability, but above all departs from its primary objective of safeguarding rights by making just decisions and promoting the unity of law.

PART II

NEW CHALLENGES AND THEIR VARIOUS ASPECTS

Transnational Cooperation in Cross-Border Insolvency

TRANSNATIONAL COOPERATION AND COORDINATION IN CROSS-BORDER INSOLVENCY

China, South Korea and Japan

Junichi Matsushita[*]

1. Introduction 187
2. Reciprocity.. 188
3. Cooperation between Courts 190
4. The Meaning and Effects of Recognition........................... 191

1. INTRODUCTION

This chapter is General Report for Session 3, "Transnational Cooperation in Cross-Border Insolvency," of XVI World Congress of Civil Procedure.

Because of the increasing volume of international trade and investment, we are now finding more and more cross-border insolvency cases than ever. The purposes of insolvency law are equal distribution among creditors, maximization of the value of a debtor's assets, promoting effective reorganization of a debtor's business in a rehabilitation proceeding, and ultimately enhancing certainty in the market and promoting economic stability and growth. There is no doubt that these purposes should also apply to multinational insolvency cases to the greatest extent possible. Nowadays, it is widely accepted that each country is expected to have a fair and harmonized legal framework for transnational cooperation in cross-border insolvency cases.

For Session 3, the other General Report is submitted, which is written by Professor Georg Kodek (hereinafter "Kodek Report"). The Kodek Report is quite comprehensive, is organized systematically, and covers almost all issues and arguments that are theoretically and/or practically important. In consideration

---

[*]   Professor of Law, Graduate Schools for Law and Politics, University of Tokyo.

Intersentia

of these characteristics of the Kodek Report, this chapter will be rather short and supplemental in relation to the Kodek Report in the following two senses. First, it will mainly focus on three countries – China, South Korea, and Japan – taking into account that this Congress was held in East Asia for the first time. Secondly, it will rely on country reports from the three countries shown above, which are answers to the Questionnaires,[1] because the Kodek Report seems to be based mainly on already published literature such as academic articles and legislative materials. These three reports were written by the following distinguished colleagues:

- Hon. Bingkun Ye (China), Head of the Six Civil (Financial& Bankruptcy) Division, Xiamen Intermediate People's Court, Fujian Province, China
- Hon. Young Seok Kim (South Korea), Seoul Bankruptcy Court, South Korea
- Prof. Jin Chun, Doshisha University, Japan.

Each report will be cited as the "China Report," the "Korea Report," and the "Japan Report" respectively. This chapter will pick up three topics, that is, reciprocity (section 2), then cooperation between courts (section 3), and, finally, the meaning and effects of recognition (section 4).

2. RECIPROCITY

According to the China Report, judicial cooperation in cross-border insolvency cases is established based upon the principle of reciprocity under Chinese insolvency law. This means that Chinese courts will not grant any assistance to the request from a court of a country that has refused the request for recognition or cooperation from China previously. China has not adopted the United Nations Commission on International Trade Law (UNCITRAL) Model Law on Cross-Border Insolvency (1997) (hereinafter "Model Law") for some historical reasons. By contrast, South Korea and Japan do not require a reciprocal relationship between themselves and a requesting country in the context of recognition of a decision commencing an insolvency proceeding in that country. In this sense, the insolvency laws of South Korea and Japan are similar to the Model Law.

The principle of reciprocity does not matter in countries where the proper legal basis for international cooperation in the area of cross-border insolvency is an international agreement (for example, a bilateral or multilateral treaty or an exchange of letters between the cooperating authorities), because reciprocity is usually built into such an international agreement. The European Insolvency Regulation is one such legal framework. Therefore, the principle of reciprocity

---

[1]   The questionnaires were written by Professor Kodek and me.

really matters not in a closed world like the European Union (EU), but in an open-ended multinational community.

It is interesting that reciprocity is one of the requirements of recognition of a foreign civil judgment in China, South Korea, and Japan. For example, Article 118, item 4 of the Code of Civil Procedure of Japan provides that a final and binding judgment rendered by a foreign court is valid only if a guarantee of reciprocity is in place.[2] When making a comparison between the recognition of a decision commencing a foreign insolvency proceeding and the recognition of a foreign judgment, China takes a parallel attitude regarding the two issues, and South Korea and Japan provide for different rules.

Reciprocity is based on the concept of equality of sovereign states. However, it could cause a kind of standstill, where two countries will refuse recognition of each other forever, which could prevent the establishment of harmonized cross-border insolvency proceedings.

Two recent movements should be mentioned here. The first of these is "presumptive reciprocity." YE (China) states as follows:

> The initiation of "presumptive reciprocity." The situation is changing especially after the initiation of "belt and road." The SPC has indicated a more and more positive attitude toward the cooperation in cross-border insolvency in recent years. A new mechanism namely "presumptive reciprocity" has been stated in a judicial document to improve the judicial cooperation in "belt and road" countries and officially announced firstly by the Chief Justice Zhou Qiang in China-ASEAN Nanning Judicial Summit Forum 2017. The main point of the norm is, when facing a judicial cooperation request from a jurisdiction where has no reciprocal cases with this country previously, the existence of the reciprocity should be recognized except [when] the law of the jurisdiction refuse to provide cooperation to China's court, the cooperation sought should be provided when other conditions contained are satisfied. Obviously, the list of the jurisdictions [which] meets the reciprocity condition will be extended significantly and, an obvious step toward universality could easily be seen.

This brand-new mechanism will hopefully work as a breakthrough in terms of traditionally rigid reciprocity as far as "belt and road" countries are concerned.

Second, it was quite recently reported that a New York bankruptcy court had recognized a Chinese insolvency proceeding in the face of creditor objections in the first ruling of its kind.[3] Detailed information on this is not available yet, but this could have a great impact on practice with respect to international cooperation in cross-border insolvency cases in China. As far as I know, thus far, a Chinese court has never recognized an U.S. bankruptcy proceeding.

---

2   On this point, South Korea seems similar to Japan. KIM (South Korea).

3   B. CLARKE, "First Recognition Granted for Chinese Company's Contested Chapter 15," October 11, 2019, https://globalrestructuringreview.com/article/1209502/first-recognition-granted-for-chinese-company's-contested-chapter-15.

3. COOPERATION BETWEEN COURTS

Traditionally courts in civil law jurisdictions have tended to be reluctant to communicate directly with foreign courts. For example, Japan has basically adopted the Model Law, but did not adopt Article 25, which provides for cooperation and direct communication between a national court and foreign courts.

In this regard, much attention should be paid to the recent developments in South Korea. First, the Seoul Bankruptcy Court (SBCourt) established "Procedural Guideline No. 504 (Cooperation between Courts in Cross-Border Insolvency Matters)" (hereinafter "Guideline No. 504"). In addition, in order to improve the efficiency and effectiveness of cross-border insolvency, the SBCourt concluded a Memorandum of Understanding (MoU) with the U.S. Bankruptcy Court for the Southern District of New York (SDNY) and the Supreme Court of Singapore in 2018.[4] All of these courts are members of the Judicial Insolvency Network (JIN), meaning that these MoUs are expected to facilitate cooperation between the courts. After concluding these MoUs, the SBCourt adopted JIN Guidelines and added Article 7 to Guideline No. 504 in July 2018, which provides as follows:

> Article 7 (Others) With regard to anything relating to the cooperation between courts not specified in Procedural Guideline No. 504, SBCourt may order to apply the "Guidelines for Communication and Cooperation between Courts in Cross-Border Insolvency Matters" established by Judicial Insolvency Network (JIN) to individual cases, in whole or in part, following an application by the parties or on its own motion.

South Korea, being categorized as a civil law country, is now quite positively attempting to change insolvency practice in order to establish an institutional framework for cooperation between courts. It is true that a few issues still remain to be discussed for future attempts to establish such systems, including eligible parties of an MoU. Whether Supreme Court of a particular country or an individual court of that country is eligible of an MoU still seems unclear. Nonetheless, these endeavors of South Korea are significant materials for other civil law countries.

The second development of note is a recent case in which the Korean judge directly communicated with the judge of the U.S. Bankruptcy Court for the Eastern District of Virginia in English. This case is introduced in the latter half of section 6.4.3 of the Kodek Report. This actual case is a good example of overcoming language barriers and is fairly suggestive to countries where English

---

[4] The details of the MoU between SBCourt and the U.S. Bankruptcy Court for the Southern District of New York are available at: http://www.nysb.uscourts.gov/outreach.

is not officially used. We should concretely learn from this actual case how the Korean judges succeeded in communicating by phone and/or via emails with the U.S. judges in English.

4. THE MEANING AND EFFECTS OF RECOGNITION

With respect of the effects of recognition, the Kodek Report analyzes the assimilation-of-effect theory and the extension model (sections 4.2.1 and 4.2.2). Assuming this dichotomy, the legal system of Japan for the recognition of foreign insolvency proceedings could be regarded as a third way. The legal framework for the recognition of and assistance for foreign insolvency proceedings is provided by the Act on Recognition of and Assistance for Foreign Insolvency Proceedings (Act No 129, 2000, hereinafter RAFIP). Under the RAFIP, a recognition order of a foreign insolvency proceeding, regardless of whether it is a main proceeding or not, does not have any automatic effects. The recognition order is a kind of "entrance ticket" or simply a general condition of granting individual assistance measures. The RAFIP provides for the following assistance measures:

- Stay Order, etc. on Other Procedures and Proceedings (Article 25).
- Prohibition of Disposition of Property, Prohibition of Payment and Other Dispositions (Article 26).
- Stay Order on Procedures for Exercising Security Interests, etc. (Article 27).
- Prohibition Order on Compulsory Execution, etc. (Article 28).[5]
- Administration Order (Article 32). This order includes the appointment of a recognition trustee.

The Tokyo District Court which has an exclusive jurisdiction over recognition cases will grant, on its discretion, assistance measures which are necessary and appropriate for the case in question. In this sense, this Japanese system could be categorized as a "Tailor-Made Relief" Model (section 4.3.3 of the Kodek Report).

In relation to "recognition," the following extract contains quotations from the Japan Report (JIN):

> Despite the RAFIP's emphasis on cooperation and coordination, it only addresses the recognition of the decision opening the foreign insolvency proceeding rather than the recognition ... of foreign insolvency decisions relating to ... confirming plans of reorganization.
>
> ...

---

5   Both Article 25 and Article 28 provide for stay on compulsory execution; the former provides for individual stay, and the latter provides for comprehensive stay.

Academic discussion in Japan suggests that the approach in Article 118 of [the] Civil Procedure Code which governs the matter of recognition of foreign Judgment should apply mutatis mutandis to the aforesaid matters. Item (ii) of Article 118 of [the] Civil Procedure Code requires, among other things, that "the defeated defendant has been served (excluding service by publication or any other service similar thereto) with the requisite summons or order for the commencement of litigation, or has appeared without being so served." However it is not clear whether the notice to creditors in foreign insolvency proceedings satisfied the requirement of "service" in Item (ii) of Article of 118. Academics now emphasize that the requirement of "service" under Item (ii) of Article 118 of [the] Civil Procedure Code should be interpreted in a flexible manner with regards to the recognition or enforcement of a decision confirming a plan of reorganization or a discharge of debts. The approach here should take into account elements, for example whether the plan has been sufficiently disclosed to the creditors, whether the creditors may appeal against the decision confirming the plan, and whether the creditors have the right to formulate and submit a plan of reorganization.

The "flexible" interpretation shown above might be unavoidable given the current Japanese insolvency law. This discussion reminds me of the Chapter 15 case of Elpida,[6] where a U.S. bankruptcy court recognized the confirmation of a reorganization plan confirmed in a Japanese insolvency proceeding. However, in order to enhance foreseeability, explicit legislation regarding the recognition of a foreign confirmation order of rehabilitation plans is certainly preferable. We need to discuss more about to what extent and in what way creditors' procedural rights to be noticed and to be heard should be protected.

---

[6]   In *re Elpida Memory, Inc.* No. 12-10947 (CSS) (Bankr. D. Del. filed March 19, 2012).

TRANSNATIONAL COOPERATION IN CROSS-BORDER INSOLVENCY

Georg KODEK*

1.	Introduction		195
2.	Sources and Methodology		198
3.	The Legal Basis for Cooperation		199
	3.1.	Introduction	199
	3.2.	UNCITRAL Model Laws	201
		3.2.1. The Model Law on Cross-Border Insolvency	201
		3.2.2. The UNCITRAL Model Law on Recognition and Enforcement of Insolvency-Related Judgments (2018)	203
		3.2.3. The UNCITRAL Model Law on Enterprise Group Insolvency	203
	3.3.	Europe	204
		3.3.1. The European Insolvency Convention (The Istanbul Convention)	204
		3.3.2. The European Insolvency Regulation	205
		3.3.3. Other EU Norms	206
	3.4.	Other Regional Developments	207
		3.4.1. The Scandinavian Insolvency Convention of 1933	207
		3.4.2. Latin America	208
		3.4.3. Central Africa	208
	3.5.	"Soft" Rules: Guidelines and Principles	209
	3.6.	The Singapore Convention	210
4.	Recognition of Foreign Decisions		211
	4.1.	Introduction	211
	4.2.	The Effects of Recognition	214
		4.2.1. Concepts of Recognition	214
		4.2.2. The Extension Model	215

---

* Judge at the Austrian Supreme Court (Oberster Gerichtshof) in Vienna and Professor of Civil and Commercial law at the Vienna University of Business and Economics (Wirtschaftsuniversität Wien (WU)).

Georg Kodek

4.2.3. The Scope of Effects of Recognition: Automatic
versus "Tailor-Made" Relief 217
4.2.4. Special Provisions for Assistance in the Foreign
Proceedings of Certain Countries 219
4.2.5. Impact on the Debtor's Status 220
4.2.6. The Powers of the Administrator 220
4.2.7. Evidentiary Consequences 223
4.3. Automatic Recognition versus Exequatur Proceedings 223
4.3.1. Exequatur Proceedings 223
4.3.2. Interim Relief 225
4.3.3. Automatic Recognition 226
4.4. Types of Decisions Recognised 228
4.4.1. Introduction 228
4.4.2. Judgments Opening the Proceeding 229
4.4.2.1. The Importance of Judgments Opening
the Proceedings 229
4.4.2.2. The Types of Proceedings Recognized 229
4.4.2.3. Retroactive Effects? 232
4.4.3. Other Administration Orders 233
4.4.4. Closure of Proceedings and Discharge 233
4.4.5. Preliminary Measures 235
4.4.6. Judgments in Related Proceedings 237
4.4.6.1. The Traditional View 237
4.4.6.2. The UNCITRAL Model Law on Recognition
and Enforcement of Insolvency-Related
Judgments 238
4.4.6.3. The EU 239
4.5. Prerequisites for Recognition 240
4.5.1. The Required Documents 240
4.5.2. *Res Judicata* Requirement? 241
4.5.3. Reciprocity 242
4.5.4. Jurisdiction of the Court Opening the Proceeding 243
4.6. Grounds for Non-Recognition 244
4.6.1. Public Policy 244
4.6.1.1. Opening Decisions and Administration
Orders 244
4.6.1.2. Related Judgments 248
4.6.2. Other Grounds 248
5. Enforcement of Foreign Decisions 249
5.1. Introduction 249
5.2. Opening of Insolvency Proceedings 250
5.3. Seizure and Sale of the Debtor's Assets 251

6. Coordination of Proceedings 251
  6.1. Introduction 251
  6.2. The "Hotchpot Rule" 252
  6.3. Cooperation between Administrators........................ 253
  6.4. Cooperation between Courts............................... 255
    6.4.1. Traditional Forms of Judicial Cooperation 255
    6.4.2. Direct Communication and Soft Law 255
    6.4.3. Selected Examples.................................... 257
    6.4.4. Joint Hearings 257
    6.4.5. Formalization of Cooperation......................... 258
    6.4.6. Civil Law Countries 259
7. Other Forms of Cooperation................................... 260
8. Conclusion.. 261

1. INTRODUCTION

The title of this chapter is "Transnational Cooperation in Cross-Border Insolvency."[1] Cooperation, of course, is much broader than just the "recognition" or "enforcement" of judgments. Indeed, many forms of cooperation have developed, in addition to recognition and enforcement, both between administrators and, even, between courts. Also, it will be shown that in insolvency law "recognition" of a judgment means something different from the recognition of "ordinary" judgments.

Let me start with a few impressions from news headlines from the corporate world: "First Recognition of Chinese Insolvency in New York,"[2] "Spanish Court

---

[1] The information available in existing publications was kindly supplemented by a number of people from around the world who deserve special credit and without whose generous support this report would not have been possible. All of them have completed questionnaires or have contributed in many other ways, e.g., by supplying articles or other information on their legal system. I would like to mention, in alphabetical order, Gert-Jan Boon, LL.M., MSc, Leiden University, the Netherlands; Professor Andre Boraine, University of Pretoria, South Africa; Professor Indrajit Dube, Rajiv Gandhi School of Intellectual Property Law, Indian Institute of Technology Kharagpur; Professor Jin Chun (金春) from Doshisha University, Japan; Young Seok Kim from the Seoul Bankruptcy Court; Professor Héctor José Miguens, Universidad Austral, Buenos Aires, Argentina, who supplied a host of information on South American law; Dr. Olha Stakheyeva-Bogovyk, Hillmont Partners, Kiev, Ukraine; Professor Roman Tomasic, University of South Australia; and, last but not least, Bingkun Ye, Senior Judge, Head of the Six Civil (Financial & Bankruptcy) Division at the Xiamen Intermediate People's Court, Fujian Province, China.

[2] B. CLARKE, "First Recognition Granted for Chinese Company's Contested Chapter 15" [2019] *Global Restructuring Review*, https://globalrestructuringreview.com/article/1209502/first-recognition-granted-for-chinese-company%E2%80%99s-contested-chapter-15. See also B. CLARKE, "Chinese Judgments Recognised and Enforced in BVI" [2020] *Global Restructuring Review*, https://globalrestructuringreview.com/article/1214566/chinese-judgments-recognised-and-enforced-in-bvi.

Blocks David Guetta Arbitration under EIR,"[3] or "Corporate Restructuring Summit in Dubai: Cross-Border Restructuring Saved Disgraced Abraaj's Assets."[4] Similarly, the Delaware Bankruptcy Court recently recognized an Indian textile company's bankruptcy case, in what counsel have called a vote of confidence in India's new restructuring regime.[5] An article appropriately entitled "The Epitome of a Cross-Border Restructuring" discusses the restructuring of Noble, a Bermuda-incorporated company, listed in Singapore, with a center of main interest (COMI) in Hong Kong.[6] Clearly, since the second half of the twentieth century, the modern world has been characterized by the increasing economic interdependence of various states. This makes it more likely that the insolvency of a debtor has effects in more than one country. Possible examples range from a debtor having some property in a foreign country (e.g., a bank account) to big corporations with production plants and facilities worldwide. Responses to cross-border insolvency issues include uniform insolvency laws, uniform choice of law rules, and uniform recognition rules.[7] Yet, the harmonization of substantive insolvency law is difficult, if not impossible, except for countries linked by a common legal tradition and close economic cooperation. In addition, states are reluctant to accept truly universal proceedings. States are jealous when dealing with insolvency cases due to political reasons and, accordingly, they are less willing to yield their sovereignty.[8] Consequently, for the foreseeable future, we are likely to have different national laws and concurrent proceedings. In light of this, it makes sense to focus on the recognition and enforcement of "foreign proceedings" and the coordination and cooperation between concurrent proceedings.[9]

---

[3] D. LAWSON, "Spanish Court Blocks David Guetta Arbitration under EIR" [2019] *Global Restructuring Review*, https://globalrestructuringreview.com/article/1209498/spanish-court-blocks-david-guetta-london-arbitration-under-eir.

[4] K. KARADELIS, "Corporate Restructuring Summit, Dubai: How a Cross-Border Restructuring Saved Disgraced Abraaj's Assets" [2019] *Global Restructuring Review*, https://globalrestructuringreview.com/article/1197520/corporate-restructuring-summit-dubai-how-a-cross-border-restructuring-saved-disgraced-abraaj%E2%80%99s-assets.

[5] D. BUSH, "India's SEL Manufacturing Obtains First Chapter 15 Recognition of IBC Bankruptcy" [2019] *Global Restructuring Review*, https://globalrestructuringreview.com/article/1210814/india%E2%80%99s-sel-manufacturing-obtains-first-chapter-15-recognition-of-ibc-bankruptcy.

[6] D. LAWSON, ""The Epitome of a Cross-Border Restructuring': Noble Unpacked" [2020] *Global Restructuring Review* https://globalrestructuringreview.com/article/1214694/%E2%80%809Cthe-epitome-of-a-cross-border-restructuring%E2%80%9D-noble-unpacked.

[7] R. MASON, "Cross-Border Insolvency and Legal Transnationalisation" (2012) 21 *International Insolvency Review* 105, 112 f.

[8] R. BORK and R. MANGANO, *European Cross-Border Insolvency Law*, Oxford University Press, Oxford 2016, para. 1.04; F.M. MUCCIARELLI, "Not Just Efficiency: Insolvency Law in the EU and its Political Dimension" (2013) 14 *European Business Organisation Law Review* 175.

[9] R. MASON, above n. 7, 117.

Cooperation in cross-border insolvency is part of a relatively young area of the law: international insolvency law. Writing more than 100 years ago, the famous German lawyer Heinrich Dernburg described cross-border insolvency as "one of the darkest and most controversial areas of the law."[10] More recently, an Australian judge stated that international insolvency law was "not an area for the faint hearted."[11] International insolvency can be defined as a situation "in which an insolvency occurs in circumstances which in some way transcend the confines of a single legal system, so that a single set of domestic insolvency law provisions cannot be immediately and exclusively applied without regard to the issues raised by the foreign elements of the case."[12] For the existence of such "foreign elements," it may suffice that the debtor has "assets in more than one State or some of his creditors are not from the State where the insolvency proceedings take place."[13]

The focus of this chapter will be on procedural questions, primarily the recognition and enforcement of foreign decisions, although other forms of cooperation will also be taken into account. While this author obviously comes from a civil law (and European) background, I will also attempt to give due regard to other legal systems. International insolvency law has developed radically in the past 30 years or so. There is the United Nations Commission on International Trade Law (UNCITRAL) Model Law and related texts, the European Insolvency Regulation (EIR) and other rules at the European Union (EU) level, there are regional international conventions, as well as developments in national law. In addition, there are various texts with recommendations which may constitute a source of "soft law." Therefore, the subject is vast. In light of the sheer amount of research already available,[14] it would be presumptuous to even remotely attempt

---

10   H. DERNBURG, *Preußisches Privatrecht*, 5th ed., Verlag der Buchhandlung des Waisenhauses, Halle 1894, §290 fn. 16.

11   N. PERRAM, "Issues in Recognition and Enforcement of Foreign Insolvency Judgments: An Australian Perspective" [2016] *Federal Judicial Scholarship* 13.

12   I.F. FLETCHER, "International Insolvency: The Way Ahead" (1993) 2 *International Insolvency Review* 15. It should be noted that this definition is by no means universally accepted. According to B. WESSELS, *International Insolvency Law*, 3rd ed., Kluwer, Deventer 2012, para. 1001, international insolvency law describes "a body of rules concerning certain insolvency proceedings or measures, which cannot be fully enforced, because the applicable law cannot be executed immediately and exclusively without consideration being given to the international aspect of a given case." A similar definition is proposed by R. BORK and R. MANGANO, above n. 8, para 1.04. R. GOODE, *Principles of Corporate Insolvency Law*, 4th ed., Sweet & Maxwell, London 2011, p. 78 fn. 5 describes international insolvencies as "insolvencies which arise from cross-border trading or which involve the application, or possible application, of the insolvency laws to two or more jurisdictions." J.L. WESTBROOK, "A Global Solution to Multinational Default" (2000) 98 *Michigan Law Review* 2276, 2278 defines international insolvency somewhat narrowly as "the management of the general financial default of a multinational enterprise."

13   Guide to the UNICTRAL Model Law on Cross-Border Insolvency.

14   See below section 2 of this chapter.

to summarize what has been written on the subject. Therefore, I had to narrow my subject accordingly. This chapter will focus primarily on the UNCITRAL Model Law, because it is the most widely used recognition scheme, and on the EIR, because it provides for the highest level of cooperation and the most liberal recognition regime. Rather than just discussing these documents one after the other, this chapter will attempt a "horizontal" description, i.e., a discussion of particular aspects of international cooperation not country by country or instrument by instrument, but issue by issue. After a brief discussion of the available sources (section 2), I will first describe the legal basis for recognition (section 3), ranging from domestic law to bilateral treaties to multilateral conventions, the UNCITRAL Model Law (or, to be precise, Model Laws) and various "soft" law instruments. The text will then proceed to a discussion of the recognition of foreign decisions (section 4) and their enforcement (section 5). The subsequent sections will deal with the coordination of proceedings (section 6) and other forms of cooperation (section 7). At the end, a brief conclusion will be drawn (section 8).

2. SOURCES AND METHODOLOGY

Traditionally, General Reports of the World Congress are prepared on the basis of country reports. In light of the vast amount of information already available on this subject, it was decided to modify this procedure. There is a wealth of publications, both in the form of books and articles, as well as online, by practitioners and academics covering every aspect of international insolvency law.[15] In addition to many works dealing with the various forms of cooperation in international insolvency laws, there are comparative country-by-country descriptions of insolvency laws worldwide. Also, a lot of useful information is available online from the International Insolvency Institute (III)[16] and

---

[15] In addition to the sources cited below, see, e.g., J.W. Boone (ed.), *International Insolvency: Jurisdictional Comparisons*, 3rd ed., Thomson Reuters, London 2012; R. Bork, *Principles on Cross-Border Insolvency Law*, Intersentia, Cambridge 2017; R.M. Buxbaum, "Trans-border Insolvency: A Generation Later" in W. Moll (ed.), *Festschrift für Hans-Jochem Lüer*, C.H. Beck, Munich 2008, p. 349; I.F. Fletcher, *Insolvency in Private International Law*, 2nd ed., Oxford University Press, Oxford 2005; L.C. Ho, *Cross-Border Insolvency: Principles and Practice*, Sweet & Maxwell, London 2016; L.C. Ho (ed.), *Cross-Border Insolvency: A Commentary on the UNCITRAL Model Law*, 4th ed., Globe Publishing, London 2017; J.R. Silkenat and C.D. Schmerler, *The Law of International Insolvencies and Debt Restructuring*, Oceana, Dobbs Ferry 2006; B. Wessels, B.A. Markell, and J.J. Kilborn, *International Cooperation in Bankruptcy and Insolvency Matters*, Oxford University Press, Oxford 2009. For a more conceptual approach, see I. Merovach, *The Future of Cross-Border Insolvency: Overcoming Biases and Closing Gaps*, Oxford University Press, Oxford 2018.
[16] www.iiiglobal.org.

INSOL International.[17] In addition, there are specialized research projects such as the University of Leyden project on insolvency protocols.[18] Thus, it would not make sense to duplicate the efforts that have already been undertaken by others in other contexts.[19] Rather, it was decided to base the report in large measure on existing sources and try to present a compact overview of the research that has been undertaken in this field so far.[20] In addition, we received a number of country reports and other valuable information from contributors around the world.[21]

3. THE LEGAL BASIS FOR COOPERATION

3.1. INTRODUCTION

In the common law, there is a long tradition of recognizing and assisting foreign insolvency proceedings.[22] There, courts have recognized foreign insolvency proceedings taking place in the jurisdiction in which the debtor was domiciled for over 200 years.[23] Similarly, English courts sought from an early stage to protect the effective administration of insolvency proceedings taking place in England.[24] Recognition in appropriate cases entailed not only allowing such a person to come before English courts to recover property, but also the "active assistance of the court."[25] Also, the U.S. courts have long been open to cooperation with foreign bankruptcy proceedings.[26]

However, in most countries, the regulation of collective insolvency proceedings has historically been statutorily based with little regard for connections with other jurisdictions.[27] Traditional positions in national legal systems in some cases limited the effects of proceedings opened in their country

---

[17]   www.insol.org.

[18]   www.universiteitleiden.nl/en/research/research-projects/law/insolvency-protocols-project.

[19]   Indeed, the amount of research already available may well make it difficult to organize conferences on so broad a topic in the future. Perhaps more limited topics would be preferable in order to achieve a more thorough discussion and actual progress.

[20]   For the benefit of international readers, I tried to use English-language sources whenever possible.

[21]   See supra note 1.

[22]   See T. SMITH, "Recognition of Foreign Corporate Insolvency Proceedings at Common Law" in R. SHELDON (ed.), *Cross-Border Insolvency*, 4th ed., Bloomsbury, London 2015, paras. 6.1 f.

[23]   The earliest case seems to be *Solomons v. Ross* [1764] 1 H Bl 131n, Wallis 59n. See R. SHELDON, "Introduction" in R. SHELDON, above n. 20, para. 1.2.

[24]   Ibid., para. 1.3.

[25]   Ibid., para. 1.5.

[26]   The first case cited is *Canadian S Ry v. Gebhard* [1883] 109 US 527.

[27]   R. MASON, above n. 7, 106; for an outline of English and Australian recognition of international elements, see R. MASON, "Cross-Border insolvency: Adoption of CLERP 8 as an Evolution of Australian Insolvency Law" (2003) 11 *Insolvency Law Journal* 62.

Intersentia

to its own territory.[28] Others, while claiming the universal effect of their own proceedings, at the same time denied recognition to foreign proceedings. The latter position was aptly described as "robbery system" ("système de pillage").[29]

Occasionally, there were bilateral treaties providing for the recognition of insolvency proceedings.[30] The earliest such treaties were entered into in the middle of the nineteenth century. Examples include treaties between Austria-Hungary and Wurttemberg, Baden, Prussia, and some Swiss cantons.[31] An example is the Mutual Declaration (Gegenseitige Deklaration) of the imperial royal Austrian government and the Small Council of the canton of St. Gallen, Switzerland, of June 1, 1842.[32] Some of these treaties may still be in force.[33] Such treaties were entered into up to the 1970s.[34] In 1925, an international model bankruptcy treaty proposed by the Hague Conference was not adopted.[35] Also, in the first half of the twentieth century, regional insolvency treaties were entered into in South America and Scandinavia.[36]

Thus, for a long time, international insolvency law was to a large degree a matter of national law, or, at most, regulated by bilateral treaties. This changed in the 1980s. These years marked a turning point, as the Swiss delegation put it at the conference of European Ministers of Justice in Madrid in 1984: "la faillite se trouve à un tournant historique."[37] The reasons for this are the internationalization of national economies and the spectacular collapses over the last 25 years (Bank of Credit and Commerce International (BCCI), Robert Maxwell, Barings Bank, Lehman Brothers, Bernie Madoff).[38] These developments contributed to the concept of "universalism" of insolvency proceedings becoming more widely accepted. In general, universalism would ideally treat a multinational bankruptcy

---

[28]   An example is Austria. See OGH 8 Ob 580/93 *ÖBA* 1994, 567 = *RdW* 1994, 247; OGH 7 Ob 663/85; OGH 2 Ob 517/89 *IPRE* 3/5; OGH 2 Ob 316/99f; see also R. Keppelmüller, *Österreichisches Internationales Konkursrecht*, Verlag Österreich, Vienna 1997, paras. 46 f (citing further authority at para. 41).

[29]   Ibid., para. 73.

[30]   See, e.g., G. Graf, *Die Anerkennung ausländischer Insolvenzentscheidungen*, Mohr Siebeck, Tübingen 2003, p. 171; K. Nadelmann, "Bankruptcy Treaties" (1944) 93 *University of Pennsylvania Law Review* 58, 67.

[31]   See F. Meili, *Moderne Staatsverträge über das internationale Konkursrecht*, Orell Füssli, Zürich 1907; B. Wiesbauer, "Internationales Insolvenzrecht" [1983] *(Austrian) Richterzeitung* 266, 268; see also R. Keppelmüller, above n. 28, para. 18.

[32]   The text is reprinted in F. Meili, above n. 31, pp. 32 f.

[33]   See V. Boll, *Die Anerkennung des Auslandskonkurses*, Manz, Vienna 1990, p. 53.

[34]   On the treaty between France and Austria of 1979, see G. Graf, above n. 28, p. 126.

[35]   K. Nadelmann, above n. 30, 67.

[36]   It has been pointed out, correctly, that regional insolvency treaties are only successful where states share generally close legal and cultural affinities. See S. Jackson and R. Mason, "Developments in Court-to-Court Communications in International Insolvency Cases" (2014) 37 *UNSW Law Journal* 507, 537.

[37]   "Tendances récentes et perspectives d'avenir en matière de droit de la faillite," Rapport présenté par la délégation de la Suisse, Conseil de l'Europe, Strasbourg 1984, MJU-14 (84) 1.

[38]   R. Mason, above n. 7, 105.

as a unified global proceeding administered by a single court assisted by courts in other countries, while territorialism is the traditional approach by which each court in a country in which assets are found seizes them (the "grab rule").[39]

While there have been tendencies toward international cooperation in the past, the efforts to institutionalize such cooperation dramatically gained momentum from the 1980s. Examples include the work on the European Insolvency Convention (which was later to become the EIR) and on the Istanbul Convention and later work on the UNICTRAL Model Law. These truly international efforts in large measure superseded the traditional approach of bilateral treaties.

3.2. UNCITRAL MODEL LAWS

3.2.1. *The Model Law on Cross-Border Insolvency*

In 1966, the United Nations Organization (UNO) established the UNCITRAL in order to further the harmonization and unification of international trade law. The Commission, which is based in Vienna, has since formulated harmonized rules on commercial transactions and, among them, has prepared conventions, model laws, legal and legislative guides, and recommendations.[40] The most important document for the present purposes is the UNCITRAL Model Law on Cross-Border Insolvency,[41] which was published in 1997 together with a Guide to Enactment and Interpretation. In addition, UNCITRAL published Legislative Guides[42] and Recommendations and Explanatory Texts. The latter include "Model Law on Cross-Border Insolvency: The Judicial Perspective" and "Practice Guide on Cross-Border Insolvency Cooperation".

The UNCITRAL Model Law, as the name suggests, is not a binding instrument, but a template for national legislatures. They do not have to adopt it, or can adopt it entirely or in part in a way which best fits into their existing national law. Because the Model Law is to serve as a model worldwide, it goes

---

[39]   J.L. WESTBROOK, "Chapter 15 at Last" (2005) 79 *American Bankrutpcy Law Journal* 713.

[40]   R. BORK and R. MANGANO, above n. 8, para. 1.19.

[41]   On this, see G. HERMANN, "The Role of UNICTRAL," in I.F. FLETCHER, L. MISTELIS, and M. CREMONA (eds.), *Foundations and Perspectives of International Trade Law*, Sweet & Maxwell, London 2001, 28; C. TOBLER, "Managing Failure in the New Global Economy: The UNCITRAL Model Law on Cross-Border Insolvency" (1999) 22 *Boston College International and Comparative Law Review* 383. A skeptical position is taken by S.C. MOHAN, "Cross-Border Insolvency: Is the UNCITRAL Model Law the Answer?" (2012) 21 *International Insolvency Review* 199 f.

[42]   These Legislative Guides comprise four parts. Two deal with "Insolvency Law" in general, the third part deals with groups of companies, and the fourth part with directors' obligations in the period approaching insolvency.

Intersentia

less far than the EIR. It does not contain provisions on jurisdictions or applicable law; rather, it only addresses issues concerning access, recognition, relief (assistance), and cooperation.[43] Therefore, the Model Law has been described as an important but modest stride toward the fair and efficient management of cross-border insolvencies.[44]

Four key principles of the UNCITRAL Model Law have been identified.[45] The *access* principle establishes the circumstances in which a "foreign representative" has rights of access to the receiving court in the enacting state from which recognition and relief are sought. Under the *recognition* principle, the receiving court may make an order recognizing the foreign proceedings (either as a foreign main or non-main proceeding). Under the *relief* principle, interim relief may be granted to protect assets within the jurisdiction of the receiving court, automatic relief applies if a receiving court recognizes the foreign proceedings as main proceedings, discretionary relief is available in certain circumstances. The *cooperation and coordination* principle places obligations on both courts and administrators in different jurisdictions to communicate and cooperate in order to ensure that the single debtor's estate is administered fairly and efficiently.

The UNCITRAL Model Law establishes simplified rules for recognition and gives liquidators and creditors a right of access to the courts of an enacting state in order to seek assistance. Also, it provides for interim relief between the filing of an application for recognition and the decision. Finally, it allows courts to cooperate in the areas covered by the Model Law and to communicate directly with foreign counterparts.[46] Notably, the Model Law only provides for the recognition of the judgment opening proceedings, but not of other judgments rendered in the course of insolvency proceedings such as a discharge.[47]

The Model Law was adopted by 47 states,[48] including a number of EU Member States (Greece, Poland, Slovenia), the United Kingdom, Australia,[49] and the United States.[50] While some states have enacted separate laws (e.g., the United Kingdom),

---

[43]   R. BORK and R. MANGANO, above n. 8, para. 1.22.

[44]   L.C. HO, "Overview" in L.C. HO (ed.), *Cross-Border Insolvency: A Commentary on the UNCITRAL Model Law*, above n. 15, p. 14; see also J.L. WESTBROOK, above n. 39, 713 fn. 23: "A journey of a 1000 miles begins with a single step."

[45]   R. MASON, above n. 7, 119 f.

[46]   Guide to the UNCITRAL Model Law on Cross-Border Insolvency, para. 19.

[47]   J.L. WESTBROOK, "Chapter 15 and Discharge" (2005) 13 *American Bankruptcy Institute Law Review* 503.

[48]   For the current status of adoption of the Model Law, see, https://uncitral.un.org/en/texts/insolvency/modellaw/cross-border_insolvency/status.

[49]   In Australia, the text of the Cross-Border Insolvency Act is somewhat unusual, in that the Model Law is included as a Schedule to the Act. This method of enactment is described as "clumsy" by S. MAIDEN, "A Comparative Analysis of the Use of the UNCITRAL Model Law on Cross-Border Insolvency in Australia, Great Britain and the United States" (2010) 18 *Insolvency Law Journal* 63, 64.

[50]   Chapter 15 of the US Bankruptcy Code.

others have incorporated the Model Law into their insolvency codes (e.g., the United States) or companies acts (e.g., Singapore). Some other countries seem to have adopted the Model Law in all but name.[51]

For EU Member States, the Model Law offers a complementary regime for cases not covered by the EIR, in particular cases where the COMI is outside the EU.[52] It was also suggested that the Model Law should be adopted by the EU as it was not in conflict with existing EU regulations.[53] Furthermore, Recital 48 EIR states that in the cooperation between insolvency practitioners and courts involved in main and secondary proceedings, "insolvency practitioners and courts should take into account best practices for cooperation in cross-border insolvency cases ... and in particular relevant guidelines prepared by the United Nations Commission on International Trade Law (UNCITRAL)".

3.2.2. The UNCITRAL Model Law on Recognition and Enforcement of Insolvency-Related Judgments (2018)

In 2018, UNCITRAL published a Model Law on Recognition and Enforcement of Insolvency-Related Judgments together with a Guide on Enactment. The Model Law on Recognition and Enforcement of Insolvency-Related Judgments (MLIJ) is designed to address those situations and provide States with a simple, straightforward, and harmonized procedure for the recognition and enforcement of insolvency-related judgments, thus complementing the Model Law on Cross-Border Insolvency (MLCBI) to further assist the conduct of cross-border insolvency proceedings.[54]

3.2.3. The UNCITRAL Model Law on Enterprise Group Insolvency

In 2019, an advance copy of the UNCITRAL Model Law on Enterprise Group Insolvency was published.[55] According to Article 1, the purpose of this Law is to provide effective mechanisms to address cases of insolvency affecting the members of an enterprise group in order to promote the objectives of: (a) cooperation between courts and other competent authorities of this state and foreign states involved in those cases; (b) cooperation between insolvency representatives appointed in this state and foreign states in those cases; (c) the development

---

51   See, e.g., for the Cayman Islands *Re Straumur-Burduras Investment Bank hf* [2010] 2 CILR 146.

52   See Guide to the UNCITRAL Model Law on Cross-Border Insolvency, para. 11.

53   See INSOL Europe, *Revision on the European Insolvency Regulation* (2012) 15.

54   See also INSOL International, *UNCITRAL's Model Law on Recognition and Enforcement of Insolvency-Related Judgments: A Universalist Approach to Cross-Border Insolvency* (2019).

55   https://uncitral.un.org/sites/uncitral.un.org/files/media-documents/uncitral/en/mlegi_-_advance_pre-published_version_-_e.pdf.

of a group insolvency solution for the whole or part of an enterprise group and cross-border recognition and implementation of that solution in multiple states; (d) the fair and efficient administration of insolvencies concerning enterprise group members that protects the interests of all creditors of those enterprise group members and other interested persons, including the debtors; (e) the protection and maximization of the overall combined value of the assets and operations of enterprise group members affected by insolvency and of the enterprise group as a whole; (f) the facilitation of the rescue of financially troubled enterprise groups, thereby protecting investment and preserving employment; and (g) the adequate protection of the interests of the creditors of each enterprise group member participating in a group insolvency solution and of other interested persons. The Model Law provides for cooperation and direct communication between courts, insolvency representatives, and any group representative appointed (Article 9) and, among other things, for the coordination of hearings (Article 12). The key term of the Model Law is "planning proceeding", which is defined as a main proceeding commenced in respect of an enterprise group member provided (inter alia) that one or more other enterprise group members are participating in that main proceeding for the purpose of developing and implementing a group insolvency solution (Article 2(g)). The recognition of a foreign planning proceeding is regulated in Article 23.

3.3. EUROPE

3.3.1. *The European Insolvency Convention (The Istanbul Convention)*

In 1980, following an initiative taken by Switzerland, the Council of Europe commenced work at a European Insolvency Convention.[56] At that time, the project looked promising because the parallel efforts of the EU did not make progress.[57] The Convention was signed in Istanbul in 1990, but never entered into force because it failed to achieve the required ratification by three states. The Convention did not contain direct rules on jurisdiction; rather, it addressed international jurisdiction only as a requirement for recognition. It provided for the automatic recognition of foreign decisions opening a main proceeding (provided the decision was rendered in the country of the debtor's COMI) and allowed the administrator in all contracting states, without formal recognition proceedings, to take any acts to administer, manage, or dispose of the debtor's assets, including removing them from the territory of the state where they are situated.

---

[56] See I.F. FLETCHER, above n. 15, paras. 6.01 ff.
[57] See below, section 3.3.2.

3.3.2. The European Insolvency Regulation

In the EU, work on a European Insolvency Convention started in 1963. Drafts published in 1980 and 1984, respectively, turned out to be too complicated. It took until 1995 to come up with a text that was ready for adoption. A further delay resulted from political disagreements. Reportedly, because of the continental European ban on the import of British beef as a consequence of a break-out of bovine spongiform encephalopathy (BSE), the United Kingdom refused to sign the Convention. The official explanation was that the status of Gibraltar was not clear. Only after the Treaty of Amsterdam enabled the EU to issue regulations (inter alia) in the area of international private law and international civil procedure (and after the import ban for beef had been lifted) was the EIR issued in 2000.[58] It has since been replaced by the recast EIR.[59]

In essence, the EIR brought a system of modified universalism with secondary proceedings being permitted in states where the debtor has an establishment. Because secondary proceedings are still permissible, the system of the EIR has been described as "limited" or "cropped" universalism.[60] Notably, it also contains direct rules on international jurisdiction (*compétence directe*) and choice-of-law provisions.

As to the recognition of foreign decisions, the EIR basically provides for automatic recognition. It expressly forbids any formal procedures as requirements for recognition.[61] Therefore, there is no exequatur or similar proceeding.[62] The provisions of the EIR concerning recognition have been described by many observers as its centerpiece.[63] The EIR is built on the principle of mutual trust[64] and seeks to afford universality to (main) insolvency proceedings.[65] It does not

---

[58] Council Regulation (EC) 1346/2000 of 29 May 2000 on insolvency proceedings [2000] OJ L160/1.

[59] Regulation (EU) 2015/848 of the European Parliament and of the Council of 20 May 2015 on insolvency proceedings [2015] OJ L141/19.

[60] J. Taupitz, "Das (zukünftige) europäische Internationale Insolvenzrecht – insbesondere aus international-privatrechtlicher Sicht" (1998) 111 *Zeitschrift für Zivilprozess* 315, 325; see also G.W. Johnson, "The European Union Convention on Insolvency Proceedings: A Critique of the Convention's Corporate Rescue Paradigm" (1996) 5 *International Insolvency Review* 80, 83: "controlled universalism."

[61] See Art. 19(1), providing for recognition from the point at which the judgment becomes effective. See also Arts. 20(1) and 32(1), providing for recognition without "further formalities".

[62] R. Goode, above n. 12, paras. 15 ff; M. Virgós and F. Garcimartín, *The European Insolvency Regulation: Law and Practice*, Kluwer, Deventer 2004, para. 344; R. Bork and R. Mangano, above n. 8, para. 5.06.

[63] See G. Moss and T. Smith, in G. Moss, I.F. Fletcher and S. Isaacs (eds.), *The EC Regulation on Insolvency Proceedings: A Commentary and Annotated Guide*, 3rd ed., Oxford University Press, Oxford 2016, para. 8.288; K. Pannen and S. Riedemann, in K. Pannen (ed.), *European Insolvency Regulation*, De Gruyter, Berlin 2007, Art. 16, para. 1.

[64] Cf. Recital 65 EIR; B. Wessels, above n. 12, para. 10466.

[65] R. Bork and R. Mangano, above n. 8, para. 5.04.

Intersentia

contain provisions about the recognition of insolvency proceedings opened in non-Member States. As to non-Member States, recognition and cooperation is governed by national law.

The effects of Brexit on international cooperation in insolvency law are not yet clear. The Withdrawal Agreement[66] does not contain any rules in this respect. Therefore, the long-term impact of Brexit will depend on whether the EU and the United Kingdom will be able to work out an agreement on this area of the law.[67]

3.3.3. Other EU Norms

In addition to the EIR, there are a number of other EU norms dealing with various aspects of international insolvency law. These acts have been described as a "system of cross-border insolvency" which was claimed to form a "hermeneutic circle within which interpretation should be made".[68] These rules include Directive 2001/17/EC of the European Parliament and of the Council of March 19, 2001 on the reorganization and winding-up of insurance undertakings,[69] Directive 2014/59/EU of the European Parliament and of the Council of May 15, 2014 establishing a framework for the recovery and resolution of credit institutions and investment firms and amending Council Directive 82/891/EEC, Directives 2001/24/EC, 2002/47/EC, 2004/25/EC, 2005/56/EC, 2007/36/EC, 2011/35/EC, 2012/30/EU and 2013/36/EU, and Regulation (EU) Nos. 1093/2010 and (EU) 648/2012 of the European Parliament and of the Council.[70] These rules primarily deal with two fields which fall outside the scope of application of the EIR, namely insurance and banking law. The EU Bank Recovery and Resolution Directive (BRRD, 2014/59/EU) governs resolution, while liquidation is regulated by national insolvency laws.

For sake of completeness, it should be added that there are a number of other EU norms which, while not primarily addressing international insolvency law, may have a bearing on international insolvency law as well. These documents include the "Communication from the Commission to the European Parliament, the Council and the European Economic and Social Committee on a new European approach to business failure and insolvency" and the "Commission Recommendation on a new approach to business failure and insolvency".[71]

---

66   Agreement on the withdrawal of the United Kingdom of Great Britain and Northern Ireland from the European Union and the European Atomic Energy Community (2019/C 384 I/01).
67   See C. UMFREVILLE et al., "Recognition of UK Insolvency Proceedings Post-Brexit: The Impact of a 'No Deal' Scenario" (2018) 27 *International Insolvency Review* 422.
68   M. VIRGÓS and F. GARCIMARTÍN, above n. 62, paras. 8 ff.
69   [2001] OJ L110/38.
70   [2014] OJ L173/190.
71   C(2014)1500 final.

Both documents express the Commission's intention to place greater emphasis on rescuing businesses. Recently, these efforts culminated in the Directive on restructuring and insolvency.[72] Finally, general procedural provisions such as the Service Regulation[73] and the Evidence Regulation[74] may also be applied in cross-border insolvency proceedings.

3.4. OTHER REGIONAL DEVELOPMENTS

3.4.1. *The Scandinavian Insolvency Convention of 1933*

From a European perspective, the Scandinavian Insolvency Convention of 1933, concluded between Denmark, Finland, Iceland, Norway, and Sweden, clearly marks the beginning of closer multinational cooperation in insolvency law.[75] These countries are quite homogeneous, which is also reflected by the rule that in all five countries, the languages of the proceeding is to be Norwegian, Swedish, or Danish. The Convention was revised in 1977 (the Copenhagen Convention Amendment) and in 1982 (the Copenhagen Convention Amendment). While the Convention provides for the recognition of insolvency proceedings opened in other signatory countries, it does not contain rules about jurisdiction. Thus, from a typological point of view, the Convention is a "single" convention.

The Convention only applies if the domicile or seat of the debtor is in the country where the proceedings are opened. The opening of insolvency proceedings in any of the Nordic countries is immediately recognized in all of the other contracting states, without the need of any exequatur proceedings.[76] Unless otherwise provided for in the Convention, the *lex fori concursus* determines the effects of the bankruptcy.

---

[72] Directive (EU) 1023/2019 of the European Parliament and of the Council of June 20, 2019 on preventive restructuring frameworks, on discharge of debt and disqualifications, and on measures to increase the efficiency of procedures concerning restructuring, insolvency and discharge of debt, and amending Directive 2017/1132 [2019] OJ L172/18.

[73] Regulation (EC) 1393/2007 of the European Parliament and of the Council on the service in the Member States of judicial and extrajudicial documents in civil or commercial matters (service of documents), and repealing Council Regulation (EC) 1348/2000 [2007] OJ L324/79.

[74] Council Regulation (EC) 1206/2001 of 28 May 2001 on cooperation between the courts of the Member States in the taking of evidence in civil or commercial matters [2001] OJ L174/1.

[75] An English and French translation of the Convention is published in *The League of Nations Treaty Series* (1935) 133. On the Convention, see C.H. PARMENT, "The Nordic Bankruptcy Convention: An Introduction" (2004), https://www.iiiglobal.org/sites/default/files/2-_Nordic_Bankruptcy.pdf2019; and I.F. FLETCHER, above n. 15, paras. 5.30 ff.

[76] Article 1(1) of the Convention.

Intersentia

3.4.2. Latin America

South America is an example of an area where steps toward closer multinational cooperation in insolvency matters were taken quite quickly.[77] Already in 1889, Argentina, Bolivia, Columbia, and Peru signed the Montevideo Convention.[78] The Convention deals with international commercial law. Title X (with 14 articles) deals with "Bankruptcies". In 1928, 15 Latin American states signed the Havana Convention on International Private Law, which is commonly referred to as Code Bustamante, named after Dr. Bustamante, its "spiritus rector". Originally there were to be separate insolvency proceedings in each country; however, the Montevideo Convention provided for judicial assistance for securing the debtor's assets. A genuine "universal" effect of the proceedings was only provided for by the Havana Convention of 1928, which also includes some rules on international private law. Although the Code Bustamante provides for cross-border enforcement of bankruptcy matters, it does not address the relationship among insolvency proceedings taking place in a number of countries, nor does it provide a means of coordination among courts or administrators.

3.4.3. Central Africa

In 1993, in Sub-Saharan Africa, OHADA was founded. OHADA is the acronym for the French "Organisation pour l'harmonisation en Afrique du droit des affaires", which translates into English as "Organization for the Harmonization of Business Law in Africa". Its 14 Member States have a population of approximately 170 million. OHADA drafted a Uniform Code which also contained provisions on international insolvency law.[79] While the Code provided for the recognition of proceedings from other Member States and the administrator could exercise, within the OHADA territory, all the powers conferred on him/her by the Uniform Act, the opening of an insolvency proceeding in one state would not constitute a bar to secondary proceedings. More recently, in 2015 the OHADA states introduced a new Uniform Act on Insolvency which basically enacted the UNCITRAL Model Law on Cross-Border Insolvency.[80]

---

[77] For the following, see J.M. DOBSON, "Treaty Developments in Latin America" in I.F. FLETCHER (ed.), *Cross-Border Insolvency: Comparative Dimensions*, United Kingdom National Committee of Comparative Law, London 1990, p. 237; see also T.B. FELSBERG, "Cross-Border Insolvencies and Restructurings in Brazil 2003" (2003), https://www.iiiglobal.org/sites/default/files/9-_Cross%20Border%20%28012703%29%202.pdf.

[78] I.F. FLETCHER, above n. 15, paras. 5.01 and 5.20 ff.

[79] Acte uniforme portant organization des procedures collectives d'apurement du passif, adopted April 10, 1998 in Libreville (Gabon). On this law, see S.M. ZOUNGRANA, *Les Faillites Internationales dans l'espace OHADA: Ou les Faillites internationales en droit OHADA*, Editions Universitaires Européennes, Saarbrücken 2012.

[80] OHADA Acte Uniforme portant Organisation des Procédures collectives d'Apurement du Passif 2015. See C. VAN ZUYELEN, "South Africa and OHADA member states" in

3.5. "SOFT" RULES: GUIDELINES AND PRINCIPLES

In addition to the instruments mentioned above, a number of documents aim to achieve the cooperation or harmonization of insolvency law in a "soft", i.e., non-binding way. While all of these texts are not binding in the technical sense, they paved the way for binding provisions such as the UNCITRAL Model Laws and the recast version of the EIR.

One of the first such attempts to institutionalize cooperation in cross-border insolvency proceedings was the International Bar Association's Model International Insolvency Cooperation Act 1989 (MIICA). This was a draft model law which did not contain rules on jurisdiction for insolvency proceedings, but encouraged auxiliary proceedings and provided mechanisms by which courts would act in aid of foreign proceedings.[81] Although it was a useful step in the evolution of modern approaches to deal with cross-border insolvency cases, no state adopted MIICA as domestic legislation.[82] In 1996, the IBA adopted an approach of encouraging uniform recognition through the action of the parties themselves. It approved a Cross-Border Insolvency Concordat[83] that provided some generalized principles intended to guide practitioners (and courts) in harmonizing cross-border insolvencies. The Concordat was applied in several cases by courts, in one case even before it had been finally adopted.[84] In a broader sense, the International Monetary Fund (IMF)'s "Orderly and Effective Insolvency Procedures" and the World Bank's "Principles and Guidelines for Building Effective Insolvency Systems and Debtor-Creditor Regimes" (2005) could also be mentioned here, even though they, for the most part, deal with domestic rather than international bankruptcy law.

A number of recommendations and guidelines specifically aim at the resolution of cross-border insolvency issues by way of agreement between the parties themselves and direct cooperation between courts. Often, these documents reflect existing "best practice".[85] In 2000, the American Law Institute (ALI)

L.C. Ho (ed.), *Cross-Border Insolvency: A Commentary on the UNCITRAL Model Law*, above n. 15, p. 576; A. FENEON, "Les aspects internationaux des procedures collectives OHADA" [2017] *Penant* 397.

[81] T.E. POWERS, R.R. MEARS, and J.A. BARRET, "The Model International Insolvency Co-operation Act" in E.B. LEONARD and C.W. BESANT (eds.), *Current Issues in Cross-Border Insolvency and Reorganisations*, Graham & Trotman and International Bar Association, London 1994.

[82] R. MASON, above n. 7, 118.

[83] M. PERRY, "Lining up at the Border: Renewing the Call for a Canada-US Insolvency Convention in the 21st Century" (2000) 10 *Duke Journal of Comparative & International Law* 469, 581 fn. 61.

[84] See R. MASON, above n. 7, 119 fn. 81.

[85] B. WESSELS and M. VIRGÓS, "Accommodating Cross-Border Coordination: European Communication and Cooperation Guidelines for Cross Border Insolvency" (2007) 10 *International Corporate Rescue* 1.

and the International Insolvency Institute (III) published "Guidelines Applicable to Court-to-Court Communication in Cross-Border Cases".[86] In 2007, a group of practitioners proposed "European Communication and Cooperation Guidelines for Cross-Border Insolvency (CoCo Guidelines)".[87] These Guidelines were adopted by INSOL Europe in 2007.[88] The CoCo Guidelines provide non-binding rules for, inter alia, direct access by an insolvency practitioner to a foreign court, the duty of practitioners to communicate, and the coordination of sales and cross-border rescues. It also annexes a Draft Protocol for use in cross-border cases. Its terms have been considered in cases such as *BenQ Holding, Automold, Pin AG, Landsbanki-Icesave, Kaupthing, Lehman Brothers Holdings* (where the global protocol made express mention of the text) and *Nortel Network*.[89] Currently, a revised version of these guidelines (CoCo 2.0) is being worked out.[90]

In 2009, the UNCITRAL "Practice Guide on Cross-Border Insolvency Cooperation" was adopted.[91] Also in 2009, the International Insolvency Institute (III)'s Committee on International Jurisdiction and Cooperation worked out a Prospective Model International Cross-Border Insolvency Protocol.[92] In 2012, ALI developed Global Principles for Cooperation in International Insolvency Cases and Global Guidelines for Court-to-Court Communications in International Insolvency Cases.[93]

3.6. THE SINGAPORE CONVENTION

For the sake of completeness, the UN Convention on International Settlement Agreements Resulting from Mediation (hereinafter "the Singapore Mediation Convention")[94] also has to be mentioned. While clearly not primarily aimed

---

[86]   https://www.iiiglobal.org/sites/default/files/7-_ali.pdf.

[87]   See W.J.B. VAN NIELEN, "European Communication and Cooperation ("CoCo') Guidelines for Cross-border Insolvency Proceedings" (2007) 4 *European Company Law* 560.

[88]   See, https://www.insol.org/_files/pdf/Press%20Release%20JudgeCo%20Project.pdf.

[89]   See B. WESSELS, "CoCo Guidelines Apply to Nortel Networks Coordination Protocol" [2015], http://www.bobwessels.nl/blog/2015-05-doc5-coco-guidelines-apply-to-nortel-networks-coordination-protocol.

[90]   See B. WESSELS, "CoCo Guidelines 2.0 on its Way," http://www.bobwessels.nl/links/coco-guidelines-2.0.

[91]   http://www.uncitral.org/pdf/english/texts/insolven/Practice_Guide_english.pdf.

[92]   E.B. LEONARD and J.J. BELLISSIMO, "Prospective Model International Cross-Border Insolvency Protocol [Annotated]" [2009] *International Insolvency Institute*, http://bobwessels.nl/site/assets/files/1256/iii-model-cross-border-protocol-annotated-june-2009-draft.pdf.

[93]   See I.F. FLETCHER and B. WESSELS, "A First Step in Shaping Rules for Cooperation in International Insolvency Cases," http://bobwessels.nl/site/assets/files/1365/icr-proof.pdf.

[94]   T. SCHNABEL, "The Singapore Convention on Mediation: A Framework for the Cross-Border Recognition and Enforcement of Mediated Settlements" (2019) 19 *Pepperdine Dispute Resolution Law Journal* 1.

at insolvency proceedings, the Convention may affect the recognition and enforcement of mediated settlements achieved in an insolvency context.[95] The Convention was signed on August 7, 2019 and was adopted by the UN General Assembly on December 20, 2018 following several years of work by UNCITRAL. The Convention entered into force on September 12, 2020. So far, the Convention was ratified by Ecuador, Fiji, Qatar, Saudi Arabia, Singapore and Belarus. In addition, it is anticipated that the United States, Israel, Colombia, Thailand, Turkey, Mexico, China, Kuwait, Sri Lanka, and Canada will become early signatories, given that these countries strongly advocated a convention from the commencement of the project. Also, the Council of Europe's European Commission for the Efficiency of Justice has recommended that Member States of the Council of Europe "consider ratifying" the Singapore Convention.[96]

The Convention aims to provide a unified framework for the enforcement of cross-border settlement agreements arising from mediation. Under Article 3, each party to the Convention shall enforce a settlement agreement in accordance with its rules of procedure and under the conditions laid down in the Convention. Article 5 sets out grounds where relief is sought or the subject matter of the dispute is not capable of settlement by mediation under the law of the state where relief is sought (Article 5(2)). In addition, an agreement is not enforced if the settlement agreement is null and void, not binding, or has been modified since the initial agreement; the obligations in the settlement agreement have already been performed or are not clear; or if there are reasonable doubts about the mediator's impartiality.

4. RECOGNITION OF FOREIGN DECISIONS

4.1. INTRODUCTION

Recognition is the solution to a problem integral to cross-border contexts: how does the legal system of state A (the "recognizing" state) respond to the insolvency proceedings opened in state B (the "opening state")?[97]

The recognition of judgments in international insolvency law differs from the recognition of ordinary judgments in a number of respects.[98] While a judgment

---

[95] See F. Assaf, "The Use of Mediation Cross-Border Insolvency and Restructuring: Possible Implications of the Singapore Convention on Mediation" [3rd Quarter 2019] *INSOL World* 26.

[96] T. Schnabel, above n. 94.

[97] R. Bork and R. Mangano, above n. 8, para. 5.03.

[98] Occasionally judges have regarded foreign insolvencies as a type of foreign judgment and thus have applied the rules governing these judgments. See per Lord Romilly MR in *Re Blithman* [1866] LR 2 Eq 23, 26; and per Faucett J in *Proudfoot v. Stubbins* [1886] 7 LR 131, 133 (NSW).

in an ordinary civil lawsuit only concerns two (or, occasionally, a few) parties and typically only concerns one claim (or a few claims), an insolvency order has a broader impact:[99] The status of the debtor is likely to be affected. The opening of an insolvency proceeding imposes disabilities upon the debtor which tend in the direction of an impairment of his/her status.[100] Thus, the opening of insolvency proceedings also affects the dealings between the debtor and all other persons in the future.[101] A corporation may even cease to exist.[102] Also, the rights of third parties against the debtor are affected. It restricts the ordinary legal remedies of creditors,[103] and the debtor's assets will be distributed in a manner which may well purport to bind all the creditors.[104]

It is these differences which have led to judgments in insolvency proceedings being treated differently from judgments in ordinary civil cases.[105] Thus, insolvency decisions are typically excluded from the Hague Conference[106] instruments, on the grounds, for example, that those matters may be seen as very specialized and best dealt with by specific international arrangements, or that they are closely intertwined with issues of public law.[107] Article 1(5) of the 1971 Hague Convention on the Recognition and Enforcement of Foreign Judgments in Civil and Commercial Matters, for example, provides that the Convention does not apply to "questions of bankruptcy, compositions or analogous proceedings, including decisions which may result therefrom and which relate to the validity of the acts of the debtor". Article 2(2)(e) of the 2005 Choice of Court Convention provides that it does not apply to "insolvency, composition and analogous matters". This approach is followed in the work to develop a global judgments convention, with the additional exclusion of "resolution of financial institutions".[108] Similarly, the Brussels I *bis* Regulation[109] excludes

---

[99] J. BRIGGS, "Recognition of Foreign Bankruptcies at Common Law" in R. SHELDON, above n. 22, para. 9.3.

[100] Innes JP in *Ex parte Stefmann*, 1902 TS 40, at 42, cited by J. BRIGGS, ibid.

[101] Innes JP in *Ex parte Stefmann*, above n. 100, at 42.

[102] J. BRIGGS, above n. 99, para. 9.3.

[103] Innes JP in *Ex parte Stefmann*, above n. 100, at 42.

[104] J. BRIGGS, above n. 99, para. 9.3.

[105] See again Innes JP in *Ex parte Stefmann*, above n. 97, at 42: "To enforce such a decree absolutely and entirely in this country, as if it were a foreign judgment, is, therefore, out of the question".

[106] The Hague Conference on Private International Law (http://www.hcch.net/index_en.php) is an international organization that was established in the nineteenth century to work toward the progressive unification of private international law.

[107] Guide to the UNCITRAL Model Law on Recognition of Insolvency Related Judgments, para. 6.

[108] See Art. 2(1)(e) of the draft Convention of May 2018. This additional exclusion refers to the new legal framework enacted in various jurisdictions under the auspices of the Financial Stability Board to prevent the failure of financial institutions.

[109] Regulation (EU) 1215/2012 of the European Parliament and of the Council of December 12, 2012 on jurisdiction and the recognition and enforcement of judgments in civil and commercial matters [2012] OJ L351/1.

(as did its predecessor version) "bankruptcy, proceedings relating to the winding-up of insolvent companies or other legal persons, judicial arrangements, compositions and analogous proceedings".[110]

Recognition of decisions in insolvency proceedings is also central to implementing the principle of universality.[111] Indeed, the recognition of judgments opening an insolvency proceeding, at least in theory, avoids conflicting decisions as to jurisdiction.[112] Under the EIR, there can only be one set of main proceedings. This follows from the rules on jurisdiction because a debtor can only have one COMI. Once an insolvency proceeding is opened in one country, this decision is recognized in all other Member States. Therefore, there is no more room for any other main proceeding. Once a judgment opening main proceedings has taken effect, all other Member States are (in principle)[113] precluded from opening main proceedings.[114] Rather, any proceeding opened in another country can only be a secondary proceeding pursuant to Article 3(3) EIR.[115] Thus, the recognition of a foreign judgment opening a main proceeding ensures that the principle of (limited) universalism is followed.

One final preliminary point: it is necessary to distinguish between whether a foreign decision is recognized and the effects that such recognition brings about.[116] Recognition as such only means that the foreign decision will in some way be respected,[117] but it does not tell us what precise effects the recognition of a judgment entails. These effects may be the same as in the country where the judgment was handed down or the same as in the country where recognition is sought, or may be some particular effects accorded to the foreign judgment in the law of the country where recognition is sought. In the latter case, there may

---

[110] Article 1(2)(b) of the Brussels I *bis* Regulation.

[111] K. PANNEN and S. RIEDEMANN, above n. 63, Art. 16 para. 2; M. VIRGÓS and F. GARCIMARTÍN, above n. 62, para. 339; M. VIRGÓS and E. SCHMIT, *Report on the Convention on Insolvency Proceedings* (1996), para. 154, http://aei.pitt.edu/952/1/insolvency_report_schmidt_1988. pdf; R. BORK and R. MANGANO, above n. 8, para. 5.01. See also B. WESSELS, above n. 12, para. 10732; R. GOODE, above n. 12, paras. 15 ff.

[112] For instances where the recognition of judgments was refused on the ground that the court opening the proceeding did not have jurisdiction, see below, section 4.6.1.

[113] Sometimes insolvency proceedings have been opened in another country because the courts there were not aware that a proceeding had already been opened elsewhere. These cases were sometimes solved by non-recognition of the first decision and sometimes by "downgrading" the second opening decision to the opening of secondary proceedings. This was the approach taken by the Vienna Court of Appeals and, subsequently, the Austrian Supreme Court in the famous *Stojevich* case. See OLG Wien 9.11.2004, 28 R 225/04w; subsequently confirmed by OGH 17.3.2005, 8 Ob 135/04t. For another interesting aspect of the *Stojevic* case, see *Stone & Rolls Ltd v. Moore Stephens* [2009] UKHL 39.

[114] BGH 29.5.2008, IX ZB 103/07 para. 26; R. BORK and R. MANGANO, above n. 8, para. 5.10.

[115] See Case C-116/11, *Bank Handlowy w Warszawie SA* and *PPHU "ADAX"/Ryszard Adamiak v. Christianapol sp. zo. o.*, ECLI:EU:C:2012:739, para. 40.

[116] See below, section 4.2.

[117] G. GRAF, above n. 30, p. 327.

Intersentia

213

be a set of effects predetermined by law, or the court, when recognizing a foreign decision, has to decide on a case-by-case basis what effects the recognition of the foreign judgment should have in the country where recognition is sought. Whenever some effects of a foreign judgment are "exported" to the recognizing state, recognition in essence serves as a substitute for choice-of-law rules.[118]

4.2. THE EFFECTS OF RECOGNITION

4.2.1. *Concepts of Recognition*

If a foreign decision is recognized, the question remains as to what effects such recognition has.[119] In the recognition of judgments (outside an insolvency context), one approach is to treat the foreign judgment like a domestic judgment; it is "equated" with a domestic judgment. Under this approach, the foreign decision is afforded all the effects that a domestic judgment would bring about. This concept is referred to as the assimilation-of-effects theory (*Gleichstellungstheorie* in German). This concept is hardly feasible for insolvency proceedings. First, an order opening a bankruptcy proceeding could produce different effects in the country of origin and in the country where recognition is sought. Second, the same decision could produce different effects in different countries, in such a way that the rights of the parties may vary according to the country they are in, and if the decision has to produce various effects vis-à-vis various third parties, then the consequences for each of them may be different, also depending upon which country they are in.[120] In spite of these disadvantages, it seems that some states still use this concept also for the recognition of insolvency proceedings. A possible example for such a model, in the case of insolvency proceedings opened in non-Member States of the EU, is Italy. Also, the UNICTRAL Model Law on Cross-Border Insolvency in some respects adopts the assimilation-of-effects theory. It does not extend the effects of the foreign proceeding as they may be prescribed by the law of the foreign state.[121] Instead, recognition of a

---

[118] C. VON BAR, *Internationales Privatrecht*, vol. 1, C.H.Beck, Munich 1987, para. 353 ("kollisionsrechtsersetzende Wirkung").

[119] For an overview of the different approaches to recognition, see J. BLITZ, *Sonderinsolvenzverfahren im Internationalen Insolvenzrecht*, Tenea, Berlin 2002, pp. 16 ff.; S. HOMANN, *System der Anerkennung eines ausländischen Insolvenzverfahrens und die Zulässigkeit der Einzelrechtsverfolgung*, LIT Verlag, Münster 2000, pp. 23 ff.; D. LUDWIG, *Neuregelungen des deutschen Internationalen Insolvenzrechts*, Peter Lang, Bern 2004, pp. 61 ff.; M. VIRGÓS and F. GARCIMATÍN, above n. 62, para. 353.

[120] M. VIRGÓS and F. GARCIMATÍN, above n. 62, para. 353.

[121] UNCITRAL Model Law on Cross-Border Insolvency Guide to Enactment, para. 159. An earlier draft had provided for relief "which may be available under the laws of the State of the foreign proceeding," but ultimately the possibility that the court could grant measures under foreign law was regarded as unrealistic. See Report of the Working Group on Insolvency Law,

foreign proceeding entails attaching to the foreign proceeding consequences envisaged by the law of the state where recognition is sought.[122] Thus, under Article 20(2), the scope, and the modification or termination, of the stay and suspension referred to in Article 20(1) are subject to the law of the enacting (i.e. recognizing) state.

On the other hand, true "recognition" would mean recognition of all effects that the foreign judgment has in its country of origin; thus, in other words, the effects the foreign judgment has in its country of origin are "exported" to the country where recognition is sought. This concept is aptly called the "extension model".[123] Under this approach, the foreign decision is accepted as it is, on its own terms, and with its own effects. From a formal point of view, this model respects the foreign decision and acknowledges it as it stands. Indeed, a decision can only be understood in the sense and with the scope with which it was rendered in the country of origin. The extension model ensures that all of the parties affected by the same foreign decision have equal rights and obligations, regardless of where recognition of that decision is sought.[124]

The more recent UNCITRAL Model Law on Insolvency-Related Judgments provides an option: The adopting state can either extend the effects the judgment has in its state of origin or, alternatively, can give it the same effects it would have had if it had been issued by a court of the state where recognition is sought.[125] If the insolvency-related judgment provides for relief that is not available under the law of this state, that relief shall, to the extent possible, be adapted to relief that is equivalent to, but does not exceed, its effects under the law of the originating state.[126]

4.2.2. The Extension Model

The EU has opted for the extension model in its Brussels I (later Brussels I *bis*) and II Regulations dealing with the recognition of judgments in civil and commercial cases and in divorce and certain other family cases. The EIR adopts the same approach for insolvency proceedings.[127] Thus, pursuant to Article 20(1) EIR, the decision opening (main) insolvency proceedings shall produce the same effects in the recognizing Member State as it produces under

---

20th Session, A/CN.9/433, October 24, 1996, 25 and 30. For a discussion of this important change, see R. Fisher and A. Al-Attar, "The UNCITRAL Model Law" in R. Sheldon, above n. 22, p. 143.

[122] Ibid.
[123] M. Virgós and E. Schmit, above n. 111, para. 153; B. Wessels, above n. 12, para. 10747.
[124] M. Virgós and F. Garcimatín, above n. 62, para. 353.
[125] Article 15(1) of the UNCITRAL Model Law on Insolvency-Related Judgments. The heading of Art. 15 is "Equivalent effect."
[126] Ibid., Art. 15(2).
[127] R. Bork and R. Mangano, above n. 8, para. 5.08.

the law of the opening Member State. As the Virgós-Schmit Report puts it, recognition in the context of the EIR is the act of "admit[ting foreign judgments] for the territory of the recognizing State the authority which they enjoy in the State where they were handed down". Therefore, in order to determine the effects that the recognition of a foreign decision has, it is necessary to analyze the effects the decision has in its country of origin.[128] According such broad effects to the recognition of judgments is only possible because the EU Member States have achieved a high level of economic, cultural, and legal integration, which should, at least in theory, reduce any reservations that may exist in certain countries vis-à-vis the legal systems of other countries.[129]

There is a debate among academic authors[130] whether the extension model applies to *all* effects (i.e., substantive and procedural effects) arising from a judgment opening main proceedings[131] or whether the extension model should only apply to the immediate procedural effects of the judgment, with all other (indirect) effects being governed by choice-of-law rules.[132] Under the latter approach, divestment of the debtor would not be the result of the decision opening the proceeding as such, but would only follow from the conflict-of-law rules (Article 7 EIR), which provide for the application of the law of the Member State where the proceedings were opened. Because under this concept, all substantive effects of the opening of proceedings is determined according to Articles 7–18 EIR, this can explain the exceptions to the application of the *lex fori concursus* in Articles 8–18.[133] On the other hand, if the extension model is understood in a wider sense that also encompasses the substantive effects of the decision, one would have to read Articles 8–18 EIR as imposing restrictions on the extension effects pursuant to Article 20 EIR.[134] Thus, the debate only concerns the proper

---

[128] Ibid., para. 5.11.

[129] It should be added that the fundamental assumption underlying the EU recognition scheme is that the legal systems of all Member States are equal not just on paper, but also in practice. The accuracy of this assumption may well be questioned.

[130] The following summary of this debate is based on R. BORK and R. MANGANO, above n. 8, para. 5.09.

[131] See R. GOODE, above n. 12, paras. 15 ff.; M. VIRGÓS and F. GARCIMATÍN, above n. 62, para. 355; B. WESSELS in G. MOSS, I.F. FLETCHER, and S. ISAACS, above n. 63, para. 8.300; B. WESSELS, above n. 12, para. 10747.

[132] J. AMBACH, *Reichweite und Bedeutung von Art. 25 EuInsVO*, Duncker & Humblot, Berlin 2009, pp. 46 ff.; J. BLITZ, above n. 116, p. 20; S. HOMANN, above n. 119, pp. 34 ff.; D. LUDWIG, above n. 119, pp. 59 ff.

[133] While the private international law provisions of the EIR are beyond the scope of this chapter, it should be stressed that under Art. 18 EIR, the effects of the opening of a proceeding on pending litigation and enforcement proceedings are determined not by the *lex fori concursus*, but by the law of the country where the respective litigation or enforcement proceeding takes place.

[134] R. GOODE, above n. 12, paras. 15 ff.; M. VIRGÓS and F. GARCIMATÍN, above n. 62, para. 356; B. WESSELS, above n. 131, para. 8.300; B. WESSELS, above n. 12, para. 10747.

Transnational Cooperation in Cross-Border Insolvency

reason for the extension of effects of the judgment recognized, not the scope of the effects of a recognition as such. Therefore, it has been pointed out, correctly, that this debate is irrelevant for practical purposes.[135]

While there is no express rule in the EIR as to how recognition of "other" judgments (i.e., other than judgments opening insolvency proceedings) is to be effected, the accepted view is that the effects they have in their country of origin are also to be extended to other countries.[136]

4.2.3. The Scope of Effects of Recognition: Automatic versus "Tailor-Made" Relief

If the foreign judgment is neither extended as to its effects to the country where recognition is sought nor equated with a local judgment, another distinction concerns the question whether recognition brings about a predetermined set of effects or requires the court to decide on the type of relief granted on a case-by-case basis.

Under the UNCITRAL Model Law, the effect of recognition depends on whether the foreign proceeding is a main or a non-main proceeding. Upon recognition of a foreign main proceeding, certain *automatic relief* ensues. Article 20 expressly enumerates the effects of recognition of a foreign main proceeding.[137] This includes a stay of individual actions or individual proceedings concerning the debtor's assets, rights, obligations, or liabilities of individual creditors against the debtor, a stay of execution against the debtor's assets, and suspension of the debtor's right to transfer, encumber, or otherwise dispose of its assets.[138] The enacting state is given plenty of freedom to define and modify the automatic relief.[139]

The stay does not affect the right to commence individual actions to preserve claims against the debtor, or to commence or file claims in local insolvency proceedings. The English law specifically preserves the rights to enforce security, repossess goods the subject of a hire purchase agreement, and set off claims. It also provides a broad discretionary power in the court to modify or terminate the Article 20 stays.

Article 21(1)(a) and (b) of the UNCITRAL Model Law provides for the same relief to be granted at the court's discretion in relation to a foreign non-main proceeding, but only at the request of the foreign representative.

---

[135] J. AMBACH, above n. 132, pp. 55 ff.; R. BORK and R. MANGANO, above n. 8, para. 5.09.
[136] R. BORK and R. MANGANO, above n. 8, para. 5.40.
[137] In Poland, there is an argument that the recognition of a foreign non-main proceeding may also ensue in an automatic stay of proceedings. See L.C. HO, above n. 44, p. 12.
[138] Article 20 of the UNCITRAL Model Law.
[139] L.C. HO, above n. 44, p. 12.

Intersentia

217

While most states provide for automatic relief, there are significant differences as to the scope of the automatic relief.[140] Thus, in the United States, the automatic relief includes a stay on the enforcement of security interests,[141] whereas in the United Kingdom, secured creditors are free to enforce their security.[142] Under Ukrainian law, even though Ukraine has adopted the UNCITRAL Model Law, the recognition of a foreign proceeding does not entail an automatic stay; rather, the foreign administrator has to apply separately for an order granting individual relief.[143] In Japan, the recognition order of foreign insolvency proceedings, including main proceedings, does not have any automatic effect. The court will act according to its discretion in order to determine whether to render assistance such as to grant a stay order for the benefit of the foreign insolvency proceedings.[144] This modification was adopted in Japan because of the concern that otherwise the courts may be excessively cautious and strict when reviewing the conditions for recognition of foreign proceedings.[145]

In addition to the automatic relief brought about by any recognition of a foreign main proceeding, Article 21 of the UNCITRAL Model Law allows the court to grant "discretionary relief" upon the recognition of a foreign main or non-main proceeding. When granting or denying relief under Article 19 or 21, or modifying or terminating relief, the court must be satisfied that the interests of the creditors and other interested persons, including the debtor, are adequately protected.[146] It may subject relief granted under Article 19 or 21 to conditions it considers appropriate.[147] It may also, at the request of the foreign representative or a person affected by relief granted under Article 19 or 21, or on its own initiative, modify or terminate such relief.[148]

By contrast, the EIR follows the extension model and thus, for the most part, the consequences of recognition of a decision opening bankruptcy proceedings triggers the application of the *lex fori concursus*. There is a notable exception, though, in that under Article 18 EIR the effects of the opening of a proceeding on pending litigation and enforcement proceedings is determined not by the *lex fori concursus*, but by the law of the country where the respective litigation or enforcement proceeding takes place. Yet, this is a general reference to the law of the forum where the respective litigation is pending; there is no need for an individualized court ruling ordering a stay as a result of a recognition of a foreign proceeding.

---

[140] L.C. Ho, above n. 44.
[141] Section 1521 of the Bankruptcy Code.
[142] Article 20 of the British Model Law.
[143] See the national report by STAKHEYEVA-BOGOVYK (Ukraine) pp. 1 et seq.
[144] See the national report by JIN (Japan), p. 1.
[145] See ibid., p. 4.
[146] Article 22(1) of the UNCITRAL Model Law.
[147] Ibid., Art. 22(2).
[148] Ibid., Art. 22(3).

4.2.4. Special Provisions for Assistance in the Foreign Proceedings of Certain Countries

In some countries, there are special provisions for assistance of foreign proceedings. Interestingly, these provisions sometimes apply only to certain "designated" or "prescribed" countries, usually countries belonging to the same family of legal system and to which close historical, cultural, and economic ties exist.[149] Therefore, these countries draw a distinction between the degree of cooperation afforded by courts from "prescribed states" and those from other states.

For example, in the United Kingdom, section 426 of the Insolvency Act 1986 authorizes the court to assist the foreign proceedings of certain "designated" countries (which essentially comprise current or former members of the Commonwealth). Under this section, a wide range of measures is available to the court.[150] The court is authorized to "apply, in relation to any matters specified in the request, the insolvency law which is applicable by either court in relation to comparable matters falling within its jurisdiction". Under this provision, the court can make an order binding creditors, whose debts were subject to English law, to the terms of an arrangement approved by an Irish court under sections 22–24 of the Irish Companies (Amendment) Act of 1990, even though there were no equivalent provisions under English law.[151] In another case, the English court, at the request of an Australian court, ordered the examination, by an Australian judge, of an individual resident in England under Division 1 of Part 5.9 of the Australian Corporations Law, even though such a measure had not been granted in a purely domestic context.[152] In another case, an English court, again at the request of an Australian court, ordered the production of documents and examination by an Australian judge of seven individuals, some of whom worked or lived in Poland.[153] Also, the House of Lords in one decision directed the English provisional liquidators of four insolvent Australian insurance companies to remit the proceeds of realization of assets in England to the Australian liquidators for distribution in accordance with Australian law, in spite of the fact that Australian law differed significantly from English law and that certain classes of creditors would be prejudiced as a result.[154]

---

[149] In the United Kingdom, "designated" states for purposes of s. 426(11) of the Insolvency Act 1986 include Australia, Bermuda, Canada, the Cayman Islands, Hong Kong, Malaysia, New Zealand, the Republic of Ireland, and the Republic of South Africa. In Australia, Corporations Regulation 5.6.74 prescribes the Bailiwick of Jersey, Canada, Papua New Guinea, Malaysia, New Zealand, Singapore, the United Kingdom, the United States, and, interestingly, Switzerland.

[150] The following examples rely on L. TAMLYN, "Assistance Pursuant to Section 426 of the Insolvency Act 1986," in R. SHELDON, above n. 22, para. 4.4.

[151] *Re Business City Express Ltd* [1997] 2 BCLC 510.

[152] *England v. Smith* [2001] Ch 4198 (CA).

[153] *Duke Group Ltd v. Carver et al.* [2001] BPIR 459.

[154] *McGrath v. Riddel, Re HIH Casualty and General Insurance Ltd.* [2008] UKHL 21, [2008] 1 WLR 852 (HL).

Intersentia

4.2.5. Impact on the Debtor's Status

Under Article 20(1)(c) of the UNCITRAL Model Law, upon recognition of a foreign proceeding that is a foreign main proceeding, the right to transfer, encumber, or otherwise dispose of any assets of the debtor is automatically suspended. In addition, under Article 21(1)(c), the court has the discretion to suspend dispositions following the recognition of a foreign non-main proceeding on application of the foreign representative. In the EU, because of the EIR's extension model,[155] the impact that the opening of an insolvency proceeding has on the debtor's status depends on the *lex fori concursus*.

4.2.6. The Powers of the Administrator

One of the most important effects of recognition of a foreign proceeding concerns the powers of the administrator. In the Guide to the UNICTRAL Model Law on Cross-Border Insolvency, access to local courts for representatives of foreign insolvency proceedings is mentioned even before the recognition of certain orders is addressed.[156] Similarly, the Scandinavian Insolvency Convention and the Istanbul Convention focus on the administrator's ability to exercise his/her powers in other countries, without even expressly mentioning recognition of the judgment opening insolvency proceedings. Also under the Code Bustamante, while a decision opening a bankruptcy or reorganization proceeding is effective in other signatory countries only after it has been recognized, the powers and functions of the representatives of the bankrupt estate extend to all Member States without requiring any special judicial or other executory action (although the trustee would be required to prove his/her capacity).[157] However, any actions which implement bankruptcy decisions, such as the collection and sale of assets, may only be performed after the issuance of the exequatur and shall be governed by domestic law of the Member State where the respective measure is to be taken.[158]

Article 9 of the UNCITRAL Model Law on Cross-Border Insolvency provides foreign representatives with the right to apply directly to a local court. Article 10 is a "safe conduct" rule which provides that an application for recognition does not create jurisdiction over the applicant in the courts of the enacting state, except for the purposes of the application.[159] According to Article 11, a foreign representative can commence a local insolvency proceeding if the conditions for

---

[155] See above, section 4.2.2.
[156] Guide to the UNCITRAL Model Law on Cross-Border Insolvency, para. 24.
[157] T.B. FELSBERG, above n. 77.
[158] Ibid., above n. 77.
[159] UNICTRAL Model Law on Cross-Border Insolvency, para. 109.

commencing such a proceeding are otherwise met. Article 12 entitles the foreign representative of a proceeding which has been recognized under the Model Law to participate in local insolvency proceedings regarding the debtor. Under Article 15(1), a foreign representative may apply to the court for recognition of the foreign proceeding in which he/she has been appointed. This direct access of the foreign representative to local courts is an important improvement compared to the traditional mechanism of judicial assistance.[160]

Finally, under Article 23(1) of the UNCITRAL Model Law, the foreign representative has standing to initiate avoidance actions. U.S. law excludes avoidance relief which might otherwise be available to a trustee in bankruptcy,[161] in order to corral all such requests for relief into local proceedings opened under other chapters of the Bankruptcy Code.[162] Under English law, if a proceeding under English insolvency law is taking place in relation to the debtor, the foreign representative may not commence avoidance proceedings under Article 23 of the Model Law without the court's permission.[163]

Article 21(1)(e) of the UNCITRAL Model Law enables the court to entrust the administration or realization of all or part of the debtor's assets located in the recognizing state to the foreign representative or another person designated by the court.[164] According to Article 21(2), following the recognition of a foreign proceeding (whether main or non-main), the court may, at the request of the foreign representative, entrust the distribution of all or part of the debtor's assets located in the respective state to the foreign representative or another person designated by the court, provided that the court is satisfied that the interests of creditors in this state are adequately protected. Where the request is made by a representative of a foreign non-main proceeding, the court must also be satisfied that the relief relates to assets that, under the law of the recognizing state, should be administered in the foreign non-main proceeding. In the United States, Article 21(1)(e) has been used to justify additional relief in the form of attachments against assets.[165]

According to Article 7(2)(c) EIR, the law of the state opening the proceeding determines "the respective powers of the debtor and the insolvency practitioner". For secondary proceedings, Article 35 EIR refers to the law of the state of the opening of secondary proceedings. These laws determine the administrator's

---

[160]   In *Re McGrath & Honey as Liquidators of HIH Insurance Ltd.* [2008] NSWC 881, the judge inquired of counsel whether consideration had been given to a direct approach to the English courts and was advised that the liquidators preferred to adopt the procedure of letters of request from court to court that they has successfully used in the past.
[161]   11 U.S.C § 1521(a)(7).
[162]   S. MAIDEN, above n. 49, p. 72.
[163]   Cross-Border Insolvency Regulation 2006 (UK), Sch. 1, Art. 23 (6). See S. MAIDEN, above n. 49, p. 73.
[164]   See R. FISHER and A. AL-ATTAR, above n. 120, paras. 3.84 f.
[165]   *Re Atlas Shipping A/S* 404 BR 726 (Bankr. S.D.N.Y. 2009).

powers, duties, and liabilities.[166] Under Article 21(1) EIR, the administrator may exercise all the powers conferred on him/her, by the law of the state of the opening of proceedings, in another Member State. In particular, the administrator may remove the debtor's assets from the territory of the Member State in which they are situated.[167] Important exceptions to this rule for rights in rem and reservation of title are stated in Articles 8 and 10 EIR. In contrast, under the domestic law of many countries, a foreign administrator would require the approval of the domestic court for seizing or selling assets located in the respective country. For example, under British law, the power to entrust the distribution of local assets to the foreign representative or another person is subject to the court being satisfied "that the interests of creditors in Great Britain are adequately protected".[168]

According to Article 7(3) EIR, in exercising its powers, the insolvency practitioner shall comply with the law of the Member State within the territory of which it intends to take action, in particular with regard to procedures for the realization of assets. Those powers may not include coercive measures, unless ordered by a court of that Member State, or the right to rule on legal proceedings or disputes.

Under the Scandinavian Insolvency Convention, bankruptcy officers (as they are called in the Convention) are authorized to dispose of all the assets of the bankruptcy estate, regardless of in which Nordic country the assets are situated. When bankruptcy administrators are acting in respect of property that is situated in other states than the state in which the bankruptcy was declared, then the administrators may request the assistance of the authorities of these states to the same extent as domestic bankruptcy administrators.[169]

Under the former OHADA Uniform Act, the administrator was allowed to exercise within the OHADA territory, all the powers conferred on him/her by the Uniform Act as long as no other collective proceedings had been initiated in any contracting state.[170] This Act has been replaced by a new Uniform Insolvency Act in 2015 which introduced the UNCITRAL Model Law.

In South Korea, the courts have developed an interesting "work-around" avoiding the traditional restrictions of domestic law.[171] In principle, a foreign representative of a foreign proceeding has no power or authority to dispose of the assets located in South Korea. However, in practice, the Seoul Bankruptcy Court has resolved this theoretical problem by appointing the foreign administrator as a local "Cross-Border Insolvency Administrator". Such a Cross-Border Insolvency

---

[166]   R. BORK and R. MANGANO, above n. 8, para. 6.24.
[167]   Article 21(1) EIR.
[168]   S. MAIDEN, above n. 49, p. 72.
[169]   Article 3 of the Scandinavian Insolvency Convention.
[170]   Article 249 of the OHADA Uniform Act.
[171]   See the national report by KIM (South Korea).

Administrator has the exclusive authority to dispose of national assets and return proceeds to the foreign country. Once a foreign representative is appointed as a Cross-Border Insolvency Administrator by the Seoul Bankruptcy Court, he/she can withdraw money from a bank, sell chattels or real estate, or conduct general civil proceedings on behalf of the debtor's estate, provided that he/she has received a prior approval from the court.

4.2.7. Evidentiary Consequences

Article 31 of the UNCITRAL Model Law on Cross-Border Insolvency is headed "Presumption of insolvency based on recognition of a foreign main proceeding". According to this provision, in the absence of evidence to the contrary, recognition of a foreign main proceeding is, for the purposes of commencing a secondary proceeding under domestic law, proof that the debtor is insolvent. The EIR goes even further. Under Article 34 EIR, where main insolvency proceedings have been opened by a court of a Member State and recognized in another Member State, a court of that other Member State may open secondary insolvency proceedings if the debtor has an establishment there. Where the main insolvency proceedings require that the debtor be insolvent, the debtor's insolvency shall not be re-examined in the Member State in which secondary insolvency proceedings may be opened. Thus, the opening of an insolvency proceeding (if it required that the debtor be insolvent) constitutes an irrebuttable presumption that the debtor is insolvent.

4.3. AUTOMATIC RECOGNITION VERSUS EXEQUATUR PROCEEDINGS

4.3.1. Exequatur Proceedings

Traditionally, recognition of a foreign decision requires a decision by a court in the country where recognition is sought: an exequatur decision. The level of court involvement in the recognition of foreign proceedings depends on the degree of trust accorded to foreign systems. If states are similar in terms of culture, the economy, and the legal system, they are more likely to accept a foreign decision. On the other hand, the more diverse legal systems are (and the less is known about them in the country where recognition is sought), the less likely states are to retain at least some degree of control by requiring approval of recognition by their own courts. Of course, one disadvantage of exequatur proceedings is that they may take considerable time – in one reported case, getting exequatur of a U.S. decision in France took four years.[172]

---

[172] G. GRAF, above n. 30, p. 126.

Intended to be a worldwide model law, the UNCITRAL Model Law on Cross-Border Insolvency takes a conservative position and retains the traditional model of exequatur proceedings, although it attempts to limit both the formalities required and the grounds which enable a local court to refuse recognition to a foreign proceeding. Under Article 15 (1), a foreign representative may apply to the court for recognition of the foreign proceeding in which he/she has been appointed. The required paperwork is set out in Articles 15 and 16 of the UNCITRAL Model Law. In the absence of evidence to the contrary, the court is entitled to presume that the statements of the foreign court regarding the status of the proceeding as a foreign proceeding and of the representative as a foreign representative are correct, and that the documents relied upon are authentic.[173] If the procedural and evidentiary requirements to demonstrate that the proceedings are foreign proceedings and that the application is made by a foreign representative are satisfied, the court is bound to recognize the foreign proceeding,[174] unless doing so would be manifestly contrary to public policy.[175] The decision recognizing a foreign proceeding can be modified or terminated when circumstances change or new information becomes available.[176]

The UNCITRAL Model Law on Recognition of Insolvency-Related Judgments specifically provides for a decision on recognition and enforcement not only upon an application for recognition and enforcement by the foreign representative, but also when the question of recognition arises by way of defense or as an incidental question before such a court.[177]

As to the "scope of examination" in exequatur proceedings, nowadays it is settled that there should not be a full re-examination of the foreign decision de novo, i.e., there is no "révision au fond". Under the UNCITRAL Model Law, recognition of foreign judgments is essentially a certification procedure. However, since the recognition of a foreign main proceeding requires that the proceeding was opened in the country where the debtor has his/her COMI, this aspect may be re-examined by the court in recognition proceedings. Even in this respect, the court can rely on a presumption that the COMI is in the state opening the proceedings.[178] Under the EIR, the court only has to examine whether the Regulation applies and whether the decision is one of the decisions mentioned in Articles 19 and 31. No further examination is required or, indeed, permitted.[179]

In some countries, recognition of foreign insolvency decisions is entrusted to "specialized courts". In the United States, a single bankruptcy court coordinates

---

[173] Article 16(1) and (2) of the UNCITRAL Model Law.
[174] Ibid., Art. 17.
[175] Ibid., Art. 6.
[176] Article 17(4) MLCBI.
[177] Article 13 of the UNCITRAL Model Law on Recognition of Insolvency-Related Judgments.
[178] See below, section 4.5.4.
[179] For the public policy exception, see below, section 4.6.1.

all ancillary proceedings.[180] The purpose of this concept is to "concentrate the recognition and deference process in one United States court, ensure against abuse and empower a court that will be fully informed of the current status of all foreign proceedings involving the debtor".[181] In Japan, recognition and assistance cases shall be subject to the exclusive jurisdiction of the Tokyo District Court, since such cases are highly specialized and exclusive jurisdiction is advantageous in accumulating practical experience and maintaining consistency across judgments. Furthermore, Tokyo as an international transport hub could provide foreign representatives with greater convenience when they file for recognition.[182]

Outside the scope of application of the UNCITRAL Model Law or the EIR, some countries still retain quite cumbersome recognition schemes. Thus, Article 431 of the Dutch Code of Civil Procedure provides for a procedure for "recognition" of foreign judgments, which is also applied for judgments opening insolvency proceedings. While recognition in the true sense of the word requires a European regulation or a treaty, similar results may be obtained by initiating a proceeding in the Netherlands.[183] In theory, the Dutch court then has to rule on the principal matter again, but according to case law and doctrine, this new proceeding may be summary when the criteria for recognition of foreign decisions, developed by case law and doctrine, are met. These criteria for recognition are derived from international standards on jurisdiction, fair trial, public policy, and irrevocability of the decision. Although technically this will be a separate Dutch judgment, it will indirectly give effect to the foreign decision. Such a summary judgment by a Dutch court based on a foreign decision is also referred to as an "exequatur in disguise" because there is no full re-examination de novo, but the Dutch court only checks whether the foreign proceedings are consistent with basic principles and formalities.[184]

4.3.2. Interim Relief

In legal systems where the recognition of a foreign judgment requires a decision by a domestic court, typically some form of interim relief is available between the time of the application and the decision of the court.[185] An example is Article 10 of the UNCITRAL Model Law. Under this provision, the court, at the foreign

---

[180]   11 U.S.C. §1509.
[181]   Bankruptcy Abuse Prevention and Consumer Protection Act of 2005, Report of the Committee on the Judiciary Hourse of Representatives 110, cited by S. MAIDEN, above n. 49, p. 68 fn. 48.
[182]   See the national report by JIN (Japan), p. 4.
[183]   See the national report by BOON (the Netherlands), p. 3.
[184]   See ibid.
[185]   The interim relief available while an application for recognition of a foreign insolvency decision is pending has to be distinguished from the question of recognition of foreign interim measures. On the latter aspect, see below, section 4.4.5.

Intersentia

225

Georg Kodek

representative's request, can grant interim relief when this is urgently needed to protect the debtor's assets or the creditor's interests. In some countries, interim relief can also be requested by other interested parties.[186]

Ukrainian law, while adopting the UNCITRAL Model Law on Cross-Border Insolvency, significantly departs from its provisions. Thus, the "provisional relief" that may be granted upon application for recognition of a foreign proceeding (before the application is decided upon) is much narrower (and less effective) than in the UNCITRAL Model Law. There is no possibility of staying the execution against the debtor's assets; rather, only court orders facilitating the collection of evidence or obtaining the information on assets, commercial operations, rights, and obligations or responsibility of the debtor are available.[187]

4.3.3. Automatic Recognition

The most liberal approach to recognition of foreign judgments in international insolvency is taken by the EIR. The EIR provides for the automatic recognition of judgments rendered within the course of insolvency proceedings. Under the EIR, recognition is based on mutual trust and is crucial for the maintenance of the universality of (main) insolvency proceedings.[188] Recognition operates "ipso iure"[189] or "automatically". Therefore, no decision on recognition and no exequatur proceeding is required; rather, the question of recognition will be determined incidentally whenever the issue arises.[190]

It has been pointed out that this approach has disadvantages because there is no express ruling that binds all authorities, which may result in a lack of legal certainty.[191] The need to examine recognition arises whenever the opening of a foreign proceeding may have an impact on the outcome of proceedings in another country. Thus, when a creditor seeks (individual) enforcement regarding assets located in state A and the debtor (or, more likely, the administrator) presents a defense based on the grounds that the main proceedings have been opened in state B, and therefore individual enforcement proceedings are barred in state A, the courts of state A will have to examine whether proceedings opened in state B should be recognized (and, if so, what effects would arise from recognition with regard to the possibility of individual enforcement proceedings).[192]

---

[186]   For Japan, see S. Abe in L.C. Ho (ed.), *Cross-Border Insolvency: A Commentary on the UNCITRAL Model Law*, above n. 15, p. 327.

[187]   See the national report by Stakheyeva-Bogovyk (Ukraine), p. 1.

[188]   R. Bork and R. Mangano, above n. 8, para. 5.01.

[189]   M. Virgós and F. Garcimatín, above n. 62, para. 344; M. Virgós and E. Schmit, above n. 111, para. 152; B. Wessels, above n. 12, para. 10733; R. Bork and R. Mangano, above n. 8, para. 5.06.

[190]   R. Bork and R. Mangano, above n. 8, para. 5.06.

[191]   M. Virgós and F. Garcimatín, above n. 62, para. 344.

[192]   R. Bork and R. Mangano, above n. 8, para. 5.06 fn. 13.

Outside the scope of application of the EIR, automatic recognition under national law is rare. An example of the automatic recognition of insolvency decisions from non-EU countries can be found in Germany. Under German law,[193] a foreign insolvency proceeding is recognized (subject to a public policy exception) if the courts of the country where the proceeding was opened have international jurisdiction under the "mirror image" rule and if the foreign insolvency law extends its effects to other countries. Another example is Austria, which provides for the automatic recognition of insolvency proceedings opened in non-EU Member States.[194] In principle, all foreign proceedings are recognized if the debtor's COMI lies in a country other than Austria. However, a foreign proceeding is not recognized if this would violate Austrian public policy or if a proceeding is already pending in Austria. Thus, a proceeding in Austria can be introduced in order to block the effects of a foreign proceeding. This relatively liberal approach to recognition is also remarkable because Austria traditionally follows a very restrictive approach to recognition of foreign judgments, generally requiring a bilateral or multilateral treaty or a domestic regulation.[195] The reason for this is simply that while the traditional rule is laid down in the Enforcement Act (Exekutionsordnung) of 1895, the recognition of insolvency proceedings belongs to a newer layer of the law, only having been introduced in 2003.

Apart from these instances, examples of automatic recognition of foreign proceedings with full extension of their effects are rare. However, for certain effects, the opening of a foreign bankruptcy proceeding may well be recognized "automatically". For example, under British law, a foreign insolvency does not require any formal process of registration; it has been settled for more than two centuries that, in appropriate circumstances, a foreign bankruptcy will immediately vest the debtor's movable property in England in the foreign assignee.[196]

Another example of "automatic" recognition can be found in Dutch law.[197] Under Dutch case law, the consequences a foreign insolvency proceeding (when the EIR is not applicable) are considered to be recognized "automatically". This is the case since the insolvency practitioner will be granted certain powers to act in the Netherlands without prior formal court approval/recognition.[198] However, such "recognition" only has limited effects because, as a consequence of the Netherlands still following the territoriality principle, a foreign bankruptcy's attachment on the assets of the debtor does not include any of the debtor's assets in the Netherlands.[199] Also, the legal effects of the foreign bankruptcy

---

[193]   Section 343 of the German Insolvency Act (Insolvenzordnung).
[194]   Section 240 of the Austrian Insolvency Act (Insolvenzordnung).
[195]   Section 406 of the Austrian Enforcement Act (Exekutionsordnung).
[196]   J. Briggs, above n. 99, para. 9.4.
[197]   For the so-called "exequatur in disguise" under Dutch law, see above, section 4.3.1.
[198]   See the national report by Boon (the Netherlands), p. 3.
[199]   Dutch Supreme Court, *Hiret v. Chiotakis* [1967] ECLI:NL:HR:1967:AB3520.

proceeding cannot be invoked in the Netherlands, inasmuch as the legal effects would result in unpaid creditors having no recourse against the assets located in the Netherlands.[200]

4.4. TYPES OF DECISIONS RECOGNISED

4.4.1. Introduction

The wording of Article 15 of the UNCITRAL Model Law on Cross-Border Insolvency suggests that what is recognized is the "proceeding" as such rather than a particular decision. The same holds true for the EIR. There, it is universally accepted that, notwithstanding the wording of the EIR,[201] the object of recognition is not "insolvency proceedings" as such, but rather individual court decisions handed down during the proceedings.[202] This is clear from Article 32 EIR, which distinguishes between opening decisions and other decisions taken during the course of proceedings. This somewhat imprecise language may be due to the fact that what is "recognized" is not so much the decision opening the proceedings, but the effects brought about by such a proceeding.[203]

An insolvency may even occur without the intervention of a foreign court;[204] indeed, there may be some type of voluntary liquidation with, or without, the assistance of a tribunal.[205] While these proceedings may well be capable of "recognition" in other countries,[206] clearly this is no longer a form of recognition in the traditional sense which is limited to decisions of foreign courts.

Judgments rendered in the course of insolvency proceedings may fall under different recognition regimes. Thus, the UNCITRAL Model Law only applies to decisions opening a proceeding, but arguably not to other decisions such as a discharge. Judgments rendered in separate proceedings, even though related to the insolvency proceeding, may be covered by a different recognition regime. Sometimes there may even be different avenues for the recognition of decisions rendered within the insolvency proceeding itself. For example, in South Korea, a decision affecting a substantive right has to be recognized as a "foreign judgment", whereas decisions such as stay orders or return of assets from

---

[200] Dutch Supreme Court, *Coppoolse v. De Vleeschmeesters* [1996] ECLI:NL:HR:1996:ZC2091, with commentary by T.M. DE BOER.

[201] See the heading of Chapter 2 EIR, as well as Arts. 20(2) and 33.

[202] M. VIRGÓS and F. GARCIMARTÍN, above n. 62, para. 341; R. BORK and R. MANGANO, above n. 8, para. 5.07.

[203] See above, section 4.1.

[204] J. BRIGGS, above n. 99, para. 9.5.

[205] Ibid. For an example, see *Pitts v. Hill* (1987) 66 CBR (NS) 273, or *Modern Terminal (Berth 5) Ltd. v. States SS Co.* [1979] HKLR 512.

[206] J. BRIGGS, above n. 99, para. 9.5.

Transnational Cooperation in Cross-Border Insolvency

South Korea to foreign countries are regarded as execution matters, recognition of which is dealt with in a special provision on Korean insolvency law.[207]

The EIR, for the purposes of recognition and enforcement, distinguishes between different types of judgments. While Article 19 EIR is devoted to the recognition of judgments opening insolvency proceedings, Article 32 EIR applies to judgments concerning the closure and conduct of proceedings (including court-approved composition), judgments based on and closely related to the proceedings ("related judgments"), judgments concerning preservation measures, and "other" judgments.[208] The latter are governed not by the EIR, but by the Brussels I *bis* Regulation.

4.4.2. Judgments Opening the Proceeding

4.4.2.1. The Importance of Judgments Opening the Proceedings

Clearly, when one examines the recognition of judgments in insolvency proceedings, the decision opening a proceeding is the most important one.[209] If this decision[210] were not recognized, a discussion of a possible recognition of subsequent decisions rendered in the course of the proceedings would be moot. Because of its paramount importance, the EIR regulates the recognition of the decision opening the proceeding separately in Article 19 EIR, while the recognition of all other decisions is dealt with in Article 32 EIR.

4.4.2.2. The Types of Proceedings Recognized

One difficulty in international insolvency is to determine what kind of proceedings would be accorded recognition.[211] Since national laws differ and there are many different kinds of proceedings available, rules on recognition also have to provide criteria as to what types of proceedings would be recognized, e.g., whether recognition is accorded only to proceedings involving companies

---

[207] See the national report by KIM (South Korea), p. 3; see Supreme Court of Korea, [2010] 2009-Ma-1600.

[208] R. BORK and R. MANGANO, above n. 8, para. 5.07.

[209] Occasionally it has been argued that the same principles applying to recognition of judgments opening proceedings should also apply to judgments refusing to open proceedings because of a lack of jurisdiction. See R. GOODE, above n. 12, paras. 15 ff.; P. OBERHAMMER, "Von der EuInsVO zum europäischen Insolvenzrecht. Eine Zwischenbilanz über rechtspolitische Gestaltungsmittel und Ziele" [2009] *KTS – Zeitschrift für Insolvenzrecht* 27, 54.

[210] It has already been pointed out that, in spite of the language of Arts. 19 and 32 EIR, what is recognized is not a "proceeding" as such, but a decision opening a proceeding. See above, section 4.4.1. Also, occasionally "proceedings" can be "recognized" even though there was no court decision at all. See also above, section 4.4.1.

[211] See, e.g., G. GRAF, above n. 30, p. 262.

Intersentia

229

or certain types of debtors such as "merchants" or also to consumer insolvency proceedings, whether recognition is limited to traditional bankruptcy proceedings or also includes restructuring or reorganization proceedings, etc.

Under the UNCITRAL Model Law, "foreign proceedings" can be recognized. Under Article 2(a), "foreign proceeding" means a "collective judicial or administrative proceeding in a foreign state, including an interim proceeding, pursuant to a law relating to insolvency in which proceeding the assets and affairs of the debtor are subject to control or supervision by a foreign court, for the purpose of reorganization or liquidation". "Foreign main proceeding" means a foreign proceeding taking place in the state where the debtor has the center of its main interests; "foreign non-main proceeding" means a foreign proceeding, other than a foreign main proceeding, taking place in a state where the debtor has an establishment. Occasionally, however, implementing legislation intentionally omits a definition of what an "establishment" is in order to give courts more freedom to recognize in appropriate circumstances a foreign proceeding from a jurisdiction where the debtor does not even have an establishment.[212]

While in principle the UNCITRAL Model Law on Cross-Border Insolvency applies to insolvency proceedings in relation to all types of debtors, Article 1(2) permits the exclusion of certain types of entity from the scope of application, such as banks and insurance companies, as they are usually subject to special insolvency regimes.[213] Also, the Guide to the UNICTRAL Model Law on Cross-Border Insolvency contemplates, for jurisdictions that have not enacted provisions for consumers or non-traders, the exclusion of insolvencies that relate to natural persons residing in the enacting state whose debts have been incurred predominantly for personal or household purposes.[214]

Under the U.S. definition,[215] "foreign proceeding" means "proceeding, whether judicial or administrative and whether or not under bankruptcy law, in a foreign country in which the debtor's domicile, residence, principal place of business, or principal assets were located at the commencement of such proceeding, for the purpose of liquidating an estate, adjusting debts by composition, extension, or discharge, or effecting a reorganization". In the United States, the UNCITRAL Model Law does not apply to certain entities that are already subject to a specialized insolvency regime such as banks and railroads, although it does apply to insurance undertakings.[216] In contrast, in the United Kingdom, the UNCITRAL Model Law does not apply to credit institutions and insurance undertakings.

---

[212]   S. GOLICK, P. RIESTERER, and M. WASSERMAN in L.C. HO (ed.), *Cross-Border Insolvency: A Commentary on the UNCITRAL Model Law*, above n. 15, p. 92.
[213]   Guide to the UNICTRAL Model Law on Cross-Border Insolvency, paras. 55 f; L.C. HO, above n. 44, p. 9.
[214]   Guide to the UNICTRAL Model Law on Cross-Border Insolvency, para. 61.
[215]   11 U.S.C. §101 (23).
[216]   L.C. HO, above n. 44, p. 9.

The ill-fated European Convention on Certain International Aspects of Bankruptcy (hereinafter "the Istanbul Convention") would have applied to all collective insolvency proceedings which entail a divestment of the debtor and the appointment of a liquidator and which may entail the liquidation of the assets. The recast EIR applies to:

> public collective proceedings, including interim proceedings, which are based on laws relating to insolvency and in which, for the purpose of rescue, adjustment of debt, reorganisation or liquidation, (a) a debtor is totally or partially divested of its assets and an insolvency practitioner is appointed, (b) the assets and affairs of a debtor are subject to control or supervision by a court; or (c) a temporary stay of individual enforcement proceedings is granted by a court or by operation of law, in order to allow for negotiations between the debtor and its creditors, provided that the proceedings in which the stay is granted provide for suitable measures to protect the general body of creditors, and, where no agreement is reached, are preliminary to one of the proceedings referred to in point (a) or (b).[217]

However, for the purposes of recognition, the EIR defines the proceedings listed in Annex A as "insolvency proceedings".[218] Therefore, Annex A is the ultimate deciding factor as to whether the provision on recognition (Article 19 EIR) applies.[219] Any proceeding not listed in Annex A will not be considered an insolvency proceeding within the scope of Article 19 EIR. Therefore, at present, restructuring proceedings such as the English scheme of arrangement proceedings pursuant to sections 895 et seq. of the Companies Act 2006 probably cannot be recognized under the EIR.[220]

In addition to the definition of insolvency proceedings, Article 2(7) EIR defines the "judgment opening insolvency proceedings" as "any decision by a court to open insolvency proceedings, to confirm the opening of such proceedings,[221] or to appoint an insolvency practitioner". Since insolvency proceedings can be opened only once, it seems that these alternatives are exclusive and the first decision of the kind mentioned in Article 2(7) should be regarded as the judgment opening proceedings. Any subsequent decisions (e.g., if the IP is appointed only after opening the proceedings) is a decision regarding

---

[217] Article 1 EIR.

[218] Ibid., Art. 2(4).

[219] M. VIRGÓS and E. SCHMIT, above n. 111, para. 145; B. WESSELS, above n. 11, para. 10734; R. BORK and R. MANGANO, above n. 8, para. 5.15.

[220] See C. KUSCHE, *Die Anerkennung des Scheme of Arrangement in Deutschland*, Carl Heymanns, Cologne 2014, pp. 46 f.

[221] This alternative takes into account that apparently there are legal systems where no formal initial opening order is made. See Recital 41 EIR; and R. BORK and R. MANGANO, above n. 8, para. 5.19 fn. 41, citing a decision of a Czech court.

the "course" of proceedings and would be recognized not under Article 19, but under Article 32.[222]

Annex B contains a list of IPs whose appointment constitutes a judgment opening the proceedings. This Annex also includes provisional administrators. Therefore, the appointment of a provisional IP (if this type of IP is listed in Annex B) already constitutes the opening of insolvency proceedings,[223] even if under national law this would not be the case.[224] The result of this rule is that if a provisional administrator is appointed e.g., while the court still examines its jurisdiction or whether the debtor is indeed insolvent, this would already be regarded as a judgment opening proceedings and would have to be recognized as such by all other Member States. The soundness of this rule has been rightly questioned.[225]

4.4.2.3. Retroactive Effects?

Occasionally it is difficult to determine the exact time when insolvency proceedings should be regarded as opened. Thus, in some countries, it is possible that the decision opening proceedings can have retroactive effects. The prevailing view seems to be that such effects are irrelevant for the purposes of Article 19 EIR and so would not be recognized.[226] Similar problems arise when the opening of proceedings has been agreed on by the creditors and/or shareholders, but still requires court approval. Since the decision of the court in this case is believed to serve evidentiary purposes only, most observers regard the decision by the competent body rather than by the court as decisive.[227]

In addition, under the UNICTRAL Model Law, it seems that the prevailing view is that the suspension of the debtor's capacity to "transfer, encumber or otherwise dispose of" his/her assets brought about by a foreign decision opening an insolvency proceeding only takes effect in the country recognizing the foreign proceeding after recognition and does not relate back.[228]

---

[222] R. BORK and R. MANGANO, above n. 8, para. 5.20.

[223] See Case C-341/04, *Eurofood IFSC Ltd.*, ECLI:EU:C:2006:281, para. 54 on the previous version of the EIR.

[224] An example is Germany, where a provisional liquidator can be appointed for a preliminary proceeding (*vorläufiges Insolvenzverfahren*) pursuant to s. 21(2)(1) of the German Insolvency Act (Insolvenzordnung), but this appointment would not be regarded a decision opening insolvency proceedings under national law. From the perspective of German national law, proceedings will not be considered opened until the formal judgment opening proceedings has been handed down (see s. 27 of the German Insolvency Act).

[225] E.g., R. BORK and R. MANGANO, above n. 8, para. 5.17 fn. 37.

[226] S. RIEDEMANN in K. PANNEN, above n. 63, Art. 2, para. 28; G. MOSS and T. SMITH, above n. 63, para. 8.84; K. PANNEN in K. PANNEN, above n. 63, Art. 3, paras. 89 ff. A contrary position is taken by R. GOODE, above n. 12, paras. 15 ff.

[227] R. GOODE, above n. 12, paras. 15 ff; G. MOSS and T. SMITH, above n. 63, para. 8.294; M. VIRGÓS and F. GARCIMATÍN, above n. 62, para. 348; S. RIEDEMANN, above n. 226, Art. 2, para. 27.

[228] See R. FISHER and A. AL-ATTAR, above n. 121, para. 3.77.

4.4.3. Other Administration Orders

While most decisions concerning the conduct of the proceeding (other than the decisions on opening and closing the proceeding), as a practical matter, may not require recognition in other countries, such recognition is, in principle, possible. Under the EIR, Article 32(1)(1) provides for the recognition of all judgments concerning the conduct[229] and closure of insolvency proceedings. These are judgments on procedural issues concerning the body of creditors.[230] Such decisions may include court decisions on hearings, lodgment of claims, dismissal of the administrator, and the introduction or closure of certain stages of the proceedings.[231] Decisions in separate lawsuits may only be recognized under Article 32(1)(2).[232]

It should be noted that the recognition of such decisions under the EIR requires that the judgment opening the proceeding is recognized pursuant to Article 19 EIR. As in the case of the judgment opening the proceeding, recognition is automatic, i.e., there is no exequatur or similar proceeding.

There is no similar provision in the UNICTRAL Model Law; rather, the Model Law limits recognition to the decision opening an insolvency proceeding. Nonetheless, occasionally countries that have adopted the Model Law include express provisions on the recognition of other decisions as well. Thus, in Ukraine, the recognition of a foreign insolvency proceeding includes the recognition of court decisions rendered by a foreign court during such a proceeding, and also the decisions on the appointment, dismissal, or replacement of the foreign representative, as well as the decision on the course of the foreign proceeding, its stay, suspension or termination.[233]

4.4.4. Closure of Proceedings and Discharge

While nowadays most states recognize foreign judgments opening insolvency proceedings, the same is not true for a discharge obtained in insolvency proceedings. Under the EIR, the closure of proceedings is recognized in the same way as the opening of proceedings. Recognition of the closure of proceedings is expressly provided for by Article 32(1) EIR. This includes all decisions concerning the closure of proceedings, regardless of the reasons for doing so.[234]

---

[229] Article 32 (1)(1) speaks of the "course" of insolvency proceedings.
[230] S. RIEDEMANN, above n. 226, Art. 25, para. 10; R. BORK and R. MANGANO, above n. 8, para. 5.25.
[231] S. RIEDEMANN, above n. 226, Art. 25, para. 10; R. BORK and R. MANGANO, above n. 8, para. 5.25 fn. 54.
[232] On these, see below, section 4.6.1.2.
[233] See the national report by STAKHEYEVA-BOGOVYK (Ukraine).
[234] S. RIEDEMANN, above n. 226, Art. 25, para. 10.

The CJEU has held that the requirements for and the effects of the closure of proceedings are determined according to the *lex fori concursus*.[235]

Under the EIR, judgments recognized pursuant to Article 32(1)(1) EIR include court-approved compositions, regardless of whether the composition was suggested by the debtor, the administrator, or the creditors. Since the EIR expressly requires that the composition is approved by the court, it is argued that an arrangement merely between the debtor and (a majority of) creditors will not be afforded recognition. Therefore, some observers from civil law countries have argued that schemes of arrangement would not be recognized under the EIR.[236]

The wording of Article 32(1)(1) EIR includes discharge orders by the court which are not based on a plan approved by the majority of creditors, since this is also a form of "closure" of proceedings. However, the wording of the Regulation does not address legal systems where the proceedings result in a discharge *ipso jure* without an express court decision. Yet, from Article 7(2)(k) EIR, which provides that the *lex fori concursus* governs creditors' rights after the closure of insolvency proceedings, it seems that such a discharge would also be recognized. Whether this is only the result of the applicable substantive law being the *lex fori concursus* or an effect of the recognition of the decision closing the proceeding (which includes the discharge *ipso jure*) is only an academic question.[237]

In the UNCITRAL Model Law, there is no express provision for recognition of a discharge. This is unfortunate because nowadays the focus of insolvency proceedings has clearly shifted from their traditional purpose of liquidation to restructuring. By not providing for a recognition of a discharge, the UNCITRAL Model Law is not in line with this development in modern insolvency law. However, some countries adopting the Model Law have introduced more liberal recognition provisions which also include a discharge – examples are the United States and Ukraine.

Under the common law, a foreign discharge is only recognized when it was in accordance with the proper law of the obligation. Thus, if foreign law applies to an obligation and a discharge is obtained under that law, the discharge will be recognized in England. Conversely, if English law applies to an obligation, a foreign discharge will not be recognized, not even if it was obtained under the law of the domicile, the seat of the corporation, or a debtor's residence or place of business.[238] The leading case in this respect is *Gibbs*.[239] In this case, the Court of Appeal rejected the defendant's argument that a discharge under French law

---

[235] Case C-116/11, *Bank Hadlowy w Warszawie SA and PPHU "ADAX"/Ryszard Adamiak v. Christianopol sp. zo. o.*, ECLI:EU:C:2012:739, paras. 50 f.

[236] S. RIEDEMANN, above n. 226, Art. 25, para. 11; R. BORK and R. MANGANO, above n. 8, para. 5.26.

[237] For a similar discussion on the effects of the opening of proceedings, see above, section 4.2.2.

[238] J. GOLDRING, "Discharge of Debts by Foreign Insolvency Proceeding" in R. SHELDON, above n. 22, para. 13.7 (citing further authority).

[239] *Gibbs v. Societe Industrielle des Métaux* [1890] 25 QBD 399.

was a defense to the English action as suggesting "a principle for which there is no foundation in law or reason". The rationale rests in the assumption that the parties have agreed to the application to the debt of all elements of the debt's proper law, including that governing discharge.[240] While clearly the rule aims at protecting creditors' expectations, it has been criticized by academic authors[241] and, occasionally, courts.[242] Obviously, this law rule hinges on characterizing bankruptcy discharge solely as a contractual matter, and one point of criticism was that bankruptcy discharge is not a consensual matter.[243] The *Gibbs* rule may have dramatic consequences in light of "Brexit": because many banks are located in the United Kingdom and grant loans under English law, in the future, a discharge of such loans obtained in a proceeding in an EU country would not be recognized in the United Kingdom. This may significantly impede, if not indeed make impossible, a restructuring of continental European debtors with loans under English law.

It should be noted that the *Gibbs* rule is not followed in all common law jurisdictions. Notably, U.S. courts recognize a discharge in foreign proceedings even if it involves rights or privileges under U.S. law. In spite of the shortcomings of the *Gibbs* rule, it appears that a similar theory is occasionally adopted in civil law countries. Thus, in Switzerland (which is not an EU Member State), a foreign discharge is recognized if the law of that country is also the law governing the respective claim.[244]

Under the Code Bustamante, a decision regarding the reorganization of insolvent companies has effect in all member countries, except for secured creditors who did not consent to the reorganization.[245]

4.4.5. *Preliminary Measures*

Many countries provide for preliminary measures issued by the court both before or, occasionally, during insolvency proceedings.[246] Under the EIR, such

---

[240] For practical limits of the effect of the *Gibbs* rule, see J. GOLDRING, above n. 238, para. 13.8.

[241] See, e.g., *Dicey, Morris & Collins on the Conflict of Laws*, 15th ed., Sweet & Maxwell, London 2012, para. 31-097; P.S.J SMART, *Cross-Border Insolvency*, 2nd ed., Butterworths, London 1998, pp. 259–260; I.F. FLETCHER, above n. 15, para. 2.127; L.C. HO, *Cross-Border Insolvency: Principles and Practice*, Sweet & Maxwell, London 2016, paras. 4-096 f. See also R. MOKAL, "Shopping and Scheming, and the Rule in *Gibbs*" [2017] *South Square Digest* 58; K. RAMESH, "The *Gibbs* Principle: A Tether on the Feet of Good Forum Shopping" (2017) 29 *Singapore Academy of Law Journal* 42.

[242] See Singapore High Court in *Pacific Andes Resources Development Ltd.* [2016] SGHC 210.

[243] L.C. HO, above n. 241, paras. 4-096 f.

[244] Example: a debtor takes a loan in Austria. He obtains a discharge in Austria. When he relocates to Switzerland, this discharge will be recognized. The result would be different if, e.g., Swiss law governed the loan.

[245] T.B. FELSBERG, above n. 77.

[246] This aspect is not to be confused with the question of whether a court can grant preliminary relief while an application for recognition of a foreign decision is pending. On this, see above, section 4.3.2.

preliminary measures are recognized if they were issued after a request to open insolvency proceedings.[247] According to at least one decision, this applies only to interim relief requested by the administrator or by a creditor, but not to applications made by the debtor himself/herself.[248]

The EIR does not define "preservation measures," which differ from state to state.[249] Some countries provide for the appointment of a preliminary administrator with varying powers to be determined by the court on a case-by-case basis[250] or, somewhat vaguely, just provide for "useful" measures to be taken by the court (which may well include the appointment of a provisional administrator).[251] According to some authors, at least two prerequisites have to be met: (i) the measure has to be an interim measure (because Article 32(1)(3) EIR only mentions measures taken before the opening of proceedings); and (ii) preservation measures must endeavor to protect the debtor's assets (cf. Article 52 EIR) and ensure the effectiveness of future proceedings.[252] If this view is followed, "preservation measures" in this sense should only include measures ordered on behalf of the creditors.[253]

There is disagreement as to whether only preliminary measures issued by a court which claims jurisdiction under Article 3 EIR fall under this provision[254] or whether preliminary measures by other courts are also included.[255] Preliminary measures issued after the opening of the proceeding do not fall under Article 32(1)(3) EIR, but under Article 32(1)(1) EIR, being decisions relating to the "course and closure" of proceedings.[256]

---

[247] Article 32(1)(3) EIR. For a similar provision (for non-EU cases) in domestic law, see, e.g., s. 344 of the German Insolvency Act (Insolvenzordnung).

[248] High Court of Ireland, *Danske Bank A/S Trading as National Irish Bank v. McFadden* [2011] IEHC 551.

[249] See A. GEROLDINGER, *Verfahrenskoordination im Europäischen Insolvenzrecht*, Manz, Vienna 2010, p. 103; S. RIEDEMANN, above n. 226, Art. 25, para. 33.

[250] This is the approach taken by German law.

[251] This is the approach, e.g., under Austrian law. See O. WINTER, *Sicherungsmaßnahmen in Insolvenzeröffnungsverfahren*, Linde, Vienna 2008.

[252] M. VIRGÓS and E. SCHMIT, above n. 111, para. 198; R. BORK and R. MANGANO, above n. 8, para. 5.29.

[253] R. BORK citing the High Court of Ireland, *Danske Bank A/S Trading as National Irish Bank v. McFadden*, above n. 248, where it was held that an interim protection order issued by the High Court of England and Wales did not constitute a preservation measure within the scope of the former Art. 25 of the old EIR, as it was not designed to protect creditors.

[254] This position seems to be the majority view. See, e.g., M. VIRGÓS and F. GARCIMATÍN, above n. 62, para. 391; M. VIRGÓS and E. SCHMIT, above n. 111, para. 198. The question is left open by R. BORK and R. MANGANO, above n. 8, para. 5.28 fn. 58.

[255] This is the position taken by T. LINNA, "Protective Measures in European Cross-Border Insolvency Proceedings" (2014) 5 *International Insolvency Law Review* 6, 8, who speaks of "a court which has jurisdiction to open the main proceedings" and "the courts of a Member State where the measures have to be put into effect".

[256] S. RIEDEMANN, above n. 226, Art. 25, para. 25; R. BORK and R. MANGANO, above n. 8, para. 5.28 fn. 59.

While the EIR expressly mentions preservation measures taken after a request for the opening of proceedings was filed, it has been suggested that recognition should also be afforded to preliminary measures taken before such an application if they relate to insolvency proceedings in order to avoid a gap between the Insolvency Regulation and the Brussels I *bis* Regulation.[257]

While under domestic law in many countries, the appointment of a provisional administrator does not amount to the opening of proceedings, but is only a preliminary measure until the court decides on the opening of proceedings, for the purposes of the EIR, such a preliminary step taken by a court may already be regarded as the "opening" of proceedings and thus constitute a bar to the opening of proceedings in other EU Member States. Under the prior Insolvency Regulation, the Court of Justice of the European Union (CJEU) has held that a judgment was to be regarded as opening insolvency proceedings if a request to open proceedings listed in Annex A to the EIR had been filed, an administrator had been appointed, and the court was seeking to divest the debtor of assets (even though a formal decision opening insolvency proceedings had not yet been made).[258] The recast EIR adopts this approach in a simplified manner, stating that the appointment of an insolvency practitioner pursuant to Annex B was a judgment opening insolvency proceedings in accordance with Article 2(7)(2) EIR.[259] Also, it should be noted that in the domestic law of some countries, a local preliminary measure may constitute a bar to the recognition of foreign (non-EU) proceedings.[260]

4.4.6. Judgments in Related Proceedings

4.4.6.1. The Traditional View

Often questions connected with an insolvency proceeding are decided not in the insolvency proceeding itself, but by way of separate litigation. An example of this is cases where detrimental acts of the debtor are challenged.[261]

---

[257] T. Linna, above n. 255, pp. 9 f.; S. Riedemann, above n. 226, Art. 25, para. 26; M. Virgós and F. Garcimatín, above n. 62, para. 391; R. Bork and R. Mangano, above n. 8, para. 5.28. According to the CJEU's decision in Case 120/79, *Louise de Cavel v. Jacques de Cavel*, ECLI:EU:C:1980:70, para. 8, preservation measures fall within the scope of the Regulation as being applicable to the claim which the measures seek to preserve.

[258] Case C-341/04, *Eurofood IFSC Ltd.*, ECLI:EU:C:2006:281. For an insightful discussion of this case, see T. Bachner, "The Battle over Jurisdiction in European Insolvency Law" (2006) 3 *European Company and Financial Law Review* 310.

[259] R. Bork and R. Mangano, above n. 8, para. 5.18 fn. 38 rightly question whether from a policy point of view, it makes sense to consider a preliminary decision which does not necessarily entail divestment of the debtor to be a judgment opening insolvency proceedings.

[260] See, e.g. s. 240(2)(1) of the Austrian Insolvency Act (Insolvenzordnung).

[261] It has been observed, correctly, that avoidance laws have the purpose and effect of reordering the distribution of a debtor's assets, erasing the results of debtor and creditor actions in favor

The traditional view is clearly that these judgments would fall not under the insolvency regime, but under the recognition scheme for ordinary judgments. In *Rubin v. Eurofinance SA*,[262] the Supreme Court held that the rules at common law governing the recognition and enforcement of foreign judgments apply to judgments given in transaction avoidance proceedings forming part of a foreign insolvency, and that there is no different rule governing the recognition and enforcement of such judgments. The Court also reasoned that recognition and enforcement of such judgments could not be effected under the Cross-Border Insolvency Regulations 2006 (enacting the UNCITRAL Model Law) or under section 426 of the Insolvency Act 1986. Therefore, the Court refused recognition of a judgment of the U.S. Bankruptcy Court because the defendants had not appeared in the proceedings. On the other hand, in a joined case,[263] where the issue was whether an order made by an Australian court, setting aside certain payments as preferences, should be enforced by the English court at the request of the Australian court, the Supreme Court enforced the judgment on the basis that the judgment debtors had submitted to the Australian court's jurisdiction.

In some countries, the law as to the recognition of insolvency-related judgments is not clear. For example, in Ukraine (where the problem is not expressly addressed in domestic law), such judgments arguably could not be accorded recognition since they fall outside the scope of the notion of "insolvency proceedings". On the other hand, recent practice in Ukraine provides for a more integrated insolvency proceeding in which all claims against the debtor and all claims of the debtor or the estate, including the avoidance transaction actions, are determined *within* the bankruptcy proceeding (instead of opening separate adversarial proceedings). This domestic practice may well contribute to a different understanding of what an "insolvency proceeding" entails and thus may lead to an expanded notion of what kinds of judgments can be recognized.

4.4.6.2. The UNCITRAL Model Law on Recognition and Enforcement of Insolvency-Related Judgments

Under the recently proposed UNCITRAL Model Law on Recognition and Enforcement of Insolvency-Related Judgments (MLIJ),[264] an insolvency-related

---

of the collective priorities established by the distribution statute; see *In re Condor Insurance Ltd.* [2010] 601 F.3d 319 (holding that a U.S. court had jurisdiction to apply avoidance relief under a foreign law by virtue of Chapter 15). In light of this, it has been suggested that they should be treated as an integral part of the entire bankruptcy system.

262 *Rubin v. Eurofinance SA* [2013] 1 AC 236.
263 *New Cap Reinsurance Corp Ltd. v. A.E. Grant* [2012] Ch 538.
264 See above, section 3.2.2.

judgment is defined as a judgment that arises "as a consequence of or is materially associated with an insolvency proceeding" (whether or not that proceeding has been closed) and was issued on or after the commencement of the insolvency proceeding. It does not include a judgment commencing an insolvency proceeding. The MLIJ addresses the relationship between the MLIJ and treaties that might address the same subject matter; the procedure for applying for recognition and enforcement, including the availability of provisional relief; grounds for refusing recognition and enforcement; the effect and enforceability of an insolvency-related judgment; the effect on the recognition and enforcement of review of the judgment in the originating state; the equivalent effect of a judgment in the recognizing state; and the severability of parts of the judgment for the purposes of recognition and enforcement. Recognition of a judgment can be sought directly by way of an application under Article 11 or as part of a defense to a claim, or as incidental to another question already before the court.

4.4.6.3. The EU

In Europe, the CJEU has held that the regime of the former Insolvency Regulation also extended to certain "related" proceedings which were closely "linked" with the insolvency proceeding.[265] The recast version of the EIR, picking up the formulation of the CJEU in these decisions, extends the recognition scheme provided for insolvency decisions in Article (32)(1)(1) EIR to judgments "derived directly from and closely linked to insolvency proceedings".[266] It is not necessary that these judgments are rendered by the court conducting insolvency proceedings. This takes into account systems in which local rules for jurisdiction provide for these "related proceedings" to be decided by a different court.[267]

Related proceedings (for which Article 6(1) EIR provides jurisdiction of the state where insolvency proceedings were opened)[268] include[269] avoidance

---

[265] See, e.g., Case 133/78, *Henri Gourdain v. Franz Nadler*, ECLI:EU:C:1979:49; Case C-339/07, *Christopher Seagon v. Deko Marty Belgium NV*, ECLI:EU:C:2009:83 (both dealing with international jurisdiction).

[266] Article 32(1)(2) EIR. See also Z. FABÓK, "Grounds for Refusal of Recognition of (Quasi-) Annex Judgements in the Recast European Insolvency Regulation" (2017) 26 *International Insolvency Review* 295.

[267] An example is Germany, where, at the time that Case C-339/07, *Christopher Seagon v. Deko Marty Belgium NV*, ECLI:EU:C:2009:83 was decided, the court conducting the insolvency proceedings did not have jurisdiction under domestic law to decide avoidance actions.

[268] This rule also subjects parties without domicile or seat in the state where the proceeding has been opened (and also without domicile or seat in the EU) to the jurisdiction of the state where the insolvency proceeding was opened. This results in a much stronger concentration of insolvency-related proceedings in the state where the proceeding has been opened compared to other countries such as the United States.

[269] See the list in Guide to the UNICTRAL Model Law on Cross-Border Insolvency, paras. 9 and 60; see also P. MANKOWSKI, "Insolvenznahe Verfahren im Grenzbereich zwischen EuInsVO

actions; insolvency law-related lawsuits on the personal liability of directors and officers; lawsuits concerning the priority of a claim; disputes between an insolvency representative and a debtor on the inclusion of an asset in the insolvency estate; approval of a reorganization plan; discharge of residual debt; actions on the insolvency representative's liability for damages, if exclusively based on the carrying out of the insolvency proceedings; action by a creditor aiming at the nullification of an insolvency representative's decision to recognize another creditor's claim; and claims by an insolvency representative based on specific insolvency law privilege. Judgments held not to fall into that category have included actions by and against an insolvency representative which would also have been possible without the insolvency proceedings; criminal proceedings in connection with insolvency; an action to recover property in the possession of the debtor; an action to determine the legal validity or amount of a claim pursuant to general laws; claims by creditors with a right to segregation of assets; claims by creditors with a right to separate satisfaction (secured creditors); and an avoidance action filed not by an insolvency representative, but by a legal successor or assignee. Most recently, the CJEU held that a lawsuit as to whether a creditor indeed had a valid claim would not fall under the Brussels I *bis* Regulation (and hence should probably fall under the Insolvency Regulation regime).[270] This is remarkable because it departs (unfortunately without discussion) from the general rule that the opening of insolvency proceedings should not affect the question of which courts have jurisdiction to determine whether a creditor has a claim against the debtor. In light of these developments, it is likely that the CJEU would also regard proceedings seeking the return of assets to the estate as "closely linked" to the insolvency proceedings.

4.5. PREREQUISITES FOR RECOGNITION

4.5.1. *The Required Documents*

According to Article 15 of the UNCITRAL Model Law on Cross-Border Insolvency, an application for recognition shall be accompanied by: (a) a certified copy of the decision commencing the foreign proceeding and appointing the foreign representative; or (b) a certificate from the foreign court affirming the existence of the foreign proceeding and of the appointment of the foreign representative; or (c) in the absence of evidence referred to in subparagraphs (a) and (b), any other evidence acceptable to the court of the existence of the foreign

---

und EuGVVO – Zur Entscheidung des EuGH in Sachen German Graphics (NZI 2009, 741)" [2010] *Neue Zeitschrift für Insolvenz- und Sanierungsrecht* 508.

[270] Case C-47/18, *Skarb Pánstwa Rzeczpospolitej Polskiej v. Generalny Dyrektor Dróg Krajowych i Autostrad v. Stephan Riel*, ECLI:EU:C:2019:754.

proceeding and of the appointment of the foreign representative. In addition, under Article 15(3) an application for recognition shall also be accompanied by a statement identifying all foreign proceedings in respect of the debtor that are known to the foreign representative. The court is entitled to presume that documents submitted in support of the application for recognition are authentic, whether or not they have been legalized.[271] The court may require a translation of documents supplied in support of the application for recognition into an official language of this state.[272]

The requirements under Article 11(2) of the UNCITRAL Model Law on Recognition and Enforcement of Insolvency-Related Judgments are similar. Under the UNCITRAL Model Law on Enterprise Group Insolvency, in addition to the documents mentioned above, Article 21(3) requires: (a) a statement identifying each enterprise group member participating in the foreign planning proceeding; (b) a statement identifying all members of the enterprise group and all insolvency proceedings that are known to the group representative that have been commenced in respect of enterprise group members participating in the foreign planning proceeding; and (c) a statement to the effect that the enterprise group member subject to the foreign planning proceeding has the centre of its main interests in the state in which that planning proceeding is taking place and that that proceeding is likely to result in added overall combined value for the enterprise group members subject to or participating in that proceeding.

Some countries, even though they have adopted the UNCITRAL Model Law on Cross-Border Insolvency, require more documents. Thus, under Ukrainian law, the foreign representative also has to submit: (i) a document stating that the foreign court decision has come into force (unless indicated in the decision itself); (ii) a document attesting that the debtor concerned (which did not take part in the court proceeding) was duly notified of the date and place of the court hearing; and (iii) a document confirming the authority of the foreign representative.[273]

Under the EIR, recognition of a foreign decision in an insolvency proceeding is automatic. The only requirements are that the judgment falls within the scope *ratione materiae* of the EIR and that the judgment has taken effect in its country of origin.

4.5.2. Res Judicata *Requirement?*

Under the UNCITRAL Model Law on Cross-Border Insolvency, it is not necessary that the judgment sought to be recognized is final. However, under

---

[271]   Article 16(2) of the UNCITRAL Model Law on Cross-Border Insolvency.

[272]   In India, a study group recommended that translation be mandatory. See the national report by DUBE (India), p. 7.

[273]   See the national report by STAKHEYEVA-BOGOVYK (Ukraine).

Article 10 of the UNCITRAL Model Law for Recognition of Insolvency-Related Judgments, recognition or enforcement of an insolvency-related judgment may be postponed or refused if the judgment is the subject of review in the originating state or if the time limit for seeking ordinary review in that state has not expired. In such cases, the court may also make recognition or enforcement conditional on the provision of such security as it shall determine.

Also, under the EIR, a judgment need not be final in the sense of *res judicata*; rather, the test is only if the judgment is already effective in the country where it was rendered.[274] Typically, in insolvency proceedings, no appeal with a suspensive effect is available.

Article 247 of the former OHADA Uniform Act provided that when a decision initiating or closing collective proceedings pronounced in a contracting state had become irrevocable, it should be *res judicata* in the other states. In 2015, this provision was replaced by the introduction of the UNCITRAL Model Law by the new OHADA Uniform Insolvency Act.

4.5.3. Reciprocity

Reciprocity is a requirement for recognition in bilateral treaties and under the domestic law of some countries. Under the UNCITRAL Model Law on Cross-Border Insolvency, reciprocity is not a requirement. Nonetheless, reciprocity has been imposed de jure or de facto by a number of states, namely the British Virgin Islands, Mauritius, Mexico, Romania, and South Africa.[275] In Ukraine, reciprocity is required and has to be guaranteed by an international treaty. In India, a study group recommended that the UNCITRAL Model Law be adopted on a reciprocal basis initially. Subsequently, with the development of an adequate infrastructure for corporate insolvency in India, the requirement of reciprocity may be withdrawn.[276]

While not establishing a reciprocity requirement in the strict sense of the word, it should be noted that the scope of available assistance under the common law was dramatically reduced by a decision of the Privy Council.[277] According to this decision, common law assistance may only be given to provide relief which is available both in the administrator's own (foreign) jurisdiction and under the domestic common law of the country in which assistance is sought. This decision in essence limits the court's powers to assist a foreign proceeding to the "common denominator" of the two legal systems concerned.

---

[274] See Art. 19 EIR; R. Bork and R. Mangano, above n. 8, para. 5.22; K. Pannen and S. Riedemann, above n. 63, Art. 16, para. 11; B. Wessels, above n. 12, para. 10734.

[275] L.C. Ho, above n. 44, p. 9.

[276] See the national report by Dube (India), p. 7.

[277] *Singularis Holdings Ltd. v. PricewaterhouseCoopers* [2014] UKPC 36. For a discussion of this decision, see R. Sheldon, above n. 23, paras. 1.6, 1.18, and 1.30.

4.5.4. Jurisdiction of the Court Opening the Proceeding

Under the UNICTRAL Model Law on Cross-Border Insolvency, recognition of a foreign main proceeding requires that the proceeding was opened in the country of the debtor's COMI.[278] As a result, recognition was sometimes refused in well-known cases.[279] Similarly, a non-main proceeding can only be recognized if the debtor has an establishment in the state where the non-main proceeding was opened.[280] In contrast, under the EIR, despite Article 19(1) stating that the judgment opening insolvency proceedings has to be handed down by a court which has jurisdiction pursuant to Article 3, the court in the country where recognition is sought is not allowed to re-examine whether the court opening the proceedings had jurisdiction.[281]

Under domestic law, many countries employ a kind of "mirror image rule."[282] According to this rule, the test is whether, if one applies the rules on jurisdiction of the country where recognition is sought, the court opening the insolvency proceedings has jurisdiction.[283] Only if this question is answered in the affirmative will the decision be recognized.

Under the UNCITRAL Model Law on Cross-Border Insolvency, the court's task in deciding upon the recognition of a foreign main proceeding is assisted by a presumption. According to Article 16 of the UNCITRAL Model Law, if the decision or certificate referred to in Article 15(2) indicates that the foreign proceeding is a main proceeding and that the foreign representative is a person or body within the meaning of Article 2(d), the court is entitled to so presume. Perhaps more importantly, in the absence of proof to the contrary, the debtor's registered office (or habitual residence in the case of an individual) is presumed to be the center of the debtor's main interests. Interestingly, U.S. law substituted the word "proof" with "evidence".[284] In Ukraine, even though this country has adopted the UNICTRAL Model Law, recognition of the "foreign main proceeding" depends not on the location of the debtor's COMI, but on its place of incorporation.[285]

---

[278] Article 17(2)(a) of the UNCITRAL Model Law.

[279] See, e.g., *In re Bear Stearns High-Grade Structures Credit Strategies Master Fund, Ltd.* and *In re Bear Stearns High-Grade Structures Credit Strategies Enhanced Leverage Master Fund, Ltd.*, US Bankruptcy Court Southern District of New York Case 07-12383 (BRL) and 07-12384 (BRL) (Bankr. S.D.N.Y. 2007).

[280] Article 17(2)(b) of the UNCITRAL Model Law.

[281] For a discussion of whether the opening of bankruptcy proceedings by a court lacking jurisdiction may constitute a violation of public policy, see below, section 4.6.1.

[282] See, e.g, G. GRAF, above n. 30, p. 289.

[283] See, e.g., s. 343 of the German Insolvency Act (Insolvenzordnung); s. 240 of the Austrian Insolvency Act (Insolvenzordnung).

[284] See S. MAIDEN, above n. 49, p. 69.

[285] See the national report by STAKHEYEVA-BOGOVYK (Ukraine).

4.6. GROUNDS FOR NON-RECOGNITION

4.6.1. *Public Policy*

4.6.1.1. Opening Decisions and Administration Orders

Virtually all recognition schemes recognize that an exception in case recognition would be contrary to public policy.[286] Under the UNCITRAL Model Law on Cross-Border Insolvency, recognition can only be refused if it would be manifestly[287] contrary to public policy.[288] Similarly, under the EIR, any Member State may refuse to recognize insolvency proceedings opened in another Member State or to enforce a judgment handed down in the context of such proceedings where the effects of such recognition or enforcement would be manifestly contrary to that state's public policy, in particular its fundamental principles or the constitutional rights and liberties of the individual.[289] This is the only ground for a refusal of non-recognition under the EIR. Since the wording of the provision is identical to Article 34(1) of the former Brussels I Regulation and Article 45(1)(a) of its successor, the Brussels I *bis* Regulation, precedents dealing with these two regulations can also provide guidance here. It is generally accepted that the public policy exception has to be interpreted restrictively[290] and should only be invoked in extreme circumstances.[291]

Recognition of a foreign decision does not involve a review of the merits of the decision.[292] Therefore, the mere fact that foreign law is different from the

---

[286] See M.A. Garza, "When is Cross-Border Insolvency Recognition Manifestly Contrary to Public Policy?" (2015) 38 *Fordham International Law Journal* 1587.

[287] Some countries adopting the Model Law have omitted the word "manifestly". See ibid., 1596.

[288] Article 6 of the UNCITRAL Model Law. See, e.g., M.A. Garza, above n. 286, 1587; G. Mccormak, "Foreign Law and Public Policy in the UNCITRAL Model Law on Cross-Border Insolvency: A Transatlantic Perspective" (2015) 3 *Nottingham Insolvency and Business Law e-Journal* 477.

[289] On the application of the ECHR on insolvency proceedings, see J.C. van Apeldoorn, *Human Rights in Insolvency Proceedings*, Kluwer, Deventer 2012; G.E. Kodek, "The Impact of the European Convention of Human Rights and Fundamental Liberties on Insolvency Proceedings" in H. Peter, N. Jeandin, and J. Kilborn (eds.), *The Challenges of Insolvency Reform in the 21st Century: Facilitating Investment and Recovery to Enhance Economic Growth*, Schulthess, Zürich 2006, p. 569; K. Puschner, *Konkurs und EMRK*, Manz, Vienna 2000; L. Vallens, "Droit de la faillite et droits de l'homme" [1997] *Revue trimestrielle de droit commercial* 567.

[290] Case C-444/07, *MG Probud Gdynia sp. z. o.o.*, ECLI:EU:C:2010:24, para. 34; Case C-341/04, *Eurofood IFSC Ltd.*, ECLI:EU:C:2006:281, para. 62; G. Corno, "Enforcement of Avoidance Claims Judgments in Europe: Present Rules and (Reasonable) Future Reforms" [2013] *International Insolvency Law Review* 417, 424.

[291] R. Bork and R. Mangano, above n. 8, para. 5.43; M. Virgós and E. Schmit, above n. 111, para. 204 (stressing that recognition is mandatory unless it is "manifestly" against the public policy of a Member State).

[292] G. Moss and T. Smith, above n. 63, para. 8.364. See also section 4.3.1 above.

law of the state where recognition is sought is not sufficient to trigger a public policy exception. Nor is it sufficient that local creditors receive less if the foreign proceeding was recognized[293] or if in the foreign proceeding creditors are ranked differently.[294] However, discrimination of creditors based on nationality runs counter to Article 18 of the Treaty on the Functioning of the European Union (TFEU).[295]

Also, national laws protecting key areas of a Member State's economy, such as the availability of a minimum quantity of energy (oil and gas),[296] must be taken into account.[297] When the former EIR was adopted, Portugal made a reservation, without a legal basis in the EIR, for the protection of domestic creditors, employees, and business partners that recognition of the conversion of a local settlement proceeding into a winding-up proceeding pursuant to Article 37 of the old version of the EIR can be refused based on the public policy exception.[298]

Occasionally it has been suggested that recognition of a discharge could be refused on public policy grounds if the creditors receive no or insufficient payments. However, in light of recent developments in insolvency law with more focus being placed on restructuring in most countries, it seems unlikely that a foreign discharge should trigger the public policy exception.[299] This is indeed the result achieved by the German Supreme Court.[300] A U.S. court denied recognition of a prepackaged Mexican plan ("concurso") which provided for the extinction of a third-party guarantee as manifestly contrary to public policy, holding that protection of third-party claims was a fundamental policy of the United States.[301]

Personal freedom and postal secrecy constitute parts of public policy.[302] In *Re Toft*, a U.S. bankruptcy court refused to enforce a German court order that would have allowed the foreign administrator unrestrained access to emails of the debtor that were being stored on internet servers in the United States.[303] According to the court, recognizing the foreign mail interception order would undermine U.S. public policy and in particular the fundamental principles of

---

[293]   *In re Ernst Young, Inc.*, 383 BR 773, 776 (Bankr. D. Colo. 2008).

[294]   *In re Quimonda AG*, 2011 Bankr LEXIS 4191 (Bankr. ED Va 2011).

[295]   S. Riedemann, above n. 226, Art. 26 para. 10; M. Virgós and F. Garcimatín, above n. 62, para. 407.

[296]   G. Moss and T. Smith, above n. 63, para. 8.237.

[297]   P. Mankowski, "Der ordre public im europäischen und im deutschen Internationalen Insolvenzrecht" [2011] *KTS – Zeitschrift für Insolvenzrecht* 185, 202 ff.; B. Wessels, above n. 131, para. 8.367.

[298]   Declaration by Portugal concerning the application of Articles 26 and 37 of Council Regulation (EC) No 1346/2000 of 29 May 2000 on insolvency proceedings [2000] OJ C183/1.

[299]   G. Graf, above n. 30, p. 308.

[300]   BGH 27.5.1993, *BGHZ* 122, 373.

[301]   *In re Vitro S.A.B. de CV*, B.R. 571 (Bankr. N.D. Texas 2011). See M.A. Garza, above n. 286, 1618.

[302]   R. Bork and R. Mangano, above n. 8, para. 5.5.4, citing further authorities.

[303]   *In re Toft*, 453 B.R. at 189 (SDNY 2011).

protecting the secrecy of electronic communications. In stark contrast to this decision, the English courts had no problem recognizing the order, concluding that it was proportionate to the legitimate aim pursued.[304] This completely opposite result was reached despite the fact that both countries adopted the Model Law.[305]

A violation of the right to be heard will normally constitute a violation of public policy.[306] Thus, a U.S. court denied recognition to an Italian insolvency proceeding on the ground that a creditor had not received a notice of the proceeding.[307] On the other hand, insolvency proceedings involve a number of participants with diverse (procedural) interests and rights regarding the different decisions handed down during an insolvency proceeding. Therefore, it seems that while the debtor must always be heard, this is not necessarily also true for individual creditors; rather, their rights may be protected by the availability of an appeal or of applications to be made later in the course of proceedings.[308] Also, it is accepted that the absence of procedural rights that may be available in a domestic context, such as a jury trial, in and of itself is not sufficient to refuse recognition.[309]

A spectacular case dealing with the public policy exception is the *Yukos* case,[310] in which the Dutch Supreme Court held that the powers of the Russian liquidator could in principle be recognized in the Netherlands and referred the case back to the court of appeal. The court of appeal then held that the Russian insolvency proceeding was contrary to the principle of a fair trial and that the behavior of the Russian authorities was such as to intentionally trigger the bankruptcy of Yukos Oil.[311] This decision was upheld in 2019 by the Dutch Supreme Court.[312]

Sometimes it is argued that the recognition of a judgment obtained by "fraud" would violate public policy. The UNCITRAL Model Law on Recognition of Insolvency-Related Judgments mentions fraud as a separate ground for non-recognition.[313]

---

[304] Order of the Chancery Division of the High Court, January 28, 2011, https://lettersblogatory. com/wp-content/uploads/2011/08/toft-uk-order.pdf. See I. KOKORIN and B. WESSELS, "Recognition of Foreign Insolvency Judgments: The Case of Yukos" (2017) 14 *European Company Law Journal* 226, 231.

[305] I. KOKORIN and B. WESSELS, above n. 304, 231.

[306] See Case C-341/04, *Eurofood IFSC Ltd.*, ECLI:EU:C:2006:281.

[307] *In re Sivex Srl*, Case No. 11-80799-TRC, 2011 WL 3651250, at *3 (Bankr. E.D. Okl. 2011). See M.A. GARZA, above n. 286, 1615 f.

[308] See R. BORK and R. MANGANO, above n. 8, para. 5.53.

[309] *In re RSM Richter v. Aguilar* (*In re Ephedra Products Liability Litigation*), 349 BR 333 (Southern District of New York 2006).

[310] See I. KOKORIN and B. WESSELS, above n. 304, 226.

[311] Gerechtshof Amsterdam, May 9, 2017, ECLI:NL:GHAMS:2017:1695.

[312] See "Bankruptcy of Yukos Oil in Russia Not Recognized in the Netherlands – Supreme Court", https://www.reuters.com/article/netherlands-russia-yukos/bankruptcy-of-yukos-oil-in-russia-not-recognized-in-the-netherlands-supreme-court-idUSA5N1TF02P.

[313] Article 14(b) of the UNCITRAL Model Law on Insolvency-Related Judgments.

Under domestic law, the notion of public policy may be broader. Thus, under English law, an expanded notion of public policy has developed in cross-border cases.[314] The right of English creditors to set off under English insolvency law has been described as a fundamental principle of justice.[315] In one case, a U.S. court has refused recognition to a proceeding commenced in violation of the worldwide stay imposed by the U.S. Bankruptcy Code.[316]

While courts have occasionally refused recognition on public policy grounds if the court opening insolvency proceedings did not have jurisdiction,[317] the majority view is that lack of jurisdiction does not give rise to a public policy exception, not even if the decision does not contain reasons as to why the court opening proceedings assumed jurisdiction.[318] It is debated whether Article 33 EIR applies in the case of a purported shift of COMI involving a deception of the court.[319]

In the *Brochier* case, a German district court held that the opening of an English main proceeding against an English limited liability company almost exclusively doing business in Germany violated German procedural public policy and was not to be recognized if the court did not examine its jurisdiction itself, but opened the insolvency proceeding solely based on the unsubstantiated allegations of the applicant debtor.[320] The German court held that the decision in England was based on the factually wrong allegations of the debtor, that it did not contain reasons as to why the court had jurisdiction, and that the administrator was not independent because he was appointed on the application of the director of the debtor and was advised by lawyers who had advised the debtor for a long time.

---

[314] R. FISHER and A. AL-ATTAR, above n. 121, para. 3.70.

[315] See *HIH, McGrath v. Riddell* [2008] UKHL 21; [2008] 1 WLR 852.

[316] *In re Gold & Honey Ltd.*, 410 BR 357, 371 (2009).

[317] This result was obtained, e.g., in the *Brochier* case by the AG Nürnberg 15.8.2006, 8004 INS 1326/06. The background of this and similar cases was that, from a European perspective, English courts tended to assume jurisdiction over insolvency cases in which there were closer ties to European countries and failed to give reasons in their decisions as to why they considered the COMI to be in England. See H. DUURSMA-KEPPLINGER, "British Courts are Satisfied, Continental Europe is Not Amused" [2003] *Zeitschrift für Insolvenzrecht & Kreditschutz* 182.

[318] See, e.g., the famous *Stojevic* case (concerning recognition of an English bankruptcy in Austria): OLG Wien 9.11.2004, 28 R 225/04w; subsequently confirmed by OGH 17.3.2005, 8 Ob 135/04t.

[319] For the application of the public policy exception in this case, see OLG Düsseldorf 23.8.2013, I-22 U 37/13; *contra* OLG Nürnberg 15.12.2011, 1 U 2/11. For additional authorities, see R. BORK and R. MANGANO, above n. 8, para. 5.48 fn. 118.

[320] AG Nürnberg 15.8.2006, 8004 IN 1326-1331/06 = ZIP 2007, 81. On this decision, see G.E. KODEK, "Zuständigkeit des deutschen Insolvenzgerichts im Verfahren der Brochier Holdings Ltd. trotz satzungsmäßigen Sitzes in England ('Brochier IV')" [2007] *EWiR – Entscheidungen zum Wirtschaftsrecht* 179.

4.6.1.2. Related Judgments

The EIR also extends its liberal recognition regime to judgments in related cases.[321] Therefore, recognition of such judgments can only be denied if this would be manifestly against the public policy of the state where recognition is sought.

On the other hand, the UNCITRAL Model Law on Insolvency-Related Judgments follows a more traditional approach. Under Article 14, recognition and enforcement of an insolvency-related judgment may be refused if the defendant was not notified properly of the proceeding, if the judgment was obtained by fraud, or if the judgment is inconsistent with a judgment issued in the state where recognition is sought in a dispute involving the same parties. In addition, a judgment will not be recognized if recognition and enforcement would interfere with the administration of the debtor's insolvency proceedings, including by conflicting with a stay or other order that could be recognized or enforced in this state.

Also, a judgment will not be recognized if it materially affects the rights of creditors generally, such as determining whether a plan of reorganization or liquidation should be confirmed, a discharge of the debtor or of debts should be granted, or a voluntary or out-of-court restructuring agreement should be approved, and the interests of creditors and other interested persons, including the debtor, were not adequately protected in the proceeding in which the judgment was issued. Finally, a judgment will only be recognized if the court exercised jurisdiction on the basis of consent or submission, or if the court exercised jurisdiction on a basis on which a court in the state where recognition is sought could have exercised jurisdiction. There is also an optional provision that insolvency-related judgments from a state whose insolvency proceedings are not recognized would not be afforded recognition.[322]

4.6.2. Other Grounds

Recognition of judgments in civil cases will ordinarily[323] be refused if the defendant was not served properly or if the judgment is irreconcilable with a judgment given between the same parties. Similarly, lack of jurisdiction may constitute a ground for non-recognition.[324] It has already been pointed out that the recognition of judgments in insolvency cases is often more generous compared to ordinary civil cases. The available grounds for non-recognition

---

[321] Article 32(1)(2) EIR.
[322] Article 14(h) of the UNCITRAL Model Law on Insolvency-Related Judgments.
[323] See, e.g., Art. 45(1) of the Brussels I *bis* Regulation.
[324] See ibid., Art. 45(1)(e).

depend on the degree of integration and cooperation achieved. Thus, it is hardly surprising that the EIR only allows recognition to be refused on the grounds of a manifest violation of public policy. The position of the UNCITRAL Model Law on Cross-Border Insolvency is similar, although it has been shown that under the Model Law, there is the additional requirement for the recognition of foreign main proceedings that the proceeding was opened in a state where the debtor has its COMI.

Outside the regime of the UNCITRAL Model Law or the EIR, the grounds for non-recognition may well be broader. In Ukraine, for example, even though this country has adopted the Model Law, recognition of a foreign insolvency proceeding is, inter alia, also refused (in addition to violations of public policy) if the party against which the foreign insolvency proceeding was opened had not been duly notified of the hearing of the case, if the foreign insolvency proceeding concerns a debtor which is incorporated in accordance with the legislation of Ukraine, or if the debtor has already been the subject of an insolvency proceeding in Ukraine and this proceeding has been closed.

While in some countries insolvency proceedings are only available for "merchants" or for companies, the EIR specifically provides that it does not constitute a bar to recognition if, on account of a debtor's capacity, insolvency proceedings cannot be brought against that debtor in the state where recognition is sought.[325]

5. ENFORCEMENT OF FOREIGN DECISIONS

5.1. INTRODUCTION

While sometimes the terms "recognition" and "enforcement" seem to be used interchangeably, recognition has to be distinguished from enforcement. Enforcement of a judgment implies its execution via the coercive powers of a state's authorities.[326] The territorial sovereignty of states is exclusive in the sense that no foreign authority may exercise such coercive powers within the respective state's jurisdiction.[327] Therefore, normally the enforcement of a judgment must be carried out by the competent national authorities and according to the domestic law of the state where enforcement is sought.[328] Even in the EU, enforcement has to be carried out by the national authorities of the state where enforcement

---

[325] Article 19(1)(2) EIR.

[326] M. VIRGÓS and F. GARCIMATÍN, above n. 62, para. 345; M. VIRGÓS and E. SCHMIT, above n. 111, para. 190; R. BORK and R. MANGANO, above n. 8, para. 5.12.

[327] M. VIRGÓS and F. GARCIMATÍN, above n. 62, para. 345; M. VIRGÓS and E. SCHMIT, above n. 111, para. 190; R. BORK and R. MANGANO, above n. 8, para. 5.12.

[328] R. BORK and R. MANGANO, n. 8, para. 5.12.

is sought. Therefore, the extension model of recognition under the EIR does not include the enforcement of the judgment in the sense described above;[329] rather, the EIR refers to the respective provisions on the enforcement of judgments in civil and commercial cases of the Brussels I *bis* Regulation. Pursuant to Article 32(1), the enforcement of judgments relating to insolvency is to be carried out pursuant to Articles 39–44 and 47–57 of the Brussels I *bis* Regulation.

Under the Brussels I *bis* Regulation, decisions from other Member States are enforced without exequatur proceedings, provided they are enforceable in their country of origin. If the judgment contains a measure or an order which is not known in the law of the Member State addressed, that measure or order shall, to the extent possible, be adapted to a measure or an order known in the law of that Member State which has equivalent effects attached to it and which pursues similar aims and interests. Such adaptation shall not result in effects going beyond those provided for in the law of the respective Member State.[330] Significantly, Articles 45 and 46 of the Brussels I *bis* Regulation on refusal of enforcement do not apply. This does not mean that states have to enforce foreign decisions even if they violate public policy; rather, Article 32(1) EIR, by exempting Articles 45 and 46 of the Brussels I *bis* Regulation, only ensures that the procedural mechanism established in Articles 45 and 46 for asserting a public policy defense in enforcement proceedings does not apply to insolvency proceedings. However, in insolvency proceedings, courts can still refuse the enforcement of foreign decisions if they are not recognized pursuant to Article 33 EIR on the grounds of public policy.[331]

5.2. OPENING OF INSOLVENCY PROCEEDINGS

Sometimes it is argued that a decision opening insolvency proceedings does not contain enforceable elements.[332] While this may be true in most cases, there are cases where the judgment opening insolvency proceedings can be enforced under national law.[333] Thus, in Germany, the administrator can use the opening decision to initiate enforcement proceedings against the debtor seeking the handing over of assets belonging to the debtor.[334]

---

[329] M. Virgós and F. Garcimatín, above n. 62, para. 342; R. Bork and R. Mangano, above n. 8, para. 5.12.

[330] Article 54 of the Brussels I *bis* Regulation.

[331] R. Bork and R. Mangano, n. 8, para. 5.62.

[332] U. Gruber in D. Hass et al. (eds.), *EuInsVO*, C.H. Beck, Munich 2005, Art. 25, para. 1; P. Mankowski, above n. 269, 511; S. Reinhart in R. Stürmer et al. (eds.), *Münchener Kommentar zur Insolvenzordnung*, C.H.Beck, Munich 2016, Art. 25, para. 1.

[333] J. Blitz, above n. 119, p. 148; A. Geroldinger, above n. 249, p. 101; R. Bork and R. Mangano, above n. 8, para. 558 fn. 152.

[334] Section 148, para. 2 of the German Insolvency Act (Insolvenzordnung).

5.3. SEIZURE AND SALE OF THE DEBTOR'S ASSETS

While the opening of insolvency proceedings may result in the debtor's rights being vested in the administrator (if the foreign law so provides), the administrator, even if he/she is allowed to collect and sell the debtor's assets, may not use force. Whenever force is necessary, he has to apply to the local courts for relief. In some countries, the decision opening proceedings already contains enforceable elements which can be used as the basis for enforcement proceedings against the debtor for the return of assets belonging to the estate.[335] In this case, the administrator has to apply for recognition (unless there is automatic recognition such as under the EIR) and has to initiate local enforcement proceedings.

6. COORDINATION OF PROCEEDINGS

6.1. INTRODUCTION

In spite of the principle of (modified or limited) universalism, for a number of reasons there can be parallel (concurrent) proceedings concerning both the same debtor and different debtors. Both the EIR and the UNCITRAL Model Law on Cross-Border Insolvency permit local proceedings in addition to the main proceeding opened in the country where the debtor has its COMI. Under the EIR, this is only possible in a country where the debtor has an establishment.[336] Under Article 28 of the UNCITRAL Model Law, a local proceeding is possible in every country where the debtor has assets. Also, in a non-technical sense, concurrent proceedings can be the result of proceedings opened against different members of a group of companies in different countries. In all these cases, cooperation and coordination of the proceedings is desirable.

Historically, in many countries, cross-border judicial cooperation has been limited or even non-existent. The UNCITRAL Model Law on Cross-Border Insolvency mandates local courts and insolvency representatives to "cooperate to the maximum extent possible with foreign courts or foreign representatives".[337] Local courts and insolvency representatives are authorized to communicate directly with foreign courts and foreign representatives. Article 27 of the UNCITRAL Model Law contains a non-exclusive list of types of cooperation: (a) the appointment of a person or body to act at the direction of the court; (b) the communication of information by any means considered appropriate by the court; (c) the coordination of the administration and supervision of the debtor's assets and affairs; (d) the approval or implementation by courts of agreements

---

[335] See above, section 5.2.
[336] Article 3(2) EIR.
[337] See Arts. 25 and 26 of the UNCITRAL Model Law.

concerning the coordination of proceedings; (e) the coordination of concurrent proceedings regarding the same debtor. Recently, the draft of an UNCITRAL Model Code on Enterprise Group Insolvency provides for cooperation and direct communication between courts, insolvency representatives, and any group representative appointed (Article 9). Similarly, already under the former OHADA Uniform Act, there was a mutual duty of administrators to exchange information.[338] The more recent Uniform Insolvency Act of 2015 introduced the UNCITRAL Model Law.

Although the UNCITRAL Model Law on Cross-Border Insolvency restricts the recognition scheme to foreign proceedings opened in a state where the debtor has either its COMI or at least an establishment, the cooperation provisions in Articles 25–27 of the UNCITRAL Model Law extend to all foreign proceedings. This includes foreign proceedings opened on the sole basis of the presence of assets within that state.[339]

Under the EIR, the administrator of the main proceeding has a dominant role. He may apply for the opening of secondary proceedings (Article 37(1a) EIR), give an "undertaking" to avoid the opening of secondary proceedings (Article 36 EIR), request a temporary stay of execution proceedings (Article 38(3) EIR), request a conversion of secondary proceedings to be opened or already opened (Articles 38(4) and 51 EIR), lodge claims in the secondary proceeding (Article 45(2) EIR), or propose a restructuring plan (Article 47 EIR). Nevertheless, the smooth running of parallel insolvency proceedings requires cooperation.[340]

6.2. THE "HOTCHPOT RULE"

Article 32 of the UNCITRAL Model Law establishes the "hotchpot rule," which requires that before a creditor who has received part-payment in respect of its claim in a proceeding pursuant to a law relating to insolvency in a foreign state may not receive a payment for the same claim in a proceeding regarding the same debtor, so long as the payment to the other creditors of the same class is proportionately less than the payment the creditor has already received. Thus, when an unsecured creditor has received 5% of its claim in a foreign insolvency proceeding and then participates in another insolvency proceeding where the rate of distribution is 15%, the creditor will only receive 10% of its claim in order to put it in a position equal to other creditors in this state.[341] A similar rule is expressed in Article 23 EIR.[342] This rule tends to mitigate differences between national insolvency laws.

---

[338]   Article 252 of the OHADA Uniform Act.

[339]   L.C. Ho, above n. 44, p. 14.

[340]   R. Bork and R. Mangano, above n. 8, para. 6.29.

[341]   Guide to the UNICTRAL Model Law on Cross-Border Insolvency, para. 198.

[342]   See R. Bork and R. Mangano, above n. 8, paras. 6.58 f.

Transnational Cooperation in Cross-Border Insolvency

While the hotchpot rule under Article 32 of the UNCITRAL Model Law only applies to non-secured creditors, some countries seem to have extended the rule to secured creditors.[343]

6.3. COOPERATION BETWEEN ADMINISTRATORS

Even before legal rules addressed the subject of cross-border cooperation, administrators have taken the initiative and worked out solutions. The earliest example can be seen in the *Maxwell Communications Corporation plc* case in 1991. In this case, concurrent principal insolvency proceedings in the United States (Chapter 11) and England (administration proceedings) were coordinated by way of an "Order and Protocol" approved by the courts in the respective jurisdictions.[344]

Nowadays, such protocols or agreements are routine in big cross-border cases.[345] These agreements can be defined as arrangements agreed upon by the parties to facilitate cross-border cooperation and the coordination of multiple insolvency proceedings in different jurisdictions, whether these concern a single debtor or an enterprise group.[346] They represent a commercial response to international insolvency issues that complements domestic insolvency and private international laws, which are proving inadequate to produce a timely and effective outcome for a globalized business community.[347] Indeed, such protocols have become so routine that it has been suggested that the use of such protocols is already part of an international law merchant.[348] For example, in the *Lehman* case, various trustees, administrators, and receivers of numerous entities around the world reached an agreement to enter into a cross-border insolvency protocol that, amongst other things, sets out an efficient claims process which includes a consistent and measured approach toward intercompany claims. In terms of claims, the guideline is that if there are two or more proceedings pending for the same debtor, consisting of one or more main proceedings and/or one or

---

[343] Possible examples include Canada, Japan, and South Korea. See L.C. Ho, above n. 44, p. 14.

[344] E.D. Flaschen and R.J. Silverman, "The Role of the Examiner as Facilitator and Harmonizer in the Maxwell Communication Corporation International Insolvency" in J.S. Ziegel (ed.), *Current Developments in International and Comparative Corporate Insolvency Law*, Clarendon Press, Oxford 1994, p. 629.

[345] See E.D. Flaschen and R.J. Silverman, "Cross-Border Insolvency Cooperation Protocols" (1998) 33 *Texas International Law Journal* 587; E. Braun and A. Tashiro, "Cross-Border Insolvency Protocol Agreements between Insolvency Practitioners and Their Effect on the Rights of Creditors," https://www.iiiglobal.org/sites/default/files/BraunTashiroandBraunCBProtocols.pdf; R. Mason, above n. 7, 105; A. Geroldinger, "Ausgewählte Fragen zur Zusammenarbeit und Kommunikation der Verwalter unter der EuInsVO 2015" in B. Nunner-Krautgasser, T. Garber and C. Jaufer (eds.), *Grenzüberschreitende Insolvenzen im europäischen Binnenmarkt*, Manz, Vienna 2017, p. 207.

[346] UNCITRAL Practice Guide on Cross-Border Insolvency Cooperation 2010, pp. 27 f and 87 f.

[347] R. Mason, above n. 7, 108.

[348] Ibid., 105.

Intersentia

253

more secondary or ancillary proceedings, a claim should be filed only in the proceeding that is designated by the official representative of the debtor.

While most cases in which protocols have been used involved common law jurisdictions, some cases where protocols have been used also involved civil law countries such as Germany, France, Israel, and Switzerland. The EIR now expressly mentions protocols[349] and provides for their approval by the court.[350] Specifically, Article 41 EIR deals with cooperation and communication between insolvency practitioners,[351] directing the administrators of the main and secondary proceedings to cooperate. Such cooperation may take any form, including the conclusion of agreements or protocols. The duty to cooperate includes providing information which may be relevant to the other proceedings, in particular any progress made in lodging and verifying claims, and all measures aimed at rescuing or restructuring the debtor or at terminating the proceedings, provided appropriate arrangements are made to protect confidential information; the exploration of the possibility of restructuring the debtor and coordination of the elaboration and implementation of a restructuring plan; and the coordination of the administration of the realization or use of the debtor's assets and affairs. These rules are supplemented by Article 43, which deals with the cooperation and communication between insolvency practitioners and the courts.

The recast EIR also contains express rules about cooperation in proceedings concerning groups of companies.[352] This cooperation may take any form, including the conclusion of agreements or protocols. Cooperation includes the exchange of information and an exploration as to whether possibilities exist for coordinating the administration and supervision of the affairs of the group members which are subject to insolvency proceedings, and whether possibilities exist for restructuring group members which are subject to insolvency proceedings. The insolvency practitioners involved may agree to grant additional powers to an insolvency practitioner appointed in one of the proceedings where such an agreement is permitted by the rules applicable to each of the proceedings. They may also agree on the allocation of certain tasks amongst them. These rules are supplemented by Article 58, which deals with cooperation and communication between insolvency practitioners and courts.

In the insolvency case of Air Berlin group, proceedings were pending in Germany and (as to one member of the Fly Niki group) in Austria.[353]

---

[349]   Articles 41(1) and 56(1) EIR.

[350]   See ibid., Arts. 42(3)(e) and 57(3)(e).

[351]   Article 41(3) EIR, somewhat cryptically, provides that: "Paragraphs 1 and 2 shall apply mutatis mutandis to situations where, in the main or in the secondary insolvency proceedings or in any territorial insolvency proceedings concerning the same debtor and open at the same time, the debtor remains in possession of its assets."

[352]   Ibid., Art. 57.

[353]   For an English-language account of the case, see, e.g., M. WELLER, "NIKI, COMI, Air Berlin and Art. 5 EIR Recast" [2018], http://conflictoflaws.net/2018/niki-comi-air-berlin-and-art-4-eir-recast.

Originally, the German court in Berlin had also opened a main proceeding against Fly Niki, but this decision was appealed by a creditor under Article 5 EIR[354] on the ground that the COMI of this company was in Austria. In the meantime, the Austrian court had also opened a main proceeding, holding that the COMI was in Austria. Later, the German intermediate appellate court reversed the decision, holding that the COMI was in Austria. Against this decision, an appeal was filed with the German Supreme Court. Thus, for some time, it was unclear whether the proceeding would continue in Austria or in Germany. In the meantime, the Austrian and German administrators cooperated and sold the debtor's assets, obtaining the approval of both the Austrian and German courts. Therefore, the sale could be approved by the court regardless of the outcome of the jurisdictional dispute.[355]

6.4. COOPERATION BETWEEN COURTS

6.4.1. Traditional Forms of Judicial Cooperation

As in other cases, whether civil or criminal, in insolvency cases courts can cooperate by way of traditional forms of judicial assistance. Under Article 21(1)(d) of the UNCITRAL Model Law, a court, following the application of the foreign representative, can provide for the examination of witnesses, the taking of evidence, and the delivery of information concerning the debtor's assets, affairs, rights, obligations, or liabilities. In the *Madoff* case, it was held that this provision includes a jurisdictional and a discretionary component.[356] In the EU, this form of cooperation is governed by the Evidence Regulation.[357]

6.4.2. Direct Communication and Soft Law

However, in recent years, other forms of cooperation between courts have arisen.[358] These include direct court-to-court communication and even

---

[354]   Under Art. 5(1) EIR, the debtor or any creditor may challenge before a court the decision opening main insolvency proceedings on the grounds of international jurisdiction. The *Air Berlin* case was the first case in which Art. 5 of the recast European Insolvency Regulation was applied.

[355]   The appeal to the German Supreme Court was subsequently withdrawn.

[356]   *Bernhard L. Madoff Investment Securities LLC; Irving H. Picard v. FIM Advisers LLP and Others* [2010] BCC 328.

[357]   Council Regulation (EC) 1206/2001 of 28 May 2001 on cooperation between the courts of the Member States in the taking of evidence in civil or commercial matters [2001] OJ L174/1.

[358]   S. JACKSON and R. MASON, above n. 36, 507. See also S.A. LUTKUS, "Court-to-Court Communication in Cross-Border Insolvency Cases" (Eighteenth Annual International Insolvency Conference, New York, September 2018), https://www.iiiglobal.org/sites/default/files/Court-to-Court%20Communication%20%28Stacy%20Lutkus%29.pdf.

joint hearings. Again, the earliest example is probably the *Maxwell* case. In this case, practitioners recall that "Judge Brozman and Chancellor Hoffman very often were in communication directly and sometimes with the parties involved".[359] A few years later, in 1996, unlike the *Maxwell* Protocol, the *Nakash* Protocol specifically contemplated court-to-court communication.[360]

In subsequent years, court-to-court communication became more frequent.[361] This development has also been furthered by the "soft law" measures described above,[362] such as the Guidelines Applicable to Court-to-Court Communication in Cross-Border Cases published by ALI and III in 2000,[363] the European Communication and Cooperation Guidelines for Cross-Border Insolvency adopted by INSOL Europe in 2008,[364] and the UNCITRAL Practice Guide on Cross-Border Insolvency Cooperation adopted in 2009.[365] In *Lehman*, the ALI Guidelines were cited in the protocol.[366]

Under the ALI Guidelines, communications from court to court may take place through the court sending or transmitting copies of decisions, transcripts of proceedings, or directing counsel or an administrator to transmit copies of documents, pleadings, affidavits, etc. participating in two-way communications with the other court by telephone or video conference call or other electronic means.[367] Counsel for all affected parties should be entitled to participate in person during the communication and advance notice of the communication should be given to all parties.[368] Therefore, the informal contacts between the judges that reportedly took place in *Maxwell* would not be authorized under the ALI Guidelines.

Yet, some observers remained skeptical. As late as 2008, a high-ranking Australian judge described the possibility of direct communication between courts as something which "remains controversial".[369]

---

[359] 01/14/09 Hr'g Tr. 78:14-16 (Miller, Harvey), *In re Lehman Brothers Holdings, Inc., et al.,* No. 08-13555 (SCC) Bankr. S.D.N.Y. 2009), cited by S.A. LUTKUS, above n. 358, p. 2.

[360] Stipulation and Order Implementing Cross Border Protocol, *In re Nakash*, No. 94-44840 (BRL) (Bankr. S.D.N.Y. 1996), reprinted in E.D. FLASCHEN and R.J. SILVERMAN, "Cross-Border Insolvency Cooperation Protocols" (1998) 33 *Texas International Law Journal* 587, 601–612.

[361] See the interview with Judge M. NASTASIE, "Judicial Communication in Cross-Border Insolvency" [3rd Quarter 2019] *INSOL World* 24.

[362] See above, section 3.5.

[363] https://www.iiiglobal.org/sites/default/files/7-_ali.pdf.

[364] See, https://www.insol.org/_files/pdf/Press%20Release%20JudgeCo%20Project.pdf; B. WESSELS and M. VIRGÓS, above n. 85.

[365] http://www.uncitral.org/pdf/english/texts/insolven/Practice_Guide_english.pdf.

[366] See S.A. LUTKUS, above n. 358, p. 6.

[367] Guidelines Applicable to Court-to-Court Communication in Cross-Border Cases, Guideline 6.

[368] Ibid., Guideline 7.

[369] S. JACKSON and R. MASON, above n. 36, 520.

6.4.3. Selected Examples

It is not surprising that direct court-to-court communication is most often found between courts of countries with a common language and belonging to the same family of legal systems. Both language barriers and a lack of understanding of foreign institutions and proceedings make direct communication difficult in other instances. Thus, most such cases seem to occur between the United States and Canada, and the United States and the United Kingdom. Recently, in the insolvency proceeding of the Air Berlin group, the Austrian and German judges communicated directly. After the appeal to the German Supreme Court had been brought, the Austrian judge contacted the German Supreme Court inquiring as to when the appeal would be decided. Subsequently, the Austrian judge opened main proceedings.[370]

Another case involved the Seoul Bankruptcy Court and the U.S. Bankruptcy Court for the Eastern District of Virginia.[371] In this case, the Korean judge sought information from the U.S. judge regarding: (i) the Korean creditors (such as name, address, allowed claims, etc.); (ii) how the Korean creditors were classified and treated in the liquidation plan; (iii) how the Korean creditors were served, notified, and given any chance to participate in the voting of the liquidation plan by due process; and (iv) the possibility for Korean creditors to participate in the proceeding by subsequent filing of their claims even after the confirmation of the liquidation plan in the event of requests from Korean creditors who belatedly get to know the existence of the proceeding, and, if not, whether there are any ways to protect Korean creditors in good faith.[372] The Korean judge and the U.S judge communicated in English. The Korean judge has also communicated in English with the Federal Court of Australia and the High Court in London.[373] While at present it seems that no jurisdiction provides interpreters or translators attached to the courts to assist such direct cooperation, such assistance would clearly be desirable.[374]

6.4.4. Joint Hearings

Perhaps the closest form of court-to-court cooperation is joint hearings. In 1995, the first U.S.–Canada cross-border joint hearing took place.[375] Nowadays, joint

---

[370] For another aspect of this case, the cooperation of the Austrian and German administrators, see above, section 6.3. See also A. Konecny, "EuInsVO 2015 und der Fall 'NIKI'" in C. Jaufer, B. Nunner-Krautgasser, and G. Schummer (eds.), *Unternehmenssanierung mit Auslandsbezug*, Linde, Vienna 2019, pp. 55–72.

[371] See the national report by Kim (South Korea) pp. 5 f.

[372] See ibid., p. 5.

[373] See ibid., p. 8.

[374] See ibid.

[375] *In re Everfresh Beverages, Inc.*, Case No. 95-B-45405-06 (Bankr. S.D.N.Y., December 20, 1995); see B. Wessels, B.A. Markell, and J.J. Kilborn, above n. 15, p. 185; S.A. Lutkus, above n. 358, p. 4.

Intersentia

257

hearings are routinely provided for in many court rules.[376] Recently, the UNCITRAL Model Code on Enterprise Group Insolvency published in 2019 also expressly provides for the coordination of hearings (Article 12).

In 2019, the Federal Court of Australia (FCA) held that it could make a request to the New Zealand High Court that there could be a joint hearing of those courts in respect of applications relating to the pooling of various funds held by companies subject to Australian and New Zealand liquidations, respectively.[377] Such a "letter of request" could be issued by the FCA to a foreign court in the context of an Australian insolvency process pursuant to section 581 of the Corporations Act 2001 (Cth). Referring to a prior decision,[378] the court noted that cooperation between courts will generally occur within a framework or protocol that has previously been approved by the court and is known to the parties in the particular proceeding. In this case, the application or the issue of a letter of request had been made on an *ex parte* basis, which meant that the framework was not yet known to all potential parties. For this reason, the Australian court did not issue a letter of request to the New Zealand High Court at this stage of the proceedings, but noted that the liquidators could make a further application for a letter of request to be issued in due course.

6.4.5. Formalization of Cooperation

In recent years, a clear trend toward somehow formalizing cooperation between courts seems to have emerged. Already in 1999, the chief judges of 25 countries, including Australia, China, Hong Kong, India, Indonesia, Japan, Kazakhstan, Korea, New Zealand, and Russia, signed the Seoul Statement on Mutual Judicial Assistance. More recently, several courts have signed memoranda of understanding.[379] In these memoranda, which are expressly stated as not

---

[376]   See, e.g., the Local Rules for the United States Bankruptcy Court District of Delaware, which provides for joint hearings (Annex A).

[377]   *Kelly, in the Matter of Halifax Investment Services Pty Ltd. (In Liquidation) (No. 5)* [2019] FCA 1341. See J. Opperman, K. Smith, and C. Crawford, "Cross-Border Cooperation: Federal Court of Australia Considers 'Classic Candidate' for Coordination with High Court of New Zealand," (2019), https://i.emlfiles4.com/cmpdoc/8/7/4/8/2/2/files/7931_kl-gates-article.pdf?dm_i=4WAM,7HJC,19L5WF,SQ1I,1.

[378]   Jacobsen J in *Parbery, in the Matter of Lehman Brothers Australia Ltd. (In Liquidation)* [2011] FCA 1449.

[379]   E.g., Memorandum of Understanding between the Supreme Court of Singapore and the United States Bankruptcy Court for the District of Delaware of September 24, 2018; Memorandum of Understanding between the Supreme Court of Singapore and the Seoul Bankruptcy Court of May 16, 2018; Memorandum of Understanding between the Seoul Bankruptcy Court and the United States Bankruptcy Court for the Southern District of New York of April 22, 2018. There is also a similar Memorandum of Understanding between the Seoul Bankruptcy Court and the Supreme Court of Singapore (see the national report by Kim (South Korea), p. 7).

being legally binding, the courts undertake to work together in transnational proceedings in order for this memorandum to be implemented based on the principles of mutual understanding and respect. Any differences arising from the interpretation, operation, and implementation of this memorandum are to be settled amicably between the courts. Cooperation in this sense may include communication and coordination for the efficient and fair administration of insolvency proceedings in both jurisdictions, communication and coordination for the efficient and timely recognition of insolvency proceedings before the courts and relief with respect to them, and communication and assistance in order to improve the mutual understanding of insolvency proceedings.[380]

Also, many courts have adopted the Judicial Insolvency Network's Guidelines for Communication and Cooperation between Courts in Cross-Border Matters. Examples include the Eastern Caribbean Supreme Court (effective May 18, 2017), the Supreme Court of New South Wales (effective September 15, 2017)[381] and the U.S. Bankruptcy Court Southern District of Florida (effective February 1, 2018).[382]

In order to overcome institutional and perhaps language barriers, on July 25, 2019, the Judicial Insolvency Network recommended that courts appoint judges as "facilitators" in cross-border cases as one of several new proposals for court-to-court communication.[383] This approach should be compatible with both the EIR[384] and the UNCITRAL Model Law.[385]

6.4.6. Civil Law Countries

In civil law countries, courts appear to have been more reluctant than common law countries to engage in direct court-to-court communications.[386] For the EU,

---

[380] Memorandum of Understanding between the Supreme Court of Singapore and the United States Bankruptcy Court for the District of Delaware of September 24, 2018. The other Memoranda mentioned in the previous footnote are worded similarly.

[381] Practice Note SC EQ 6.

[382] In the meantime, a number of other countries have also adopted the guidelines. See, Judicial Insolvency Network (jin-global.org).

[383] D. LAWSON, "JIN Recommends 'Facilitators' to Aid Parallel Court Proceedings" [2019] *Global Restructuring Review*, https://globalrestructuringreview.com/article/1195557/jin-recommends-"facilitators"-to-aid-parallel-court-proceedings.

[384] Article 42(2) EIR expressly mentions "any appointed person or body acting on their [the courts'] behalf."

[385] See Art. 27(a) of the UNCITRAL Model Law mentioning the "[a]ppointment of a person or body to act at the direction of the court".

[386] For South Korea, see C. RIM, "South Korea" in L.C. HO (ed.), *Cross-Border Insolvency: A Commentary on the UNCITRAL Model Law*, above n. 15, p. 585 (mentioning language difficulties and difficulties in understanding foreign systems). On the restrictive attitude in this regard of courts in Brazil, see G. GORNATI, "Court-to-Court Communication in Cross-Border Insolvency Cases" (Eighteenth Annual International Insolvency Conference,

this may change in the near future.[387] Unlike its predecessor version,[388] the recast EIR has express rules for cooperation and communication between courts. For this purpose, the courts may appoint an independent person or body acting on its instructions. The courts are now expressly authorized to communicate directly with, or request information or assistance directly from, each other, provided that such communication respects the procedural rights of the parties to the proceedings and the confidentiality of information. Possible coordination measures include: coordination in the appointment of the insolvency practitioners; communication of information by any means considered appropriate by the court; coordination of the administration and supervision of the debtor's assets and affairs; coordination of the conduct of hearings; and coordination in the approval of protocols. Article 57 EIR contains similar rules for insolvencies concerning groups of companies.

In an effort to facilitate cooperation and communication with the Dutch courts, in the case of a cross-border insolvency case, the Dutch judiciary has created a website with information and contact details.[389] Here, the use of the EU JudgeCo Principles is recommended. Furthermore, in 2019, the District Court Midden-Nederland adopted the JIN Guidelines on communication and cooperation with courts outside of the EU.[390]

7. OTHER FORMS OF COOPERATION

For the sake of completeness, other forms of cooperation should be mentioned. Thus, the EIR (in Articles 25–27) envisages a number of implementing acts aimed at establishing and interconnecting national insolvency registers. Also, national registers will communicate with the European e-Justice Portal (Article 26 EIR).[391] Another aspect of cross-border information is the information of creditors.[392] This is, of course, assisted by electronic registers. Finally, if one understands "cooperation" broadly, the participation of foreign creditors also

---

New York, September 2018), https://www.iiiglobal.org/sites/default/files/Court-to-Court%20 Communication%20%28Gilberto%20Gornati%29.pdf. For Germany, a skeptical position was also expressed by U. Ehricke, "Probleme der Verfahrenskoordination – Eine Analyse der Kooperation von Insolvenzverwaltern und Insolvenzgerichten bei grenzüberschreitenden Insolvenzverfahren im Anwendungsbereich der EuInsVO" in P. Gottwald (ed.), *Europäisches Insolvenzrecht – Kollektiver Rechtsschutz*, Gieseking, Bielefeld 2007, p. 127.

[387] For an example involving Austria and Germany, see above, section 6.4.3.
[388] The former EIR only contained rules for the cooperation of administrators. In light of this, many authors were skeptical as to whether court-to-court communication was authorized under this regime. See U. Ehricke, above n. 386, p. 127.
[389] https://www.rechtspraak.nl/English/Pages/International-Insolvency.aspx.
[390] See the national report by Boon (the Netherlands), p. 6.
[391] See R. Bork and R. Mangano, above n. 8, paras. 6.76 f.
[392] See ibid., paras. 6.01 f.

falls within this topic. While this is beyond the scope of this chapter, it should be noted that both the UNCITRAL Model Law[393] and European law prohibit the discrimination of foreign creditors. In order to facilitate the lodging of claims by foreign creditors, the EIR permits them to do so in any of the official languages of the EU.

Also, in addition to the forms or cooperation discussed in this chapter which focus on specific proceedings, there may be cooperation on a more abstract level, e.g., in the form of seminars, conferences, publications, etc. While these forms of cooperation are beyond the scope of this chapter, their possible effect should not be underestimated as they may contribute to a better understanding and, consequently, to a reduction of reservations often encountered in cross-border contexts.

8. CONCLUSION

This chapter has shown that there are considerable differences between the recognition of ordinary judgments in civil cases and the recognition of insolvency proceedings. The growing internationalization of economies and a series of spectacular failures of multinational companies have contributed to a more open attitude toward cooperation in cross-border insolvency cases. Newer recognition regimes are remarkably liberal compared to traditional rules on the recognition of judgments. In addition, practitioners have stepped in and have, by way of agreements between administrators of concurrent proceedings, solved many practical problems which were not (or not adequately) addressed by national or international laws.

However, in spite of all the efforts at harmonization, for the foreseeable future, substantial differences between national insolvency laws are likely to remain. Indeed, in light of fundamental inconsistencies across jurisdictions in both bankruptcy and related laws, harmonization was described as virtually "unattainable".[394] Paradoxically, in some areas of international insolvency law, legal systems even seem to move further apart because countries tend to fill out the leeway granted to them under the UNCITRAL Model Law or EU law differently. Thus, while complete harmonization or unification of insolvency laws seems unlikely, further efforts as to the harmonization of rules on international jurisdiction and choice of law may be worthwhile. This could be accomplished by a revised version of the UNCITRAL Model Law. For pragmatic reasons,

---

[393] Article 13 of the UNCITRAL Model Law on Cross-Border Insolvency.

[394] H.L. BUXBAUM, "Conflict of Economic Laws: From Sovereignty to Substance" (2002) 42 *Virginia Journal of International Law* 931, citing L.M. LOPUCKI, "Cooperation in International Bankruptcy: A Post-Universalist Approach" (1999) 84 *Cornell Law Review* 696.

Intersentia

UNCITRAL has adopted a different approach of retaining the well-accepted original Model Law, but developed additional optional instruments addressing certain aspects, such as insolvency-related litigation or groups of companies.

Arguably the most significant defect in the current UNCITRAL Model Law is that it only provides for the recognition of the opening of proceedings, but not of one of its most important results, i.e., a discharge. This is unfortunate because modern insolvency law very often provides for (and indeed aims at) such a discharge. Without the recognition of a discharge obtained in one country, a debtor with international assets would have to seek a discharge in several countries, which significantly impairs international restructuring efforts. Fortunately, many countries already do provide for the recognition of a discharge in their national laws. The same holds true for regional regimes like the European Regulation or the Code Bustamante.

The time is probably not yet ripe for a truly unified insolvency law or at least an unlimited universality principle. In the meantime, generous recognition of foreign decisions and cross-border cooperation in the form described in this chapter may indeed be the best possible and the only realistic approach for now.

PART II

NEW CHALLENGES
AND THEIR VARIOUS ASPECTS

Recognition and Enforcement of Foreign Titles

REGIONALISM IN THE PROCESS OF RECOGNITION AND ENFORCEMENT OF FOREIGN TITLES

Ronald A. Brand*

1. Introduction 266
2. The Function of Public Policy as a Ground for the Refusal
   of Recognition and Enforcement of Foreign Judgments................ 267
   2.1. The Global Perspective 267
   2.2. Regionalism and Common Law Countries 271
        2.2.1. The Brussels Regime: Ireland and the United Kingdom 271
        2.2.2. The Trans-Tasman Regime: Australia and New Zealand ... 273
   2.3. National Common Law Approaches........................... 274
        2.3.1. Statutory Law in Common Law States.................. 274
        2.3.2. The Content and Application of the Public Policy Ground
               for Non-Recognition 276
               2.3.2.1. The Content of Public Policy: The Overlap between
                        Judgment Recognition and Applicable Law...... 276
               2.3.2.2. Examples of Successful Applications of Public
                        Policy to Prevent the Recognition and
                        Enforcement of Judgments.................... 278
3. The Function of Public Policy as a Ground for the Refusal
   of Recognition and Enforcement of Foreign Arbitral Awards 280
   3.1. The Global Perspective 280
   3.2. National Common Law Approaches........................... 282
4. Jurisdiction in Actions to Recognize and Enforce Foreign Decisions..... 287
   4.1. Indirect Jurisdiction.. 287
        4.1.1. The Global Perspective............................... 287
        4.1.2. National Law Approaches 288

---

* Chancellor Mark A. Nordenberg University Professor, Director, Center for International Legal Education, University of Pittsburgh.

Intersentia

4.1.3.	The United Kingdom	290
4.1.4.	Canada	293
4.1.5.	Other Countries	294

4.2. Recognition Jurisdiction ... 294

| 4.2.1. | The United States. | 294 |

4.2.1.1. Option 1: No Personal Jurisdiction Required 296
4.2.1.2. Option 2: Requiring Full Personal Jurisdiction..... 298
4.2.1.3. Option 3: Requiring Either Personal Jurisdiction or Quasi-in Rem Jurisdiction 299
4.2.1.4. Sorting Out the Options 300

| 4.2.2. | Singapore | 304 |
| 4.2.3. | The United Kingdom | 307 |

5. Enforcement Following Recognition ... 308
6. Injunctive Relief ... 309
6.1. Global Injunctive Relief Generally. ... 309
6.2. The Recognition and Enforcement of Injunctive Relief ... 312
7. Searching and Seizing Foreign Assets ... 313
7.1. The United States ... 313
7.2. Singapore. ... 314
8. Conclusions ... 316

1. INTRODUCTION

In this chapter, I address three major questions relating to the recognition and enforcement of foreign titles in common law jurisdictions:

1. Public policy as a ground for the refusal of recognition and enforcement of foreign titles (both judgments and arbitral awards);
2. Jurisdiction in actions to recognize and enforce foreign titles; and
3. Enforcement: searching and seizing foreign assets.

In addressing the public policy question, I pay attention first to the global framework for each, and then move to regionalism and national law through discussion of the law in each of the national reports prepared for use in compiling this general report. In addressing enforcement jurisdiction and searching and seizing foreign assets, the focus is on the law of the states represented in the national reports, as there is no real global framework for these issues. For common law states, the process of regionalism has only had a limited impact on the matters being considered. Parts of this chapter provide a broad overview, while others focus on a more limited set of countries given the information available.

I am indebted to the authors of the following national reports on which this chapter is based:

- Australia, Richard Garnett
- Canada, H. Scott Fairley and Ruzbeh Hosseni
- England and Wales, Wendy Kennett
- Ireland, M Ni Shúlleabháin
- Israel, Ehud Brosh
- Singapore, Tiong Min Yeo
- United States, Ronald A. Brand

2. THE FUNCTION OF PUBLIC POLICY AS A GROUND FOR THE REFUSAL OF RECOGNITION AND ENFORCEMENT OF FOREIGN JUDGMENTS

As a matter of law, public policy is perhaps the most common ground found for the denial of recognition and enforcement of foreign judgments. It is contained in every global instrument and in every national law surveyed for this chapter. Nonetheless, as a matter of practice, it seldom results in the actual denial of recognition or enforcement.

2.1. THE GLOBAL PERSPECTIVE

The Hague Conference on Private International Law has produced three multilateral conventions in the last 50 years that deal with the recognition and enforcement of foreign judgments. The first of these is the Hague Convention of February 1, 1971 on the Recognition and Enforcement of Foreign Judgments in Civil and Commercial Matters.[1] While that Convention has technically entered into force in Albania, Cyprus, Kuwait, the Netherlands, and Portugal, no bilateral Supplementary Agreement, as required under the Article 21 opt-in process, has been completed, so it has no effect.[2]

The second Hague Convention is the Convention of June 30, 2005 on Choice of Court Agreements.[3] The Choice of Court Convention is in force for the

---

[1] https://www.hcch.net/en/instruments/conventions/full-text/?cid=78 (hereinafter "the 1971 Judgments Convention").

[2] See the status report at https://www.hcch.net/en/instruments/conventions/status-table/?cid=78.

[3] https://www.hcch.net/en/instruments/conventions/full-text/?cid=98 (hereinafter "the Choice of Court Convention").

Intersentia

267

European Union (EU) and its 27 Member States (including Denmark, which acceded separately), Montenegro, Singapore, and the United Kingdom, with China, Israel, the Republic of North Macedonia, Ukraine, and the United States having signed but not ratified it.[4] This Convention is limited to the recognition and enforcement of judgments from other Contracting States for which jurisdiction in the court of origin was based on an exclusive choice of court agreement.[5] Article 9(e) of the Convention provides that recognition or enforcement of a judgment may be refused if "recognition or enforcement would be manifestly incompatible with the public policy of the requested State, including situations where the specific proceedings leading to the judgment were incompatible with fundamental principles of procedural fairness of that State."[6]

The Explanatory Report to the Choice of Court Convention provides two paragraphs elaborating on the public policy exception to recognition and enforcement:

> 189 The fifth exception: public policy. The fifth exception, set out in sub-paragraph e), is that recognition or enforcement would be manifestly incompatible with the public policy of the requested State, including situations where the specific proceedings leading to the judgment were incompatible with fundamental principles of procedural fairness of that State. The first part of this provision is intended to set a high standard in accordance with the provisions of Article 6. The second part is intended to focus attention on serious procedural failings in the particular case at hand.

> 190 It will be seen that there is considerable overlap among the last three exceptions, since they all relate, partly or wholly, to procedural fairness. Thus, for example, if, owing to the plaintiff's fraud, the writ was not served on the defendant and (s)he was unaware of the proceedings, the exceptions set out in sub-paragraphs c), d) and e) would all be potentially applicable. The reason for this emphasis on procedural fairness is that in some countries fundamental principles of procedural fairness (also known as due process of law, natural justice or the right to a fair trial) are constitutionally mandated. In such countries, it might be unconstitutional to recognise a foreign judgment obtained in proceedings in which a fundamental breach of these principles occurred.[7]

This language provides only limited guidance in determining the boundaries of the public policy ground for non-recognition. Given its still-recent entry into force, no cases have yet arisen to require the interpretation of this or any other provision of the Convention.

---

4   See the status report at https://www.hcch.net/en/instruments/conventions/status-table/?cid=98.
5   Choice of Court Convention, above n. 3, Art. 8.
6   Ibid., Art. 9(e).
7   T. Hartley and M. Dogauchi, "Explanatory Report", https://assets.hcch.net/upload/expl37final.pdf (hereinafter "the Hartley-Dogauchi Report").

The third Hague Convention is the Convention of July 2, 2019 on the Recognition and Enforcement of Foreign Judgments in Civil or Commercial Matters.[8] This is a more general judgments recognition Convention, providing in Article 5(1) 13 bases on which a judgment may qualify for circulation under the Convention.[9] Once a judgment is determined to be qualified for circulation, Article 7 lists six discretionary grounds on which recognition or enforcement may be refused. The third of these, found in Article 7(c), provides that recognition or enforcement may be refused if "recognition or enforcement would be manifestly incompatible with the public policy of the requested State, including situations where the specific proceedings leading to the judgment were incompatible with fundamental principles of procedural fairness of that State and situations involving infringements of security or sovereignty of that State."[10] While the language differs somewhat from that used in the Choice of Court Convention, the intent is the same. The 2018 Draft Explanatory Report for the 2019 Judgments Convention discusses this provision, with greater elaboration than was provided in the 2005 Explanatory Report, as follows:

Sub-paragraph (c) – public policy

258. Introduction. The public policy defence to recognition and enforcement of foreign judgments is widely admitted across legal systems. Internationally, it has been included in relevant HCCH Conventions for decades and is found in the 1958 New York Convention. The text in the Convention replicates the formulation used in the 2005 HCCH Choice of Court Convention.

259. Manifestly incompatible with public policy. The public policy defence is a final safeguard against recognition or enforcement of a foreign judgment that is considered to be "manifestly incompatible with the public policy of the requested State." It is widely accepted that the concept of public policy must be "interpreted strictly" and recourse thereto "is to be had only in exceptional cases." Recognition or enforcement of the judgment in question "would have to constitute a manifest breach of a rule of law regarded as essential in the legal order of the State in which enforcement is sought or of a right recognised as being fundamental within that legal order."

260. "Manifestly" is a high threshold, intended to ensure judgments of States are recognised and enforced by other States unless there is a compelling public policy reason not to do so in a particular case. The word "manifestly" has been used in previous cases to discourage the overuse of the public policy exception and to limit its use to situations where recognition and enforcement would lead to an "intolerable result."

---

[8] https://www.hcch.net/en/instruments/conventions/full-text/?cid=137 (hereinafter "2019 Judgments Convention").

[9] Ibid., Art. 5(1).

[10] Ibid., Art. 7(c).

261. Principles of procedural fairness. The formulation of the defence in sub-paragraph (c) is more specific than the one found in previous HCCH instruments save for the 2005 HCCH Choice of Court Convention. Under sub-paragraph (c), public policy expressly includes "situations where the specific proceedings leading to the judgment were incompatible with fundamental principles of procedural fairness" of the requested State. The Hartley/Dogauchi Report explains that in some States, fundamental principles of procedural fairness (also known as due process of law, natural justice or the right to a fair trial) are constitutionally mandated. In such States, it might be unconstitutional to recognise a foreign judgment obtained in proceedings in which a fundamental breach of these principles occurred. The reference in sub-paragraph (c) overlaps with procedural safeguards and fundamental principles regarding notification in sub-paragraph (a) and concerns regarding procedural fairness in the face of fraud in sub-paragraph (b). This should ensure that adequate procedural protection is provided to parties facing recognition and enforcement proceedings regardless of the particular way in which those issues are dealt with in the requested State.

262. Content of public policy. The content of the public policy defence is notoriously difficult to define. However, its scope in the Convention should be understood in relation to other provisions in the text. As mentioned above, other defences under paragraph 1 overlap with the public policy defence and that defence should be interpreted accordingly, extending beyond the specifics of the particular defences only where doing otherwise would be a "manifest" contradiction with essential policies of the requested State.

263. The exceptional character of the public policy defence means that it is not sufficient for the party opposing recognition or enforcement to point to a mandatory rule of the law of the requested State that the foreign judgment fails to uphold. Indeed, this mandatory rule may be considered imperative for domestic cases but not for international situations. The public policy defence of sub-paragraph (c) should be triggered only where such a mandatory rule reflects a fundamental value whose violation would be manifest if enforcement of the foreign judgment was permitted. In this sense, the defence relates to "international public policy" and not to domestic public policy.

264. Sub-paragraph (c) does specify that it refers to the public policy of the requested State. This means that there is no expectation of uniformity as to the content of public policy in each State. While the general purpose of the Convention to facilitate the circulation of judgments should limit recourse to this defence, as should the narrow scope of its application described in the previous paragraphs, it remains up to each State to define the public policy defence. The provision refers to infringements of sovereignty or security of the State as a situation in which recognition and enforcement may be manifestly incompatible with public policy. Despite this addition, the scope of this provision is no different from the scope of the equivalent provision in the 2005 HCCH Choice of Court Convention. The addition simply reflects the greater potential for issues involving infringements of security or sovereignty of the State to arise in the context of this Convention than under the 2005 HCCH Choice of Court Convention.

Regionalism in the Process of Recognition and Enforcement of Foreign Titles

265. Damages. The Convention allows a requested State to refuse to enforce a judgment to the extent that it involves an award of punitive or exemplary damages (Art. 10). In some States where punitive or exemplary damages are not typically allowed, refusals to enforce such awards have been assessed under the public policy defence. Because Article 10 addresses punitive or exemplary damages, however, the public policy defence in sub-paragraph (c) should not be used to address challenges to the recognition or enforcement of judgments on that basis. This further narrows the scope of the public policy defence under the Convention.

266. Although the availability of the public policy defence is widely accepted, it is rarely successful as a means of denying recognition or enforcement to a foreign judgment, particularly in civil or commercial matters. Examples where it has succeeded include: where the foreign court enforced a contract to commit an illegal act (smuggling), where the foreign judgment impinged on constitutionally guaranteed fundamental rights (freedom of speech), and where the foreign judgment enforced a gambling debt.[11]

Other Hague Conventions have similar public policy provisions dealing with judgment recognition in specific types of cases and on some matters of applicable law. These include the Convention of April 15, 1958 concerning the recognition and enforcement of decisions relating to maintenance obligations towards children (Article 2); the Convention of October 5, 1961 concerning the powers of authorities and the law applicable in respect of the protection of infants (Article 16); the Convention of June 1, 1970 on the Recognition of Divorces and Legal Separations (Article 10); the Convention of March 14, 1978 on Celebration and Recognition of the Validity of Marriages (Articles 5 and 14); the 1985 Trusts Convention, at Article 18; the Convention of May 29, 1993 on Protection of Children and Co-operation in Respect of Intercountry Adoption (Article 24); the 1996 Child Protection Convention (Articles 22 and 23); the 2000 Protection of Adults Convention (Articles 21 and 22); the 2005 Choice of Court Convention (Articles 6 and 9); and the 2007 Child Support Convention (Article 22).

2.2. REGIONALISM AND COMMON LAW COUNTRIES

2.2.1. *The Brussels Regime: Ireland and the United Kingdom*

While the United Kingdom has exited the EU, its history as a Member State is important to current law, and Ireland remains an EU Member State. This has made them parties to the Brussels I regime that has been effective through the Brussels I (Recast) Regulation, as well as a number of other EU instruments

---

[11] F. GARCIMARTÍN and G. SAUMIER, "Draft Explanatory Report" (hereinafter "Garcimartín-Saumier Draft Report").

Intersentia

271

which provide for the circulation of judgments within the EU. The case law of the Court of Justice of the European Union (CJEU), along with these instruments, suggests a public policy basis for the non-recognition of judgments which is much narrower than is the case under the common law in the United Kingdom and Ireland. This was demonstrated in particular in the cases of *Krombach v. Bamberski*[12] and *Renault v. Maxicar*.[13]

Under the Brussels I regime, public policy cannot be invoked simply because the court of origin made an error of fact or law, or because the court of origin applied a law which is substantially different from that applied in the recognizing state. It is only in exceptional cases where recognition would be at variance to an "unacceptable degree" with the legal order of the recognizing State – or where it would infringe a fundamental principle of that State and constitute a "manifest breach" of an essential rule of law – that recognition and enforcement may be refused on public policy grounds. The CJEU has also emphasized (and this is reaffirmed by Article 45(1)(b) of the Brussels I (Recast) Regulation) that the judgment-debtor is ordinarily expected to raise any concerns before the court of origin and not at the recognition stage.

The application of the public policy defense in Ireland is instructive, as the Irish case law on public policy under the EU instruments is very much in line with the expectations laid down in *Krombach* and *Renault*. For instance, in *Emo v. Mulligan*,[14] the Irish High Court ruled (in the context of the Insolvency Regulation) that forum shopping was not sufficient to raise a public policy defense. The judge emphasized the exceptionality of the defense – and noted that "the exceptions which have given rise to a refusal to recognise appear to be exceptions in which a fundamental right of an individual or entity has been engaged, such as the right to a fair trial."[15] The judge also emphasized the need for an aggrieved litigant to seek a remedy in the jurisdiction of origin where that was still feasible. Similarly, in *Westpac v. Dempsey*,[16] the Irish High Court emphasized that the public policy exception could not be used to raise substantive arguments which ought to have been put before the court of origin.

The exceptionality of the public policy doctrine was also emphasized in *Fairfield v. Citco*,[17] where the Irish High Court refused to accept that the principle of *pari passu* distribution amongst unsecured creditors was a fundamental principle of Irish law so as to justify the invocation of the public policy defense.

---

[12]   [2000] ECR I-1935.
[13]   [2000] ECR I-3009.
[14]   [2011] IEHC 552.
[15]   Ibid.
[16]   [1993] 3 IR 331 (a Brussels Convention case).
[17]   [2012] IEHC 81.

Thus, Dutch orders would be recognized notwithstanding their propensity to interfere with *pari passu* distribution.[18]

However, in some Brussels I Regulation cases, the Irish courts have been relatively lenient in sanctioning reliance on the public policy defense – perhaps more lenient than EU law permits. In *Sporting Index v. O'Shea*,[19] for example, the Irish High Court accepted that the enforcement of an English order for the collection of a gambling debt would be contrary to public policy because under the Irish Gaming and Lotteries Act 1956, the enforcement of betting contracts was prohibited. This judgment sits uneasily alongside the *Renault* principle that differences in substantive law should not of themselves justify a public policy defense. In *Celtic Atlantic Salmon v. Aller Acqua*,[20] differences in procedural laws appeared to trigger a public policy defense when an Irish judgment-debtor was allowed to resist enforcement of a Danish negative declaration on the basis that Danish law precluded reliance on an expert report which was central to the Irish party's case.[21]

2.2.2. The Trans-Tasman Regime: Australia and New Zealand

The Agreement between the Government of Australia and the Government of New Zealand on Trans-Tasman Court Proceedings and Regulatory Enforcement (hereinafter "the Trans-Tasman Agreement") was signed by both countries in Christchurch, New Zealand in 2008.[22] The Agreement provides for the reciprocal recognition and enforcement of final money judgments and of final non-money judgments, except for: (1) orders about probate, letters of administration, or the administration of an estate; (2) orders about the guardianship or management of property of someone who is incapable of managing their personal affairs or property; (3) orders about the care, control, or welfare of a child; and (4) orders that, if not complied with, may lead to conviction for an offense in the place where the order was made.[23]

---

[18] The case law on recognition of family law judgments under Brussels II *bis* also emphasizes the exceptionality of the public policy defense and the "high hurdle" laid down. See, e.g., *Belfast Health and Social Care Trust v. DS* [2011] IEHC 468; *Carmarthenshire County Council v. CD* [2016] IEHC 418.

[19] [2015] IEHC 407.

[20] [2014] IEHC 421.

[21] Interestingly, the High Court in *Sporting Index* accepted that while the English order for the enforcement of a gambling debt was contrary to public policy, the associated order for costs did not raise any public policy concerns and was enforceable in Ireland.

[22] Agreement between the Government of Australia and the Government of New Zealand on Trans-Tasman Court Proceedings and Regulatory Enforcement (hereinafter "the Trans-Tasman Agreement"), http://www.austlii.edu.au/au/other/dfat/treaties/ATS/2013/32.html.

[23] Ibid., Art. 3.

Article 5(6) of the Trans-Tasman Agreement includes the standard public policy ground for non-recognition, stating that: "The registration of a judgment pursuant to this Article may only be set aside in the registering court, and the judgment refused recognition and enforcement in the country of registration, if registration of the judgment would be contrary to the public policy of that country." This is followed in Article 5(7) with a reversal of the standard revenue rule, stating specifically that: "Judgments registered under this Article shall not be refused recognition and enforcement on the grounds that to do so would involve the direct or indirect enforcement of a foreign public or revenue law."

2.3. NATIONAL COMMON LAW APPROACHES

2.3.1. Statutory Law in Common Law States

In all common law states, courts declare public policy to be a limitation on the recognition and enforcement of judgments. In some states, this ground for non-recognition has made its way into a statute. For example, in approximately two-thirds of the states of the United States, this requirement is a matter of statutory law through the adoption of either the 1962 Uniform Foreign Money-Judgments Recognition Act[24] or the 2005 Uniform Foreign-Country Money Judgments Recognition Act.[25]

In the United Kingdom and Ireland, membership in the EU has subjected the courts to the Brussels I (Recast) Regulation, which provides for the recognition and enforcement of judgments from other EU Member States, and includes a specific provision in Article 45(1)(a) that a judgment "shall be refused … if such recognition is manifestly contrary to public policy (order public) in the Member State addressed."[26] However, the Brussels I (Recast) Regulation does not apply to judgments from courts outside the EU.[27]

---

[24] Section 4(b)(3). While this Act remains in effect in a number of states, it appears to have been removed from the website of the Uniform Law Commission.

[25] Uniform Foreign-Country Money Judgments Recognition Act, https://www.uniformlaws. org/HigherLogic/System/DownloadDocumentFile.ashx?DocumentFileKey=f6461fc7-183e-598b-d960-055343811a2f&forceDialog=0 (hereinafter "the 2005 Recognition Act"). Section 4(c)(3) of the Act provides that: "A court of this state need not recognize a foreign-country judgment if … the judgment or the [cause of action/claim for relief] on which the judgment is based is repugnant to the public policy of this state or of the United States." This makes public policy a discretionary ground for non-recognition.

[26] Regulation (EU) No 1215/2012 of the European Parliament and of the Council of 12 December 2012 on jurisdiction and the recognition and enforcement of judgments in civil and commercial matters (recast), Art. 45(1) [2019] OJ L351/1 (20 December 2019) (hereinafter "the Brussels I (Recast) Regulation").

[27] Other EU instruments regulating aspects of judgment recognition include the Brussels II *bis* Regulation 2201/2003, the Maintenance Regulation 4/2009, the European Small Claims

Outside of the EU framework, the United Kingdom has two acts which govern the recognition and enforcement of foreign judgments. The Administration of Justice Act (AJA) 1920 establishes a scheme for the enforcement in the United Kingdom from colonial and Commonwealth countries, providing for the registration of the foreign judgment "if in all the circumstances of the case [the court] think[s] it just and convenient that the judgment should be enforced in the United Kingdom."[28] The Foreign Judgments (Reciprocal Enforcement) Act 1933 applies to judgments from countries to which it has been extended by an Order in Council and provides for preclusive effect of those judgments, as well as for enforcement.[29]

In Israel, judgment recognition is one of the few areas of private international law that is governed by statute. The Foreign Judgments Enforcement Law of 1958 takes a unique approach to judgment recognition, setting out "conditions of enforcement" in section 3, which apparently must be demonstrated by the party seeking recognition and enforcement, and "protection against enforcement" in section 6, for which the burden appears to be on the judgment debtor.[30] Under section 3(3), a condition of enforcement is that "the tenor of the judgment is not repugnant to the laws of the State of Israel or to public policy in Israel."[31]

Singapore has a statutory regime for the recognition of judgments under the Reciprocal Enforcement of Foreign Judgments Act (REFJA),[32] the Reciprocal Enforcement of Commonwealth Judgments Act (RECJA),[33] and the Choice of Court Agreements Act (CCAA).[34] While the REFJA and the CCAA focus on whether the recognition and enforcement would be contrary to the public policy of Singapore, the RECJA requires a determination of whether the judgment was in respect of a cause of action which for reasons of public policy could not have been entertained by the Singapore court. Thus, the former focuses on the effect of recognition and enforcement, while the latter focuses on the underlying substantive claim.[35]

Regulation 861/2007, the European Enforcement Order Regulation 805/2004, the European Order for Payment Regulation 1896/2006, and the Insolvency Regulation 2015/848.

28 Administration of Justice Act (AJA) 1920, §9(1).

29 The countries involved include Australia, Canada (except Quebec), India, Pakistan, and Israel.

30 Israel, Foreign Judgments Enforcement Law, 5718-1958.

31 Ibid., §3(3).

32 Singapore, Cap 265, 2001 Rev Ed. Hong Kong is the only jurisdiction gazetted.

33 Singapore, Cap 264, 1985 Rev Ed. Gazetted jurisdictions are: New Zealand, Sri Lanka, Malaysia, the Windward Islands, Pakistan, Brunei Darussalam, Papua New Guinea, India (except the State of Jammu and Kashmir), and Australia and its constituent states and territories.

34 Singapore, Cap 39A, 2017 Rev Ed.

35 *Poh Soon Kiat v. Desert Palace Inc. (Trading as Caesar's Palace)* [2010] 1 SLR 1129; [2009] SGCA 60.

2.3.2. The Content and Application of the Public Policy Ground for Non-Recognition

2.3.2.1. The Content of Public Policy: The Overlap between Judgment Recognition and Applicable Law

The principal agreement among common law legal systems is that public policy for the purposes of the denial of recognition and enforcement of a foreign judgment is a limited concept. It cannot be based simply on different laws or different approaches to an issue. Moreover, the same limitation on public policy seems to govern the applicability of foreign law. Most common law countries will also deny the recognition of judgments in revenue and penal matters.[36]

In the United States, the overlap between judgment recognition and applicable law is demonstrated by the fact that the most cited statement on what constitutes sufficient public policy grounds for the denial of recognition of a foreign judgment is Judge Cardozo's comment in *Loucks v. Standard Oil*, which was a case dealing with a determination of applicable law. In this case, Cardozo stated: "We are not so provincial as to say that every solution of a problem is wrong because we deal with it otherwise at home."[37] This makes public policy a narrow ground for the denial of recognition of a foreign judgment. A simple difference in policy (e.g., differing statutory positions on an issue) is not enough. The Uniform Law Commissioners have stated that "a difference in law, even a marked one, is not sufficient to raise a public policy issue."[38] The Third Circuit U.S. Court of Appeals stated the test as follows: "A judgment is necessarily offensive to public policy when it 'tends clearly to injure the public health, the public morals, the public confidence in the purity of the administration of the law, or to undermine that sense of security for individual rights, whether of personal liberty, or of private property, which any citizen ought to feel, is against public policy.'"[39]

A similar relationship regarding public policy exists in Canada. In *Beals v. Saldanha*,[40] the Canadian Supreme Court stated that in order to amount to a public policy violation justifying non-recognition, the laws of the originating state must "offend the Canadian concept of justice."[41] Thus:

> The use of the defence of public policy to challenge the enforcement of a foreign judgment involves impeachment of that judgment by condemning the foreign law on

---

[36] See, e.g., *Bank of Ireland v. Meeneghan* [1995] 1 ILRM 96 (an English freezing order in the context of suspected tax evasion was denied recognition in Ireland).

[37] *Loucks ex rel. Loucks v. Standard Oil Co. of N.Y.*, 120 N.E. 198, 201 (N.Y. 1918).

[38] 2005 Recognition Act, above n. 25, §4, cmt. 8.

[39] *Somportex Ltd. v. Philadelphia Chewing Gum Corp.*, 453 F.2d 435, 443 (3d Cir. 1971, cert. denied, 405 U.S. 1017 (1972), quoting *Goodyear v. Brown*, 155 Pa. 514, 26 A. 665, 666 (1893).

[40] [2003] 3 SCR 416.

[41] Ibid. ¶ 76.

which the judgment is based. It is not a remedy to be used lightly. The expansion of this defence to include perceived injustices that do not offend our sense of morality is unwarranted. The defence of public policy should continue to have a narrow application.[42]

The notion of public policy in Canada is directed "at the concept of repugnant laws and not repugnant facts."[43] It is a companion to the defenses of fraud and a failure of natural justice, and is thus narrower than public policy alone might be in other legal systems which may include these other two matters within the concept of public policy.[44]

In Australia, courts similarly apply a narrow definition of public policy for judgment recognition purposes, accepting public policy as a defense to recognition only where a fundamental question of moral and ethical policy, fairness of procedure, or illegality is involved.[45] As in other common law systems, a judgment may not be refused recognition merely because the law of the state of origin differs from that of Australia.[46]

In Ireland, denial of recognition of foreign judgments has occurred most often in family law matters, where fraud, collusion, and duress constitute grounds for non-recognition which may or may not be subsumed within the concept of public policy.[47]

In Israel, in order to prevent the recognition of a foreign judgment based on public policy, there must be some violation of "fundamental values of state and society, of morals, justice and fairness."[48] This has been applied to defeat a public policy argument against the recognition of a New York judgment which included $1.5 million in punitive damages.[49] While Israel's Foreign Judgments Enforcement Law has a separate provision barring the enforcement of a foreign judgment which is prejudicial to state sovereignty or security, this provision does not appear to have been applied yet.[50]

---

[42]   Ibid. ¶ 74.

[43]   Ibid. ¶ 71.

[44]   See J. WALKER, *Castel & Walker: Canadian Conflict of Laws*, 6th ed., Butterworths, Toronto 2005, p. 2.

[45]   *Stern v. National Australia Bank* [1999] FCA 1421, ¶ 143. See also *Jenton Overseas Investment Pte Ltd. v. Townsing* [2008] 221 FLR 398, ¶ 22 (stating that the defense is available only where there is "substantial injustice, either because [the judgment involves] a repugnant foreign law or a repugnant application of the law in a particular case").

[46]   *Kok v. Resorts World at Sentosa Pte Ltd.* [2017] WASCA 150, ¶¶ 22–23.

[47]   See, e.g., *Gaffney v. Gaffney* [1975] IR 133 (refusing recognition of a divorce obtained in England where the spouses had lied about their place of residence in order to provide an apparent basis for jurisdiction).

[48]   *Boulus Gad Ltd. v. Globe Master Management Ltd.*, 59(5) PD 616, 619–20 (CA 4949/03) (2005).

[49]   *Greenberg v. Bamira*, CA 1268/07.

[50]   Israel, Foreign Judgments Enforcement Law, §7.

Singapore also acknowledges a more limited concept of public policy for private international law purposes than for domestic law, with the Court of Appeal having stated that "public policy in the conflict of laws operates with less vigour than public policy in the domestic law."[51]

2.3.2.2. Examples of Successful Applications of Public Policy to Prevent the Recognition and Enforcement of Judgments

The limited nature of the public policy basis for the denial of recognition of a foreign judgment can be seen in the very rare cases that have resulted in non-recognition. In the United States, the one area in which the public policy exception has provided the most successful source of challenges to the recognition of a foreign judgment is that of Constitutional First Amendment rights and, in particular, the law of defamation.[52] This basis for non-recognition is now codified in the federal SPEECH Act,[53] which provides that:

> a domestic court shall not recognize or enforce a foreign judgment for defamation unless the domestic court determines that—
>
> (A) the defamation law applied in the foreign court's adjudication provided at least as much protection for freedom of speech and press in that case as would be provided by the first amendment to the Constitution of the United States and by the constitution and law of the State in which the domestic court is located; or
>
> (B) even if the defamation law applied in the foreign court's adjudication did not provide as much protection for freedom of speech and press as the first amendment to the Constitution of the United States and the constitution and law of the State, the party opposing recognition or enforcement of that foreign judgment would have been found liable for defamation by a domestic court applying the first amendment to the Constitution of the United States and the constitution and law of the State in which the domestic court is located.[54]

In *Trout Point Lodge, Ltd. v. Handshoe*,[55] the court applied the SPEECH Act to prevent the recognition of a Canadian defamation judgment.

Cases prior to the SPEECH Act set the stage for its enactment. In *Bachchan v. India Abroad Publications Inc.*,[56] an Indian plaintiff sued a foreign news agency in the United Kingdom for libel based on the reporting of events that

---

51   *Liao Eng Kiat v. Burswood Nominees Ltd.* [2004] 4 SLR(R) 690; [2004] SGCA 45, ¶ 41.
52   The First Amendment to the U.S. Constitution states that "Congress shall make no law … abridging the freedom of speech."
53   28 U.S.C. §§4101–4105.
54   28 U.S.C. §4102(a)(1).
55   729 F.3d 481, 4860496 (5th Cir. 2013).
56   585 N.Y.S.2d 661 (Sup. Ct. 1992).

had occurred in India. The court found that under U.K. libel law, "any published statement which adversely affects a person's reputation, or the respect in which that person is held, is prima facie defamatory" and the "Plaintiffs' only burden is to establish that the words complained of refer to them, were published by the defendant, and bear a defamatory meaning."[57] This was determined to be contrary to U.S. First Amendment jurisprudence, which places the burden on the plaintiff to prove the words to have been false and protects the right of the press to "publish speech of public concern."[58] The court in *Bachchan* based its decision to deny recognition both on the difference in the burden of proof in U.K. libel law and the determination that enforcement of a foreign judgment in which constitutional standards were not met would have the same "chilling effect" on speech as would an equivalent determination of liability in a U.S. court.[59]

The *Bachchan* case was followed in *Telnikoff v. Matusevitch*,[60] where a libel judgment had been obtained in England by one Russian émigré against another regarding a dispute over a letter published by one of them in the *Daily Telegraph*. The Maryland court, on certification from the Federal District Court, determined that Maryland public policy prevented the recognition of the English libel judgment because of the reversed burden of proof in England and the failure to consider the public context of the statements made.[61]

Bachchan and *Telnikoff* demonstrate that defects in foreign proceedings that would give rise to a constitutional level if the case had originated in the United States trigger the public policy ground for non-recognition of the resulting judgment. In *Bachchan*, the New York court noted that public policy is usually a discretionary ground for non-recognition, but went on to state that "if … the public policy to which the foreign judgment is repugnant is embodied in" the Constitution, "the refusal to recognize the judgment should be, and it is deemed to be, 'constitutionally mandatory.'"[62]

In addition to the First Amendment grounds, U.S. courts have denied recognition to a foreign judgment on the basis of public policy when a Luxembourg

---

[57]   Ibid., at 663.

[58]   Ibid., at 664.

[59]   Ibid., at 664–65.

[60]   347 Md. 561, 702 A.2d 230 (1997), aff'd (table), 159 F.3d 636 (D.C. Cir. 1998).

[61]   See also *Sarl Louis Feraud Int'l v. Viewfinder, Inc.*, 489 F.3d 474 (2d Cir. 2007) (remanding for a decision on whether the facts demonstrated fair use under copyright laws that would be protected by the First Amendment); *Yahoo!, Inc. v. La Ligue Contre Le Racisme et L'Antisemitisme*, 169 F. Supp. 2d 1181, 1189–90 (N.D. Cal. 2001) (holding that the French judgment rendered under a law prohibiting Nazi propaganda because such a law would violate the First Amendment and would not be recognized), rev'd on other grounds, 433 F.3d 1199 (9th Cir. 2006) (*en banc*).

[62]   *Bachchan v. India Abroad Publications Inc.*, 585 N.Y.S.2d 661, 662 (N.Y. Sup. Ct. 1992) (quoting from Siegel, *Practice Commentaries, McKinney's Cons. Laws of N.Y.*, Book 7B, C.P.L.R. C5304:1).

court approved an insolvency plan treating the U.S. Internal Revenue Service as a general (rather than a priority) creditor,[63] when a judgment for attorney's fees covered services that the client did not authorize,[64] when a Nicaraguan judgment was based on an irrefutable presumption of causation,[65] when a Canadian judgment granted attorney fees based on a contingent fee arrangement in a custody dispute,[66] and when a Mexican judgment awarded alimony after remarriage.[67]

In other countries, most denials of recognition and enforcement of judgments based on public policy grounds appear to be in family law cases.[68] A second area in which the defense has been successful has been in efforts to enforce gambling debts, but this seems to be becoming a relic of history.[69] In Ireland, a foreign judgment enforcing a champertous contract was denied recognition on public policy grounds.[70]

3. THE FUNCTION OF PUBLIC POLICY AS A GROUND FOR THE REFUSAL OF RECOGNITION AND ENFORCEMENT OF FOREIGN ARBITRAL AWARDS

3.1. THE GLOBAL PERSPECTIVE

All of the countries surveyed for this chapter are parties to the United Nations Convention on the Recognition and Enforcement of Foreign Arbitral Awards

---

[63]   *Overseas Inns, SA P.A. v. United States*, 911 F.2d 1146, 1149 (5th Cir. 1990).

[64]   *Ackermann v. Levine*, 788 F.2d 820 (2d Cir. 1986).

[65]   *Osorio v. Dole Food Co.*, 665 F. Supp. 2d 1307, 1347 (S.D. Fla. 2009), aff'd sub nom. *Osorio v. Dow Chem. Co.*, 635 F.3d 1277 (11th Cir. 2011).

[66]   *Maxwell Schuman & Co. v. Edwards*, 663 S.E.2d 329, 332–333 (N.C. Ct. App. 2008).

[67]   *Pentz v. Kuppinger*, 31 Cal. App. 3d 590, 597, 107 Cal. Rptr. 540, 545 (1973).

[68]   See, e.g., Garcimartín-Saumier Draft Report, above n. 11, ¶ 296 n. 203: "In a 1998 decision of the England and Wales Court of Appeal, only three refusals to enforce on public policy grounds were noted, two of which were in family law matters, excluded under the draft Convention (see *Soleimany v. Soleimany* [1998] EWCA Civ 285. In the most recent edition of the *Jurisclasseur de droit international*, almost all of the examples of refusal by French courts arise in family law matters (divorce, filiation and adoption) – see Fascicule 584–640."

[69]   See ibid. ¶ 296 n. 206. See also, *Sporting Index Limited v. John O'Shea* [2015] IEHC 407 (Irish High Court); *The Ritz Hotel Casino Ltd. v. Datuk Seri Osu Haji Sukam* [2005] 6 *Malayan Law Journal* 760 (High Court of Malaysia). But other courts have rejected this use of public policy if gambling was legal where the debt was incurred: see for example *Boardwalk Regency Corp. v. Maalouf* (1992), 6 O.R. (3d) 737 (Ontario C.A.); *G.N.L.V. Corp. v. Wan* [1991] B.C.J. No. 3725 (British Columbia S.C.); *Liao Eng Kiat v. Burswood Nominees Ltd.* [2004] 4 S.L.R. 690 (Singapore C.A.). For the diversity of approaches to gambling debts see Z.S. TANG, "Cross-Border Enforcement of Gambling Contracts: A Comparative Study" (2014) 7 *International Journal of Private Law* 1.

[70]   *Fraser v. Buckle* [1994] 1 IR 1.

(hereinafter "the New York Convention"). Article III of the Convention sets forth the basic rule requiring recognition and enforcement:

> Each Contracting State shall recognize arbitral awards as binding and enforce them in accordance with the rules of procedure of the territory where the award is relied upon, under the conditions laid down in the following articles. There shall not be imposed substantially more onerous conditions or higher fees or charges on the recognition or enforcement of arbitral awards to which this Convention applies than are imposed on the recognition or enforcement of domestic arbitral awards.

The public policy ground for non-recognition is found in Article V(2)(b), which provides as follows:

> 2. Recognition and enforcement of an arbitral award may also be refused if the competent authority in the country where recognition and enforcement is sought finds that:
>
>   ...
>
>   (b) The recognition or enforcement of the award would be contrary to the public policy of that country.

While the grounds for non-recognition in Article V(1) must be raised by a party to the dispute, the Article V(2) grounds may be raised *sua sponte* by the court.

The same format is true for the Inter-American Convention on International Commercial Arbitration (hereinafter "the Panama Convention"),[71] Article 4 of which provides the basic rule on recognition and enforcement:

> An arbitral decision or award that is not appealable under the applicable law or procedural rules shall have the force of a final judicial judgment. Its execution or recognition may be ordered in the same manner as that of decisions handed down by national or foreign ordinary courts, in accordance with the procedural laws of the country where it is to be executed and the provisions of international treaties.

The public policy rule then follows in Article 5(2)(b):

> 2. The recognition and execution of an arbitral decision may also be refused if the competent authority of the State in which the recognition and execution is requested finds:
>
>   ...
>
>   b. That the recognition or execution of the decision would be contrary to the public policy ("ordre public") of that State.

---

[71] See http://www.oas.org/en/sla/dil/inter_american_treaties_B-35_international_commercial_arbitration.asp.

Like the New York Convention, the public policy ground for non-recognition may be applied with or without its being raised by a party to the relevant proceedings.

Under both the New York and Panama Conventions, the relevant public policy is that of the state in which recognition and enforcement is requested. Neither Convention provides a definition of "public policy." The use of the permissive term "may" in both Convention statements of the public policy ground for non-recognition implies that non-recognition is discretionary and not required by treaty.

3.2. NATIONAL COMMON LAW APPROACHES

All states surveyed for this chapter apply a narrow definition of public policy for the purposes of interpretation and application of the New York and Panama Conventions (of the states surveyed, only the United States is a party to the Panama Convention).[72]

Section 10 of the U.S. Federal Arbitration Act puts forward the grounds for vacating an arbitral award by a federal district court in the district in which the award was made.[73] These grounds are as follows:

(1) where the award was procured by corruption, fraud, or undue means;
(2) where there was evident partiality or corruption in the arbitrators, or either of them;
(3) where the arbitrators were guilty of misconduct in refusing to postpone the hearing, upon sufficient cause shown, or in refusing to hear evidence pertinent and material to the controversy; or of any other misbehavior by which the rights of any party have been prejudiced; or
(4) where the arbitrators exceeded their powers, or so imperfectly executed them that a mutual, final, and definite award upon the subject matter submitted was not made.[74]

While these grounds do not include public policy, courts considering challenges to international arbitral awards rendered in the United States nonetheless also consider public policy under Article V(2)(b) of the New York Convention.[75]

In the United States, the 2019 *Restatement of the Law, The US Law of International Commercial and Investor-State Arbitration* defines the "scope and nature of public policy" as follows:

As with other grounds for granting or denying recognition or enforcement, public policy is interpreted in light of the presumption in favor of effectuating awards.

---

[72] See the status report at http://www.oas.org/juridico/english/Sigs/b-35.html.
[73] 9 U.S.C. §10.
[74] Ibid.
[75] See, e.g., *RZS Holdings AVV v. PDVSA Petroleos S.A.*, 598 F. Supp. 2d 762 (E.D. Va. 2009) (refusing vacatur based on a challenge on the grounds that the arbitrator was allegedly biased and that such bias was a violation of public policy under Art. V(2)(b) of the NY Convention).

Regionalism in the Process of Recognition and Enforcement of Foreign Titles

To overcome the presumption, the award must violate a policy that is well-defined, deeply held, and rooted in basic notions of morality and justice. Public policy is not offended, for example, simply because an award misapplies governing law or gives effect to a law or policy at variance with U.S. law or U.S. foreign policy, provided that the award does not require contractual performance or other acts that violate U.S. public law. Nor is public policy properly implicated merely because the arbitral tribunal followed procedural, evidentiary, or discovery practices unknown in the United States, or because it applied a rule of law different from U.S. law or the law that a U.S. court would have applied to the dispute.[76]

The *Restatement* comments also note that: "The public policy ground is often invoked, but rarely with success. Nonetheless, it remains an important safeguard for protecting fundamental policies of the United States."[77] This is also the case for the other countries surveyed for this chapter. The same comment gives the following as possible examples of conditions that might be considered to breach the public policy of the United States:

punishing compliance with U.S. economic laws, stemming from arbitral procedures that are fundamentally unfair, facilitating corruption or the evasion of fiscal regulations, or promoting other widely condemned criminal conduct such as arms smuggling, human trafficking, or terrorist activity. Additionally, awards made in arbitral proceedings that ignore or circumvent U.S. court orders regarding the dispute, or which are duplicative of a U.S. court judgment adjudicating the same dispute, may be denied recognition or enforcement on the basis of public policy.[78]

The case most often cited in the United States for describing public policy is *Parsons & Whittemore Overseas Co. v. Société Generale de L'Industrie du Papier (RAKTA)*,[79] which states that the recognition of an arbitral award should be denied on public policy grounds only if recognition "would violate the forum state's most basic notions of morality and justice."[80]

In the United States, it is easy to find cases in which the public policy ground for the non-recognition of an arbitral award was rejected. These often deal with arguments involving mere differences in the applicable law or likely outcome. For example, courts have held that public policy is not offended where the tribunal admitted testimony that would not be admitted in U.S. courts,[81] where

---

76   *Restatement of the Law The U.S. Law of International Commercial and Investor-State Arbitration*, ¶ 4.16, cmt. b (2019).
77   Ibid. cmt. c.
78   Ibid.
79   508 F.2d 969 (2d Cir. 1974).
80   Ibid., at 974.
81   *Indus. Risk Insurers v. M.A.N. Gutehoffnungshütte GmbH*, 141 F.3d 1434, 1443 (11th Cir. 1998).

Intersentia

the tribunal limited or excluded the cross-examination of witnesses,[82] where the court was asked to substitute its own opinion as to whether evidence was fraudulently prepared,[83] where a tribunal did not give preliminary rulings on every issue,[84] where the tribunal independently investigated collateral facts,[85] and where arbitrator impartiality was challenged after an award was rendered.[86]

Two U.S. cases demonstrate instances in which an arbitral award was denied recognition and enforcement based on public policy grounds. In *Hardy Exploration & Production (India), Inc. v. Government of India*,[87] the D.C. District Court refused to enforce a specific performance order that required India to restore private exploration activities within its territory. The court in this case found itself faced with "two important US public policy values: respect for the sovereignty of other nations and respect for foreign arbitral agreements"[88] and determined that "forced interference with India's complete control over its territory violates public policy to the extent necessary to overcome the United States' policy preference for the speedy confirmation of arbitral awards."[89]

The second U.S. case found to deny the recognition and enforcement of an arbitral award based on public policy grounds is *Victrix S.S. Co., S.A. v. Salem Dry Cargo, A.B.*,[90] where the Second Circuit focused on a countervailing strong policy favoring deference to foreign bankruptcy proceedings and the fact that the award recipient had pursued London arbitration after a Swedish bankruptcy court had appointed an administrator and suspended creditors' suits against the debtor in bankruptcy. Thus, the court bowed to the "public policy of ensuring equitable and orderly distribution of local assets of a foreign bankrupt."[91]

In Canada, the public policy ground for the non-recognition of arbitral awards is similarly limited, applying only when the award "offends our local principles of justice and fairness in a fundamental way."[92]

---

[82]   *Generica Ltd. v. Pharm. Basics, Inc.*, 1996 U.S. Dist. LEXIS 13716 (N.D. Ill., September 18, 1996), aff'd, 10 125 F.3d 1123 (7th Cir. 1997).

[83]   *Nordell Int'l Res. v. Triton Indon.*, 1993 U.S. App. LEXIS 12 19616, at *3–4 (9th Cir., July 23, 1993).

[84]   *Trans Chem. Ltd. v. China 15 Nat'l Mach. Imp. & Exp. Corp.*, 978 F. Supp. 266, 308 (S.D. Tex. 1997).

[85]   *Avraham v. Shigur Express Ltd.*, 1991 U.S. Dist. LEXIS 12267, at *7–9, 17 (S.D.N.Y., September 4, 1991).

[86]   See, e.g., *Imperial Eth. Gov't v. Baruch-Foster Corp.*, 535 F.2d 334, 337 (5th Cir. 1976) (where the arbitrator had years earlier helped draft a local civil code for the government involved); *Brandeis Intsel Ltd. v. Calabrian Chems. Corp.*, 656 F. Supp. 160, 169 (S.D.N.Y. 1987) (where an arbitrator had been a member of the same metals exchange as one party's representatives); and *Fertilizer Corp. of India v. IDI Mgmt., Inc.*, 517 F. Supp. 948, 954–55 (S.D. Ohio 1981) (where an arbitrator did not disclose having done prior work as an advocate for a party).

[87]   314 F. Supp. 3d 95, 109, 114 (D.D.C. 2018).

[88]   Ibid., at 109.

[89]   Ibid., at 113.

[90]   825 F.2d 709 (2d Cir. 1987).

[91]   Ibid., at 714.

[92]   *Corporacion Transnacional de Inversiones, SA de CV et al v. Stet International SpA (2000)*, 45 OR (3d) 183 (CA), quoting from *Schreter v. Gasmac Inc. (1992)*, 7 OR (3d) 608 (Gen Div).

In Australia, section 8(7A) of the International Arbitration Act of 1974,[93] which implements the New York Convention, provides a non-exhaustive definition of public policy:

> without limiting (the scope of the defence) enforcement of an award would be contrary to public policy if (a) the making of the award was induced by fraud or corruption or (b) a breach of the rules of natural justice occurred in the making of the award.[94]

Australian judicial decisions follow the international approach of a narrow interpretation of the public policy ground for non-recognition of arbitral awards, limiting it to situations where recognition or enforcement would constitute an offense to the fundamental notions of fairness and justice.[95] Thus, an error of law in an award would not be contrary to public policy, but an award that provided for "double recovery" would.[96]

In Singapore, the courts have drawn on the public policy analysis in arbitration in order to find a limited public policy ground for the recognition and enforcement of foreign judgments.[97] The regime for international arbitration awards is separate from that for domestic awards and is governed by the International Arbitration Act.[98] A foreign arbitration award from the relevant countries may also be registered to be enforced under the RECJA[99] or the REFJA[100] if the award has become enforceable in the same manner as a judgment under the law of the place where the award was made, on which there is also no case law. In principle, under this regime, the award is deemed to be a judgment for the purposes of enforcement, so the same principles and approaches that apply to the enforcement of foreign judgments would apply. Singapore is a party to the New York Convention and has adopted the 1985 Model Law, and practically all international arbitration awards have been dealt with under these two regimes.

Public policy operates at two points in the context of international arbitration in Singapore: in the supervisory jurisdiction of the court where the seat of the arbitration is Singapore; and where the Singapore court is asked to enforce a foreign arbitral award. The Court of Appeal has stated that "public policy" has the same meaning in both contexts; whether the seat of arbitration is in Singapore or elsewhere, the arbitration has an international focus.[101] In both cases, the question is whether "exceptional circumstances" exists which would call for the court to

---

[93]   (Cth), s. 8 Sch. 1 (IAA).
[94]   Ibid., §8(7A).
[95]   *Castel Electronics Pty Ltd v. TCL Air Conditioner (Zhongshan) Co. Ltd. (No. 2)* [2012] FCA 1214, ¶¶ 33, 177.
[96]   *Indian Farmers Fertiliser Cooperative Ltd v. Gutnick* [2015] VSC 724.
[97]   *Liao Eng Kiat*, above n. 69.
[98]   Cap 143A, 2002 Rev Ed, s 5(2).
[99]   RECJA, above n. 33, §2(1).
[100]   REFJA, above n. 32, §10(a).
[101]   *AJU v. AJT* [2011] 4 SLR 739; [2011] SGCA 41.

intervene in a Singapore arbitration or to refuse the enforcement of a foreign award because of a violation of "the most basic notions of morality and justice."

In the context of the court's supervisory jurisdiction, the Singapore Court of Appeal has adopted a narrow approach to challenging the findings of the arbitration tribunal, an approach that it will also apply when it comes to enforcement of foreign awards. The Singapore court will not review the findings made by an arbitration tribunal when a challenge is made to set aside the award on the basis of illegality in the underlying transaction. The Court of Appeal refused to follow the English Court of Appeal decision in *Soleimany v. Soleimany*,[102] which held that in appropriate circumstances where the court regarded the award as unsafe, the court will review the tribunal's findings. Instead, the court followed the approach of the majority in the English Court of Appeal case of *Westacre Investments Inc v. Jugoimport-SPRR Holding Co. Ltd.*,[103] ruling that the court will consider the illegality challenge, despite the tribunal's finding that the contract was not illegal, only if the challenge was based on matters not placed before the tribunal. Even if the tribunal's findings of fact or law are wrong, such errors would not by themselves engage the public policy of Singapore. However, an erroneous finding of the tribunal as to the public policy of Singapore could be a ground for setting aside the award if there was indeed a contravention of Singapore public policy. The rationale for this narrow approach was the primacy of the autonomy of the arbitration process as embodied in the New York Convention and the Model Law. Consequently, parties need to live by their choice of arbitrators.

The Singapore courts have also taken a narrow approach to the content of public policy. A specific public policy objection must be identified and it must be shown how the award conflicts with it.[104] Arguments not sufficient to support a public policy objection include that the tribunal made errors of fact or law,[105] that the tribunal made an excessive costs award,[106] or that the tribunal made an award that was perverse, irrational, or unreasonable.[107] In order to succeed in the public policy argument, the party raising the objection must "cross a very high threshold and demonstrate egregious circumstances such as corruption, bribery or fraud, which would violate the most basic notions of morality and justice."[108]

The other countries surveyed tend to interpret public policy for the purposes of the recognition and enforcement of arbitral awards in much the same way as

---

[102]   [1999] QB 875.

[103]   [2000] 1 QB 288.

[104]   *John Holland Pty Ltd v. Toyo Engineering Corp (Japan)* [2001] 1 SLR(R) 443; [2001] SGHJC 48, at 25.

[105]   *PT Asuransi Jasa Indonesia (Persero) v. Dexia Bank SA* [2007] 1 SLR(R) 597 at [55]; *AJU v. AJT* (n. 101).

[106]   *VV v. VW* [2008] 2 SLR(R) 929.

[107]   *Sui Southern Gas Co. Ltd v. Habibullah Coastal Power Co. (Pte) Ltd.* [2010] 3 SLR 1; [2010] SGHC 62, at 47.

[108]   Ibid., at 48.

for the recognition and enforcement of judgments. This is true in Ireland under the Arbitration Act 2010.[109]

4. JURISDICTION IN ACTIONS TO RECOGNIZE AND ENFORCE FOREIGN DECISIONS

The question of jurisdiction poses itself in two ways in actions to recognize and enforce foreign decisions. With both judgments and arbitral awards, an initial question is whether the court addressed for the purposes of recognition and enforcement has jurisdiction to consider the effect of the foreign decision in the country asked to recognize. This is referred to below as the question of "recognition jurisdiction." For the recognition and enforcement of judgments, there is the more basic jurisdictional question, often referred to as the question of "indirect jurisdiction." In most legal systems, a foreign judgment will not be recognized or enforced unless the court from which the judgment originates had jurisdiction on a basis considered appropriate in the state in which recognition is being sought. This section of the chapter deals first with the question of indirect jurisdiction and then with the question of recognition jurisdiction.

4.1. INDIRECT JURISDICTION

While all of the countries surveyed for this chapter consider whether the court from which the judgment originates ("court of origin") had jurisdiction, the test differs in ways that may often be important. This will change on the multilateral level if, and when, the 2019 Hague Judgments Convention becomes widely ratified.[110]

4.1.1. The Global Perspective

The question of indirect jurisdiction presents itself in two different ways in both international instruments and national law. One approach makes the existence of jurisdiction in the court of origin a gateway to the recognition and enforcement of a judgment. Thus, it is a necessary element for the judgment to be considered for recognition. The second approach makes the existence of jurisdiction in the court of origin a basis for non-recognition. The effect is largely the same, but the distinction may result in important differences. For example, a gateway approach

---

[109] A. Dowling-Hussey and D. Dunne, *Arbitration Law*, 2nd ed., Thomson Reuters, London 2014.

[110] 2019 Judgments Convention, above n. 8.

Intersentia

generally appears to place the burden on the party seeking recognition to prove that the indirect jurisdictional basis has been met, while the other approach places the burden on the party seeking to prevent recognition to prove that no acceptable basis of indirect jurisdiction existed.

The 2019 Hague Judgments Convention takes the gateway approach, providing in Article 5(1) 13 bases on which a judgment may qualify for circulation under the Convention. Article 7 then lists the bases for non-recognition. While the Convention does not explicitly address the matter, this division of functions appears to place the burden of proving a relevant indirect jurisdiction basis on the party seeking recognition and enforcement.

4.1.2. National Law Approaches

There are two basic approaches to the question of indirect jurisdiction in the countries surveyed in this chapter. The first is for the country in which recognition is sought to simply apply its direct jurisdiction rules as the relevant indirect jurisdiction rules. Thus, any basis on which jurisdiction would exist in the recognizing court would be considered legitimate for the court of origin. By using the direct jurisdiction bases also as the bases for testing indirect jurisdiction, there is no gap between the two. The other approach involves a jurisdiction gap between direct and indirect bases of jurisdiction. In jurisdiction gap countries, the courts will hear cases on a broader set of jurisdictional bases than they will accept as appropriate when used in the foreign court whose judgment is being considered for the purposes of recognition and enforcement.

The 2019 Judgments Convention does not address the question of jurisdiction gap directly. The list of 13 bases of indirect jurisdiction in Article 5(1) is relatively inclusive, but likely not co-extensive with any potential Contracting State's list of direct jurisdictional bases. Thus, it will incorporate a jurisdiction gap. In some states, this will be filled through Article 15, which allows for recognition and enforcement under national law, even when it would not occur under the Convention requirements. However, in states with an existing jurisdiction gap, it is likely that this will not bridge the existing differences between direct and indirect jurisdictional bases, resulting in a continued set of indirect jurisdiction rules which may be more limited than a contracting state's corresponding set of direct jurisdiction rules. This will allow Member States to continue to allow the use of what are otherwise considered to be exorbitant bases of jurisdiction against foreign defendants in their own courts, while at the same time refusing to recognize and enforce judgments brought on the same bases in foreign courts.[111]

---

[111] Such a discriminatory approach is clearly rejected in the internal EU system for the recognition and enforcement of judgments through the operation of Art. 5 of the Brussels I Recast Regulation, which allows defendants domiciled in Member States to be sued in other Member States only if one of the bases of jurisdiction listed in ss. 2–7 of the Regulation exists.

A study carried out for the Hague Conference Judgments Convention Working Group in 2015 listed the following countries as using the same test for direct jurisdiction as for indirect jurisdiction, and thus having no jurisdiction gap:[112] Albania, Argentina, Austria, Bulgaria, Canada, Chile, Germany, Greece, Hungary, Ireland, Israel, Italy, Japan, South Korea, Latvia, Luxembourg, Mexico, Slovakia, and the United States.

The same study found a jurisdiction gap in which direct bases of jurisdiction were more extensive than were indirect bases of jurisdiction in the following countries: Australia, Cyprus, Denmark, Egypt, Finland, Ghana, Iceland, Indonesia, Jordan, Kazakhstan, Kenya, New Zealand, Nigeria, Norway, Sweden, the United Arab Emirates, the United Kingdom, and the United States. Of the common law countries surveyed for this chapter, the absence of a jurisdiction gap can be demonstrated by the judgment recognition system in the United States, where the general rule for the recognition of judgments is found most often in state law in the form of a uniform act.[113] The 2005 Uniform Foreign-Country Money Judgments Recognition Act[114] provides that a foreign money judgment which is final and enforceable in the country in which it is rendered shall be recognized and enforced,[115] subject to a limited list of grounds for non-recognition.[116] One of the mandatory grounds for non-recognition is that "the foreign court did not have personal jurisdiction over the defendant."[117] U.S. courts have uniformly interpreted this provision of the Uniform Act (and the common law test without the Uniform Act) to mean that the foreign court must have had jurisdiction according to U.S. tests of personal jurisdiction.[118]

With the resulting exclusive list of direct bases of jurisdiction, recognition and enforcement under Art. 36 then occurs without consideration of jurisdiction in the court of origin, thus making the bases for direct and indirect jurisdiction exactly the same under the Regulation. Brussels I (Recast) Regulation, above n. 26.

[112] "Comparative Study of Jurisdictional Gaps and Their Effect on the Judgments Project," memo of July 1, 2015 to Permanent Bureau of the Hague Conference on Private International Law, prepared by Mr. Charles Kotuby, partner at the law firm Jones Day, Washington, DC (hereinafter "Comparative Study"). See also Comparative Table on Grounds of Jurisdiction Prepared by the Permanent Bureau, January 2015.

[113] For more complete information on the U.S. system for the recognition of foreign judgments, see R.A. BRAND, "Federal Judicial Center International Litigation Guide: Recognition and Enforcement of Foreign Judgments" (2013) 74 *U. Pitt. L. Rev.* 491, https://papers.ssrn.com/sol3/papers.cfm?abstract_id=2443977.

[114] National Conference of Commissioners on Uniform State Laws, Uniform Foreign-Country Money Judgments Recognition Act, https://www.uniformlaws.org/committees/community-home/librarydocuments?communitykey=ae280c30-094a-4d8f-b722-8dcd614a8f3e&tab=librarydocuments.

[115] Ibid., Art. 4(a).

[116] Ibid., Art. 4(b) and (c).

[117] Ibid., Art. 4(b)(2).

[118] "The prevailing view is that, even if the rendering court had jurisdiction under the laws of its own state, a court in the United States asked to recognize a foreign judgment should scrutinize the basis for asserting jurisdiction in the light of American concepts of jurisdiction to adjudicate. International Shoe and its progeny govern this determination." R.A. BRAND,

Intersentia

This means that if the facts before the foreign court would have satisfied the tests that a U.S. court would apply in determining direct jurisdiction, then the U.S. court addressed for the purposes of recognition and enforcement will accept that judgment, subject to other specifically listed grounds for non-recognition. There is no difference between the test for direct jurisdiction and the test for indirect jurisdiction.[119]

4.1.3. The United Kingdom

This is not the case in those countries which have a broader list for direct jurisdiction than for indirect jurisdiction purposes. An example of such a discriminatory jurisdiction gap is found in the United Kingdom, in which the direct jurisdiction rules are found in Practice Direction 6B, which accompanies Part 6 of the Civil Procedure Rules 1998 of the Supreme Court of England and Wales (CPR). The Practice Direction provides a court with discretion to order service outside the jurisdiction of the United Kingdom in a number of specific situations.[120] The Practice Direction lists 21 connecting factors, each

---

International Business Transactions Fundamentals 2nd ed., Wolters Kluwer, Alphen aan den Rijn 2018, ch. 6. See, e.g., *Mercandino v. Devoe & Raynolds, Inc.*, 181 N.J. Super. 105, 108, 436 A.2d 942 (App. Div. 1981): "In determining whether the Italian court had jurisdiction we deem it appropriate to apply the minimum contacts test."

[119]   The same is true in German courts faced with a request for the recognition and enforcement of a judgment from outside the EU. Judgments from within the EU are governed by the Brussels I Recast Regulation (Brussels I Recast Regulation, above n. 26). Section 328(I) of the German Code of Civil Procedure includes a requirement that the foreign court from which a judgment originates had "jurisdiction under German law." See I PHILIP WEEMS, *Enforcement of Money Judgments Abroad* FRG-29, 1993. In Italy, Art. 64(1)(a) of Law 218/1995 is similar in this respect, requiring that in order for recognition of a foreign judgment to occur, "the authority rendering the judgement had jurisdiction pursuant to the criteria of jurisdiction in force under Italian law." In each of these instances, the rules of direct jurisdiction are applied as the rules of indirect jurisdiction. This means that so long as the case could have been brought in the recognizing state on similar jurisdictional facts, the court addressed will accept that jurisdiction was proper in the court of origin.

[120]   Practice Direction 6:

Service out of the jurisdiction where permission is required

3.1 The claimant may serve a claim form out of the jurisdiction with the permission of the court under rule 6.36 where—

General Grounds

(1)   A claim is made for a remedy against a person domiciled within the jurisdiction.

(2)   A claim is made for an injunction (GL) ordering the defendant to do or refrain from doing an act within the jurisdiction.

(3)   A claim is made against a person ("the defendant") on whom the claim form has been or will be served (otherwise than in reliance on this paragraph) and—
   (a)   there is between the claimant and the defendant a real issue which it is reasonable for the court to try; and
   (b)   the claimant wishes to serve the claim form on another person who is a necessary or proper party to that claim.

of which may justify service outside the jurisdiction and thus constitute an acceptable basis of jurisdiction over a foreign defendant. The same is not true when a U.K. court tests the jurisdiction of a foreign court when a judgment is brought for recognition and enforcement. In the latter event, U.K. courts apply "the Dicey Rule," which can be found in the most recent edition of

---

(4)   A claim is an additional claim under Part 20 and the person to be served is a necessary or proper party to the claim or additional claim.

(4A)   A claim is made against the defendant in reliance on one or more of paragraphs (2), (6) to (16), (19) or (21) and a further claim is made against the same defendant which arises out of the same or closely connected facts.

Claims for interim remedies

(5)   A claim is made for an interim remedy under section 25(1) of the Civil Jurisdiction and Judgments Act 1982.

Claims in relation to contracts

(6)   A claim is made in respect of a contract where the contract—
    (a)   was made within the jurisdiction;
    (b)   was made by or through an agent trading or residing within the jurisdiction;
    (c)   is governed by English law; or
    (d)   contains a term to the effect that the court shall have jurisdiction to determine any claim in respect of the contract.

(7)   A claim is made in respect of a breach of contract committed within the jurisdiction.

(8)   A claim is made for a declaration that no contract exists where, if the contract was found to exist, it would comply with the conditions set out in paragraph (6).

Claims in tort

(9)   A claim is made in tort where—
    (a)   damage was sustained, or will be sustained, within the jurisdiction; or
    (b)   damage which has been or will be sustained results from an act committed, or likely to be committed, within the jurisdiction.

Enforcement

(10)   A claim is made to enforce any judgment or arbitral award.

Claims about property within the jurisdiction

(11)   The subject matter of the claim relates wholly or principally to property within the jurisdiction, provided that nothing under this paragraph shall render justiciable the title to or the right to possession of immovable property outside England and Wales.

Claims about trusts etc.

(12)   A claim is made in respect of a trust which is created by the operation of a statute, or by a written instrument, or created orally and evidenced in writing, and which is governed by the law of England and Wales.

(12A)   A claim is made in respect of a trust which is created by the operation of a statute, or by a written instrument, or created orally and evidenced in writing, and which provides that jurisdiction in respect of such a claim shall be conferred upon the courts of England and Wales.

(13)   A claim is made for any remedy which might be obtained in proceedings for the administration of the estate of a person who died domiciled within the jurisdiction or whose estate includes assets within the jurisdiction.

(14)   A probate claim or a claim for the rectification of a will.

The Conflict of Laws.[121] This test provides for only four grounds of indirect jurisdiction.[122] The result could be interpreted either as an acknowledgment that the longer list of direct bases of jurisdiction found in Practice Direction 6B contains otherwise questionable bases of jurisdiction or that there is a desire to discriminate against judgments from foreign courts.

---

(15) A claim is made against the defendant as constructive trustee, or as trustee of a resulting trust, where the claim arises out of acts committed or events occurring within the jurisdiction or relates to assets within the jurisdiction.

(16) A claim is made for restitution where—
   (a) the defendant's alleged liability arises out of acts committed within the jurisdiction; or
   (b) the enrichment is obtained within the jurisdiction; or
   (c) the claim is governed by the law of England and Wales.

Claims by HM Revenue and Customs

(17) A claim is made by the Commissioners for H.M. Revenue and Customs relating to duties or taxes against a defendant not domiciled in Scotland or Northern Ireland.

Claim for costs order in favour of or against third parties

(18) A claim is made by a party to proceedings for an order that the court exercise its power under section 51 of the Senior Courts Act 1981 to make a costs order in favour of or against a person who is not a party to those proceedings. (Rule 46.2 sets out the procedure where the court is considering whether to exercise its discretion to make a costs order in favour of or against a non-party.).

Admiralty claims

(19) A claim is—
   (a) in the nature of salvage and any part of the services took place within the jurisdiction; or
   (b) to enforce a claim under section 153, 154,175 or 176A of the Merchant Shipping Act 1995.

Claims under various enactments

(20) A claim is made—
   (a) under an enactment which allows proceedings to be brought and those proceedings are not covered by any of the other grounds referred to in this paragraph; or
   (b) under the Directive of the Council of the European Communities dated 15 March 1976 No. 76/308/EEC, where service is to be effected in a Member State of the European Union.

Claims for breach of confidence or misuse of private information

(21) A claim is made for breach of confidence or misuse of private information where
   (a) detriment was suffered, or will be suffered, within the jurisdiction; or
   (b) detriment which has been, or will be, suffered results from an act committed, or likely to be committed, within the jurisdiction.

[121] DICEY and MORRIS, *The Conflict of Laws*, Rule 43 (14R-054) 15th ed., 2012. See, e.g., *Rubin v. Eurofinance SA* [2012] UKSC 46, at ¶¶ 7–10, in which Lord Collins, the General Editor of DICEY AND MORRIS, follows the "Dicey Test" and traces its history.

[122] DICEY and MORRIS, above n. 121, Rule 43:

   Rule 43 – Subject to Rules 44 to 46, a court of a foreign country outside the United Kingdom has jurisdiction to give a judgment *in personam* capable of enforcement or recognition as against the person against whom it was given in the following cases:

4.1.4. Canada

In Canada, early twentieth-century jurisprudence incorporated a limited set of bases of indirect jurisdiction, similar to the current U.K. model. Thus, the foreign judgment creditor had the burden of proving that: (1) the defendant was a subject of the foreign country; (2) the defendant was a resident of the foreign country; (3) the defendant had sued as a plaintiff in the foreign country and the judgment resulted from a successful counterclaim in the foreign action; (4) the defendant voluntarily attorned to the jurisdiction of the foreign court; or (5) the defendant contracted for disputes to be submitted to the foreign court.[123] This changed with the adoption of the "real and substantial connection" test in the 1990 decision in *Morguard Investments Ltd. v. De Savoye*,[124] which dealt with the internal recognition of judgments between provinces. In the 2002 case of *Muscutt v. Courcelles*,[125] the Ontario Court of Appeal refined the real and substantial connection test. Judge Sharpe noted that the connection could be either between the court and the defendant or the court and the claim, and then set out what have become known as the Muscutt factors in determining the existence of a real and substantial connection between the foreign court and the case:

1. The connection between the forum and the plaintiff's claim;
2. The connection between the forum and the defendant;
3. Unfairness to the defendant in assuming jurisdiction;
4. Unfairness to the plaintiff in not assuming jurisdiction;
5. The involvement of other parties to the suit;
6. The court's willingness to recognize and enforce an extra-provincial judgment rendered on the same jurisdictional basis;
7. Whether the case is inter-provincial or international in nature; and
8. Comity and standards of jurisdiction, recognition and enforcement prevailing elsewhere.[126]

First Case – If the person against whom the judgment was given was, at the time the proceedings were instituted, present in the foreign country.

Second Case – If the person against whom the judgment was given was claimant, or counterclaimed, in the proceedings in the foreign court.

Third Case – If the person against whom the judgment was given, submitted to the jurisdiction of that court by voluntarily appearing in the proceedings.

Fourth Case – If the person against whom the judgment was given, had before the commencement of the proceedings agreed, in respect of the subject matter of the proceedings, to submit to the jurisdiction of that court or of the courts of that country.

[123] *Emanuel v. Symon* [1908] 1 KB 302, 309 (CA).
[124] [1990] 3 SCR 1077.
[125] 60 O.R. (3d) 20, at para. 75 (CA) (2002).
[126] Ibid., ¶¶ 74–100.

This test has replaced the limited set of indirect jurisdictional filters in Canada and appears to parallel the Canadian test for direct jurisdiction, leaving little if any jurisdictional gap at this point in Canada.

4.1.5. Other Countries

Australia was reported in the 2015 study carried out for the Hague Conference to have a jurisdiction gap similar to that in the United Kingdom.[127] Israel is reported to have no jurisdiction gap.[128] Singapore appears to follow the British approach, with courts applying an indirect jurisdiction test that requires that the judgment debtor has been present or resident in the state of the court of origin at the time of commencement of the proceedings, or otherwise has agreed to or submitted to the jurisdiction of the court of origin.[129]

4.2. RECOGNITION JURISDICTION

Some countries allow an action to be brought for the recognition or enforcement of a judgment or arbitral award only if separate jurisdiction exists in the recognizing court for the purposes of bringing the recognition and enforcement action. This aspect of the process of recognition and enforcement has been the subject of jurisprudence and commentary, most notably in the United States and Singapore. The following discussion therefore focuses on these two countries, followed by additional comments about the law in other countries.

4.2.1. The United States[130]

In the United States, there are separate federal and state judicial systems, so an initial question is whether to bring any action in a state or a federal court. In order to bring a matter in a federal court, there must be federal subject matter jurisdiction as well as personal jurisdiction over the defendant (federal courts are courts of limited subject matter jurisdiction, but state courts are, for the most part, courts of general subject matter jurisdiction). In proceedings relating to arbitration, federal courts have subject matter jurisdiction through Chapter II of the Federal Arbitration Act, which implements the New York Convention.

---

[127]   "Comparative Study," above n. 112.
[128]   Ibid.
[129]   Singapore Report, at 1.
[130]   This subsection is developed from the author's earlier writings in R.A. BRAND, "Understanding Judgments Recognition" (2014) 40 N. Car. J. Int'l L. & Com. Reg. 878; and R.A. BRAND, "The Circulation of Judgments under the Draft Hague Judgments Convention" (2019), https://papers.ssrn.com/sol3/papers.cfm?abstract_id=3334647.

"An action or proceeding falling under the Convention shall be deemed to arise under the laws and treaties of the United States."[131]

Even where the action is brought in a federal court, the applicable law may be state law. Rule 64 of the Federal Rules of Civil Procedure effectively borrows state remedies and enforcement procedures whenever property is seized:

> Rule 64. Seizing a Person or Property
>
> (a) Remedies Under State Law-In General. At the commencement of and throughout an action, every remedy is available that, under the law of the state where the court is located, provides for seizing a person or property to secure satisfaction of the potential judgment. But a federal statute governs to the extent it applies.[132]

The resulting importance of state law means that three overlapping elements are important for bringing both pre- and post-arbitration enforcement proceedings:

1. The likelihood that assets of the respondent will be within the relevant jurisdiction;
2. The state statute(s) providing for judicial assistance in aid of arbitration; and
3. The likelihood that jurisdiction will be available for purposes of the desired relief in the relevant jurisdiction.

The role of New York City as a financial center makes it more likely that a party to an international arbitration will have assets that pass through New York than through most other U.S. states. Moreover, New York has one of the clearest state statutes on pre-arbitration attachment relief. Thus, it is the most useful example when considering state law on the matter. The most important New York statute on the matter is New York Civil Practice Law and Rules (CPLR) §7502(c), which reads as follows:

> (c) Provisional remedies. The supreme court in the county in which an arbitration is pending or in a county specified in subdivision (a) of this section, may entertain an application for an order of attachment or for a preliminary injunction in connection with an arbitration that is pending or that is to be commenced inside or outside this state, whether or not it is subject to the United Nations convention on the recognition and enforcement of foreign arbitral awards, but only upon the ground that the award to which the applicant may be entitled may be rendered ineffectual without such provisional relief.[133]

---

[131]   9 U.S.C. §203.

[132]   Federal Rules of Civil Procedure, Rule 64(a).

[133]   New York Civil Procedure Law and Rules (CPLR), §7502(c).

The Uniform Law Commissioners promulgated a Uniform Asset-Preservation Orders Act in 2012 (amended in 2014), which would clarify and unify state law on attachments and injunctions in aid of arbitration (as well as providing for the recognition and enforcement of asset preservation orders from other countries), but this Act has not yet been enacted in any US state.

While the issue of personal jurisdiction over the judgment debtor in judgment recognition cases (recognition jurisdiction) is a matter of constitutional law and could thus be resolved by the U.S. Supreme Court, this has not happened and may not happen for some time. The closest the Supreme Court has come to the question is a footnote in the celebrated case of *Shaffer v. Heitner*.[134] *Shaffer* raised the question of whether a court may proceed when the defendant is without sufficient contacts with the forum state to support personal jurisdiction, but the property of the defendant is located in the forum state.[135] In its footnote 36, the Court stated:

> Once it has been determined by a court of competent jurisdiction that the defendant is a debtor of the plaintiff, there would seem to be no unfairness in allowing an action to realize on that debt in a State where the defendant has property, whether or not that State would have jurisdiction to determine the existence of the debt as an original matter.[136]

Because this footnote is as near as the Supreme Court has come to touching on the question of recognition jurisdiction, it is the language on which lower courts have focused when faced with jurisdictional challenges in judgment recognition cases. The same issue arises whether it is a foreign judgment or a foreign arbitral award for which recognition is being sought, so the cases from both of these areas are instructive.

4.2.1.1.   Option 1: No Personal Jurisdiction Required

Cases and commentary have demonstrated three possible approaches to the question of recognition jurisdiction.[137] The first approach is to determine that due process is an appropriate matter for the court deciding the rights of the parties, and that a court that is being asked only to recognize and enforce a judgment is simply implementing that decision rather than making decisions

---

[134]   433 U.S. 186 (1977).
[135]   For a complete discussion of *Shaffer v. Heitner*, see L.J. SILBERMAN, "*Shaffer v. Heitner*: The End of an Era" (1978) 53 *N.Y.U. L. Rev.* 33.
[136]   433 U.S. at 210 fn. 36.
[137]   For a more detailed discussion of recognition jurisdiction issues, see R.A. BRAND, "Recognition Jurisdiction and the Hague Choice of Court Convention" *Liber Amicorum Kresimir Sajko*, HRVOJE SIKIRIĆ, VILIM BOUČEK and DAVOR BABIĆ eds., Pravni fakultet Sveučilišta u Zagrebu, 2012, pp. 155–187, from which this discussion is developed: http://papers.ssrn.com/sol3/papers.cfm?abstract_id=1629360.

of "life, liberty, or property." This approach does not require a full personal jurisdiction analysis in a judgment recognition action and – as a practical matter – facilitates pre-emptive recognition so that enforcement may occur quickly if, and when, the judgment debtor's assets are later found in the recognizing state. A proponent of this approach would argue that the judgment debtor has had his or her day in court in the court of origin, and that the application of due process principles is most important in that forum.

This approach is demonstrated by the decision of the New York Appellate Division in *Lenchyshyn v. Pelko Electric, Inc.*,[138] in which the court stated:

> that the judgment debtor need not be subject to personal jurisdiction in New York before the judgment creditor may obtain recognition and enforcement of the foreign country money judgment, as neither the Due Process Clause of the United States Constitution nor New York law requires that the New York court have a jurisdictional basis for proceeding against a judgment debtor.[139]

While the facts may not have gone so far as the language of the case,[140] the New York court went on to state that:

> even if defendants do not presently have assets in New York, plaintiffs nevertheless should be granted recognition of the foreign country money judgment pursuant to [the New York version of the Uniform Foreign Money-Judgments Recognition Act], and thereby should have the opportunity to pursue all such enforcement steps *in futuro*, whenever it might appear that defendants are maintaining assets in New York.[141]

The *Lenchyshyn* analysis was followed in *Abu Dhabi Commercial Bank PJSC v. Saad Trading, Contracting and Co.*[142] In this case, the First Department Appellate Division quoted from the *Lenchyshyn* opinion, stating:

> "a party seeking recognition in New York of a foreign money judgment (whether of a sister state or a foreign country) need not establish a basis for the exercise of personal

---

[138]   281 A.D.2d 42, 723 N.Y.S.2d 285 (2001).
[139]   Ibid., at 43, 723 N.Y.S.2d at 286.
[140]   In *Lenchyshyn*, the plaintiff alleged that the defendant had assets within the forum state, but that fact was not specifically established.
[141]   281 A.D.2d at 50, 723 N.Y.S.2d at 291. While *Lenchyshyn* is a New York decision, it is notable that the International Commercial Disputes Committee of the Association of the Bar of the City of New York rejected its approach in favor of requiring either personal jurisdiction or the presence of the judgment debtor's assets in order to support an action. INTERNATIONAL COMMERCIAL DISPUTES COMMITTEE OF THE ASSOCIATION OF THE BAR OF THE CITY OF NEW YORK, "Lack of Jurisdiction and *Forum Non Conveniens* as Defenses to the Enforcement of Foreign Arbitral Awards" (2005) ABCNY Committee Report 15, http://www.nycbar.org/pdf/report/ForeignArbitral.pdf.
[142]   986 N.Y.S.2d 454 (1st Dep't 2014).

jurisdiction over the judgment debtor by the New York courts," because "[n]o such requirement can be found in the CPLR, and none inheres in the Due Process Clause of the United States Constitution, from which jurisdictional basis requirements derive." Although CPLR 5304(a) provides that the trial court may refuse recognition of the foreign country judgment if the foreign country court did not have personal jurisdiction over the judgment debtor, it does not provide for non-recognition on the ground that the New York court lacks personal jurisdiction over the judgment debtor in a CPLR article 53 proceeding.[143]

However, this position was significantly limited in the 2019 decision in *AlbaniaBEG Ambient Sh.p.k. v. Enel S.p.A.*[144] In *AlbaniaBEG*, the judgment debtor raised five non-frivolous grounds for the non-recognition of a judgment from an Albanian court. This distinguished the case from *Abu Dhabi*, in which the only defense was jurisdictional. The court in *AlbaniaBEG* relied on this difference to limit *Abu Dhabi* to its facts, noting that in *AlbaniaBEG*, "there is something to defend, and the court's function ceases to be merely ministerial."[145] Moreover, "[t]o require a defendant to litigate such substantive issues in a forum where it maintains no property, and where it has no contacts that would otherwise subject it to personal jurisdiction, would 'offend [the] traditional notions of fair play and substantial justice' at the heart of the Due Process Clause."[146] Thus, if the judgment debtor defends only on the grounds of personal jurisdiction and does not raise any substantive defenses to recognition, a New York court may proceed, even without jurisdiction over the defendant or the defendant's assets. On the other hand, so long as a non-frivolous substantive defense to recognition is raised, either personal or quasi-in rem jurisdiction will be required.

4.2.1.2. Option 2: Requiring Full Personal Jurisdiction

The second approach is to determine that each judicial proceeding requires a separate due process determination and thus full personal jurisdiction analysis is required in any action to recognize a foreign judgment. Unless there is personal jurisdiction over the judgment debtor, no recognition action may be maintained and no recognition judgment may be granted.

---

[143] 986 N.Y.S.2d at 457–58 (internal citations omitted). See L.J. Silberman and A.D. Simowitz, "Recognition and Enforcement of Foreign Judgments and Awards: What Hath Daimler Wrought?", http://papers.ssrn.com/sol3/papers.cfm?abstract_id=2639820, in which the authors criticize the *Abu Dhabi* opinion on the grounds that: "The New York appellate court in *Abu Dhabi* overlooked the requirement of the New York statute that recognition of a foreign judgment proceed by an action. Its erroneous interpretation reinforced a divide between the recognition and enforcement of foreign judgments and the requirements imposed by U.S. federal appellate courts on judgment creditors attempting to recognize or enforce foreign arbitral awards."

[144] 160 A.D.3d 93, 73 N.Y.S.3d 1 (N.Y.A.D. 2018).

[145] Ibid., at 160 A.D.3d 108.

[146] Ibid., at 108, quoting *International Shoe Co. v. Washington*, 326 U.S. 310, 316 (1945).

This approach was adopted by the Fourth Circuit Federal Court of Appeals in *Base Metal Trading, Ltd. v. OJSC "Novokuznetsky Aluminim Factory,"*[147] which involved an action to recognize and enforce a foreign arbitral award. The court held that even quasi-in rem jurisdiction through the attachment of assets of the judgment debtor within the state is not sufficient and that personal jurisdiction over the judgment debtor is always required in an action to recognize an arbitral award.[148] A court adopting this logic for the recognition of arbitral awards would seem to do the same for judgment recognition.

4.2.1.3. Option 3: Requiring Either Personal Jurisdiction or Quasi-in Rem Jurisdiction

The third approach is to acknowledge that the presence of the judgment debtor's assets within the state of the court asked to recognize the foreign judgment is also sufficient to allow a court to adjudicate on the question of recognition and enforcement, at least to the extent and value of the assets present in the state of the recognizing court. This approach essentially adopts the language of footnote 36 from *Shaffer v. Heitner*,[149] with the effect of recognition being limited to the value of the judgment debtor's assets in the forum if full personal jurisdiction does not exist. Thus, due process is considered to be satisfied if either: (1) the defendant has sufficient personal contacts to satisfy standard minimum contacts analysis; or (2) there are assets of the defendant in the forum state, even if those assets are unrelated to the claim in the underlying judgment.[150]

This approach is adopted in both the *Restatement (Fourth) Foreign Relations Law*[151] and the American Law Institute's 2005 *Recognition and Enforcement of Foreign Judgments: Analysis and Proposed Federal Statute ALI Proposed Federal Statute*.[152] The *Restatement*, relying on footnote 36 in *Shaffer*, states that while "the presence of assets will suffice to establish personal jurisdiction in a proceeding that simultaneously recognizes and enforces a foreign money judgment ... the

---

[147]   283 F.3d 208 (4th Cir. 2002), cert. denied, 537 U.S. 822 (2002).
[148]   283 F.3d 213 ("when the property which serves as the basis for jurisdiction is completely unrelated to the plaintiff's cause of action, the presence of property alone will not support jurisdiction").
[149]   See above n. 135 and accompanying text.
[150]   See, e.g., *Pure Fishing, Inc. v. Silver Star Co. Ltd.*, 202 F. Supp. 2d 905, 910 (N.D. Iowa 2002) ("the minimum contacts requirement of the Due Process Clause does not prevent a state from enforcing another state's valid judgment against a judgment-debtor's property located in that state, regardless of the lack of other minimum contacts by the judgment-debtor"); *Electrolines v. Prudential Assurance Co. Inc.*, 260 Mich. App. 144, 163, 677 N.W.2d 874, 885 (2003) ("in an action brought to enforce a judgment, the trial court must possess jurisdiction over the judgment debtor or the judgment debtor's property").
[151]   *Restatement (Fourth) Foreign Relations Law* §482 cmt. b (2018).
[152]   ALI, *Recognition and Enforcement of Foreign Judgments: Analysis and Proposed Federal Statute*, §9 (2005).

effect of recognition in a proceeding in which personal jurisdiction is based solely on the presence of assets is limited to the property that supports jurisdiction."[153]

The ALI Proposed Federal Statute similarly provides in section 9 that:

> (b) An action to recognize or enforce a judgment under this Act may be brought in the appropriate state or federal court
> (i) where the judgment debtor is subject to personal jurisdiction; or
> (ii) where assets belonging to the judgment debtor are situated.

In each of these ALI texts, it would seem that the language would be limited by traditional jurisprudence on quasi-in rem jurisdiction and that the extent of recognition would go no further than the value of the judgment debtor's assets present within the forum state.[154]

4.2.1.4. Sorting Out the Options

Unlike the 1962 Recognition Act, section 6 of the 2005 Recognition Act specifically provides that the question of recognition of a foreign judgment is to be raised either by filing a separate new action "seeking recognition of the foreign-country judgment" or through a "counterclaim, cross-claim, or affirmative defense" in a pending action.[155] While this makes the procedure for judgment recognition clear, the Uniform Law Commissioners took no position on the question of recognition jurisdiction if offensive recognition is sought in the first of these two manners.[156]

Other courts have rendered decisions that seem only to add to the uncertainty existing through non-uniformity when considering recognition jurisdiction. In the language of its decision in *Pure Fishing Inc. v. Silver Star Co. Ltd.*,[157] the Federal District Court for the Northern District of Iowa appears to follow the

---

[153] *Restatement (Fourth) Foreign Relations Law* §482 Reporters' fn. 3 (2018).

[154] See, e.g., *CME Media Enterprises B.V. v. Zelezny*, 2001 WL 1035138 (S.D.N.Y. 2001) (ultimately limiting the enforcement of an arbitration award to $.05 in the judgment debtor's bank account within the state).

[155] 2005 Recognition Act, above n. 25, §6.

[156] Ibid., cmt. 4: "While this Section sets out the ways in which the issue of recognition of a foreign-country judgment may be raised, it is not intended to create any new procedure not currently existing in the state or to otherwise effect existing state procedural requirements. The parties to an action in which recognition of a foreign-country judgment is sought under Section 6 must comply with all state procedural rules with regard to that type of action. Nor does this Act address the question of what constitutes a sufficient basis for jurisdiction to adjudicate with regard to an action under Section 6. Courts have split over the issue of whether the presence of assets of the debtor in a state is a sufficient basis for jurisdiction in light of footnote 36 of the U.S. Supreme Court decision in *Shaffer v. Heitner*, 433 U.S. 186, 210 n. 36 (1977). This Act takes no position on that issue."

[157] 202 F. Supp. 2d 905 (N.D. Iowa 2002).

Lenchyshyn analysis[158] by requiring neither contacts sufficient to find personal jurisdiction over the judgment debtor nor the presence in the forum state of assets of the judgment debtor. But the facts in both *Pure Fishing* and *Lenchyshyn* indicated that the judgment debtor in each case had assets in the forum state, leaving it unclear whether the language of each decision that would not require that condition is part of the holding or merely dicta.[159]

In *Electrolines Inc. v. Prudential Assurance Company Ltd.*,[160] the Michigan Court of Appeals rejected the less stringent jurisdictional approach in *Lenchyshyn*, stating that "in an action brought to enforce a judgment, the trial court must possess jurisdiction over the judgment debtor or the judgment debtor's property."[161] Two cases in Texas specifically rejected the *Electrolines* approach in favor of the New York language in *Lenchyshyn*, finding a requirement of personal jurisdiction for the purposes of judgment recognition neither in the United States Constitution nor in the Texas version of the 1962 Recognition Act. In *Haaksman v. Diamond Offshore (Bermuda) Ltd.*,[162] the Texas Court of Appeal held that "the United States Constitution does not require in personam jurisdiction over the judgment debtor in the state in which a foreign judgment is filed."[163] Thus, "even if a judgment debtor does not currently have property in Texas, a judgment creditor should be allowed the opportunity to obtain recognition of his foreign-money judgment and later pursue enforcement if or when the judgment debtor appears to be maintaining assets in Texas"[164] and "a trial court does not have to possess jurisdiction over the judgment debtor or the judgment debtor's property in order to rule on a motion for nonrecognition under the Uniform Act."[165] A second Texas Appeals Court opinion in *Beluga Chartering B.V. v. Timber S.A.*[166] went further in its analysis of the 1962 Recognition Act

---

[158] Ibid., at 910: "The Iowa [Foreign Money-Judgments Recognition Act] itself contains no requirement of personal jurisdiction over the judgment debtor. The court notes that in the context of the recognition and enforcement of other state judgments, the minimum contacts requirement of the Due Process Clause does not prevent a state from enforcing another state's valid judgment against a judgment-debtor's property located in that state, regardless of the lack of other minimum contacts by the judgment-debtor."

[159] See above, n. 140.

[160] 260 Mich. App. 144, 677 N.W.2d 874 (Mich. App. 2003).

[161] *Electrolines*, above n. 150, at 260 Mich. App. 163, 677 N.W.2d 885.

[162] 260 S.W.3d 476 (Tex. App. 2008).

[163] Ibid., at 480 (determining that the language in *Shaffer v. Heitner* regarding full faith and credit to sister state judgments applies equally to the recognition of foreign judgments).

[164] Ibid., at 481: "the plain language of the Uniform Act does not require the judgment debtor to maintain property in the state in order for that state to recognize a foreign-money judgment. [The Act] provides a list of specific reasons why the trial court may refuse recognition of the foreign-country judgment; however, lack of property in the state is not a ground for nonrecognition."

[165] Ibid.

[166] 294 S.W.3d 300 (Tex. App. 2009).

as enacted in Texas, finding that the Act in fact prohibited a requirement of personal jurisdiction in an action to recognize a foreign judgment.[167]

Cases dealing with the recognition of foreign arbitral awards provide useful analysis of the same recognition jurisdiction issue as that in judgment recognition actions. While judgment recognition law currently is dispersed at the state level and thus suffers significant non-uniformity, arbitration law is governed by federal law as a result of the Federal Arbitration Act[168] and the New York Convention.[169] Under this combination of federal sources, the Second, Third, Fourth, Fifth, and Ninth Federal Circuit Courts of Appeal have all held that there must be personal jurisdiction over the award debtor – or presence of the award debtor's assets in the forum state – in order to confirm a foreign arbitral award.[170]

The Second Circuit decision in *Frontera Resources Azerbaijan Corp. v. State Oil Co. of the Azerbaijan Republic*[171] demonstrates the federal court analysis and

---

[167]   294 S.W.3d at 305: "Under the [Texas Uniform Foreign Money-Judgments Recognition Act's] express language, the trial court 'may not, under any circumstances, review the foreign country judgment in relation to any matter not specified in Section 36.005.' ... Section 36.005 provides that the trial court may refuse recognition if the foreign country court did not have personal jurisdiction over the judgment debtor in connection with the underlying action giving rise to the foreign country judgment for which enforcement is sought. The trial court does not entertain claims against the judgment debtor in the enforcement proceeding, and does not exercise personal jurisdiction over the judgment debtor. Therefore, lack of personal jurisdiction over the judgment debtor is not an available basis for resisting the subsequent UFCMJRA proceeding in Texas."
While the court did not specifically address the question of quasi-in rem jurisdiction, the judgment debtor had argued that there must be either *in personam* or quasi-in rem jurisdiction, suggesting that the judgment debtor did not have assets within Texas. Ibid., at 304.

[168]   9 U.S.C. §1 *et seq.*

[169]   United Nations Convention on the Recognition and Enforcement of Foreign Arbitral Awards (New York Convention).

[170]   *Frontera Res. Azer. Corp. v. State Oil Co. of Azer. Rep.*, 582 F.3d 393, 397–398 (2d Cir. 2009) (personal or quasi-in rem jurisdiction required for confirmation proceedings under the New York Convention); *Telcordia Tech Inc. v. Telkom SA Ltd.*, 458 F.3d 172, 178–179 (3d Cir. 2006) ("the New York Convention does not diminish the Due Process constraints in asserting jurisdiction over a nonresident alien"); *Base Metal Trading, Ltd. v. OJSC "Novokuznetsky Aluminum Factory,"* 283 F.3d 208, 212 (4th Cir. 2002) ("while the [New York] Convention confers subject matter jurisdiction over actions brought pursuant to the Convention, it does not confer personal jurisdiction when it would not otherwise exist"); *First Inv. Corp. of Marshall Islands v. Fujian Mawei Shipbuilding, Ltd.*, 703 F.3d 742 (5th Cir. 2012) ("Congress could no more dispense with personal jurisdiction in an action to confirm a foreign arbitral award than it could under any other statute"); *Glencore Grain Rotterdam B.V. v. Shivnath Rai Harnarain Co.*, 284 F.3d 1114, 1122 (9th Cir. 2002) (determining that the Federal Arbitration Act requires personal jurisdiction because dispensing with such a requirement would raise question about the statute's constitutionality). See also *Emp'rs Ins. of Wausau v. Banco De Seguros Del Estado*, 199 F.3d 937, 941–943 and fn. 1 (7th Cir. 1999) (requiring personal jurisdiction in a dispute arising under the Inter-American Convention on International Commercial Arbitration, but observing that the result would be the same under the New York Convention).

[171]   582 F.3d 393 (2d Cir. 2009).

302

reviews the earlier cases from other Circuits. In rejecting the argument that no limitations outside the bases for non-recognition found in Article V of the New York Convention were available to avoid recognition of a foreign arbitral award, the Second Circuit stated:

> [T]he need for personal jurisdiction is fundamental to "the court's power to exercise control over the parties ... Some basis must be shown, whether arising from the respondent's residence, his conduct, his consent, the location of his property or otherwise, to justify his being subject to the court's power."
>
> ... Article V's exclusivity limits the ways in which one can challenge a request for confirmation, but it does nothing to alter the fundamental requirement of jurisdiction over the party against whom enforcement is being sought.[172]

The jurisprudence in arbitral award recognition thus holds that there must be either personal jurisdiction over the award debtor or the presence in the forum state of assets of the award debtor in order to recognize and enforce a foreign arbitral award under the New York Convention and the Federal Arbitration Act. A similar position is found in commentary as well. The draft *ALI Restatement on International Commercial Arbitration*,[173] the International Commercial Disputes Committee of the Association of the Bar of the City of New York,[174] and Gary Born's leading commentary on international commercial arbitration[175] all consider it to be necessary to have either personal jurisdiction over the award debtor or quasi-in rem jurisdiction over assets of the award debtor for purposes of an action for enforcement of a foreign arbitral award.[176]

---

[172] Ibid., at 397 (citations omitted).

[173] ALI, *Restatement of the Law (Third) U.S. Law of International Commercial Arbitration*, §5-19 and Reporters' Notes (Tentative Draft No. 1, March 29, 2010) (stating a requirement of either statutory personal jurisdiction and compliance with "general constitutional due-process requirements under the Fifth and Fourteenth Amendments," or quasi-in rem jurisdiction, but also noting that "a court remains free to predicate jurisdiction on consent where the parties entering into an agreement selecting that court as a forum for the enforcement of an award," citing *D.J. Blair & Co. v. Gottdiener*, 462 F.3d 95, 104 (3d Cir. 2006)).

[174] INTERNATIONAL COMMERCIAL DISPUTES COMMITTEE OF THE ASSOCIATION OF THE BAR OF THE CITY OF NEW YORK, above n. 141.

[175] G.B. BORN, *International Commercial Arbitration*, 2nd ed., Kluer Law International, Dordrecht 2014, pp. 2981–2984. Born takes the position that "customary jurisdictional limitations on the judicial powers of Contracting States" are sufficient grounds to deny recognition and enforcement of an arbitral award under the New York Convention, but that the application of the doctrine of *forum non conveniens* to avoid recognition and enforcement (being, in his analysis, substantive and not procedural) is not reconcilable with Arts. III and V of the New York Convention. Ibid., at 2984–2987.

[176] Note, however, that §5-19 of the Restatement Tentative Draft No. 1 carries the title "Personal Jurisdiction in Actions to Enforce International Arbitral Awards," leaving out the word "recognition" in its text, comments, and Reporters' Notes. ALI, above n. 173, §5-19. One might infer from this that the discussion applies only to enforcement (for the purposes of which there would necessarily have to be property of the award debtor within the jurisdiction

Ronald A. Brand

As noted in the above discussion, the majority rule in the United States is that either personal jurisdiction over the award debtor or quasi-in rem jurisdiction resulting from the presence of that debtor's assets within the jurisdiction will be sufficient to bring the action for recognition and enforcement. However, jurisdiction based on the presence of assets will be limited to the value of those assets.

4.2.2. Singapore[177]

There are no specific rules on where a foreign judgment should be enforced or executed in Singapore. Enforcement under the common law is by way of an action on the debt represented by the foreign judgment. Thus, the judgment creditor must sue the judgment debtor and seek to establish the Singapore court's *in personam* jurisdiction over the judgment debtor. *In personam* jurisdiction may be established by service of process on the defendant within the jurisdiction or service out of the jurisdiction. Service within the jurisdiction can take one of several forms. If the defendant is a natural person who is physically present in Singapore, he or she may be served personally in Singapore to establish jurisdiction. If the defendant is a body corporate incorporated in Singapore or a foreign company that is registered in Singapore, jurisdiction can be established through service by registered mail to its registered office. If the defendant is a foreign body corporate that is not registered in Singapore, then service may be effected on an officer or agent in Singapore if the company is carrying on business in Singapore, i.e., it is carrying on its business from a fixed place of business for more than a temporary period of time. If the defendant cannot be served within the jurisdiction, then the defendant may be served outside the jurisdiction with the leave of the court.

Leave of the court may be granted if there is a sufficient legal nexus – as defined by the law – between the defendant, or the cause of action, or the subject matter of the suit, and Singapore. Enforcing a foreign judgment in Singapore is a specific nexus mentioned in the law. Whether the service is within or without the jurisdiction, usually the Singapore court will only exercise jurisdiction if it is the natural forum. However, this is usually not an issue because the defendant usually has assets in Singapore in an enforcement case and that is normally a good enough reason for the Singapore court to regard itself as a natural forum. One court has suggested that perhaps the natural forum is simply irrelevant in

---

of the forum state) and not to recognition. However, the absence of any separate discussion of recognition also operates at the same time to weaken this implicit result – if §5-19 applied only to enforcement and not to recognition, then there would necessarily be other discussion of recognition jurisdiction in the draft, and that is not the case.

[177] This section is taken pretty much verbatim from the Singapore National Report by Tiong Min Yeo.

relation to the enforceability of a foreign judgment.[178] Under the common law, what is eventually executed is a judgment of the Singapore court.

Where the judgment is successfully registered under the RECJA or the REFJA, or a successful application is made to enforce a judgment under the CCAA, the judgment can be executed as if it were a Singapore judgment. There is no need to establish *in personam* jurisdiction over the judgment debtor.

In all cases involving the enforcement of foreign judgments, the execution process is the same as for judgments given by the Singapore court and, as a general rule, the execution process kicks in only after it has been established that the judgment is enforceable under the respective regimes. Because the initial court order is the result of an *ex parte* application under the statutory regimes, there is a further qualification that execution should be delayed until the expiry of the time allowed for the judgment debtor to challenge the court order giving effect to the application to register (the RECJA and the REFJA) or the application to enforce (the CCAA) the foreign judgment, or until the challenge has been dismissed.[179]

In appropriate circumstances, the Singapore court may order the judgment creditor to provide security for costs under all four legal regimes.

For money judgments, the execution process includes: writs of seizure and sale; writs of possession of immovable property; appointment of a receiver; garnishment orders; and applications for the examination of judgment debtors. There is no legal requirement that the defendant should have any assets in Singapore, though the absence of assets within the territory will clearly pose practical difficulties. Writs of seizure and sale and writs of possession are only effective against property within the territory of Singapore.

A garnishment order is made against a third party (the garnishee) who owes money to the judgment debtor to pay the judgment creditor instead in order to satisfy (partially or fully) the judgment debt. The result of the court order under Singapore law is to discharge the obligation owed by the third party to the judgment debtor to the extent of the payment.[180] A garnishment order may only be made against a third party who is within the jurisdiction.[181] This means that the third party must be present within the jurisdiction or must have submitted to the jurisdiction of the court.[182]

---

[178]   *Alberto Justo Rodriguez Licea v. Curacao Drydock Co, Inc.* [2015] 4 SLR 172; [2015] SGHC 136, ¶ 20.

[179]   Rules of Court, Order 67, Rule 10(1) and (2) (RECJA and REFJA); Rules of Court, Order 111, Rule 8 (CCAA).

[180]   Singapore Rules of Court, Order 49, Rule 8.

[181]   Ibid., Rule 1(1).

[182]   As the judgment creditor has no substantive cause of action against the third party, there is no basis for service out of jurisdiction to bring the third party within the jurisdiction of the court.

Intersentia

The law on garnishment orders in Singapore is practically the same as in English law.[183] There is indirect approval of the English common law position that the garnishment order operates like the enforcement of a judgment in rem against a debt, and its effect is characterized as the involuntary transfer of title to a chose in action governed by the *lex situs*,[184] which in this context usually means the residence of the (third-party) debtor where the debt is recoverable. The English position, which is likely to be persuasive under Singapore law, is that the court does not have (subject matter) jurisdiction to make a garnishment order in respect of debts situated outside the jurisdiction unless the order would be recognized under the law applicable in that place.[185] The main consideration is that the garnishee should not be practically subject to double liability under the law of its own residence in addition to the garnishment order. In principle, in the converse case, a foreign garnishment order may be recognized if it is from the court of the *lex situs* of the debt that is the subject matter of the order.[186]

A receiver may be appointed by the court to enforce a judgment by way of equitable execution. The appointment of a receiver does not create rights over the property that is subject to an equitable interest or any other interest in property. This is a useful means of enforcing judgment debts when other methods of enforcement are not effective, e.g., if the assets are overseas.[187] However, whether such a receiver will be recognized in foreign countries or be effective in calling in foreign assets are matters beyond the control of the Singapore court. In considering whether it is just and equitable to make such an appointment, the court will consider the amount claimed by the judgment creditor relative to the amount likely to be collected by the receiver and the probable costs of the appointment. Where appropriate, the appointment may be accompanied by injunctions restraining the judgment debtor from dealing with certain assets (where non-compliance by the judgment debtor could be punishable as contempt of court).

Under the Debtors Act, a judgment debtor may be committed to prison if "there is probable reason for believing, having regard to his conduct, or the state of his affairs, or otherwise, that he is likely to leave Singapore with a view to avoiding payment" of such money that remains owing under a judgment debt.[188]

---

183   *Telecom Credit Inc v. Midas United Group Ltd.* [2018] SGCA 73, ¶ 29.
184   *The Republic of the Philippines v. Maler Foundation* [2014] 1 SLR 1389; [2013] SGCA 66 (hereinafter *Maler Foundation*), ¶ 89.
185   *Taurus Petroleum Ltd v. State Oil Marketing Co. of the Ministry of Oil, Republic of Iraq* [2017] UKSC 64; [2018] AC 690.
186   *Maler Foundation*, above n. 184.
187   A Singapore court is likely to find the reasoning of the English Court of Appeal (*Masri v. Consolidated Contractors International (UK) Ltd. (No. 2)* [2009] QB 450; [2008] EWCA Civ 303) on this issue highly persuasive, i.e., that there is no rule that the court could never make a receivership order by way of equitable execution in relation to foreign debts.
188   Cap 73, 2014 Rev Ed, §3.

Any imprisonment under this statute does not extinguish the debt or prejudice the execution process against the property of the debtor.

Foreign injunctive relief in the context of execution of a judgment is not recognized or enforced under any of the four legal regimes in Singapore. They are not money judgments and cannot be enforced under the common law, the RECJA or the REFJA. They are not decided on the merits and so cannot be recognized or enforced under the common law, the RECJA, the REFJA, or the CCAA. However, a foreign court order that executes a transfer of property in the course of enforcing a judgment may well take effect as an involuntary transfer of property, which could be effective under the *lex situs* (or possibly the applicable law of the debt where the property in question is a debt).[189]

4.2.3. The United Kingdom

In the United Kingdom, the recognition and enforcement of judgments outside the Brussels I and Lugano regimes is governed by the Administration of Justice Act (AJA) 1920 and the Foreign Judgments (Reciprocal Enforcement) Act (FJ(RE)A) 1933. The main role of the legislation is to provide a registration procedure rather than requiring a new action to be brought. Recognition is justified by the principle of reciprocity rather than the doctrine of obligation. The 1920 Act establishes a scheme for the enforcement in the United Kingdom of certain judgments from colonial and Commonwealth countries to which Part II of the Act extends.[190] The 1933 Act provides rules for the registration in the United Kingdom of money judgments from countries to which Part I of the Act has been extended by an Order in Council.[191] A distinctive feature of the AJA 1920 is that following the application by the foreign judgment creditor, the court may order the registration of the judgment "if in all the circumstances of the case they think it just and convenient that the judgment should be enforced in the United Kingdom."[192]

The issue of recognition jurisdiction has presented itself in the United Kingdom in the form of actions seeking freezing orders in aid of foreign proceedings. If a freezing order is sought in aid of foreign proceedings, and the assets are not located in the United Kingdom, the order will be granted only if

---

[189]   *Maler Foundation*, above n. 184.
[190]   These include a considerable number of Caribbean and African states and several South-East Asian states: e.g., the British Virgin Islands, the Cayman Islands, Ghana, Hong Kong, Kenya, Malaysia, Nigeria, Singapore, Tanzania, Uganda, and Zambia. New Zealand is also covered by the 1920 Act.
[191]   These include Australia, Canada (except Quebec), India, Pakistan, Israel, and some European countries to the extent that the judgment is not within the Brussels I (Recast) Regulation or the Lugano Convention (Austria, Belgium, France, Germany, Italy, the Netherlands, and Norway).
[192]   §9(1).

the respondent or the dispute has a sufficiently strong link with the jurisdiction or if there is some other factor justifying the court's intervention.[193] Thus, in *Banco Nacional de Comercio Exterior SNC v. Empresa de Telecomunicaciones de Cuba SA*,[194] the court refused the grant of a worldwide order because the judgment debtor was outside the jurisdiction, the original judgment was granted in Italy, and although assets within England and Wales were covered by a domestic freezing order, granting a worldwide order would be likely to give rise to disharmony and confusion.

5. ENFORCEMENT FOLLOWING RECOGNITION

It is not always clear whether recognition and enforcement are a single concept within a legal system or are treated as separate events. In the United States, they are clearly separate concepts. Once recognition occurs, the question of enforcement of either a judgment or an arbitral award is largely a matter of state law in the United States. This is a result of Federal Rule of Civil Procedure 64.[195] This means that state law must be consulted. New York law is probably the best developed in this regard, with the general law of attachment found in Articles 60–63 of the New York Civil Practice Law and Rules (NYCPLR). Under this framework, §7502(c) of the New York Civil Procedure Law and Rules was enacted specifically to address aiding attachment in aid of arbitration.[196]

In accordance with §7502(c) CPLR, the New York Appellate Division rendered a decision allowing attachment in *Matter of Sojitz Corp. v. Prithvi Info. Solutions Ltd.*,[197] even though there were no other connections to New York, the parties were from Japan and India, and the contract was performed and payments were made in India. Moreover, the contract was governed by English law and the arbitration was to be held in Singapore. The only connection the case had to New York was the fact that a New York customer owed money to the buyer.

Under §6201(5) CPLR, an attachment may be granted in any cause of action, and such action can be based on a judgment, decree, or order of a court of the United States or of any other court which is entitled to full faith and credit, or on a judgment which qualifies for recognition under the provisions of Article 53 of the CPLR. Most state laws authorize provisional remedies in aid of arbitration.[198]

---

[193]   *Mobil Cerro Negro Ltd v. Petroleos de Venezuela SA* [2008] 1 Lloyd's Rep 684.
[194]   [2007] 2 All ER 1093.
[195]   See text above at n. 132.
[196]   See CPLR, above n. 133, §7502(c).
[197]   82 A.D.3d 89, 921 N.Y.S.2d 14, 2011 N.Y. App. Div. LEXIS 1709 (2011).
[198]   See *Stemcor USA Inc. v. CIA Siderurgica Do Para Cosipar*, 870 F.3d 370, 374–379 (5th Cir. 2017) (where pre-arbitration attachment was available under Louisiana law in aid of an arbitration subject to the Convention to be filed in New York).

In general, UK law has been more restrictive in its approach to the enforcement of foreign judgments than in relation to the recognition of such judgments. For enforcement, an action on the judgment is required (subject to the procedural changes made by the AJA 1920 and the FJ(RE)A 1933), whereas the courts have been prepared to recognize preclusive effects to a foreign judgment where it has been raised in the course of litigation without the need for any special "recognition" procedure.

6. INJUNCTIVE RELIEF

The circulation of injunctive relief brings with it issues that differ from the rather more simple concept of the recognition and enforcement of monetary judgments and awards. Injunctions often have a rather territorial scope when they deal with restrictions on the transfer of assets within the granting jurisdiction, prohibitions on the use of intellectual property rights within the granting jurisdiction, the use of immovable property within the granting jurisdiction, and similar matters. However, the last half-century has seen the development of injunctions designed to have global effect. This raises the question of whether such injunctions issued in one jurisdiction are subject to recognition and enforcement in other jurisdictions.

6.1. GLOBAL INJUNCTIVE RELIEF GENERALLY

Global injunctive relief is often referred to as a *Mareva* injunction. A *Mareva* injunction, first available in U.K. courts, temporarily freezes assets which may be required to satisfy a judgment or expected judgment in order to prevent the dissipation of assets or their removal from the jurisdiction during the pendency of the case.[199] In the United Kingdom, the authority for the *Mareva* injunction is now found in a statute at section 37(1) of the Supreme Court Act 1981. Most Commonwealth and other Anglo-American legal systems have adopted the *Mareva* injunction in some form. The Canadian Supreme Court has defined such an injunction as:

> the right to freeze exigible assets when found within the jurisdiction, wherever the defendant may reside, providing, of course, there is a cause between the plaintiff and the defendant which is justiciable in the courts of England. However, unless there is a genuine risk of disappearance of assets, either inside or outside the jurisdiction, the injunction will not issue.[200]

---

[199]   *Mareva Compania Naviera SA v. International Bulk Carriers SA* [1975] 1 WLR 1093 (CA).
[200]   *Aetna Financial Services v. Feigelman* [1985] 1 SCR 2, ¶ 26.

Intersentia

309

Mareva injunctions, now known as freezing injunctions in the United Kingdom, restrain a party from removing assets located within the jurisdiction out of the country, or from dealing with assets whether they are located within the jurisdiction or not.[201] However, it does not give the claimant any security or any priority in relation to other creditors. Given the risk against which protection is sought, an application for a freezing injunction in the United Kingdom will be made without notice to the defendant and before service of the claim form. The application must be supported by evidence in the form of a sworn statement, with supporting documentation, and must give "full and frank disclosure" of all material facts – including those that are not in the applicant's favor. The jurisdiction of the UK High Court to grant a freezing injunction is part of its inherent jurisdiction.

In Canada, a *Mareva* injunction is a discretionary equitable remedy typically obtained by an *ex parte* motion, without notice being given to other parties. It is considered "an exceptional form of interlocutory relief."[202] *Mareva* injunctions operate *in personam* and do not attach to the property itself.[203] The granting of a *Mareva* injunction does not give priority of execution to the successful party and it does not affect insolvency laws.[204] A *Mareva* injunction is distinguishable from execution because a party obtaining a *Mareva* injunction is required to give an undertaking to pay damages in the event that any are suffered due to the defendant's inability to deal with the property.

In *Grupo Mexicano de Desarrollo, S.A. v. Alliance Bond Fund Inc.*,[205] the US Supreme Court specifically rejected the idea that U.S. federal courts have the authority to issue *Mareva*-type injunctions. Finding that English courts in equity had no authority to issue such injunctions at the time of the incorporation of English equity practice into U.S. law by the Judiciary Act of 1789, Justice Scalia followed the "historical principle that before judgment (or its equivalent) an unsecured creditor has no rights at law or inequity in the property of his debtor,"

---

[201] See CPR, Rule 25.1(1)(f):

Orders for interim remedies

25.1

(1) The court may grant the following interim remedies—
....
(f) an order (referred to as a "freezing injunction (GL)")—
(i) restraining a party from removing from the jurisdiction assets located there; or
(ii) restraining a party from dealing with any assets whether located within the jurisdiction or not;

[202] *R. v. Consolidated Fastfrate Transport, Inc.*, 1995 Carswell Ont. 993, ¶ 130.
[203] *Aetna Financial Services v. Feigelman* [1985] 1 SCR 2, ¶ 28.
[204] Ibid.
[205] 527 U.S. 308 (1999).

determining that "[t]he requirement that the creditor obtain a prior judgment is a fundamental protection in debtor-creditor law – rendered all the more important in our federal system by the debtor's right to a jury trial on the legal claim."[206] Justice Ginsburg, joined by three other Justices in dissent, would have allowed such a preliminary injunction, noting that "increasingly sophisticated foreign-haven judgment proofing strategies, coupled with technology that permits the nearly instantaneous transfer of assets abroad, suggests that defendants may succeed in avoiding meritorious claims in ways unimaginable before the merger of law and equity."[207] While the *Grupo Mexicano* case does not address whether a federal district court has authority to grant *Mareva*-style injunctions under state law pursuant to Rule 64 of the Federal Rules of Civil Procedure or whether the result might be different when the relief sought on the merits is equitable rather than legal in nature (the *Grupo Mexicano* claim was for breach of contract), it does place clear limits on the availability of such injunctions in U.S. federal courts.

In Australia, a freezing order is available to restrain dissipation of foreign assets by a debtor or third-party bank in support of the enforcement of an Australian judgment, provided that such a person is subject to the personal jurisdiction of the Australian court. Service outside Australia of an application for a freezing order is permissible in such a case, but only where there are local assets sought to be frozen as well as foreign assets.[208] A freezing order may be accompanied by an order requiring a defendant to disclose the nature, location, and details of its assets.[209]

In Singapore, a freezing injunction may be available in the appropriate circumstances. It is a particularly powerful remedy because it can be applied for *ex parte* in the first instance (subject to discharge in subsequent *inter partes* proceedings). It can also be made in respect of foreign assets, with ancillary orders made to compel the disclosure of the whereabouts of assets in Singapore or overseas; it can be made against parties complicit with the defendant in potential dissipation of the assets. Non-parties with notice can be liable for contempt of court for assisting in the breach of the injunction or orders.

The freezing injunction in Singapore is not an attachment order against property and gives no priority in the case of insolvency. It is a personal order restraining the defendant from dealing with assets in a way that could defeat the enforcement of a judgment, or a judgment that has not yet been obtained. Third parties with notice of the injunction may be held in contempt of court if they assist the defendant in breaching the injunction. The injunction may also

---

[206] 527 U.S. at 329–330.
[207] Ibid., at 339.
[208] See, e.g., Uniform Civil Procedure Rules (New South Wales), Rule 25.16.
[209] *Universal Music Australia Pry Ltd v. Sharman License Holdings Ltd.* (2005) 228 ALR 474, ¶ 20.

be granted against third parties who are complicit in assisting the defendant to defeat the enforcement of the judgment. In addition, disclosure orders may be made ancillary to the freezing orders in relation to assets both within and outside Singapore. The freezing injunction may be granted in respect of foreign assets (since the order is made against the defendant personally) and some injunctions may have worldwide effect, though courts are generally cautious about the extraterritorial effect of such injunctions. In particular, third parties in a foreign country are not to be liable for contempt of court unless the order has been made enforceable in the foreign country.

There are two types of freezing injunctions in Singapore: pre-judgment and post-judgment. The pre-judgment freezing injunction is available where: (1) the defendant can be brought within the *in personam* jurisdiction of the Singapore court; (2) the plaintiff has a substantive cause of action against the defendant that is justiciable in the Singapore court; (3) the plaintiff has a good arguable case on the merits; (4) the defendant has assets within or outside of Singapore that are available to meet any judgment debt; and (5) there is a real risk of dissipation of the assets to defeat the enforcement of the impending judgment if the injunction is not granted.[210] However, the plaintiff must give an undertaking to the court to pay damages to the defendant in the event that the claim turns out to be unfounded. The post-judgment freezing injunction may be available where: (1) there is a real risk of the debtor dissipating or disposing of its assets with the intention of depriving the judgment creditor of any satisfaction of the judgment debt; and (2) the injunction will act as an aid to the execution of the judgment.[211] In both cases, the remedy is discretionary and will be granted only if it would be in the interests of justice to do so.

6.2. THE RECOGNITION AND ENFORCEMENT OF INJUNCTIVE RELIEF

In the United States, the recognition and enforcement of injunctive relief is available only under common law. Both the 1962 Uniform Foreign Money-Judgments Recognition Act and the 2005 Uniform Foreign-Country Money Judgments Recognition Act apply only to money judgments.

In Singapore, foreign injunctive relief in the context of execution of a judgment is not recognized or enforced under any of the four legal regimes. They are not money judgments and cannot be enforced under the common law, the RECJA, or the REFJA. They are not decided on the merits and so cannot be recognized or enforced under the common law, the RECJA, the REFJA, or the CCAA. However, a foreign court order that executes a transfer of property in the course

---

[210]   *China Medical Technologies, Inc. (in Liquidation) v. Wu Xiaodong* [2018] SGHC 178.
[211]   *Hitachi Leasing (Singapore) Pte Ltd. v. Vincent Ambrose* [2001] 1 SLR(R) 762; [2001] SGHC 76.

of enforcing a judgment may well take effect as an involuntary transfer of property, which could be effective under the *lex situs* (or possibly the applicable law of the debt where the property in question is a debt).[212]

7. SEARCHING AND SEIZING FOREIGN ASSETS

7.1. THE UNITED STATES

The more extensive nature of discovery in U.S. litigation generally means that the United States is a more liberal legal system for searching and seizing assets. The process comes with limitations when addressed in conjunction with foreign litigation and arbitration. As noted earlier,[213] Rule 64 of the Federal Rules of Civil Procedure makes state law applicable in federal court for seizing property to secure satisfaction of a judgment. This means that the process may vary on a state-by-state basis.

The law of the state of New York is perhaps most developed in regard to seizing assets in international litigation. In 2010, in *Hotel 71 Mezz Lender LLC v. Falor*,[214] the Court held that CPLR §6201 permits pre-judgment seizure of an out-of-state debtor's assets, citing its decision in *Koehler v. Bank of Bermuda*,[215] for the proposition that one of the purposes of attachment is to keep a judgment debtor over whom the court has personal jurisdiction from freely using or transferring property that could be applied in satisfaction of the judgment creditor's judgment. The Court further noted that because a court could "compel observance of its decrees by proceedings in personam against the owner within the jurisdiction," the trial court was within its power to attach the defendants' out-of-state assets since they had submitted voluntarily to the court's jurisdiction. The Court also found that the intangible and uncertificated assets at issue were "property" within the meaning of Article 62 of the CPLR. In support of this interpretation, the Court cited CPLR §5201(b), which provides that "a money judgment may be enforced against any property that may be assigned or transferred, whether it consists of a present or future right or interest and whether or not it is vested."

The *Hotel 71* Court also cited *ABKCO Industries v. Apple Films*,[216] which held that an absent debtor's intangible contract right to net profits from a future film promotion was a "debt or property" within CPLR §5201 and could be attached for the purpose of securing quasi-in rem jurisdiction, despite the fact that the

---

[212]   *Maler Foundation*, above n. 184.
[213]   See above n. 132.
[214]   14 N.Y.3d 303, 926 N.E.2d 1202, 900 N.Y.S.2d 698 (2010).
[215]   12 N.Y.3d 533 (2009).
[216]   39 N.Y.2d 670 (1976).

value of the contract right was uncertain. Using the *ABKCO* decision's definition of property, the Court found that the 22 out-of-state intangible interests were akin to the contract rights at issue in the *ABKCO* case and thus constituted "property" under CPLR §6202. The Court next addressed the issue of whether the defendants' intangible interests had a situs in New York, a determination made more difficult by the fact that the interests were not evidenced by a certificate or other negotiable instrument. Following the U.S. Supreme Court's guidance in *Harris v. Balk*, the Court of Appeals found that the situs of intangible property "clings to and accompanies [the debtor] wherever he goes" for the purposes of attachment. It thus rejected the view that the situs of intangible property is the domicile of the debtor.

New York has reaffirmed the "separate entity rule," which holds that assets held at a foreign office of a bank that has a branch or representative office in New York are not considered in-state assets for the purpose of garnishment in *Motorola Credit Corp v. Standard Chartered Bank*.[217] However, the *Motorola* approach to the separate entity rule was not followed by the Appellate Division, First Department, in *B & M Kingstone, LLC v. Mega Intern. Commercial Bank Co. Ltd.*,[218] where it allowed broad discovery of a New York branch so as to reach information about assets in branches of the same bank abroad.

7.2. SINGAPORE

In Singapore, the normal method for ascertaining the location of the assets of the judgment debtor is by way of examination in court. This process is only available as part of the execution of the Singapore judgment (common law) or deemed Singapore judgment (the RECJA, the REFJA, and the CCAA), so the enforceability of the foreign judgment under Singapore law must first be established under the respective regimes.

Because the primary function of this process is the collection of information only, an examination order may be made under the RECJA and REFJA regimes before an application to set aside the registration has been heard and dismissed (or the expiry of time for such an application if no application has been made to set it aside),[219] because it is not considered "execution" for the purposes of its postponement under the Rules of Court.[220] However, while under the RECJA and the REFJA, the foreign judgment has the same legal effect as a Singapore judgment upon registration (subject to being set aside subsequently), under the

---

[217]   24 N.Y.3d 149, 163 (2014).
[218]   131 A.D.3d 25915 N.Y.S.3d 318 (App. Div. 1st Dept. 2015).
[219]   *PT Bakrie Investindo v. Global Distressed Alpha Fund 1 Ltd. Partnership* [2013] 4 SLR 1116; [2013] SGCA 51.
[220]   Singapore Rules of Court, Order 67 Rule 10(1) and (2).

common law, the foreign judgment only gives rise to a civil obligation until a Singapore judgment is pronounced upon it, so that there is no basis for such an order until the Singapore judgment has been granted. Under the CCAA, the Singapore court order giving effect to the foreign judgment "does not take effect" until the time for challenge has expired or a challenge has been dismissed.[221] It is likely that the Singapore court will adopt the same approach taken under the RECJA and the REFJA, and will hold that the purpose of the provision is to delay the physical process of execution against assets and that it does not necessarily delay the process of the examination of the judgment debtor.

A judgment debtor (or in the case of a body corporate, an officer of the judgment debtor) may be ordered to attend court to be orally examined on whatever property the judgment debtor has wherever they are situated, and may be ordered to produce any books or documents in the possession of the judgment debtor that are relevant to such questions. The summons must be properly served on the party to be examined and, if necessary, service out of jurisdiction may be obtained with leave of court on non-parties (e.g., a company officer).[222] Discretion to grant such leave would be exercised sparingly on company officers, and the court would consider whether an officer was so closely connected to the substantive claim, and the extent of his/her knowledge of the company's financial affairs and extent of his/her involvement in matters relating to the claim.[223] The Singapore court is very cautious about the extraterritorial reach of its orders.

In Singapore, freezing orders have been developed to expedite the execution of Singapore judgments and there is some uncertainty about how they apply in the context of the enforcement of foreign judgments. The starting point is that a foreign judgment per se cannot be executed in Singapore. The execution process kicks in only after a Singapore judgment has been given (common law) or the foreign judgment has been statutorily deemed to have the same legal effect as a Singapore judgment (the RECJA, the REFJA, and the CCAA).

The pre-judgment freezing injunction (and all the incidents thereof) is only available under common law enforcement because it is the only enforcement regime where the plaintiff is bringing a substantive cause of action (a debt) to the Singapore court. Under the statutory regimes, there is no substantive cause of action as such, only a right to apply for the foreign judgment to be registered and enforced (the RECJA and the REFJA) or to apply to have the foreign judgment enforced (the CCAA). Under the RECJA and the CCAA (but not the REFJA),

---

[221]   Ibid., Order 111, Rule 8.
[222]   Leave may be dispensed with in the case of parties to the proceedings who have already been property brought within the jurisdiction of the Singapore court, either by service within jurisdiction or service out of jurisdiction with leave of court.
[223]   *Burgundy Global Exploration Corp. v. Transocean Offshore International Ventures Ltd.* [2014] 3 SLR 381; [2014] SCGA 24.

the judgment creditor is not prohibited from enforcing the foreign judgment under the common law. However, it is not clear whether the plaintiff can start a common law action simply to obtain a freezing injunction to protect the enforcement of the foreign judgment under the respective statutory regimes because the statutorily deemed local judgment for execution is a different legal creature from the Singapore judgment resulting from the substantive cause of action relied on in the common law action. Yet, there is no issue if the plaintiff elects to pursue the common law route all the way to the Singapore judgment, although this defeats the purpose of the statutory regimes to facilitate enforcement. On the other hand, in practice it will be rare for there to be an urgent need for a pre-judgment freezing injunction under the statutory regimes because the application of the judgment creditor is *ex parte* and usually the judgment debtor would not know about the proceedings until the court order has been granted.

There is also no legal difficulty with invoking a post-judgment freezing injunction (and all the incidents thereof) after the foreign judgment has become executable under Singapore law. In common law, the Singapore judgment (on the debt arising from the foreign judgment) is executable once granted. Under the RECJA, the REFJA, and the CCAA, the foreign judgment is executable on the same basis as a Singapore judgment only after a failed challenge or after the time for challenge has expired if there is no challenge. This means that there could be a window of opportunity for the dissipation of assets once the judgment debtor is notified of the judgment creditor's successful application under the statutory regimes. Whether the Singapore court will grant a post-judgment freezing injunction before the foreign judgment has become executable as a deemed local judgment has not been tested in the Singapore court. But it is possible to find the basis for such jurisdiction and power if the Singapore court takes its cue from its position on the examination of judgment debtors and holds that a post-judgment injunction given from the moment of successful *ex parte* registration (under the RECJA and the REFJA) or application (under the CCAA), but before the expiry of the time for challenge or dismissal of such a challenge, is one that aids "execution" in the broader sense.

8. CONCLUSIONS

From the above discussion, a few very simple conclusions can be drawn about public policy and the recognition and enforcement of judgments and arbitral awards. They begin with a near-global consensus among common law states on the following:

1. The public policy ground for non-recognition always exists (globally, regionally, and nationally);

2. Public policy for this purpose is always narrowly defined;
3. Public policy for this purpose is seldom successfully asserted;
4. The test of public policy generally is the same for recognition as for applicable law; and
5. The public policy ground for non-recognition is crucial to the negotiation of international and regional conventions.

The two major jurisdiction issues that arise in judgment and arbitral award recognition cases are the question of indirect jurisdiction and the question of recognition jurisdiction. Some common understanding of rules of indirect jurisdiction was acknowledged in the 2019 Hague Convention on the Recognition and Enforcement of Judgments in Civil or Commercial Matters. With its Article 5(1) set of jurisdictional filters that operate as indirect bases of jurisdiction used to test a judgment for the purposes of determining whether it will circulate under the Convention. However, even with the 2019 Hague Convention, there remain two categories of states: those in which there is no gap between direct and indirect jurisdictional bases, and those in which there is a gap and the list of indirect bases of jurisdictional generally is smaller than the list of direct bases of jurisdiction.

No clear conclusion may be drawn regarding recognition jurisdiction; it remains a matter of differing national law. U.S. developments in this area have seen particularly development in recent years toward an understanding that an action for recognition of a judgment or arbitral award may be brought only if there exists either a clear basis of personal jurisdiction over the judgment or award debtor, or the presence of assets of that debtor within the forum state.

Regarding enforcement following recognition, national law remains important as there are no clear global or regional instruments on the matter. This is also true for injunctive relief and for the process of searching and seizing foreign assets.

The end game of any litigation or arbitration is not just a judgment or arbitral award, and it is not just recognition of the judgment or award in another state – it is satisfaction of the remedy ordered, often through the collection of a money judgment or arbitral award. This ultimately may require the seizure of assets, either pre- or post-judgment. It may be time to move the end game to the forefront of the development of procedural law on a regional and global basis.

REGIONALISM IN THE PROCESS OF RECOGNITION AND ENFORCEMENT OF FOREIGN TITLES

Civil Law Jurisdictions

Tanja Domej*

1. Introduction 320
2. National and Regional Approaches to Public Policy 322
3. Europe as a Breeding Ground for a Regionalized Concept of Public Policy? 331
   3.1. The Operation of the Brussels and Lugano Systems 331
   3.2. Successful and Failed Attempts at Abolishing the Public Policy Exception within the EU 334
   3.3. A Tale of Two Cities: Strasbourg and Luxembourg 337
   3.4. Public Policy as a National Concept and Tendencies Toward Regionalization 344
4. Intensity of Review 350
5. Public Policy and Specific Grounds for Refusal of Recognition and Enforcement 355
6. Jurisdiction and Public Policy 356
7. The Double Function of Public Policy 357
8. Arbitral Awards 358
9. Implementing Regional Public Policy: Possible Ways Forward 363
10. Enforcement 366
    10.1. Attachment of Assets 366
    10.2. Recognition and Enforcement of Foreign Garnishee Orders 369

---

*　Professor of Civil Procedure, Private Law, Private International Law and Comparative Law at the University of Zurich, Switzerland. I thank Nico Ravazzolo and Patrick Honegger-Müntener for their research assistance and help with compiling the footnotes. A short version of this report has been published as T. Domej, 'Regionalism in the Recognition and Enforcement of Foreign Titles: Implications for Public Policy Scrutiny" [2019] *IJPL* 235.

Intersentia

10.3. Managing Risks for Third-Party Debtors 371
10.4. Search and Disclosure of Assets 372
10.5. Obligations to Perform or to Refrain from Acting 374

1. INTRODUCTION

The recognition and local enforcement of foreign judgments by a court of
the state of enforcement at the request of a party has become the prototype
mechanism for "importing" foreign judgments. Alternative methods seem to
have largely lost their significance, at least outside the common law world. Such
alternative methods are enforcement at the request of a foreign court and an
action upon the foreign judgment that leads to the creation of a new domestic
judgment. The recognition and enforcement of foreign judgments does not
imply cooperation at the enforcement level. The judgment creditor must initiate
enforcement proceedings in every jurisdiction whose authorities need to take
action to enforce the judgment. Instruments providing for the free movement of
judgments only remove the requirement of obtaining a new title for enforcement
in each jurisdiction whose enforcement authorities the judgment creditor wishes
to engage.

The recognition and enforcement of foreign judgments can either operate
ipso iure or require a separate procedure, i.e., *delibation* with respect to
recognition[1] and/or exequatur with respect to enforceability. Where it operates
ipso iure, it is generally up to every court or other authority for whose decision
the foreign judgment is relevant to assess whether the prerequisites for
recognition and enforcement are met. From the perspective of the party relying
on the foreign judgment, the optimal solution is if a separate procedure in which
a court issues a binding decision on whether the judgment can be recognized
and enforced in the state addressed is available but not mandatory.[2]

---

[1] One of the jurisdictions that have a special recognition procedure in place that is compulsory
in most cases to give any effects to foreign judgments is Brazil (N. DE ARAUJO and
M. DE NARDI (Brazil), p. 1).

[2] This is, e.g., the approach followed by the Brussels I *bis* Regulation (Regulation (EU)
No 1215/2012 of the European Parliament and of the Council of 12 December 2012 on
jurisdiction and the recognition and enforcement of judgments in civil and commercial
matters [2012] OJ L351/1). Meanwhile, under the Brussels I Regulation (Council Regulation
(EC) No 44/2001 of 22 December 2000 on jurisdiction and the recognition and enforcement
of judgments in civil and commercial matters [2001] OJ L12/1), the declaration of
enforceability was a prerequisite for cross-border enforcement, while a recognition procedure
was optional. The same is still the case for the Lugano Convention of 2007. However, not all
states bound by the Lugano Convention insist that the judgment creditor obtain a declaration

Regardless of the procedural framework, rules on the recognition and enforcement of foreign judgments generally require that the judgment fulfils certain prerequisites. In addition, they provide for grounds for refusal. The consequences of the distinction between prerequisites and grounds for refusal may vary and are not always completely clear.[3]

This report's main focus is on public policy and its function in the rules on the recognition and enforcement of judgments and arbitral awards in civil and commercial matters. It discusses whether this function is or should be different within the framework of regional instruments as opposed to the global level. Enforcement can be difficult and cumbersome if the judgment debtor's assets are widely dispersed – even more so if the judgment creditor does not know the location of such assets. This leads to the questions of enforcement jurisdiction and of the possibility to obtain information about the existence and location of assets abroad, and, ideally, to prevent further dissipation of such assets. These are addressed in the final part of the chapter.

I am greatly indebted to the following national reporters for valuable information and insight:

- Ece ALPAY (Turkey), MEF University
- Nadia DE ARAUJO (Brazil), Pontifícia Universidade Católica do Rio de Janeiro (PUC-Rio)
- Marcelo DE NARDI (Brazil), Universidade do Vale do Rio dos Sinos
- Yosr EL-BENNA (Tunisia), Ouerfelli Attorneys & Counsels
- Qisheng HE (China), Peking University Law School
- Jerca KRAMBERGER ŠKERL (Slovenia), University of Ljubljana
- Ahmed OUERFELLI (Tunisia), Ouerfelli Attorneys & Counsels
- Hakan PEKCANITEZ (Turkey), Galatasaray University
- Keisuke TAKESHITA (Japan), Hitotsubashi University
- Dimitrios TSIKRIKAS (Greece), University of Athens
- Guangjian TU (China – Macau SAR), University of Macau
- Denise WIEDEMANN (Germany), Max Planck Institute for comparative and international private law Hamburg

---

of enforceability. In Switzerland, for example, the declaration of enforceability is generally considered to be optional (see G. WALTER and T. DOMEJ, *Internationales Zivilprozessrecht der Schweiz*, 5th ed., Haupt, Berne 2012, pp. 514 f.).

3   A typical difference would be that the person relying on the judgment bears the burden of proof with respect to prerequisites, whereas the burden of proof with respect to facts that establish a ground for refusal is on the person opposing recognition and enforcement. See, e.g., P GOTTWALD, "Commentary on §328 of the German Code of Civil Procedure (ZPO)" in T. RAUSCHER and W. KRÜGER (eds.), *Münchener Kommentar zur Zivilprozessordnung*, 6th ed., vol. 1, C.H. Beck, Munich 2020, marginal no. 81.

2. NATIONAL AND REGIONAL APPROACHES TO PUBLIC POLICY

Public policy is notoriously difficult to define[4] and views on it are, as the Turkish national report rightly remarks, "changeable and shifting."[5] Recently, they seem to have shifted more than ever in many states and regions. Some of these shifts concern particular issues of compatibility or incompatibility of certain outcomes with a state's public policy.[6] Others relate to the concept of public policy itself and the justification and purpose of retaining it as a ground for refusing recognition and enforcement of judgments in the global or regional context.

When defining public policy for the purposes of recognition and enforcement of foreign judgments, the most common approach in civil law jurisdictions seems to be to refer to fundamental principles of procedural or substantive law that are essential and indispensable from the perspective of the state where recognition and enforcement is sought.[7] Often such principles are enshrined in the respective state's constitution, but this is neither sufficient[8]

---

[4]   N. DE ARAUJO and M. DE NARDI (Brazil). See also, e.g., N. TROCKER, "Procedural Differences, Ordre Public and Recognition of Foreign Judgments. An Impressionistic Account" (2010) 9 *Int'l Lis* 26, 27.

[5]   H. PEKCANITEZ and E. ALPAY (Turkey), p. 1. See also A. ANTHIMOS, "Der verfahrensrechtliche ordre public im internationalen Zivilprozessrecht Griechenlands" [2000] *IPRax* 327, 327; M.D. BEGLEITER, "Taming the 'Unruly Horse' of Public Policy in Wills and Trusts" (2012) 26 *Quinn. Prob. Law Jour.* 125, 135; M. BERGER, "Conflicts Law and Practice in Egyptian Family Law: Islamic Law through the Backdoor" (2002) *50 Am. J. Comp. L.* 555, 567; L.E. TRAKMAN, "Aligning State Sovereignty with Transnational Public Policy" (2018) 93 *Tulane Law Review* 207, 215; G. WALTER and S. BAUMGARTNER, "General Report: The Recognition and Enforcement of Judgments outside the Scope of the Brussels and Lugano Conventions" in G. WALTER and S. BAUMGARTNER (eds.), *The Recognition and Enforcement of Judgments outside the Scope of the Brussels and Lugano Conventions, Civil Procedure in Europe Volume 3*, Kluwer Law International, The Hague 2000, p. 1, 29.

[6]   D. MARTINY, "Anerkennung ausländischer Entscheidungen nach autonomem Recht" in *Max-Planck-Institut für Ausländisches und Internationales Privatrecht, Handbuch des Internationalen Zivilverfahrensrechts*, vol. III/1, Mohr Siebeck, Tübingen 1984, marginal no. 994; J. VON HEIN, "Commentary on Article 6 of the German Introductory Act to the Civil Code (Einführungsgesetz zum Bürgerlichen Gesetzbuch)" in F. SÄCKER, R. RIXECKER, H. OETKER, and B. LIMPERG (eds.), *Münchener Kommentar zum Bürgerlichen Gesetzbuch*, 8th ed., vol. 12, C.H. Beck, Munich 2020, marginal nos. 218 f. (with examples from case law).

[7]   See, e.g., A. ANTHIMOS, above n. 5, p. 328; M. FREY and L. PFEIFER, "Der ordre public – die öffentliche Ordnung: derselbe Begriff, verschiedene Funktionen – ein Rechtsprinzip?" [2015] *EuR* 721, 728; J. HUANG, *Interregional Recognition and Enforcement of Civil and Commercial Judgments, Lessons for China from US and EU Law*, Hart Publishing, Oxford 2014, pp. 89 ff.; F. SARGIN, "A Critical Analysis of the Requirements of Recognition and Enforcement of Foreign Judgments under Turkish Law" [2008] *IPRax* 354, 356 f.; L. SHMATENKO, "Die Auslegung des anerkennungsrechtlichen ordre public in der Ukraine" [2013] *IPRax* 473, 474; L.E. TRAKMAN, above n. 5, p. 215; G. WALTER and S. BAUMGARTNER, above n. 5, p. 28.

[8]   The fundamental rights enshrined in a state's constitution typically represent the basic ideas of justice in that state's legal system. However, constitutional standards that would be binding

nor necessary. Sometimes the purported essential principles are even unwritten,[9] presumably because they are considered to be so self-evident that they need not be put down explicitly in legislation. Another element of public policy that seems to be widely recognized is the state's sovereignty and security,[10] which is explicitly mentioned in Article 7(1)(c) of the 2019 HCCH Judgments Convention.[11]

Sometimes, public policy is defined more broadly and is considered to encompass crucial economic and political interests,[12] basic moral rules[13] or social cohesion.[14] However, it does not seem completely clear whether this is supposed to mean that recognition and enforcement could be denied purely on the basis of extralegal norms or values, or whether only norms (whether written or unwritten) that are also legally binding can stand as part of public policy. This might not least be due to the complex interplay of law and morality that exists in some systems.

In the field of civil and commercial matters, the protection of elementary procedural rights seems to be the primary function of public policy today. The right to be heard (as far as it is not covered by specific rules such as those on the defective service of process) is at the core of procedural public policy in

---

for domestic courts cannot necessarily be directly transplanted to the field of recognition and enforcement of foreign judgments. See, in more detail, C. Völker, *Zur Dogmatik des ordre public: die Vorbehaltsklauseln bei der Anerkennung fremder gerichtlicher Entscheidungen und ihr Verhältnis zum ordre public des Kollisionsrechts*, Duncker & Humblot, Berlin 1998, pp. 117 ff.; see also I. Bach, "Commentary on §328 of the German Code of Civil Procedure" in V. Vorwerk and C. Wolf (eds.), *BeckOK ZPO*, 36th ed., C.H. Beck, 2020 [online], marginal no. 38; P. Georganti, *Die Zukunft des ordre public-Vorbehalts im Europäischen Zivilprozessrecht*, Herbert Utz, Munich 2006, p. 68.

[9]   M. Frey and L. Pfeifer, above n. 7, pp. 730 ff.

[10] This is highlighted, e.g., by Q. He (China), p. 1. See also A. Radjuk, "Grenzen der Anwendung des ausländischen Rechts in Russland" [2010] *IPRax* 370, 372; L.E. Trakman, "Domestic Courts Declining to Recognize and Enforce Foreign Arbitral Awards: A Comparative Reflection" (2018) 6 *Chinese Journal of Comparative Law* 174 ff.

[11] Convention of July 2, 2019 on the Recognition and Enforcement of Foreign Judgments in Civil or Commercial Matters.

[12] This aspect is mentioned by J. Kramberger Škerl (Slovenia), p. 2 and H. Pekcanitez and E. Alpay (Turkey), p. 1. See also K. Bälz, "Die Anerkennung und Vollstreckbarerklärung von ausländischen Schiedssprüchen im Irak" [2011] *SchiedsVZ* 27, 29; K. Bälz, "Das internationale Vertragsrecht der Vereinigten Arabischen Emirate" [2019] *IWRZ* 215, 217 f.; M. Berger, above n. 5, p. 567; J. Fröhlingsdorf, "Verletzung des wirtschaftlichen ordre public als Aufhebungsgrund eines inländischen Schiedsspruchs in Spanien" [2016] *SchiedsVZ* 246, 248.

[13] This is mentioned by J. Kramberger Škerl (Slovenia), p. 2. See also K. Bälz, "Das internationale Vertragsrecht der Vereinigten Arabischen Emirate" [2019] *IWRZ* 215, 217 f.; M. Berger, above n. 5, p. 567; J. Huang, above n. 7, p. 91; D. Marenkov, "Zur Anerkennung und Vollstreckung von ausländischen Schiedssprüchen in Russland" [2011] *SchiedsVZ* 136, 138.

[14] This is mentioned by Q. He (China), p. 1 and H. Pekcanitez and E. Alpay (Turkey), p. 1. See also K. Bälz, above n. 13, p. 217 f.; J. Huang, above n. 7, p. 90.

many systems today.[15] It is well established that a procedure is not unfair simply because it differs, even if significantly, from the one adhered to in the state where recognition and enforcement is sought.[16] However, even if this basic approach seems to be broadly recognized, it is rather difficult to predict on this basis which stance national courts will take when assessing the compatibility of particular procedural features alien to their domestic system with their public policy.

From the perspective of German case law, for example, the requirement is that the proceedings that led up to the judgment deviated from the German fundamental principles of civil procedure to an extent that the proceedings cannot be considered as based on the rule of law from a German perspective.[17] The public policy exception has been rejected by German courts, e.g., in the following instances:[18] suspension of the defendant from the proceedings as a sanction for contempt of court;[19] a worldwide freezing order;[20] the lack of a possibility to recover costs from the losing party;[21] and judgment by lay judges.[22] The lack of a requirement to be represented by a lawyer in foreign divorce proceedings does not violate German public policy,[23] but the fact that the foreign procedural law does not enable the (economically) weaker party to have a lawyer may amount to such a violation.[24] Mere differences in the rules on admissible evidence (e.g., with respect to party's testimony[25] or pre-trial discovery)[26] do not

---

[15] This aspect is highlighted by D. WIEDEMANN (Germany), p. 2 f. and D. TSIKRIKAS (Greece), p. 9. See also A. ANTHIMOS, above n. 5, p. 328; A. ÇIVI, *Die Anerkennung und Vollstreckung ausländischer familienrechtlicher Entscheidungen in der Türkei*, PhD thesis, Fribourg 2007, p. 51; I. THOMA, *Die Europäisierung und die Vergemeinschaftung des nationalen ordre public*, Mohr Siebeck, Tübingen 2007, p. 159; N. TROCKER, above n. 4, p. 27.

[16] S. LEIBLE, "Commentary on Article 45 Brussels I *bis* Regulation" in T. RAUSCHER (ed.), *Europäisches Zivilprozess- und Kollisionsrecht*, vol. 1, 4th ed., Otto Schmidt, Cologne 2016, marginal no. 15; F. GARCIMARTÍN ALFÉREZ and G. SAUMIER, *Draft Explanatory Report on the 2019 HCCH Judgments Convention*, 2019, marginal no. 263.

[17] Bundesgerichtshof, September 21, 2017 – IX ZB 5/17, BeckRS 2017, 126763; June 4, 1992 – IX ZR 149/91, NJW 1992, 3096; D. WIEDEMANN (Germany), p. 2.

[18] The following case references are taken from D. WIEDEMANN (Germany), pp. 2 f. See also R. STÜRNER, "Anerkennungsrechtlicher und europäischer Ordre Public als Schranke der Vollstreckbarerklärung – der Bundesgerichtshof und die Staatlichkeit in der Europäischen Union" in C.W. CANARIS, A. HELDRICH, K.J. HOPT, C. ROXIN, K. SCHMIDT, and G. WIDMAIER (eds.), *50 Jahre Bundesgerichtshof: Festgabe aus der Wissenschaft*, vol. 3, C.H. Beck, Munich 2000, pp. 677, 680 ff.

[19] Bundesgerichtshof, September 2, 2009 – XII ZB 50/06 (judgment from Australia); October 18, 1967 – VIII ZR 145/66, NJW 1968, 354 (judgment from the United Kingdom).

[20] Oberlandesgericht Nürnberg, December 22, 2010 – 14 W 1442/10, BeckRS 2011, 2567.

[21] Bundesgerichtshof, June 4, 1992 – IX ZR 149/91, NJW 1992, 3096, 3099.

[22] Oberlandesgericht Saarbrücken, August 3, 1987 – 5 W 102/87, NJW 1988, 3100.

[23] Bayerisches Oberstes Landesgericht, October 3, 1973 – BReg. 2 Z 29/73, NJW 1974, 418.

[24] Bundesgerichtshof, November 25, 1993 – IX ZR 32/93, NJW 1994, 1413.

[25] Bundesgerichtshof, April 6, 2017 – IX ZB 19/16, EuZW 2017, 623; R. GEIMER, "Commentary on §328 of the German Code of Civil Procedure" in R. ZÖLLER, *Zivilprozessordnung*, 33rd ed., Otto Schmidt, Cologne 2020, marginal no. 237.

[26] R. GEIMER, above n. 25, marginal no. 238.

constitute a violation of public policy. However, an incompatibility with the fundamental principles of fact-finding in the relevant field may amount to a violation of public policy (e.g., a determination of paternity without statement of the father and without medical expert opinion).[27] The parties' right to be heard has public policy status in Germany.[28] However, this only means that the party must have had an opportunity to participate in the proceedings; if it did have such an opportunity but failed to make use of it, public policy is not violated.[29] The principle of proceedings in public (open justice) is a fundamental principle of German procedural law. However, this does not mean that it is always a breach of public policy if the foreign proceedings were not public to the same extent as they would have been under German law.[30] Greek courts, when assessing the compatibility of limitations to the right to be heard, tend to look not only at the rules in themselves but also at whether they apply in a discriminatory way.[31] In some jurisdictions, it is considered to be incompatible with public policy if a foreign judgment does not contain any reasons, at least in certain circumstances.[32] In Turkey, however, such judgments can be recognized and enforced, even though the Turkish Constitution contains a rule according to which a judgment must contain reasons for the decision.[33] In Tunisia, the lack of the possibility of an appeal against the judgment in the state of origin is considered to be incompatible with procedural public policy.[34] In Greece, anti-suit injunctions are considered to be incompatible with the right of access to court and therefore contrary to Greek public policy.[35] In Slovenia, the right of a party to use their own language in the proceedings (which is enshrined in Article 62 of the Slovenian Constitution) has been considered to have public policy status.[36]

---

27 Bundesgerichtshof, August 26, 2009 – XII ZB 169/07, NJW 2009, 3306.
28 Bundesgerichtshof, September 10, 2015 – IX ZB 39/13, NJW 2016, 160, 161.
29 Bundesgerichtshof, June 4, 1992 – IX ZR 149/91, NJW 1992, 3096.
30 Oberlandesgericht Saarbrücken, August 3, 1987 – 5 W 102/87, NJW 1988, 3100.
31 D. TSIKRIKAS (Greece), p. 11.
32 For a detailed analysis of the French approach, see G. CUNIBERTI, "The Recognition of Foreign Judgments Lacking Reasons in Europe: Access to Justice, Foreign Court Avoidance, and Efficiency" (2008) 57 *Int'l & Comp.L.Q.* 25, 34 ff.; see also I. THOMA, above n. 15, p. 158. The Swiss Federal Court did not consider a default judgment without reasons as incompatible with Swiss public policy (BGE 116 II 631 consideration 4d). According to German case law, judgments lacking reasons can only be recognized and enforced if other documents, such as the statement of claim, enable the court to identify the subject matter of the dispute; see Bundesgerichtshof, September 10, 2015 – IX ZB 39/13. As regards the limits of a refusal for lack of reasons from the perspective of the Brussels I Regulation, see Case C-619/10, *Trade Agency Ltd v. Seramico Investments Ltd.*, ECLI:EU:C:2012:531.
33 H. PEKCANITEZ and E. ALPAY (Turkey), p. 2. The Greek courts seem to take a similar approach; see P. GEORGANTI, above n. 8, p. 83.
34 A. OUERFELLI and Y. EL-BENNA (Tunisia), p. 2.
35 D. TSIKRIKAS (Greece), p. 10.
36 Judgment No. Cp 11/2001 of November 8, 2001. The judgment (given before Slovenia entered the EU and thus the Brussels regime) concerned a case where a default judgment was given

Where a state follows the principle that foreign judgments have the same effects that they would have in the state of origin, public policy can also operate as a limit of this extension of effects.[37] For example, public policy might potentially be used to refuse the recognition of an issue preclusion effect of a U.S. judgment in a state where such an effect would be incompatible with fundamental procedural principles.[38]

Issues of substantive public policy arise rather less frequently than those of procedural public policy in most civil law jurisdictions today,[39] especially outside family law.[40] Nevertheless, there are some principles of substantive law that are still widely regarded as so essential that foreign judgments contravening them cannot be recognized or enforced. The most important and practically relevant issue of substantive public policy outside family law could be the enforceability of judgments awarding damages that are perceived as excessive.[41] The incompatibility of punitive damages with public policy is addressed, for example, in the national reports for Germany[42] and Japan.[43]

---

after the document instituting the proceedings had been served on a Slovenian party by an Austrian court without a translation into Slovenian, and there was no documentary proof that the Slovenian court effecting the service at the Austrian court's request had informed the defendant of the right to refuse acceptance of the document.

[37] P. GOTTWALD, above n. 3, marginal no. 5; G. WALTER and T. DOMEJ, above n. 2, p. 414.

[38] D. TSIKRIKAS (Greece), p. 4.

[39] P. BEAUMONT and E. JOHNSTON, "Can Exequatur Be Abolished in Brussels I Whilst Retaining a Public Policy Defence?" (2010) 6 *JPIL* 249, 263 f.; see also J. BASEDOW, "Die Verselbständigung des europäischen ordre public" in M. COESTER, D. MARTINY, and K.A. PRINZ VON SACHSEN GESSAPHE (eds.), *Privatrecht in Europa: Vielfalt, Kollision, Kooperation. Festschrift für Hans Jürgen Sonnenberger zum 70. Geburtstag*, C.H. Beck, Munich 2004, p. 291, 299; A. BRUNS, "Der anerkennungsrechtliche ordre public in Europa und den USA" (1999) 54 *JZ* 278, 282 f.; P. GEORGANTI, above n. 8, p. 105 f.; C. VÖLKER, above n. 8, p. 290.

[40] See, however, H. ROTH, "Commentary on §328 of the German Code of Civil Procedure" in R. BORK and H. ROTH (eds.), *Stein/Jonas Kommentar zur Zivilprozessordnung*, 23rd ed., vol. 5, Mohr Siebeck, Tübingen 2015, marginal no. 102.

[41] For a recent comparative analysis, see C. VANLEENHOVE, "The Current European Perspective on the Exequatur of U.S. Punitive Damages: Opening the Gate But Keeping a Guard" (2015) 35 *Polish Y.B. Int'l L.* 235 ff.

[42] D. WIEDEMANN (Germany), p. 3. See also Bundesgerichtshof, June 4, 1992 – IX ZR 149/91, NJW 1992, 3096; J.C. SPINDLER, *Anerkennung und Vollstreckung ausländischer Prozessvergleiche unter besonderer Berücksichtigung der US-amerikanischen Class action settlements*, Hartung-Gorre, Constance 2001, p. 49; R. STÜRNER, above n. 18, pp. 678 ff.

[43] K. TAKESHITA (Japan), pp. 1 f. See also N.T. BRASLOW, "The Recognition and Enforcement of Common Law Punitive Damages in a Civil Law System: Some Reflections on the Japanese Experience" (1999) 16 *Arizona Journal of International and Comparative Law* 285 ff.; Y. NISHITANI, "Anerkennung und Vollstreckung US-amerikanischer punitive damages-Urteile in Japan" [2001] *IPRax* 365 ff.; P. MACHNIKOWSKI and M. MARGONSKI, "Anerkennung von punitive damages- und actual damages-Urteilen in Polen" [2015] *IPRax* 453, 453 ff.; C. TRIADAFILLIDIS, "Anerkennung und Vollstreckung von 'punitive damages'-Urteilen nach kontinentalem und insbesondere nach griechischem Recht" [2002] *IPRax* 236, 238. In Switzerland, the Federal Court used to refuse the recognition of punitive damages on

The Greek national report mentions a case where the recognition and enforcement of an arbitral award was refused as incompatible with Greek public policy because an insurance company had been ordered to pay the entire insurance sum even though insurance coverage exceeded the value of the insured ship.[44] However, at first glance, this seems to be a rather strict approach. It should also be noted that a debate has been going on for a considerable time about the justification of the idea that tort law is only there to compensate the victim's loss and not to regulate behavior,[45] and it remains to be seen how far attitudes toward non-compensatory damages will shift as a result of this process. An infringement of essential constitutional rights (e.g., freedom of opinion[46] and the principle of equality[47]) may also violate substantive public policy,[48] as may an incompatibility with the receiving state's competition law or environmental law standards.[49] Meanwhile, the unenforceability of gambling debts that used to be regarded as an important principle in many legal systems and that used to have implications beyond gambling in the strict sense seems to have largely (albeit not necessarily completely)[50] lost its significance in most Western legal systems.[51]

As already mentioned, in the field of family law, substantive public policy still tends to play an important role. Marriage and divorce,[52] same-sex

---

the basis of the understanding that such a judgment is criminal in nature (Bundesgericht BGE 116 II 376). More recently, the question was left open (BGer 4A_663/2018, consideration 4). Lower instance courts have taken a more generous approach in recent case law; see Obergericht Zürich, November 5, 2018 – RV170015, consideration 6.2. On this development, see also J. KREN KOSTKIEWICZ, *Schweizerisches Internationales Privatrecht*, 2nd ed., Stämpfli, Berne 2018, marginal nos. 984 f.

[44] D. TSIKRIKAS (Greece), p. 19. In Greece, the same public policy standard seems to apply to judgments and arbitral awards.

[45] On this debate, see G. WAGNER, "Prävention und Verhaltenssteuerung durch Privatrecht – Anmaßung oder legitime Aufgabe?" (2006) 206 *AcP* 352, 352 ff.

[46] Bundesgerichtshof, July 19, 2018 – IX ZB 10/18, NJW 2018, 3254.

[47] Bundesverfassungsgericht, September 12, 2006 – 2 BvR 2216/05.

[48] D. WIEDEMANN (Germany), pp. 3 f.; M. KLÖPFER and P. RAMIC, "Ablehnung der Vollstreckbarerklärung eines ausländischen Urteils – Meinungsfreiheit" [2018] *NJW* 3254, 3258.

[49] P. GEORGANTI, above n. 8, p. 105.

[50] With respect to Germany, see P. GOTTWALD, above n. 3, marginal no. 125; H.C. LAUGWITZ, *Die Anerkennung und Vollstreckung drittstaatlicher Entscheidungen in Zivilsachen*, Mohr Siebeck, Tübingen 2016, p. 250. From the Russian perspective, see E. GERASIMCHUK, *Die Urteilsanerkennung im deutsch-russischen Rechtsverkehr*, Mohr Siebeck, Tübingen 2007, p. 132. With respect to Korean law, see D. STILLER, *Das internationale Zivilprozessrecht der Republik Korea*, Mohr Siebeck, Tübingen 1989, p. 176.

[51] See, e.g., Bundesgericht BGE 126 III 534, consideration 2c. In this judgment, contrary to previous case law, the court did not classify the mandatory unenforceability of gambling debts under national law as part of public policy.

[52] Some cases are mentioned by K. TAKESHITA (Japan), pp. 4 f. See also Bundesgericht BGE 131 III 182, consideration 4.2; J. ANTOMO, "Kinderehen, ordre public und Gesetzesreform" [2016] *NJW* 3558, 3560 ff.; A. BÜCHLER, "Islamisches Familienrecht und

relationships,[53] child custody,[54] adoption,[55] and surrogacy[56] are areas where strong and diverging views are held, often within the same jurisdiction. In many jurisdictions, attitudes have shifted and are still shifting, sometimes so much that approaches that used to be treated as incompatible with public policy come to be considered as that policy's very embodiment.[57] When facing such developments, courts adopt varying degrees of flexibility toward foreign solutions. The Macau report, for example, mentions that in cases where the outcome of a judgment is not compatible with Macau law, Macau courts would still consider recognizing it if it conformed to modern international developments.[58] The Supreme Court of Slovenia, in 2010, decided that recognition of an adoption by a same-sex couple pronounced by a U.S. court was not contrary to Slovenian public policy. While such an adoption would not have been possible under Slovenian law at that time, the Slovenian courts did not consider it to be incompatible with the vital principles of the Slovenian legal system.[59] In Japan, a U.S. judgment

---

ordre public in Europa" in I. GÖTZ, I. SCHWENZER, K. SEELMANN, and J. TAUPITZ (eds.), *Familie – Recht – Ethik: Festschrift für Gerd Brudermüller zum 65. Geburtstag*, C.H. Beck, Munich 2014, pp. 61, 64 f.

[53] Bundesgericht BGE 119 II 264; F. BATES, "Same-Sex Marriages, Conflict of Laws and Public Policy: A Modern Commentary" (1999) 21 *Liverpool L. Rev.* 49 ff.; M. FORKERT, *Eingetragene Lebenspartnerschaften im deutschen IPR: Art. 17b EGBGB*, Mohr Siebeck, Tübingen 2003, pp. 83 ff.; X. KRAMER, "Same-Sex Marriage, Conflict of Laws, and the Unconstitutional Public Policy Exception" (1997) 106 *Yale L.J.* 1965 ff.; L. SILBERMAN, "Same-Sex Marriage: Refining the Conflict of Laws Analysis" (2005) 153 *U. Pa. L. Rev.* 2195, 2209 ff. For a recent comparative perspective on the shifting attitudes in this field, see F. WOLLENSCHLÄGER and D. COESTER-WALTJEN, *Ehe für alle: die Öffnung der Ehe für gleichgeschlechtliche Paare aus verfassungsrechtlicher und rechtsvergleichender Perspektive*, Mohr Siebeck, Tübingen 2018.

[54] Again, K. TAKESHITA (Japan), p. 5 gives several examples.

[55] M. BERGER, above n. 5, p. 578.

[56] See the restrictive stance taken by the Swiss Bundesgericht in BGE 141 III 312 and BGE 141 III 328. Meanwhile, the German Bundesgerichtshof (December 10, 2014 – XII ZB 463/13, NJW 2015, 479) considers foreign judgments establishing the parentage of intended parents to be compatible with German public policy. See also the judgment of the ECtHR's Grand Chamber of 24 January 2017, *Paradiso and Campanelli v. Italy*, Application No. 25358/12, http://hudoc.echr.coe.int/eng?i=001-170359; most recently, see ECtHR, November 19, 2019, *C and E v. France*, Application Nos. 1462/18 and 17348/18, http://hudoc. echr.coe.int/eng?i=001-199497.

[57] See, in particular, the French Cour de cassation's judgment of January 28, 2015, https://www. legifrance.gouv.fr/affichJuriJudi.do?idTexte=JURITEXT000030174434, according to which the right to enter into a same-sex marriage has international public policy status in France.

[58] G. TU (Macau), p. 2. However, recognition and enforcement of a Hong Kong judgment allowing adoption of a girl by a couple, one of whom was the child's biological mother, was denied on the grounds that it is incompatible with Macau public policy for a biological mother to become her own child's adoptive mother.

[59] Slovenian Supreme Court, No. II Ips 462/2009 of January 28, 2010, English translation available at http://www.sodisce.si/mma_bin.php?static_id=20110413133235; J. KRAMBERGER ŠKERL (Slovenia), pp. 2 f. Furthermore, J. KRAMBERGER ŠKERL (Slovenia), p. 3 mentions a

declaring the parenthood of a Japanese couple (who had donated the egg and sperm) with respect to a child that had been born by a surrogate mother was not recognized in Japan, even though the Japanese court indicated that this is a developing field of law and that there was a need to discuss whether the current approach of the national legal system should be changed.[60] In Switzerland, a U.S. judgment recognizing the intended same-sex parents as legal parents of a child born by a surrogate mother was only recognized in relation to the man who had donated the sperm, as the prohibition of surrogacy was considered to be a matter of public policy. The Swiss Federal Court considered whether such a stance violated Article 8 of the European Convention on Human Rights (ECHR) (the right to respect for private and family life), but concluded that it did not, as there was a possibility for the other partner to adopt the child.[61] In Turkey, courts sometimes even go as far as to directly refuse recognition and enforcement in adoption and child custody matters, apparently on the assumption that public policy is so strongly involved in such cases that they should only be decided by domestic courts for the purpose of enforcement in Turkey.[62]

Another controversial issue that is often addressed in the context of public policy is *talaq* (Islamic divorce by repudiation).[63] However, views in this respect may shift or depend on the specific situation. Thus, in Tunisia, a divorce without a court judgment used to be considered to be incompatible with public policy, but this view has been abandoned.[64] In Germany[65] and Switzerland,[66] the courts have taken a flexible approach, looking at the circumstances of the individual case. In Greece, recognition was granted in a recent case where the application had been filed by the repudiated wife.[67]

While traditional and, particularly, religiously inflected approaches to public policy have been on the decline in much of the civil law world and, instead, human rights and anti-discrimination have become important elements of

---

     judgment pointing out that differences in the rules for calculating the amount of maintenance do not in themselves lead to refusal on the grounds of public policy in Slovenia.

60   K. TAKESHITA (Japan), pp. 2 ff.

61   Bundesgericht BGE 141 III 312.

62   See H. PEKCANITEZ and E. ALPAY (Turkey), p. 2.

63   P. KRUINIGER, *Islamic Divorces in Europe: Bridging the Gap between European and Islamic Legal Orders*, Eleven International Publishing, The Hague 2016, p. 5.

64   A. OUERFELLI and Y. EL-BENNA (Tunisia), p. 2.

65   See R. HAUSMANN, *Internationales und Europäisches Familienrecht*, 2nd ed., C.H. Beck, Munich 2018, marginal no. 295.

66   Bundesgericht BGE 103 Ib 69; 122 III 344; 126 III 327; see also C. WACK, "La réception du droit musulman dans l'ordre juridique Suisse: la reconnaissance des mariages polygames et de la répudiation" [2019] *FamPra.ch* 1148, 1166 ff.

67   A. ANTHIMOS, "Talaq Reloaded: Repudiation Recognized if Application Filed by the Wife," http://conflictoflaws.net/2019/talaq-reloaded-repudiation-recognized-if-application-filed-by-the-wife.

public policy, a different development might be taking place in parts of the Islamic and Arab world. The Tunisian report suggests that under regional treaties between Islamic and Arab countries, public policy tends to be associated with public morality and sometimes with Sharia (Islamic law).[68] However, the overall impact of this development seems unclear. In particular, it does not seem completely certain whether such an understanding of public policy would also apply toward judgments and arbitral awards coming from states outside the region or whether it would be restricted to the relationship between contracting states of the respective regional treaties.[69] The picture is further complicated by the fact that Islamic law is not a monolithic bloc, but that there are very diverse approaches and schools.[70] From an outside perspective, it is therefore difficult to assess whether an alternative or competing regional concept of public policy that is largely founded on Sharia (Islamic law) could indeed be emerging and what the consequences would be.[71] However, it does appear that the concept of divine law is of the utmost importance for the definition of public policy in jurisdictions that consider Sharia as a part of their legal system.[72] This can have significant consequences for public policy in fields like family law and inheritance law.[73] For example, a mixed marriage between a Muslim and a non-Muslim might be considered invalid,[74] and a non-Muslim might be unable to inherit from a Muslim.[75] The unenforceability of gambling debts is also still upheld as a principle of public policy in jurisdictions adhering to Islamic law.[76] Those jurisdictions also refuse to recognize and enforce judgments conflicting

---

[68] A. OUERFELLI and Y. EL-BENNA (Tunisia), p. 3. See also K. BÄLZ, "Die Anerkennung und Vollstreckbarerklärung von ausländischen Schiedssprüchen im Irak" [2011] *SchiedsVZ* 27 ff.; K. BÄLZ and A. SHAHOUD ALMOUSA, "Reform des Schiedsrechts in Saudi-Arabien" [2013] *SchiedsVZ* 248, 252; M. BERGER, above n. 5, pp. 569 ff.; H. KRÜGER and W. SAAD, "Internationales Privatrecht des Sultanats Oman" [2014] *IPRax* 370, 372; M. TAVANA, "The Role of Sharia in International Commercial Arbitration: An Enquiry into Potential Convergence," PhD thesis, Zurich 2017, pp. 112 ff.

[69] See A. OUERFELLI and Y. EL-BENNA (Tunisia), p. 4; K. BÄLZ and A. SHAHOUD ALMOUSA, above n. 68, p. 252.

[70] For an overview from a Western perspective, see M. ROHE, *Das islamische Recht. Geschichte und Gegenwart*, 3rd ed., C.H. Beck, Munich 2011.

[71] In this context, see M. AL-NASAIR and I. BANTEKAS, "The Effect of Public Policy on the Enforcement of Foreign Arbitral Awards in Bahrain and UAE" (2013) 16 *Int. A.L.R.* 88, 89; G. BLANKE, "The Enforcement of International Commercial and Investment Arbitration Awards in the MENA Region" (2017) 83 *Arbitration* 71, 78.

[72] M. AL-NASAIR and I. BANTEKAS, above n. 71, at 89.

[73] See A. BÜCHLER, above n. 52, p. 65; A. SHAHOUD ALMOUSA, "IPR und Ordre Public im Recht Arabischer Staaten" (2014) 2 *EJIMEL* 63 f.

[74] M. BERGER, above n. 5, p. 573.

[75] A. BÜCHLER, above n. 52, p. 65; A. SHAHOUD ALMOUSA, above n. 73, p. 63 f.

[76] M. MALACKA, "Die rechtliche, politische und kulturelle Bedeutung des ordre public im Internationalen Privatrecht" [2019] *ZfRV* 61, 69; A. SHAHOUD ALMOUSA, above n. 73, p. 67.

with the rules of Islamic law on the prohibition of interest.[77] Furthermore, in jurisdictions adhering very strictly to Islamic law, such as Saudi Arabia,[78] the recognition of a foreign judgment or arbitral award might even be declined because it was given by a woman or a non-Muslim.[79] However, this approach seems to be the exception rather than the rule and, in any case, it appears to be in decline.[80]

In some jurisdictions, substantive and procedural public policy are treated in separate rules. For example, Article 27(1) of the Swiss Private International Law Act (PILA) provides for the refusal of recognition if recognition would be manifestly incompatible with Swiss public policy. This provision is not explicitly limited to substantive public policy, but it is interpreted that way, as Article 27(2)(b) PILA contains a separate ground for refusal for cases where the judgment was given in a way that violated the fundamental principles of Swiss procedural law, in particular where the party opposing recognition was deprived of the right to be heard.

However, it seems to be more common not to make such a distinction and to cover substantive and procedural public policy in a single rule. For example, this is the case in the Brussels and Lugano instruments, in the 2019 HCCH Judgments Convention, and in the national laws of China,[81] Germany,[82] Greece,[83] Japan,[84] and Slovenia.[85] However, the potential of separating these categories and, perhaps, of providing for different procedural treatment should be kept in mind.

3. EUROPE AS A BREEDING GROUND FOR A REGIONALIZED CONCEPT OF PUBLIC POLICY?

3.1. THE OPERATION OF THE BRUSSELS AND LUGANO SYSTEMS

In Europe, the first multilateral regional instrument on the recognition and enforcement of foreign judgments was the Brussels Convention,[86] if we do

---

[77] K. Bälz and A. Shahoud Almousa, above n. 68, p. 252; A. Shahoud Almousa, above n. 73, p. 67.
[78] See, e.g., G. Blanke, above n. 71, p. 78.
[79] K. Bälz and A. Shahoud Almousa, above n. 68, p. 252; A. Shahoud Almousa, above n. 73, p. 67.
[80] M. Al-Nasair and I. Bantekas, above n. 71, p. 89.
[81] Q. He (China), p. 2.
[82] D. Wiedemann (Germany), p. 2 f.
[83] D. Tsikrikas (Greece), p. 8.
[84] K. Takeshita (Japan), p. 6.
[85] J. Kramberger Škerl (Slovenia), p. 1.
[86] 1968 Brussels Convention on jurisdiction and the enforcement of judgments in civil and commercial matters.

Intersentia

331

not count the Scandinavian and Benelux instruments that were concluded by groups of neighboring states with strong economic and cultural ties. The Brussels Convention was a treaty under public international law, but at the same time an instrument of European integration. Therefore, membership of the Brussels Convention was considered to be limited to Member States of the European Community. A separate convention, the Lugano Convention, had to be concluded to enable states that were not members of the EU to join the European judicial area, or at least a segment of it.[87]

Both the Brussels and the Lugano Conventions were innovative in some respects. The most striking feature was that they were "double conventions," i.e., they contained rules not only on the recognition and enforcement of foreign judgments, but also on direct jurisdiction.[88] Anyone who has followed the work that culminated in the 2019 HCCH Judgments Convention will appreciate that this was a big achievement. It required a significant extent of pre-existing common ground as regards the jurisdictional systems of the contracting states. One might speculate whether a similar result would have been achieved had the United Kingdom already been an EU Member State at the time that the Brussels Convention was concluded. After the United Kingdom joined the Brussels system, several cases decided by the European Court of Justice (ECJ) that concerned the very fundamentals of the Brussels system originated in the United Kingdom. Consider the *Turner v. Grovit*,[89] *Owusu*,[90] and *West Tankers*[91] cases. The ECJ's judgments in these cases greatly restricted the ability of U.K. courts to rely on *forum non conveniens* or to issue anti-suit injunctions. How these judgments were received on the two sides of the Channel shows that what was considered as perfectly reasonable by most on the Continent was deplored by some in the United Kingdom.[92] It is probably fair to say that the Brussels

---

[87]   P. GROLIMUND, "Allgemeine Einleitung" in A.K. SCHNYDER (ed.), *Lugano-Übereinkommen zum internationalen Zivilverfahrensrecht: Kommentar*, Dike, Zürich/St. Gallen 2011, marginal no. 4; C. OETIKER and T. WEIBEL, "Einleitung LugÜ" in C. OETIKER and T. WEIBEL (eds.), *Basler Kommentar zum Lugano Übereinkommen*, 2nd ed., Helbing Lichtenhahn, Basel 2016, marginal no. 10; G. WALTER and T. DOMEJ, above n. 2, p. 173 f.

[88]   See, e.g., A. STAUDINGER, "Der ordre public-Einwand im Europäischen Zivilverfahrensrecht" (2004) 5 *European Legal Forum* 273, 273.

[89]   Case C-159/02, *Gregory Paul Turner v. Felix Fareed Ismail Grovit, Harada Ltd and Changepoint SA*, ECLI:EU:C:2004:228.

[90]   Case C-281/02, *Andrew Owusu v. N.B. Jackson*, ECLI:EU:C:2005:120.

[91]   Case C-185/07, *Allianz SpA v. West Tankers Inc.*, ECLI:EU:C:2009:69.

[92]   See, e.g., T. KRUGER, "The Anti-suit Injunction in the European Judicial Space: *Turner v. Grovit*" (2004) 53 *ICLQ* 1030 ff.; MENDELOWITZ and ROSE, "West Tankers – Disharmonious Variations in the European Dispute Resolution Process?" (2012) 17 *IBA Arb. News* 43 ff.; P. SHERRINGTON and C. ROBERT, "Jurisdiction and Judicial Discretion: A Clash of Approaches between the European Court of Justice and the English Courts?" (2008) 2 *Disp. Resol. Int'l* 225 ff.

system in its original form was not a bridge-building project between civil law and common law.[93] This may have been mitigated to some degree, though not decisively, by the changes introduced by the 2012 recast, particularly with respect to jurisdiction agreements and to *lis pendens* in the relationship with third states.

The uniform rules on direct jurisdiction together with the mutual trust[94] between the courts of Member (or Contracting) States that is expected, or, as some would say, decreed in the Brussels/Lugano system were the basis for the almost total abolition of the review of jurisdiction of the court of the state of origin in the state where recognition and enforcement is sought.[95]

In other respects, the Brussels and Lugano Conventions were quite traditional, and some of the conservative features have survived to this day. In particular, the Brussels I *bis* Regulation of 2012 and the Lugano Convention of 2007[96] still allow the requested state to refuse the recognition and enforcement of foreign judgments based on public policy.[97]

In the Brussels and Lugano systems, it is up to the party against whom recognition and enforcement is sought to oppose it. Under the Lugano Convention of 2007,[98] as was the case under the Brussels I Regulation of 2001, there is no review of grounds for refusal, including public policy, in the exequatur proceedings at first instance. These grounds can only be invoked at the appellate stage. However, it is not clear whether they must be invoked by the debtor or whether the appellate court may rely on public policy to refuse recognition and

---

[93] However, the perceived divide among common law and civil law jurisdictions with respect to *forum non conveniens* is often overstated. In this respect (and others), see the study (JLS/C4/2005/07-30-CE)0040309/00-37) on residual jurisdiction in civil and commercial matters in EU jurisdictions (2007) led by ARNAUD NUYTS, available at https://ec.europa.eu/civiljustice/news/docs/study_residual_jurisdiction_en.pdf, pp. 70 ff.

[94] For a critical assessment, see C. ALTHAMMER and M. LÖHNIG, "Zwischen Realität und Utopie: Der Vertrauensgrundsatz in der Rechtsprechung des EuGH zum europäischen Zivilprozessrecht" (2004) 9 *ZZPInt* 23 ff.; F. BLOBEL and P. SPÄTH, "The Tale of Multilateral Trust and the European Law of Civil Procedure" (2005) 30 *E.L. Rev.* 528 ff.; see also S. ESSLINGER, *Gegenseitiges Vertrauen: Zur grenzüberschreitenden Beurteilung des Grundrechtsschutzes im Raum der Freiheit, der Sicherheit und des Rechts*, Mohr Siebeck, Tübingen 2018; A.-K. KAUFHOLD, "Gegenseitiges Vertrauen" [2012] *EuR* 408 ff.

[95] See, most recently, H. SCHACK, "Anerkennungs- und Vollstreckungsversagungsgründe im Europäischen Zivilprozessrecht" [2020] *ZVglRWiss* 237 ff.

[96] Convention on jurisdiction and the recognition and enforcement of judgments in civil and commercial matters of 30 October 2007 [2007] OJ L339/3.

[97] On the operation of the public policy exception in the European judicial area, see the comprehensive study commissioned by the European Parliament and led by B. HESS and T. PFEIFFER, PE 453.189, http://www.europarl.europa.eu/RegData/etudes/STUD/2011/453189/IPOL-JURI_ET(2011)453189_EN.pdf.

[98] The Brussels Convention and the Lugano Convention of 1988 took a different approach in this respect. The judgment debtor was not heard in the exequatur proceedings at first instance, but the court was authorized to perform an *ex officio* review of the grounds for refusal (see Art. 34(1) and (2) of the Brussels Convention and the Lugano Convention 1988).

Tanja Domej

enforcement even though the judgment debtor only addresses other grounds for refusal.[99]

The recast Brussels I *bis* Regulation no longer requires an exequatur. Therefore, it is no longer the appeal against the declaration of enforceability where the public policy exception can be raised. Instead, the debtor must initiate proceedings for the refusal of recognition (Article 45 of the Brussels I *bis* Regulation) or enforcement (Article 46). Nevertheless, the public policy exception itself continues to exist, as does the uncertainty about whether the court may refuse recognition or enforcement based on public policy if the judgment debtor does not raise this objection.[100] Nor is it clear whether a court of the state addressed that becomes aware of the probable existence of a ground for refusal may inform the judgment debtor that there could be a chance of making a successful application for the refusal of recognition and enforcement.[101]

3.2. SUCCESSFUL AND FAILED ATTEMPTS AT ABOLISHING THE PUBLIC POLICY EXCEPTION WITHIN THE EU

For quite some time, the abolition of the public policy exception in EU instruments on recognition and enforcement was an important goal of European institutions. I say "was" and not "has been," as apparently it has meanwhile been realized that getting completely rid of this ground for refusal is not politically feasible at this stage. Attempts to proceed beyond what was once only seen as a "first step" of this process have become much less intense, at least for the time being.

In October 1999, the European Council held a special meeting in Tampere "on the creation of an area of freedom, security and justice in the European Union."

---

[99] See, e.g., P. OBERHAMMER, "Commentary on Article 34 Brussels I Regulation" in *Stein/Jonas Kommentar zur Zivilprozessordnung*, 22nd ed., vol. 10, Mohr Siebeck, Tübingen 2011, marginal no. 4; A. STAUDINGER, above n. 88, p. 279.

[100] At least in the German-speaking literature, it seems to be the prevailing view that the court may rely on a violation of public policy even if the debtor did not raise it; see T. PFEIFFER, "Die Fortentwicklung des Europäischen Prozessrechts durch die neue EuGVO" (2014) 127 *ZZP* 409, 426; A. STADLER, "Commentary on Article 45 Brussels I *bis* Regulation" in H-J. MUSIELAK and W. VOIT (eds.), *Zivilprozessordnung*, 17th ed., Vahlen, Munich 2020, marginal no. 1 n. 1; see also R. GEIMER, "Unionsweite Titelvollstreckung ohne Exequatur nach der Reform der Brüssel I-Verordnung" in R. GEIMER, A. KAISSIS, and R. THÜMMEL (eds.), *Ars aequi et boni in mundo: Festschrift für Rolf A. Schütze zum 80. Geburtstag*, C.H. Beck, Munich 2015, 109, 114 f.

[101] In a recent judgment, the ECJ made clear that the court of the state of origin where a certificate according to Art. 53 of the Brussels I *bis* Regulation is requested is not authorized to ascertain *ex officio* whether there has been a breach of the jurisdictional rules for the protection of consumers that might enable the judgment debtor to make a successful application for a refusal of recognition and enforcement; see Case C-347/18, *Avv. Alessandro Salvoni v. Anna Maria Fiermote*, ECLI:EU:C:2019:661.

334

Intersentia

In the conclusions of the presidency,[102] the goals for European legislation were set out as follows:

> 34. In civil matters the European Council calls upon the Commission to make a proposal for further reduction of the intermediate measures which are still required to enable the recognition and enforcement of a decision or judgement in the requested State. As a first step these intermediate procedures should be abolished for titles in respect of small consumer or commercial claims and for certain judgements in the field of family litigation (e.g. on maintenance claims and visiting rights). Such decisions would be automatically recognised throughout the Union without any intermediate proceedings or grounds for refusal of enforcement. This could be accompanied by the setting of minimum standards on specific aspects of civil procedural law.

The EU legislature took the "first step" mentioned in this commitment in the Enforcement Order Regulation,[103] the Order for Payment Regulation,[104] the Small Claims Procedure Regulation,[105] the Maintenance Regulation,[106] and the Regulation on jurisdiction, recognition, and enforcement in matrimonial and parental responsibility matters.[107] These regulations, in various ways and degrees, removed or reduced exequatur proceedings and/or grounds for refusal at least for some judgments, partly replacing them by specific uniform remedies in the state of origin.[108]

Already in its preparatory work for the Brussels I Regulation (Regulation 44/2001), the Commission had proposed to remove the public policy exception in that flagship instrument as well. However, this idea was soon abandoned, as it was not endorsed by the working group in which at that time

---

102 http://www.europarl.europa.eu/summits/tam_en.htm.

103 Regulation (EC) No 805/2004 of the European Parliament and of the Council of 21 April 2004 creating a European Enforcement Order for uncontested claims [2004] OJ L143.

104 Regulation (EC) No 1896/2006 of the European Parliament and of the Council of 12 December 2006 creating a European order for payment procedure [2006] OJ L399/1.

105 Regulation (EC) No 861/2007 of the European Parliament and of the Council of 11 July 2007 establishing a European Small Claims Procedure [2007] OJ L199/1.

106 Council Regulation (EC) No 4/2009 of 18 December 2008 on jurisdiction, applicable law, recognition and enforcement of decisions and cooperation in matters relating to maintenance obligations [2009] OJ L7/1.

107 Council Regulation (EC) No 2201/2003 of 27 November 2003 concerning jurisdiction and the recognition and enforcement of judgments in matrimonial matters and the matters of parental responsibility, repealing Regulation (EC) No 1347/2000, replaced by Council Regulation (EU) 2019/1111 of 25 June 2019 on jurisdiction, the recognition and enforcement of decisions in matrimonial matters and the matters of parental responsibility, and on international child abduction as of 1 August 2022 [2019] OJ L178/1.

108 See, e.g., D. MARTINY, "Die Zukunft des europäischen ordre public im Internationalen Privat- und Zivilverfahrensrecht" in M. COESTER, D. MARTINY, and K.A. PRINZ VON SACHSEN GESSAPHE (eds.), *Privatrecht in Europa: Vielfalt, Kollision, Kooperation. Festschrift für Hans Jürgen Sonnenberger zum 70. Geburtstag*, C.H. Beck, Munich 2004, pp. 523, 541 ff.; B. SUJECKI, "Die Möglichkeiten und Grenzen der Abschaffung des ordre public-Vorbehalts im Europäischen Zivilprozessrecht" [2008] *ZEuP* 458 ff.

the Brussels I Regulation and the parallel reform of the Lugano Convention were discussed.[109] The next and more serious, but also more nuanced, attempt was made in the proposal for the Brussels I *bis* Regulation.[110] The Commission wanted to abolish the public policy exception, but to introduce a new rule that would pick up some elements of procedural public policy. Violations of procedural fair trial principles were meant to be addressed with remedies split between the state of origin and the state of enforcement. The Commission proposed that the lack of proper service of the document instituting the proceedings should only be challengeable in the state of origin (Article 45 of the Commission's proposal). Other cases where "recognition or enforcement would not be permitted by the fundamental principles underlying the right to a fair trial" should remain within the jurisdiction of the courts of the requested state (Article 46 of the Commission's proposal). However, the reference to public policy would have been removed. This would have invited a fully autonomous interpretation of the provision. The proposal would also have led to a total removal of substantive public policy as a ground for refusal.[111]

In 2011, BURKHARD HESS and THOMAS PFEIFFER led a study for the European Parliament's Directorate-General for Internal Policies on the "Interpretation of the Public Policy Exception as Referred to in EU Instruments of Private International and Procedural Law."[112] On the basis of statistical data and of an analysis of available national case law and literature, the study looked into how the public policy exception operates in the context of EU instruments. As public policy continues to be a national concept even within the EU, the study also provides important insights into the handling of public policy in the relationship between EU Member States and third states, even though in the relationship with third states, the autonomous limits imposed by the ECJ for the intra-EU relationship do not apply. The study undertook to find out whether there was a tendency toward a uniform concept of European public policy.[113] The authors looked at public policy clauses then existing in EU instruments on cross-border enforcement and on private international law. These were the Brussels I Regulation 44/2001 (now replaced by Regulation 1215/2012),[114] the Insolvency Regulation 1346/2000 (now replaced by Regulation 2015/848), Regulation 2201/2003 on jurisdiction and recognition, and enforcement in matrimonial matters and the matters of parental responsibility (which will be replaced by Regulation 2019/1111 with effect from 1 August 2022), the Rome I

---

[109]   S. LEIBLE, above n. 16, marginal no. 5.

[110]   COM(2010) 748.

[111]   See T. DOMEJ, "Die Neufassung der EuGVVO: Quantensprünge im europäischen Zivilprozessrecht" (2014) 78 *RabelsZ* 508, 511 f. with further references.

[112]   PE 453.189, http://www.europarl.europa.eu/RegData/etudes/STUD/2011/453189/IPOL-JURI_ET(2011)453189_EN.pdf.

[113]   Ibid., p. 16.

[114]   And that Regulation's predecessor, the Brussels Convention; see ibid., pp. 17 f.

and Rome II Regulations (593/2008 and 864/2007), and the Maintenance Regulation 4/2009.[115]

The proposal to remove the public policy ground for refusal met with strong opposition.[116] Those who advocated retaining it pointed out that abolition could not be justified on the basis that public policy is hardly ever successfully invoked. They compared it to an emergency brake that is not intended for everyday use, but for the prevention of catastrophic, if rare, accidents.[117] In the end, the Commission did not prevail on this point, and the grounds for refusal were basically retained as they were. The decisive innovation happened at the procedural level with the removal of exequatur as a prerequisite for enforcement. The onus of initiating proceedings that can eventually lead to a refusal of recognition and enforcement is now entirely on the judgment debtor.[118]

3.3. A TALE OF TWO CITIES: STRASBOURG AND LUXEMBOURG

According to the case law of the European Court of Human Rights (ECtHR), there is a human rights dimension to the scrutiny of foreign judgments entering a jurisdiction bound by the ECHR. In the case of *Pellegrini v. Italy*, the ECtHR ruled that the courts of a Contracting State of the ECHR, before authorizing the enforcement of a foreign judgment, must duly satisfy themselves that the relevant proceedings fulfilled the guarantees of Article 6 ECHR (the right to a fair trial).[119] The ECtHR also said:

> A review of that kind is required where a decision in respect of which enforcement is requested *emanates from the courts of a country which does not apply the Convention.*[120] Such a review is especially necessary where the implications of a declaration of enforceability are of capital importance for the parties.

---

[115] The Maintenance Regulation only provides for a public policy exception in cases where the judgment comes from a Member State that is not party to the Hague Maintenance Protocol of 2007, i.e. the United Kingdom, as long as the Maintenance Regulation continues to apply to it.

[116] See P. BEAUMONT and E. JOHNSTON, above n. 39, pp. 259 ff.; G. CUNIBERTI and I. RUEDA, "Abolition of Exequatur: Addressing the Commission's Concerns" (2011) 75 *RabelsZ* 286, 288; J.F. JÜNGST, *Der europäische verfahrensrechtliche ordre public – Inhalt und Begrenzung*, Peter Lang, Frankfurt am Main 2011, pp. 194 ff., 260; P. GEORGANTI, above n. 8, pp. 143 ff.; X. KRAMER, "Abolition of Exequatur under the Brussels I Regulation: Effecting and Protecting Rights in the European Judicial Area" [2011] *NIPR* 633, 640; P. OBERHAMMER, "The Abolition of Exequatur" [2010] *IPRax* 197, 201; P. SCHLOSSER, "The Abolition of Exequatur Proceedings – Including Public Policy Review?" [2010] *IPRax* 101 ff. See also A. BRUNS, "Der anerkennungsrechtliche ordre public in Europa und den USA" (1999) 54 *JZ* 278, 287.

[117] P. OBERHAMMER, above n. 116, pp. 201 f.; see also P. GEORGANTI, above n. 8, p. 145; M. THÖNE, *Die Abschaffung des Exequaturverfahrens und die EuGVVO*, Mohr Siebeck, Tübingen 2016, p. 204.

[118] H. SCHACK, above n. 95, p. 239.

[119] ECtHR 20 July 2001, *Pellegrini v. Italy*, App. No. 30882/96, http://hudoc.echr.coe.int/eng?i=001-59604, marginal no. 40.

[120] Emphasis added.

Intersentia

While the ECtHR emphasized the duty to scrutinize judgments coming from non-ECHR states, this does not necessarily imply that judgments from Contracting States of the ECHR can simply be implemented without any safeguards being available in the state addressed. In the subsequent case law, it indeed turned out that the relationship between European instruments on the free movement of judgments and the ECHR is complex. Even after the judgments given in *Bosphorus v. Ireland*[121] and *Avotiņš v. Latvia*[122] that concerned the relationship between the duties of EU Member States under EU law and these states' duties under the ECHR, there are still open questions. The situation is further complicated by the tensions existing between the ECJ and the ECtHR as regards scrutinizing the application of EU law from a human rights perspective. In general, the ECtHR tends to exercise self-restraint in this respect, but the possibility remains that the application of EU rules imposing mutual trust and forbidding courts to address even severe fundamental rights violations at the recognition and enforcement stage could lead to the requested state being held to account in Strasbourg.[123]

In *Bosphorus*, a case that concerned the impounding of a leased aircraft on the basis of EU law and the compatibility of such a measure with Article 1 of Protocol No. 1 to the ECHR (i.e., the protection of the right to property), the ECtHR established what has become known as the "Bosphorus presumption":

> 156. If ... equivalent protection [of fundamental rights, as regards both the substantive guarantees offered and the mechanisms controlling their observance] is considered to be provided by [an international, including supranational] organisation [to whom a Contracting State has transferred sovereign power in order to pursue cooperation in certain fields of activity], the presumption will be that a State has not departed

---

[121] ECtHR June 30, 2005, *Bosphorus Hava Yolları Turizm ve Tivaret v. Ireland*, App. No. 45036/98, http://hudoc.echr.coe.int/eng?i=001-69564. For an analysis of this judgment, see, e.g., J. Bröhmer, "Die Bosphorus-Entscheidung des Europäischen Gerichtshofs für Menschenrechte. Der Schutz der Grund- und Menschenrechte in der EU und das Verhältnis zur EMRK" [2006] *EuZW* 71 ff. C. Costello, "The *Bosphorus* Ruling of the European Court of Human Rights: Fundamental Rights and Blurred Boundaries in Europe" (2006) 6 *Human Rights L. Rev.* 87 ff.; A. Hinarejos, "*Bosphorus v. Ireland* and the Protection of Fundamental Rights in Europe" (2006) 31 *E.L. Rev.* 251 ff.; K. Kuhnert, "*Bosphorus*: Double Standards in European Human Rights Protection" (2006) 2 *Utrecht L. Rev.* 177 ff.

[122] ECtHR 23 May 2016, *Avotiņš v. Latvia*, App. no. 17502/07, http://hudoc.echr.coe.int/eng?i=001-163114.

[123] For a more detailed analysis, see, e.g., G. Biagioni, "*Avotiņš v. Latvia*: The Uneasy Balance between Mutual Recognition of Judgments and Protection of Fundamental Rights" (2016) 1 *European Papers* 579 ff.; D. Düsterhaus, "The ECtHR, the CJEU and the AFSJ: A Matter of Mutual Trust" (2017) 42 *E.L. Rev.* 388, 396; L.R. Glas and J. Krommendijk, "From Opinion 2/13 to Avotiņš: Recent Developments in the Relationship between the Luxembourg and Strasbourg Courts" (2017) 17 *Human Rights L. Review* 567 ff.; P. Gragl, "An Olive Branch from Strasbourg? Interpreting the European Court of Human Rights' Resurrection of *Bosphorus* and Reaction to Opinion 2/13 in the *Avotiņš* Case" (2017) 13 *European Constitutional Law Review* 551 ff.

from the requirements of the Convention when it does no more than implement legal obligations flowing from its membership of the organisation.

However, any such presumption can be rebutted if, in the circumstances of a particular case, it is considered that the protection of Convention rights was manifestly deficient. In such cases, the interest of international cooperation would be outweighed by the Convention's role as a *'constitutional instrument of European public order'* in the field of human rights.[124]

After describing the mechanisms for ensuring compliance with EU law, the ECtHR further stated:

164. Moreover, it is essentially through the national courts that the Community system provides a remedy to individuals against a member State or another individual for a breach of Community law …

The ECJ maintains its control on the application by national courts of Community law, including its fundamental rights guarantees, through the procedure for which Article 177 of the EC Treaty provides … It is further noted that national courts operate in legal systems into which the Convention has been incorporated, albeit to differing degrees.

165. In such circumstances, the Court finds that the protection of fundamental rights by Community law can be considered to be, and to have been at the relevant time, "equivalent" (within the meaning of paragraph 155 above) to that of the Convention system.

In *Avotiņš*, the ECtHR dealt with the relationship between the mutual trust required by EU instruments on the cross-border circulation of judgments and obligations under the ECHR. It said:

113. In general terms, the Court observes that the Brussels I Regulation is based in part on mutual recognition mechanisms which themselves are founded on the principle of mutual trust between the Member States of the European Union … The Court is mindful of the importance of the mutual recognition mechanisms for the construction of the area of freedom, security and justice referred to in Article 67 of the TFEU [Treaty on the Functioning of the European Union], and of the mutual trust which they require … The Court has repeatedly asserted its commitment to international and European cooperation (see, among other authorities, *Waite and Kennedy v. Germany* [GC], no. 26083/94, §§63 and 72, ECHR 1999-I, and *Bosphorus*, cited above, §150). Hence, *it considers the creation of an area of freedom, security and justice in Europe, and the adoption of the means necessary to achieve it, to be wholly legitimate in principle from the standpoint of the Convention.*[125]

---

[124] Emphasis added.
[125] Emphasis added.

114. Nevertheless, *the methods used to create that area must not infringe the fundamental rights of the persons affected by the resulting mechanisms*,[126] as indeed confirmed by Article 67(1) of the TFEU. However, it is apparent that the aim of effectiveness pursued by some of the methods used results in the review of the observance of fundamental rights being tightly regulated or even limited. Hence, the CJEU [Court of Justice of the European Union] stated recently in Opinion 2/13 that "when implementing EU law, the Member States may, under EU law, be required to presume that fundamental rights have been observed by the other Member States, so that … save in exceptional cases, they may not check whether that other Member State has actually, in a specific case, observed the fundamental rights guaranteed by the EU" (see paragraph 49 above). *Limiting to exceptional cases the power of the State in which recognition is sought to review the observance of fundamental rights by the State of origin of the judgment could, in practice, run counter to the requirement imposed by the Convention according to which the court in the State addressed must at least be empowered to conduct a review commensurate with the gravity of any serious allegation of a violation of fundamental rights in the State of origin, in order to ensure that the protection of those rights is not manifestly deficient.*[127]

115. Moreover, the Court observes that where the domestic authorities give effect to European Union law and have no discretion in that regard, the presumption of equivalent protection set forth in the *Bosphorus* judgment is applicable. This is the case where the mutual recognition mechanisms require the court to presume that the observance of fundamental rights by another Member State has been sufficient. The domestic court is thus deprived of its discretion in the matter, leading to automatic application of the *Bosphorus* presumption of equivalence. The Court emphasises that this results, paradoxically, in a *twofold limitation* of the domestic court's review of the observance of fundamental rights, due to the *combined effect of the presumption on which mutual recognition is founded and the Bosphorus presumption of equivalent protection.*[128]

116. In the *Bosphorus* judgment, the Court reiterated that the Convention is a "constitutional instrument of European public order" (ibid., §156). Accordingly, the Court must satisfy itself, where the conditions for application of the presumption of equivalent protection are met (see paragraphs 105–106 above), that the mutual recognition mechanisms do not leave any gap or particular situation which would render the protection of the human rights guaranteed by the Convention manifestly deficient. In doing so it takes into account, in a spirit of complementarity, the manner in which these mechanisms operate and in particular the aim of effectiveness which they pursue. Nevertheless, it must verify that the principle of mutual recognition is not applied automatically and mechanically (see, mutatis mutandis, *X v. Latvia* [GC], no. 27853/09, §§98 and 107, ECHR 2013) to the detriment of fundamental rights – which, the CJEU has also stressed, must be observed in this context (see, for instance, its judgment in *Alpha Bank Cyprus Ltd*, cited at paragraph 48 above). In this spirit,

---

[126] Emphasis added.
[127] Emphasis added.
[128] Emphasis added.

> *where the courts of a State which is both a Contracting Party to the Convention and a Member State of the European Union are called upon to apply a mutual recognition mechanism established by EU law, they must give full effect to that mechanism where the protection of Convention rights cannot be considered manifestly deficient. However, if a serious and substantiated complaint is raised before them to the effect that the protection of a Convention right has been manifestly deficient and that this situation cannot be remedied by European Union law, they cannot refrain from examining that complaint on the sole ground that they are applying EU law.[129]*

It seems fair to say that this reasoning is ambivalent and that it strikes, at best, an "uneasy balance"[130] between mutual trust and human rights. It may have been intended as an "olive branch"[131] offered to the ECJ after that court had delivered its much-criticized opinion[132] on the EU's accession to the ECHR. However, it also signals that the ECtHR would consider a complete and unqualified prohibition against a review of incoming judgments in respect of human rights violations as unacceptable even in the relationship between EU Member States.[133]

In its above-mentioned Opinion 2/13, the ECJ famously said that:

> The agreement on the accession of the European Union to the European Convention for the Protection of Human Rights and Fundamental Freedoms is not compatible with Article 6(2) TEU or with Protocol (No 8) relating to Article 6(2) of the Treaty on European Union on the accession of the Union to the European Convention on the Protection of Human Rights and Fundamental Freedoms.

With respect to the principle of mutual trust and its relationship with fundamental rights, it stated:

> 191. In the second place, it should be noted that the principle of mutual trust between the Member States is of fundamental importance in EU law, given that it allows an area without internal borders to be created and maintained ...

---

[129] Emphasis added.

[130] See G. Biagioni, above n. 123, pp. 579 ff.

[131] See P. Gragl, above n. 123, pp. 551 ff.

[132] ECJ, December 18, 2014, Opinion 2/13, ECLI:EU:C:2014:2454. See, e.g., H.P. Aust, "Eine völkerrechtsfreundliche Union? Grund und Grenze der Öffnung des Europarechts zum Völkerrecht" (2017) *EuR* 106, 114 ff.; M. Breuer, "'Wasch mir den Pelz, aber mach mich nicht nass!': Das zweite Gutachten des EuGH zum EMRK-Beitritt der Europäischen Union" (2015) *EuR* 330 ff.; B. de Witte and Š. Imamović, "Opinion 2/13 on Accession to the ECHR: Defending the EU Legal Order against a Foreign Human Rights Court" (2015) 40 *E.L. Rev.* 683 ff.; T. Isiksel, European Exceptionalism and the EU's Accession to the ECHR" (2016) 27 *Eur. J. Int'l L.* 565 ff.; M. Wendel, "Der EMRK-Beitritt als Unionsrechtsverstoß: Zur völkerrechtlichen Öffnung der EU und ihren Grenzen" [2015] *NJW* 921 ff; J. Wolber, "Der Beitritt der Europäischen Union zur EMRK im Lichte des Europäischen Zivilprozessrechts" [2017] *ZEuP* 936 ff.

[133] See G. Biagioni, above n. 123, p. 594; D. Düsterhaus, above n. 123, p. 396.

192. *Thus, when implementing EU law, the Member States may, under EU law, be required to presume that fundamental rights have been observed by the other Member States, so that not only may they not demand a higher level of national protection of fundamental rights from another Member State than that provided by EU law, but, save in exceptional cases, they may not check whether that other Member State has actually, in a specific case, observed the fundamental rights guaranteed by the EU.*[134]

193. The approach adopted in the agreement envisaged, which is to treat the EU as a State and to give it a role identical in every respect to that of any other Contracting Party, specifically disregards the intrinsic nature of the EU and, in particular, fails to take into consideration the fact that the Member States have, by reason of their membership of the EU, accepted that relations between them as regards the matters covered by the transfer of powers from the Member States to the EU are governed by EU law to the exclusion, if EU law so requires, of any other law.

194. In so far as the ECHR would, in requiring the EU and the Member States to be considered Contracting Parties not only in their relations with Contracting Parties which are not Member States of the EU but also in their relations with each other, including where such relations are governed by EU law, require a Member State to check that another Member State has observed fundamental rights, even though EU law imposes an obligation of mutual trust between those Member States, accession is liable to upset the underlying balance of the EU and undermine the autonomy of EU law.

However, the ECJ has meanwhile made clear that there are limits to mutual trust where a proper foundation for such trust is manifestly lacking.[135] Such a situation may lead to a reinstatement of "entry checks" for measures taken by other Member States even in areas where they would normally be prohibited. In a case concerning a European arrest warrant,[136] the ECJ ruled:

Article 1(3) of Council Framework Decision 2002/584/JHA of 13 June 2002 on the European arrest warrant and the surrender procedures between Member States, as amended by Council Framework Decision 2009/299/JHA of 26 February 2009, must be interpreted as meaning that, where the executing judicial authority, called upon to decide whether a person in respect of whom a European arrest warrant has been issued for the purposes of conducting a criminal prosecution is to be surrendered, has material, such as that set out in a reasoned proposal of the European Commission adopted pursuant to Article 7(1) TEU, indicating that there is a real risk of breach of

---

[134] Emphasis added.
[135] Case C-216/18 *PPU, LM*, ECLI:EU:C:2018:586. See also D. Düsterhaus, "Konstitutionalisiert der EuGH das Internationale Privat- und Verfahrensrecht der EU?" [2018] *ZEuP* 10, 22 ff.; F. Korenica and D. Doli, "No More Unconditional 'Mutual Trust' between the Member States: An Analysis of the Landmark Decision of the CJEU in Aranyosi and Caldararu" (2016) 5 *E.H.R.L.R.* 542 ff.; M. Wendel, "Rechtsstaatlichkeitsaufsicht und gegenseitiges Vertrauen" [2019] *EuR* 111 ff.
[136] *LM*, above n. 135.

the fundamental right to a fair trial guaranteed by the second paragraph of Article 47 of the Charter of Fundamental Rights of the European Union, on account of *systemic or generalised deficiencies*[137] so far as concerns the independence of the issuing Member State's judiciary, that authority must *determine, specifically and precisely*,[138] whether, having regard to his personal situation, as well as to the nature of the offence for which he is being prosecuted and the factual context that form the basis of the European arrest warrant, and in the light of the information provided by the issuing Member State pursuant to Article 15(2) of Framework Decision 2002/584, as amended, there are substantial grounds for believing that that person will run such a risk if he is surrendered to that State.

This was a reaction to measures taken in Poland that undermined the independence of the Polish judiciary. It seems that from the ECJ's perspective, systemic deficiencies in a Member State do not create a presumption against recognition and enforcement of acts of that state. However, they do trigger an obligation to assess whether there is a real threat to fundamental rights of the person against whom the act is directed. The ECJ is not willing to uphold the principle of mutual trust at all costs and in the face of a situation in a Member State where such trust would appear unjustified.[139]

It should be noted that the above-cited judgment concerned an arrest warrant and thus a particularly sensitive measure, and it is not clear how the ECJ would deal with the issue in the context of civil and commercial matters. However, there may also be indications in other recent case law that the ECJ increasingly perceives it as its task to ensure that the integrity and independence of the judiciary in the Member States is protected.[140] While the judicial dialogue[141] between the ECtHR and the ECJ might be characterized as a fight for judicial supremacy in matters involving both EU law and human rights,[142] both courts seem to share the basic assumption that regional integration can justify a reduction of human rights scrutiny at the enforcement stage only if there is a

---

[137] Emphasis added.

[138] Emphasis added.

[139] See F. KORENICA and D. DOLI, above n. 135, pp. 542 ff.

[140] M. BONELL and M. CLAES, "Judicial Serendipity: How Portuguese Judges Came to the Rescue of the Polish Judiciary: ECJ 27 February 2018, Case C-64/16, *Associação Sindical dos Juízes Portugueses*" (2018) 14 *European Constitutional Law Review* 622 ff.

[141] See the title of a speech given by D. SPIELMANN in March 2017, "The Judicial Dialogue between the European Court of Justice and the European Court of Human Rights. Or How to Remain Good Neighbours after the Opinion 2/13," http://www.fp7-frame.eu/wp-content/uploads/2017/03/ECHRCJUEdialog.BRUSSELS.final_.pdf. See also, e.g., P. EECKHOUT, "Opinion 2/13 on EU Accession to the ECHR and Judicial Dialogue: Autonomy or Autarky?" (2015) 38 *Fordham International Law Journal* 955 ff.

[142] See, e.g., U. KRANENPOHL, "Kompetenzgerangel oder Interpretationsdiskurs? Intrajustizielle Kontrolle im Mehrebenensystem" (2016) 26 *Zeitschrift für Politikwissenschaft* 149 ff.; C. TOMUSCHAT, "Der Streit um die Auslegungshoheit: die Autonomie der EU als Heiliger Gral. Das EuGH-Gutachten gegen den Beitritt der EU zur EMRK" (2015) 42 *EuGRZ* 133 ff.

Intersentia

solid basis for the assumption that human rights are properly protected in the state of origin. That the state of origin is itself bound by the ECHR or equivalent norms is an important building block for this assumption, but it does not completely remove the duty to assess whether the state of origin actually lives up to the standards set by the relevant instruments. However, the exact extent and limits of this duty still need to be clarified, presumably on a case-by-case basis.

3.4. PUBLIC POLICY AS A NATIONAL CONCEPT AND TENDENCIES TOWARD REGIONALIZATION

It seems to be the general view that the content of public policy is determined by national law, even with respect to the interpretation of public policy clauses in bilateral or multilateral treaties[143] and the European regional instruments on the free movement of judgments.[144] However, to prevent the handling of the public policy exception from upsetting the balance in the relationship among contracting parties of an international instrument or of member states of a supranational organization, there must be autonomous boundaries to this ground for refusal. If, in the context of binding international or supranational instruments, every state were entirely free in determining which features of its legal system it considers to be matters of public policy, judicial cooperation could be undermined. If nothing else, the principle of good faith must set limits in this regard. It is therefore not surprising that the ECJ, in its famous *Krombach*[145] judgment where it laid down the basic guidelines for public policy review within the European judicial area, made it clear that Member States must respect autonomous limits of public policy review:

> While the Contracting States in principle remain free, by virtue of the proviso in Article 27, point 1, of the Convention of 27 September 1968 on Jurisdiction and the Enforcement of Judgments in Civil and Commercial Matters, to determine, according to their own conceptions, what public policy requires, the limits of that concept are a matter for interpretation of the Convention. Consequently, *while it is not for the Court to define the content of the public policy of a Contracting State, it is none the less required to review the limits*[146] within which the courts of a Contracting State may have recourse to that concept for the purpose of refusing recognition to a judgment emanating from a court in another Contracting State.

---

[143] N. DE ARAUJO and M. DE NARDI (Brazil), p. 4; L.E. TRAKMAN, above n. 10, pp. 174 ff.

[144] J. BASEDOW, above n. 39, pp. 291 ff.; P. GOTTWALD, "Commentary on Article 45 Brussels I *bis* Regulation" in T. RAUSCHER and W. KRÜGER (eds.), *Münchener Kommentar zur Zivilprozessordnung*, 5th ed., vol. 3, C.H. Beck, Munich 2017, marginal no. 12; A. STAUDINGER, above n. 88, p. 274.

[145] Case C-7/98, *Dieter Krombach v. André Bamberski*, ECLI:EU:C:2000:164. On this judgment and its influence, see also P. GEORGANTI, above n. 8, pp. 85 ff; I. THOMA, above n. 15, pp. 129 ff.

[146] Emphasis added.

Regionalism in the Process of Recognition and Enforcement of Foreign Titles

In *Krombach* and some subsequent judgments,[147] the ECJ had the opportunity to outline some of those limits and, especially, to discuss the conditions in which breaches of fundamental procedural rights can constitute manifest breaches of public policy. In *Krombach*, it said:

> 38 With regard to the right to be defended, to which the question submitted to the Court refers, this occupies a prominent position in the organisation and conduct of a fair trial and is one of the fundamental rights deriving from the constitutional traditions common to the Member States.
>
> ...
>
> 43 The Court has also held that, even though the Convention is intended to secure the simplification of formalities governing the reciprocal recognition and enforcement of judgments of courts or tribunals, it is not permissible to achieve that aim by undermining the right to a fair hearing (Case 49/84 *Debaecker and Plouvier v. Bouwman* [1985] ECR 1779, paragraph 10).
>
> 44 It follows from the foregoing developments in the case-law that recourse to the public-policy clause must be regarded as being possible in exceptional cases where the guarantees laid down in the legislation of the State of origin and in the Convention itself have been insufficient to protect the defendant from a manifest breach of his right to defend himself before the court of origin, as recognised by the ECHR. Consequently, Article II of the Protocol cannot be construed as precluding the court of the State in which enforcement is sought from being entitled to take account, in relation to public policy, as referred to in Article 27, point 1, of the Convention, of the fact that, in an action for damages based on an offence, the court of the State of origin refused to hear the defence of the accused person, who was being prosecuted for an intentional offence, solely on the ground that that person was not present at the hearing.

In the ECJ's judgment in the *Gambazzi* case,[148] the relationship between fair trial and public policy was further elaborated on, specifically with respect to cases where a party is excluded from the proceedings as a sanction for contempt of court. The ECJ gave rather detailed guidelines for assessing whether this amounts to an unacceptable violation of fair trial rights, before stating the following:

> 46 It must be underlined that verifying those points, to the extent that the sole purpose is to identify any manifest and disproportionate infringement of the right to

---

[147] Case C-38/98, *Régie nationale des usines Renault SA v. Maxicar SpA and Orazio Formento*, ECLI:EU:C:2000:225; Case C-394/07, *Marco Gambazzi v. DaimlerChrysler Canada Inc. and CIBC Mellon Trust Company*, ECLI:EU:C:2009:219; Case C-420/07, *Meletis Apostolides v. David Charles Orams and Linda Elizabeth Orams*, ECLI:EU:C:2009:271; Case C-619/10, *Trade Agency Ltd. v. Seramico Investments Ltd.*, ECLI:EU:C:2012:531; Case C-302/13, *flyLAL-Lithuanian Airlines AS v. Starptautiskā lidosta Rīga VAS and Air Baltic Corporation AS*, ECLI:EU:C:2014:2319; Case C-681/13, *Diageo Brands BV v. Simiramida-04 EOOD*, ECLI:EU:C:2015:471; Case C-559/14, *Rūdolfs Meroni v. Recoletos Ltd.*, ECLI:EU:C:2016:349.

[148] *Marco Gambazzi*, above n. 147.

Intersentia

345

be heard, does not mean reviewing the High Court's assessment of the merits, which would constitute a review as to the substance of the judgment expressly prohibited by Article 29 and the third paragraph of Article 34 of the Brussels Convention. The referring court must confine itself to identifying the legal remedies which were available to Mr. Gambazzi and to verifying that they offered him the possibility of being heard, in compliance with the adversarial principle and the full exercise of the rights of defence.

47 Following completion of such verification, it is for the national court to carry out a balancing exercise with regard to those various factors in order to assess whether, in the light of the objective of the efficient administration of justice pursued by the High Court, the exclusion of Mr Gambazzi from the proceedings appears to be a manifest and disproportionate infringement of his right to be heard.

A similar approach was adopted in the *Trade Agency*[149] case, where the ECJ ruled as follows:

Article 34(1) of Regulation No 44/2001, to which Article 45(1) thereof refers, must be interpreted as meaning that the courts of the Member State in which enforcement is sought may refuse to enforce a judgment given in default of appearance which disposes of the substance of the dispute but which does not contain an assessment of the subject-matter or the basis of the action and which lacks any argument of its merits, only if it appears to the court, after an overall assessment of the proceedings and in the light of all the relevant circumstances, that that judgment is a manifest and disproportionate breach of the defendant's right to a fair trial referred to in the second paragraph of Article 47 of the Charter of Fundamental Rights of the European Union, on account of the impossibility of bringing an appropriate and effective appeal against it.

It might be questioned whether the application of a ground for refusal that only aims at preventing "manifest" incompatibility with the fundamental legal principles of the requested state's legal order should really require such delicate balancing. After all, it might be considered as a contradiction in itself to require such balancing to determine whether recognition and enforcement would be manifestly incompatible with fundamental principles. However, requiring the court of the requested state to take a closer look at the proceedings and their context can prevent conclusions being jumped to in cases where, at first glance, the incompatibility does appear to be manifest. In the context of public policy, features of the foreign procedural system should not be looked at in isolation. The court of the state addressed needs to consider the context in which they operate.[150] However, the "balancing" approach can also be understood as

---

[149]   Case C-619/10, *Trade Agency Ltd. v. Seramico Investments Ltd.*, ECLI:EU:C:2012:531.
[150]   B. SUJECKI, "Unverhältnismäßige Beeinträchtigung des Anspruchs auf rechtliches Gehör" (2009) *EuZW* 422, 425 notes that the court of the receiving state must have a detailed knowledge of foreign procedural law in order to comply with the standard of review under the *Gambazzi* judgment.

a consequence of the realization that the function of procedural policy is no longer, and perhaps never has been, primarily the protection of the sovereignty of the state addressed, but that the individual interests of the parties to the case have a decisive role to play.[151]

Another opportunity to elaborate on the relationship between fair trial rights and public policy arose in the *Rüdolfs Meroni*[152] case, which concerned the protection of third parties affected by a worldwide freezing order.[153] In this case, the ECJ ruled:

> Article 34(1) of Council Regulation (EC) No 44/2001 of 22 December 2000 on jurisdiction and the recognition and enforcement of judgments in civil and commercial matters, considered in the light of Article 47 of the Charter of Fundamental Rights of the European Union, must be interpreted as meaning that, in circumstances such as those at issue in the main proceedings, the recognition and enforcement of an order issued by a court of a Member State, without a prior hearing of a third person whose rights may be affected by that order, cannot be regarded as manifestly contrary to public policy in the Member State in which enforcement is sought or manifestly contrary to the right to a fair trial within the meaning of those provisions, in so far as that third person is entitled to assert his rights before that court.

The *Rüdolfs Meroni* judgment is remarkable and indeed problematic.[154] Its reasoning not only seems to indicate that a third party whose rights are affected by a judgment carries the burden of challenging that judgment in the state of origin, but also seems to imply that the prohibition of a review as to the substance carries with it a sort of *erga omnes* effect of judgments. In this, it demonstrates that the position of third parties in international civil procedure is and remains perilous and uncertain, all the more so because there are no clear rules about the jurisdictional prerequisites of placing procedural burdens on third parties. However, it is beyond the scope of this chapter to explore this issue further.

The ECJ's case law on the public policy ground for refusal of the European Insolvency Regulation (now Article 33 of the recast Insolvency Regulation 2015/848) also recognizes the importance of fair trial rights in this regard. Indeed, the provision on public policy contained in the Insolvency Regulation explicitly mentions "fundamental principles or the constitutional rights and liberties of the individual" as an element of public policy.

---

[151] See also P. GEORGANTI, above n. 8, pp. 106 f.
[152] Case C-559/14, *Rüdolfs Meroni v. Recoletos Ltd.*, ECLI:EU:C:2016:349.
[153] See also Case C-350/13, *Antonio Gramsci Shipping Corp. v. Aivars Lembergs*, ECLI:EU:C:2014:1516, in which the ECJ did not have to give a ruling as the initial decision was annulled.
[154] See also D. TSIKRIKAS (Greece), pp. 9 f., p. 13.

Intersentia

In the *Eurofood*[155] case, the ECJ ruled that the case law on public policy concerning the Brussels Convention and the Brussels I Regulation is transposable to the interpretation of the Insolvency Regulation's public policy clause. It stated:

> 65 In the procedural area, the Court of Justice has expressly recognised the general principle of Community law that everyone is entitled to a fair legal process (Case C-185/95 P *Baustahlgewebe v. Commission* [1998] ECR I-8417, paragraphs 20 and 21; Joined Cases C-174/98 P and C-189/98 P *Netherlands and Van der Wal v. Commission* [2000] ECR I-1, paragraph 17; and *Krombach*, paragraph 26). That principle is inspired by the fundamental rights which form an integral part of the general principles of Community law which the Court of Justice enforces, drawing inspiration from the constitutional traditions common to the Member States and from the guidelines supplied, in particular, by the European Convention for the Protection of Human Rights and Fundamental Freedoms, signed in Rome on 4 November 1950.

> 66 Concerning more particularly the right to be notified of procedural documents and, more generally, the right to be heard, referred to in the referring court's fifth question, these rights occupy an eminent position in the organisation and conduct of a fair legal process. In the context of insolvency proceedings, the right of creditors or their representatives to participate in accordance with the equality of arms principle is of particular importance. Though the specific detailed rules concerning the right to be heard may vary according to the urgency for a ruling to be given, any restriction on the exercise of that right must be duly justified and surrounded by procedural guarantees ensuring that persons concerned by such proceedings actually have the opportunity to challenge the measures adopted in urgency.

> 67 In the light of those considerations, the answer to the fifth question must be that, on a proper interpretation of Article 26 of the Regulation, a Member State may refuse to recognise insolvency proceedings opened in another Member State where the decision to open the proceedings was taken in flagrant breach of the fundamental right to be heard, which a person concerned by such proceedings enjoys.

Within the EU, rules of EU law can, in principle, also have public policy status. Indeed, the majority of cases decided by the ECJ with respect to substantive public policy concerned the (mis)application of EU law. The ECJ has made it clear that not every violation of EU law constitutes a manifest incompatibility with public policy. In the *Renault Maxicar*[156] case, the ECJ ruled:

> 30 Recourse to the clause on public policy in Article 27, point 1, of the Convention can be envisaged only where recognition or enforcement of the judgment delivered in another Contracting State would be at variance to an unacceptable degree with

---

[155]   Case C-341/04, *Eurofood IFSC Ltd.*, ECLI:EU:C:2006:281.
[156]   *Régie nationale des usines Renault SA*, above n. 147.

the legal order of the State in which enforcement is sought inasmuch as it infringes a fundamental principle. In order for the prohibition of any review of the foreign judgment as to its substance to be observed, the infringement would have to constitute a manifest breach of a rule of law regarded as essential in the legal order of the State in which enforcement is sought or of a right recognised as being fundamental within that legal order (*Krombach*, paragraph 37).

…

32 *The fact that the alleged error concerns rules of Community law does not alter the conditions for being able to rely on the clause on public policy.*[157] It is for the national court to ensure with equal diligence the protection of rights established in national law and rights conferred by Community law.

33 The court of the State in which enforcement is sought cannot, without undermining the aim of the Convention, refuse recognition of a decision emanating from another Contracting State solely on the ground that it considers that national or Community law was misapplied in that decision. On the contrary, it must be considered whether, in such cases, the system of legal remedies in each Contracting State, together with the preliminary ruling procedure provided for in Article 177 of the Treaty, affords a sufficient guarantee to individuals.

This position was reaffirmed in the *flyLAL*[158] and *Diageo Brands*[159] judgments.

In *Apostolides*,[160] a case concerning a Greek judgment against a British couple ordering them to vacate a property in Northern Cyprus, the ECJ took a restrictive stance concerning a Member State's ability to rely on the public policy ground for refusal in politically charged situations. The ECJ ruled that a U.K. court could not refuse recognition and enforcement on the basis of public policy:

The fact that a judgment given by the courts of a Member State, concerning land situated in an area of that State over which its Government does not exercise effective control, cannot, as a practical matter, be enforced where the land is situated does not constitute a ground for refusal of recognition or enforcement under Article 34(1) of Regulation No 44/2001 and it does not mean that such a judgment is unenforceable for the purposes of Article 38(1) of that regulation.

Even with respect to fair trial rights, where there is a lot of common ground between EU (and Lugano) states, the ECJ nevertheless sticks to the idea that every national court needs to examine the compatibility with its own public policy independently and cannot simply adopt the position taken by a foreign

---

[157]   Emphasis added.
[158]   *flyLAL-Lithuanian Airlines AS*, above n. 147.
[159]   *Diageo Brands BV*, above n. 147.
[160]   *Meletis Apostolides*, above n. 147.

court that also conducted a public policy review. In the *Gambazzi* case,[161] it pointed out:

> 38 With regard to the specific assessment of the conflict with Swiss public policy carried out in the present case by the Tribunal fédéral in its abovementioned judgment, it should be noted that that assessment cannot formally bind the national court. That is especially true in this case because the latter court must carry out its assessment with regard to Italian public policy.

An even more crucial consequence of public policy being a matter of national law is that there is no minimum public policy standard that a state must enforce against foreign judgments by virtue of the Lugano Convention, of EU instruments on the free movement of judgments, or of a bilateral or multilateral convention. This is the case even with respect to serious violations of fair trial rights. However, the consequences should not be overstated. There are other rules of national, international and EU law that can create an obligation to rely on the public policy exception.[162] Furthermore, in the European system of free movement of judgments, the refusal ground of lack of service of the document instituting the proceedings is not discretionary. Despite these mitigating factors, the way in which the public policy exception operates does not seem particularly well suited to a regional system of free movement of judgments that wants to strike a fair balance not only between the interests of states, but also between those of private persons. One may therefore regret that the idea to replace procedural public policy with an autonomous standard of fair trial rights in the Brussels I *bis* Regulation did not succeed. In any case, the more the essential values and fundamental procedural standards that are protected by public policy clauses become subject to regional integration, the more the concept of public policy itself necessarily becomes "regionalized." Sooner or later, this development could also lead to the reappreciation of the operation of the public policy clause itself and not just of its content.

4. INTENSITY OF REVIEW

It seems universally accepted that mere differences between foreign and domestic law do not suffice to establish a violation of public policy,[163] and that

---

[161] *Marco Gambazzi*, above n. 147.
[162] With regard to the ECHR, see, e.g., T. CORTHAUT, *EU Ordre Public*, Wolters Kluwer, Alphen aan den Rijn 2009, p. 157.
[163] D. WIEDEMANN (Germany), p. 1; H. PEKCANITEZ and E. ALPAY (Turkey), p. 1; Bundesgerichtshof, June 22, 2017 – IX ZB 61/16, WM 2017, 1428; Bundesgericht BGE 126 III 101, consideration 3b; G. FRANGOU, *Vollstreckung ausländischer Entscheidungen in Griechenland: Die Anwendung des europäischen Zivilprozessrechts durch die griechische Rechtsprechung*, Nomos, Baden-Baden 2017, p. 80.

not all rules that are internally mandatory also belong to public policy for the purposes of denying recognition and enforcement of foreign judgments.[164] Nor does a misapplication of the law per se constitute a violation of public policy.[165] According to the ECJ's judgment in *Krombach*, the foreign judgment must be "at variance to an unacceptable degree with the legal order of the state in which enforcement is sought inasmuch as it infringes a fundamental principle."[166] In Brazil, an incompatibility with essential values of justice and fundamental constitutional rights is required.[167] Other systems adopt similar stances.[168] While the degree of generosity that courts apply in this context does vary from jurisdiction to jurisdiction and from court to court, this basic approach seems to be very broadly recognized.

In the area of recognition and enforcement of foreign judgments, it is necessary to reconcile the prohibition of *révision au fond*, which has been implemented in most jurisdictions, with the public policy exception.[169] This is achieved by asking not whether the content of the judgment is incompatible with public policy, but whether *recognition and enforcement* would be so.[170] It is therefore not relevant whether the court of the requested state would have decided or proceeded in the same way as the court that gave the judgment. The application of a different law than the one applicable under the conflict-of-laws rules of the requested state also seems to have largely lost its significance either as an element of public policy or as a self-standing ground for refusal.[171] Along similar lines, it is said that only the operative part of the judgment and not the court's reasoning can constitute an incompatibility with substantive public policy.[172] Refusing recognition and enforcement based on public policy does not even necessarily require that there is a policy difference or a difference of general legal rules between the state of origin and the requested state. It is quite possible that a judgment whose recognition and enforcement would be incompatible with public policy in the requested state is also defective from the perspective of the state of origin. However, where that is the case, the possibility to rely on

---

[164] This well-established principle is explicitly mentioned, e.g., by J. KRAMBERGER ŠKERL (Slovenia), p. 1; see also H. PEKCANITEZ and E. ALPAY (Turkey), p. 1.

[165] P. OBERHAMMER, above n. 99, marginal no. 32 f.

[166] *Dieter Krombach v. André Bamberski*, above n. 145, marginal no. 37.

[167] N. DE ARAUJO and M. DE NARDI (Brazil), p. 2.

[168] See, e.g., Bundesgericht BGE 122 III 344, consideration 4a; G. FRANGOU, above n. 163, pp. 79 f.; C. VÖLKER, above n. 8, pp. 110 ff.

[169] From the German perspective, see Bundesgerichtshof, June 22, 2017 – IX ZB 61/16, WM 2017, 1428 with further references; D. WIEDEMANN (Germany), p. 3.

[170] In Turkey, the same aim is pursued by limiting public policy review (presumably mainly with respect to substantive public policy) to the operative part of the judgment, ruling out a public policy review of the reasoning; see H. PEKCANITEZ and E. ALPAY (Turkey), pp. 1 f.

[171] R. GEIMER, above n. 25, marginal no. 239; D. MARTINY, above n. 108, p. 530.

[172] Bundesgerichtshof, July 19, 2018 – IX ZB 10/10, NJW 2018, 3254, n. 14.

public policy in the requested state instead of addressing the issue in the state of origin can be limited.[173]

Nevertheless, it would often be difficult or impossible to decide whether recognition and enforcement would be incompatible with public policy without looking at the content of the judgment or at the proceedings that led up to it. The requirement of a "manifest" breach of public policy[174] and the prohibition of *révision au fond* serve to ensure that this examination does not amount to relitigating the case. The ECJ's reasoning in the *Krombach*[175] judgment illustrates this relationship between the prohibition of *révision au fond* and the requirement of a sufficiently serious violation:

> 36 By disallowing any review of a foreign judgment as to its substance, Article 29 and the third paragraph of Article 34 of the [Brussels] Convention prohibit the court of the State in which enforcement is sought from refusing to recognise or enforce that judgment solely on the ground that there is a discrepancy between the legal rule applied by the court of the State of origin and that which would have been applied by the court of the State in which enforcement is sought had it been seised of the dispute. Similarly, the court of the State in which enforcement is sought cannot review the accuracy of the findings of law or fact made by the court of the State of origin.
>
> 37 Recourse to the public-policy clause in Article 27, point 1, of the Convention can be envisaged only where recognition or enforcement of the judgment delivered in another Contracting State would be at variance to an unacceptable degree with the legal order of the State in which enforcement is sought inasmuch as it infringes a fundamental principle. In order for the prohibition of any review of the foreign judgment as to its substance to be observed, the infringement would have to constitute a manifest breach of a rule of law regarded as essential in the legal order of the State in which enforcement is sought or of a right recognised as being fundamental within that legal order.

As pointed out in the General report for the common law jurisdictions, a popular reasoning given for restrictions on public policy scrutiny is that "we are not so provincial as to say that every solution of a problem is wrong because we deal with it otherwise at home."[176] This is undoubtedly an important consideration. However, if taken at face value, it might suggest a rather too generous reading of the public policy exception in the field of recognition and enforcement. Asking whether recognition and enforcement would be in manifest contradiction to the fundamental values of the state where recognition and enforcement is

---

[173] See *Diageo Brands BV*, above n. 147.

[174] However, if a jurisdiction does not explicitly call for a "manifest" incompatibility, this does not necessarily mean that the concept of public policy is interpreted more broadly; see, e.g., J. KRAMBERGER ŠKERL (Slovenia), p. 4.

[175] *Dieter Krombach v. André Bamberski*, above n. 145.

[176] R. BRAND, General report on common law jurisdictions, pp. 12 f.

sought is quite a different test from asking whether the decision reached by the foreign court is "just as good" as or "not much worse" than one that would have been made by a domestic court. The public policy test is not whether, from a "tolerant" perspective, the foreign solution is of equal or even similar value as the domestic solution. Recognition and enforcement of the judgment must be entirely unacceptable to justify relying on the public policy exception. As the ECJ said in *Krombach*:[177]

> 37 Recourse to the public-policy clause in Article 27, point 1, of the Convention can be envisaged only where recognition or enforcement of the judgment delivered in another Contracting State would be at variance to an unacceptable degree with the legal order of the State in which enforcement is sought inasmuch as it infringes a fundamental principle. In order for the prohibition of any review of the foreign judgment as to its substance to be observed, the infringement would have to constitute a manifest breach of a rule of law regarded as essential in the legal order of the State in which enforcement is sought or of a right recognised as being fundamental within that legal order.

Even if the proceedings before the foreign court diverged from the procedural law of the state where recognition and enforcement is sought in a way that would be considered as a breach of a rule of fundamental importance, had the proceedings taken place in the state addressed, this does not necessarily justify resorting to the public policy exception. Instead, the court of the state addressed must look at the big picture, taking into account all relevant aspects of the proceedings before the court in the state of origin, as the ECJ ruled in the *Eurofood*[178] case:

> 68 Should occasion arise, it will be for the referring court to establish whether, in the main proceedings, that has been the case with the conduct of the proceedings before the Tribunale civile e penale di Parma. In that respect, it should be observed that the referring court cannot confine itself to transposing its own conception of the requirement for an oral hearing and of how fundamental that requirement is in its legal order, but must assess, having regard to the whole of the circumstances, whether or not the provisional liquidator appointed by the High Court was given sufficient opportunity to be heard.

With respect to public policy as a ground for refusal, many systems place the bar higher than in the field of choice of law.[179] The reasoning behind this is that

---

[177]   *Dieter Krombach v. André Bamberski*, above n. 145.
[178]   *Eurofood IFSC Ltd.*, above n. 155.
[179]   Bundesgerichtshof, April 21, 1998 – XI ZR 377–97, NJW 1998, 2358; D. Wiedemann (Germany), pp. 1, 4; D. Tsikrikas (Greece), p. 11; H. Pekcanitez and E. Alpay (Turkey), pp. 1, 2. See also Bundesgericht BGE 142 III 355, consideration 3.2. However, it is difficult to assess the extent to which public policy is more restrictive in the area of recognition; see J. Basedow, above n. 39, pp. 298 ff.

choice-of-law rules determine the domestic court's judgment on the substance of the case, while the law of recognition and enforcement addresses situations where a court has already decided the matter. Moreover, the rules on jurisdiction should presumably ensure that there were sufficient contacts either of the defendant or of the case with the state of origin. Another argument advanced in favor of this approach is that one should be very careful about creating "limping" judgments.[180] However, the idea that public policy scrutiny is more lenient at the recognition and enforcement stage than in the choice-of-law context does not seem to be universally endorsed. In Brazil, China, and Tunisia, for example, no difference seems to be made between public policy in private international law and public policy as a ground for the refusal of recognition and enforcement.[181]

For the intra-EU situation, it has been argued that the uniform handling of the public policy clauses in conflict-of-laws rules and procedural instruments would promote direct enforceability.[182] This has been illustrated by referring to the Maintenance Regulation, where public policy can only be invoked as a ground for refusal of recognition and enforcement if the judgment comes from a Member State not bound by the Hague Protocol which establishes uniform conflict-of-laws rules.[183]

One important difference between conflict of laws and recognition and enforcement is that in the conflict of laws, public policy is said to have not only a negative but also a positive function, leading to the application of "lois d'application immédiate" or "lois de police" – a function that is not present in the field of recognition and enforcement, at least not directly.[184] However, in some cases, the refusal of recognition and enforcement on the basis of a violation of public policy can indirectly open the door to the exercise of such a "positive function," as it enables the courts of the state where recognition and enforcement is sought to make their own judgment in the case, which is not possible if the *res judicata* effect of the foreign judgment is recognized. However, in the European judicial area, this is not as easy as it is outside it, as this would require that there is a basis for jurisdiction in the state whose public policy was violated. It is unclear whether the refusal of recognition and enforcement would allow the refusing state to make its own judgment on the matter regardless of whether there is a basis for jurisdiction under EU law.[185]

---

[180] D. TSIKRIKAS (Greece), p. 11; see further Bundesgericht BGE 141 III 312, consideration 4.1.
[181] See N. DE ARAUJO and M. DE NARDI (Brazil), p. 2 f.; Q. HE (China), p. 1; A. OUERFELLI and Y. EL-BENNA (Tunisia), p. 3. See also G. TU (Macau), p. 2.
[182] Public policy study, above n. 112, p. 27.
[183] Ibid., p. 27.
[184] D. WIEDEMANN (Germany), p. 4. See also I. THOMA, above n. 15, p. 18; C. VÖLKER, above n. 8, pp. 58 ff.; Bundesgericht BGE 128 III 201, consideration 1b.
[185] See R. GEIMER, *Internationales Zivilprozessrecht*, 8th ed., Otto Schmidt, Cologne 2020, marginal nos. 1030, 1054, who advocates in favor of a *forum necessitatis* in the state where recognition and enforcement was refused.

In some jurisdictions, courts also take into account whether and to what degree there is a domestic nexus when determining whether a deviation from fundamental legal principles or constitutional rights of the respective jurisdiction amounts to a violation of its public policy.[186]

5. PUBLIC POLICY AND SPECIFIC GROUNDS FOR REFUSAL OF RECOGNITION AND ENFORCEMENT

Alongside the general public policy clause, bilateral and multilateral instruments as well as national laws usually contain specific grounds for refusal of recognition and enforcement that can be considered as specific elements of public policy.[187] For example, defective service is often a specific ground for refusal with respect to default judgments and can be classified under this category.[188] The same goes for the refusal grounds addressing conflicts between judgments.[189] Another provision that can be classified in this category is Article 12 of the 2019 HCCH Judgments Convention, according to which the recognition or enforcement of a judgment may be refused if and to the extent that the judgment awards damages, including exemplary or punitive damages, that do not compensate a party for actual loss or harm suffered. Another issue that might be regulated separately or in the context of public policy is the prevention of fraud.[190]

Creating specific refusal grounds addressing what might be considered as specific types of public policy violations,[191] particularly in bilateral or multilateral treaties or supranational instruments, can carry implications for the margin of state discretion and potentially also for the parties' situation. This can be illustrated by looking at the differences between the public policy ground for refusal in Article 45(1)(a) of the Brussels I *bis* Regulation and the specific grounds for refusal dealing with defective service (Article 45(1)(b)) and conflicting judgments (Article 45(1)(c) and (d)). With respect to such issues, there is no room for a subsidiary application of general public policy.[192]

---

[186] D. WIEDEMANN (Germany), p. 3; H. ROTH, above n. 40, marginal nos. 101 f.; see also Bundesgericht BGE 141 III 312, consideration 4.1.

[187] The Tunisian reporters take the view that every ground for refusal except for lack of reciprocity ultimately relates to public policy; see A. OUERFELLI and Y. EL-BENNA (Tunisia), p. 5.

[188] See N. DE ARAUJO and M. DE NARDI (Brazil), p. 4.

[189] An example of a jurisdiction that deals with this issue as a matter of public policy is Japan; see K. TAKESHITA (Japan), p. 5.

[190] See, e.g., J. KRAMBERGER ŠKERL (Slovenia), p. 2; D. WIEDEMANN (Germany), p. 6.

[191] See D. WIEDEMANN (Germany), p. 5.

[192] Bundesgerichtshof, May 17, 2018 – IX ZB 26/17, IWRZ 2019, 80; D. WIEDEMANN (Germany), p. 5. With respect to the delineation between the special ground for refusal concerning defective service and the public policy exception, see also Bundesgerichtshof, September 10, 2015 – IX ZB 39/13, NJW 2016, 160; Bundesgerichtshof, March 21, 1990 – XII ZB 71/89, NJW 1990, 2201.

Intersentia

Tanja Domej

While public policy is defined by national law, if within autonomous limits, no scope of discretion is left for national law in handling the above-mentioned specific grounds for refusal in the European judicial area. The criteria for these grounds for refusal are autonomous. If they are met, an application for refusal of recognition and enforcement must be granted, without any discretion of the requested state or the court to which the application is addressed.[193] These grounds for refusal do not create a national prerogative, but a uniform standard. Yet, obviously, this is not a strictly necessary consequence of outsourcing certain issues of public policy into specific refusal grounds, as is demonstrated by the 2019 HCCH Judgments Convention, where there are also specific grounds for refusal for defective service and conflicting judgments, but they are discretionary and not mandatory for the requested state.

6. JURISDICTION AND PUBLIC POLICY

The European instruments on the free movement of judgments explicitly rule out the possibility to rely on public policy to justify the refusal of recognition and enforcement for lack of jurisdiction of the court of the state of origin. Outside the specific rules on indirect jurisdiction (such as Article 45(1)(e) of the Brussels I *bis* Regulation), refusal on jurisdictional grounds is not permitted, even if the rules on direct jurisdiction were manifestly misapplied.[194]

The approaches to the relationship between jurisdiction and public policy in national laws vary. Many jurisdictions contain positive requirements of indirect jurisdiction that go far beyond public policy considerations. This is also the approach of the HCCH 2019 Judgments Convention, under which it is a positive requirement for recognition and enforcement that the criteria of a jurisdictional filter set out in the Convention are met. There are also some national laws, such as in Switzerland, that set out specific rules on indirect jurisdiction that need to be complied with to make a foreign judgment eligible for recognition and enforcement.[195] Other states, such as Germany[196] or Greece,[197] adhere to the "mirror principle," meaning that the indirect jurisdiction of the foreign court is assessed by asking whether that court would have had jurisdiction under the requested state's rules on direct jurisdiction.

---

[193]   Case C-80/00, *Italian Leather SpA/WECO Polstermöbel GmbH & Co.*, ECLI:EU:C:2002:342.
[194]   P. GOTTWALD, above n. 144, marginal no. 57; A. STADLER, above n. 100, marginal no. 16.
[195]   G. WALTER and T. DOMEJ, above n. 2, pp. 424 ff.
[196]   J. BASEDOW, "Variationen über die spiegelbildliche Anwendung des deutschen Zuständigkeitsrechts" [1994] *IPRax* 183 ff.; H.C. LAUGWITZ, above n. 50, pp. 104 ff. As regards the operation of the "mirror principle" in relation to multi-unit states, see C. SCHÄRTL, *Das Spiegelbildprinzip im Rechtsverkehr mit ausländischen Staatenverbindungen*, Mohr Siebeck, Tübingen 2005.
[197]   D. TSIKRIKAS (Greece), p. 5.

In contrast, some states take an approach to indirect jurisdiction in their national laws that may be characterized as public policy oriented. Brazil seems to be an example of this, as the Brazilian Superior Court of Justice, a senior court that has a monopoly to decide upon the recognition and enforcement of foreign judgments in Brazil,[198] may only "examine if the foreign authority has not invaded the exclusive jurisdiction of the Brazilian national judge."[199] A similar approach is taken in Tunisia.[200] The Brazilian Superior Court of Justice seems to handle this criterion rather generously. For example, it has allowed the recognition and enforcement of a foreign judgment ordering the expropriation of immovable property situated in Brazil as a civil consequence of criminal conviction for transnational organized crime.[201] The Turkish national report also indicates that the scrutiny of jurisdiction in the context of recognition and enforcement carries strong public policy elements.[202] In Greece, the "mirror principle" applies, but the national report indicates that in addition, there might be a room for public policy to step in if suing the defendant in an exorbitant forum resulted in an impairment of the right to be heard.[203]

Another approach is to ask whether reasonable connecting factors were present in the state of origin that justified the foreign court's acceptance of jurisdiction. This can be combined with a requirement that the foreign court did not interfere with the requested state's exclusive jurisdiction.[204]

7. THE DOUBLE FUNCTION OF PUBLIC POLICY

It seems to be broadly recognized that public policy has a double function: it protects not only the public interest of the requested state, but also individual rights.[205] This is most apparent with respect to procedural public policy whose main purpose today is the protection of the right to a fair trial. But there are also cases where substantive public policy serves to protect individual rights that the requested state considers to be of fundamental importance. In particular, at least in some parts of the world, gender equality and non-discrimination on

---

[198] N. DE ARAUJO and M. DE NARDI (Brazil), p. 1.
[199] Ibid., p. 6.
[200] A. OUERFELLI and Y. EL-BENNA (Tunisia), p. 5.
[201] N. DE ARAUJO and M. DE NARDI (Brazil), p. 6.
[202] H. PEKCANITEZ and E. ALPAY (Turkey), p. 3 f.
[203] D. TSIKRIKAS (Greece), p. 13.
[204] Indeed, this seems to be the approach in Turkey; H. PEKCANITEZ and E. ALPAY (Turkey), p. 4.
[205] The relationship between the parties', third parties', and public interests is explored, e.g., by F. GHODOOSI, "The Concept of Public Policy in Law: Revisiting the Role of the Public Policy Doctrine in the Enforcement of Private Legal Arrangements" (2016) 94 *Neb. L. Rev.* 685, 710 ff.

the grounds of ethnicity, religion, sexuality, or disability are matters of public policy.[206] Where rules on the freedom of expression[207] or on privacy have public policy status, individual interests and the way in which the requested state strikes a balance between them also play an important role.

Statutory rules on public policy and case law usually do not seem to draw a clear distinction between cases where individual interests predominate and those where the public interest is primarily at stake. In most cases, this will not be of too much consequence, as usually the party against whom the judgment ruled will have an interest in invoking the public policy ground for refusal. However, there may be instances where none of the parties is interested in relying on the public policy exception: money laundering, corruption, or the financing of terrorism spring to mind. Where rules to combat such practices are given public policy status, the question may arise whether refusal of recognition and enforcement of contravening judgments should depend on a party's initiative.[208]

8. ARBITRAL AWARDS

In the field of arbitration, the New York Convention,[209] today the only globally operational international instrument on recognition and enforcement, is of prime importance.[210] Regional instruments are much less relevant in this field than in the field of the recognition and enforcement of judgments.[211] For example, the Brazilian national report points out that the Brazilian Superior Court of Justice has so far never relied on the Inter-American Convention on International Commercial Arbitration of 1975.[212] Instead, it consistently uses

---

[206] See, e.g., M. MÜLLER-CHEN, "Commentary on Article 27 of the Swiss Private International Law Act" in M. MÜLLER-CHEN and C. WIDMER LÜCHINGER (eds.), *Zürcher Kommentar zum IPRG*, 3rd ed., vol. 1, Schulthess, Zürich 2018, marginal no. 7.

[207] See Bundesgerichtshof, July 19, 2018 – IX ZB 10/18, NJW 2018, 3254.

[208] An *ex officio* review of public policy in cases where supra-individual legal interests are affected is favored, e.g., by T. PFEIFFER, above n. 100, p. 426; A. STADLER, above n. 100, marginal no. 1 n. 1. See also R. GEIMER, above n. 100, pp. 114 f.

[209] Convention on the Recognition and Enforcement of Foreign Arbitral Awards, New York, June 10, 1958.

[210] As of June 2020, the New York Convention has 164 Contracting States. The complete list of contracting states is available at https://treaties.un.org.

[211] However, the New York Convention does not affect the validity of such regional instruments (Art. VII(1)).

[212] N. DE ARAUJO and M. DE NARDI (Brazil), p. 8. According to a survey conducted in Latin America in 2008, most states that are parties to both the New York Convention and the Inter-American Convention on International Commercial Arbitration of 1975 rely exclusively on the New York Convention for the recognition and enforcement of foreign arbitral awards (see E. GAILLARD and G.A. BERMANN, *Guide on the Convention on the Recognition and Enforcement of Foreign Arbitral Awards*, Brill Online, Leiden 2017, p. 313, with reference to C. CONEJERO ROOS, "The New York Convention in Latin America: Lessons from Recent Court Decisions" [2009] *Arbitration Review of the Americas* 21).

the national arbitration act of 1996 whose provisions on the recognition and enforcement follow the New York Convention.[213] Many jurisdictions base their national rules on the New York Convention.[214]

The predominant approach seems to be that the concept of public policy is no different with respect to foreign arbitral awards than with respect to judgments.[215] Some jurisdictions make a stronger distinction between judgments and arbitral awards, and tend to take the view that in relation to arbitral awards, a restrictive concept of "international public policy" should apply.[216] Even in those jurisdictions where such an approach is not followed, there are often at least nuances, either with respect to public policy in general or specific grounds for refusal intended to protect fundamental procedural principles. One issue where this indeed seems essential for the smooth functioning of the arbitral process is the service of documents. Thus, the Brazilian national report notes that the criteria for the effectiveness of service (see Article V(1)(b) of the New York Convention) are more generous for arbitral awards than they are for judgments; mail service or service in a form provided for in the parties' agreement is sufficient.[217] The German Bundesgerichtshof has made it clear that it does not violate German public policy if communications during arbitral proceedings take place by fax.[218]

Public policy scrutiny of arbitral awards can be relevant not only in the context of the recognition and enforcement of foreign arbitral awards, but also with respect to setting aside a domestic arbitral award.[219] There are considerable divergences between jurisdictions as to whether the same, a stricter, or a more lenient standard should apply to the setting aside of an arbitral award given by a tribunal within the jurisdiction, compared with the recognition and enforcement of foreign arbitral awards.

In France, the recognition and enforcement of a foreign arbitral award can only be refused if it is obviously incompatible with the "ordre public

---

[213]   N. DE ARAUJO and M. DE NARDI (Brazil), p. 8.

[214]   See, e.g., K. TAKESHITA (Japan), p. 8. More favorable national rules may be applied on the basis of Art. VII(1) of the New York Convention; see E. GAILLARD and A. BERMANN, above n. 212, p. 7.

[215]   N. DE ARAUJO and M. DE NARDI (Brazil), p. 7, p. 8; Q. HE (China), p. 3; D. WIEDEMANN (Germany), p. 6; G. TU (Macau), p. 3; A. OUERFELLI and Y. EL-BENNA (Tunisia), p. 6; Bundesgerichtshof, October 6, 2016 – I ZB 13/15, NZG 2017, 227.

[216]   From a comparative perspective, see P. HOLLANDER, "Report on the Public Policy Exception in the New York Convention" (2016) 10 *Disp. Resol. Int'l* 35 ff.; P. SCHLOSSER, "Annex to the Commentary on §1061 of the German Code of Civil Procedure" in R. BORK and H. ROTH (eds.), *Stein Jonas Kommentar zur Zivilprozessordnung*, 23rd ed., vol. 10, Mohr Siebeck, Tübingen 2015, marginal no. 317.

[217]   N. DE ARAUJO and M. DE NARDI (Brazil), p. 5 f., p. 7.

[218]   Bundesgerichtshof, February 1, 2001 – III ZR 332/99, NJW-RR 2001, 1059.

[219]   Q. HE (China), p. 4; D. WIEDEMANN (Germany), p. 7; D. TSIKRIKAS (Greece), p. 19 f.; J. KRAMBERGER ŠKERL (Slovenia), p. 6; H. PEKCANITEZ and E. ALPAY (Turkey), p. 6.

Intersentia

international."[220] The "ordre public international" includes rules and values which, from the French perspective, must be reinforced and upheld even in international cases.[221] The same standard applies to arbitral awards given in cross-border disputes by arbitral tribunals seated in France (Article 1514 of the French Code of Civil Procedure). However, in purely domestic cases, the stricter standard of national public policy applies (Article 1488 of the French Code of Civil Procedure).

With respect to setting aside an arbitral award by a tribunal seated in Switzerland, the Swiss Federal Court has ruled that the award is incompatible with public policy (Article 190(2)(e) of the Swiss Private International Law Act) only if it violates the essential and broadly recognized values that, from the Swiss perspective, must be the basis of every legal system,[222] and that an international perspective must be taken into account in making this assessment.[223] If both parties to the arbitration are domiciled abroad, they can even completely avoid public policy scrutiny by agreeing on a waiver of remedies (Article 192(1) of the Swiss Private International Law Act). However, in the case of such a waiver, the New York Convention applies analogously to any enforcement of the arbitral award in Switzerland.[224] It should be noted that with respect to arbitral proceedings before tribunals seated in Switzerland, there are separate legal regimes for cases with an international element, which are governed by the Private International Law Act, and for purely domestic cases, which are governed by the Code of Civil Procedure. However, parties may switch between these regimes (Article 353(2) of the Swiss Code of Civil Procedure and Article 176(2) of the Swiss Private International Law Act). Under the regime for domestic cases, a party can apply for the setting aside of the award on the basis of arbitrariness (Article 393(e) of the Swiss Code of Civil Procedure).[225]

For the purposes of the recognition and enforcement of foreign arbitral awards under the New York Convention (Article 194 of the Swiss Private

---

[220] On the development of this approach, see most recently E. LOQUIN, "L'ordre public et l'arbitrage" (2018) 4 *Revue de Jurisprudence Commerciale* 1, 12 ff.; see also U. HAAS, *Die Anerkennung und Vollstreckung ausländischer und internationaler Schiedssprüche*, Duncker & Humblot, Berlin 1991, pp. 220 f.

[221] M.-E. ANCEL, P. DEUMIER, and M. LAAZOUZI, *Droit des contrats internationaux*, 2nd ed., Dalloz, Paris 2020, marginal no. 578.

[222] Bundesgericht BGE 132 III 389, c. 2.2.3; BGE 144 III 120, c. 5.1.

[223] Bundesgericht BGE 120 II 155.

[224] It is unclear whether, in such cases, the grounds for refusal provided for in the New York Convention apply in full or whether only those grounds for refusal that are also grounds for setting aside under the Private International Law Act can be asserted; see P.M. PATOCCHI and C. JERMINI, "Commentary on Article 192 of the Swiss Private International Law Act" in H. HONSELL, N.P. VOGT, A.K. SCHNYDER, and S. BERTI (eds.), *Basler Kommentar Internationales Privatrecht*, 3rd ed., Helbing Lichtenhahn, Basel 2013, marginal nos. 30 f.

[225] The concept of arbitrariness is broader than that of public policy; see Bundesgericht BGE 132 III 389, consideration 2.2.2.

International Law Act), the Swiss Federal Court has taken the position that the same principles apply as for foreign judgments.[226] Accordingly, the attenuated standard that generally applies in the field of recognition and enforcement (*ordre public atténué*) applies, but it is sufficient that recognition and enforcement would be incompatible with the fundamental principles of the Swiss legal system.[227] It is not required that the violation is so serious that, from the Swiss perspective, no civilized legal system could tolerate it.[228] However, it is important not to overestimate the practical differences between the "transnational" public policy standard used in setting aside proceedings and the standard used in recognition and enforcement cases.[229]

In Germany, a distinction is often made between a stricter public policy standard (*ordre public interne*, internal public policy) with respect to awards given by tribunals seated in Germany (§§1059(2)(2)(a) and 1060 of the German Code of Civil Procedure) and a more generous standard (*ordre public international*, international public policy) with respect to the recognition and enforcement of foreign arbitral awards (§1061 of the German Code of Civil Procedure and Article V(2)(b) of the New York Convention).[230] However, it is unclear how much difference there actually is in practice between "internal" and "international" public policy.[231] Unlike in France or Switzerland, no distinction is made between domestic and cross-border cases with respect to awards issued by tribunals seated in Germany.[232] Yet, some scholars argue that the public policy standard should be more lenient in cases with a cross-border element.[233]

---

[226] Bundesgericht 4A_233/2010, consideration 3.2.1; 5A_427/2011, considerations 7, 7.1.
[227] Bundesgericht 4A_233/2010, consideration 3.2.1; 5A_427/2011, considerations 7, 7.1; 5A_165/2014, consideration 5.
[228] On the distinction between public policy scrutiny with respect to setting aside Swiss arbitral awards and with respect to recognition and enforcement of foreign arbitral awards, see B. BERGER and F. KELLERHALS, *International and Domestic Arbitration in Switzerland*, 3rd ed., Stämpfli, Berne 2015, marginal no. 2097. Meanwhile, equal treatment is advocated by T. GÖKSU, *Schiedsgerichtsbarkeit*, Dike, Zurich 2014, marginal no. 2446.
[229] See, e.g., BGE 141 III 229, where the Bundesgericht, while referring to its "transnational" public policy standard, set aside an arbitral award on the basis of a violation of the *res judicata* principles of the forum.
[230] D. WIEDEMANN (Germany), p. 7; Bundesgerichtshof, January 29, 2009 – III ZB 88/07, BGHZ 179, 304; W. VOIT, "Commentary on §1061 of the German Code of Civil Procedure" in H.-J. MUSIELAK and W. VOIT (eds.), *Zivilprozessordnung*, 17th ed., Vahlen, Munich 2020, marginal no. 23; I. SAENGER, "Commentary on §1061 of the German Code of Civil Procedure" in I. SAENGER (ed.), *Zivilprozessordnung*, 8th ed., Nomos, Baden-Baden 2019, marginal no. 15; C. VÖLKER, above n. 8, pp. 265 f.
[231] See K.H. SCHWAB and G. WALTER, *Schiedsgerichtsbarkeit: Kommentar*, 7th ed., C.H. Beck, Munich 2005, chapter 30 marginal no. 21; C. VÖLKER, above n. 8, pp. 266 f.
[232] C. VÖLKER, above n. 8, p. 270.
[233] See P. SCHLOSSER, above n. 216, marginal no. 317.

Intersentia

Like Switzerland, Tunisia[234] seems to treat arbitral awards given by tribunals seated within the jurisdiction more generously, while Greece[235] and Turkey,[236] like Germany and France, seem to be stricter with respect to domestic awards than with respect to foreign ones. In Slovenia, meanwhile, no difference is made between domestic and foreign arbitral awards with respect to public policy scrutiny.[237]

An international public policy standard seems to apply to foreign arbitral awards in Turkey.[238] However, it is difficult to tell to what extent this concept is indeed different from the *ordre public attenué* that is recognized in many jurisdictions in the field of recognition and enforcement of judgments, where it is well accepted that not every incompatibility with mandatory rules of internal law ("ordre public interne") will result in a refusal of recognition and enforcement.[239] Even where the idea of a truly transnational public policy is advocated, the perspective taken is generally still whether certain principles should be considered as essential for every civilized society or every state following the rule of law from the perspective of the state whose judge decides about setting aside or recognition and enforcement.[240]

It is unclear whether an international or transnational approach to public policy could lead to the result that an arbitral award might be set aside even if it is not incompatible with the public policy of the state of the seat of the arbitral tribunal. Arguably, this could prevent limping awards, where there is an incompatibility with the public policy of a state where recognition or enforcement is or presumably will be sought. However, arbitration-friendly jurisdictions might be expected to be very cautious in taking such an approach. Instead, applying a specific kind of "international" public policy to arbitral awards will generally operate as a mitigating factor, meaning that courts will be more cautious in setting aside the award. There is an aspect of preventing limping awards in this context as well. There is a possibility that an award that has been set aside at the seat of the arbitration can still be recognized and enforced elsewhere.[241] By applying an international concept of public policy, situations where this actually comes to pass can be minimized (though admittedly, they would probably be very exceptional as it is).

---

[234]   A. OUERFELLI and Y. EL-BENNA (Tunisia), p. 6 f.

[235]   D. TSIKRIKAS (Greece), p. 21.

[236]   H. PEKCANITEZ and E. ALPAY (Turkey), p. 6. The national report mentions a judgment, critically received by the Turkish doctrine, according to which an arbitral award can be set aside if it results in a reduction in government revenue.

[237]   J. KRAMBERGER ŠKERL (Slovenia), p. 6.

[238]   H. PEKCANITEZ and E. ALPAY (Turkey), p. 5.

[239]   See above section 4.

[240]   For a critical assessment, see C. VÖLKER, above n. 8, pp. 283 f.

[241]   Article IX of the European Convention on International Commercial Arbitration of 21 April 1961 explicitly envisages this possibility.

9. IMPLEMENTING REGIONAL PUBLIC POLICY: POSSIBLE WAYS FORWARD

It is sometimes understood to be a specific feature of the European judicial area that the parties' and not states' interests should be at the forefront of the law of cross-border recognition and enforcement, including the operation of the public policy exception. According to the European public policy study of 2011:

> Lastly and most importantly, the perspective has changed: cooperation among courts and other judicial authorities in civil matters is aimed at implementing the substantive and procedural rights of the parties. This concept transgresses the traditional forms of judicial assistance under public international law which are mainly based on the concept of judicial assistance between sovereign states.[242]

However, the differences between EU law and the rules on the recognition and enforcement that operate outside the intra-EU relationship should not be overstated. Both within and outside the EU, there is an uneasy balance between sovereignty on the one hand, and individual rights and interests on the other hand.

It seems that in most European jurisdictions today, the opinion prevails that there is no difference in the content of public policy in the relationship with other Brussels or Lugano states as opposed to the relationship with third states.[243] It could be assumed that even if there were a regionalization of public policy in the sense that a uniform European concept of public policy were implemented, this would then also operate on a global level, perhaps with minor modifications.

Creating a uniform standard for the protection of fundamental fair trial principles at the enforcement stage would have fit in quite well with the development of the other grounds for refusal that address procedural problems. The rules of the Brussels and Lugano system on lack of proper service and on conflicting judgments, which can be understood as specific uniform rules on a facet of procedural public policy,[244] create an obligation for the state addressed to refuse recognition and enforcement.[245]

In other words, the Brussels/Lugano instruments, as opposed to the 2019 HCCH Judgments Convention, create not only a "floor" but also a "ceiling" for

---

[242] Public policy study, above n. 112, p. 24.

[243] D. WIEDEMANN (Germany), p. 5; J. KRAMBERGER ŠKERL (Slovenia), p. 4; H. DÖRNER, "Commentary on Article 45 Brussels I *bis* Regulation" in I. SAENGER (ed.), *Zivilprozessordnung*, 8th ed., Nomos, Baden-Baden 2019, marginal no. 3; A. STADLER, above n. 100, marginal no. 3. See, however, from the Swiss perspective, Bundesgericht BGE 142 III 180.

[244] P. OBERHAMMER, above n. 99, marginal nos. 29 f.

[245] With respect to the rule on conflicting judgments, see *Italian Leather SpA v. WECO Polstermöbel GmbH & Co.*, above n. 193.

the recognition and enforcement of judgments falling within their scope.[246] The operation of the public policy exception may be considered as a deviation from this basic concept, as it leaves some freedom for the states bound by those instruments to set the standards that a foreign judgment must comply with in order to benefit from the free movement of judgments established by these instruments. Where the public policy exception only protects the regulatory public interests of the state where recognition or enforcement is sought, this is not problematic. However, as procedural public policy also covers violations of fundamental fair trial principles that are not addressed by other grounds for refusal, it is not self-evident that it should remain a national concept. This is especially true in an "area of freedom, security and justice" with a largely common understanding of fundamental fair trial rights, underpinned by Article 6(1) ECHR and Article 47 of the Charter of Fundamental Rights.[247] Therefore, the idea that procedural public policy should be replaced by a set of uniform minimum standards of fair trial seems appealing within the framework of a European regional instrument on the free circulation of judgments,[248] though it must be recognized that it is not an easy task to define such standards.

When considering how such minimum standards should be enforced, the basic question is whether there should be a remedy in the state of origin[249] or in the state of enforcement,[250] or possibly both. In European civil procedure, the basic approach today is that the judgment debtor is expected to take the opportunity of addressing violations of fair trial rights in the state of origin. This is addressed explicitly in Article 45(1)(b) of the Brussels I *bis* Regulation with respect to a lack of proper service of the document instituting the proceedings. Where the judgment debtor could have challenged the judgment in the state of origin but failed to do so, this ground for refusal cannot subsequently be invoked in the state of enforcement. With respect to public policy, it seems to be accepted that the person against whom recognition and enforcement is sought cannot rely successfully on public policy if they did not take the opportunities available in the state of origin to challenge the judgment.[251] However, mutual trust does not go so far as to exclude the possibility of seeking refusal of recognition and enforcement if a remedy was unsuccessfully brought in the state of origin.

---

[246] Somewhat ironically, however, Member States are considered to be free with respect to the recognition and enforcement of provisional measures that were issued *ex parte* and are meant to be enforced without prior service on the debtor, as these judgments are out of the scope of the Brussels I *bis* Regulation (see the second subparagraph of Art. 2(a) of the Brussels I *bis* Regulation and Recital 33 of that Regulation).

[247] See, however, B. SUJECKI, above n. 108, p. 466, who points out that even the fair trial principles enshrined in the ECHR are interpreted differently in the Member States.

[248] See G. CUNIBERTI and I. RUEDA, above n. 116, pp. 290, 296 ff.

[249] This is favored by P. OBERHAMMER, above n. 116, p. 202.

[250] In favor of such an approach, see G. CUNIBERTI and I. RUEDA, above n. 116, p. 312.

[251] P. OBERHAMMER, above n. 99, marginal nos. 28, 40.

In particular, the court of the state where recognition or enforcement is sought is not even bound by the findings of fact or the legal assessment of the court in the state of origin when examining the proper service of the document instituting the proceedings.[252] Nor is it bound by findings of fact or law in relation to a violation of public policy.

It should be mentioned that with respect to conflicting judgments, the refusal of recognition and enforcement does not depend on whether the debtor brought a challenge in the state of origin or could have done so. The grounds for refusal dealing with conflicting judgments are perhaps the purest expression of procedural public policy. It is not only, perhaps not even mainly the debtor's individual interest that is protected by the rules on conflicting judgments, but also the requested state's interest of not having to enforce "a" and "non-a" simultaneously.[253] However, this is not necessarily easy to reconcile with the fact that recognition and enforcement must nevertheless take place if no opposition is made by the debtor.

The Brussels I *bis* Regulation and the Lugano Convention do not contain any rules on whether a judgment that violated fundamental fair trial principles, and whose recognition and enforcement can therefore be refused in other Member (or Contracting) States, can also be challenged in the state of origin. With respect to what is now Article 45(1)(a) of the Brussels I *bis* Regulation, i.e., the general public policy clause, this situation would be no different had the Commission's original proposal be adopted. The remedy envisaged in the draft Article 46 of the Commission's proposal for the Brussels I recast was, as mentioned previously, intended to operate in the state addressed. Probably there are still good reasons to provide for such a safety net in the state addressed, even within the European judicial area. This is true particularly (but not only) in cases where the judgment does not originate from proceedings that were conducted under uniform European procedural rules. However, as mentioned previously,[254] in some European instruments, public policy review in the state addressed has indeed been abolished.

It might be a shortcoming of the Brussels I *bis* Regulation and the Lugano Convention that there are no uniform rules on the possibility to challenge a judgment in the state of origin if there was a violation of fundamental fair trial rights in the proceedings. Within a judicial area with common rules on direct jurisdiction, this can lead to even greater problems than in a less integrated context. After all, the judgment creditor cannot necessarily obtain a new judgment

---

[252]   Case 166/80, *Peter Klomps v. Karl Michel*, ECLI:EU:C:1981:137, marginal nos. 15 f.; Case 228/81, *Pendy Plastic v. Pluspunkt*, ECLI:EU:C:1982:276.

[253]   See P. JENARD, "Report on the Convention on jurisdiction and the enforcement of judgments in civil and commercial matters (Signed at Brussels, 27 September 1968)' OJ 1979 C 59/1, 45; *contra*, P. OBERHAMMER, above n. 99, marginal no. 81.

[254]   See above section 3.2.

Intersentia

365

in the state where recognition or enforcement was refused, as there may not be a suitable basis for jurisdiction in that state. If one were to assume that in such cases, there is an unwritten *forum necessitatis* in the state addressed for creating a new title,[255] this could provoke conflicting judgments. There is therefore a case for creating uniform rules on challenging judgments that were made in violation of fair trial rights in the state of origin.[256] The first steps in this direction have been made in Article 19(4) of the European Service Regulation, Article 19 of the European Enforcement Order Regulation, Article 20 of the European Order for Payment Regulation and Article 18 of the European Small Claims Regulation. However, these rules are far from being sufficiently comprehensive. Having such rules would not necessarily preclude having a corresponding ground for refusal in the state addressed as well. The party opposing recognition or enforcement could either be given a choice between attacking the judgment in the state of origin or in the state addressed, or a priority of a challenge in the state of origin could be established. Implementing such parallel remedies might even be a viable first step toward a fully integrated system, as it would avoid the controversial measure of simply abolishing the refusal ground before giving citizens, businesses, and courts the opportunity to gather experience with remedies operating in the state of origin.

10. ENFORCEMENT

10.1. ATTACHMENT OF ASSETS

While there is a large body of law and doctrine on the recognition and enforcement of foreign judgments, the cross-border aspects of the enforcement procedure itself are subject to much less explicit regulation and there is great legal uncertainty in this regard. The enforcement procedure itself remains a matter for national law and there is little cross-border cooperation. This may indirectly contribute to the fact that there is significantly less cross-border litigation and enforcement than one might expect considering the volume of cross-border transactions.

Even within the EU, there are hardly any uniform rules in this field, apart from the European Account Preservation Order (EAPO) Regulation. It is widely accepted that Article 24(5) of the Brussels I *bis* Regulation is no rule on

---

[255] This is advocated by R. Geimer, "Introduction to Regulation 44/2001" in R. Geimer and R. Schütze (eds.), *Europäisches Zivilverfahrensrecht*, 3rd ed., C.H. Beck, Munich 2010, marginal no. 80; P. Oberhammer, "Commentary on Article 33 Regulation 44/2001" in *Stein/Jonas Kommentar zur Zivilprozessordnung*, 22nd ed., vol. 10, Mohr Siebeck, Tübingen 2011, marginal no. 16.
[256] See also P. Oberhammer, above n. 116, p. 202.

jurisdiction for enforcement measures.[257] It is also the general understanding that the Brussels I *bis* Regulation is not a basis for the recognition or enforcement of foreign enforcement measures,[258] with the exception of judgments ordering a payment by way of penalty (Article 55). The EAPO Regulation only has a limited scope of application and leaves measures available under national law untouched. So far, it seems to have had little practical impact. The lack of cooperation at the enforcement level might be an impediment to the functioning of the European judicial area, where the uniform rules on jurisdiction have made it more difficult to sue the debtor at the place where enforcement can presumably be carried into effect.

Particularly with respect to movable and especially to non-corporeal assets, this uncoordinated situation can create significant difficulties for the judgment creditor and serious risks of inappropriate outcomes for third-party debtors, particularly but not only the risk of being forced to pay twice (to the judgment debtor and the judgment creditor).[259]

It seems universally accepted that enforcement authorities are only entitled to act on the territory of their own state. There is also a widely shared view that only assets located within the jurisdiction can be attached,[260] but this is much less clear and often based on mistaken premises. Upon a closer look, it is not possible to establish public international law limits on actions of enforcement authorities beyond the prohibition of physical constraint on a foreign territory.[261] Therefore, in the absence of bilateral or multilateral agreements, it is a matter for national law whether the jurisdiction of enforcement authorities also covers the attachment of foreign assets, as far as such attachment is possible without performing physical acts abroad.

The issue mainly arises with respect to non-corporeal assets.[262] In many jurisdictions, the debtor's domicile is the primary forum for the attachment of

---

[257] See e.g. T. DOMEJ, *Internationale Zwangsvollstreckung und Haftungsverwirklichung*, Mohr Siebeck, Tübingen 2016, pp. 267 ff.; J. WOLBER, "Die Pfändbarkeit eines Gesellschaftsanteils an einer britischen LLP im Inland: Zugleich ein Beitrag zu den Grundlagen des Europäischen Zwangsvollstreckungsrechts" (2019) *EuZW* 863, 864.

[258] T. DOMEJ, above n. 257, pp. 446 ff.

[259] See T. DOMEJ, "Internationale Zwangsvollstreckung zwischen Territorialitätsprinzip, Gläubigerinteressen und Schuldnerschutz" in B. HESS (ed.), *Die Anerkennung im Internationalen Zivilprozessrecht – Europäisches Vollstreckungsrecht*, Gieseking, Bielefeld 2014, pp. 109, 118.

[260] N. DE ARAUJO and M. DE NARDI (Brazil), p. 10; A. OUERFELLI and Y. EL-BENNA (Tunisia), pp. 8 f. This also seems to be the view taken by the German Bundesgerichtshof; see most recently its judgment of April 3, 2019 – VII ZB 24/17, NJW-RR 2019, 930.

[261] See, in detail, T. DOMEJ, above n. 257, pp. 165 ff.

[262] It is well established that corporeal assets can only be attached if they are located in the state where enforcement is sought (see, e.g., D. WIEDEMANN (Germany), p. 9), regardless of whether the place of physical constraint or the location of assets is the decisive connecting factor. If only the place of physical constraint is relevant, one might still ask whether the debtor could be ordered to bring the assets into the jurisdiction, and indeed some jurisdictions provide for possibilities to make orders to such an effect.

such assets, and the third party's domicile or other specific connecting factors relating to the asset in question are only referred to as the relevant basis for jurisdiction in cases where the judgment debtor is domiciled abroad.[263] Nevertheless, as indicated above, it is often assumed that the location of assets, whether corporeal or not, is always a prerequisite for enforcement jurisdiction. However, it is also broadly recognized that it is a matter for national law to determine the situs of (at least) non-corporeal assets. Many jurisdictions seem to take a flexible approach, considering it to be sufficient that there is a reasonable link between the assets and the jurisdiction.[264] Therefore, a restriction of jurisdiction to assets within the territory does little to remove risks for (especially) the third party.[265]

There seems to be a tendency, also followed by the EAPO Regulation, to restrict the attachment of debts in cross-border cases to the courts at the third party's domicile or relevant branch.[266] However, this is by no means a settled matter. There are jurisdictions like Germany, where a much more flexible (if also unsettled) approach is followed by the courts and where the prevailing doctrinal opinion advocates a generous approach to jurisdiction for the garnishment of debts in cross-border situations.[267] In Japan and Switzerland,[268] garnishment is possible if the debtor is domiciled within the jurisdiction, even if the third-party debtor is domiciled abroad. However, in Japan, the courts have the power to look at the circumstances of the case and consider whether it is reasonable to issue a garnishee order against the foreign third party.[269]

Where a generous approach to enforcement jurisdiction is taken, practical difficulties often arise with respect to the service of garnishee orders out of the jurisdiction, particularly on the third party. Some take the view that under the Hague Service Convention, a request for such service may be refused on the basis of Article 13 of that Convention (infringement of sovereignty and security).[270] This issue does not arise within the European judicial area, as the European

---

[263] See, e.g., §828(2) of the German Code of Civil Procedure; §18(3) of the Austrian Enforcement Act (Exekutionsordnung). Concerning the Swiss approach, see T. DOMEJ, above n. 257, pp. 16 ff.

[264] N. DE ARAUJO and M. DE NARDI (Brazil), p. 10.

[265] DOMEJ, above n. 259, pp. 109 ff.

[266] See, e.g., D. TSIKRIKAS (Greece), pp. 26 f. For a particularly generous approach in this respect, see R. GEIMER, above n. 185, marginal no. 3212.

[267] D. WIEDEMANN (Germany), p. 10. For a detailed discussion of German doctrine and case law in this respect, see T. DOMEJ, above n. 257, pp. 47 ff., 71 ff.

[268] On the Swiss approach, see in detail T. DOMEJ, above n. 257, pp. 31 ff.

[269] K. TAKESHITA (Japan), pp. 12 ff.

[270] See D. GAUTHEY and A. MARKUS, L'entraide judiciaire internationale en matière civile, Stämpfli, Berne 2014, marginal no. 306; A. MARKUS, "Drittschuldners Dillema" in M. JAMETTI GREINER, B. BERGER, and A. GÜNGERICH (eds.), Rechtsetzung und Rechtsdurchsetzung. Festschrift für Franz Kellerhals zum 65. Geburtstag, Stämpfli, Berne 2005, pp. 177, 188; for further references, see T. DOMEJ, above n. 257, p. 191 fn. 40.

Service Regulation does not contain such a ground for refusal to comply with a request for service.[271] Nevertheless, it can cause friction if garnishee orders are served in jurisdictions that consider this as an intrusion upon their sovereignty.

In Germany, the prevailing view is that garnishee orders can be served on third parties abroad. Where the third party is domiciled in another EU Member State, the European Service Regulation is considered to apply.[272] Germany does not oppose to service of foreign garnishee orders to third parties in Germany (see section 84(6) of the Rechtshilfeordnung in Zivilsachen). However, if a request for service is made to a German authority in such a case, the third party is informed that nothing can be inferred from the service concerning whether or to what extent the garnishee order is effective in Germany, and whether or to what extent the third-party debtor is obliged to pay to the creditor.[273]

It seems that in most jurisdictions, at least those belonging to the civil law world, it is not a requirement for the possibility to enforce that the judgment debt itself (or the judgment debtor personally) is connected to the jurisdiction.[274] In many jurisdictions, there are mechanisms that can make it more difficult for foreign creditors to attach assets, particularly assets belonging to a debtor domiciled outside the state where the assets are located. In particular, this can be the effect of some principles that have been developed to limit the operation of exorbitant fora by requiring a connecting factor – which is then, in effect, often the creditor's domicile. However, these mechanisms usually do not seem to apply in cases where the creditor has an enforceable title against the judgment debtor.

10.2. RECOGNITION AND ENFORCEMENT OF FOREIGN GARNISHEE ORDERS

The issue of extraterritorial effects of garnishee orders can arise in various contexts. In practice, the most salient issue from the third party's perspective

---

[271] T. DOMEJ, above n. 257, p. 192.

[272] D. WIEDEMANN (Germany), pp. 13 f. See also F. BAUR, R. STÜRNER, and A. BRUNS, *Zwangsvollstreckungsrecht*, 13th ed., C.F. Müller, Heidelberg 2006, marginal no. 55.30; T. DOMEJ, above n. 257, pp. 58, 77, 192 fn. 41; B. HESS, *Europäisches Zivilprozessrecht*, C.F. Müller, Heidelberg 2010, §10 marginal no. 151; J. RIEBOLD, *Die Europäische Kontenpfändung*, Mohr Siebeck, Tübingen 2014, pp. 264 ff.

[273] D. WIEDEMANN (Germany), p. 14.

[274] See, however, Art. 13(2) of the 2019 HCCH Judgments Convention, according to which "[t]he court of the requested State shall not refuse the recognition or enforcement of a judgment under this Convention on the ground that recognition or enforcement should be sought in another State" – a provision that aims at preventing resort to *forum non conveniens* in the enforcement context and that is implicitly based on the assumption that there is a probability of jurisdictions relying on *forum non conveniens* in this context. In this context, see also R. BRAND, above n. 176, pp. 33 ff.

Intersentia

369

is the recognition or acceptance of the discharge effect of a payment to the garnishor. Meanwhile, from the garnishor's perspective, the question arises whether they can enforce the garnished debt against the third party. While in some systems, a title for enforcement is created against the third party in the course of the garnishment proceedings,[275] in others (such as Germany), the garnishor has to bring a separate lawsuit against the third party to obtain such a title.[276] Depending on the procedure in which a title against the third party is created, that title might be eligible for recognition and enforcement as a judgment.[277] However, some take the view that this could be refused on the basis of public policy, at least if giving the garnishee order is considered as an inappropriate exercise of enforcement jurisdiction.[278]

Particularly in cases where no judgment or equivalent title is created against the third party but only the claim or the right to enforce it is transferred to the judgment creditor, there is significant legal uncertainty concerning the possibility of cross-border recognition of the effects of the garnishment.[279] This, in turn, can lead to a risk of double jeopardy, particularly in cases where the third party can be sued both in the state where the garnishee order was issued and in one where that order is not recognized.

While some jurisdictions seem to refuse outright to contemplate the recognition or enforcement of foreign garnishee orders,[280] others could be more open toward such a possibility.[281] Realistically speaking, the matter probably has not been given a great deal of thought in many jurisdictions.[282] However, in German doctrine, there has been a rather broad discussion of it. Several avenues have been explored with respect to the recognition of foreign garnishee orders.[283] Some scholars advocate applying the rules on recognition and enforcement of judgments by analogy.[284] Others prefer an application of the rules of §343 of the German Insolvency Act (Insolvenzordnung), which governs the recognition of

---

[275] This is, for example, the case in Greece; see D. Tsikrikas (Greece), p. 28.

[276] T. Domej, above n. 257, pp. 383 f.

[277] From the perspective of the Brussels and Lugano regimes, see T. Domej, above n. 257, pp. 528 f., with further references.

[278] On this discussion, see T. Domej, above n. 257, pp. 532 ff.

[279] For more details, see T. Domej, above n. 257, pp. 490 ff.

[280] A. Ouerfelli and Y. El-Benna (Tunisia), pp. 8 f.; H. Pekcanitez and E. Alpay (Turkey), p. 9.

[281] N. de Araujo and M. De Nardi (Brazil), pp. 11 f.

[282] On the doctrine and case law in various European jurisdictions, see Domej, above n. 257, pp. 457 ff.

[283] D. Wiedemann (Germany), pp. 14 f.; T. Domej, above n. 257, pp. 460 ff.; L. Sonnabend, *Der Einziehungsprozess nach Forderungspfändung im internationalen Rechtsverkehr*, Otto Schmidt, Cologne 2007, p. 49; J. Wolber, *Schuldnerschutz im Europäischen Zwangsvollstreckungsrecht*, Mohr Siebeck, Tübingen 2015, pp. 156, 237, 240.

[284] T. Domej, above n. 257, pp. 504 ff.; R. Geimer, above n. 185, marginal no. 3288 with further references.

foreign insolvency decrees.[285] Case law is scarce and inconclusive.[286] The Higher Regional Court of Oldenburg took the position that foreign garnishee orders can be recognized according to the rules on the recognition and enforcement of foreign judgments, but in the case at hand, recognition was refused on the basis of public policy because the garnishee order had not been served on the third-party debtor.[287] The Federal Labour Court,[288] the Higher Regional Court of Frankfurt,[289] and the Labour Court of Berlin[290] refused to recognize foreign garnishee orders. Even if a foreign garnishee order cannot be procedurally recognized, it may be appropriate to take it into consideration at the substantive law level.[291]

10.3. MANAGING RISKS FOR THIRD-PARTY DEBTORS

Trying to reduce the risks for the third party by creating restrictive rules on jurisdiction (in particular, restricting jurisdiction to the third party's domicile or relevant branch) might seem tempting, but it also creates opportunities for abuse and can make enforcement very difficult. It might be a possible way to address such problems to focus on developing *in personam* enforcement measures that only operate against the judgment debtor for cross-border situations.[292] In England and Wales, receivership orders have been used for this purpose in an ingenious way,[293] which might serve as an inspiration for civil law jurisdictions, even though one should not set one's hopes too high in this respect. In any case, it is necessary to be aware that cross-border enforcement on the basis of creative use of existing instruments is probably not a viable option for most everyday cases, but rather one for high-profile cases where large amounts of money are involved.[294] Where effective protection for the third party cannot be guaranteed, it seems appropriate to refrain from giving garnishee orders outside the state of the third party's domicile or residence, unless the attached debt is closely connected with the state of garnishment.[295]

---

[285] J. LANGE, *Internationale Rechts- und Forderungspfändung*, Duncker & Humblot, Berlin 2004, pp. 343 ff.

[286] D. WIEDEMANN (Germany), p. 15; T. DOMEJ, above n. 257, pp. 460 ff.

[287] Oberlandesgericht Oldenburg, April 25, 1995 – 1 U 161/94; H. SCHACK, "Zur Anerkennung ausländischer Forderungspfändungen" [1997] *IPRax* 318 ff.

[288] German Bundesarbeitsgericht, March 19, 1996 – 9 AZR 656/94, NZA 1997, 334.

[289] Oberlandesgericht Frankfurt, February 16, 2011 – 17 U 234/10, WM 2011, 693.

[290] Arbeitsgericht Berlin, September 29 2004 – 86 Ca 10240/04, BeckRS 2004, 300803263.

[291] P. GOTTWALD, above n. 3, marginal no. 79; T. DOMEJ, above n. 257, pp. 525 f.

[292] See, in more detail, T. DOMEJ, above n. 257, pp. 355 ff., 440; T. DOMEJ, above n. 259, p. 122.

[293] For a more detailed analysis and references to the relevant case law, see T. DOMEJ, above n. 257, pp. 124 ff.

[294] T. DOMEJ, above n. 257, pp. 129 f.; T. DOMEJ, above n. 259, pp. 122 f.

[295] T. DOMEJ, above n. 257, p. 564.

There will be those who think that creating an international convention would be the best way to address the issues of cross-border circulation and the effects of garnishee orders. While this might theoretically appear to be a good solution, it is unrealistic at this stage that this could be addressed in an appropriate fashion by binding multilateral rules, particularly at the global scale. Even at the European level,[296] it has so far been impossible to create a satisfactory set of rules for cross-border issues of enforcement. Addressing the issue on a case-by-case basis seems to be preferable for the time being. However, it seems necessary to stop looking at such issues primarily from a sovereignty or territoriality perspective.[297]

10.4. SEARCH AND DISCLOSURE OF ASSETS

In general, there are two basic approaches to uncovering the debtor's assets, which may of course also be used in combination. One is to oblige the debtor to give disclosure and the other is to allow the creditor access to information provided by authorities (e.g., tax statements, social security information, and entries in public registers) or third parties (in particular, potential third-party debtors such as employers or banks).[298] Regardless of which approach is taken, prerequisites and modalities can vary greatly from jurisdiction to jurisdiction.

The ingenious use of rules on the disclosure of assets can be a tool to determine in which jurisdiction it is best to introduce enforcement proceedings. However, where information must be obtained from the debtor, which will often be the case with respect to assets whose location is unknown, there is an obvious risk that assets might be taken elsewhere before enforcement can effectively take place. Most civil law jurisdictions do not provide for counterparts of worldwide freezing orders,[299] which would, however, seem to be a necessary accompaniment to disclosure obligations in the cross-border context.

---

[296] There have been multiple suggestions to create a European instrument on cross-border enforcement; see, e.g., A.K. BITTER, *Vollstreckbarerklärung und Zwangsvollstreckung in der Europäischen Union*, Mohr Siebeck, Tübingen 2009, pp. 229 ff.; W. KENNETT, *The Enforcement of Judgments in Europe*, Oxford University Press, Oxford 2000, pp. 283 ff.; M. SCHIMRICK, *Die unmittelbar grenzüberschreitende Forderungsvollstreckung im internationalen und europäischen Rechtsraum*, Dr. Kovač, Hamburg 2012, pp. 253 ff.; for further references, see T. DOMEJ, above n. 257, p. 3 fn. 8.

[297] See T. DOMEJ, above n. 259, p. 118.

[298] From the EU perspective, see COM(2008) 128, pp. 3 f.

[299] See, e.g., F. SARANOVIC, "Jurisdiction and Freezing Injunctions: A Reassessment" (2019) 68 *ICLQ* 639; B. GIROUD, "Do You Speak Mareva? How Worldwide Freezing Orders are Enforced in Switzerland" (2012/2013) 14 *Yearbook of Private International Law* 443.

The European Commission commissioned a study, delivered in 2004, on the transparency of a debtor's assets[300] and subsequently published a Green Paper on this matter.[301] Several proposals were made to enhance legal certainty and uniformity of approaches in this field, but to comparatively little avail. However, in the EAPO Regulation, the EU legislator took a modest step toward creating European minimum standards for access to information (Article 14):

> 5. Each Member State shall make available in its national law at least one of the following methods of obtaining the information referred to in paragraph 1:
>
> (a) an obligation on all banks in its territory to disclose, upon request by the information authority, whether the debtor holds an account with them;
>
> (b) access for the information authority to the relevant information where that information is held by public authorities or administrations in registers or otherwise;
>
> (c) the possibility for its courts to oblige the debtor to disclose with which bank or banks in its territory he holds one or more accounts where such an obligation is accompanied by an in personam order by the court prohibiting the withdrawal or transfer by him of funds held in his account or accounts up to the amount to be preserved by the Preservation Order; or
>
> (d) any other methods which are effective and efficient for the purposes of obtaining the relevant information, provided that they are not disproportionately costly or time-consuming.
>
> Irrespective of the method or methods made available by a Member State, all authorities involved in obtaining the information shall act expeditiously.

In Germany, the debtor today can be ordered to disclose all their assets if they do not satisfy the judgment claim within two weeks after being requested by the *Gerichtsvollzieher* (enforcement officer) to do so (§§802c and 802f of the German Code of Civil Procedure). Where there has been an unsuccessful attempt at enforcement, disclosure can be ordered immediately (§807 of the German Code of Civil Procedure). Switzerland takes a similar approach, obliging the debtor to disclose all their assets, including those in the hands of third parties, to the enforcement officer, as far as this is necessary to satisfy the debt (Article 91(1)(2) of the Schuldbetreibungs- und Konkursgesetz). Yet, in some jurisdictions, it is a prerequisite for obtaining a disclosure of assets from the debtor that an unsuccessful attempt at enforcement has been carried out.[302]

---

[300] Study JAI/A3/2002/02; general report (prepared by BURKHARD HESS) available at http://www2.ipr.uni-heidelberg.de/studie/General%20Report%20Version%20of%2018%20Feb%202004.pdf, pp. 20 ff.

[301] COM(2008) 128.

[302] See, e.g., D. TSIKRIKAS (Greece), p. 28 f.

In Germany, all assets (including those located abroad) must be disclosed.[303] This is also the position in Greece[304] and China.[305] In Turkey, meanwhile, the debtor's disclosure obligation is considered to be limited to assets located within the jurisdiction.[306] Third parties' obligations to disclose information about the debtor's assets may also extend to assets situated abroad.[307]

In Brazil, there is no duty of the judgment debtor to disclose assets, whether domestic or foreign.[308] Instead, assets are generally searched for in public registers.[309] Enquiries to tax registries are also frequently used.[310] Obviously, such registries only provide information that is stored in them, which means that often only assets within the jurisdiction will be covered. However, tax authorities may possess information about foreign assets owned by the judgment debtor.[311]

10.5. OBLIGATIONS TO PERFORM OR TO REFRAIN FROM ACTING

The cross-border enforcement of judgments ordering injunctive relief can raise a host of questions and difficulties. Many of these arise in situations where the relief is not ordered in a final judgment, but as a provisional measure. This issue will not be addressed in detail in this chapter. Even if final judgments ordering the debtor to behave or to refrain from behaving in a certain way are looked at, frictions and uncertainties abound when it comes to cross-border enforcement. In civil law jurisdictions, judgments ordering permanent injunctive relief are generally considered to be eligible for recognition and enforcement subject to the same conditions as money judgments,[312] but there are many open questions as to how they should be enforced in cross-border situations.

There are different methods of enforcing obligations to perform or to refrain from acting. Where the judgment debtor is obliged to carry out an activity

---

[303] D. WIEDEMANN (Germany), p. 19; Landgericht Frankfurt am Main, September 29, 2008 – 2-09 T 327/08; C.W. HERGENRÖDER, "Das Vermögensverzeichnis: Auskunftspflichtige und Auskunftspflichten" [2018] *DGVZ* 221, 225; M. WÜRDINGER, "Commentary on §802c of the German Code of Civil Procedure" in R. BORK and H. ROTH (eds.), *Stein/Jonas Kommentar zur Zivilprozessordnung*, 23rd ed., vol. 8, Mohr Siebeck, Tübingen 2017, marginal no. 12.
[304] D. TSIKRIKAS (Greece), p. 29.
[305] Q. HE (China), p. 18.
[306] H. PEKCANITEZ and E. ALPAY (Turkey), p. 10.
[307] See, e.g., A. OUERFELLI and Y. EL-BENNA (Tunisia), p. 9.
[308] N. DE ARAUJO and M. DE NARDI (Brazil), p. 14.
[309] Ibid.
[310] Ibid., pp. 14 f.
[311] See ibid., p. 15.
[312] I. BACH, above n. 8, marginal no. 4.1; R. GEIMER, above n. 185, marginal no. 2853.

that could also be performed by another person, the judgment creditor can be authorized to commission substitute performance at the judgment debtor's expense. Where only the debtor personally can comply with the judgment, either by doing something only they can do or by refraining from acting in a certain manner, this is of course not an option. In some cases, direct compulsion (in particular, measures directly preventing the debtor from committing certain infringements) may still be possible. Mostly, however, indirect compulsion is used to enforce such obligations. The judgment debtor may be punished for contempt of court or ordered to pay a fine to the state. In other systems, a civil fine (*astreinte*) can be made payable to the judgment creditor.[313] Such enforcement measures might be ordered in the judgment itself or in separate enforcement proceedings.

The main issues that arise in this context are how foreign judgments ordering a certain behavior are to be enforced, whether enforcement measures are allowed with respect to behavior abroad, and whether orders made for the purpose of enforcing a certain behavior (either abroad or within the jurisdiction) can themselves circulate.

Even within the EU, significant legal uncertainty persists around these issues. One of the provisions aimed at resolving it is Article 55 of the Brussels I *bis* Regulation, which states that "[a] judgment given in a Member State which orders a payment by way of a penalty shall be enforceable in the Member State addressed only if the amount of the payment has been finally determined by the court of origin." While this provision seems straightforward enough at first glance, it raises a number of difficult issues.[314] Another rule designed to overcome difficulties in this context is Article 54 of the Brussels I *bis* Regulation, introduced by the 2012 recast, which provides that: "If a judgment contains a measure or an order which is not known in the law of the Member State addressed, that measure or order shall, to the extent possible, be adapted to a measure or an order known in the law of that Member State which has equivalent effects attached to it and which pursues similar aims and interests."

The Greek national report states that from the Greek perspective, it is the task of the court giving the judgment to decide about the measures that should be taken to enforce it and that in cross-border situations, Greek courts will enforce the measures of constraint that were ordered by the court in the state of origin.[315] In Germany, both enforcing the fine imposed by the foreign court

---

[313]   On the different models, see in detail O. Remien, *Rechtsverwirklichung durch Zwangsgeld*, Mohr Siebeck, Tübingen 1992.

[314]   See, e.g., P. Mankowski, "Commentary on Article 55 Brussels I *bis* Regulation" in T. Rauscher, above n. 16, marginal nos. 1 ff.

[315]   D. Tsikrikas (Greece), pp. 25 f.

Intersentia

and issuing an order imposing a fine in Germany are considered as viable options.[316]

In the *Realchemie*[317] case, which concerned the enforcement of a fine payable to the state ("Ordungsgeld" pursuant to §888 of the German Code of Civil Procedure) for breach of an order prohibiting certain patent infringements, the ECJ ruled:

> The concept of "civil and commercial matters" in Article 1 of Council Regulation (EC) No 44/2001 of 22 December 2000 on jurisdiction and the recognition and enforcement of judgments in civil and commercial matters must be interpreted as meaning that that regulation applies to the recognition and enforcement of a decision of a court or tribunal that contains an order to pay a fine in order to ensure compliance with a judgment given in a civil and commercial matter.

While this case may serve as a door-opener for cooperation at the enforcement level beyond the cross-border enforcement of fines payable to the creditor, many issues remain unresolved, such as who can apply for enforcement of fines payable to the state[318] and where the proceeds of enforcement should go.

Risks for the judgment debtor, not least the risk of multiple enforcement, can arise from the fact that enforcement jurisdiction remains subject to national law. Even if the judgment debtor can avert additional burdens arising out of multiple enforcement actions by complying with the judgment, the risks of abuse and of upsetting the balance between the parties arising from the possibility of enforcing the same judgment in multiple jurisdictions should not be taken too lightly. On the other hand, the lack of coordinated rules on where judgments ordering injunctive relief should be enforced can also create the risk of negative conflicts of jurisdiction. As there are usually no explicit statutory provisions on these matters, it is mainly left to doctrine and case law to develop appropriate approaches. The Greek national report notes that it is difficult to say whether judgments prescribing a certain behavior should be enforced at the debtor's domicile or at the place where the behavior should take place.[319] The Greek reporter favors the judgment debtor's residence.[320] In German doctrine, meanwhile, there is a view that only where the coercive penalty payment is to be enforced in Germany can German courts have enforcement jurisdiction.[321] However, this does not seem

---

[316] D. WIEDEMANN (Germany), p. 16; P. GOTTWALD, "Commentary on Article 55 Brussels I *bis* Regulation" in T. RAUSCHER and W. KRÜGER above n. 142, marginal no. 8, with further references.

[317] Case C-406/09, *Realchemie Nederland BV v. Bayer CropScience AG*, ECLI:EU:C:2011:668.

[318] The Swiss Bundesgericht (BGer 4A_75/2014) has ruled out the possibility of an application by the court in the state of origin that ordered the fine.

[319] D. TSIKRIKAS (Greece), p. 25.

[320] Ibid.

[321] D. WIEDEMANN (Germany), p. 11.

to square very well with the ECJ's *Realchemie* judgment, even if strictly speaking that judgment does not deal with jurisdiction to make coercive payment orders. In China, the perception seems to be that injunctive relief is only possible with respect to behavior within the jurisdiction.[322] In Brazil, it is assumed that orders imposing a coercive fine can be recognized and enforced in the same way as a judgment on the merits.[323]

---

[322] Q. HE (China), p. 7.
[323] N. DE ARAUJO and M. DE NARDI (Brazil), p. 13.

PART II

NEW CHALLENGES
AND THEIR VARIOUS ASPECTS

Electronic Technologies in Judicial Proceedings

APPLICATION OF NEW TECHNOLOGIES IN JUDICIAL PROCEEDINGS

Francisco VERBIC*

1. Introduction 381
2. The First Dimension: Electronic Proceedings and the Tendency
   to Abandon Paper as Communication Support 382
3. The Second Dimension: Online Dispute Resolution 385
4. The Third Dimension: Artificial Intelligence in Case Management 387
5. The Fourth Dimension: New Technologies and Citizens' Access
   to Public Information. 390
6. Advantages, Risks, and Challenges Created by the Use of New
   Technologies in Judicial Proceedings. 392
7. Overall Assessment and a Look into the Future. 393

1. INTRODUCTION

This chapter analyzes electronic proceedings, online disputes resolution, artificial intelligence and access to public information. It is divided into six main sections.

Section 2 refers to electronic proceedings and the general tendency to abandon paper as a form of communication support, examining the Small Claims Procedure and the European Order for Payment Procedure.

Section 3 is dedicated to the analysis of online disputes resolution mechanisms, paying particular attention to the recent experience of the United Kingdom with the "Online Court."

---

* Lawyer (UNLP), LL.M. in International Legal Studies (NYU), Adjunct Professor of Civil Procedure (UNLP). Academic Secretary of the LL.M. in Procedural Law (UNLP). This chapter was presented in the XVI World Congress of the IAPL, held in Kobe on November 2–5, 2019, under the title "Aplicación de nuevas tecnologías al proceso judicial: proceso electrónico, resolución de controversias online, inteligencia artificial y acceso a información pública." It was translated into English by Milagros Garozzo. Special thanks to Yasmín Aguirre and María Victoria Feito Torrez for their assistance and great help in revising the translation and editing its final version.

Intersentia

Section 4 focuses on the scope and challenges of artificial intelligence as an instrument in case management and issues resolution, highlighting examples of its application within the framework of Brazil's and Colombia's Constitutional Courts.

Section 5 points towards the implication of these new technologies for citizens in terms of access to public information, offering as an example the experience of the Justice Studies Center of the Americas and its Index of Online Access to Judicial Information.

Section 6 comprises a sort of review involving some of the advantages, risks, and challenges posed by the implementation of new technologies in judicial proceedings.

Finally, section 7 aims at presenting some reflections in terms of assessment and looks into the future.

Before proceeding, some clarification is required. There are a number of issues that, although considered to be within the framework of "application of new technologies in judicial proceedings", are not addressed in this chapter. Prominent among these are the problems related to e-discovery, the management of evidence by the parties in preliminary instances, the use of information acquired by cameras placed inside vehicles and other similar devices, and the evaluation of evidence through artificial intelligence. The reason for not addressing such issues is that they are addressed by Professors Sugiyama and Picó in their contributions in this book.

2. THE FIRST DIMENSION: ELECTRONIC PROCEEDINGS AND THE TENDENCY TO ABANDON PAPER AS COMMUNICATION SUPPORT

As explained by Talmadge at the beginning of 2000 regarding the U.S. Courts of Appeal, the work by then was developed in a similar fashion to what happened in many courts around the world at the dawn of the twenty-first century: "they process written documents ... Judges of Appeal and their work teams read memorials in paper. After a written judgement is published, the paper is filed in a repository. Very often, due to the resistance of lawyers, work teams and judges themselves, and due to the fact that the resources needed were not available to move towards an electronic environment, Courts of Appeal did not use new technologies that could have made their work easier."[1]

---

[1] P.A. TALMADGE, "Briefing and Oral Argument: New Technologies and Appellate Practice" (2000) 2 *J. App. Prac. & Process* 363.

Application of New Technologies in Judicial Proceedings

In particular, at that time, Talmadge identified four aspects in which the use of new technologies could improve the work done at the Courts of Appeal. We believe that these aspects apply to all courts in general:

1. Electronic filings, motions, and pleadings: emails, fax, and shared documents can be used for communicating files containing the parties' positions. Also, videoconferences and telephone communications could prove useful to carrying out pleadings and oral defenses.[2]
2. Digital records: this could include paper-scanned documents or electronic documents. In this matter, the ease of handling the transmission of files, the possibility of remote consultation and simultaneous analysis, the possibility of searching through keywords in order to facilitate the analysis, and, of course, the saving of economic resources linked to the storage and transfer of files were all emphasized.[3]
3. Dissemination of judgments: this was traditionally done via hardcopy printed books, with clear limitations in terms of distribution and the scope of audience reach. Talmadge also noted that, by then, judgments had already started to be published on each court's webpage. This caused some problems regarding how to cite such judgments, but we consider it a minor matter compared to the great advantages in terms of the transparency and publicity generated by online outreach.
4. Recording digital files: once again, this relates to bearing the problem of storage costs.

The situation has changed greatly since the beginning of the millennium regarding the availability of technological resources, the focus and objectives of public policies in this field, and the attitude of system operators regarding the new possibilities and advantages with which these technological resources contribute.

The current opportunities to make progress in these four areas are clear, as is the need to do it in a context of general austerity in relation to worldwide systems of justice administration.

---

[2]   Regarding the situation in Costa Rica, see K.M. NAVARRO, "La inclusión de las tecnologías en la gestión judicial. Poder Judicial de República de Costa Rica", in *Revistas Sistemas Judiciales*, Centro de Estudios de Justicia de las Américas – CEJA, Año 9, N° 16, pp.48–55, which explains that: "To date, 100% of judicial offices at the national level have been interconnected with the institutional network. Besides, all legal agents have computers. Approximately 80% of court case processing is done by using the Management System of Costa Rica's Judicial Offices, and new ways of processing based on oral speech and on the concept of 'paperless' electronic courts were implemented in experimental offices in matters of payments, allowance for food, constitutional, labor, criminal, agricultural and disciplinary matters."

[3]   Regarding the situation in Paraguay, see A. MARTINEZ, "Reporte de la situación del expediente electrónico judicial en el Paraguay," in *Revista Sistemas Judiciales*, Centro de Estudios de Justicia de las Américas – CEJA, Año 9, N°16, pp. 70–72.

Intersentia

Further, it is clear that these fields of work do not apply only to appellate courts, but can also be promoted as a way to tackle tasks in all judicial branches.

In this sense, an interesting example of progress in the field of public policies can be seen in the United Kingdom, where an ambitious reform program has been launched. One of its fundamental objectives is to digitalize the civil justice system and modernize the way in which the courts operate.[4]

This program, which is supposed to be completed by 2023, involves the investment of £1 trillion, £700 million of which have already been spent on to the purposes outlined above.[5]

The European Union (EU) scenario also offers concrete examples in this respect, with years of practical experience and effective implementation. Among them, particular reference should be made to the "European Small Claims Procedure," which was set up to deal with cross-border claims of up to €5,000.[6] This procedure is initiated through the use of a standard form with all the documents relevant to hold the claim attached to it. This procedure does not require legal advice in order for the case to be heard. As informed by the European e-Justice Portal:

> Form A (application form) must be sent to the court that has the jurisdiction. Once the court receives the application form, it must fill in its part of the "Answer Form." Within 14 days of receiving the application form, the court should serve a copy of it, along with the Answer Form, on the defendant. The defendant has 30 days to reply, by filling in his or her part of the Answer Form. The court must send a copy of any reply to the plaintiff within 14 days. Within 30 days of receiving the defendant's answer (if any) the court must either give a judgment on the small claim, or request further details in writing from either party or summon the parties to be represented by a lawyer and, if the court has appropriate equipment, the hearing should be carried out through videoconference or teleconference.[7]

It should be noted that this is a procedure that, in spite of not qualifying as an online resolution method, it is almost completely digitalized. The purpose

---

[4] HMCTS, "Guidance: The HMCTS Reform Programme" (2018), available at https://www.gov.uk./guidance/the-hmcts-reform-programme.

[5] See P. CORTÉS and T. TAKAGI, "The Civil Money Claims Online: The Flagship Project of Court Digitalization in England and Wales" (2019) 25(8) *Computer and Telecommunications Law Review* 207, in which the authors explain that the modernization program goes beyond civil justices and also involves criminal justice, family justice, and the organizational structure of the courts. Among the numerous individual (although related) projects that make up the program, there are initiatives connected to online judicial filing, online expenses management, online hearings, and the creation of new services centers related to the topic.

[6] Council Regulation (EC) No 861/2007 of the European Parliament and of the Council of July 11, 2007 establishing a European Small Claims Procedure (latest consolidated version July 14, 2017). For more information on the topic, see X. KRAMER, "The European Small Claims Procedure: Striking the Balance between Simplicity and Fairness in European Litigation" (2008) 2 *Zeitschrift für Europäisches Privatrecht*, 355.

[7] See https://e-justice.europa.eu/content_small_claims-42-es.do.

of its creation was to lower costs and streamline these kinds of claims in the region.

However, particularly during the first year following its implementation, the need for taking into account certain factors that go "against this procedural streamlining" was noted.[8]

A similar development is the European Payment Order.[9] As explained by Pérez Ragone, its regulation "is simple and easy to access, and it does not require legal advice or advice from any other professional; and a set of standardized form attached as annexes of the regulation warrant it. Ease or simplicity that also allow for a uniform and automatic processing of data."[10]

3. THE SECOND DIMENSION: ONLINE DISPUTE RESOLUTION

Another of the most relevant issues at present concerning the application of new technologies to court proceedings is connected to the possibility of solving disputes virtually, exclusively through the internet.

Among the various definitions offered by the literature, one general conceptual approximation of the idea of "Online Dispute Resolution Systems" requires us to think of "Internet-based platforms that enable parties in a dispute to complete the entire resolution process, from filing through final determination, in an online environment."[11]

According to Rabinovich and Katsh, the first contact between the internet and the world of online dispute resolution took place at the beginning of the 1990s.[12] What was later called "online dispute resolution" was an initial response to new problems posed by what was, at that time, a novel environment: the – cyberspace.[13]

---

[8]   N.V. PELLEJERO, "Algunas reflexiones acerca del proceso europeo de escasa cuantía" (2011) 2(2) *Revista Chilena de Derecho y Ciencia Política* 65; among them, the author highlights some legal loopholes that make it necessary to resort to the law of each of the Member States, as well as the need for the procedure to respect the parties' human rights, which are enshrined in Art. 6 of the European Convention on Human Rights.

[9]   Council Regulation (EC) No 1896/2006 of 12 December 2006 creating a European order for payment procedure [2006] as amended by Regulation (EU) 2015/2421.

[10]   Á.P. RAGONE, "Un monitorio para la Argentina desde la experiencia comparada," delivered at "Jornadas de Profesores de la Asociación Argentina de Derecho Procesal," Mendoza, September 7–8, 2018. See also Á.P. RAGONE, "En torno al procedimiento monitorio desde el derecho procesal comparado europeo: caracterización, elementos esenciales y accidentales" (2006) 19(1) *Revista de Derecho (Valdivia)* 205.

[11]   A. SELA, "Can Computers Be Fair? How Automated and Human-Powered Online Dispute Resolution Affect Procedural Justice in Mediation and Arbitration" (2018) 33 *Ohio State Journal on Dispute Resolution* 91.

[12]   In 1994, e-commerce did not exist: sites like eBay, Amazon, and Google were yet to appear.

[13]   O.R. EINY and E. KATSH, "Technology and the Future of Dispute Systems Design" (2009) 17 *Harv. Negotiation L. Rev.* 151.

In this context, Rabinovich and Katsh say, while an increasing number of people used networks in order to interact and trade, it was unavoidable that they would start having conflicts as well. This raised an interesting question: should networks themselves promote new and better ways of solving disputes relating to their use?

The first examples of these mechanisms were born in the main e-commerce platforms. The case of eBay is the most frequently cited in terms of its success and the volume of solved disputes since its implementation.[14]

At first, the system focused on using traditional alternative means of dispute resolution, i.e., a human mediator who communicated with the parties. Therefore, innovation was limited to the way in which such communication was performed. The parties did not meet the mediator face to face; exchanges took place by email. This pilot test solved 200 cases in two weeks, achieving a high degree of satisfaction among participants.[15]

Then, the system escalated and, even though it allowed for the possibility of resorting to a human mediator, it began requiring a computer-controlled process as a first compulsory step, which in some cases could have led to an agreement without any human intervention at all.

It is no coincidence that the origin of this kind of dispute resolution mechanism can be found in consumer disputes. Later developments in this procedural field have been particularly deep in this area of substantive law.[16]

On the other side of the ocean, the United Kingdom provides one of the most interesting experiences currently developing regarding online dispute resolution, which is part of the general modernization program discussed in section 2 above. This is the system of online civil money claims, also known informally as the "Online Court."[17]

The initiative involves a simplified procedure to solve small claims through the use of technology as the main communication medium. Currently, this online proceeding comprehends not only small claims (less than £10,000), but also medium range claims (between £10,000 and £100,000). Some cases which are more complex, such as personal injury and real estate possession recovery, are excluded from its scope of application.[18]

---

[14]   https://resolutioncenter.ebay.com.

[15]   E. Katsh et al., "E-commerce, E-disputes and E-resolution: In the Shadow of 'eBay Law'" (2000) 15 *Ohio St. J. on Disp. Resol.* 705, 708.

[16]   See C. Rule and A.J. Schmidtz, "The New Handshake: Online Dispute Resolution and the Future of Consumer Protection," *Faculty Book Gallery* (2008), https://scholarcommons.scu. edu./faculty_books/406; A.J. Schmitz and C. Rule, "Online Dispute Resolution for Smart Contracts" (2019) 2 *Journal of Dispute Resolution* 103.

[17]   See at https://www.gov.uk/make-money-claim.

[18]   Ibid.

As Cortés and Takagi explain,[19] the system is much more than the digitalization of the existing process considering it brings with it important structural changes. In this context, they note that the court process is divided into three stages.

During the first stage, the Web platform helps litigants make claims and defenses. It also encourages parties to participate proactively in the negotiation of an agreement through the exchange of non-binding offers. During the second stage, legal assistance is assigned either to help litigants reach an agreement, if this has not yet been achieved, or to help them manage what is necessary for the preliminary stage of the case's adjudicatory stage. Finally, the cases that go through these two stages without reaching an agreement are processed and solved by the district judge.[20]

According to Cortés, changing from "face-to-face" judges to online judges "provides the opportunity to think justice in another way." In the context of the Online Court, he holds that it creates better conditions for judges to specialize and that the need for generalist judges to serve in the local communities disappears, resulting in more efficient and consistent ways of solving disputes.[21]

4. THE THIRD DIMENSION: ARTIFICIAL INTELLIGENCE IN CASE MANAGEMENT

In general terms, artificial intelligence has been qualified as "the most disruptive technology in the modern age."[22] However, those who put forward this argument are also aware of that, contrary to what some might think, technology is not objective. This is because algorithms and decision-making processes built on their basis are designed by those who build them, which generates the risk of (even unintentionally) transmitting their biases and personal choices and values to judicial proceedings.

In other words, this design involves discretionary choices (sometimes clearly and simply arbitrary) on the code used and the information selected to "train" the machine. Through these choices, the programmers transfer their "values,

---

[19] See P. CORTÉS and T. TAKAGI, "The Civil Money Claims Online: The Flagship Project of Court Digitalization in England and Wales" (2019) 25(8) *Computer and Telecommunications Law Review* 207.

[20] See C. RULE and A.J. SCHMIDTZ, "The New Handshake: Online Dispute Resolution and the Future of Consumer Protection," *Faculty Book Gallery* (2008), https://scholarcommons.scu.edu./faculty_books/406; A.J. SCHMITZ and C. RULE, "Online Dispute Resolution for Smart Contracts" (2019) 2 *Journal of Dispute Resolution* 103.

[21] P. CORTÉS, "Using Technology and ADR Methods to Enhance Access to Justice" (2019) 5(1) *International Journal of Online Dispute Resolution* 103.

[22] K. MANHEIM and L. KAPLAN, "Artificial Intelligence: Risks to Privacy and Democracy" (2019) 21 *Yale Journal of Law and Technology* 106.

slants and human failings,"[23] a fact that has a direct impact on the possible results of such logical processes.

In criminal courts, for example, the use of artificial intelligence has been justified as a way to produce more consistent results and to save resources.[24] However, its use has also produced discriminatory outcomes that have already been proved. A study carried out by Pro Publica showed this problem in the state of Florida in the United States and claimed, controversially, that its results were "somewhat more accurate than a coin flip."[25] In what ways had the systems failures developed? In accordance with such study, these failures resulted mostly against black people. Why did this occur? The answer to this question is due to the biases (unconscious or not) in the building and developing of the algorithms responsible for the decision-making process.

Artificial intelligence works by recognizing patterns coming either from the data provided by those who build its algorithms or from data that it itself acquires or generates autonomously, on certain assumptions, from the data with which it is provided.

Corvalán presents the link between judicial proceedings and artificial intelligence, which is based upon a basic premise of our discipline:

> Judicial proceedings are viewed as systems that aim to be "an ordered, completed whole composed by interconnected elements." The proceeding is a system presented as a finite number of operations set forth in procedural law, which allows for legal solutions to problems through the application of rules and principles. In this way, if it is a system of concatenated and coherent rules and orders to achieve an aim, then it works with a very similar logic to that of algorithms. That is to say, there are instructions to follow based on rules to attain a goal. This is where the connection between artificial intelligence (hereinafter "AI") and procedural law arises: design algorithms and train them to learn and execute procedural rules, to the extent that different conditions related to the data and the digital ecosystem present in certain proceedings are given.[26]

In this context, the limitations of artificial intelligence in judicial proceedings are clearly shown when the cases in which it is used demand a consideration of principles and not the application of a certain rule (even when such a rule derives from relatively consolidated precedents turned into a kind of binding positive law, as is the case in Brazil with the *súmulas*). The same can be said

---

[23] Ibid.

[24] S. LEVIN, "Imprisoned by Algorithms: The Dark Side of California Ending Cash Bail," *The Guardian*, September 7, 2018.

[25] J. ANGWIN et al., "Machine Bias," <https://www.propublica.org/article/machinebias-ris k-assessments-in-criminal-sentencing.

[26] J.G. CORVALÁN, "Inteligencia artificial y proceso judicial. Desafíos concretos de aplicación," *Diario DPI – Diario Civil y Obligaciones*, September 30, 2019.

about specific issues in such cases (for example, requirements of admissibility in extraordinary remedies to access the highest institutional levels).[27] Nieva Fenoll is absolutely clear in his view regarding this when he highlights certain limits: "artificial intelligence is human because it has been built by humans, even if it is able to 'learn' from the collected data. But artificial intelligence does not deliver judgements, at least not typically. It just helps to give them."[28]

Under this light, Corvalán holds that "it is not advisable to train AI systems to interpret and weight principles drawn from decision trees. This means that the automation, in this respect, is not conducive to solve the cases in which there is a tension among principles." However, according to him, it would be possible to use artificial intelligence to "set precedents or provisions regarding cases in which there are multiple principles at stake."[29]

The development of this topic in Argentina finds one of its main institutional actors in the Innovation and Artificial Intelligence Laboratory, an initiative created by the University of Buenos Aires and the Public Prosecution Ministry of the City of Buenos Aires.[30]

This Laboratory built and developed the "Promethean" system, which is currently being applied in the Colombian Constitutional Court for an intelligent and quick detection and selection of urgent and priority cases, as well as for the provision of intelligent assistance in report making, automation of files, and advanced systematization of jurisdiction.[31]

The Colombian Constitutional Court receives around 2,700 "acciones de tutela" a day, the majority of which relate to fundamental rights such as health. On the first use of the Promethean system, it has made it possible to read, analyze, detect, and suggest the 32 most urgent cases to be dealt with out of a total number of 2,016 cases.

---

[27]   D.G. Ribeiro, "Las reformas procesales en Brasil: hacia un nuevo código procesal civil," in E. Oteiza (ed.), *Sendas para la reforma de la justicia a principios del siglo XXI*, Marcial Pons, Madrid 2018, pp. 115–133.

[28]   J.G. Corvalán, *Inteligencia artificial y proceso judicial*, Marcial Pons, Madrid 2018, Introduction.

[29]   J.G. Corvalán, above n. 25.

[30]   https://ialab.com.ar. The work at the laboratory focuses on four strategic axes: (i) artificial intelligence to improve the relationship between citizens and justice administration; (ii) automation; (iii) predictive artificial intelligence; and (iv) applied research.

[31]   When asked about the impact of the use of this artificial intelligence model at the Court, Dr. Grenfieth Sierra Cadena, Director of the Public Law Research Group of the University of Rosario and Director of Specialization in Administrative Law, said that "with Promethean we have already proved that the Court improves by 900% the case management of the "acciones de tutela" filed for protecting the right to health, which means that it would be possible to answer requests in real time. Changes would also involve judges, who would have greater analysis capacity, more time and the possibility to research decisions on the substance of the matter. These changes, I repeat, do not modify the judge's decision; they simply help them in terms of legal precision." See G. Sierra Cadena, "Promethean, Artificial Intelligence for the Revision of Custody at the Constitutional Court," https://www.ambitojuridico.com/noticias/informe/constitucional-y-derechos-humanos/prometea-inteligencia-artificial-para-la.

Francisco Verbic

In this task, in a few minutes and without human intervention, the artificial intelligence system "elaborated detailed reports with statistics; detected and selected a group of priority cases; extracted the most relevant paragraphs of the cases involving disadvantaged people; automatically uploaded in 2 minutes and 46 seconds 38 judgments to Blockchain, which would take a person 43 minutes to complete; and automatically created 14 files in 16 minutes, which manually would have required 2 hours and 40 minutes of work."[32]

Another example of this can be found in Brazil, where the Supreme Federal Court is using an artificial intelligence system called "Víctor," which has been described by some as the first artificial intelligence project implemented in supreme courts on a global scale. Its main use relates to the analysis and detection of "general repercussion" cases, facilitating the determination of said constitutional court's jurisdiction to hear extraordinary appeals.[33]

The relevance of this tool in the context of Brazil is clear in the light of the statistics being handled in terms of litigation and congestion: approximately 100 million proceedings in progress and the initiation of around 30 million new proceedings every year.[34] Within the Supreme Federal Court, the statistics show that its 11 members resolved around 140,000 cases in 2016, which is the approximate equivalent to 12,727 cases a year for each member.[35]

5. THE FOURTH DIMENSION: NEW TECHNOLOGIES AND CITIZENS' ACCESS TO PUBLIC INFORMATION

In many countries around the world, the judicial branch is the most distant in relation to the people in terms of access to public information. This problem, in turn, generates serious deficiencies regarding social control and accountability from system operators.[36]

---

[32] "¿Analizar 2016 sentencias en 2 minutos? Prometea en la Corte Constitucional de Colombia," <https://ialab.com.ar/prometeacolombia.

[33] N.C. DA SILVA, "Notas iniciais sobre a evolução dos algoritmos do VICTOR: o primeiro projeto de inteligência artificial em supremas cortes do mundo" in R. VIEIRA DE CARVALHO FERNANDES and A. GAMBA PRATA DE CARVALHO (eds.), *Tecnologia jurídica & direito digital*, Belo Horizonte, 2018, pp. 89–94.

[34] CONSELHO NACIONAL DE JUSTIÇA, *Justiça em Números 2018*, 2018, available at <https://www.cnj.jus.br/wp-content/uploads/conteudo/arquivo/2018/08/44b7368ec6f888b383f6c3de40c32167.pdf.

[35] CONSELHO NACIONAL DE JUSTIÇA, *Supremo em ação 2017: ano-base 2016*, 2017, available at https://www.conjur.com.br/dl/relatorio-supremo-acao.pdf.

[36] The 2018 Latinobarometro confidence index showed an average of 24% for the judicial branch in the Latin American region. In the data disaggregation, it was pointed out that "there are countries in the region where the judicial branch does not even have the confidence of one-third of the population. The countries with lower levels of trust in the judiciary are El Salvador with 14%, Nicaragua with 15%, Peru with 16%, followed by Venezuela with 18%.

Different factors come together for this to happen. Among them, particular emphasis is given to the complexity of the language used in everyday work and the non-use of new technologies to facilitate citizenship access to relevant information about what is going on inside the justice administration system.

An experience that deserves to be mentioned for being innovative and necessary in the Latin American region is the Index of Online Access to Judicial Information, which was created by the Justice Studies Centre of Americas and which has already published its eleventh issue. This Index measures judicial branches and public ministries of the 34 member countries of the Organization of American States (OAS) based on standards of active transparency.[37] The indicators and variables used in this measurement are as follows:

1. The existence of an institutional website that provides information about the institution, with some minimum content (for example, a list of contacts).
2. The publishing and updating of court judgments, classified according to subject matter, jurisdiction, and the hierarchy of the court that delivered them (only for judicial branches).
3. The publishing and updating of the institution's internal agreements, tutorials, and regulations.
4. Statistics on integrated, solved, and pending cases.
5. A schedule of hearings, ordered either according to the hierarchy of the court in which the hearing is taking place or to the territory in which the hearing is located (only for judicial branches).
6. The physical and material resources of these institutions.
7. Financial budgets.
8. Relevant aspects of judges and other officers of the court or public ministry, such as salary, resumés, patrimonial status and disciplinary record.
9. The publishing of conferences and contract biddings, both regarding the staff and infrastructure.
10. The access regime – that is, to see if the access to the services provided by the website is free and universal or if it is required to pay for it.

The analysis of all these variables results in a ranking system that allows for the objective evaluation of transparency and accessibility of these institutional spaces, as well as for the promotion of appropriate public polices to improve the situation.

On the other hand, the countries with higher levels of trust in the judiciary are Costa Rica with 49%, Uruguay with 39% and Brazil with 33%" (see http://www.latinobarometro.org/latdocs/INFORME_2018_LATINOBAROMETRO.pdf).

[37] The 11th edition of the report (August 2019) can be found at: http://biblioteca.cejamericas.org/handle/2015/5633.

Francisco Verbic

6. ADVANTAGES, RISKS, AND CHALLENGES CREATED BY THE USE OF NEW TECHNOLOGIES IN JUDICIAL PROCEEDINGS

In general, it is possible to find a number of convergence points regarding certain advantages that the use of new technologies in judicial proceedings brings about, which include the following:

1. Greater speed in solving incidental or substantive matters.
2. Reducing the cost of proceedings and, hence, greater economic efficiency derived from the impact created by saving in both human and material resources for the different justice administration systems.
3. Further progress in creating a greater degree of judicial security, certainty and equality (mainly by using artificial intelligence systems that allow for even better contextualization, analysis, and weighting of characteristics, implications, and consequences of the cases to be solved).
4. Improving access to justice and human rights for those lacking resources, as well as in small claim cases, and for those who live far from the urban centers where the main courts are located.
5. The visibility of online public information for citizens concerning the operations of the judicial branches and about relevant issues dealt with in courts which, in turn, generates greater transparency and better conditions for effective accountability of system operators.
6. A favorable environmental impact in terms of eliminating paper use.

As a counterpart to the advantages of new technologies when applied to judicial proceedings, some of the risks and disadvantages that may be caused should be noted, which include the following:

1. The "dereliction of human justice": blindly trusting in artificial intelligence as a decision-making instrument despite cognitive distortions and other limitations pointed out in this chapter.
2. The structural inequality in some states in terms of citizen access to the Internet and other computer resources. The barriers created by this inequality cannot be avoided when discussing two of the main (and almost undisputed) arguments generally wielded for the use of technology in judicial proceedings: simplification and cost lowering of digital access to justice.
3. The limitation that these technologies present in terms of access and understanding for the elderly.
4. Regarding artificial intelligence, the almost blind trust of some sectors on its reliability, overlooking (or minimizing) the risks underlying system building and its algorithms.

392

Intersentia

5. The inadequacies of budgets, especially in underdeveloped countries, to fund infrastructure costs entailed in the implementation of new technologies and the computer security measures needed to guarantee its inviolability, authorship, authenticity and immutability.
6. The protection of personal data that is incorporated in managing systems and online dispute resolution.

7. OVERALL ASSESSMENT AND A LOOK INTO THE FUTURE

In 2002, Ortells Ramos argued that the use of new technologies in judicial proceedings could be seen in three different ways: first, new technologies could be seen as an auxiliary means for the development of certain procedural acts (for example, videotaping of hearings); second, they could be a means of facilitating new ways in the performance of procedural acts (electronic notifications, electronic filing, videoconferences, etc.); and, third, they could lead to a real, pure digital or online proceeding.[38]

The decision over the extent to which new technologies are used to deal with dispute resolutions depends, first and naturally, on a public policy choice. For many years, even while recognizing their benefits in the procedural law field, the use of new technologies has been restricted -in terms of their implementation- by a slow and gradual technological development (with the impact this has had on the costs of its acquisition, maintenance, and updating), and also by the limited reach of internet.

These constraints no longer exist. However, we are witnessing a turning point -in historical terms- where, beyond public policy decisions, the cultural factor also plays a determining role when it comes to the success of the implementation of new technologies.

In this sense, for example in Latin America, one of the findings made by the Justice Studies Center of the Americas when following that implementation in the region was that "even though a decision process and a deep intense regulatory change has taken place, rule implementation processes demands cultural changes of practices and knowledges, citizenship participation and trust in these instruments. Policies on those factors have been rather weak and little planned."[39]

---

[38] M.O. Ramos, "Incidencia de las nuevas tecnologías en el proceso jurisdiccional," *XVIII Jornadas Iberoamericanas y XI Uruguayas de Derecho Procesal*, Uruguay, September 2002.

[39] Ricardo Lillo L. "Indicadores de CEJA: El rol de las TIC en una justicia para ciudadanos", in *Revista Sistemas Judiciales*, Centro de Estudios de las Américas – CEJA, Año 9, N° 16, pp. 6–17.

Also Piché makes reference to this issue in her analysis of the situation in Canada, highlighting that for a better implementation of new technologies in the field of procedural law, "it is necessary that judges' and lawyers' attitudes evolve and that such actors decide to trust in technology so that they can see it as a vehicle for change, since, together with it, it would be possible to move towards greater efficiency and a fairer dispute resolution, both inside and outside courts."[40]

I share her viewpoint in that "the main key" to changing our justice administration systems relies on a greater use of new technologies in courts and in the provision of other judicial services. Accordingly, Piché holds that technology is useful to "challenge and transform the provision of legal services, as well as producing greater efficiency in the management of disputes resolution systems." All this would result in the strengthening of the access to justice and human rights.[41]

It is indisputable that the use of new technologies in general, and of artificial intelligence in particular, is a of absolute relevance for the improvement of case management in any procedural system around the world.[42] It would result in significant savings in terms of human and material resources, as well as progress and improvement of opinion's drafts.

What is apparently not very clear is up to what extent we are willing to hand over the decision-making power to computer systems. This does not mean that new technologies, especially artificial intelligence, are not relevant instruments to be used in the making of decisions – the experiences of the Constitutional Court of Colombia and the Federal High Court of Brazil discussed above show, to some extent, evidence of it working successfully.

One of the challenges seems to be how to find a way of developing judicial branches that use new technologies and exploit all their potential, but that do not separate the adjudication, the act of doing justice (or least trying to do so), from its social, historical, and anthropological essence.

---

[40] C. PICHÉ, "Administering Justice and Serving the People. The Tension between the Objective of Judicial Efficiency and Informal Justice in Canadian Access to Justice Initiatives," (2017) 3 *Erasmus Law Review*, DOI: 10.5553/ELR.000078.

[41] Ibid. The author states that even though there is an increased use of online filing, digital records, centralized information management systems, digital recording equipment, and videoconferences, there is still much to be done.

[42] On case management in general, although without the analysis of artificial intelligence as a working tool in this context, see the exhaustive work of A. CABRAL, "New Trends and Perspectives on Case Management: Proposals on Contract Procedure and Case Assignment Management" (2018) 6(1) *Peking University Law Journal* 5, DOI: 10.1080/20517483.2018.1603636.

THE APPLICATION OF ELECTRONIC TECHNOLOGIES IN JUDICIAL PROCEEDINGS

Ho Moon-hyuck*

1. Introduction 396
   1.1. Access to Justice and the Application of Electronic Technologies 396
   1.2. Litigation Practice Situation and AET 397
   1.3. The Introduction of AET in Judicial Proceedings 399
2. Recording as a Means of Ensuring Transparency of Proceedings 400
   2.1. Recording as a Court Protocol 400
        2.1.1. Conventional Court Protocol 401
        2.1.2. Recording of the Hearing 401
   2.2. Expansion of the Principle of Public Trial 402
        2.2.1. Disclosing of the Hearing 402
        2.2.2. Disclosing of the Litigation Records 404
3. The Handling of Electronic Documents 405
   3.1. Online Filing of Petition and Defense 405
        3.1.1. Admissibility 405
        3.1.2. Preference of the Parties 406
        3.1.3. Advantages 407
        3.1.4. Problem 408
   3.2. Online Service 409
        3.2.1. Problem of the Traditional Service of Documents
               or Written Statements 409

---

* Professor Emeritus, Seoul National University School of Law. The reports I based the text on are briefly stated in the footnote as follows:

K.-L. Shen and C.-L. Wang, "Application of Technologies in Judicial Proceedings": Taiwanese Report

Z. Wang, "Application of Electronic Technologies in Civil Judicial Proceedings in China": Chinese Report

K.B. Agrawal and K. Kumwat, "Application of Electronic Technologies in Judicial Proceedings": Indian Report

Intersentia

	3.2.2.	Admissibility 410
	3.2.3.	Advantages and Disadvantages 411
3.3.		Documents in the Main Hearing 411
3.4.		Electronic Documents as Evidence 412
3.5.		Non-Documentary Objects 412
3.6.		Electronic Data as Evidence in China 413
4. The Process of Using Video Devices 415		
4.1.		Statements of the Parties 415
4.2.		Witnesses 415
4.3.		Experts 416
4.4.		Interrogation of Parties as Evidence 417
5. Online Dispute Resolution 417		
5.1.		ADR in General 417
5.2.		ODR as a Means of ADR 417
5.3.		Judicial Proceedings with ODR 418
	5.3.1.	Taiwan 419
	5.3.2.	Korea 419
	5.3.3.	China 420
6. The Future of the Judiciary 423		
6.1.		AI Lawyer and AI Judge? 423
6.2.		Access to Justice without Any Limitations? 424
7. Conclusion 426		

1. INTRODUCTION

1.1. ACCESS TO JUSTICE AND THE APPLICATION OF ELECTRONIC TECHNOLOGIES

As seen in the formulary system of ancient Roman civil proceedings, litigation is a procedure that is heavily focused on form and formality. Of course, in the Roman era, the formality of litigation was necessary because legal concepts had not yet been established, but in the modern system of litigation, the form of litigation was necessary to prevent arbitrary judgment by a powerful judge. As Rudolf von Jhering said in the nineteenth century, form is the sworn enemy of arbitrariness and the twin sister of freedom.[1] This did not change much in the legal and litigation system until the end of the twentieth century, when communication via email entered the mainstream due to transformations in communication technology. Previously, it had been important in legal

---

[1]   R. VON JHERING, *Geist des römischen Rechts auf den verschiedenen Stufen seiner Entwicklung*, Teil 2, Abt. 2, 5. Aufl., Leipzig 1898, S. 471.

proceedings that paper documents or other material objects were delivered or appeared in the presence of judges. Hearing had to be held face to face in the presence of judges in the courtroom. These regulations were essential to ensure the stability of proceedings, the prevention of arbitrary judgment by judges, and the legitimate consequences of litigation.

However, in the twenty-first century, electronic technology has developed radically and has had a revolutionary effect on human life, so that machines have even acquired artificial intelligence (AI), and this phenomenon has affected the litigation system and the activities of judges and lawyers. The recording of sound and video footage, already a familiar feature in our everyday lives, made it possible in some countries to check whether the court proceedings were conducted transparently and fairly. As e-commerce, which is actively used in everyday life, is not found to create any problems in terms of the safety of transactions due to the development of security technology, the perception has become common that there is little risk in the electronic service of legal documents. The development of video transmission technology also raised questions about whether judges should have to give parties or witnesses face-to-face hearing in courtroom like they have done before. It may be assessed that the application of these electronic technologies (AET) would contribute significantly (if not inherently) to access to justice. However, the traditional litigation system, which respects the personal autonomy of the parties, adopted the principle of party disposition and adversary system. To back this up, the legal aid system was prepared, and it will guarantee the parties' access to justice from an economic perspective. Until now, people thought that was enough. This belief ignored the reality that physical access to courts could be very difficult or could take a long time, especially in Asia, where citizens find it difficult to get help from lawyers because the number of them is insufficient and the cost of them is pretty high. In this situation, AET has the advantage of significantly increasing accessibility to courts. It could also help ease the burden of judges' and lawyers' work.

Conversely, there may still be problems with AET, which reduces the accuracy of judges' judgments by intervening of electronic devices between judges and parties, as well as between judges and evidence. And for citizens who are not familiar with these electronic technologies, AET could be a hindrance to their access to the courts. These issues should also be considered when discussing AET.

1.2. LITIGATION PRACTICE SITUATION AND AET

The advantages of AET include the ability of citizens to protect their rights by using litigation easily, cheaply, and quickly, and the fact that it relieves judges of some of the burden involved in the exercise of their duties. Submitting a complaint or other document in the proceedings is often inconvenient, especially since the service is cumbersome and the success rate is low, so this could be improved through AET.

The work burden shouldered by judges seems to be so great in Taiwan and Korea that it is difficult for judges to deliberate on single cases. In Taiwan, for example, the average number of "cases closed by each judge per month in District Court is 68.29 (28 civil litigation cases), in the high court and its branches, it is 12.30, and in the Supreme Court, where there are 34 judges dealing with civil cases, it is 13.18.[2]

In Korea, for instance, the number of first instance judges stood at 2,406 as of 2018, with the number of litigations totaling 6,313,863. The average number of cases before first instance judges was 2,624.22 cases per year, and the average number of cases handled per month was 218.68.[3] This means that Korean judges have to deal with far more cases than judges in Taiwan.

In China, the number of cases (including first instance, second instance and retrial cases) dealt with by Chinese courts at all levels increased from 613,000 in 1978 to 16.7 million in 2015, an increase of 27.3 times, and civil cases experienced an even faster increase in both rate and total numbers – from 318,000 to 11.05 million (34.7 times) in the same timeframe. Meanwhile, the number of Chinese judges also increased (from about 60,000 in 1981 to 196,000 in 2015, a more than threefold increase), but this growth rate is far less than the increase in case numbers. Such uneven growth in the number of cases and the number of judges necessarily means that the annual workload per judge in China has greatly increased, from 20 in 1981 to 85 in 2015.[4]

Delays in legal proceedings resulted in numerous complaints from the parties involved. In Taiwan, based on the general public survey of judicial cognition in 2018 carried out by the Judicial Yuan, it is considered that the proceedings are too time-consuming. Specifically, regarding the reasons why people are unwilling to go to court to resolve disputes, according to the number of the options selected by the general public, the most popular one is "the litigation process is suffering" (91.2%).[5] AET is expected to help solve these problems to some extent, but it remains to be seen whether this will actually help facilitate and quickly end lawsuits. For those who are familiar with AET, it is clear that litigation using AET is convenient. So far, however, the statistics do not show that lawsuits using AET are proceeding quickly.

---

[2]   K.-L. SHEN and C.-L. WANG, Taiwanese Report, p. 3 (quoting https://www.judicial.gov.tw/juds).

[3]   Yearbook of Judiciary 2019, National Court Administration, p. 562.

[4]   Z. WANG, Chinese Report, pp. 7–8 (quoting H. ZHANG, "Coping the Difficulties of 'Too Many Cases But Not Enough Judges' in Chinese Courts – An Analysis of Civil Cases" (2018) 2 *Journal of Shandong University (Philosophy and Social Sciences)*.

[5]   SHEN and WANG, Taiwanese Report, p. 4 (quoting https://www.judicial.gov.tw/juds/u107.pdf).

1.3. THE INTRODUCTION OF AET IN JUDICIAL PROCEEDINGS

AET began relatively early in Korea and Taiwan, and Japan has taken a very cautious stance and is now pushing it in earnest. China started late, but is actively advancing its use of AET.

In Korea, the Act on the Special Cases Concerning Remote Video Trials was enacted in December 1995. This was designed to reduce inconveniences for residents living in areas where travelling to court is very difficult. Under this Act, such procedures were implemented in February 1996 on Ulleung Island, far from mainland Korea, followed by two areas in the mountainous Gangwon Province. However, the online lawsuits on Ulleung Island were suspended in 1998, while those in the mountainous Gangwon Province area were suspended in 2001. The main reasons for these suspensions included the excessive cost of dealing with small cases to operate the system and the obsolescence of relay equipment.[6] Then, the Framework Act on Electronic Documents and Electronic Transactions enacted in January 2002 enables all government agencies to work using electronic documents. And the use of electronic documents was implemented in the summary payment order procedure in 2006, and the adjudication proceeding through electronic information processing was implemented in the Constitutional Court and Administrative Appeal proceeding in 2009. In March 2010, the Act on the Utilization of Electronic Documents in Civil Procedure, etc. (EDCPA) was enacted. The Supreme Court Rules on the Utilization of Electronic Documents in Civil Procedure, etc., which oversaw the details of the implementation of this Act, was enacted in June 2013.

In Japan, the telephone conference system was introduced in 1996 to prepare for the hearing of the civil court and has been widely used until now. In 2004, the Civil Procedure Act (CPA) was amended so that some of the application cases could be applied online (Articles 132-10 ff. CPA). Thus, in 2006, online systems were introduced to summary payment order proceedings and were actively used in the process. And the online application system began to operate on an experimental basis for some cases of civil litigation in the Sapporo District Court. However, the attempt at the online system ended in failure and were suspended in 2009. In response to the sluggish online use of Japan's legal system, there have been growing calls from the business community to promote IT. Accordingly, a Committee for Review of Informatization of Procedure was established in October 2017.[7]

In Taiwan, the Intellectual Property Case Adjudication Act of 2008 allows judges of the Intellectual Property Court (IPC) to authorize the use of equipment that enables the live transmission of voices and images of a trial at the request of the parties or on its own initiative. In terms of the software, from July 2015 to July 2017, the IPC

---

[6] S.-H. IM, "A Review on the Preparatory Proceeding Using Video Conferencing" (2018) 476 *Human Rights and Justice* 115–16.

[7] S. JUNKO, "Informatization of Civil Proceedings in Japan," paper presented at a joint symposium of Judicial Policy Research Institute and Waseda University, February 2018, Tokyo.

Intersentia

successively launched the online litigation system for administrative litigation, the online litigation system for civil litigation, and asymmetric online filing. In these systems, the online service mechanism was adopted.[8] In August 2016, the Electronic Litigation Documents (including Online Filing) Service Platform started to expand the coverage of the online filing service for actions at the first and second instances and the summary proceedings; the parties (including advocates) may file complaints and responses using the platform. In August 2018, statutory guardians of a minor were allowed to act as a proxy for the minor to initiate an action online.[9]

In China, the Law of Civil Procedure (CPL) in 2012 for the first time recognized "electronic data" as one of the eight categories of evidence that can be used in civil litigation in China (Article 63 CPL).[10] Since 2012, the Supreme People's Court of China (SPC) considered promoting judicial reforms and the construction of an "intelligent court" to be its priority. Since 2017, China has started to establish a new form of court – the Internet Court – which is a byproduct of the SPC's intelligent court project. In August 2017, the SPC established the first internet court in Hangzhou City in September 2018, while two other internet courts were established in Beijing and Guangzhou respectively.[11]

In India, the use of AET began in 2014, but to a very limited extent. The record of the court is being digitalized very slowly. The proceedings in the civil courts take on an average a minimum of ten years.[12]

Several steps could be taken in the process of introducing AET: the first is to record audio or video proceedings in the court, acknowledge the file as a court protocol, and release the files and decisions to at least a certain range of people; the second is the process of handling e-documents; the third is the process of using video devices to investigate evidence other than documents; the fourth is remote video-based court hearings; the fifth is the whole process of litigation being conducted online and mobile device-based litigation; and the sixth could perhaps be a lawsuit by an AI judge and AI lawyers.

2. RECORDING AS A MEANS OF ENSURING TRANSPARENCY OF PROCEEDINGS

2.1. RECORDING AS A COURT PROTOCOL

There can be various ways to draw up the court protocol. As it has been the case, a court clerk could summarize and document the lawsuit. Recently, the

---

8   SHEN and WANG, Taiwanese Report, p. 1.
9   Ibid., p. 2.
10   WANG, Chinese Report, p. 1.
11   Ibid., p. 18.
12   K.B. AGRAWAL and K. KUMWAT, Indian Report, p. 1.

method of recording all hearings and recognizing this recorded file as the court protocol, printing the recorded file and recognizing both as the court protocol, and recognizing the recorded video file as the court protocol has been used. Each method will have its advantages and disadvantages, so each country will have to choose the method that best suits its situation. However, when there are problems with conventional methods, it is desirable to solve them using AET.

2.1.1. Conventional Court Protocol

In Taiwan, according to Article 212 Code of Civil Procedure (CCP), the court clerk shall prepare an oral argument transcript. According to Article 213, the transcript shall indicate the purport of the argument, and Article 66 of the Precautionary Matters on Handling Civil Procedure also states that the transcript does not need to indicate every detail of the oral argument; the clerk need only record the essential part of the argument.[13]

In Korea's civil litigation, the court protocol is written by a court clerk summarizing the statements of the parties and those involved in the litigation, and the contents of the presiding made by the judge (Article 152 Civil Procedure Act (CPA)).

In India, the judge of a court must summarize the contents of the parties' arguments as a rule, but in practice, the clerk of the court provides this summary.[14]

2.1.2. Recording of the Hearing

In Taiwan, with regard to audio and video recordings in court proceedings, pursuant to Article 213-1 CCP, the court may, at the request of parties or on its own initiative, use a tape recorder or other machines or equipment in order to capture the oral argument transcript. In addition, based on Article 90 of the Court Organic Act, when the court is in session, the audio session should be recorded and, if necessary, the video session may be recorded. For further details, Article 2 of the Regulations of Audio Recording in Court issued by the Judicial Yuan states that the court shall conduct audio recording during the domestic and civil proceeding sessions, and if necessary, the court may employ video recording in order to maintain the principle of transparency and judicial accountability. These articles show that recording is already part of Taiwan's court proceedings. And according to Article 90-2 of the Court Organic Act, the recordings shall be kept for two years after the judgment is finalized.[15]

---

[13]   Shen and Wang, Taiwanese Report, p. 28.
[14]   Agrawal and Kumwat, Indian Report, p. 5.
[15]   Shen and Wang, Taiwanese Report, pp. 28–29.

Intersentia

In Korea today, all comments made during the hearing can be recorded if the judge states that this is necessary. However, the recording itself is not recognized as a court protocol. Recording files can be recognized as a part of the court protocol, but the court clerk should later prepare a separate court protocol. In this case, the court may dispose of the recording if the decision has become final or with the consent of both parties (Article 159 CPA). This discipline means that recording is only used as an auxiliary means to record the proceedings and content of the hearing.

In both Taiwan and Korea, the conventional court protocol does not properly reflect what happened in the actual oral arguments. Because the court protocol contains only the gist and results of oral arguments, it does not reveal how the judge presided over the proceedings or how the parties and representatives responded to such proceedings. Evidence also includes the intent of the entire argument, but the concrete situation is not recorded in this protocol. In addition, the situation regarding whether the judge conducted the hearing in a biased manner is not revealed at all. Thus, it is no longer reasonable to maintain such an inadequate court protocol system. The court has already begun recording arguments, and the ability to convert the contents of a recorded voice file to text and to search for certain content in a file can also be fully utilized. Therefore, it is now reasonable to ensure that the recording file is used as a court protocol, as is already done in other international courts.

2.2. EXPANSION OF THE PRINCIPLE OF PUBLIC TRIAL

The principle of public hearings and trials in the judiciary has been regarded as an important one since the establishment of the modern judicial system. However, this principle has remained almost only in form on the one hand, as in the legal practice written statements has been considered more important than oral arguments. On the other hand, there was a trend that emphasized the principle of public hearings and trials as a way to ensure transparency and fairness in litigation proceedings. Today, the scope of public hearings and trials has tended to expand. In the past, it was thought that it would be sufficient to disclose the hearing and trial to the public in a courtroom, but now it has been discussed whether to disclose the hearing to the public outside the courtroom or even to the public outside the court, or whether to allow real-time broadcasting of the hearing and trial. It is now discussed whether the court decision or even the entire litigation record will be made public for anyone to have access to.

2.2.1. Disclosing of the Hearing

In Taiwan, at the National Conference on Judicial Reform in 2017, the fourth subgroup made a resolution on the topic of "Participation in Transparent and

Accessible Justice" to broaden the scope of the application of the court live broadcast.[16] First of all, the Conference suggested that fact-finding proceedings should be broadcast live. The openness and transparency of court proceedings can raise public awareness of the operation of the judiciary and satisfy the public's right to know in major cases. It will further have a good effect on legal education for citizens.[17] However, considering that live broadcasting of court proceedings involves broadcasting technology and cost expenditure, and may probably cause damage to litigants' interests and the privacy rights of the parties, the Conference felt that court broadcasts should only be applicable in specific types of cases relating to the general public good, for example, election cases and certain cases in which harm may be cause to the public interest.[18] Furthermore, the oral-argument session held by the Supreme Court, the Supreme Administrative Court, and the Constitutional Court would also be broadcast live. By focusing on the debate on legal issues, the public's rights to know could be satisfied and this could also lead to the constructive discussion about the judiciary and effectively promote the civic legal education.[19] However, the Judicial Yuan has not yet constructed detailed regulation, so that the court broadcast has not been fully applicable, now only the oral argument sessions of the Constitutional Court and the Supreme Court have several live broadcast records.[20]

In Korea, the Supreme Court's Rules on Watching and Filming of Court Proceeding, enacted in 1973, were amended in February 2017 to allow recording, video recording, and filming for broadcast purposes under certain conditions. The Regulation allows the presiding judge to order recording, video recording, or filming to relay the hearing in the following cases: (1) in cases where it is difficult to maintain the court order because the number of litigants involved is significantly higher than the number of persons allowed to enter the courtroom in which a hearing is conducted; or (2) in cases where multiple lives have been lost due to disasters or other reasons, and it is difficult for the parties, the victims, or their legal representatives to appear in court because many of them live far away from the court where the lawsuit is taking place (Article 6, para. 1). In such a case, the presiding judge may take measures necessary to prevent the undue disclosure of personal information of the litigants by the broadcasting service.

Usually, the Supreme Court does not hold a hearing. However, when it comes to matters of great public interest or importance, it is necessary to publicize

---

[16]   For the details of the fourth subgroup's resolution at the National Conference on Judicial Reform in 2017, see https://justice.president.gov.tw/meetinggroup/4 (quoted in SHEN and WANG, Taiwanese Report, p. 31).

[17]   SHEN and WANG, Taiwanese Report, pp. 31–32.

[18]   Ibid., p. 32.

[19]   Ibid.

[20]   Ibid.

the hearing process and the issues that the case raises. In 2013, the Supreme Court enacted the Rule Concerning Hearing in the Supreme Court, allowing recording, video recording, filming, and broadcasting with the permission of the presiding judge. In this case, in order to protect the rights of the litigants or the public interest, or to maintain order in the court, the presiding judge may take necessary measures, such as limiting the time or method of the above action or attaching conditions to the permit (Article 7-2). The Supreme Court's public hearings are held several times a year, with the great advantage of giving the general public a better understanding of the legal issues that have been subject of public attention.

In contrast, trials in India are open only to the parties themselves.[21]

2.2.2. Disclosing of the Litigation Records

The disclosure of the hearing and trial means not only that anyone can watch the content in real time, but also that the proceedings and content of the hearing and trial will have to be visible to the public later on. Accordingly, the content of the trial and the litigation record should be available for anyone to read or copy and access them online as well. This will increase transparency, but it will also increase the risk of leaking personal information relating to lawsuits.

In Taiwan, according to para. 1 of Article 83 of the Court Organic Act, all courts shall in principle publish the judgment, and only if it is stipulated otherwise by other provisions, these provisions shall apply. However, in order to protect the privacy of the parties, para. 2 of Article 83 states that the publication may exclude the natural person's identification card number or other information that may easily identify him/her. Nowadays, besides the publication gathering together the judgments issued by all courts, the Judicial Yuan also developed the Law and Regulations Retrieving System for the general public to search for judgments. It can be considered that the judgments within the scope of disclosure are open to the public and can be reviewed by anyone.[22] In addition, the court dossier which involves the content of a hearing is not completely open to the public. According to Article 242 CCP, only the parties and the third party with the parties' consent or with a preliminary showing of his/her legal interests concerned may apply to the court to inspect, copy, or photograph the documents and to get the copies at cost in advance.[23]

In Korea, important Supreme Court judgments are published in hardcopy form. Selected Supreme Court judgments can also be found on the Supreme Court website or on other websites. In the case of lower courts, only decisions

---

[21]   AGRAWAL and KUMWAT, Indian Report, p. 6.
[22]   SHEN and WANG, Taiwanese Report, pp. 32–33.
[23]   Ibid., p. 33.

that are considered to be very important are published. In such published judgments, the names of the parties are made anonymous. This is done to protect privacy. More and more people, especially lawyers and legal scholars, are now calling for the full disclosure of lower court judgments. The court has responded positively, but has yet to disclose the judgments. The reason for this is that it takes a long time to redact the parties' names. Under the Civil Procedure Act, a party or a third party who declares its interest may apply for a review or copy of the litigation records, the issuing of a copy of the original, a certified copy, an abridged copy, or a certificate of the matters on the case. Anyone may apply for a review of the records of a final court decision for the purposes of protection of rights, academic research, or the public interest (Article 162 CPA). In this case, access may be granted only with the agreement of the involved person in the case.

In India, it is only the parties who can apply for review the order or judgment. The record of the procedure is not open to the public.[24]

3. THE HANDLING OF ELECTRONIC DOCUMENTS

3.1. ONLINE FILING OF PETITION AND DEFENSE

Countries that have adopted AET naturally allow for the submission of legal documents such as complaints, answers, and preparatory documents online.

3.1.1. Admissibility

Taiwan currently allows the general public to carry out online filing, and exchange the answer and litigation documents through the Electronic Litigation Documents (Including Online Filing) Service Platform. The platform will immediately transmit the litigation data to the court in which the action is pending.[25] In order to use the service platform, lawyers should first file a motion with the Judicial Yuan, and the general public should use their Citizen Digital Certificate, which is issued by the Interior Ministry Certificate Authority and contains a "digital signature" and a "public key" to obtain an account number and password for the system, and then apply to the court to activate the online facility, after which the user can send and receive legal documents online.[26]

---

[24] AGRAWAL and KUMWAT, Indian Report, p. 6.

[25] SHEN and WANG, Taiwanese Report, pp. 8–9.

[26] Ibid., p. 9 (quoting the announcement and the press release of the launch of Electronic Litigation Documents (including Online Filing) Service Platform on August 8, 2016).

Intersentia

The service platform can only be used with a computer and the platform is the only way to exchange legal documents online. But according to Articles 2, 4, and 5 of the Regulations Governing the Use of Telefax or Other Technological Device in Transmitting Civil Litigation Paper, the parties, agents, witnesses, and appraisers are allowed to send litigation documents to the court via email. However, they can only send the email after the action has been initiated and approved by the court.[27]

In Korea, the parties, litigation representatives, and other persons may submit the documents to the court in electronic form using the court-designated computerized information processing system (Article 5, para. 1 EDCPA). In order to use this system, they need to register with the system. A registered user who agrees to perform a civil litigation using the court-designated system shall, in principle, submit the documents to the court in electronic form as prescribed by the Supreme Court rules (Article 8 EDCPA).

In India, online petitions and defenses have not yet been adopted by the courts, as the courtrooms are not properly equipped to handle this. Still, it is expected that AET will make lawsuits quicker and more economical.[28]

3.1.2. Preference of the Parties

Online submission of litigation documents is a very convenient method, and parties, litigants, and others seem to be very satisfied with it. According to the survey in Taiwan, the rate of lawyers' satisfaction with the current electronic system is 60.8%,[29] while for the general public who have used online filing and electronic litigation systems, the rate of satisfaction is 96.1%.[30] The function of online answer submission is mostly used in cases in which government agencies (such as Intellectual Property Office in the intellectual property cases) are defendants.[31]

Korea's statistics show that a total of 959,270 civil suits were filed in the court of first instance in 2018, of which 760,901 (79.3%) were filed using AET. This means that plaintiffs who are active parties prefer to use AET. However, the number of cases in which both parties agreed to a lawsuit using AET shows that defendants who are passive do not prefer AET as much as plaintiffs, and the lower the value of the lawsuit, the more they avoid it.

---

[27]   SHEN and WANG, Taiwanese Report, p. 9.

[28]   AGRAWAL and KUMWAT, Indian Report, p. 2.

[29]   SHEN and WANG, Taiwanese Report, p. 10 (quoting "2018 Lawyer Satisfaction Investigation on Judicial Reform" made by the Judicial Yuan, 27).

[30]   SHEN and WANG, Taiwanese Report, p. 10 (quoting Analysis of the "Public Satisfaction Investigation on the Administrative Service Quality of the Court" made by the Judicial Yuan, 2).

[31]   SHEN and WANG, Taiwanese Report, p. 10.

Table 1. Civil cases filed in the court of first instance in 2018[32]

	Collegiate Bench	Single Judge	Small Claims Case	Total
Total filed Cases (A)	45,364	205,146	708,760	959,270
Filing with AET (B)	38,268	160,225	562,408	760,901
Ratio (B/A)	84.3%	78.1%	79.4%	79.3%
Agreed AET (C)	22,522	48,515	40,499	111,536
Ratio (C/B)	58.9%	30.3%	7.2%	14.7%

3.1.3. Advantages

People generally expect that AET will allow litigation to proceed more quickly, but this has not been the case according to the statistics so far. In Korea, there are no exact statistics yet on whether the introduction of AET will speed up proceedings. However, it may be useful to see how the duration of cases has changed. In the first instance, the average proceeding period for cases on the merits to be decided in the collegiate court in 2013 was 8.2 months, and the cases on the merits to be decided by the single judge was 4.3 months. These figures were 10.7 months and 4.5 months in 2016, and 9.8 months and 4.6 months in 2017, respectively. And there is another statistics that compares the duration of all cases with that of the cases with AET.

Table 2. Average proceeding period for cases on the merits in the first instance (in days)[33]

	Collegiate Bench	Single Judge	Small Claim
Total Cases	297.1	210.1	119.4
Cases with AET	316.0	227.4	116.9

This phenomenon can also be seen in Taiwan. According to the Judicial Yuan statistics, the average number of days involved in civil proceedings in Taiwan from 2014 to 2018 did not reduce, but gradually increased. In other words, after 2016, the year in which the electronic litigation system started to be used in civil litigation, the process of civil litigation has not been significantly accelerated.[34] This shows that the introduction of AET has the advantage of being convenient for filing litigation documents, but it does not help speed up litigation.

---

[32]   See Yearbook of Judiciary 2019 (n. 3), pp. 740, 742, 754, 756.
[33]   Ibid., p. 581.
[34]   SHEN and WANG, Taiwanese Report, p. 10 (quoting "The Survey on the Average Number of Days Required to Close a Case by Each Court" made by the Judicial Yuan).

Even if the filing of the lawsuit online does not greatly help in terms of speeding up proceedings, it is undeniable that providing convenience in a lawsuit is a huge advantage. Ensuring that documents can be submitted online, especially when the submission deadline for litigation documents is imminent, is of great help to the protection of the rights of the parties.

It is also considered that the introduction of AET has reduced litigation costs. Transcripts can be transmitted and the documents from the opposing party can be received online at any time. The parties do not need to mail or send the pleadings to the courts in person, or print the papers. The system can reduce costs and protect the environment at the same time.[35]

These advantages will be common in all countries that have adopted AET. In particular, it can reduce the direct costs of litigation, such as service of paper documents to be paid by the parties, transportation, and communication costs. In addition, it saves money on paper and office supplies. However, these costs only account for a small proportion of the total legal costs.

3.1.4. Problem

If the filing of the lawsuit documents online is to pay off, the judges, the parties, and their representatives in the case must become accustomed to online submission.

In Taiwan, when the plaintiff starts the initiation of action online, the defendant still has to send a consent form to using the electronic litigation system in hardcopy form, and the referee fee cannot be paid through the system at the same time. And if the defendant refuses to use the electronic litigation system, both parties still have to submit paper copies or photocopies to the court to reach the opposing party.[36] There is still a long way to go before complete digitization will be achieved. The Judicial Yuan is currently developing an "asymmetric (only for one party to use)" electronic litigation function for the civil litigation, which is expected to be published by the end of 2019 and can be used by the parties.[37]

In Korea, as mentioned earlier, the percentage of plaintiffs filing a lawsuit online is quite high, with the proportion of defendants agreeing to the online procedure being lower. This may be because the passive party finds it cumbersome to submit litigation documents online or to proceed with litigation proceedings online. In addition, many judges and lawyers print out and read the documents when they review online legal documents. This is because they are not used to reading documents on a computer screen – looking at a monitor for a long time creates problems with eye health, and feels uncomfortable with

---

[35] SHEN and WANG, Taiwanese Report, p. 10.
[36] Ibid., pp. 10–11 (quoting the instruction for the "Electronic Litigation Documents (including Online Filing) Service Platform").
[37] SHEN and WANG, Taiwanese Report, p. 11.

underlining or taking notes on the monitor when reviewing the documents. Therefore, the advantages of saving money from printing paper and protecting the environment by saving paper consumption are minimal.

3.2. ONLINE SERVICE

3.2.1. *Problem of the Traditional Service of Documents or Written Statements*

The traditional service of documents or written statements has been a persistently difficult question to address in almost all jurisdictions in Asia. In Korea, legal documents are served in principle by personal service (Article 178, para. 1 CPA). In the event that personal service is not feasible, supplementary service (Article 186, paras. 1 and 2 CPA), service by leaving (Article 186, para. 3 CPA), service by mail (Article 187 CPA), and service to the service-box in the court (Article 188 CPA) are accepted. In addition, if it is not known where to serve to the parties, service by public notice is permitted (Articles 194–196 CPA). However, life in modern society has become busier and more complicated, so it is not easy to serve at the address or office of the person being delivered as was previously the case. It is not uncommon for debtors to frequently change addresses or to go somewhere and live in hiding to avoid receiving the documents. In many cases, the party may refuse to receive the documents being served. This is why the service takes a long time and sometimes documents to be served are wrongly received by others, causing delays in litigation.

In Taiwan, compared to the online system, using hardcopies consumes a lot of paper and costs are higher.[38] Moreover, it often takes more time for the documents to reach the opposing party, and the possibilities of missing the documents or not reaching the opposing party is also raised.[39]

In China, traditional service methods are extremely time-consuming. Certain local courts in China reported that the work of service took up as much as 80% of the working hours of their legal assistants and law clerks. With regard to service efficiency, mailing within the jurisdiction usually requires one or two days; for cross-jurisdiction cases, service time will be longer; for service via public announcement, the completion of a process usually would take about three months.[40]

---

[38] Ibid. (quoting the Intellectual Property Court's Frequently Asked Questions of the online filing service "The Reasons for Launching the Electronic Litigation System": http://ipc. judicial.gov.tw/ipr_internet%20/index.php?option=com_content&view=article&id=1208% 3Aq9&catid=148%3Aqaa&Itemid=100076).

[39] SHEN and WANG, Taiwanese Report, p. 11.

[40] WANG, Chinese Report, p. 15 (quoting the Research Office of Wuxi Intermediate People's Court: "A Study on E-Service Based on Mobile Phone SMS," July 4, 2019, http://wxzy. chinacourt.gov.cn/article/detail/2019/07/id/4153421.shtml.

Ho Moon-hyuck

Also in India, the traditional service has been time-consuming and requires a high level of human resources.[41]

3.2.2. Admissibility

Online service is one of the core contents of AET. This is because it is a way to solve many of the problems of traditional service. Therefore, it is natural for countries that have adopted AET to admit online service.

In Taiwan, the current Electronic Litigation Documents Service Platform allows parties not only to sue and answer but also to exchange pleadings. At present, the scope of the pleadings which can be exchanged online includes: the complaint from the party or the advocate, the preparatory pleading, the answer, the pleading of amendment or addition of claims, the pleading of initiation of counterclaims, the writ petition, the instrument of appeal, reasons for appeal in writing, and a notice of appeal.[42]

Online service is also admissible in Korea. A court official may serve or notify electronically using the computer information processing system if the person receiving the service or notification falls into any of the following categories: (1) a registered user who agrees to proceed with civil litigation using the computer information processing system in advance; (2) a person who has agreed to proceed with civil litigation using the computer information processing system as a registered user after receiving a document printed from an electronic document; (3) State, local government, or other person equivalent thereto prescribed by the Supreme Court Rules as a registered user (Article 11, para. 1 EDCPA). In the case of a litigation representative, the service or notification of para. 1 shall be made to the litigation representative (Article 11, para. 2 EDCPA). The court clerk shall conduct the service by registering electronic documents to be served in the computer information processing system and electronically notifying those who shall receive the information (Article 11, para. 3 EDCPA). In the case of such online services, the person to be sent the documents shall be deemed to have been served when the person checks the registered electronic documents (Article 11, para. 4 EDCPA).

In China, a very progressive service system has been created. According to Article 87 CPL as amended in 2012, email delivery is permitted if the recipient's consent is obtained. However, this does not include judgments, rulings, and mediation results. Through the Judicial Interpretation of the SPC issued in 2015, specific rules were established on the application of e-service, including adding "mobile communication" as a legitimate means of service. On the other hand, since 2015, China has started to mandatorily require each mobile phone number bound with the real name of a resident and his/her ID card.

---

[41]   AGRAWAL and KUMWAT, Indian Report, p. 2.

[42]   SHEN and WANG, Taiwanese Report, p. 11 (quoting the Judicial Yuan Decree No. Yuan Tai Tzuyitzu 1050017623, issued July 6, 2016).

410   Intersentia

The Application of Electronic Technologies in Judicial Proceedings

Chinese courts also worked with the police departments and telecom companies to share information databases. The SPC also launched an online e-service platform at "China Judicial Process Information Online'[43] for litigants to manage their own litigation documents.[44]

Online service in India is not yet permitted. However, it is hoped that the introduction of online service will speed up litigation and reduce legal costs.[45]

3.2.3. Advantages and Disadvantages

Online service could speed up proceedings and reduce legal costs. However, the most obvious advantage of online service lies in its convenience. Service takes place quickly and accurately between the parties or their representatives registered on the court's online system.

However, there are also weaknesses in this approach. There is a clear indication as to whether a service is successful or not. However, the problem is that if the recipient does not press the confirmation button to show that he/she received the documents even after receiving them online, the service of the documents will not be effective. It is a so-called "delivered but not received" phenomenon.

To solve this problem, Korean law regulates as follows: if registration is not confirmed within one week from the date of notification, it shall be deemed that the document has been served on the date when a week has passed since the registration was notified (Proviso to Article 11, para. 4 EDCPA).

A unique solution has emerged in China. Some local Chinese courts designed and implemented a "forced pop-up notification function" for e-service via cellphones.[46] So, basically, after a litigation announcement was sent, a forced pop-up notification will immediately appear on the screen of the linked cellphone of the recipient. His/her phone will be locked and thus cannot be used at all, unless the recipient clicks the "Yes, I received" button on the screen. Practice in multiple local courts all over the country indicates that this is a very effective way of ensuring e-service.[47]

3.3. DOCUMENTS IN THE MAIN HEARING

It can be discussed whether electronic documents, PowerPoint, image files, or video files can be submitted as a form of AET or whether presentation can be done using these files.

---

[43]   See http://splcgk.court.gov.cn/splcgk-dzsd (quoted in WANG, Chinese Report, p. 16).

[44]   WANG, Chinese Report, pp. 15–16.

[45]   AGRAWAL and KUMWAT, Indian Report. p. 3.

[46]   WANG, Chinese Report, p. 16 (quoting X. LIU and M. LIU, "On the Status Quo and Improvement of the E-Service in Civil Litigations in China" (2018) 3 *Journal of Law Application*).

[47]   WANG, Chinese Report, p. 16.

Intersentia

In Taiwan, parties and judges can use PowerPoint, image files, or video files in the hearing to present written documents.[48]

In Korea, if documents such as a complaint, answer to the complaint, or preparatory writings are listed as electronic documents, the hearing shall be made by either a party to state material matters verbally or by the court to confirm such matters to the party verbally. This hearing can be made by pointing out what is needed on the display screen, where electronic documents are produced by devices equipped with information processing capabilities such as computers.

In India, only the presentation of written allegations is permissible.[49]

3.4. ELECTRONIC DOCUMENTS AS EVIDENCE

In Taiwan, there are five forms of evidence in the CCP: witness testimony, court-expert testimony, document evidence, inspection, and party testimony. Some scholars believe that since Taiwan allows for the free evaluation of evidence, electronic documents should also be accepted as evidence in courts.[50] The use of new types of evidence is not uncommon in recent court practice – for example, electronic medical records, emails, flash disk drives, image files on a CD, documents printed from a website, dashcam recordings, and documents printed from Wikipedia.[51]

According to Korean law, there are six forms of evidence in the CPA: witness, expert, document, inspection, interrogation of parties, and information containing objects. Also, the evidence investigation of electronic documents may be conducted by the following means: (1) viewing electronic documents using monitors, screens, etc. in case of investigating evidence of information in the form of letters, other symbols, drawings, photographs, etc.; (2) listening to or viewing electronic documents in case of investigating evidence of voice or video information (Article 13, para. 1 EDCPR).

3.5. NON-DOCUMENTARY OBJECTS

Electronic documents contain not only text but also photographs, and audio and video information. They can have the same function as a document – that

---

[48] SHEN and WANG, Taiwanese Report, p. 16.
[49] AGRAWAL and KUMWAT, Indian Report, p. 4.
[50] SHEN and WANG, Taiwanese Report, p. 20 (quoting K.-L. SHEN, *Civil Evidence Law and Fairness of Procedure*, Angle Publishing, Taipei 2007, p. 76).
[51] SHEN and WANG, Taiwanese Report, p. 20.

The Application of Electronic Technologies in Judicial Proceedings

is, although there is no record of the word or the symbol, it can still convey the meaning or thoughts of the person.

Thus, in Taiwan, it is provided in Article 363 CCP that non-documentary objects communicating human ideas could be viewed as "quasi-documents" and the provisions of documents apply *mutatis mutandis* to such objects. According to Article 363, para. 1 CCP, "the provisions of this item shall apply mutatis mutandis to non-documentary objects which operate as documents." Since electronic documents (such as emails) are created by humans to convey and communicate ideas, they qualify as "quasi-documents."[52]

In Korea, graphic files, audio files, and video files are recognized as electronic documents if they were created or converted in electronic form by the court-designated information processing system. Such voice or video files are recognized as documents only when they represent the essential nature of the document, i.e., the author's thoughts.

3.6. ELECTRONIC DATA AS EVIDENCE IN CHINA

The Chinese report details the concept and problems of electronic data as evidence. In particular, it is described in detail how to secure its authenticity.

According to Article 116 of the Judicial Interpretation on Civil Procedural Law of the SPC, which explains what belongs in the "electronic data" category of evidence listed in Article 63 CPL 2012, electronic data refers to "information formed or saved in certain electronic medium through an email, electronic data exchange, online conversation record, blog, microblog, cellphone text message, electronic signature or domain name, etc. This rule also applies to audio and visual recordings saved in electronic medium." Through a form of cataloging, this judicial interpretation detailed specific types of electronic data that can be used as electronic evidence in civil litigation in China.[53]

The hard part for the Chinese civil court is to determine the authenticity of such evidence. Compared to other types of evidence, electronic data (due to its nature) is easier to manipulate via computer programs or other software. When Chinese civil judges deal with this matter, they usually approve the authenticity of electronic evidence through two alternative ways – the opposing party's recognition or notarization.[54] In recent years, more methods that can provide support for judges authenticating electronic evidence have been established and have become popular. One way to do this is through activating a mechanism of cross-examinations at trial made by expert assistants to the parties. Such a

---

[52] Ibid., p. 21 (quoting K.-L. SHEN, above n. 50, p. 78).
[53] WANG, Chinese Report, p. 2.
[54] Ibid., p. 3.

Intersentia

413

mechanism was added into the CPL in the 2012 amendment. Statements made by expert assistants would be considered as statements of the parties. Such an adversarial mechanism between experts usually solves most technical issues in authenticating electronic evidence. If the problem is still not resolved, Chinese civil judges can then initiate forensic examination to determine the authenticity of such evidence. The advantage of such a mechanism is it can significantly facilitate and empower trial judges in confirming the authenticity of electronic evidence. The downside is obviously the extra costs to the litigating parties, which may be unaffordable for many.[55]

Alternatively, an eye-catching, relatively cost-effective solution is third-party independent service providers preserving (or "depositing") digital files for (potential) civil litigants, a method that has gained popularity very quickly in China in the last few years.

This service, mostly provided by private commercial tech companies in China, usually works by simulating Web browser requests, downloading the resulting website files (including images and source codes), and packing them into an archive. The archive file is then digitally signed and "hashed" (an algorithm is applied, resulting in a unique code) and the hash code is timestamped and distributed onto encrypted data platforms, e.g., a blockchain-based system. Even a miniscule change to the archive file would result in a completely different hash code. Compared to manually operated notarization, third-party e-file deposition service is cheaper and more convenient to litigants, while equally or even more reliable as an endorsement of the authenticity of the electronic evidence preserved. It could potentially significantly lower costs for the party bearing the burden of producing evidence in civil litigation, especially for plaintiffs of small claims.[56]

To follow-up quickly on such a new situation, the SPC issued Provisions on Several Issues in the Trial of Cases in Internet Courts, which for the first time recognized that electronic evidence deposited in and extracted from blockchains could be admitted as valid evidence by judges, as long as its authenticity has been verified.

The downside of third-party e-file deposition service is equally obvious. For instance, this is an area that currently is not legally disciplined, nor having any national unified technical standards in China.[57] In addition, underlying technologies like blockchain behind the e-file deposition service are always complex and difficult to explain to or to be understood by trial judges. It is also difficult for judges to verify the reliability of such technology.[58]

---

[55]   Ibid., p. 4.
[56]   Ibid., pp. 4–5.
[57]   Ibid., p. 5 (quoting G. Guo, W. Li, and Y. Shen, "Analysis of Problems of Third-Party E-Data Depository Platform and Suggestions" (2018) 138 *China Intellectual Property*).
[58]   Wang, Chinese Report, p. 6.

4. THE PROCESS OF USING VIDEO DEVICES

The question is whether video transmission can be used in proceedings. Such issues include whether a judge may listen to the statements of a party not present in the hearing on a video relay, or whether the statements of witnesses or experts on video recordings will be permitted. China, as mentioned earlier, is already moving in the direction of installing and operating the Intelligent Court and the Internet Court, so it is a natural assumption that video technology will be used in a hearing. Therefore, only the situation in Korea and Taiwan will be dealt with here.

4.1. STATEMENTS OF THE PARTIES

At present in Korea, it is not permitted for both parties to speak to judges through video transmission without appearing in the competent court. However, there is a debate over whether one party can make a video argument without attending a hearing. This is not permitted in practice, where oral hearing is mandatory. This is because it is not fair that only one party appears in court and the other pleads in another court via a video.[59] However, some argue that the development of technology has resolved these problems sufficiently and that online arguments should now be allowed.[60]

4.2. WITNESSES

In Taiwan, in principle, the witnesses who are legally notified have an obligation to appear at the court in person. However, Article 305 CCP allows the court to examine a witness via the medium of a technological device if the court considers it appropriate to do so.[61] With regard to cross-examination, only a one-to-one connection between the court and the place of technological device located is acceptable.[62] It is not necessary for witnesses to go to another court to use a technological device for interrogation; instead, there are several means of interrogation. First, in accordance with Article 305, para. 1 CCP, when the witness cannot appear at the court or when there are other necessary circumstances, the witness may be examined at the place where he/she is presently located.[63]

---

[59] See H.-J. KANG, "On the Civil Procedure Using Electronic Technology" (2019) 479 *Human Rights and Justice* 141.

[60] Ibid., pp. 141–47.

[61] SHEN and WANG, Taiwanese Report, pp. 17, 23.

[62] Ibid., p. 25.

[63] Ibid., p. 24.

Furthermore, based on Article 3 of the Regulations Governing the Court's Handling of Remote Interrogation in Civil Cases, if no technological device is available for the remote interrogation at the place where the witness is located, he/she may use the device in a nearby court. Currently, the generally accepted locations of remote interrogation include the court and specific government agencies, such as prisons and shelters.[64]

In Korea, a witness may appear at a location where video or other relay facilities are installed, and may be interrogated by video or audio transmission in the following cases: (1) where it is difficult for a witness to appear in court directly due to the fact that he/she lives far away, in a place where travel is inconvenient, or for other reasons; (2) the psychological burden significantly damages mental tranquility of the witness in case that the witness testifies in court in the presence of a party (Article 327-2 CPA). The relay device to be used by the witness shall, in principle, be installed in the court, but exceptions may be granted in this respect.

4.3. EXPERTS

According to Article 324 CCP in Taiwan, the provisions regarding the examination of witnesses shall apply *mutatis mutandis* to expert testimony. And according to Article 305, para. 5 CCP, the court may remotely examine a witness directly between the location of a witness and the court by using any available technological audio/visual device if the court considers it appropriate to do so. Therefore, the court may order expert witnesses to state their opinions using a technological device if it is appropriate to do so (based on Article 335 CCP).[65]

In Korea, the court may, by listening to the opinions of the parties, have the expert present at the place where there is a relay device or an internet video device, and examine the expert by video and sound in the following cases: (1) where there are special circumstances in which it is difficult for the expert to appear in court; or (2) in order to interrogate a person residing in a foreign country as an expert (Article 339-3 CPA). In these cases, there is no requirement that an internet video device should be installed in a court. Therefore, the expert can make a statement sitting in front of the computer in his/her office or home. Previously, the process of verifying the credibility of expert's opinion took a long time because it was done in writing, but now it is expected that video-based interrogation will help speed up the litigation process. This regulation is also applicable to translators who translate for foreigners (Article 143 CPA).

---

[64] Ibid.
[65] Ibid., p. 25.

4.4. INTERROGATION OF PARTIES AS EVIDENCE

In Korea, the interrogation of parties as evidence is admissible because the provisions regarding examination of witnesses shall apply *mutatis mutandis* to the examination of parties (Articles 372-2 and 373 CPA).

In Taiwan, where the interrogation of parties as evidence was only permitted in 2000 following the amendment of the CCP, according to Article 367-3, the provisions regarding examination of witnesses shall apply *mutatis mutandis* to the examination of parties. And pursuant to Article 305, para. 5, the court may examine a party directly between the location of a party and the court by using any available technological device if the court considers it appropriate to do so.[66] Furthermore, Article 11 of the Regulations Governing the Court's Handling of Remote Interrogation in Civil Cases shows that the regulation regarding examination of witnesses shall also apply *mutatis mutandis* to the examination of parties.[67]

5. ONLINE DISPUTE RESOLUTION

5.1. ADR IN GENERAL

There are many different kinds of alternative dispute resolution(ADR); settlement, conciliation, and arbitration are the most frequently used. ADR in the form of mediation has also frequently been employed in recent years.[68] The characteristics of these proceedings are that they are not formal and are flexible. It is common that the settlement, conciliation, and mediation processes bring about a consensus among the parties involved in the dispute. Unlike litigation procedures that value strict formality, these ADR features have little problem with online proceedings.

5.2. ODR AS A MEANS OF ADR

Online dispute resolution (ODR) means proceedings conducted through informal online communication. It refers to the online process of the parties' main communication in ADR – that is, the concept of conducting ADR online. ODR is based on the idea that disputes arising from online transactions are

---

[66]   Ibid., p. 26.

[67]   Ibid., p. 27.

[68]   The relationship between mediation and conciliation is not clear. *Black's Law Dictionary* describes the two as being the same, while others explain that conciliation is a mixture of mediation and arbitration (see M. WENDLAND, *Mediation und Zivilprozess*, Mohr Siebeck, Tübingen 2017, p. 136).

appropriate to resolve online, which is understood as an extension of online business. In particular, it is recognized as a useful dispute settlement mechanism for international e-commerce. It is suitable for disputes involving small amounts that occur in large quantities. It is used to resolve disputes as quickly as possible at a lower cost. And this is effective if the parties to the dispute do not need to or do not want to face each other in court. ODR began to be discussed by the Organisation for Economic Co-operation and Development (OECD) in the late 1990s, and the International Chamber of Commerce drew up the ODR working guidelines in 2003. The United Nations Commission on International Trade Law (UNCITRAL)'s Working Group III then created UNCITRAL Technical Notes on Online Dispute Resolution in 2017.[69]

The United States is a country where ODR is actively used. For example, the eBay Dispute Resolution Center receives about 60 million different disputes a year and solves them through the use of answers, negotiations, and mediation. If these do not resolve the dispute, it shall be settled within ten days after it is handed over to arbitration. The European Union has created an ODR platform that resolves disputes by communicating remotely with the ODR method if consumers in the EU have product or service problems in all retail sectors.[70]

In Taiwan, some commentators believe that online arbitration has obvious technical advantages for e-commerce. The entire process of online arbitration can be carried out using electronic technology and the internet. Therefore, it is recommended to establish an online arbitration procedure for e-commerce in Taiwan.[71]

In Korea, ODR is thought to be used more actively in settlement and conciliation. There is little possibility of using ODR for settlement and conciliation in court. This is because this is part of the court proceedings. However, it is highly likely that ODR will be used in settlement and conciliation proceedings made outside the court, because there are few legal regulations in relation to such proceedings. Also, settlement, conciliation, and arbitration using ODR are expected to be widely used in disputes arising in e-commerce.

5.3. JUDICIAL PROCEEDINGS WITH ODR

Whether ODR, which has great advantages in relation to ADR, could be used in the future in court proceedings is a subject of debate.

---

[69]   I.-K. KAY, *The Research on the Online Dispute Resolution (ODR)*, Judicial Policy Research Institute, New York 2018.

[70]   Ibid.

[71]   SHEN and WANG, Taiwanese Report, p. 35 (quoting J.-H. LIN, "Preliminary Discussion of the E-commerce Disputes and Online Arbitration" (2015) 101 *Arbitration Quarterly*, 119–20, http://www.arbitration.org.tw/upload/publication/pub_Logo31486015683101__4%E6%9E%97%E4%BF%8A%E5%AE%8F.pdf.

5.3.1. Taiwan

In Taiwan, there is no express provision in the Constitution as to whether or not the judicial process should be material. It is only prescribed that the "organization of the Judicial Yuan and of the law courts of various grades shall be prescribed by law" (Article 82 of the Constitution). Therefore, it could be possible to apply ODR to judicial proceedings in the future.[72] Taiwan is developing an e-court system, though not necessarily ODR system. There are four key aspects of an e-court system: (1) an online filing system; (2) an online motion and file reading system; (3) an electronic court records system; and (4) a digital file and evidence presentation system.

5.3.2. Korea

In Korea, as mentioned above, remote video trials were not successful. The reason for this was that it proved too costly to deal with minor cases. Moreover, the people who experienced this system complained that they did not feel like they were being interrogated directly and that the process became more delayed.[73]

Today, with faster internet speed and highly developed video transmission technology, the courts in Korea are re-examining the issue of online litigation. Experiments are taking place with trials using video calls at district courts in Seoul, Suwon, and Busan.[74] In order to preserve the merits of using the video facility in proceedings, judges and parties are using internet-based computers and smartphones for everyday use, not video machines installed in the courts.[75] Lawyers whose offices are far from the courts have usually responded positively to the experiment.[76] The problems encountered in this experiment are as follows. The connection status of video calls has sometimes deteriorated, sound issues have sometimes made it difficult to understand the other party's words, and the identity of the litigants and parties present can be difficult to identify.[77] Such ODR experiments are currently being conducted only in part of the litigation process due to statutory limitations. It will be necessary to revise the statute if ODR is to be used formally.

Currently, the Computer Information Management Bureau of the National Court Administration designs future models of the next-generation electronic litigation system. The first is a lawyer-less lawsuit subsidized by

---

[72] SHEN and WANG, Taiwanese Report, p. 35.
[73] S.-H. IM, above n. 6, p. 116.
[74] J.-C. SON, "Report on the Results of Trial Proceedings using Video Call" (2019) 476 *Human Rights and Justice* 92.
[75] Ibid., 93.
[76] Ibid., 95.
[77] Ibid., 98.

artificial intelligence. The system allows artificial intelligence robots to guide the parties throughout the entire proceedings, including the creation of a complaint. Therefore, anyone will be able to improve judicial accessibility by accessing easy-to-understand information 24 hours a day regardless of court hours, and simple litigation documents can be written by the parties themselves to reduce litigation costs.[78]

The second is online litigation. In the short term, the National Court Administration will push for the expansion of video trials through the internet, where the parties and their representatives can appear at a remote courtroom for trial. In the mid- to long-term, the plan is to establish an online litigation system that will ultimately allow users to appear in court online at fixed hearing times at their home or office via cellphone.[79]

Some have been critical of these plans. Given the failed experience of video litigation in 1996, it would be uncomfortable for parties who are not familiar with video litigation and would not feel like they are being heard in person. It is impossible to do all the work of a real lawsuit online. No matter how good the monitor screen is, it cannot eliminate the above-mentioned disadvantage of remote hearing. Therefore, there would be a limit to the court's thorough grasp of the entire content of the hearing.[80]

5.3.3. China

As mentioned above, the annual workload per judge in China has greatly increased in recent years. The number of civil cases has continued to surge in China after 2015, partly because in 2015, the filing system for Chinese civil cases changed from the traditional judicial review model to a so-called registration model, which makes civil case filing much easier than before. In contrast, since 2017, the number of Chinese judges has actually decreased, mostly due to a nationwide reform on purifying and selecting competent judges,[81] which makes the workload problem even worse.[82] To solve this problem, the SPC decided to introduce a new technology to allow judges to hear cases more efficiently. This is the intelligent court that the SPC has made a push for.[83]

---

[78] J.-H. CHANG, "The Age of Informatization and the Change of Litigation" (2018) 476 *Human Rights and Justice* 199.

[79] Ibid., pp. 200–201.

[80] S.-H. IM, above n. 6, p. 116.

[81] WANG, Chinese Report, p. 8 (quoting L. Feng, "Reform on Purifying and Selecting Competent Judges Has Been Implemented Nationwide, with More Than 90,000 Previous Judges Still Not Qualified," *China News*, July 5, 2017, https://www.chinanews.com/gn/2017/07-05/8269363.shtml.

[82] WANG, Chinese Report, p. 8.

[83] Ibid.

Since 2017, promoting the development of the "intelligent court" project has been a key component of Chinese judicial reforms. The People's Courts intend to establish a networking, transparent and intelligent informatization system which will support all litigation procedures (from case filing to the enforcement of the judgment) going online and make these accessible to the general public, which will improve and modernize the Chinese judicial system in a scientific way.[84] There are at least two key reasons behind the SPC's massive and determinative support for the "intelligent court" project.[85] The first of these is to address the disturbing problems of "too many cases but not enough judges." By promoting the "intelligent court" project, the SPC aims to develop an online software system for all courts and judges in China which can intelligently assist judges handling cases – e.g., digitalizing all case files, helping judges generating legal documents, online document review, an approval and transfer system, automatic generation of trial transcripts, automatic reference to similar case judgments and the text of related law and regulations, etc. The SPC anticipates that such a system could significantly improve the efficiency of trials and relieve the pressure on judges.[86] The second reason is to promote the transparency of the judiciary and public access to this. By promoting and implementing the "intelligent court" project through measures like constructing online platforms and databases, the general public could freely and easily check the litigation progress/status of any given case, watch live streaming of trials, and search and review case judgments and enforcement information at any time and anywhere. By allowing judicial activities to be more visible to the general public, the SPC also hopes that this might force Chinese judges to handle cases in a more careful manner than has been the case in the past.[87]

To support this project, China has invested hundreds of millions of RMB each year as well as enormous human resources into the construction of an intelligent court. Most of the finance has been funded by the central and local Chinese governments.[88] There are four substantive accomplishments that have been made in relation to the project:[89] the digitalization of court files,[90] the construction of multiple online platforms (China Judicial Proceeding Information Online, China Trial Online, China Enforcement Information Online),[91] developing legal

---

[84]   Ibid., p. 6 (quoting SPC Announcement on Accelerating Construction of Intelligent Court (2017) (SPC Announcement 2017 No. 12) Article 1, "Purpose, Goal and Requirements," http://gongbao.court.gov.cn/Details/5dec527431cdc22b72163b49fc0284.html).

[85]   WANG, Chinese Report, p. 7.

[86]   Ibid., p. 8 (quoting Q. XIONG, "Construction of Intelligent Court Boosting Judicial Reforms in China," *Guangming Daily*, December 7, 2017, http://epaper.gmw.cn/gmrb/html/2017-12/07/nw.D110000gmrb_20171207_3-15.htm.

[87]   WANG, Chinese Report, pp. 8–9.

[88]   Ibid., p. 10.

[89]   Ibid.

[90]   Ibid., pp. 10–11.

[91]   Ibid., pp. 11–12.

AI software and programs (using automatic speech recognition technology to generate real-time trial transcripts and developing an automatic notification system for similar judgement in similar cases),[92] and establishing the e-service of judicial documents.[93]

Plan to establish the Internet Court: Since 2017, China started to establish a new form of court – the Internet Court – which no doubt is a byproduct of the SPC's "intelligent court" project.[94] In August 2017, the SPC established the first Internet Court in Hangzhou City. Hangzhou is most prosperous city in China's e-commerce industry.[95] The Court has a team of full-time judges and is the size of an ordinary local people's court. According to official statistics published by the Court, as of August 17, 2018, one year after its establishment, it had handled 12,074 internet-related cases (mostly civil cases and a few administrative disputes) of which 10,391 cases are now closed. All these cases have some factor(s) relating to the jurisdiction of Hangzhou City. And in these cases, if the defendant responded online, the case was tried via an online platform operated by the Hangzhou Internet Court. The average duration of these online trials was 28 minutes per trial, and the average processing period from filing an online complaint to case termination was 38 days.[96] Subsequently, in September 2018, two other Internet Courts were established in Beijing and Guangzhou, respectively. According to the Provisions, Internet Courts are designated to handle disputes involving online contractual disputes over sales of goods, services, and financial loans; online copyright disputes; disputes over internet domain names; disputes over using the internet to infringe others' personal or property rights; disputes over product liability as a result of online shopping; internet-related public interest lawsuits brought by the People's Procuratorates; and administrative litigation arising out of internet management by the government (Article 2 of the Provisions of the Supreme People's Court of China on Several Issues in the Trial of Cases in Internet Courts).[97] As a general rule, the entire litigation process in the Internet Courts will be conducted online, including the service of legal documents, the presentation of evidence, and the actual trial itself. Most of the evidence in the cases heard by Internet Courts is electronic data and is stored online.[98]

---

[92] Ibid., pp. 12–15.
[93] Ibid., pp. 15–16.
[94] Ibid., p. 18.
[95] Ibid.
[96] Ibid., p. 19 (quoting G. Du and M. Yu, "China Establishes Three Internet Courts to Try Internet-Related Cases Online," *China Justice Observer*, December 16, 2018), https://www.chinajusticeobserver.com/a/china-establishes-three-internet-courts-to-try-internet-related-cases-online).
[97] Wang, Chinese Report, p. 19.
[98] Ibid., p. 20.

In relation to these Internet Courts, the following are some of the real problems that have been noted in China. All three Chinese Internet Courts are located in cities that are the home to giant tech companies. And almost all these tech companies have publicly announced their firm support for the local Internet Court. They may even have participated in the preparation of launching such courts.[99] However, Alibaba and its subsidiaries (such as Taobao and Tmall) are somehow related to most online disputes that appear before the Hangzhou Internet Court. Therefore, there are increasing public doubts as to whether these Internet Courts can maintain their impartiality rather than bias in favor of those tech giants that gave their technological support to the court.[100] In addition, according to the current Internet Court setting, the corresponding appellate court is usually the Intermediate People's Court of the same city. However, the rule designers seem to have forgotten that those intermediate courts do not have the same online trial platform or other equipment as the Internet Court does, which means the appellant has to convert an online case offline. Such incompatibility between an Internet Court and its upper appellate body in the traditional court form would thus provide trial judges of online trials with enormous discretion in their case adjudication. How to supervise and restrict the power of Internet Court judges has already become a critical issue.[101]

6. THE FUTURE OF THE JUDICIARY

6.1. AI LAWYER AND AI JUDGE?

Today, many lawyers are worried that AI lawyers and AI judges will appear in the near future. There is also debate as to whether it is desirable for this to happen.

According to the present legal system, only natural persons can become lawyer and judges. However, it is necessary to be legally prepared in advance in the event that AI lawyers emerge due to developments in technology. It is assumed that there is no regulation in Asia in this regard. The problem about letting an AI lawyer represent a party is how to control its "behaviors," how to make sure its counseling or representation would be good and honest, and how to avoid infringement of the interests of the parties by an AI lawyer.[102]

Ethical issues relating to the introduction of AI also emerge. Thus, in Taiwan, researchers have requested "the government to conduct further research on a number of relevant legal issues, such as the impact that AI has on the labor market, the necessity of setting forth AI ethic rules and ethic committees, the

---

[99] Ibid., p. 21.
[100] Ibid.
[101] Ibid., pp. 20–21.
[102] SHEN and WANG, Taiwanese Report, p. 35.

Intersentia

patentability of inventions by AI, in order to mitigate the potential impact that the application of AI will bring about and to prevent any loss of opportunity in AI development due to Taiwan's existing legal restrictions."[103]

Here we should first clarify what the activities of AI lawyers should be. The basic activity of AI lawyers is simply to provide legal information, such as existing statutes, the courts' case law, and theories applicable to the current case. The next step of activity is to present legal opinions for legal reference based on information about cases entered by lawyers. The third step would be to take legal action instead of a lawyer or to make a decision in place of a judge based on the data entered. If this becomes the situation in reality, existing judges and lawyers will become merely assistants to the AI lawyer or AI judge. What people fear not only in the legal profession but also in many professional groups is the development of AI technology to this very point. However, we are oblivious to the fact that AI technology is developed by humans; it is not evolving on its own and we do not need to be afraid of it. Thus, the speed and limitations of the technological development of AI can be controlled by humans. From this perspective, we will need to come up with measures to cope with new technological developments.

6.2. ACCESS TO JUSTICE WITHOUT ANY LIMITATIONS?

Ease of access to the court through AET is preferable, but there may be questions about whether easy access to the courts is necessarily a good thing. Given the current circumstances of each country, the easier, the better. As Taiwanese report points out, in this way, it is possible to reduce the use of the judicial system to realize substantive rights, and procedural loss of the party in terms wasted time, travel, paperwork, communication, and so on. As a result, it is hard to say whether access to justice through AET may be superfluous and excessive.[104] If the above process can be assisted by electronic technology, it will effectively reduce time and complexity of procedures, improve the efficiency of data transmission, and decrease the occurrence of errors.[105] As the Chinese report noted, online trials at the Internet Court will save litigants time, money, and other resources, as well as being more convenient. It sends out a clear message that it would be

---

[103]   Ibid., p. 36 (quoting LEE and LI, *Attorneys-at-Law* (2018), Commissioned Research Project on International Trends and Responses of Relevant Regulations on Artificial intelligence, ii–iii, https://ws.ndc.gov.tw/Download.ashx?u=LzAwMS9hZG1pbmlzdHJhdG9yLzEwL3JlbGGZ pbGUvNTc0NC8zMTk5OC8xY2MwZWFiZi1jNTMzLTQ0M2QtYjc1Mi1iM2U4MDkwZm YzMTIucGRm&n=44CM5Lq65bel5pm65oWn5LmL55u46Zec5rOV6KaP5ZyL6Zq b55m85bGV6Lao5Yui6IiH5Zug5oeJ44CN5aeU6KiX56CU56m26KiI55Wr57WQ5qGI5a Cx5ZGKLnBkZg%3D%3D&icon=.pdf).
[104]   SHEN and WANG, Taiwanese Report, p. 37.
[105]   Ibid.

a revolutionary creation which could change the rules of the game.[106] The fact that AET is of great help in terms of improving access to justice is also true other countries.

However, we cannot overlook the following problems listed in relation to online procedures in China. One great thing about the traditional courtroom setting is a sense of solemn ritual, which makes people standing in it want to speak truthfully. Unfortunately, live streaming online trials do not have such a sense of formality.[107] Another great thing about the traditional trial setting is the parties and their witnesses testifying in front of the judge is close proximity where the judge will pay close attention not just to the content of their testimony but also the facial expression, tone of voice, body language, and other behaviors of the witnesses, which in return will usually help the judge determine witnesses' honesty to a significant degree.[108] Online trials will suffer accordingly, no matter how great the technology or the network infrastructure is.[109]

And no matter how many advantages AET has in terms of access to justice, the parties should not be forced to use this process. As the Taiwanese report emphasized, we should protect the rights of the parties to choose the procedure for their own dispute resolution. Specifically, when the parties choose to resolve disputes through the traditional judicial system, and the choice will do no harm to the public interests and the interests of the other party, since the interests of the substantive and the procedural interests involved in the dispute are attributable to the parties, the pursuit of such interests should respect the choices of the parties. Therefore, based on the protection of the procedural choice, we should ensure that the parties have the option of access to justice as much as possible.[110]

Also, the plan for the lawyer-less lawsuit of the Computer Information Management Bureau of the National Court Administration in Korea presents many problems. People at the Bureau think it could be a form of judicial service to help the people to sue easily. But it is not the court's duty to induce people to sue without the help of lawyers; rather, it is normal for the parties to file lawsuits easily with the help of lawyers to protect their rights. The plan is thought to have ignored the role of the lawyer in the legal profession and that the plan, if realized, could destroy the market for lawyers. More serious is the fact that no matter how advanced AI and information processing technology are, the influence of judges in litigation may increase, resulting in the loss of the party's position as the subject of the lawsuit and becoming an object of investigation.

---

[106] WANG, Chinese Report, p. 21 (quoting S. ZHAN and Y. WANG, "Rethink the Online Trial Mechanism of the Internet Court" (2019) 6 *Jianghan Forum*).

[107] WANG, Chinese Report, p. 20 (quoting X. WANG, "Trial Must Have a Sense of Formality and Ritual," Xinjiang Court Net, October 24, 2016, http://oldwww.xjcourt.org/public/detail. php?id=25153).

[108] WANG, Chinese Report, p. 20 (quoting S. ZHAN and Y. WANG, above n. 106).

[109] WANG, Chinese Report, p. 20.

[110] SHEN and WANG, Taiwanese Report, p. 37.

7. CONCLUSION

In ADR outside the court, it is desirable to actively utilize ODR. However, in court proceedings, the use of AET, as well as ODR, needs to be somewhat cautious. Those who praise AET and ODR only emphasize convenience and efficiency in court proceedings, and the downside behind this is easy to overlook. It is questionable, to put it in extreme terms, whether the parties would be allowed to lie in bed with their cellphones, send their complaints, and even make online arguments, even if we admit it is ideal to eliminate obstacles to access to the court.

Applying AET or ODR to litigation proceedings can be two different situations. One is when people have to deal with objects in a lawsuit, and the other is when people interact with each other. The former includes the submission and service of legal documents, including the complaint and reply, and the investigation of evidence such as documentary evidence and evidence by inspection. The latter is the case in which a judge hears the parties, the parties each other make oral arguments, and the parties or the judge interrogates a witness or an expert. In the case of the former, it would be fine to allow AET in principle, since items such as documents are subject to legal regulation. There may be problems such as document forgery, but these have been overcome by the development of electronic technology. Instead, the benefits of convenience in litigation could be maximized.

However, in the latter case, it is completely different. In court, it is a very sensitive and detailed matter for the judge and the parties, the judge and the witness, and the parties and the witness to have face-to-face conversations in hearing or evidence investigations. Even if there's a transparent glass between the two people talking in their daily lives, their mood of conversation would be quite different compared to that of conversation without the glass. If the hearing in court could be a mechanical exchange of questions and answers, it would be safe to open the hearing by video call or video conversation. However, arguments and witness examinations are where the two parties are sharply divided over facts and legal issues in court. Finding facts in a lawsuit is the process to find out whose argument is correct by which at least one of the two opposing parties denies to tell the truth.

Therefore, it is desirable for judges, parties, lawyers, and witnesses to allow the machines to be used as a medium only where it is indispensable or plays a supporting role. In this sense, we should not just look at or praise AET and ODR. Legal measures should be taken to encourage what should be encouraged and to restrict what should be limited. I think the statement of Jhering still makes sense, even in part, today in the twenty-first century: "Form is the sworn enemy of arbitrariness and the twin sister of freedom."

PART II

NEW CHALLENGES
AND THEIR VARIOUS ASPECTS

New Types of Evidence

PRESENT AND FUTURE ISSUES REGARDING NEW TYPES OF EVIDENCE

Electronic and Digital Evidence in Particular

Etsuko Sugiyama[*]

1. Introduction 431
   1.1. The Purpose of this Chapter 431
       1.1.1. The Current Situation on the Use of Evidence in Civil
              Procedure 431
       1.1.2. What are "New" Types of Evidence? 433
   1.2. The Questionnaire for National Reporters and
        National Reports.. 433
2. The General Rule on Evidence in Civil Procedure.................... 435
   2.1. Various Attitudes Toward the Admissibility or the Probative
        Value of Evidence... 435
   2.2. Free Choice and Evaluation of Evidence...................... 436
       2.2.1. The Relevance or Necessity of Evidence 437
       2.2.2. Hearsay Evidence is Admissible 437
       2.2.3. The Best Evidence Rule or the Original Document Rule ... 438
       2.2.4. Illegally Obtained Evidence.......................... 438
       2.2.5. Rules on the Probative Value of a Public or Private
              Document 439
       2.2.6. Other Restrictions as to the Examination of Evidence
              for Efficient Adjudication........................... 441
   2.3. Jurisdiction with Rules on the Admissibility of Evidence.......... 441
       2.3.1. The Relevance Rule.................................. 441
       2.3.2. The Hearsay Rule................................... 442

---

[*]   Professor, Graduate School of Law, Hitotsubashi University, Japan.

		2.3.3.	Opinion Evidence	442
		2.3.4.	Character Evidence	442
		2.3.5.	The Best Evidence Rule or Original Document Rule	443
	2.4.		Initiative in Examination of Evidence	443
	2.5.		Types of Evidence Allowed in Civil Procedure	445
		2.5.1.	Admissible Types of Evidence	445
		2.5.2.	The Categorization of New Types of Evidence and the Review of Categorization Itself	445
		2.5.3.	Priorities Among Evidence: Documentary Evidence versus Oral Testimony	447
3.			New Types of Evidence	447
	3.1.		Examples of New Forms of Evidence	447
	3.2.		Rules on New Evidence in General	449
		3.2.1.	Rules on the Admissibility and Probative Value of New Types of Evidence	450
		3.2.2.	The Production of New Types of Evidence	452
		3.2.3.	Authenticity and Integrity	454
		3.2.4.	The Hearsay Rule	458
	3.3.		Other Issues Relating to Electronic Evidence: Illegally Obtained Evidence	458
	3.4.		The Fact-Finder's Access to Information Available on the Internet	460
4.			Gathering and Preserving New Types of Evidence	462
	4.1.		How to Gather Evidence in General and Electronic Evidence before or During Trial	463
		4.1.1.	The Approach Taken by Common Law Countries	463
		4.1.2.	The Approach Taken by Civil Law Countries	464
	4.2.		Preservation of Electronic Evidence	466
		4.2.1.	The Approach Taken by Common Law Countries	466
		4.2.2.	The Approach Taken by Civil Law Countries	468
	4.3.		Challenges Created by New Technology	469
5.			Future Challenges Created by New Technology	470
	5.1.		Prevalence of the IoT	470
	5.2.		Protection of Confidential Information	471
	5.3.		Assistance from a Third Party and Improving Judges' Skills	472
	5.4.		Rethinking the Definition of Evidence	473
	5.5.		Rethinking Priority Among Different Forms of Evidence: Witness versus Data	474
	5.6.		The Impact of the Electronification of Procedure	474
	5.7.		Returning to the Starting Point …	475

1. INTRODUCTION

1.1. THE PURPOSE OF THIS CHAPTER

1.1.1. *The Current Situation on the Use of Evidence in Civil Procedure*

Fact-finding is one of the most crucial processes in civil procedure. As such fact-finding should be based on evidence in order to result in objective and just decisions, examination of evidence is also a critical process in civil litigation. Traditionally, most jurisdictions have provided detailed rules for evidence that regulate the admissibility or probative value of each piece of evidence in criminal procedure. However, regarding the rules of evidence in civil procedure, most civil law jurisdictions have been relatively permissive of any type of evidence and have left the evaluation of each form of evidence to the discretion of judges. The principle of "free evaluation of the evidence" by judges is based on the presumption that professional judges are well trained and qualified to evaluate the probative value of each type of evidence and to apply it in the fact-finding process. On the other hand, some jurisdictions, especially common law jurisdictions with jury systems, have provided strict rules on the admissibility or probative value of evidence in order to avoid unjust or arbitrary fact-finding.[1]

This does not necessarily mean that jurisdictions which adopt the principle of free evaluation of evidence by judges allow "all kinds of evidence" in the process of a judge's fact-finding. Instead, the scope or the types of evidence admissible in civil procedure have also been limited. Traditionally, the types of evidence accepted in most jurisdictions are "physical" forms of evidence, such as paper documents, witnesses, and experts. Yet, recent technological developments have resulted in the emergence of new types of evidence, which is "non-physical" or "invisible" evidence. As such types of evidence have come to play a more important role in the fact-finding procedure, many jurisdictions have been facing continuous demands to prepare new rules to regulate these types of evidence. Some examples of new forms of evidence are electronic or digital documents and emails. Many jurisdictions have been struggling to modify the traditional rules of evidence in order to cover these newly emerged types of evidence.[2] Common law countries have continuously revised the rules on discovery or disclosure so as to adjust them in Electronically Stored Information (ESI), in addition to rules on the admissibility of electronic evidence. Civil law countries have mainly been concerned with how to handle, collect, and preserve electronic documents stored on a computer, hard

---

[1]   See MARCUS (United States).

[2]   The issue of electronic evidence was already discussed in the previous International Association of Procedural Law (IAPL) conferences (M. KENGYEL and Z. NEMESSÁYI, *Electronic Technology and Civil Procedure New Path to Justice from around the World*, Springer, Berlin 2012).

Intersentia

431

disk, etc. in civil procedure, as well as whether and to what extent these documents should be differentiated from traditional paper documents.

Obviously, drastic technological change has been occurring since the last century. However, this change has increased more rapidly in the past few years and we are now entering the "fourth revolution age" and the paperless age.[3] Data stored in the cloud, conversation through social media, mobile phones, smartphones, and information from Global Positioning System (GPS) data and the Internet of Things (IoT) are just a few examples of recently emerged evidence, which have slightly different characteristics from what we currently perceive as electronic evidence.

One of the features specific to current electronic evidence is the volume of the data contained and presented to court. This feature is well expressed in phrases such as "we are faced with an unprecedented explosion of data; we would thus produce as much information in two days as all humanity would have produced in two million years"[4] or "more data has been created in the last two years than in the entire previous history of the human race, and the amount of data is predicted to grow ten-fold by 2020."[5]

Another feature of current evidence is the accessibility. As more information is available through the internet, the internet has become one of the most valuable sources of information that both courts and parties can access without much difficulty, and sometimes we depend too heavily on the information on the internet. Therefore, we should consider whether or not and to what extent such information can be used in civil procedure.

Faced with the above situation, the premise that professional judges or lay juries are capable of evaluating the value of evidence and finding facts correctly has begun to collapse. Instead, new expertise or technology to deal with new evidence will be required. For instance, the use of artificial intelligence (AI) will need to be considered for the purposes of examining or sorting out evidence in the near future,[6] although the issue of using AI in civil procedure is not directly addressed here.

Rather, the aim of this chapter is to review how the procedural law of each jurisdiction has reacted to the emergence of new types of evidence from the

---

[3]   For example, Kaiser Permanente in the United States stopped using paper records a decade ago; see ANDINO (Spain).

[4]   M. HILBERT and P. LOPEZ, "The World's Technological Capacity to Store, Communicate, and Compute Information" (2011) 332(6025) *Science* 60, 60–65 (see PICHÉ and GAUTRAIS (Canada)).

[5]   In *Gordon v. T.G.R. Logistics, Inc., 321 F.R.D. 401 (D.Wyo.2017)* (see MARCUS (United States)).

[6]   The problem of using AI in civil procedure, especially in the examination of evidence, was covered in the Congress of Salamanca (N.F. FENNOLL, Proeba Cietífica, "Cuestiones de Futuro: Neurociencia e Inteligencia Artificial" in *II Conferencia Internacional & XXVI Jornadas Iberoamerianas de Derecho Procesal IIDP and IIDA "Evidence in the Process"*, Atelier LIBROS JURIDISCO, Barcelona 2018, p. 473, S. HAACK, "Proof, Probability, and Statistics: The Dangers of 'Delusive Exactness,'" in *II Conferencia Internacional & XXVI Jornadas Iberoame-rianas de Derecho Procesal IIDP and IIDA "Evidence in the Process"* (2018), p. 497.

comparative view and to present some perspectives as to we should react to the emergence of new types of evidence. Therefore, the discussion here starts by providing an overview of the general rules of evidence and then moves on to considerations of new types of evidence.

1.1.2. What are "New" Types of Evidence?

The boundary between "new" types of evidence and "old," "traditional" or "conventional" types of difference is difficult to define, since each jurisdiction has different interpretations of these terminologies. The issues that arise regarding the examination or collection of electronic documents or emails stored on the hard disk of a computer have already been discussed repeatedly, and many jurisdictions seem to have already adopted new rules for them. However, there are significant differences in terms of the approach taken by each jurisdiction to regulate new types of evidence. In addition, even a jurisdiction that has already adopted a new rule on "specific" types of evidence needs to perform a constant process of review in order to discern whether this rule can be applied to other types of newly developed evidence. Therefore, reviewing the current situations of electronic or digital evidence in civil procedure is inevitable, regardless of the fact that this issue has been tackled for decades.

The same is true with the use of experts in civil procedure. Many jurisdictions allow courts or parties to appoint experts to provide special expertise that is necessary for fact-finding. Despite the fact that many jurisdictions are accustomed to using experts in cases that require special knowledge and making efforts to determine how to evaluate their opinion, the successive development of science requires them to review whether the existing rules should be retained, modified, or abolished. Progress in the field of digital evidence in particular has generated a new demand for new expertise such as forensic science.

Therefore, physical and well-known evidence which judges or juries are able to evaluate its value without much difficulty is categorized as traditional evidence. In this chapter, the focus is on electronic or digital evidence.[7]

1.2. THE QUESTIONNAIRE FOR NATIONAL REPORTERS AND NATIONAL REPORTS

Professor Picó and I distributed questionnaires to national reporters and asked them to provide brief answers with a summary of their institutional backgrounds. The questionnaires consisted of six parts.

---

[7] The issues on the use of experts in civil procedure and the use of privileged communication are dealt with in the contribution to this volume by Professor Picó.

Intersentia

433

In Part 1 of the questionnaire, national reporters were asked to provide us with brief information on the general rules of traditional or physical evidence, for example, general rules on the admissibility or probative value of evidence, the types of admissible evidence, and the possibility of examining evidence *ex officio*, etc., within the jurisdiction of the reporters. Part 1 was intended to gather background information for the following parts.

Part 2 focused on the rules on new types of new evidence. We asked national reporters to provide brief answers on the situations and rules of new types of evidence, especially electronic or digital evidence. We asked about rules on probative values, authenticity, and the method of examining such evidence. We also inquired about the possibility of gathering and using information available on the internet by judges or juries themselves. National reporters were also asked to add any information on the situations of new types of evidence in their jurisdiction, since there might be many issues that we had not yet considered.

Part 3 focused on the methods for collecting and preserving new types of evidence. We first inquired about the general system to collect and preserve evidence and then asked about any special systems to collect and preserve new types of evidence (e-discovery, etc.). We also asked if parties have any obligations to preserve new types of evidence and, if so, how such obligations affect the strategies taken by parties and their representatives.

Part 4 was closely linked to both Part 3 and Part 6, and we asked about future issues in the area of evidence, for instance, the use of functional magnetic resonance imaging (fMRI) and the impact of the increased use of IoT.

In Part 5, we asked about the use of private communications between lawyers and the documents, or any other evidence, that are obtained in mediation and/or via other legal proceedings that try to avoid a future judicial proceeding between the parties in civil procedure. In Part 6, we asked about the use of scientific knowledge of an expert and its judicial control.

At our request, national reports were submitted from various jurisdictions covering all continents, including common law, civil law and mixed jurisdictions.[8] The scope of consideration and terminology used in this chapter.

---

[8] The discussion in this chapter is heavily indebted to and has greatly benefited from the invaluable information provided by the national reporters in the following list: *Asia*: Professor Guo Zhiyuan (China); Professor Hassan Mohseni and Professor Mostafa Elsan (Iran); Professor Hiroshi Tega (Japan), Dr. Ji Won Park,(Republic of Korea); and Professor Kuan-Ling Shen (Taiwan); *Africa*: Professor Rashri Baboolal-Frank (South Africa); *North America*: Professor Daniel Capra (United States); Professor Richard Marcus(United States)); Professor Catherine Piché and Vicent Gautrais (Canada – this report mainly refers to the rules in Quebec (mixture of common law and civil law) and Ontario (common law)); and Professor Carina Gómez Fröde (Mexico); *South America*: Professor Leandro J. Giannini (Argentina); Professor Darci Guimaraes Ribeiro (Brazil); Professor Andrés Gustavo Mazuera Zuluaga, Professor Dimaro Alexis Agudelo Mejía, Professor Liliana Damaris Pabón Giraldo, Professor Luis Orlando Toro Garzón, Professor Mónica María Bustamante Rúa, and Professor Orión Vargas Vélez (Colombia); Professor Giovanni F. Priori Posada and

The problems in Parts 1–3 are addressed in this section of the chapter and those in Parts 4–6 are included in the chapter written by Professor Picó. Although some jurisdictions do not clearly distinguish the law of evidence in civil procedure from that of criminal procedure, this chapter focuses on the use of electronic or digital evidence in civil procedure.

There is of course a difference between digital evidence and electronic evidence in a strict sense.[9] This chapter will often refer only to "electronic evidence," but this does not mean that digital evidence is excluded from it. Evidence that derives from data stored in or produced by a computer system or network will also be covered here.

2. THE GENERAL RULE ON EVIDENCE IN CIVIL PROCEDURE

2.1. VARIOUS ATTITUDES TOWARD THE ADMISSIBILITY OR THE PROBATIVE VALUE OF EVIDENCE

Before considering the rules of new evidence (including electronic evidence) closely, we will quickly review the general rules of evidence, especially those on the admissibility or probative value of evidence in general. The general approach toward the admissibility of all types of evidence has a decisive effect on the approach taken in relation to newly emerged types of evidence.

Professor Roberto Pérez-Prieto de las Casas (Peru); and Professor Santiago Campos Pereira and Professor María Virginia Barreiro (Uruguay); *Europe*: Professor Dr. Piet Taelman and Dr. Wannes Vandenbussche (Belgium); Professor Alan Uzelac (Croatia); Professor Corinne Bléry and Avoue Jean-Paul Teboul (France); Dr. Norbert Lösing (Germany); Professor Dr. Viktória Harsági (Hungary); Professor Angelo Dondi and Professor Paolo Comoglio (Italy); Professor Anna Nylund (Norway); Professor Dr. Kinga Flaga-Gieruszyńska and Dr. Aleksandra Klich (Poland); Professor Ana Paula Costa e Silva and Professor Leonor Ruivo (Portugal); Professor Francisco Ramos, Marigtrate Juan Andino, and Professor Yolanda Ríos (Spain); and Professor John Sorabji (United Kingdom – this report covers the civil justice system of England and Wales).

9   For instance, electronic evidence is defined as evidence derived from data contained in or produced by any device the functioning of which depends on a software program, or from data stored on or communicated over a computer system or network in "Draft Convention on Electronic Evidence" (2016) 13 *Digital Evidence and Electronic Signature Law Review*, https://journals.sas.ac.uk/deeslr/article/view/2321, and in the Iranian report, it "includes databases, operating systems, computer programs, computer generated models, any information stored in computer memory or exchanged, processed, recovered or generated through computer or telecommunication systems" (see MOHSENI and ELSAN (Iran)). Digital evidence is defined as data that was stored or transmitted in electronic form and could be used to prove the fact in a case according to "Electronic Evidence in China" in B. TAN, M. LEW, and B. ANG, *A Practical Guide to E-Discovery in Asia*, Lexis Nexis, Singapore 2017, p. 39.

Whereas some jurisdictions do not make any clear distinction between the rules of evidence in criminal procedure and those in civil procedure,[10] many jurisdictions adopt different rules between both procedures and tend to apply stricter rules to the former procedure than the latter. In jurisdictions where lay juries rather than professional judges play the major role in fact-finding,[11] stricter rules on the admissibility of evidence are adopted compared to jurisdictions where professional judges are responsible for fact-finding based on objective evidence. In the latter case, the evaluation of evidence is mostly left to the discretion of professional judges, but some exceptions to this principle of free evaluation have also been accepted. Differences also exist with respect to the forms of evidence law; rules of evidence can be a stand-alone law, a part of the law of civil procedure, or a part of substantive law.[12]

2.2. FREE CHOICE AND EVALUATION OF EVIDENCE

In general, civil law countries, instead of having specific rules on the admissibility of evidence, allow judges to exercise wide discretion in deciding whether a produced evidence may be admitted as a source of fact-finding (the admissibility of evidence) and to what extent it would be reliable (the probative value of evidence),[13] unless otherwise regulated. Any type of evidence is generally admissible[14] and it is the parties that choose the evidence and submit it to court. Judges may evaluate the eligibility and the value of each form of evidence "freely" (the free evaluation of evidence). More specifically, the judge decides on the basis of the probative value rather than the admissibility of evidence.[15]

---

[10]   Canada (PICHÉ and GAUTRAIS (Canada)), China (ZHIYUAN (China)).

[11]   A well-known example is the United States (see MARCUS (United States)).

[12]   In the United Kingdom, the law of evidence is an element of substantive law (see SORABJI (United Kingdom)), and in Portugal, the probative value of evidence, for instance, legal evidence of full evidentiary value and legal evidence of sufficient evidentiary value, is regulated by the Civil Code (see COSTA E SILVA and RUIVO (Portugal)). On the other hand, in the United States, the law of evidence is regulated by the Federal Rules of Evidence or a similar stand-alone rule in each state. Almost all states have evidence rule systems that are derived from the Federal Rule of Evidence; see MARCUS (United States).

[13]   The principle of free evaluation of evidence is accepted in countries like Japan (see TEGA (Japan)), Taiwan (see SHEN (Taiwan)), Argentina (see GIANNINI (Argentina)), Brazil (see GUIMARAES RIBEIRO (Brazil)), Uruguay (see PEREIRA (Uruguay)), Colombia (see BUSTAMANTE et al. (Colombia)), Germany (§286 ZPO; see LÖSING (Germany)), Belgium (see TAELMAN and VANDENBUSSCHE (Belgium)), Portugal (see COSTA E SILVA and RUIVO (Portugal)), Norway (ss 21-2 and 21-3 of the Dispute Act; see NYLUND (Norway)), Croatia (see UZELAC (Croatia)), and Hungary (see HARSÁGI (Hungary)).

[14]   Needless to say, evidence should fall into one of the categories that each procedural law admits as evidence.

[15]   See TAELMAN and VANDENBUSSCHE (Belgium).

Nevertheless, it should be noted that accepting judges' free evaluation of evidence does not necessarily entail allowing judges' "arbitrary" evaluation of evidence. Diverse exceptions to this principle have been accepted.[16]

2.2.1. The Relevance or Necessity of Evidence

The first exception is that evidence on which a judge relies when fact-finding must be relevant or useful for confirming a controversial fact (relevance).[17] The decision as to whether the evidence is relevant also falls under the ambit of free evaluation by a judge.[18] Indeed, the system by which the court decides on the application for examination of evidence submitted by the parties on the basis of necessity and relevancy functionally play the role of the admissibility rule.[19]

It should be emphasized that the evaluation of evidence should be "reasonable" and should not widely diverge from the "common sense" of ordinary people.[20]

2.2.2. Hearsay Evidence is Admissible

As there are no specific rules on the admissibility of evidence, evidence based on hearsay[21] is usually admissible;[22] that is, there is no specific "hearsay rule" to exclude hearsay evidence. Judges can freely evaluate the credibility of hearsay evidence.

The fact that a rule on hearsay evidence will not necessarily mean that the written statement of a witness is permitted as evidence. For instance, in Norway, circumstantial evidence, including hearsay evidence, is permitted when there

---

[16] In Germany, ZPO §286, para 2 opens the door to an exception to the principle of free assessment of evidence, by regulating as follows; The court shall be bound to statutory rules of evidence only in the cases designated in the present code; see Lösing (Germany).

[17] For instance, in Spain, evidence must be relevant, useful, legal, and licit before freely evaluated by a judge (Article 281–283 of the Spanish Code of Civil procedure), See Andino (Spain).

[18] See Shen (Taiwan), Tega (Japan), Giannini (Argentina), Priori and Pérez-Prieto (Peru), and Pereira (Uruguay, the court may reject evidence that is manifestly unnecessary, irrelevant), Lösing (Germany), Taelman and Vandenbussche (Belgium).

[19] Articles 290 and 190 of the Korean Code of Civil Procedure; see Park (Korea).

[20] In Japan, a judge can evaluate probative value of evidence freely, but this evaluation should be based on reasonable empirical laws. A deviation from the reasonable empirical laws in a judgment can be a ground of an appeal as a violation of Art. 247 CCP; see Tega (Japan).

[21] Hearsay is defined as evidence offered to "prove the truth of the matter asserted (Rule 801(c)(2) of the Federal Rules of Evidence), or any out-of-court statement – verbal, non-verbal or implied – offered for the truth of its contents"; see Piché and Gautrais (Canada).

[22] Hearsay evidence is admissible in some case law in BGH.01.03.2018-IX ZR179/17 in Germany (see Lösing (Germany)) and Oda v. Minami, 6 Minshu 1117 (Sup. Ct., December 5, 1952) in Japan. See Tega (Japan). Hearsay evidence is also admissible in Belgium; see Taelman and Vandenbussche (Belgium). See also Uzelac (Croatia), and Harsági (Hungary). On the contrary, in France since 2009, hearsay evidence is no longer admissible; see Bléry (France).

are no direct witness observations, and producing the written statement of a witness as evidence is prohibited.[23]

2.2.3. *The Best Evidence Rule or the Original Document Rule*

The best evidence rule, which is common knowledge in common law countries, or a similar original document rule is also accepted in civil law countries.

For example, in Norway, evidence law is also based on the principle of the best evidence available. According to this principle, the parties must strive to present the best evidence, which is the evidence with the closest possible link to the circumstance that is to be verified.[24] The above-described rule in which circumstantial evidence is allowed only when there are no direct witness observations also reflects this principle.

As regards documentary evidence for which a copy can be easily produced, different approaches can be seen as to whether the original should be submitted in court or a copy can be submitted instead. One approach is that the original should be submitted as documentary evidence and that the original evidence has more probative value than its derivative evidence. Only one exception is allowed in the case where the submission of the original is difficult. In that event, the submission of photocopies or extracts is allowed.[25] Another approach is that a document should be submitted either in its original or copy form, but the copy should be accompanied with some proof of authentication,[26] otherwise the party has to show the location of the original. If the requirement is satisfied, the copy generally has the same value as the original.[27]

2.2.4. *Illegally Obtained Evidence*

Even if evidence is relevant to the fact in dispute and is of the best quality it is commonly recognized that illegally obtained evidence will not be admissible

---

[23] Because, unlike a witness, paper does not blush, the judge has difficulty in evaluating the trustworthy nature of the statement; see NYLUND (Norway).

[24] See NYLUND (Norway).

[25] Articles 70 and 77 of the Chinese Civil Procedure Law; see ZHIYUAN (China).

[26] In Uruguay, Article 165 of the General Code of Procedure (CGP): document in file should be presented in original or copy with authentication of their fidelity regarding the original one by a notary or public official (Article 163 CGP). See PEREIRA (Uruguay). In Japan, a copy can be produced instead of the original or "as an original" (see Y. MACHIMURA and Y. USUI, *Theory and Practice of Electronic Evidence*, Minjiho-kenkyukai, Japan 2016, pp. 158-, N. SAKURABA, "The Problems of Electronic Data for Factfinding under Electronification of Erocedure" *NBL* 1132, p. 27, 28).

[27] In Colombia, the party has to provide the original if it has this in its possession. If there is any reliable guarantee that the integrity of the information has been preserved from the moment it was generated for the first time in its final form, as a data message or in some other way, the requirement of originality is satisfied; see BUSTAMANTE et al. (Colombia).

either explicitly or implicitly.[28] While the doctrine of illegally obtained evidence in civil procedure is expected to play a much more significant role in deciding the admissibility or probative value of electronic evidence than before, the criteria for applying this doctrine to each case have not necessarily been clearly regulated.[29]

Some jurisdictions, such as Argentina and Germany, do not allow evidence obtained in a manner which infringes constitutionally protected rights or fundamental rights.[30] Germany also adopts the balancing test, according to which the judge may decide on the admissibility of illegally obtained evidence by balancing infringed interests against the importance of the evidence, etc.[31]

In other jurisdictions, evidence is considered "inadmissible" when it is obtained contrary to law or when it is obtained in a manner contrary to the rules of social coexistence and ethical norms that are commonly accepted.[32] For example, Belgian civil procedure was reformed in 2008 and since then, illegally obtained evidence has been admissible subject to following exceptions: where the legislation explicitly prescribes nullity as a sanction for the failure to comply with a relevant provision, where the illegality or irregularity has made the evidence unreliable, or where the use of the illegally obtained evidence is not compatible with the principle of a fair trial.[33] On the other hand, in Norway, evidence that is against any rule prohibiting the disclosure of information is illegal and inadmissible.[34]

2.2.5. Rules on the Probative Value of a Public or Private Document

A number of jurisdictions that do not have any general rules on the admissibility of evidence and instead adopt the principle of free evaluation of evidence have some exceptions to this principle in the case of examination of public or private documents.

---

[28]   See Dondi and Comoglio (Italy), Tega (Japan), Pereira (Uruguay), Bustamante et al. (Colombia; Art. 168 CCP), etc. The general problem of illegally obtained evidence was discussed at the Salamanca Congress (G. Priori, "Posadam Reglas de Exclusión Probatoria y Prueba Ilícita en Iberoamérica: Un Reporte Desde El Derecho Fundamental a Probar" in *II Conferencia Internacional & XXVI Jornadas Iberoamerianas de Derecho Procesal IIDP and IIDA "Evidence in the Process,"* 2018, p. 153; L. PASSANANTE, "Illegally Obtained Evidence in Civil Litigation; A Comparative Perspective" in *II Conferencia Internacional & XXVI Jornadas Iberoamerianas de Derecho Procesal IIDP and IIDA "Evidence in the Process,"* 2018, p. 175).

[29]   For instance, in Hungary, 269 of the Hungarian Code of Civil Procedure(HCCP), illegally obtained evidence may not be used in civil proceedings if the condition of 4 requirement are met; see Harsági (Hungary).

[30]   See Giannini (Argentina) and Lösing (Germany).

[31]   BVerfG JA 2003, 274; BGH JA 2003, 625.

[32]   See Flaga-Gieruszyńska and Klich (Poland).

[33]   See Taelman and Vandenbussche (Belgium). Whereas the use of illegally obtained evidence was previously automatically rejected, the rule was changed in 2008.

[34]   See Nylund (Norway).

Intersentia

439

For instance, in Germany, the Code of Civil Procedure provides the evidentiary value of some types of evidence, such as a hearing record (§165 *Zivilprozeßordnung* (ZPO)), a public record (§415 ZPO), and a private document (§416 ZPO). Public documents are given full probative value, while private documents are also given full probative value with a signature or certification by a notary according to the below provisions:[35]

> §415 Evidentiary value of public records and documents regarding declarations
>
> (1) Records and documents that have been prepared, in accordance with the requirements as to form, by a public authority within the scope of its official responsibilities, or by a person or entity vested with public trust within the sphere of business assigned to him or it (public records and documents), shall establish full proof, provided they have been executed regarding a declaration made before the public authority or the public official issuing the deed.
> (2) Evidence verifying that the transaction has been improperly recorded is admissible.
>
> §416 Evidentiary value of private records and documents
>
> To the extent that private records and documents are signed by the parties issuing them, or have been signed using a mark that has been certified by a notary, they shall establish full proof that the declarations they contain have been made by the parties who prepared such records and documents.

Similar rules are applied in Spain[36] and Hungary. In Hungary, a paper or electronic document issued by a court, a notary public, or other authority or administrative organ has full probative value (Article 323 HCCP). The public document is deemed to be authentic unless otherwise proven otherwise. A private document shall have a full probative value if the document was written and signed by the issuing person. The authenticity of a private document of full probative value needs to be verified only if it is questioned by the other party. The rules on the authenticity of a document can be found elsewhere.[37] For instance, Japanese civil procedure presumes the authenticity of a private document with a signature or stamp.[38] In South Africa, a private document should be proven by a witness or a handwriting expert.[39]

---

[35] See Lösing (Germany).
[36] A private document has full probative value if its authenticity is not challenged; see Andino (Spain).
[37] See Shen (Taiwan), Priori and Pérez-Prieto (Peru), and Pereira (Uruguay).
[38] Article 228(4) of the Code of Civil Procedure; see Tega (Japan).
[39] See Baboolal-Frank (South Africa). Exceptions are when the document is produced under a discovery order, judicially noticed by a court, handed in from the bar, produced under a *subpoena duces tecums*, or an affidavit in interlocutory proceedings, or admitted by the opposite party.

2.2.6.   Other Restrictions as to the Examination of Evidence for Efficient Adjudication

The timing of the production of evidence is regarded as one of the elements which a judge may consider in deciding whether to accept the evidence produced. For instance, in Argentine, documents, electronic data storage devices, etc. must be presented at the initial statement.[40]

The cost of obtaining the evidence could be one of the grounds for a judge to disallow evidence, for instance, in Norway.[41]

2.3.   JURISDICTION WITH RULES ON THE ADMISSIBILITY OF EVIDENCE

By contrast, there are jurisdictions which provide rules on the admissibility or probative value of evidence in a general or specific form.

In Asia, China has general rules on admissibility and probative value in the Code of Civil Procedure and Interpretation by the Supreme Court. It also has a limited hearsay rule.[42] The Iranian Civil Code and Code of Civil Procedure also have a general rule on admissibility.[43] Furthermore, common law systems may well be characterized as having rules on the admissibility of evidence, which are described below.

2.3.1.   The Relevance Rule

The first important element required to allow an evidence to be admissible in court is "relevance." According to Rule 401(a) of the Federal Rules of Evidence (FRE) in the United States, relevance is allowing the consideration of any evidence that "has any tendency to make a fact more or less probable." At the same time, the relevancy rule excludes the evidence if it distorts judicial fact-finding (hearsay) or if it unnecessarily prolongs the duration of a trial, confuses the issues, or undermines some important value other than fact-finding.[44]

In the United States, where the jury system is adopted, the judge may refuse to admit relevant evidence "if its probative value is substantially outweighed by a danger of … unfair prejudice" or "misleading the jury" (Rule 403 FRE). This

---

[40]   See Giannini (Argentina).

[41]   Da 21-8. See Nylund (Norway).

[42]   Article 77 of the Chinese Code of Civil Procedure; see Zhiyuan (China).

[43]   See Mohseni and Elsan (Iran).

[44]   See Piché and Gautrais (Canada), and Baboolal-Frank (South Africa). In Canada, the evidence should be relevant, material, and without any ground for exclusion to be admissible in court.

is because a very broad relevance standard can include a variety of forms of evidence that would be much more likely to prompt the jury to decide on an improper basis than to decide according to the applicable legal rules.[45]

2.3.2. The Hearsay Rule

Hearsay evidence is generally inadmissible.[46] Since there are often arguments that the statement offered is relevant for some other purpose, there are also a number of explicit exceptions to the ban on hearsay evidence to prove the fact in dispute. For instance, recorded recollections, public records, etc. are not excluded by the rule against hearsay, regardless of whether the declarant is available as a witness (Rule 803 FRE), and former testimony etc. is not excluded by this rule if the declarant is unavailable as a witness (Rule 804 FRE).

On the contrary, the United Kingdom, where the admissibility and probative value of evidence is governed by common law, abolished the hearsay rule in 1995. Therefore, as a general rule, hearsay is no longer inadmissible.[47]

2.3.3. Opinion Evidence

In Canada, witnesses must testify as to what was observed and must not give their opinion on what was observed. Opinion evidence is thus generally inadmissible, subject to two exceptions. First, non-experts may provide opinion evidence that is "within common knowledge and based on multiple perceptions that can best be communicated in compendious format." Second, expert opinion is admissible if the information sought to be presented by this expert is "relevant and reasonably necessary," that is, likely to be outside the experience and knowledge of the judge or jury, and the expert is "properly qualified" because he/she has a special or peculiar knowledge through study or experience. Lastly, all information presented by the expert must be otherwise admissible.[48]

2.3.4. Character Evidence

Character evidence refers to a testimony or document submitted for the purpose of proving that a person acted in a particular way on one occasion based on his/her traits, propensities, and dispositions to behave in a particular way. In civil litigation, good character evidence is generally inadmissible, except where the party's character is directly at issue, such as in a defamation case.

---

[45] See CAPRA (United States), MARCUS (United States).
[46] See PICHÉ and GAUTRAIS (Canada), BABOOLAL-FRANK (South Africa), CAPRA (United States), and MARCUS (United States); see Rule 820 of FRE.
[47] See SORABJI (United Kingdom).
[48] See PICHÉ and GAUTRAIS (Canada).

However, this type of evidence may be admissible as circumstantial proof of a fact where the probative value of the evidence outweighs the prejudicial effect.[49]

2.3.5. *The Best Evidence Rule or Original Document Rule*

The best evidence rule, more accurately called the original document rule, is likewise adopted to protect the document from fraud and manipulation.

In the United States, this rule is found in Article X FRE, according to which, an original writing, recording, or photograph is required in order to prove its content unless these rules or a federal statute provide otherwise (Rule 1002 FRE). However, there are some exceptions. First, a duplicate is admissible to the same extent as the original, unless a genuine question is raised about the original's authenticity or the circumstances make it unfair to admit the duplicate (Rule 1003 FRE). Second, the proponent can forgo the original if there is a good reason for not having it, such as when all the originals are lost or destroyed, or an original cannot be obtained by any available judicial process (Rule 1004 FRE).[50]

2.4. INITIATIVE IN EXAMINATION OF EVIDENCE

Generally, it is parties who are authorized to produce evidence in ordinary civil cases. Parties are also responsible for producing evidence in order to win the case. Then can judges or juries examine evidence *ex officio* or of their own initiative? Or do they have to examine evidence if the parties do not produce any evidence at all?

In most jurisdictions, neither judges nor jurors are obliged to examine evidence; in fact, they are prohibited from examining evidence on their own initiative.[51] They are not allowed to apply their own knowledge for the case either. Judges are only allowed to encourage parties to produce evidence.[52] Nevertheless, various exceptions have been accepted.

First, judges may examine certain types of evidence *ex officio*, such as expert witnesses in some jurisdictions.[53] Second, the judges are allowed to investigate

---

[49] See Piché and Gautrais (Canada).

[50] South Africa also has a similar rule (see Baboolal-Frank (South Africa)). This rule is likely to be a problem only if the proponent is unprepared or has acted in an improper way before trial (see S. Scheindlin and D. Capra, *Electronic Discovery and Digital Evidence, Cases and Materials*, 3rd ed., Cengage, Detroit 2015, p. 967).

[51] See Tega (Japan), Shen (Taiwan), Nylund (Norway), Flaga-Gieruszyńska and Klich (Poland), Uzelac (Croatia), Sorabji (United Kingdom), etc. In the United States, a judge is not allowed to examine evidence unless it is a bench trial and the judge is the fact-finder (see Capra (United States)).

[52] DA s. 11-5 (Nylund (Norway)), and Flaga-Gieruszyńska and Klich (Poland).

[53] For instance, in Canada, expert witnesses are examined *ex officio* (see Piché and Gautrais (Canada)), and in Germany, the court is allowed to collect documents, visual inspection,

evidence in its motion in specific cases relating to family matters, labor matters, and administrative litigation, partly in order to protect the public interest.[54] For instance, in Article 288 of the Taiwanese Code of Civil Procedure, civil courts may investigate evidence on their own initiative to protect the public interest in environmental lawsuits or consumer group lawsuits, or to ensure a fair and just trial in special lawsuits, such as medical malpractice lawsuits so as to amend inequality of resources and capacity among parties. The court's investigation works as a supplement to the adversary system.[55]

Third, the judges are also allowed to investigate matters which parties do not have to prove and which judges are usually expected to know, such as legal rules,[56] notorious or obvious facts,[57] and empirical laws including rules to evaluate the value of evidence.[58]

Even though *ex officio* examination of evidence is possible, there are limitations on this. The principle that *ex officio* examination should be carried out as a last resort is one example of such limitations.[59] Respecting the principle of contradiction and allowing the judge to rely only on evidence for which both parties have had the opportunity to discuss is another example.[60]

In contrast, several numbers of jurisdictions allow the judge to examine evidence on his/her own motion.[61] In such a case, *ex officio* examination of evidence is regarded as a duty of the judge.[62]

---

    expert reports, and party examination on its motion (§§142–144 and 448 ZPO) (see Lösing (Germany)). It is also the duty of the judge to examine them (The OLG Münich (judgment of January 10, 2014 – 10 U 2231/13). In Japan, examination of the parties (Art. 207(1) CCP), commissioning of examinations (Art. 186), commissioning of expert testimony (Art. 218), examination of the authenticity of an official document's provenance to a public office (Art. 228(3)), expert testimony during an inspection of evidence (Art. 233), and preservation of evidence relating to a pending litigation (Art. 237) can be carried out *ex officio* (see Tega (Japan)).

[54]   For instance, judges are allowed to investigate evidence on their own motion concerning personal status litigation, domestic relations case procedure, and administrative litigation in Japan, see Tega (Japan)), labor case in Italy (see Dondi and Comoglio), in un dispositive case in Norway,(Nylund (Norway)), and in small claim cases and securities related actions in Korea (see PARK (Korea). *Ex officio* examination is also allowed in Spain (see Andino (Spain)).

[55]   See Shen (Taiwan).

[56]   See Uzelac (Croatia). In Spain, a judge may examine foreign law on his/her motion (see Andino (Spain)).

[57]   See Lösing (Germany; see §291 ZPO), Tega (Japan), Giannini (Argentina), Guimaraes Ribeiro (Brazil), Pereira (Uruguay), and Costa e Silva and Ruivo (Portugal).

[58]   See Park (Korea). In Japan, a judge is not allowed to undertake research on empirical laws (see Tega (Japan)).

[59]   See Nylund (Norway).

[60]   French Code of Civil Procedure146II; see Bléry (France).

[61]   See Baboolal-Frank (South Africa) and Zhuyun (China, if parties cannot produce evidence).

[62]   See Giannini (Argentina), Guimaraes Ribeiro (Brazil), Mohseni and Elsan (Iran), Priori and Pérez-Prieto (Peru), Pereira (Uruguay), Bustamante et al. (Colombia), Taelman and Vandenbussche (Belgium), Harsági (Hungary; Art. 276(2) HCCP), and Costa e Silva and Ruivo (Portugal).

2.5. TYPES OF EVIDENCE ALLOWED IN CIVIL PROCEDURE

2.5.1. Admissible Types of Evidence

Both in jurisdictions where general rules on the admissibility of evidence exist and in jurisdictions where judges are freely able to evaluate the admissibility or credibility of evidence, the types of evidence which are admissible in court are limited.

Traditionally, the types of evidence acceptable in civil procedure have been divided into two groups: oral evidence and real evidence.[63] Witness testimony, expert testimony, and party testimony are classified as oral evidence. Oaths[64] and confessions,[65] if allowed as evidence, may also be categorized as oral evidence. Documents and items for judicial inspection[66] are classified as real evidence.

2.5.2. The Categorization of New Types of Evidence and the Review of Categorization Itself

How to categorize electronic evidence or new types of evidence differs from jurisdiction to jurisdiction, and depends on whether the list of evidence is limited or not.[67] One approach is to add a new category of evidence to a current list and explicitly indicate that digital or electronic evidence falls into this new category of evidence.[68] The other approach is to regulate that the rules on documentary evidence apply to electronic evidence, such as photographs, audiotapes, videotapes, etc.,[69] or to broaden the definition of document to cover electronic documents.[70] These approaches presuppose that the list of evidence

---

[63] Canada divides evidence into oral or testimonial evidence, documentary evidence, and real evidence, but it also has five subcategories: sworn statement, unsworn statement, things, experiments, and documents; see PICHÉ and GAUTRAIS (Canada).

[64] See BUSTAMANTE et al. (Colombia), BLÉRY (France), and TAELMAN and VANDENBUSSCHE (Belgium).

[65] See MOHSENI and ELSAN (Iran), GÓMEZ FRÖDE (Mexico), GUIMARAES RIBEIRO (Brazil), BUSTAMANTE et al. (Colombia), BLÉRY (France), COSTA E SILVA and RUIVO (Portugal), and TAELMAN and VANDENBUSSCHE (Belgium).

[66] In France, bailiffs can make an inspection of items by using drones; see BLÉRY (France).

[67] The problem of categorization is more apparent in civil law countries rather than common law countries. I thank Professor Richard Marcus for his comment on this point at the Kobe Congress.

[68] See MOHSENI and ELSAN (Iran), BABOOLAL-FRANK (South Africa), GUIMARAES RIBEIRO (Brazil), ZHIYUAN (China), GÓMEZ FRÖDE (Mexico), and HARSÁGI (Hungary; Art. 268 HCCP).

[69] See TEGA (Japan; Art. 231 CCP) and SHEN (Taiwan; Art. 363, para. 1 CCP).

[70] Civil Procedure Rules (CPR) r.31.4 and Practice Directions (PD) 31 para. 2A.1 in the United Kingdom cover not only emails and electronic communications accessible from computer systems, but also those stored on servers and back-up systems and metadata; see SORABJI (United Kingdom).

is specific or limited. They require the addition of new evidence to this list whenever it emerges.

Different approaches are taken by other jurisdictions, where a list of evidence such as documents, witnesses, etc. is regarded as illustrative.[71] For instance, Argentina has a category of "generic evidence" into which new types of evidence fall. Korea allows for the possibility of extending the admissible evidence by listing "other evidence" as one category of evidence.[72] This approach does not necessarily exclude the application of traditional rules on evidence rule (such as that relating to documents) to new types of evidence. However, the problem with this approach is how to set the boundaries for admissible evidence.

If the first approach is taken (or even if not), it is inevitable that the traditional categorization of evidence will be reviewed, since it becomes more difficult to draw clear distinctions between traditional categories as new technologies make the boundaries between them difficult to identify.[73] Reviewing the definition of documentary evidence is particularly important.[74]

Regarding this problem, a definition adopted in some civil law countries might be of great help. In these countries, documents are defined as the "written embodiment of human thought or idea";[75] conversely, images, sounds, or videos are not embodiment of thought. Thus, they are not purely documents and are therefore categorized as either an object of visual inspection by a judge[76] a "quasi-document.",[77] or a document.[78] According to the Canadian report, it is important to classify these new documents (technology) according to the existing means of proof, e.g., writing, testimony, or real evidence. Then, if the types of evidence are distinguished in accordance with their functions, writings are pre-constitution documents that have the virtue of being valid for the future. The testimony is a statement of a past event. Real evidence is the recognition of a present moment, contemporary to the occurrence of the fact, and corresponding to a recording, a photograph, or a screenshot; a "polaroid" of a moment "t."[79]

---

[71]   See GIANNINI (Argentina), PEREIRA (Uruguay), NYLUND (Norway), and FLAGA-GIERUSZYŃSKA and KLICH (Poland). France divides evidence into named evidence and unnamed evidence, and audio recordings, etc. fall into the second category; see BLÉRY (France). In Croatia, electronic evidence is admissible by interpretation, but it is not clear how admissibility is interpreted; see UZELAC (Croatia).

[72]   See PARK (Korea, Civil Procedure Act (CRA) 3 74).

[73]   See PICHÉ and GAUTRAIS (Canada).

[74]   See HARSÁGI (Hungary).

[75]   For instance, H. KANEKO et al., *Commentary on Civil Procedure*, 2nd ed., Kobundo, Japan 2011, p. 1176.

[76]   LÖSING (Germany).

[77]   SHEN (Taiwan).

[78]   In Poland, they are categorized as document or objects of judicial inspection; see FLAGA-GIERUSZYŃSKA and KLICH (Poland).

[79]   See PICHÉ and GAUTRAIS (Canada).

Most of the new evidence produced by parties – for instance, a screenshot of an SMS conversation, or a website – will probably fall into the category of writing according to the definition adopted in some civil law jurisdictions. However, it can be categorized as an object of judicial inspection from the functional point of view. This kind of consideration reminds us of the necessity to scrutinize the content of evidence for the purpose of ensuring that new evidence cannot be categorized as a document without careful consideration.

2.5.3. *Priorities Among Evidence: Documentary Evidence versus Oral Testimony*

Parties or their representatives usually choose by themselves which evidence should be produced among the various types of evidence available. Judges generally evaluate the admissibility and the probative value of each type of evidence produced[80] and then choose the appropriate evidence that they think is useful for fact-finding. However, diverse views are expressed regarding which types of evidence should have more probative value than others or which evidence should be examined first.

One view is that documentary evidence is more reliable than live testimony from witnesses. It might be better to say that live testimony is less favored or feared because of the risk of mendacity.[81] Another view, adopted by the United States, is that live testimony and cross-examination in court are the greatest guarantors of just outcomes.[82] The same seems to be true in Canada, where items for judicial inspection can only be submitted to the court after testimonial evidence or an admission.[83]

3. NEW TYPES OF EVIDENCE

3.1. EXAMPLES OF NEW FORMS OF EVIDENCE

Nowadays, digital evidence or electronic evidence is said to be offered in virtually every trial.[84] Below is a (non-exhaustive) list of examples of electronic or digital evidence that were used quite often in the civil proceedings of jurisdictions of the national reporters.

---

[80] Even in jury systems, it is the role of a judge to decide on the issue of admissibility of evidence (Rule 104(a) FRE).

[81] See MARCUS (United States), GUIMARAES RIBEIRO (Brazil), and HARSÁGI (Hungary). As to a fact that can be proved by documents, the court may ignore other evidence, especially the witness which often lacks trustworthiness.; see BLÉRY (France).

[82] See MARCUS (United States).

[83] See PICHÉ and GAUTRAIS (Canada).

[84] S. SCHEINDLIN and D. CAPRA, above n. 50, p. 925.

Intersentia

Those which are not necessarily new but are commonly used are:

- copies of emails or electronic documents;
- electronic documents stored on a computer, a hard disk, a flash drive, or external disks such as CDs or DVDs – examples of electronic documents that are often used in court are electronic business records and electronic medical records;
- image, video, or sound data digitally stored in the above-mentioned disks.

More recently, the following forms of evidence have also been used:

- dashcam recordings, motor vehicle Event Data Recorder (EDT) footage, and black box evidence;
- video surveillance data;[85]
- digitally enhanced photographs;
- electronic documents or images located in cloud storage, Web servers, or Personal Digital Assistants (PDAs);
- information (letters or pictures) on social media[86] (for example, information from Wikipedia,[87] Google Maps[88] or Google Earth, YouTube,[89] or postings or communication through Social Networking Services (SNS) (Twitter, Facebook, LINE, Telegram Messengers, WhatsApp,[90] Webchat, QQ, etc.);[91]
- GPS data;[92]
- metadata.[93]

---

[85] In Hungary, video surveillance is used in labor cases; see HARSÁGI (Hungary).

[86] However, there are no cases addressing this issue in Belgium (see TAELMAN and VANDENBUSSCHE (Belgium)). In the United Kingdom, these are not at issue (see SORABJI (United Kingdom)).

[87] See SHEN (Taiwan). In Argentina, generally the information from WIKI is not reliable and cannot be used, but can be used in defamation case; see GIANNINI (Argentina).

[88] In Japan, there is case law (X1-X5 v. Y, 1899 Jinho Journal 1, Tokyo High Court Mart. 13. 2013), which admits GPS data as evidence; see TEGA (Japan).

[89] It is used in defamation cases and copyright cases. See CAPRA (United States), MOHSENI and ELSAN (Iran), and HARSÁGI (Hungary).

[90] The example of a WhatsApp transcript is given in the Mexican report; see GÓMEZ FRÖDE (Mexico).

[91] In Belgium, Facebook photos are used to demonstrate that the damage suffered by its opponent is less serious than the opponent asserts, and Facebook messages are also used to prove adultery.; see TAELMAN and VANDENBUSSCHE (Belgium).

[92] The use of GPS information by an employer has occurred in labor cases in Norway (LH-2011-26141); see NYLUND (Norway).

[93] R. MARCUS, "Introduction" in S. SCHEINDLIN and D. CAPRA, above n. 50, p. 12. The audit trail of medical records is one example of this.

New types of evidence that are used for the purpose of explanation include:

- computerized animations illustrating how a disputed event may have occurred;
- digital presentations to illustrate an expert's opinion.[94]

3.2. RULES ON NEW EVIDENCE IN GENERAL

Facing a sharp increase in the use of new types of evidence described above, which is especially the result of increased reference to social media and the increased usage of search engines, the traditional rules on evidence need to be adjusted to these new forms. Here we will first look at the situations and the problems concerning the use of electronic evidence in court, and then we will examine the means of collecting electronic evidence (e-discovery) in various countries. While the focus of discussion tends to be placed on the former point in civil law countries, more attention has been paid to the latter point in common law countries. As already mentioned above, variations exist in terms of the general rules on evidence. Therefore, differences also exist in the regulations on new types of evidence. It should also be noted that while there are jurisdictions which already have specific rules on electronic evidence, other jurisdictions have adapt the traditional rules on "documentary" evidence to apply to newly emerged electronic evidence.

Issues relating to the use of electronic documents as evidence in civil procedure have been addressed for years. For instance, in civil law countries such as Germany, issues concerning electronic documents were summarized as follows:

(1) Does the law of evidence or civil procedure permit the use of electronic evidence as evidence?
(2) What category of evidence should electronic documents be assigned to in cases where there is a difference in the rules relating to different types of evidence?
(3) How do judges consider questions of authenticity and credibility or the probative value of electronic documents and how parties present them?[95]

---

[94] S. Scheindlin and D. Capra, above n. 50, p. 925. Digital presentations may reduce the relevance of the evidence and raise a risk of unfair prejudice under Rule 403 FRE.

[95] H. Rüssmann, "Electronic Documents: Security and Authenticity Electronic Evidence and Civil Procedure" in M. Kengyel and Z. Nemessáyi, above n. 2, p. 248.

In Hungary, the debate on electronic documents has related to the presentation and safe storage of electronic documents, in addition to the integrity of their contents and their authenticity.

The same issues would arise whenever other types of digital evidence emerged. Therefore, the discussion here will focus on the admissibility, the probative value, the means of presentation, and the authenticity or integrity of electronic evidence, including the issue of how new evidence is categorized.

3.2.1. *Rules on the Admissibility and Probative Value of New Types of Evidence*

Regardless of the existence or non-existence of specific rules, new types of evidence (see section 3.1 above) are somehow considered to be admissible in many jurisdictions.[96] As noted above, not all jurisdictions have specific rules on each new type of evidence; instead, the rules on traditional or conventional evidence apply to new types of evidence.[97] Therefore, in jurisdictions where the admissibility and probative value of evidence is freely evaluated by judges, the admissibility and probative value of new types of evidence are also evaluated in the same way.[98] As for the probative value of electronic evidence, the fact that it can be easily modified does not deprive it of its value.[99]

Again, regarding categorization, electronic evidence is often categorized as a document or an item for judicial inspection. Alternatively, it is often dealt with in a similar manner as a paper document or item for judicial inspection.[100] For example, the Canadian Act had established a legal framework for information technology (Act to establish a legal framework for information technology (ATLFIT)) (2001), which is based on the notion of a "document" without introducing new means of evidence.

Electronic evidence (or documents) may be categorized as a sub-category of documentary evidence in some jurisdictions. For instance, in Taiwan, a document which is not physical in form, but which communicates human ideas (such as an email) is classified as a "quasi-document"[101] and the evidence rules relating

---

[96]   Exceptionally, Italy is rather negative in terms of accepting new types of evidence; see DONDI and COMOGLIO (Italy).

[97]   For instance, in the United States, the FRE referred mainly to hardcopy, but the courts have not treated digital evidence any differently from any kind of evidence; all evidence must be reliable, probative, and authentic (see S. SCHEINDLIN and D. CAPRA, above n. 50, p. 935). In addition, the FRE were amended to cover electronically stored information (Rule 101(6)); see CAPRA (United States)). Other examples can be seen in Iran, Japan, Spain, Mexico, China, Italy, Korea, and the United Kingdom.

[98]   See SHEN (Taiwan).

[99]   See FLAGA-GIERUSZYŃSKA and KLICH (Poland).

[100]   See GIANNINI (Argentina), MOHSENI and ELSAN (Iran), HARSÁGI (Hungary), BLÉRY (France; electronic writing is equivalent to paper writing, if integrity and identification of author are satisfied.). In the United Kingdom, electronic documents are included in a broad definition of a document CPR r.31.4 and PD 31 para. 2A.1; see SORABJI (United Kingdom).

[101]   Rule 363 CCP (see SHEN (Taiwan)).

to physical document applies *mutatis mutandis*. In Japan, electronic documents are also deemed to be documents or objects equivalent to a document,[102] but an object that does not contain any human ideas and is classified as a "quasi-document." In addition, video tape and audio tape are also classified as "quasi-documents" (Rule 321 of the Code of Civil Procedure(CCP)). Therefore, the boundary between a document and a quasi-document or an object seems to have become blurred.

In any case, the general framework of the law of evidence or the general rule of documentary evidence also applies to electronic evidence. Thus, electronic evidence should satisfy the requirement of admissibility if it is required to do so and should also have the probative value.[103] However, some special considerations are also required regarding authenticity and probative value. Therefore, a couple of special rules on probative value on electronic documents exist.

For example, according to §371(3) ZPO in Germany, the rules concerning the evidentiary value of public records and documents will be applied *mutatis mutandis* to electronic documents created in accordance with the requirements as to form (public electronic documents), by a public authority within the purview of its official responsibilities, or by a person or entity vested with public trust within the sphere of business assigned to him/her/it. §416a ZPO regulates the evidentiary value of the hardcopy printout of a public electronic document, according to which a certified hardcopy printout of an electronic document has the same value as a certified copy of a public record or document (§371a ZPO). A certified scan from a public electronic document also has the same value as a public document (§371b ZPO). Therefore, these documents have full probative value:

> §416a
>
> The certified hard-copy printout of an electronic document pursuant to Section 371a (3) that a public authority has created, in accordance with the requirements as to form, within the scope of its official responsibilities, or a person or entity vested with public trust within the sphere of business assigned to him or it, as well as the hard-copy printout of an electronic document issued by a court bearing an endorsement by the competent court pursuant to Section 298 (2) shall be equivalent to the certified copy of a public record or document.

On the contrary, a simple private electronic document is subject to the free assessment of a judge. However, a private electronic document with a qualified

---

[102]   Rule 231 CCP (see TEGA (Japan)).
[103]   The introduction of the notion of "integrity" does not change the probative value that a document must satisfy (*Bensity v. Kloda*, 2018 QCCA 608)); see PICHÉ and GAUTRAIS (Canada).

electronic signature (§371a ZPO) has the same value as a private document signed by the author.[104]

A similar rule can be found in Hungary, where a public document in electronic form itself has full probative value to verify that the issuing entity adopted the decision and that the data or facts confirmed by the public document are true.[105] This rule is different from German law in the sense that it mentions only the probative value of a document in electronic form before being printed out.

In contrast, the Colombian Code of Civil Procedure explicitly regulates that data messages are admissible. These fall into the category of documentary evidence, but at the same time, their value is regulated separately. According to this rule, documents that have been provided in the same format in which they were generated, sent, or received, or in some other format that reproduces it with accuracy are referred to as data messages. The simple printing on paper of a data message will be valued in accordance with the general rules on documents (Article 247 of the General Code of Procedure (GCP)). If the requirements of authenticity and integrity are fulfilled, the data message has full probative value. However, it is not clear why the legislator explicitly regulated the probative value of the data message when it should be regarded as documentary evidence, regardless of the fact that data messages are deemed to be documentary evidence (Article 243 GCP).[106] This is one example which shows the difficulties involved in the categorization of electronic evidence.

3.2.2. *The Production of New Types of Evidence*

The next issue is the way in which forms of electronic evidence can be presented in court and how judges can examine them. The difficulty in deciding the means of producing electronic evidence is often pointed out.[107] In practice, the presentation of new types of evidence can be presented in forms borrowed from other conventional types of evidence. Indeed, it is often the case that the printed version of an electronic document or other digital data is presented,[108] partly because of technical difficulties of presenting or receiving digital evidence in court. For instance, emails are printed out and presented in court,[109] as are

---

[104]   See LÖSING (Germany).

[105]   See HARSÁGI (Hungary).

[106]   See BUSTAMANTE et al. (Colombia). The general rule on probative value also applies to data messages.

[107]   See COSTA E SILVA and RUIVO (Portugal).

[108]   See UZELAC (Croatia), ANDINO (Spain), and COSTA E SILVA and RUIVO (Portugal). According to B. TAN et al., above n. 9, p. 8, in many countries, parties and lawyers are still reluctant to use e-discovery and would rather disclose hardcopies.

[109]   See GÓMEZ FRÖDE (Mexico), and MOHSENI and ELSAN (Iran). In Uruguay, the exception is allowed when the other party questions its authenticity; see PEREIRA (Uruguay).

printed screenshots of websites.[110] In other words, electronic evidence is converted into conventional types of evidence and is then produced in court.

A printed version of electronic evidence is sometimes required to be ready for online inspection[111] or should be accompanied with a validation of its authenticity and digital data itself that both parties can access.[112] For instance, in Korea, when a printed screenshot (such as a text message screen) is submitted, it is recommended to capture the entire screen, including the URL.[113] Alternatively, it is possible to produce digital evidence either in a printed form or on external devices such as USB flash drives and CD.[114]

Producing only digital data by using a digital media is subject to the court's ability to receive such technological means.[115] In addition, data is required to be presented in a usable format in court. In Korea, electronic documents are not only produced in printed forms, but also examined on a screen or display devices in court; therefore, there are special rules regarding the submission of multimedia.[116]

Sound, image, or video files can be also produced on an external device (for example, CD) and shown in court.[117] The submission of a transcript or description of the content of an audio or video recording is sometimes required.[118]

A couple of points should be noted in this context. First, regardless of the difference in the degree of the electronification of civil procedure (filing a complaint electronically, etc.), there is preference for hardcopy form in general. A printed document is submitted in court and then a judge reads and examines it.[119] Second, there are different views on what will be proven by the "printout" of data. In Poland, where Article 308 of the CCP assigns a probative value to printouts of emails, etc., a printout of data constitutes "a different means of evidence" to indicate the existence of a computer record of a specific content at the time of printing.[120] However, generally a printout of data is produced with the intention to prove the content of the data itself when requirements of authenticity and integrity are satisfied.

---

[110]   See GÓMEZ FRÖDE (Mexico), PICHÉ and GAUTRAIS (Canada), and CAPRA (United States). In Uruguay, however, website is not allowed to be presented in a printed form, as it requires intervention of a computer expert; see PEREIRA (Uruguay).
[111]   See LÖSING (Germany).
[112]   See GUIMARAES RIBEIRO (Brazil), TEGA (Japan).
[113]   See PARK (Korea).
[114]   See PEREIRA (Uruguay), TEGA (Japan), SORABJI (United Kingdom), etc.
[115]   See PICHÉ and GAUTRAIS (Canada), GÓMEZ FRÖDE (Mexico), and MOHSENI and ELSAN (Iran).
[116]   See PARK (Korea).
[117]   See ANDINO (Spain) and PEREIRA (Uruguay). Image or sound files are produced on CD with corresponding copies for the parties. In Portugal, a party brings devices in court to display cinematographic reproduction and phonographic register (Art. 428); see COSTA E SILVA and RUIVO (Portugal).
[118]   See PARK (Korea).
[119]   Ibid.
[120]   See FLAGA-GIERUSZYŃSKA and KLICH (Poland; Art. 308 of the Polish CCP).

Presenting a printout of digital data entails a conflict with the original document rule or the best evidence rule where such rules exist. Moreover, there is a problem in deciding what is "original" in the case of electronic evidence when various ways of presenting evidence are admitted.[121] Generally, a document may be reproduced either by generating a copy in the same medium or in a medium that is based on the same technology, or by transferring the information contained in the document to a medium based on different technology. Therefore, the variety of forms (copy or transfer) makes it more difficult to identify what is the original version of a reproduced form of evidence.[122]

Efforts have been made to overcome these difficulties by proving that the copy or transfer has not been modified compared to the original data (integrity).[123] For instance, in Colombia, if the integrity of the information is preserved from the moment it was generated for the first time in its final form (as a data message or in some other way), the requirement of originality is satisfied.[124]

Third, using a hardcopy form as the means of submitting digital data is a transitional and tentative method. If technologically possible, digital documents should be presented and handled in court instead of using printouts of such documents. The new mechanism to enable the production of data without conversion into conventional evidence should also be taken into consideration.

3.2.3. Authenticity and Integrity

One of the most difficult issues regarding electronic evidence seems to be proof of authenticity and the integrity of electronic documents. An electronic document is more easily destroyed or manipulated than a paper document, and it is much weaker than a paper document from the point of view of its integrity.[125] Therefore, these are critical elements that need to be addressed in order for such evidence to have probative value.

It should be noted that some jurisdictions explicitly distinguish authenticity from integrity, while others assume that integrity is a component of authenticity.[126] According to the former view, authenticity implies only the link

---

[121] For instance, in Canada, there are two different types of documents (copy and transfer), and it is often difficult to identify the original of a reproduced document; see Piché and Gautrais (Canada). This problem also exists in Uruguay; see Pereira (Uruguay).

[122] Art. 2841 of the Civil Code of Quebec (C.C.Q); see Piché and Gautrais (Canada).

[123] According to Art. 5-1 of the Draft Convention on Electronic Evidence, the printout or other physical manifestation shall be considered the best evidence and admitted as evidence subject to satisfactory proof of its integrity.

[124] See Bustamante et al. (Colombia).

[125] See Piché and Gautrais (Canada). A paper document has autonomy (that is, its quality is intrinsically linked to the physical medium), but technological evidence requires "double proof."

[126] The notion of authenticity is sometimes mixed with the notion of integrity; see Piché and Gautrais (Canada).

between a document and the author. Conversely, the latter view understands that authenticity implies both: (1) a link between a document and the author; and (2) the integrity of the document. In private writing, the link with the author is made using a signature. It should also be noted that the integrity of a copy with the original data is also required, in addition to a link with the original by the author ("double proof").

Usually, it is the parties that need to prove the authenticity of electronic evidence[127] and authenticity only matters when it is contested. In practice, the authenticity of electronic documents is rarely contested.[128] However, if contested, the investigating authenticity seems to be difficult due to the difference between digital evidence and traditional evidence, especially documents. Nevertheless, it is also said that this weakness can be overcome and some solutions may be found by using various technological tools (electronic signature, hash value, timestamp, blockchain, etc.), managerial processes, and some legal practices (e.g., vault system).[129]

To begin with, the rules on the authenticity of a traditional paper document often apply to electronic evidence itself. For instance, if a document is authenticated by the signature of the author, then the electronic document or data could also be authenticated by a digital signature or certification of a notary public. An electronic signature is increasingly and widely used to secure the authenticity and integrity of an electronic document,[130] although it does not necessarily resolve all of these problems because it is only effective before its expiration data and there is a potential that the signature key can be stolen by someone else.[131]

Here are some examples: in Germany, a private electronic document with a qualified electronic signature has the same evidentiary value as a private document which has been signed by its author or issuer or certified by a notary

---

[127] See TEGA (Japan), SORABJI (United Kingdom), etc. Article 4 of the Draft Convention on Electronic Evidence also states that the party seeking to introduce electronic evidence in any legal proceeding has the burden of proving it is what is claims to be.

[128] See PICHÉ and GAUTRAIS (Canada), CAPRA (United States), and ANDINO (Spain). In United Kingdom, any document is deemed to be authentic unless a party challenges its authenticity (Rule 32.19(1) CPR); see SORABJI (United Kingdom).

[129] See PICHÉ and GAUTRAIS (Canada). In the United States, because of the possibility of manipulation of electronic data, authenticity issues present extra challenges, but the courts have generally managed to deal with the authenticity of electronic data without much trouble; see MARCUS (United States).

[130] In Uruguay, Taiwan, Japan, Belgium, France, China, Argentina, Portugal, Brazil, the United Kingdom, Spain, Hungary, Norway, Croatia, Portugal, etc. Many European countries follow EU Directive 1999/93/EC, the European Regulation on electronic identification and trust service for electronic transaction (eIDAS Regulation), even outside the EU.

[131] Y. MACHIMURA and Y. USUI, above n. 26, p. 249. Electronic signatures might not be the safest solution in the near future; see https://www.nytimes.com/2019/10/23/technology/quantum-computing-google.html and https://ai.googleblog.com/2019/10/quantum-supremacy-using-programmable.html.

Intersentia

455

public (§371a, para. 1 ZPO (the Electronic Signature Act)).[132] The opposing party may only prove the inauthenticity of a document by verifying facts that raise serious doubts about the declaration having been made by the holder of the signature key. Certain emails that an individual has registered securely for a "Demail" account also enjoy the presumption of authenticity (§371a, para. 2 ZPO).

It is also pointed out that an electronic document may be authenticated by a signature through the document authentication based on the identification service, specified by an act or government decree, etc. If the electronic data is signed or stamped, it is deemed authentic based on the certification of the storage service provider.[133]

In contrast, the difficulty of meeting the requirement for the integrity and accountability of emails or text messages should be noted, because emails are not reliably signed or encrypted[134] without the existence of the above-mentioned register of emails in other jurisdictions.

In the United States, the FRE were recently amended in 2017 to allow electronic evidence to be authenticated without the need to call a witness to testify (FRE 902(13) and (14), self-authentication);[135] the new rules require no extrinsic evidence of authenticity in order to be admitted – for instance, a record generated by an electronic process or system that produces an accurate result, and data copied from an electronic device, storage medium, or file, as shown by the certification of a qualified person that complies with the certification requirements of Rule 902(11) or (12). The proponent must also meet the notice requirements (Rule 902(11)).[136]

Apart from this, a general rule on authentication applies. According to Rule 901(a), in order to satisfy the requirement of authenticating or identifying an item of evidence, the proponent must produce evidence sufficient to support a finding that the item is what the proponent claims it is. Emails, chat room conversations, social media evidence etc. are some examples where the issue on authentication needs to be resolved. For instance, the trustworthiness of a website is assessed based on the length of time the data were posted on the website, etc. Important evidence for authenticity is normally available from the personnel managing the website (the webmaster personal). There is also a rule

---

[132] According to RÜSSMANN, above n. 95, §371a ZPO is a developmental error in the system of the law of evidence.

[133] See HARSÁGI (Hungary).

[134] In France, the judge carries out the written verification of Article 283 CCP (Cass.1re Civ. September 30, 2010, No. 09-68555); see BLÉRY (France).

[135] P. GRIMM et al., *Best Practice Manual for Authenticating Electronic (Digital?) Evidence*, West Academic Publication, United States 2016, p. 26.

[136] According to Rule 902(11) FRE, before the trial or hearing, the proponent must give an adverse party reasonable written notice of the intent to offer the record and must make the record and certification available for inspection, so that the party has a fair opportunity to challenge them.

on self-authentication in the case of an official website (Rule 902(5) FRE). Emails may be authenticated by reference to their appearance, contents, substance, internal patterns, or other distinctive characteristics, taken together with all the circumstances under Rule 901(a).[137]

If authenticity cannot be presumed, it should be verified by the parties. Various methods of proof are indicated: the use of an expert,[138] especially a digital forensic science expert;[139] witness testimony;[140] judicial inspection;[141] or other means.[142] In some jurisdictions, the parties are even obliged to disclose information relating to the authenticity of electronic data, such as the date of the printout, the date and time of recording, the title and the author of the electronic document, and the date of its creation in an oral hearing.[143] Metadata would be very useful in terms of solving the issue of the authenticity of electronic evidence; however, as far as it is produced paper format, the authenticity does not matter.[144] Moreover, judges or parties are sometimes reluctant to deal with metadata.[145]

Obviously, it is useful to prevent parties from manipulating digital data itself. An electronic signature, coupled with a hash value[146] is one example of how to do this. In addition, some jurisdictions make use of notaries public to certify

---

[137] S. SCHEINDLIN and D. CAPRA, above n. 50, pp. 1002~1008, 1011~1013.

[138] According to B. TAN et al., above n. 9, p. 5, in a few special cases, parties may have to engage digital forensic experts to assist in the collection of ESI – for instance, they may be called in to retrieve computer files and data from hard drives that have been deleted, or GPS data from smartphones and satellite navigation systems, or data from hard drives that have been encrypted. In cases where employees secretly copied documents or emails from the original company onto a storage media before leaving, digital forensics experts collect and analyze the deleted evidence from the storage media and report their findings. However, in many cases, e-discovery involves common business records and does not require digital forensic science. See https://capsicumgroup.com/digital-forensics-and-e-discovery-where-one-stops-the-other-begins-2.

[139] See TEGA (Japan), PRIORI and PÉREZ-PRIETO (Peru), BLÉRY (France; writing verification by a judge or an expert), BUSTAMANTE et al. (Colombia), ANDINO (Spain; a graphologist if the authenticity of a private document is challenged), and MOHSENI and ELSAN (Iran; the use of IT experts in criminal cases).

[140] See PEREIRA (Uruguay).

[141] G. KODEK, "Modern Communications and Information Technology and the Taking of Evidence" in M. KENGYEL and Z. NEMESSÁYI, above n. 2, p. 261. Article 809 of the Civil Code allows for the inspection of a computer to determine whether electronic documents have been manipulated.

[142] It is possible to present a header of emails to prove their integrity; see TEGA (Japan).

[143] See PARK (Korea). In Korea, the act on the use etc. of electronic document in civil provisions and KRCP 120(2) regulates the obligation.

[144] R. MARCUS, above n. 93, p. 12.

[145] See DONDI and COMOGLIO (Italy).

[146] According to P. GRIMM et al, above n. 135, p. 31, "data copied from electronic devices, storage media, and electronic files are ordinarily authenticated by 'hash value.' A hash value is a number that is often represented as a sequence of characters and is produced by an algorithm based upon the digital contents of a drive, medium, or file. If the hash values for the original and copy are different, then the copy is not identical to the original. If the hash values for the original and copy are the same, it is highly improbable that the original and copy are not

Etsuko Sugiyama

the content of websites, etc. before filing a suit.[147] As will be discussed below, an original form of digital data can be saved to an unchangeable data carrier or secured by a trustworthy third party.[148] To prevent manipulation, it is also helpful to impose sanctions on a lawyer or parties who have altered electronic data which is or will be submitted as evidence in court.[149] This issue will again be addressed below (see section 4.2).

Yet, it should also be noted that not all jurisdictions face serious problems in terms of proving the authenticity of electronic evidence or face a number of cases where authenticity is contested.[150] For instance, in Spain, in the past, fears of a lack of authenticity or evidence manipulation existed, but over time the current litigation practice has proven them to be unfounded.[151] Norway does not have serious discussions on the authenticity of digital evidence because of the wide use of electronic documents, especially in the government, and the high level of official trust in them.[152]

3.2.4. *The Hearsay Rule*

Hearsay in digital evidence is dealt with in the same way as it is in conventional evidence (hard copy, etc.)[153] where the hearsay rule exists. The exceptions to a hearsay ban are also adopted for electronic evidence.[154]

3.3. OTHER ISSUES RELATING TO ELECTRONIC EVIDENCE: ILLEGALLY OBTAINED EVIDENCE

There are other issues many jurisdictions face in relation to examining electronic evidence. One of the most significant concerns commonly shared among

---

identical. Thus, identical hash values for the original and copy reliably attest to the fact that they are exact duplicates".

[147] See GIANNINI (Argentina), PEREIRA (Uruguay), and PRIORI and PÉREZ-PRIETO (Peru). In Hungary, before filing the case, the plaintiff obtains a notarial certification of the current content of a website, so there is no need to involve an IT specialist as an expert; see HARSÁGI (Hungary).

[148] RÜSSMANN also insisted that the situation would also change if system, program, and data access were comprehensively logged in such a way that one could tell from the records which data was accessed by whom, when, and using which program; see RÜSSMANN, above n. 95, p. 250.

[149] *King v. Fleming, 899 F.ed 1140 (10th Cir. 2018)* (sanctions on a lawyer who attached a materially altered email as an exhibit to a complaint); see MARCUS (United States).

[150] See PICHÉ and GAUTRAIS (Canada), and TEGA (Japan, the authenticity is usually contested in criminal cases.).

[151] See ANDINO (Spain).

[152] See NYLUND (Norway).

[153] S. SCHEINDLIN and D. CAPRA, above n. 50, p. 973.

[154] For instance, according to FRE803, business record exception, public record exception, are exempt from the hearsay rule. Emails may be too sporadic to qualify as business records. However, emails may be too sporadic to qualify as business record (*Id.* at 973); see CAPRA (United States).

countries is illegally obtained evidence. The admissibility or probative value of illegally obtained evidence is generally problematic and at present there does not seem to be any clear definition as to what illegally obtained evidence is (see section 2.2.4 above). Regardless of the non-existence of a uniform clear boundary between lawfully and illegally obtained evidence, many cases are reported involving the illegality of obtaining new types of evidence, its admissibility, or its probative value.

The admissibility of emails obtained without the consent of the sender or the receiver is one example that is often contested. Whereas cases are reported which do not admit such emails as illegally obtained evidence,[155] another case allowed an employer to present emails from the employee's work email account as evidence because the employer had lawful access to the employee's account.[156] That the employer may have access to the employees' device is also problematic. One case is also reported where an employer was able to use information from a GPS device for purposes other than those for which they had permission to monitor the employees – that is, the use of the GPS data is allowed to monitor whether drivers perform their works dutifully and properly.[157]

Video recorded on a dashcam (in-car camera) or surveillance camera also faces the issue of legality in the way it was obtained. In Germany, a video recorded by a dashcam was admitted after the weighing up of interests, in spite of the fact that the recording of the video violated the general personal right.[158] In a case from Norway, video material that an insurance company investigator had filmed illegally (without consent) was inadmissible in a personal injury insurance fraud case.[159] The extent to which the right of privacy is infringed also matters; the more seriously privacy is infringed, the less likely it is that the court will admit the evidence. Accordingly, video data from a surveillance camera in a shop does not violate the private life of the clients or the staff because the shop is a public place, and courts tend to admit it. Conversely, video data from a surveillance camera in a locker room would amount to a violation of private life and courts would normally not allow it to be admitted.[160]

In Belgium, where a new rule has been adopted regarding illegally obtained evidence, if digital evidence was obtained by hacking a profile page on social media, this would affect the reliability of that evidence; on the contrary, public Facebook messages could be used as evidence even though they were not

---

[155] For instance, *X v. Y*, Westlaw Japan 2009WLKPCA12168006 (Tokyo District Ct., December 16, 2009); see TEGA (Japan).

[156] HR2002-1390; see NYLUND (Norway).

[157] Norway (LH-2011-261419). The criteria is "the more blameworthy of the method used to obtain the evidence was, the more likely the court will disallow it." See NYLUND (Norway).

[158] BGH, 15.05.2018-VI Z 233/17; see LÖSING (Germany).

[159] HR-2014-1950-U (Norway). However, the investigator could be called as a witness because hidden observation is not illegal, although hidden filming is illegal; see NYLUND (Norway).

[160] Norway, Rt 1991 616; see NYLUND (Norway).

addressed personally to the person presenting them in court and no consent was given for the evidence to be obtained.[161] The point seems to be whether the message or conversation is expected to be a completely private one or one that is disclosed to third parties.

3.4. THE FACT-FINDER'S ACCESS TO INFORMATION AVAILABLE ON THE INTERNET

Facing the fact that a large volume of information is available on webpages, web pages including social media sites are often presented as evidence in court,[162] there are concerns regarding the credibility of information available on social media. Since databases and other available sources differ vastly in terms of their reliability and acceptance, the issue arises as to whether and to what extent information on the internet can be used as a source of information in court proceedings.[163] In addition, it has become problematic whether or not, or to what extent, a judge or a jury may also use information available on social media, as access to such information has become easier and more convenient than ever before. Although this concern does not necessarily seem to be a commonly shared one, it cannot be denied that a judge or juror is always exposed to the temptation to refer to information on the internet.

As a whole, the majority view disapproves of such information being used, yet not all jurisdictions provide specific rules to ban a judge or juror from using knowledge obtained from the internet. However, there is a new tendency to provide new rules to prohibit them from using such information. For instance, in the United States, juries are generally prohibited from gathering their own information, but this prohibition has generated significant difficulties in the age of the "wired juror," i.e., one who goes online to learn more about the case. Therefore, in California, the legislature provides by statute that jurors may be held in contempt of court for disobeying an order not to conduct online research about the case; however, they are allowed to use their life experience, etc. in their considerations. In addition, a judicial conference adopted a rule of judicial ethics that prohibits a judge from accessing the internet to obtain any information relating to a specific case.[164]

---

[161] Court of Appeal, Antwerp, May 6, 2015, *Rechtspraak Antwerpen Brussel Gent* 2015, 1075; Labour Court of Appeal of Brussels, September 3, 2013, *Rechtskundig Weekblad* 2013-14, 1586; Court of Appeal of Liège, February 16, 2016, *La Revue du Droit des Technologies de l'Information* 2016, 91; see TAELMAN and VANDENBUSSCHE (Belgium).

[162] S. SCHEINDLIN and D. CAPRA, above n. 50, p. 941. Admissibility is evaluated under the standard evidentiary concepts of hearsay, authenticity and Rule 403 FRE.

[163] G. KODEK, above n. 141, p. 272.

[164] Cal. Code. Civ. Proc. 1209(a)(6); see MARCUS (United States).

Many jurisdictions without a jury system also assume that a judge is prohibited from conducting his/her own research on the internet to obtain and apply the knowledge on facts regarding a pending case,[165] except in the following situations. First, a judge may conduct research to confirm facts or something else that parties are not required to prove, such as notorious or obvious facts, or officially known facts.[166] The judge may confirm whether a fact is asserted as notorious and therefore proof is not required. Yet, this does not mean that all information available on the internet is commonly known or public knowledge.[167] Other examples in which a judge may conduct his/her own research are (applicable) law,[168] doctrine or jurisprudence,[169] and empirical laws, such as rules for evaluating the value of evidence.[170] A judge can also investigate the meaning of terms or clarify the notion of new social phenomenon,[171] or can conduct judicial inspection regarding an accident that occurred on the internet if *ex officio* examination is allowed.[172] Although a judge is not necessarily obliged to undertake research on these matters, he/she is expected to possess such knowledge and, if not, he/she is expected to obtain this knowledge.

Second, it is without doubt possible for a judge to conduct research on matters that he/she can or should examine *ex officio* (see section 2.4 above).[173] Accordingly, a couple of jurisdictions, which generally allow or sometimes oblige a judge to examine evidence, do not pose any limitations on a judge's research on the internet.[174] This means that in jurisdictions where a judge is expected to play an active role in the examination of evidence and fact-finding, his/her referring to such information is embraced. Even in these jurisdictions, arguments as to whether the information obtained from the internet was reliable or not and whether or not there is any limitation on using it are inevitable. Nevertheless, these issues have not been explicitly examined.

---

[165]   See Nylund (Norway). In Korea, a judge may carry out his/her own research for the purpose of finding indirect or auxiliary facts (Park (Korea)).

[166]   See Lösing (Germany; §291 ZPO), Tega (Japan), Guimaraes Ribeiro (Brazil), Giannini (Argentina), and Costa e Silva and Ruivo (Portugal).

[167]   See Flaga-Gieruszyńska and Klich (Poland); G. Kodek, above n. 141, p. 272. In the United States, government website data are subject to mandatory judicial notice (FRE 201(b)(d)).

[168]   See Uzelac (Croatia).

[169]   See Pereira (Uruguay).

[170]   See Park (Korea).

[171]   See Harsági (Hungary), amd Costa e Silva and Ruivo (Portugal).

[172]   For instance, watching YouTube in the case of infringement of copyright; see Harsági (Hungary) and Bustamante et al. (Colombia).

[173]   See Gómez Fröde (Mexico), Pereira (Uruguay), and Bustamante et al. (Colombia; judicial inspection or expert opinion). In Brazil, a judge may seek information on the internet as to whether to grant or not legal aid; see Guimaraes Ribeiro (Brazil).

[174]   See Zhiyuan (China) and Baboolal-Frank (South Africa).

As noted above, the matters which a judge or a jury may or should do research on differ among jurisdictions. Generally, a judge and a juror may not apply his/her own knowledge to the facts in a pending case in order to maintain his/her neutrality and objectivity. Therefore, he/she is also prohibited from conducting research on the facts of the pending case on the internet. At the same time, he/she is also allowed or expected to have knowledge on the statutory laws, case law, empirical laws or common knowledge, and these can be acquired through the internet, as he/she is commonly used to doing through reading books.

Therefore, the issue of the possibility of conducting research on the internet becomes a traditional one that we have addressed before in this chapter; where are the boundaries of fact and law (statutory laws, empirical laws etc.),[175] how does a judge decide whether the information is reliable or not, and how are parties given opportunities to being made aware of and rebutting the use of information which a judge applies. To address these issues, it would be desirable for a judge to disclose information which he/she has obtained through the internet to the parties and give them the opportunity to contest the reliability of the information, etc. The same principle would apply to cases where judges can conduct research on the internet on the facts. It is true that many people believe that internet searches are very useful; at the same time, they recognize the risk of relying too heavily on these. This is why we need clearer rules on whether or to what extent a judge or a juror can rely on the information obtained from the internet.

4. GATHERING AND PRESERVING NEW TYPES OF EVIDENCE

The last but most serious problem is how to gather and preserve electronic evidence for use in a civil trial. In common law countries which have the system of discovery or disclosure, the argument on the use of electronic evidence in civil procedure seems to have been focused on how to treat digital evidence in discovery or disclosure rather than at trial. Of course, preserving electronic evidence is a serious and urgent issue in civil law countries as well, since electronic evidence can easily be destroyed or manipulated, even at the last minute. Different approaches are taken among jurisdictions, but similarities also exist.

---

[175] For example, in France, the Labor Court was not allowed to conduct research on the internet on the consumption of electricity and water necessary for the operation of a washing machine; see Bléry (France). However, this information might be evaluated as knowledge rather than fact.

4.1. HOW TO GATHER EVIDENCE IN GENERAL AND ELECTRONIC EVIDENCE BEFORE OR DURING TRIAL

4.1.1. *The Approach Taken by Common Law Countries*

Countries which have a pre-trial discovery or disclosure system[176] have been faced with problems as to how to manage the volume of evidence and the cost of collecting it. As the volume of ESI tends to be enormous, the cost and time required to collect information is substantial. Although the discovery of emails or electronic documents were an issue two decades ago, common law countries are again facing problems caused by new technology, such as social media and the IoT.[177] To overcome the problems caused by the expanding volume of information and cost of discovery, the concept of proportionality is adopted.[178]

More specifically, in the United States, under Rule 26 the Federal Rules of Civil Procedure (FRCP), a party must disclose certain information without having to receive a request from the opposing party to do so. This information includes: (1) the names and contact information of each individual likely to have discoverable information that the disclosing party may use to support its case; (2) a copy of all documents and electronic information in the party's control that the party may use to support its claims; (3) a calculation of damages; and (4) any relevant insurance agreement that might be used to satisfy the judgment. In addition, a party can demand information from an opponent or from a third party. At the same time, Rule 26(b) places special limits on the discovery of ESI if access to ESI is unduly burdensome. It generally provides that upon demand, "parties may obtain discovery regarding any nonprivileged matter that is relevant to any party's claim or defense and proportional to the needs of the case." Proportionality involves an analysis of "the importance of the issues at stake in the action, the amount in dispute, the parties' relative access to relevant information, the parties' resources, the importance of the discovery in resolving the issues, and whether the burden or expense of the proposed discovery outweighs its likely benefit." In addition, Rule 26(b)(B) states that a party answering a discovery demand "need not provide discovery of electronically stored information from sources that the party identifies as not reasonably accessible because of undue burden or cost."

---

[176] The United States, Canada, the United Kingdom, and South Africa (see Baboolal-Frank (South Africa; discovery under Rule 35 of High Court Rules of Court).

[177] See Marcus (United States).

[178] The United States and Canada. In Canada, Sedona Canada Principles show how to handle a vast majority of ESI. The central concepts of the principles are proportionality and cooperation. Parties should agree on: (1) the scope of data to be searched; (2) the use of de-duplication software to remove true duplicate documents; (3) the search tools to be used; and (4) the method for validating the results (the Guideline and Model Order published by the Ontario E-Discovery Sub-Committee of the Discovery Task); see Piché and Gautrais (Canada).

The party opposing the discovery has the burden of showing that the ESI is not reasonably accessible. Even if that burden is met, the requesting party may still be able to obtain it if there is good cause to obtain it. However, in that event, Rule 26 gives the trial court the discretion to require the seeking party to pay the costs of retrieving the ESI.[179]

Organizing a large volume of information is also an issue. In Canada, parties can agree on the sorting method of ESI.[180] In the United Kingdom, where Civil Procedure Rules (CPR) set out the basis for documentary disclosure, including electronic documents and interim remedies to preserve evidence by the court,[181] the scope of disclosure is also a subject of debate. Paragraphs 25–27 of Practice Direction (PD) 31B provide for electronic document searches to be conducted via "keyword search or other automated methods of searching." However, there seems to be no guidance on the rules concerning whether such searches may be carried out using a computer program or not.[182]

ESI is sometimes stored outside its owner's hands. In that case, whose duty is it to produce evidence? The duty to preserve and produce evidence can extend to third-party vendors of ESI. So, for example, the court held that a defendant was required to obtain electronic records (emails) from its third-party vendor, stating that the fact that the records were held by a third-party "does not obviate the defendant's obligation to produce all information that is available to them."[183]

4.1.2. The Approach Taken by Civil Law Countries

In contrast, civil law countries mostly have no discovery or disclosure, or only limited discovery or disclosure.[184] However, the necessity of gathering evidence, including electronic evidence, from the opposite party or third parties in the early stage of litigation also exists in these countries.

One example of a means to collect evidence which is widely accepted in civil law countries is a judicial order to produce evidence documents or items.[185] This order is usually issued after a suit is filed, but in exceptional circumstances, it may

---

[179] See Capra (United States).

[180] See Piché and Gautrais (Canada).

[181] Disclosure and e-disclosure take place before the action on a voluntary basis (pre-action protocols) or pursuant to a court order. Post-action disclosure is governed by CPR Pt 31 and PD 31B. Interim remedies are given when there is a strong *prima facie* case of a civil cause of action; the claimant must establish that there is a serious danger that important evidence will be destroyed or will disappear, etc.; see Sorabji (United Kingdom).

[182] See Sorabji (United Kingdom).

[183] *Carrillo v. Schneider Logistics*, 2012 WL4791614. See Capra (United States). The role of vendors has become important (R. Marcus, above n. 95, p. 20).

[184] For instance, in Norway, petition for disclosure (ss 26-5, 26-6 DA, for instance, to a bank account) is admissible, but the duty to disclosure is limited; see Nylund (Norway).

[185] See Tega (Japan), Park (Korea), Lösing (Germany), and Andino (Spain; Art. 338 CCP). In Germany, independent evidentiary proceeding is also available.

also be available prior to filing a suit. The party or the third party to which the order is issued is obliged to produce documents,[186] however, although this is subject to some exceptions. For instance, if the document contains information regarding privacy or trade secrets, the parties or the third party are exempted from producing it.[187] These systems were originally designed to gather physical evidence such as documentary evidence or items and not all jurisdictions necessarily have explicit rules for collecting electronic evidence. However, in some jurisdictions, rules governing the gathering of conventional documentary evidence from opposite parties or third parties also apply *mutatis mutandis* to electronic/digital evidence,[188] while other jurisdictions do not adjust conventional rules on gathering documentary evidence to gathering electronic evidence.[189]

The court order to produce evidence or to provide information is indeed useful in cases involving the infringement of intellectual property (IP) rights.[190] In Norway, for instance, the IP rights holder may request the court to order the infringing party to provide information on the origin of and distribution networks for goods and services. The order may only be given when the importance of enforcing the IP right exceeds the disadvantages caused to the alleged infringing party or person contributing to the infringement. Unlike in general civil cases, the court may make a disclosure order regardless of whether a case is pending or not.[191]

Another example often cited is the anticipation of evidence or preservation of evidence allowed under strict conditions.[192] Preservation of evidence allows the court to conduct an examination of the evidence following a petition by a party in a case where there is a risk that the evidence will be lost and it becomes difficult to use it in trial unless it is examined in advance.[193] As evidence must

---

[186]   See ANDINO (Spain; Art. 328 CCP).

[187]   In Norway, the matter relating to privacy is protected from this order. Most of the case law on preservation of evidence relates to whether a party has the right to obtain privileged information (HR-2017-833-A and HR-2010-1060-A, both of which concern access to information on infringement of copyrights on films through illegal file sharing); see NYLUND (Norway). Trade secrets are protected from disclosure in Japan (Rule 220(4) CCP).

[188]   See PARK (Korea), ANDINO (Spain), etc.

[189]   See UZELAC (Croatia). In Japan, a printout of an electronic document used to be produced; see Y. MACHIMURA and T. KOMUKAI, *Practical E-Discovery*, NTT Publication, Japan 2010, p. 139.

[190]   See TEGA (Japan; Rule 105 of the Patent Law), NYLUND (Norway; however, the rules in cases of infringement of IP rights are far more lenient than for other types of cases), FLAGA-GIERUSZYŃSKA and KLICH (Poland), and ANDINO (Spain).

[191]   See NYLUND (Norway; s. 28 A-1, A-2 DA) and TEGA (Japan).

[192]   See TEGA (Japan), PARK (Korea; CCP 132-4, KCPA344-351, 366), and BLÉRY (France, this proceeding is measure in futurum (Art. 14 CCP). In these countries, collection of evidence prior to filing a suit is also possible. Anticipation of evidence is used in Spain, Peru, and Argentina. See ANDINO (Spain), PRIORI and PÉREZ-PRIETO (Peru), and GIANNINI (Argentina).

[193]   In Japan, preservation of evidence is conducted in medical malpractice cases, since medical records which are under the control of doctors might be destroyed by them; see TEGA (Japan). See also NYLUND (Norway; ss 28-1-28-5 DA).

be secured immediately, prompt action is required. Accordingly, *ex parte* proceedings are also allowed if there is a risk that the opposing party will obstruct the examination of evidence or there is no time to give notice to the opposing party to be present at the examination of evidence.[194] It also functions as an order to gather evidence if evidence that is under the control of the opposite party or third party is preserved.

The next significant issue is how to organize or find related information from a large amount of ESI which may contain a large quantity of information that is irrelevant to the case,[195] as is the case in common law countries. Sometimes, a party that is obliged to disclose evidence might wish to overwhelm the court and the opposing party with evidence and to make them difficult to find proper evidence.

One solution to this problem is to appoint a neutral third party, such as a judicial officer or an enforcement officer,[196] who may organize the ESI in conjunction with an IT expert. In Norway, although there are no formal rules on this issues, the party may agree on the organization method and keywords based on which the technical staff organizes the evidence.[197] In France, a judicial officer accompanied by an IT expert can search the computers of a competitor suspected of unfair competition.[198]

4.2. PRESERVATION OF ELECTRONIC EVIDENCE

Collecting easily destroyed electronic evidence in the early stages of litigation contributes to preserving it. However, there are also other ways of preserving evidence (and especially electronic evidence). The order to preserve evidence described above is one example and obligating the party to preserve evidence is another.

4.2.1. The Approach Taken by Common Law Countries

In common law countries that have disclosure or discovery, parties are obliged to preserve essential that is evidence or relevant to the case. However, a couple of significant issues remain unresolved.

The first issue is whose duty is it to preserve and disclose evidence, and when this duty arises. In the United States, any "potential party" is under an obligation to

---

[194]   See NYLUND (Norway).
[195]   This issue has been important in common law countries.
[196]   See NYLUND (Norway) and BLÉRY (France). In Norway, in case HR-2010-1985-U, a party was obliged to give the court access to a file consisting of 800 emails to enable the court to identify emails that could serve as evidence, but appointing a neutral third party would be better.
[197]   See NYLUND (Norway).
[198]   See BLÉRY (France).

preserve "potentially discoverable evidence" from the time he/she becomes aware of a potential lawsuit (known as the "trigger" for the obligation to preserve).[199] However, because of the incredible volume of digital information and the wide variety of places in which it might be found, preserving all information could become a monumental task, and many large corporations have asserted that they have been unfairly criticized for a failure to preserve everything, and that juries were instructed that they could make an adverse inference from the company's failure to retain certain potential evidence. Therefore, new rules relating to the failure to preserve ESI came into effect in 2015.[200]

According to the new rule, if ESI that should have been preserved in the anticipation or conduct of litigation is lost because a party failed to take reasonable steps to preserve it, and it cannot be restored or replaced through additional discovery, the court:

(1) upon finding prejudice to another party from loss of the information, may order measures no greater than necessary to cure the prejudice; or

(2) only upon finding that the party acted with the intent to deprive another party of the information's use in the litigation may:

(A) presume that the lost information was unfavorable to the party;

(B) instruct the jury that it may or must presume the information was unfavorable to the party; or

(C) dismiss the action or enter a default judgment.

In the United kingdom, although there is no general procedural obligation to preserve potential evidence, according to para. 7 of PD 31 B, "as soon as litigation is contemplated, the parties' legal representatives must notify their clients of the need to preserve disclosable documents. The documents to be preserved include electronic documents which would otherwise be deleted in accordance with a document retention policy or otherwise deleted in the ordinary course of business."[201]

The second issue is how to enforce the obligation to preserve evidence. In this regard, substantive sanctions such as adverse inference and fines are possible when evidence that was subject to litigation has been destroyed.[202] It is even possible for the court to order an injunction if the parties that are obliged to preserve evidence are going to destroy it.[203] Considering these significant

---

[199] See MARCUS (United States); B. TAN et al., above n. 9, p. 8 (the parties are put on notice that they have a duty to preserve data once it can be reasonably anticipated that they might be sued).

[200] See MARCUS (United States). Rule 37(e) of FRCP.

[201] See SORABJI (United Kingdom).

[202] See CAPRA (United States). In Canada, the court has a wide level of discretion to impose suitable sanctions; see PICHÉ and GAUTRAIS (Canada).

[203] See BABOOLAL-FRANK (South Africa).

Intersentia

sanctions, the need has arisen to narrow the range of excessive duties and release the burden of preserving a large volume of evidence for all for the foreseeable future.

Who is responsible for the preservation or disclosure will be discussed in section 4.3 below.

4.2.2. *The Approach Taken by Civil Law Countries*

In civil law countries, parties and third parties are generally not obliged to preserve evidence for a pending suit or future litigation. Such a duty only arises when the court order is issued (as described above) or when the substantive law, such as company law, tax statute provides that they are obliged to preserve specific types of evidence[204] or unless otherwise regulated.[205] Whether the parties are also obliged to preserve ESI or electronic documents depends on the substantive law itself.[206]

Without explicit rules on the obligation to preserve evidence, adverse inference in the case of destruction of evidence is possible in the same way as it is in common law countries. In other words, if a party destroys or manipulates evidence, a judge may assume that the evidence destroyed is unfavorable to that party. Although this inference is not necessarily explicitly regulated, it could be derived from the general duty to collaborate with a court or an opposite party.[207] Thus, this inference indirectly forces parties to preserve evidence, including electronic evidence. However, difficulties exist in terms of applying such sanctions in the case of failure to preserve electronic evidence by negligence, considering the fact that electronic evidence can be too easily destroyed compared to other types of evidence.

To avoid the cost of maintaining electronic evidence, it is sometimes deposited with a third party. For instance, in Spain, electronic information is often stored on third-party servers in addition to the devices of the owner of information.[208] In France, some services have been established that make it possible to stockpile evidence (from emails to GPS data) before litigation occurs and to request a

---

[204] See Andino (Spain), Park (Korea), Uzelac (Croatia; business records), Bustamante et al. (Colombia), and Costa e Silva and Ruivo (Portugal; Medical Practitioner's Act regulates the duty to preserve medical records). In common law countries, like South Africa, companies are obliged to keep documentary record for five years, and in case of emails, they should be kept in archiving system or cloud. See Flaga-Gieruszyńska and Klich (South Africa).

[205] In Brazil, parties owe a duty to preserve the original version of digital documents until the deadline of motion to set aside a judgment; see Guimaraes Ribeiro (Brazil).

[206] For instance, in Croatia, substantive law regulates the duty to preserve business records, etc., but the law does not specifically regulate the duty to preserve electronic documents. However, some private companies already offer services of e-archiving, etc.; see Uzelac (Croatia).

[207] See Bustamante et al. (Columbia) and Uzelac (Croatia).

[208] See Andino (Spain).

bailiff's finding when the dispute arises.[209] Using a "vault" service offered by companies also occurs in common law countries.[210]

4.3. CHALLENGES CREATED BY NEW TECHNOLOGY

Jurisdictions with a wide range of discovery and disclosure have extended their scope to cover electronic evidence or digital data. However, they are being faced with the necessity of reducing the burden on parties and third parties caused by a wide range of obligations to preserve and disclose evidence. Conversely, jurisdictions which do not generally have discovery or disclosure have some alternatives that allow parties to gather evidence from the opposing parties or third parties or to preserve them. Regardless of the difference in terms of the starting point, most jurisdictions face the same difficulties arising from new technology: how to tackle the vast amount of data, how to find relevant information and how to protect confidential information from unnecessary disclosure.

The wide range of places where electronic data is stored causes another problem. Currently electronic data is stored not only on one computer, but other mobile devices, tablets, and mobile phones. In the case of companies, many employees use their own mobile devices for business purposes (Bring Your Own Device (BYOD)). In the case of discovery, parties need to consider whether relevant information might be stored on such devices and whether it must be preserved for use in litigation and be produced. In addition to using personal devices, many employees are given devices by their employers, which have become known as "corporate-owned personally enabled" (COPE). At the same time, employers are required to develop policies that protect the privacy of employees with respect to their personal information, but also allow the employer to preserve and produce business-related information that may be required in litigation.[211]

Cloud computing is also becoming a major challenge. Parties and lawyers are increasingly turning to "cloud computing": Web-based email, data storage,

---

[209] Examples are Filecys.fr, Mailicys.fr, and Attestis.fr. Filecys.fr is devoted to the proof of authentication, Mailicys.fr to the traceability of the exchange of mails, and Attestis.fr to the statement of building permits. Mailicy.fr. has been developed to prove the sending of an email message to a recipient and on a given date. To do this, all that needs to be done is to simply copy in the address mailicys@huissier-justice.fr at the time of sending. In the event of a dispute, the report by judicial officer is simplified. Attestis.fr enables employees to track the planning permission billboards from their desktop or smartphone using the technology to connect objects awarded by the European Space Agency: GPS or Galileo in the future. See BLÉRY (France).

[210] See PICHÉ and GAUTRAIS (Canada).

[211] S. SCHEINDLIN and D. CAPRA, above n. 50, p. 129. See also BLÉRY (France; employer's access to employees' emails is allowed).

Intersentia

469

and other applications such as Gmail, Yahoo!, Hotmail, Google Docs, Microsoft Office 365, Dropbox, and SugarSync, as well as social media platforms, such as Facebook, LinkedIn, and Instagram, rather than a hard disk, CD, or DVD. However, ESI held by a cloud provider is no different from ESI held by any other third party.[212]

5. FUTURE CHALLENGES CREATED BY NEW TECHNOLOGY

There is a huge difference in the general attitude toward the admissibility or probative value of evidence: some jurisdictions have explicit rules on the admissibility of evidence, while others allow judges to evaluate it freely. However, most jurisdictions have somehow found a way to deal with electronic evidence in civil procedure. And regardless of differences in the degree of the adoption of disclosure or discovery between common law countries and civil law countries, a number of jurisdictions currently face or will face challenging problems due to the continuing development of new technology and increases in the volume of information exchanged between parties or between courts and parties.

5.1. PREVALENCE OF THE IoT

First, the emergence and prevalence of the IoT, in combination with Big Data, brings about new challenges in evidence law. The IoT makes it possible for devices to be connected thorough the internet and to store and transmit data to each other. Data can be stored in local devices and transferred to other devices and the cloud. Internet-connected devices store and transmit an enormous volume of data.

The data in IoT devices is often important as evidence in cases involving competition law, but it is also valuable as evidence in labor cases or medical malpractice cases. One example in which the IoT is used as critical evidence in civil litigation is wage and hour litigation. Employees have recently been able to work in places other than in their offices with electronic connectivity. In lawsuits claiming overtime pay, employers have demanded discovery of the employees' digital devices, focusing on what the GPS readings show about where the employees actually were while they were supposed to be working.[213]

---

[212] S. SCHEINDLIN and D. CAPRA, above n. 50, p. 138. This is also an issue in the United Kingdom (P. HIBBERT, *Electronic Evidence and Disclosure Handbook*, Sweet & Maxwell, London 2016).

[213] MARCUS (United States) stated that "we've been able to assess billions of location and time records to understand when and where employees were during their claims of overtime."

The data on digital ingestion tracking systems which enables the patient to track the ingestion of medication with sensor on his/her smartphone is also used in civil proceedings[214]

For now, there seems to be no consensus on how to categorize information in IoT devices. However, it could be categorized as a digital or electronic document[215] or a quasi-document.[216] Using the IoT in civil proceedings generally raises the same issues as cloud computing or other types of evidence: how to acquire and organize the vast amount of data, how to protect the privacy of the owner of the data, to what extent the assistance of the expert is required to analyze the authenticity and integrity of the data, and how to redefine "document."[217]

5.2. PROTECTION OF CONFIDENTIAL INFORMATION

Confidential information, such as confidential communications and trade secrets,[218] is exempt from disclosure, discovery, or similar means to gather evidence. Also, evidence which is obtained by infringing privacy or trade secrets unduly could be illegally obtained evidence and therefore excluded, although various doctrines in relation to this subject. Recently, the protection of a user's right of privacy on their social network activity[219] or the IoT[220] has become a serious issue. However, it is not necessarily taken for granted that privacy should be protected in civil procedure.[221] Moreover, even if privacy is to be protected procedurally, it is not clear what types of information can be protected as privacy. Regarding the privacy right of users of social networks such as Facebook, a single point of view is expressed: these users limit access to selected content in the expectation that this content will not be shared beyond their group of friends, but this expectation is objectively unreasonable, because other users can disseminate the content without obtaining consent from the user who posted it.[222] This view seems to carefully restrict privacy rights. Privacy rights also matter when data from surveillance cameras is produced as evidence. In these cases, the expectation on the possibility of privacy being disclosed should be carefully examined on a case-by-case basis (see section 3.3 above).

---

[214]   See ANDINO (Spain).
[215]   See ANDINO (Spain).
[216]   See SHEN (Taiwan).
[217]   See ANDINO (Spain).
[218]   EU Directive No. 2016/943.
[219]   K.L. MIX, "Discovery of Social Media" (2011) 5 *Fed. Cts. L. Rev.* 120, 127–129.
[220]   Article 283 *bis* b of the Spanish Code of Civil Procedure (confidentiality of competition law); see ANDINO (Spain).
[221]   Generally, civil law countries in the EU protect privacy more strictly than common law countries.
[222]   It summarized that courts have not acknowledged privacy rights in social-networking information.

Intersentia

5.3. ASSISTANCE FROM A THIRD PARTY AND IMPROVING JUDGES' SKILLS

The assistance of third parties *ex ante* and *ex post* is inevitable in addressing various issues regarding new types of evidence in civil procedure. Before litigation, a number of jurisdictions actually and willingly rely on a third party's cooperation to preserve electronic evidence. Although a consensus has not necessarily been reached on when, on whom and to what extent the obligation to preserve evidence applies, a party that possesses a digital evidence inevitably faces a risk of possible sanctions for modifying easily destroyable evidence, whereas the opposing party is obliged to assume the burden of contesting the integrity and authenticity of digital data. To avoid an increase of such fragile litigation and to reduce the parties' burden and cost of preserving evidence and contesting its authenticity, other than using technological schemes (electronic signature, hash value, etc.), entrusting the data to a trustworthy third party would be very useful in order to prevent manipulation for, for example, electronic signatures.

The cooperation of experts after litigation is also crucial to solve issues (authentication, etc.) relating to electronic evidence. Especially in the case of using data in the IoT, the involvement of experts will be much more anticipated than examining electronic documents stored in a computer. At the same time, the cases where it is necessary to call experts to investigate authenticity, etc. do not seem to be quite as common, especially in civil litigation. Using experts in civil litigation inevitably entails the traditional questions on how to retain the neutrality and credibility of the experts, as well as who appoints and who bears the cost of consulting the experts.[223] Sometimes the cost of using experts will be significant. Alternatively, it would be useful to seek the knowledge and experience of ordinary persons and to avoid a situation where only one professional judge is responsible for deciding the admissibility of new types of evidence.

For instance, in the United States, Rule 104(a) FRE provides that: "The court must decide any preliminary question about whether a witness is qualified, a privilege exists, or evidence is admissible." Most decisions about the admissibility of evidence, whether digital or otherwise, are made by the judge alone. They include decisions about whether evidence is relevant, constitutes hearsay (or fits within one of the many hearsay exceptions), or is excessively prejudicial when compared to its probative value, whether experts are qualified and the extent of opinion testimony that will be allowed, and most questions regarding the application of the original writing rule. When the judge makes a ruling under Rule 104(a), he/she is the sole decision maker as to whether the evidence may be heard by the jury. If admitted, of course, the jury is free to give the evidence whatever weight (if any) they think it deserves. This is familiar territory for trial judges, but

---

[223]   E. SUGIYAMA, *Experts in Civil Procedure*, Yuhikaku, Japan 2008, pp. 341 et seq.

with digital evidence, there is a greater likelihood that the judge alone may not be the final decision maker regarding admissibility. The jury also may have a part to play in the admissibility decision, and this is where Rule 104(b) provides that "[w]hen the relevance of evidence depends on whether a fact exists, proof must be introduced sufficient to support a finding that the fact does exist. The court may admit the proposed evidence on the condition that the proof be introduced later." Actually, Rule 1008 FRE provides that "[o]rdinarily, the court determines whether the proponent has fulfilled the factual conditions for admitting other evidence of the content of a writing, recording, or photograph under Rule 1004 or 1005. But in a jury trial, the jury determines – in accordance with Rule 104(b) – any issue about whether: (a) an asserted writing, recording, or photograph ever existed; (b) another one produced at the trial or hearing is the original; or (c) other evidence of content accurately reflects the content."[224]

Thus, improving the knowledge and skills of judges and lawyers is crucial. On this point, we should also care about a generation gap that exists in relation to new technology; the younger generations tend to overly rely on technology and pay little attention to the risks involved in doing so. On the contrary, older generations are not familiar with new technology and are over-cautious about the risk it poses.[225] Therefore, they need to improve their knowledge and their consciousness depending on their situations, as well as seek the assistance of experts.

The involvement of neutral third parties (including experts) would be helpful when organizing a huge amount of electronic evidence, finding information relevant to the pending case, or finding information which should not be disclosed. In that process, it is critical to give parties and their representatives the opportunity to contest the findings.

5.4. RETHINKING THE DEFINITION OF EVIDENCE

As shown above, most jurisdictions have somehow found a way to deal with electronic evidence in civil procedure. A widely accepted approach is to slightly modify the rules on documentary evidence, especially the rules on the authenticity of paper documents, and adopt them for electronic documents. At the same time, we are now facing a much larger amount of digital data than an ordinary judge or party could manage to deal with in proceedings. In addition, most of the newly emerged data (data in GPS, IoT devices, etc.) that does not contain any "human ideas" does not necessarily fit into the traditional definition of a document. As such, another question arises: how do we define a "document"

---

[224]   P. Grimm et al, above n. 135, p. 2.
[225]   X. Kramer, "Challenges of Electronic Taking of Evidence: Old Problems in a New Guise and New Problems in Disguise" in *II Conferencia Internacional & XXVI Jornadas Iberoamerianas de Derecho Procesal IIDP and IIDA "Evidence in the Process,"* 2018, pp. 409–410.

Intersentia

or writing? In examining data that does not contain human ideas, inspection of objects can also be used. But if judicial inspection of the current data is used for the purpose of examining a past situation, then confirming the identity of the current data with the past data is inevitable.

The variety of forms of "conversion" of data must be taken into consideration in addressing the issue relating to the probative value, authenticity, and integrity of electronic evidence, especially electronic documents. Many jurisdictions have an "original document rule" or alternatively a "best evidence rule" which generally permits only original documents as evidence, and apply this rule to electronic evidence. Therefore, it is necessary to define what is original, but this is not an easy task. Instead, we should carefully compare the identity of data produced in court with that of the original version and also give parties the opportunity to carefully check and contest it.

5.5. RETHINKING PRIORITY AMONG DIFFERENT FORMS OF EVIDENCE: WITNESS VERSUS DATA

There is a difference as to which types of evidence are given more probative value than others and how much value is placed on oral evidence (see section 2.5.3 above). Many jurisdictions place more importance on documentary evidence than oral evidence, especially witness testimony, while other jurisdictions do the opposite. Nevertheless, the prevalence of new technology could possibly alter this situation completely. Even in the United States, where witness testimony is regarded as the most important form of evidence, especially in criminal cases, video evidence may be viewed as decisive and is preferred to live testimony. If video or other digital data are regarded as "objective, unbiased, transparent," a summary judgment is given based on video evidence.[226] Video data from surveillance cameras, GPS data, etc. can be more decisive than witness testimony or conventional documentary evidence. Therefore, instead of cross-examination, a careful review by judges and parties from a procedural point of view is required. For instance, the possibility of manipulation and the method of obtaining evidence should be closely examined.

5.6. THE IMPACT OF THE ELECTRONIFICATION OF PROCEDURE

The issue of how to deal with digital/electronic documents in civil procedure might be more or less dependent on the degree of electronification of the procedure

---

[226] Therefore, it is necessary that everything is recorded in order to discover the truth; see MARCUS (United States).

itself, since filing electronically generated documents or electronically converted documents depends on the technological capacity of the judicial system (i.e., technological equipment in courts). As for the electronification of procedure, there are huge disparities between jurisdictions. Some courts have already adapted to the paperless procedure,[227] while in other courts, electronification is now in progress.[228] In courts which accept only paper-based evidence, electronic documents should be converted into paper documents or hardcopies of digital data should be produced. However, even if electronification is accepted, there seems to be a greater preference for producing hardcopies rather than producing digital data itself. If digital data itself is accepted as evidence, the conversion of hardcopies into electronic evidence is necessary,[229] and conversion from digital data into a format usable in court is also required, while minimizing possible disputes about the form.[230]

5.7. RETURNING TO THE STARTING POINT …

Facing the new issues arising from the emergence of new types of evidence, we should not forget that the general traditional rules of evidence should also apply to new types of evidence, although in a modified form. Regarding electronic evidence, civil law countries overly emphasize how to fit new evidence into the traditional categorization of evidence, how to define the original or copy of digital evidence, how to authenticate it, etc. On the contrary, little attention has been paid to the rules regarding the content of evidence, such as the relevance rule, etc. As wide discretionary powers are granted to a judge to evaluate the value of evidence, the evaluation of new types of evidence seems to have been left to him/her as well. In contrast, jurisdictions which have rules on the content of oral or documentary evidence, such as the hearsay rule, make it clear that

---

[227] In Spain, all paper documentation is converted into a digital format; see ANDINO (Spain). See also PARK (Korea). In Canada, digital filing of pleadings is allowed (Article 99 of CCP). The technological repository is used in British Columbia, Alberta, Prince Edward Island, New Brunswick, Nova Scotia, Ontario, Newfoundland and Labrado; see PICHÉ and GAUTRAIS (Canada).

[228] See TEGA (Japan) and UZELAC (Croatia). In Norway, submission of electronic documents started in the fall of 2018. After that, during the main hearing, the parties may show documents, objects, images, video and audio recordings to the court, and, increasingly, parties may transmit evidence electronically; see NYLUND (Norway).

[229] In Korea, if the data are in the form of a (written) document that is converted into an electronic evidence, the title, author, and the creation date of the "original" should be disclosed; see PARK (Korea).

[230] See ANDINO (Spain). In the United States, Rule 34(b)(2)(D) FRCP directs that the responding party must state the form it intends to use before producing it, regardless of whether or not the request specified a form for production. If the parties cannot agree on the form, the court must decide what form should be used (R. MARCUS, above n. 93, p. 13).

these rules also generally apply to electronic evidence, as do its exceptions. Electronic evidence is one of the various types of evidence on which a judge or jury can rely. It might be true that it has more impact on a judge's or jury's conviction than other types of evidence, especially oral evidence, but it is still one element of the basis of his/her judgment. It should be relevant to the fact in dispute and reliable. Therefore, a judge should not be afraid of evaluating such evidence fairly in the same way as other traditional evidence, on the condition that the risk of manipulation and the illegality of obtaining it are considered closely.

THE NEW CHALLENGES OF EVIDENCE LAW IN THE FOURTH INDUSTRIAL REVOLUTION

Joan Picó*

1. Neuroscience and Evidence...479
   1.1. Introduction...479
   1.2. Worldwide Experiences in the Use of New Technologies for the
        Control of Personal Testimony Given in Civil Proceedings........482
        1.2.1. Use is not Permitted..................................482
        1.2.2. Only Allowed under Certain Conditions.................483
        1.2.3. Allowed..484
        1.2.4. There is no Debate (Either in Favor or Against)...........484
        1.2.5. Final Reflection.....................................485

---

* Full Professor of Procedural Law, Pompeu Fabra University (Barcelona, Spain). I would like to thank the national reporters for their invaluable help: Professor L. Giannini (Argentina), Professor P. Taelman and Professor W. Vandenbussche (Belgium), Professor D. Guimaraes Ribeiro (Brazil), Professor C. Piché and Professor V. Gautrais (Canada), Professor G. Zhiyuan (China), Professors M. Bustamante, A. Mazuera, D. Agudelo, L. Pabón, L. Toro, and O. Vargas (Colombia), Professor A. Uzelac (Croatia), Professor J. Sorabji (England and Wales), Professor C. Bléry and Professor Jean-Paul Teboul (France), Professor N. Lösing (Germany), Professor V. Harsági (Hungary), Professor H. Mohseni and Professor M. Elsan (Iran), Professor A. Dondi and Professor P. Comoglio (Italy), Professor H. Tega (Japan), Professor C. Gómez Fröde (Mexico), Professor A. Nylund (Norway), Professor G. Priori and Professor R. Pérez-Prieto (Peru), Professor K. Flaga-Gieruszyńska and Professor A. Klich (Poland), Professor A.P. Costa e Silva and Professor L. Ruivo (Portugal), Professor R. Baboolal-Frank (South Africa), Professor J.W. Park (South Korea), Professor J.A. Andino, Professor F. Ramos-Romeu, and Judge Y. Ríos (Spain), Professor K.L. Shen (Taiwan), Professor S. Pereira and Professor M. Virginia (Uruguay), and Professor D. Capra (United States). I also thank Professor R. Marcus for his study *US Experience with the Challenges of Electronic Evidence*. This chapter is part of the R&D project *Towards a New Regulation of Expert Evidence* (DER2016-7549-P), funded by the Spanish Ministry of Economy and Competitiveness, as well as the Consolidated Research Group *Evidence Law* (2017 SGR 2015), funded by Catalonian Agency for Management of University and Research Grants. The principal investigator of both is Professor Joan Picó.

Intersentia

2. Facial Micro-Expression Algorithms for Lie Detection: True or False? . . . 485
  2.1. The Theoretical Framework 485
  2.2. The APDP Clinical Trial (2019) 488
    2.2.1. Introduction 488
    2.2.2. Material, Method, and Results 488
3. Possible Problems Caused by the Increasing Prevalence of
  New Technologies and Especially the "Internet of Things" in
  Civil Procedure 489
  3.1. Introduction 489
  3.2. The Search for Digital Evidence: Dangers to Avoid. 491
  3.3. The Traditional Rules of Evidence: Do they Work for
    "Electronic Facts"? 493
4. The Scientific Knowledge of the Expert and its Inspection in the
  Civil Process 494
  4.1. Can the Civil Judge Appoint an Expert? 494
  4.2. The Scientific Knowledge of the Expert and Judicial Control:
    How is the Independence and Impartiality of the Expert
    Protected against Any Type of External Interference? 497
    4.2.1. Introduction: Judicial Independence and Impartiality 497
    4.2.2. Expert Impartiality 498
    4.2.3. The Independence of the Expert 500
      4.2.3.1. The Practical Significance of the Independence
        of the Expert and its Theoretical and
        Legal Basis 500
      4.2.3.2. The Minimum Necessary Conditions for the
        Existence of Expert Independence 501
        4.2.3.2.1. The Expert Must not be Answerable to
          Anyone, but Only to their Own
          Specialist Knowledge 501
        4.2.3.2.2. Effective Mechanisms Must be in Place
          to Enable the Expert to Report Any
          Possible Attacks on their Independence. . . 503
  4.3. How can the Judge Control the Scientific Knowledge of the
    Expert Stated in their Expert Opinion? 504
    4.3.1. The Preventive System 504
    4.3.2. The Reactive System 506
    4.3.3. Other Forms of Judicial Control of Expert Opinion 508
5. Private Communications between Lawyers as Evidence. 510
  5.1. Are Such Communications Covered or Protected by Legal
    Privilege between Lawyers? 510
    5.1.1. Communications between Lawyers are Always
      Confidential 510

5.1.2. Communications between Lawyers are Confidential,
but Only for Settlement Negotiations. 511
5.1.3. Communications between Lawyers are Protected,
but Only for Mediation Proceedings 512
5.1.4. The Protection of Privilege Corresponds to
Client–Attorney Communications. 512
5.1.5. Communications between Lawyers are not Confidential,
but the Lawyer has the Right to Refuse a Disclosure 513
5.1.6. Communications between Lawyers are not
Confidential 513
5.2. Regarding the Possibility for a Lawyer to Attach Private
Communications between Lawyers to a Judicial Proceeding 514
5.2.1. A Lawyer is Entitled to Attach Communications
between Lawyers to a Judicial Proceeding at the
Lawyer's or Client's Sole Discretion 514
5.2.2. Attachment is Allowed under Certain Conditions. 514
5.2.3. It is Forbidden for a Lawyer to Attach Communications
between Lawyers to a Judicial Proceeding. 515
5.3. Consequences of the Unlawful Attachment of Communications
between Lawyers 516
5.3.1. The Court may Exclude/not Admit Such Evidence 516
5.3.2. The Court will not Assess Such Evidence 517
5.3.3. The Court will Accept Such Evidence, Even if it is
Forbidden by Ethical Rules 517

1. NEUROSCIENCE AND EVIDENCE

1.1. INTRODUCTION

New technologies not only play a part in the field of evidence law as mechanisms for re-creating reality that can serve to convince the trier of fact, but are also presented as a means capable of verifying traditional forms of evidence.

We put forward for consideration here whether it is possible to check, via technology, the testimony of parties, witnesses, and experts. Neurological science appears to offer mechanisms capable of measuring the veracity of such statements such as through magnetic resonance imaging (MRI). However, it is the case that, at present, there is no unanimous consensus regarding the effectiveness or scientific validity of these mechanisms.

Every day, neuroscience provides new techniques aimed at detecting evidence of neural changes in the human brain with the aid of sophisticated brain-imaging techniques that allow us to show specific areas of the brain that

Joan Picó

execute specific functions.[1] Nevertheless, at present, we face important empirical limitations regarding the dependability of this scientific lie-detection evidence.[2] Even if it were true that it is possible to detect which area of the brain has the function of responding to an interrogation (i.e., to determine scientifically when the speaker is consciously being untruthful), this raises numerous questions, as it is possible that the speaker:

(a) is lying but has the – innate or acquired – ability to control their emotional reactions, thus preventing the activation of the area of the brain responsible for lying, and the lie is therefore undetected;

(b) is not lying, but the area of the brain stimulated by lying becomes active because their nervous system has been excessively altered as a result of discussing matters of an intimate nature, or which they have kept secret for some time and wishes to continue doing so, or that could result in particularly damaging consequences of whatever sort (affective, personal, professional, economic, etc.);

(c) is both lying and telling the truth because, for example, the lie is based on an erroneous knowledge of the facts;[3]

(d) is telling the truth in relation to facts that formally appear to be false.

I participated in a real case where in which X-ray images showed a situation in which it was objectively logical to think that pain existed when, in fact, it never did: these was the X-ray images of an 89-year-old woman who, after being hit by a car, had to undergo surgery to place an intramedullary nail as a result of a pertrochanteric fracture in her right hip. During post-operative monitoring,

---

[1] In this regard, see H.T. GREELY and A. WAGNER, "Reference Guide on Neuroscience" in *Reference Manual on Scientific Evidence*, 3rd ed., National Academies Press, Washington, D.C. 2011, pp. 807–808. And similarly, cf. different experiments designed to detect the area of the brain active in lying, published in scientific journals, described by M. PARDO and D. PATTERSON, "Philosophical Foundations of Law and Neuroscience" [2010] *University of Illinois Law Review* 1228, notes 91–93.

[2] For example, it is often argued that not all human brains are the same, that the experiments are still few, and that in many cases the area of the brain alleged to be responsible for lying is also associated with other cognitive activities beyond that of lying (cf. M. PARDO and D. PATTERSON, above n. 3, 1228, note 95).

[3] To simplify this affirmation, the following example should suffice. Let us suppose that Mr. A believes the Earth to be flat; that is to say, he holds the statement that the Earth is flat (1) to be true. Now let us suppose that Mr. A lies to Mr. B and tells him that the Earth is round (2). In this case, statement 1 is true and statement 2 is false, but Mr. A has lied to Mr. B and has told him a lie, which, curiously, is the truth. It is a truth based on erroneous knowledge of the actual facts. Mr. A is lying – as he is saying something contrary to what he believes to be true – but being mistaken (believing something false) has led him to tell the truth while lying (this example is taken from http://filosofia.laguia2000.com/creencias/sobre-verdad-y-mentira).

the patient, despite the fact that X-ray images showed that the fracture had healed, claimed to experience extreme pain in her right hip both during and after rehabilitation, which she had never experienced before the accident, and which the doctor representing the insurance company of the person responsible for the accident concluded must have existed prior to the accident, due to the evidence of coxarthrosis visible in the X-rays prior to the operation. For this reason, in this case, the insurance company refused to pay compensation to the patient for the pain (and subsequent treatment of it – which could entail, for example, further surgery for arthroplasty or a full hip replacement), given that arthrosis is a degenerative condition that us not attributable to an injury (and in fact, as we have indicated, was already perceived in the X-ray images prior to surgery). While it is true that the X-ray images showed the existence of arthrosis, which habitually causes pain, at the trial it was proved that the elderly woman had never complained of any pain in that area (as was verified, among other evidence, by the testimony of her family doctor – who had been treating her for years – and the record of her medical history, which did not show any medical prescription pertaining to hip pain or any ER visits for that reason), and it was therefore determined that the accident had triggered the pain, for which reason the insurance company was ordered to pay compensation to the woman.[4]

Ultimately, all these situations lead us to much deeper debates, such as the dichotomy between the brain and the mind (that is, whether it is possible that the mind exists beyond a mere physiological element of the brain), which is why the study of this human organ – no matter how in-depth or thorough – would seem to be incapable of detecting the speaker's mind. However, all of this is beyond the scope of this chapter.[5] In any case, the hypothesis that it is possible by means of images of the brain to detect when a person is lying continues to be refuted by numerous scientific studies, which is why it is logical to continue reflecting on the admissibility as evidence of such images of the brain as a means of determining the greater or lesser credibility of the court testimony of the parties, witnesses, and experts.

---

[4]   Similarly, the work of H.T. GREELY and A. WAGNER, above n. 1, points out the existence of studies carried out with computerized imaging which show that people can be hypnotized to feel pain without any painful external stimulus, but nevertheless the "pain matrix" is activated (ibid., p. 809), and therefore these images of the brain would give a false representation of the facts. Similarly, we may think of an amputee suffering from phantom pains, who claims to feel pain in the missing limb. In this case it is indeed possible that the speaker is telling the truth – that is to say, he or she is not lying – but that this does not agree with something that is objectively true, namely that the limb which they indicate as the source of pain does not exist. As can be seen, in both cases, the device can detect that the speaker is not lying – because the pain exists as a subjective perception of the person affected – even though the fact of the origin of the pain is manifestly false.

[5]   On this subject, see M. PARDO and D. PATTERSON, above n. 2, pp. 1218–1220.

Joan Picó

1.2. WORLDWIDE EXPERIENCES IN THE USE OF NEW TECHNOLOGIES FOR THE CONTROL OF PERSONAL TESTIMONY GIVEN IN CIVIL PROCEEDINGS

The first thing emphasized in the study of the diverse worldwide experiences in the use of new technologies (fMRI, functional magnetic resonance imaging) to verify the accuracy of personal testimony given in civil proceedings is the absence of regulation: no country provides express regulation on this point. This is evident proof that technological development always moves at a faster pace than legal development.

All of this results in a rich variety of legal situations in the various countries studied, ranging from the most extreme (permitting or refusing these new technologies) to the more intermediate (where they are either permitted or refused depending on different circumstances). And, in the same way, there are countries in which this debate has not even taken place. In the following section, we will look at the legal situations that can be found in this worldwide context.

1.2.1. Use is not Permitted

Many countries do not allow the use of new technologies to verify the testimony given in court by witnesses, parties, and experts. The reasons that are given to support this conclusion are very diverse:

(a) the express lack of regulatory provisions, which leads to these new technologies not being used in judicial practice;[6]

(b) express prohibition in civil procedural codes;[7]

(c) the lack of trust in the reliability, or lack of scientific nature of these new technologies;[8] or

---

[6] So, for example, regarding England, SORABJI (England and Wales) stresses that: "Such technology is not used. I have never heard of any suggestion that such technology could be relied upon to purport to verify the veracity of witness or party evidence in English civil procedure. I would very much doubt that its use would ever been permitted." And in the same way for China, ZHIYUAN indicates that in the absence of any regulatory provision on this point, judicial practice does not admit the use of modern technology to verify the authenticity of personal statements made before the judge.

[7] This is the case, for example, in Japan, where TEGA informs us that the Japanese CCP does not expect (and does not allow) the use of fMRI, etc., during the examination of witnesses.

[8] In this regard, for the United States, CAPRA points out the cases of *United States v. Semrau*, 693 F.3d 510 (6th Cir. 2012) and *Wilson v. Corestaff Servs. L.P.*, 28 Misc.3d 425, 900 N.Y.S.2d 639 (N.Y.Sup.Ct. 2010). In the first judgment, the court stated that the technology "had not been fully examined in real world settings"; that there was no way to determine a rate of error; and that the clinical studies did not establish reliability sufficiently for use in a trial." And the second judgment also expressed "doubts about the reliability of fMRI results as an indicator of truth telling." For England, similarly, SORABJI (England and Wales) states that the lack of confidence in this technology means that it is not used, which leads him to conclude that "its use would never be permitted."

482

Intersentia

(d) the express legal provision that the control of the veracity of the witnesses, parties, or experts is entrusted exclusively to the judge, who upon careful evaluation of the evidence must become freely convinced of that veracity, and nothing may interfere with his/his freedom to assess the evidence.[9] In similar terms, this is also formulated in common law countries where there is a jury, because an expert's report cannot substitute the jury's exclusive responsibility for giving more or less probative value to the persons who testify before it.[10]

Obviously, this does not exclude the possibility in all countries of allowing the use of fMRI of the brain as documentary evidence to prove the certainty of the facts of the case (for example, when the trial deals with neurodegenerative diseases or brain cancers).[11]

1.2.2. Only Allowed under Certain Conditions

In some countries, the use of new technologies is allowed for the purpose of verifying the truthfulness or mendacity of witnesses, provided that this is in accordance with the will of those wishing to submit to these new technologies and there is no denigrating treatment against their human dignity.[12] Therefore, the limit to the attempt to seek the truth of the facts would be full respect for

---

[9] This occurs, for example, in Italy, in relation to which DONDI and COMOGLIO, after indicating that "so far, no rules or case law, or scholarly elaboration, exist concerning this topic," go on to state that: "However, in the Italian legal system these new technologies do not seem to be allowed. In fact, more than a general rule, the widespread belief is that the veracity of a witness must be verified essentially through the careful evaluation by the judge." And also with respect to Mexico, GÓMEZ FRÖDE affirms that "it is not allowed to verify or control the veracity of statements with any system (neither lie detector nor fMRI) because the evaluation remains strictly human and under the perception and sensitivity of the judges."

[10] As a good example, the United States is noteworthy: thus, CAPRA (United States), citing *Wilson v. Corestaff Servs. L.P.*, 28 Misc.3d 425, 900 N.Y.S.2d 639 (N.Y.Sup.Ct. 2010), points out how the court stated that the expert opinion about the fMRI results "is of a collateral matter, i.e. the credibility of a fact witness" and "credibility is a matter solely for the jury and is clearly within the ken of the jury."

[11] As clearly shown by BABOOLAL-FRANK (South Africa) and TEGA (Japan).

[12] This is the case in Germany, where LÖSING states that the use of new technologies to check the veracity of court testimony does not violate art. 1 of the German Constitution and could be allowed if the request is voluntary, although he admits that "an application in a civil procedure has not taken place yet and does not seem to be imminent." However, regarding the criminal process, he puts forward the experience of the use of such technologies being allowed in the year 2000 when an expert provided his opinion regarding the possible brain damage of a witness, using these new scientific techniques to conclude from the fMRI that the witness was telling the truth, for which reason the defendant was convicted. In the same vein, for example, in Peru, PRIORI and PÉREZ-PRIETO highlight how its Constitutional Court has allowed the use of the polygraph in criminal proceedings, but always limited to the investigation phase of criminal acts (with the presence of the investigated party's lawyer and respecting their right of defense and right to a fair hearing), but not for the oral hearing or trial phase, as this is prohibited by the presumption of innocence. Finally, we must point

Joan Picó

the constitutional rights of the persons who testify at trial, and therefore, in the event of the violation of such rights, such evidence would be illegal or unlawful and, consequently, inadmissible.[13]

1.2.3. Allowed

In many countries, judges allow the probative use of fMRI to test the truth of testimony, either because the law expressly allows it or because the law refers to the free assessment of the evidence, which gives the judge a wide margin of discretion to allow and assess any probative element that they deem useful in reaching their finding on the facts of the case.[14]

In addition, there are countries in which new technologies are openly allowed in the judicial field due to the general conviction that they are effective and authentic, and the generalized use made of them by the government leads them to trust all technological advances.[15] This means that in the event that a party denounces the falsehood of testimony of the opposing party or the witnesses, prima facie, any valid technological means can be used to reveal it.

1.2.4. There is no Debate (Either in Favor or Against)

Finally, the existence of many countries in which the problem presented here has not been raised because there are no legal rules or case law on the subject must be noted.[16]

---

out a similar legal situation in South Korea, in which it is stated by PARK (South Korea) that "though polygraphs are used extensively in criminal investigations, the courts do not consistently allow them in trial."

[13] This is indicated by COSTA E SILVA and RUIVO in relation to Portugal when they affirm that "considering the principle of freely choosing the means of proof, the parties are prima facie authorized to add to the procedural action any probative elements they consider necessary or useful to the rendition of a favorable decision on the merits determined by the judge. Hence, new technologies allowed in civil procedure will be determined negatively: all evidence that is not illegal will be admissible. In turn, in assessing the lawfulness of the evidence, an analysis of the manner in which it is obtained and of its content (in particular, whether it must be considered as intrusive of the right to privacy or other constitutionally consecrated rights) is essential."

[14] This is the case in Taiwan, where, as indicated by SHEN, "since Taiwan's Code of Civil Procedure allows judges' free evaluation of evidence, judges are entitled to utilize any new technology (for example, fMRI – Magnetic Resonance Imaging – or similar) to verify or control the veracity of the personal statements of witnesses, parties, etc." And the same is indicated, with respect to Uruguay, by PEREIRA CAMPOS and BARREIRO.

[15] Nordic countries stand out as a paradigm of this way of thinking, as pointed out by NYLUND (Norway).

[16] As is the case in Argentina (cf. GIANNINI (Argentina)), Belgium (cf. TAELMAN and VANDENBUSSCHE (Belgium)), Brazil (cf. GUIMARAES RIBEIRO (Brazil)), Hungary (cf. HARSÁGI (Hungary), and Poland (cf. FLAGA-GIERUSZYŃSKA and KLICH (Poland)).

1.2.5. Final Reflection

In the absence of a rule prohibiting the use of fMRI to detect mendacity in the testimony of witnesses, parties, or experts in civil proceedings, there should be no obstacle to allowing its use, provided that the following three conditions are met:

(a) the person testifying must voluntarily submit to it;
(b) it must be used following the guidelines established by the scientific community, and must be documented in an expert report, which the opposing party must be allowed to contradict.
(c) free judicial assessment of all the evidence must be respected, i.e., both of the testimony subject to fMRI and the expert report, since, as it is not yet entirely reliable today, a margin of discretion should be left to the judge's assessment. As is well known, this freedom of assessment does not imply, under any circumstances, judicial arbitrariness, but quite the opposite: the need to give grounds in the judgment for the findings drawn from the evidence submitted, because only in this way is the person on trial allowed to know the real reason for that judgment. In any case, there is a problem here that is difficult to solve with regard to countries with a jury (basically common law countries), since the facts are tried by the jury without stating the grounds, and therefore there is a danger (already pointed out by Damaška) that the expert could come to replace the function of the judge, i.e., something that is not reliable (the expert opinion of fMRI) could unduly condition something that pertains exclusively to the jury, which is the decision to grant more or less credibility to the people who give evidence to it, and therefore it is best to reject the admissibility of its use. As we have seen, this is what happens in the United States, where the Supreme Court and the federal courts do not allow fMRI, even if it were reliable, because it is the responsibility of the jury to assess the credibility of witnesses and parties.

2. FACIAL MICRO-EXPRESSION ALGORITHMS FOR LIE DETECTION: TRUE OR FALSE?

2.1. THE THEORETICAL FRAMEWORK

As noted above, one of the fundamental aspects for the best judicial resolution of disputes is to be able to know when the litigant, a witness, or an expert is lying in his statement before the judge.

Nowadays, there is a part of clinical psychology that holds that it is possible to detect when a person is lying through their facial micro-expressions.[17] On the basis of the studies of Higgard and Isaacs, followed by the works of Paul Ekman as well as those of Porter and Brike, and ending with the most recent studies of Professor Matsumoto (a leading figure in the field of facial micro-expressions), we can reach the theoretical conclusion that there are certain areas of the face that, when properly analyzed, allow us to know when a person is lying or telling the truth.[18] For these authors, when emotions are spontaneously expressed, the same facial expressions and muscle movements appear on the face, and this appears to be due to the fact that these facial expressions are under the neural control of two distinct areas of the brain, one controlling involuntary movements and the other voluntary movements. Consequently, if a person tries to control their expressions, both systems become involved in a neuronal conflict over control of the face, which produces a very brief facial expression that is termed a "micro-expression." Based on this, there seems to be an innovative means of evidence based on the analysis of facial micro-expressions and other physical and/or physiological reactions in people, providing measurable objective data to determine whether the testimony of an individual is spontaneous or planned, whether their facial expressions are genuine or feigned, whether they are trying to hide a universal facial reaction, and even allowing us to tell whether a reported event comes from a memory of the person's actual experience, or whether it is imagined or has been induced by another person.

Based on these results, there are companies that, applying an algorithm (which they do not disclose), are capable of producing expert reports that are used in court as evidence to give greater or lesser credibility to a particular person's statement.[19] And sometimes these expert reports are admitted as evidence.[20]

---

[17] See J. Picó Junoy, C. de Miranda Vázquez and J.A. Andino López, "Examen de un nuevo método de detección judicial de la mentira" ("Examination of a New Method of Judicial Lie Detection") in J. Picó Junoy, *La prueba en acción. Estrategias procesales en materia probatoria*, 2019, J.Mª. Bosch, Barcelona, pp. 267–275.

[18] For the study of this doctrine, see D. Matsumoto and H.C. Hwang, "Micro-expressions Differentiate Truths from Lies about Future Malicious Intent" (2018) 9 *Frontiers in Psychology* 1 (see https://www.frontiersin.org/articles/10.3389/fpsyg.2018.02545/full).

[19] Especially in the field of family law, since this is where personal relationships operate in the private sphere, and can be evaluated as another element among all the evidence presented, and in the area of criminal proceedings for crimes of gender violence, since here there are usually only two contradictory statements: that of the victim and that of the alleged aggressor.

[20] Thus, for example, the divorce judgment of Court of First Instance 18 of Barcelona, July 31, 2018. And even judgments of the Spanish Supreme Court refer to non-verbal physical reactions as another indication to be weighed as part of the evidence examined (in this regard, the judgment of the Supreme Court, Division 2 (Criminal Division), 119/2019, March 6, 2019, established: "Assumptions in the analysis of the court's assessment of the victim's testimony ... allow us remember that it is possible for the court to base its finding on the victim's version, since the credibility and plausibility of his/her testimony are part of

Recently, however, an international group of experts in the field has published a study, which has turned out to be extremely significant, on the "pseudo-science" nature of all these methods of lie detection.[21] They reveal, among other things, that those with scientific experience in lie detection agree that there is no non-verbal behavior that is proper and exclusive to truthful or untruthful people. Put more simply, there are no objective indicators of a lie, as in the fabled story of Pinocchio and his nose.

As this panel of experts explains, the widespread obsession of the layperson with everything that comes "out of the mouth" of the experts has caused any supposedly scientific knowledge to be accepted uncritically. In the matter at hand, this phenomenon has been very marked, probably driven by the imperative need to find infallible methods to detect deception in a judicial scenario.

However, the truth is that there is a lack of experimental studies that give scientific validity to these methods of detecting lies.[22] One of them is the study carried out by the "Asociación de Probática y Derecho Probatorio" (APDP)[23] in Spain, which is discussed below.

---

the weighing of a series of factors to take into account in the court's process of weighing the evidence. And here we can cite the following: ... 4. [that] convincing 'body language' ... is of great importance and is characterized by the way in which the victim expresses himself from the point of view of the 'gestures' which accompany his or her testimony before the court" (and, previously, also the judgment of the same Court 282/2018, of June 13, 2018).

[21] V. DENAULT et al., "The Analysis of Nonverbal Communication: The Dangers of Pseudoscience in Security and Justice Contexts" (2020) 30 *Anuario de Psicología Jurídica* 1 (see https://journals.copmadrid.org/apj/art/apj2019a9).

[22] Therefore, there are court decisions that do not give probative value to such expert evidence. As a good example of this, the decision of section 18 of the Court of Appeal of Barcelona (Spain), May 8, 2019 (ECLI:ES:APB:2019:5002) states the following: "The report of 22-11-2017 of XX entitled *Research and Development of Micro Facial Expressions and Body Language* states ... The credibility of the story is affirmed by eye reactions and gestural chronology. As stated in the ruling, no scientific publication has been provided to support and compare the technique used. In the appeal, a bibliographic record on the subject is provided, but no accreditation is given to support the scientific validity of the technique used, and it is noted that there is literature that questions its scientific basis. We cannot consider such a technique as valid for the verification of the credibility of the statements made by the minor ... The use of this methodology is not sufficiently verified, the exact nature of the training of the people who have carried it out is unknown, and the way in which the methodology has been applied to the minor in question is considered by the Chamber to be totally inadequate. For all these reasons, the conclusions reached in the report are discarded." Along the same lines, the judgment of section 12 of the Court of Appeal of Barcelona (Spain), December 18, 2018 (ECLI:ES:APB:2018:12369) maintains: "In relation to the expert evidence provided by Ms. Gracia to support her version, the documentation of the judicial procedure includes ... an analysis by the company – of facial micro-expressions and unconscious body language, an analysis to which the Chamber does not give scientific value." And, finally, the criminal judgment of section 20 of the same Court of Appeal of Barcelona, of 13 September 2018, states: "Thus, the expert opinion on facial micro-expressions is completely unnecessary and can provide nothing relevant."

[23] Forensic Evidence and Evidence Law Association.

2.2. THE APDP CLINICAL TRIAL (2019)

2.2.1. *Introduction*

Just as if we were dealing with a new medicine, it is fundamental to test or verify the degree of effectiveness of any method offered in judicial practice as a panacea for the detection of lies through the control of facial micro-expressions, and this is especially fundamental when a court may be inclined to grant scientific validity – and consequently probative value – to expert opinions in which it is alleged that a person (party, witness, or expert) is lying or telling the truth.

For this reason, the APDP – an association of university professors, judges, lawyers, and experts–devised a clinical trial to test the degree of effectiveness of a lie detection system that a European company was presenting in court in the form of expert opinions.[24]

2.2.2. *Material, Method, and Results*

Through the APDP and the aforementioned European company, a clinical trial was devised to verify the degree of effectiveness of the system for detecting lies by means of facial micro-expressions through the oral testimony of ten women who had allegedly suffered gender-based violence.

The APDP contacted different associations for abused women and two drama schools. Finally, for the clinical trial, four actresses were chosen to lie about an episode of gender-based violence, as were six women who had to recount the real experiences as actual victims of such a crime (as documented by court rulings).

For the company that was to issue the expert reports, the identity of all the women was kept completely anonymous. They had to make an oral presentation, lasting 30 minutes, recorded by the company, recounting their episodes of gender-based violence and answering questions from the company's psychologist, their identity given only as a simple number (from 1 to 10).[25] The recordings had to be made in the presence of one of the authors of the study and the company was expressly forbidden to contact the aforementioned women afterwards.[26]

The ten women were kept from meeting one another to avoid any influence this might have on their statements. Interviews were conducted with all of them

---

[24]   See J. Picó Junoy et al., above n. 18, pp. 267–275.

[25]   The correlation of the number with the specific identity of the person, and the circumstance of whether or not she had suffered gender-based violence, was kept secret from the company, and this data was contained in escrow (in a sealed envelope) kept by a notary, who, after the delivery of the company's expert reports, was required to verify their accuracy.

[26]   For participating in this clinical trial, giving the account of gender-based violence, the women who had actually suffered it received €200, while the actresses received €100 at the time of the recording, and €100 more if they managed to avoid having their false statement detected by the company.

individually to explain the object and purpose of the clinical trial, and to obtain their express consent.

A schedule of recordings between the women and the APDP was agreed upon so that in one week (August 27–29, 2019) the women could make their statements to the company that was to provide the expert opinion indicating which women had really suffered gender-based violence and which had not.

In short, after more than four months of preparation for the clinical trial and 200 hours of work by the researchers, seven days before the recordings were due to be made, the company that was to issue the expert opinions on lie detection through facial micro-expressions sent an email in which it expressed its intention not to carry out the clinical trial, justifying its decision by the volume of work it currently had (the recordings were scheduled for the last week of August in order not to interfere with the company's normal work).[27] The company was immediately offered the option of carrying out the same clinical trial without any date restrictions so as to adapt to a schedule that would suit it better, but the response was the same: the company declined to scientifically test the method used to reach its expert opinions, claiming to have a high volume of work which would not allow it to do so. The facts speak for themselves – let everyone draw their own conclusions.

3. POSSIBLE PROBLEMS CAUSED BY THE INCREASING PREVALENCE OF NEW TECHNOLOGIES AND ESPECIALLY THE "INTERNET OF THINGS" IN CIVIL PROCEDURE

3.1. INTRODUCTION

The so-called "Age of the Fourth Industrial Revolution" in which we find ourselves is characterized by the massive use of new technologies and their involvement in almost all human activities. These new technologies are found especially in three areas of society:

(a) In the way in which people relate, through the continuous use of social networks like Facebook (with more than 2.2 billion users), YouTube (with 1.9 billion users), WhatsApp (with more than 1.5 billion users), Messenger

---

[27] Literally, the email received by the person carrying out this study on August 20, 2019 indicated: "Good morning Joan: I inform you that we have had an urgent meeting of the Board of Directors and it will be impossible for us to carry out the trial. Unfortunately, as of today, we cannot commit to making 10 simultaneous reports and meeting the stipulated dates."

(with 1.3 billion users), Instagram (with more than 1 billion users), Twitter (with 350 million users), or LinkedIn (with 260 million users),[28] and the storage and transmission of all types of information, data, or online content in one of the many virtual spaces available on the market, such as Google Drive, Dropbox, WeTransfer, Mega, Box, OneDrive, Dataprius, CloudMe, HubiC, Degoo, MediaFire, Weflio Drive, Filesharing24, PlusTransfer, and Wimi. All of these concepts have become part of our everyday vocabulary;

(b) in transactions, with the meteoric development of large multinational companies engaged in electronic commerce of any type of product or service, such as the US corporations Amazon or eBay, Alibaba or Tencent in China, Rakuten in Japan, or Vente Privee or Zalando in Europe – the rise of electronic transactions over the internet means that the turnover of online business is getting closer every day to that of traditional paper-based transactions; and

(c) in the direct interconnection of everyday electronic devices in citizens' lives through the internet, i.e. the Internet of Things (IoT). Various studies indicate that today there are some 30 billion devices connected to the internet in order to offer smart services and applications that are useful for the comfort of society (and that this figure will reach 75 billion by 2025).[29] This continuous increase in the IoT is favoring the incredible upsurge in smart contracts in which things interact autonomously, i.e., without the direct intervention of people, depending on the program for which they have been developed.[30] However, the 42 national reporters contributing to this chapter stress that there are still no evidentiary issues with regard to smart contracts in their jurisdictions.

New technologies even affect the way in which people communicate, such as through the use of symbols or images (emojis or emoticons), which, as Goldman points out,[31] also have an evidentiary impact, since it is increasingly common for such icons to be admitted in court as proof of whatever facts they might represent.

---

[28] See https://marketing4ecommerce.net/cuales-redes-sociales-con-mas-usuarios-mundo-2019-top.

[29] See https://www.researchgate.net/figure/Internet-of-Things-IoT-connected-devices-from-2015-to-2025-in-billions_fig1_325645304.

[30] A smart contract, according to the concept of its own creator SZABO (1996, 2016), is "a set of promises, specified in digital form, including protocols within which the parties perform on these promises" (see http://digitalchamber.org/assets/smart-contracts-12-use-cases-for-business-and-beyond.pdf). Its field of action is huge: thus, for example, in December 2016, the Chamber of Digital Commerce – the world's largest trade association representing the digital asset and blockchain industry, based in Washington, D.C. – in the document *Smart Contracts: 12 Use Cases for Business & Beyond*, describes 12 examples of smart contracts for areas as wide-ranging as digital identity, trade finance, securities, derivatives, financial data recording, bank transactions and mortgages, land title recording, supply chain, auto insurance, clinical trials, etc.

[31] E. GOLDMAN, 'Emojis and the Law' (2018) 9 *Washington Law Review* 1227.

The first thing that must be emphasized here is that we are dealing with a subject where, once again, technology is ahead of legislation, so that court practice has to deal with new technological problems using traditional legal instruments. In this chapter, we will only refer to evidence issues, so we will not enter into, for example, an examination of e-case management and e-courts, or any other aspects that falls outside the scope of evidence.

As far as evidence is concerned, similar and very complex problems arise in all countries. We are accustomed to proving physical facts that are easily verifiable as they exist on paper, but all this becomes much more difficult when we are facing what we might call "electronic or digital facts" (where an "electronic fact" is understood to be one that is to be found in a virtual or non-physical medium, i.e., basically through the internet). Therefore, traditional civil procedure must adapt quickly to these new technological challenges.

We will try to discover how the technological world is beginning to affect the field of judicial evidence and what future awaits us. And we will try to answer the questions that are habitually raised in courts all over the world and that are not always easy to solve: how is electronic data submitted in a trial? What limits are there on the control of electronic data? How can data be challenged and verified? What precautions should be taken to preserve electronic data? When is a computer expert necessary?

3.2. THE SEARCH FOR DIGITAL EVIDENCE: DANGERS TO AVOID

When the evidence is not in the real world, but rather in the virtual or digital sphere, it is much more complicated to locate such evidence and submit it at a trial.

The three areas of society in which new technologies have been developed especially have a similar regulatory situation throughout the world: (a) social media and electronic transactions have their own regulations in all democratic states; and (b) the IoT is usually not subject to any specific regulation in almost all countries.[32]

There are two major problems that are usually present in dealing with electronic or digital evidence, and they are very worrying: the possible interference in people's private life or innermost sphere in order to gain access

---

[32] For example, with respect to Africa, see BABOOLAL-FRANK (South Africa); for Asia, see TEGA (Japan) and ZHIYUAN (China); for North America, see PICHÉ and GAUTRAIS (Canada) and CAPRA (United States); for South America, see GIANNINI (Argentina) and GUIMARAES RIBEIRO (Brazil); and for Europe, see TAELMAN and VANDENBUSSCHE (Belgium), LÖSING (Germany), HARSÁGI (Hungary), DONDI and COMOGLIO (Italy), FLAGA-GIERUSZYŃSKA and KLICH (Poland), COSTA E SILVA and RUIVO (Portugal), and RÍOS (Spain).

to such facts, precisely because they are held in a closed area of privacy; and the ease with which the content can be manipulated or altered.

Regarding the first problem, it is true that technology has opened up certain areas in the sphere of personal privacy which previously remained private (thus, for example, a person's right to personal honor, image, or privacy can be violated by news transmitted through social media, and certain facts of a familial, personal, or intimate nature can be publicly displayed in a WhatsApp message or SMS; or the fact that, through the IoT, one can enter a house through any device that is in it and is connected to the internet). Such a digitally interconnected world tends to "depersonalize" social relationships – i.e., it forgets that behind each of the "electronic facts" there are people whose fundamental rights must always be respected (especially the right to privacy and the right to the protection of personal data, among others). Consequently, the most important danger to avoid is that in the search for and obtaining electronic evidence, a fundamental right is violated. And in this sense, both the European Court of Human Rights (ECtHR) and the Inter-American Court of Human Rights (ICtHR) have on occasion emphasized that in presenting evidence, not everything is admissible, one of their strictest limits being when such evidence is obtained unlawfully or illegally.[33] To combat this problem in the most effective way possible, it is essential that the law declares categorically that any probative element obtained by violating a constitutional right, both in the real world and the virtual world, must be inadmissible as evidence in a judicial process (and, in fact, in most international jurisdictions, there is case law and rules of exclusion regarding unlawfully obtained evidence).

The second problem is the ease of manipulating the content of a social network, an email message, or an electronic document. As noted by Piché and Gautrais, it is much easier to alter the content of a digital document than a traditional paper document, and thus they point out, for example, that it is possible without much experience to modify the textual content or the addressee of an email; that it is easy to modify the source code of an html page and then print it out, giving the impression that the document thus reproduced is the same as that found online; and that it is not difficult to modify an image file such as a photograph in order to give a distorted view of reality. However, these problems are overcome in most countries through the use of certain technological tools

---

[33]   Repeatedly, these senior international courts emphasize that in the current world of revolutionary change in information and communication technologies, fundamental rights must be respected at all costs. In this regard, I refer to the judgments of the ECtHR of January 12, 2016 (*Barbulescu v. Romania*) and April 3, 2007 (*Copland v. United Kingdom*); and the judgments of the ICtHR of September 2, 2015 (*Humberto Maldonado Vargas and Others v. Chile*), November 26, 2010 (*Cabrera García y Montiel Flores v. Mexico*), and October 30, 2008 (*Bayarri v. Argentina*).

(such as digital certification through certification companies publicly authorized to issue such certifications) and various legal practices (either through the use of different types of testimony – especially through institutions dedicated to mediating between companies – or the drafting of policies or protocols of action to which the contracting parties must agree to submit).

3.3. THE TRADITIONAL RULES OF EVIDENCE: DO THEY WORK FOR "ELECTRONIC FACTS"?

Once the existence of "electronic facts" and their full legal validity are admitted, the problem arises as to how they can be used in a trial to prove the rightfulness of claims.

In the three areas of society in which new technologies have been developed, as described in section 1.2.1 above, "electronic facts" can be introduced into a trial as follows:

(a) With reference to social media, their admission as evidence in a trial can take place, basically, through:
   – private documentary evidence: normally, conversations, data, or information collected on social media are usually printed and submitted as documents without any problem regarding their admissibility in a trial. In addition, at the request of a party, the judge may instruct the administrator or operator of a specific social network to provide the documentation that they consider of interest to the trial;
   – public documentary evidence: sometimes, a notary public or similar attesting official can be approached and asked to access a certain social network in order to certify, in a document recording the facts, a true reflection of its content for subsequent submission at the trial. In this regard, the utmost care must be taken, given the ease of manipulating the electronic data presented to the attesting official (such as making credible copies of webpages, altering the identification of the sender and recipient of an email, or the date that the electronic message was sent);
   – digital storage devices such as a USB, a pen drive, or a CD – in some countries, these devices are considered as documents, while in others they have their own separate regulation;[34]
   – questioning of the parties or witnesses. Obviously, such testimony can shed light on the contents published on a social network or the party's

---

[34] As is the case, for example, in Spain (cf. arts. 382–384 of the Code of Civil Procedure (CCP)).

Joan Picó

true participation in it (it must not be forgotten that phishing or identity fraud occurs with a certain frequency in social media communications); and

– the computer expert opinion. With this evidence, the possible alteration of the data on a social network can be proved, the date of its incorporation onto that network, etc.

(b) With respect to electronic transactions, each country usually has its own regulations governing electronic signatures, so we must turn to these national regulations to find out each type, their probative value, and how they may be challenged in a trial. In addition, it is necessary to emphasize the existence on the market of companies responsible for acting as intermediaries in all electronic transactions so that, in the event of litigation, they can intervene in the process by submitting documents or by testifying as witnesses. Similarly, the testimony of the parties is fundamental for ascertaining how willing they really are to do business.

(c) Finally, as regards the IoT, the intervention of the programmer involved in the various stages of creation and development of the smart contract will be fundamental, as well as the evidence of the computer expert, to verify the correctness of the data provided by the parties and the aforementioned programmer.

In conclusion, as we can see, the traditional means of evidence still serve to submit the "digital" or "virtual" evidence found on social media, in digital transactions, or in the world of the IoT at the trial. And this is the response that we are seeing worldwide in all countries.[35]

4. THE SCIENTIFIC KNOWLEDGE OF THE EXPERT AND ITS INSPECTION IN THE CIVIL PROCESS

4.1. CAN THE CIVIL JUDGE APPOINT AN EXPERT?

This is a question with a number of diverse solutions. We will now examine the four responses that are most commonly given and the arguments on which they are based:

(a) The first response is to reject any such possibility. There are two arguments that are most commonly used for this: (1) the validity of the adversarial

---

[35] This is clear, for example, from BABOOLAL-FRANK (South Africa) for Africa; SHEN (Taiwan) for Asia; COSTA E SILVA and RUIVO (Portugal) for Europe; PICHÉ and GAUTRAIS (Canada), and GÓMEZ FRODE (Mexico) for North America; and GIANNINI (Argentina) and GUIMARAES RIBEIRO (Brazil) for South America.

494

system or procedural freedom of the parties to request the evidence they deem most appropriate to defend their arguments; and (2) to prevent the judge's impartiality from being compromised.[36]

(b) The second response, which is along the same lines as the previous one, consists of attributing the initiative to seek this evidence to the parties and only exceptionally allowing the judge the possibility of ordering expert evidence ex officio when the initiative of the parties has been unsuccessful.[37]

(c) The third response, in complete opposition to the previous two, is to allow the judge to appoint an expert, normally with only two limitations: (1) not to alter the facts of the dispute; and (2) to allow the parties to defend themselves against the result of this expert evidence.[38] This regulatory

---

[36] For example, with respect to Africa, see BABOOLAL-FRANK (South Africa); or for Europe, see HARSÁGI (Hungary). A very clear example of this is the changing situation in Croatia, as pointed out by UZELAC (Croatia): until 2003, the Code of Civil Procedure authorized judges to request evidence *ex officio* if they consider this evidence essential for decision making. However, in spite of the permissive formulation of the statutory provision (the judges "may" request evidence *ex officio*, in the context of the socialist legal tradition and its emphasis on inquisitorial control over private transactions (even in the context of civil cases), the higher courts often quashed the judgments of lower courts, arguing that the factual basis for judgments was insufficiently established since certain evidence (not proposed by any of the parties) was missing. This led to passive behavior of the parties and to abusive strategies of their lawyers, all in all resulting in a slow and inefficient style of litigation, where judges technically felt obliged to procure most evidence *ex officio*. To put an end to this inefficiency of civil litigation, in 2003 the Code of Civil Procedure introduced the opposite rule (art. 250): general prohibition in respect of requesting evidence *ex officio*. The remaining counterweight is the right of the court to remind the parties of their duty to assert facts and propose evidence. Using this right, judges may instruct the parties about their provisional assessment of the legal case and indicate that the establishment of certain facts needs additional proof.

[37] This is the case, for example, in Japan, where, although as a general rule an expert cannot be appointed, an exception is allowed when the court considers it strictly necessary to judge the facts (art. 218.1 CPC) or to assess the evidence examined at the trial (art. 233 CPC) (see TEGA (Japan)). Similarly, in Europe, the cases of France and Belgium stand out: in the case of France (BLÉRY and TEBOUL (France)), arts. 10 and 145 of the nouveau code de procédure civile grant evidence-seeking initiative to the civil judge, but art. 146.II establishes that in no case shall an investigative measure be ordered to provide for the failure of the party in the administration of evidence, and in the Belgian case (TAELMAN and VANDENBUSSCHE (Belgium)), this evidence-seeking initiative of the civil judge is allowed, although with the limit of not substituting the negligence or unjustified inactivity of the parties, and it is therefore established that this does not entail destroying the *onus probandi* of the parties. In the same vein, see Spain (J. PICÓ JUNOY, *El juez y la prueba [The Judge and the Evidence]*, J.Mª Bosch, Barcelona 2007) or Taiwan (SHEN (Taiwan)). However, this author highlights the existence of draft amendments made by the Judicial Yuan to the Code of Civil Procedure in 2018, in which the judge is allowed to appoint an expert (art. 39-1).

[38] This is the case in Germany (LÖSING (Germany)), Brazil (DARCI GUIMARAES (Brazil)), China, (ZHIYUAN (China)), Colombia (BUSTAMANTE et al. (Colombia)), Croatia (UZELAC (Croatia)), Iran (MOHSENI (Iran)), Italy (DONDI and COMOGLIO (Italy)), Norway (NYLUND (Norway)), Poland (FLAGA-GIERUSZYŃSKA and KLICH (Poland)), Peru (PRIORI and PÉREZ-PRIETO (Peru)), Portugal (COSTA E SILVA and RUIVO (Portugal)), Uruguay (PEREIRA and BARREIRO (Uruguay)), and the United States (CAPRA (United States)). In some cases, this

Joan Picó

option is based on the judge's duty to issue a judgment in the fairest way possible, which may lead him/her to order that such evidence be sought to ensure that the facts of the dispute are judged correctly.[39] The reference to the fairness of the judicial decision usually appears in international texts on the protection of human rights (such as Article 6 of the European Convention on Human Rights and in most national constitutions).[40]

(d) And finally, the fourth response, which is along similar lines to the previous one, is to allow the expert to intervene in the process not by giving evidence, but as a mere advisor to the judge when the latter lacks the necessary scientific or technical knowledge about the facts of the dispute. In this case, the advisor provides the judge with advice (not evidence) so that they can effectively carry out their jurisdictional function. As a paradigm of this situation, we find the case of England, with rule 35 of the Civil Procedural Rules 1998, which allows the judge to have ex officio expert advisors when they must decide on highly technical matters that require specialized knowledge (rule 35.15).[41]

In conclusion, in light of the origin of all these regulatory responses, we come to the conclusion that the option chosen does not depend on a certain political ideology, but on reasons of legislative technique, as there are fully democratic countries in which the civil judge is allowed to take the evidence-seeking initiative. Likewise, we can conclude that the traditional distinction between the common law system and the civil law system has disappeared, according to which, in the former system, the judge's initiative was not allowed, while in the latter system, it was, since, as we have indicated, there are common law countries (significantly the United States and England) where the civil judge is allowed to appoint an expert (or an advisor) ex officio, and there are civil law countries where this is prohibited.[42]

---

evidence-seeking initiative of the judge is provided in particular for disputes in which a public interest is discussed (as in Argentina: GIANNINI (Argentina)).

[39] However, in some countries, even though there is a rule that allows the judge to appoint an expert, it is emphasized that in practice one is not usually designated (this is the case, for example, in the United States: CAPRA (United States)).

[40] In this regard, for example, with regard to Belgium, they refer to a fair hearing as per art. 6 of the European Convention: TAELMAN and VANDENBUSSCHE (Belgium).

[41] SORABJI (England and Wales) emphasizes that the advisor is not an expert or a witness, for which reason he should not testify orally in the trial and cannot be asked questions, although the parties should be informed of the advice given by the advisor to the court so that they can make allegations. Similarly, this occurs in Japan. As we have already indicated, in this country, in addition to expert opinion as evidence, a court can use technical advisers and obtain from them a specialized knowledge of the facts of the dispute (TEGA (Japan)).

[42] This reinforces the thesis of TARUFFO (M. TARUFFO, *La semplice verità. Il giudice e la costruzione dei fatti*, Editori Laterza, Bari 2009, pp. 172 ff.); FABIANI (FABIANI, *I poteri istruttori del giudice civile*, Edizioni Scientifiche Italiane, Naples 2008, pp. 490 ff.) and PICÓ JUNOY (J. PICÓ JUNOY, above n. 38, pp. 114 ff.), as well as the idea put forward by DAMAŠKA (M. DAMAŠKA, *Evidence Law Adrift*, Yale University Press, New Haven 1997, p. 50) that, with

496   Intersentia

For the future, from the point of view of legislative technique, the option that is currently acquiring greater prominence around the world is to allow the civil judge to appoint an expert (or technical advisor) for the best resolution of the litigation (independently of the right of the parties to designate an expert of their own), and the following two experiences provide good examples of regulatory reform involving various states: (a) at the European level, Article 11.1 of the European Parliament Resolution of July 4, 2017 with recommendations to the Commission on common minimum standards of civil procedure in the European Union[43] establishes: "Without prejudice to the possibility for the parties to produce expert evidence, Member States shall ensure that the court may at any time appoint court experts in order to provide expertise for specific aspects of the case. The court shall provide such experts with all information necessary for the provision of the expert advice";[44] and (b) internationally, Article 22.4 ab initio of the Principles of Transnational Civil Procedure of the American Law Institute and the International Institute for the Unification of Private Law (UNIDROIT) clearly indicates that, in addition to the right of the parties to appoint an expert: "The court may appoint an expert to give evidence on any relevant issue for which expert testimony is appropriate."[45]

4.2. THE SCIENTIFIC KNOWLEDGE OF THE EXPERT AND JUDICIAL CONTROL: HOW IS THE INDEPENDENCE AND IMPARTIALITY OF THE EXPERT PROTECTED AGAINST ANY TYPE OF EXTERNAL INTERFERENCE?

4.2.1. Introduction: Judicial Independence and Impartiality

One of the characteristic features of the jurisdictional function is that it is carried out by independent and impartial judges, and this is recognized in the precepts that reflect the procedural guarantees of all international human rights treaties: Article 10 of the Universal Declaration of Human Rights 1948; Article 6(1)

---

the passage of time, the difference between common law and civil law in matters of evidence is more tenuous.

[43] After multiple attempts to harmonize European civil law procedure (it will suffice to remember, for example, the Storme Report, the various studies of Professor Tarzia, the European Law Institute/UNIDROIT project on *From Transnational Principles to European Rules of Civil Procedure*, among other documents cited in the preamble of that resolution) and taking into consideration the case law of the Court of Justice of the European Union on the principles of national procedural autonomy and effective judicial protection, the European Parliament finally presented this text of minimum standards to the scientific community for discussion by the European Commission.

[44] Available at http://www.europarl.europa.eu/sides/getDoc.do?pubRef=-//EP//TEXT+TA+P8-TA-2017-0282+0+DOC+XML+V0//EN.

[45] Available at https://www.unidroit.org/instruments/transnational-civil-procedure.

Intersentia

497

Joan Picó

of the European Convention on Human Rights, 1950; Article 14.1 of the International Covenant on Civil and Political Rights 1966; and Article 8.1 of the American Convention on Human Rights 1969.

Judicial independence is usually defined as the procedural guarantee aimed at allowing the judge full freedom to act in the face of possible interference from the rest of the state's powers (both the legally established – i.e., the executive and legislative powers – and the de facto powers – i.e., the mass media and financial institutions.), as well as from the judiciary itself, being subject only to the system of law.

Judicial impartiality, on the other hand, is usually defined as the procedural guarantee that seeks to ensure that the judge is in the best psychological and emotional state to make an objective judgment on the specific case before him/her. Therefore, in an attempt to preserve such impartiality at all times, laws tend to provide for different situations in which, due to the judge's close connection with a specific case (either with the parties or with the object of the dispute), their objectivity to judge may be called into question. Consequently, they establish mechanisms aimed at both the judge himself/herself (self-recusal) and at the parties (motion to recuse) to question the possible lack of such objectivity. In this regard, the ECtHR, interpreting Article 6(1) of the European Convention on Human Rights, repeatedly defines impartiality as the "absence of prejudice or bias [necessary to achieve] the confidence that the courts must inspire in citizens in a democratic society".[46] On the basis of this concept of impartiality, the ECtHR usually distinguishes a twofold scope of impartiality: (a) a subjective one, which refers to the personal conviction of a particular judge with respect to the specific case and the parties – an impartiality that must be presumed unless proven otherwise; and (b) another objective one, which relates to sufficient guarantees that the judge must meet in his actions with respect to the very object of the proceeding, presuming a lack of impartiality in the absence of the aforementioned guarantees.[47]

As we can see, the concepts of independence and impartiality have a different scope and content, and therefore, as we have indicated, both guarantees are recognized separately in international legal instruments for the protection of human rights. Independence is effective at a time prior to the judicial process, while impartiality is to be found at the time of the judicial proceeding.

4.2.2. Expert Impartiality

Most international legal systems establish the need for experts to act with complete impartiality. As a preventive measure, some legal systems establish the

---

[46]   See *Piersack v. Belgium*, 1 October 1982 (Appl. n. 8692/79), paragraph 30 (available at https://www.conjur.com.br/dl/case-of-piersack-belgium.pdf-).

[47]   *In extenso*, see J. Picó Junoy, *La imparcialidad judicial y sus garantías: la abstención y la recusación (Judicial Impartiality and its Guarantees: Self-Recusal and Motion to Recuse)*, J.Mª. Bosch, Barcelona 1998, pp. 23–51.

498   Intersentia

circumstances that may compromise the expert's impartiality so that the expert cannot accept the undertaking and issue their opinion.[48]

In any case, in all legal systems there are control mechanisms to protect expert impartiality when any cause likely to endanger it is detected after the expert has been chosen and their report has been drawn up: these are (a) the self-recusal (ex officio) of the expert; or (b) the disqualification at the request of the parties to the proceedings. Each legal system has its own grounds for recusal and disqualification, as well as its own procedure for both circumstances. As a general rule, the grounds for recusal of judges are usually the same as for experts, especially (but not only)[49] in those legal systems where the expert is an assistant to the judge[50]

For all these reasons, expert impartiality in general does not create legal complexities beyond the specific legislative regulation that may be found in one country or another. As a general rule, all circumstances that could objectively

---

[48]   This is the case, for example, in Japan and arts. 212 and 214 CCP, in which it is stipulated which persons may not be chosen as experts, or in Colombia and art. 235 of the General Procedure Code. This has nothing to do with regulations which provide for very high or very demanding levels of admissibility of expert evidence, typical of juridical systems with juries, in which the aim is to avoid misleading jurors with pseudo-science. For a perfect example of this regulation, the case of the United States and the famous rule 702 of the Federal Rules of Evidence stands out, embodying the legal doctrine of the *Daubert* case. This type of regulation has been transferred to non-jury legal systems, as is the case, for example, with the Colombian legal system, where art. 226 of the General Procedure Code establishes criteria for the admission of expert evidence which are very similar to those laid down in the North American regulation following the *Daubert* case (cf. BUSTAMANTE et al. (Colombia)).

[49]   Thus, for example, in Spain, the expert is not an assistant to the judge, but a true means of evidence and the grounds for recusing him/her are the same as for judges when the expert has been appointed, always at the request of a party, through the procedure established in the CCP (cf. art. 124 CCP). However, incomprehensibly, if the expert's report is issued by an expert chosen directly by the party (who submits the report together with his statement of claim or defense), the expert cannot be recused, but simply challenged. The difference between the recusal and challenge lies in the fact that only the former results in the removal of the expert and their report from the process, while the latter alerts the judge of the possible lack of impartiality of the expert, but does not succeed in removing their report from the process. However, the judge must take into consideration the cause of the challenge in order to give greater or lesser probative value to the expert's report. For a harsh critique of this duality of systems of objecting to the partiality of the expert, see J. PICÓ JUNOY, *La prueba pericial en el proceso civil español* (*Expert Evidence in Spanish Civil Procedure*), J.Mª. Bosch, Barcelona 2001.

[50]   Thus, for example, with regard to Asia, see TEGA (Japan) (art. 92-6 Japanese CCP) and SHEN (Taiwan) (art. 330 CCP Taiwan); for South America, see PEREIRA and BARREIRO (Uruguay) (art. 179 Uruguayan General Code of Procedure (CGP)), and BUSTAMANTE et al. (Colombia) (art. 235 Colombian General Code of Procedure [CGP]); and for Europe, see TAELMAN and VANDENBUSSCHE (Belgium) (arts. 828 and 829 of the Belgian Judicial Code), BLÉRY and TEBOUL (France) (art. 234.I *ab initio* French Code de Procédure Civile [CPC]), LÖSING (Germany) (§406(1) ZPO), DONDI and COMOGLIO (Italy) (art. 63 Italian Codice di Procedura Civile [CPC]), FLAGA-GIERUSZYŃSKA and KLICH (Poland) (art. 281 Polish Code of Civil Procedure [CCP]); or COSTA E SILVA and RUIVO (Portugal) (art. 470 Portuguese Code of Civil Procedure [CCP]).

and subjectively compromise any type of prejudice in favor of or against a litigating party are established as causes that would prevent an expert from being appointed or, if already appointed, require that they withdraw[51] (as well as a list of causes, national legislation usually provides an open clause to cover any situation that jeopardizes expert impartiality).[52]

4.2.3. *The Independence of the Expert*

4.2.3.1. The Practical Significance of the Independence of the Expert and its Theoretical and Legal Basis

Much has been written about the independence of judges and it is logical inasmuch as they support one of the essential pillars of any democratic state and of the rule of law. However, judicial experts have not been afforded the same consideration. Consequently, the first question we must answer is: can the concept of the independence of the judge be transferred to that of the judicial expert? This is very important, as I am reminded of the words of Damaška, who, at the conclusion of his study Evidence Law Adrift, rightly points out that: "A symptom of coming trouble is the growing concern about the role of the Continental court-appointed expert. Even at this juncture judges are often unable to understand his arcane findings. The fear is spreading that courts are covertly delegating decision-making powers to an outsider without political legitimacy. Is the court's nominal servant becoming its hidden master?"[53] If this is the case, it is clear that control over the expert's activity, i.e., his loss of independence, will ultimately lead to an attack on the necessary judicial independence.

Unlike the impartiality of the expert, express reference to his independence does not usually appear in comparative law. Does this mean that such independence is not required of experts? I believe that the answer must be no – that is, that the full independence of the expert is indeed required. If by independence we understand the procedural guarantee aimed at allowing the full

---

[51]   *Ad exemplum*, see arts. 196, 201.2 and 4, and 212.2 Japanese CCP; art. 51 Italian CPC; art. 301(1) Hungarian CCP; arts. 115 and 117 Portuguese CCP; or art. 141 Colombian CGP, etc.

[52]   In this regard, for example, see art. 214.1 Japanese CCP; art. 828 of the Belgian Judicial Code; art. 301(1) Hungarian CCP, etc. There are also legal systems in which it has been decided not to list causes, but to provide for a single list with very general content (for example, art. 325 of the Uruguayan General Code of Procedure, according to which: "Any verifiable circumstance that may affect the impartiality of the [expert] due to an interest in the process in which he/she intervenes, or esteem or enmity in relation to the parties or their lawyers and solicitors, as well as having given a specific opinion on the case, shall be cause for recusal").

    However, in some countries (such as Belgium), experts, just like judges, must also be impartial, although this requirement vis-à-vis experts is interpreted less strictly compared to judges (TAELMAN and VANDENBUSSCHE (Belgium)).

[53]   M. DAMAŠKA, above n. 43, pp. 150–151.

freedom of action of the judge against the possible interferences of any power of the state, having to submit only to the system of law, the expert's independence should be conceptualized as the guarantee aimed at allowing the full freedom of action of the expert against any type of external interference, having to submit only to his scientific, technical, or specialized knowledge of the matter on which his opinion is sought. Consequently, the expert should only be subject to the lex artis of their profession. The sole duty of the expert to submit to her lex artis is what guarantees his independence, just as the judge's sole duty to submit to the rule of law is what also guarantees his independence. For this reason, the ethical codes of judicial experts do refer to their independence, along with the full objectivity of their actions, submitting only to the lex artis of their field of knowledge.

Moreover, the expert's duty of independence derives implicitly from the necessary judicial independence: if the latter requires full submission to the law and, for this reason, requires full knowledge of the facts to be examined, to the extent that such knowledge is of a scientific, technical, or specialized nature, then expert assistance will be required, and therefore the lack of independence of the expert will, indirectly, be transferred to and affect the due independence of the judge.[54]

4.2.3.2. The Minimum Necessary Conditions for the Existence of Expert Independence

Having highlighted the theoretical and legal basis of expert independence, we must ask ourselves what the minimum conditions should be to achieve the required expert independence. If judicial or expert independence is characterized as protection against any kind of external interference in the activity of the judge or expert, respectively, and, in addition, as the sole submission of the judge is to the law and of the expert is to their precise specialized knowledge, we can find two minimum conditions necessary to achieve a true independence of judicial experts.

4.2.3.2.1. The Expert Must not be Answerable to Anyone, but Only to their Own Specialist Knowledge

The expert must act in their professional capacity on the sole basis of their specialized knowledge, and therefore no one may interfere with their scientific or technical judgment on the subject matter of the ruling: neither the judge

---

[54] Along these lines, VIGNEAU, "L'indépendance de l'expert vis-à-vis du juge" (2015) 120 *Experts* 25–26 points out that the expert, in their capacity as assistant to the judge, is subject to the same obligation of independence as the judge established in art. 6.1 of the European Convention on Human Rights.

nor the parties may give instructions on how they should proceed from the perspective of their methodology, or how to examine the problematic issue, what tests or experiments should be carried out, among other aspects that have a direct bearing on the final result (at most, they may ask him/her to try, as far as possible, to be more precise or clear in the presentation of the expert opinion and/or conclusions).

However, since the expert's activity is carried out within a trial, the only limit to their activity must come from the factual area on which they are required to prepare their opinion. Due to the applicability of the principle that the parties delimit the scope of the subject matter (*Dispositionsprinzip*) and the principle of production of evidence (*Verhandlungsmaxime*), the expert's role will be limited by the facts which are the subject of the dispute, which is why no essential facts (or documents) other than those forming the subject matter of the procedural debate can be introduced through the expert's opinion. But, in any case, the formation and expression of the expert's specialized opinion must be independent within the object of their report, which, as we have indicated, is determined by the parties and/or the judge.

The expert's independence is given by the full freedom in drafting their report (within the margin of intervention marked by the parties and/or the judge), for which reason they are free to use the working method that they deem best or most appropriate for the purpose of the matter on which they are to express an expert opinion, to formulate their report as they deem most correct, and to give meaning to their conclusions based solely on their best knowledge and understanding, without prejudice to responding to any clarifications, observations, or questions from the parties and/or the judge. In order to guarantee a sufficient and standardized level of specialist knowledge for experts in a given field of knowledge, we might consider requiring that, apart from their own professional qualifications in this field, they should be members of a particular institution or professional association. And, along the same lines, in order to fully guarantee the expert's independence, which is understood as the submission solely to her specialized knowledge, the expert should also be required to undergo continuous training. Through their continuous training, it is assured that they will be able to act independently because, otherwise, if they depend on the knowledge of others, it is clear that they will lose their independence of criteria and will submit to the opinion or knowledge of a third party.

Last but not least, it is necessary to point out that the possibility of interference in the expert's independence may also come about through other, more subtle means, such as control over the expert's income. This raises the serious problem of the independence of experts working for insurance companies, large financial institutions, or any other type of institution for which the expert provides his professional services. In this case, the possibility of being adversely affected economically if they do not meet the expectations of these companies or institutions may affect their freedom to assess the scientific or technical facts on which their opinion is required.[55] Unfortunately, however, this is an aspect that is often overlooked by academics in the field of expert evidence.

4.2.3.2.2. Effective Mechanisms Must be in Place to Enable the Expert to Report Any Possible Attacks on their Independence

There is no point in providing for the necessary expert independence if no legal instruments are established to guarantee it. Here different levels of protection of expert independence can be structured:

(a) The establishment of a legal statute for the expert which, in a precise and specific manner, establishes the conditions for the independent action of the expert. Only by pre-establishing his rights and duties, including the rules on incompatibilities, disqualifications, prohibitions, irremovability, etc. (as provided, for example, for judges) is he in full control of carrying out his duties. It is essential to regulate all personal and professional situations that may affect the expert's independence, especially when the judicial expert provides services or private advice to insurance companies, financial or credit institutions, etc., which are then involved as part of the specific litigation in which the expert is expected to intervene. For this reason, at a European level, it is in the interests of judicial experts themselves to establish such a legal regime (for example, the following should be noted: the *Guide to Good Practices in Civil Judicial Expertise in the European Union* by the European Expertise & Expert Institute of October 2015[56] and the *Guidelines on the Role of Court-Appointed Experts in Judicial Proceedings of the Council of Europe's Member States* by the European Commission for the Efficiency of Justice of December 2014).[57]

(b) The establishment of public or private institutions with the power to report the possible violation of expert independence. In the case of experts designated by a party, there are usually professional associations or institutes, duly accredited or approved by the state, which could oversee the independence of their members against any allegation of violation

---

[55] We must not confuse the independence of the expert with the receipt of their fees, as they are still carrying out their professional activity. For this reason, the remuneration of the expert's services does not in itself constitute grounds for dependency: the remuneration of the expert is a necessity of their own professional activity and therefore, in principle, does not merit a negative preconception with regard to their independence.

[56] Available at https://experts-institute.eu/en/projects/the-guide-to-good-practices-in-civil-judicial-expertise-in-the-european-union.

[57] Available at https://rm.coe.int/168074827a.

of expert independence. And with reference to court-appointed experts, if they are public officials, existing institutions that currently represent them could be used to channel any such complaints; if they are independent professionals, the aforementioned associations and private institutions could be used.

(c) The establishment of a regime of sanctions against undue interference with expert independence, which here could be both procedural "sanctions" (ranging from mere warnings given by the judge to any participant in the proceedings attempting to interfere with expert independence to fines)[58] and the establishment of specific criminal offenses.[59]

4.3. HOW CAN THE JUDGE CONTROL THE SCIENTIFIC KNOWLEDGE OF THE EXPERT STATED IN THEIR EXPERT OPINION?

In comparative systems, we find two models of judicial control of scientific knowledge: one preventive (at the stage of the admission of evidence) and another reactive (when the evidence is being assessed).

4.3.1. The Preventive System

Within the preventive system, we find different ways of controlling, before the admission of the expert's report or specialized opinion, compliance with certain requirements aimed at ensuring the highest quality or excellence of the technical information that the judge may receive. In general, there are two ways – one broad and one restrictive – of preventively controlling this technical or specialized knowledge:

(a) The broad way is the one that requires that the specialized person must have undergone prior quality control, through their inclusion on a register (or list) of specialists in a certain field, usually supervised by a public body

---

[58] In this respect, for example, CAPRA (United States) notes that in the American system, the judge can protect the expert by means of an express court order prohibiting any person from influencing the normal development of the expert's work, in accordance with rule 706 of the Federal Rules of Evidence. TAELMAN and VANDENBUSSCHE (Belgium) also show how, in Belgium, their judicial code makes it possible to report to the judge of the specific case any type of problem that could compromise their independence (such as unacceptable behavior or comment by a party).

[59] Thus, for example, GÓMEZ FRODE (Mexico), with respect to Mexico, points out that although there are no protective measures for experts, in the event that they are subjected to pressure to issue their opinion in a particular way against their will, the Public Prosecutor's Office must be notified in order to prosecute a possible crime of extortion.

(normally of the judiciary itself) in order to be able to participate as an expert in a court case.[60]

(b) The preventive (and more restrictive) way of judicially controlling the specialized knowledge is not only by controlling the expert's scientific capability, but also by requiring that the opinion submitted meets certain quality criteria. In this way, as Capra indicates, the judge can be assured that the expert will give a reliable opinion. The best example of this model is the United States with rule 702 of the Federal Rules of Evidence (FRE) (originating, as is known, from the famous doctrine of the *Daubert* case). Specifically, this rule establishes:

> Testimony by Expert Witnesses. A witness who is qualified as an expert by knowledge, skill, experience, training, or education may testify in the form of an opinion or otherwise if:
>
> (a) the expert's scientific, technical, or other specialized knowledge will help the judge to understand the evidence or to determine a fact in issue;
> (b) the testimony is based on sufficient facts or data;
> (c) the testimony is the product of reliable principles and methods; and
> (d) the expert has reliably applied the principles and methods to the facts of the case.

Thus, in the United States, the aim is to prevent the jury from being misled by pseudo-scientific knowledge, with the judge acting prior to the intervention of the jury (as a gatekeeper). However, this strict form of preventive control is also found in non-jury judicial systems, as is the case for example in Colombia, where Article 226 of its new General Procedural Code states that:

> The expert must state, under oath, presumed upon signature of the document, that his opinion is independent and relies on his real professional conviction. The

---

[60] Thus, for example, with regard to Belgium, TAELMAN and VANDENBUSSCHE inform us that recently the Act of April 10, 2014 has been issued, which entered into force on December 1, 2016, introducing a national register of court-appointed experts (who can only be individuals, thus excluding businesses, companies, and organizations; art. 991 *quater* of the Belgian Judicial Code) who are required not only to have professional competences, but also a knowledge of the legal position and role of an expert witness in civil and criminal proceedings (however, this register is not yet fully operational). With regard to France, BLÉRY and TEBOUL stress that while the expert must be registered on the lists established by the courts of appeal or the Court of Cassation, the judge may appoint an expert of their choice if they deem it necessary. Similarly, GUIMARAES RIBEIRO (Brazil), regarding the new civil procedural code of Brazil, shows that Brazilian experts must not only be duly registered in the Superior Court in which the judge has jurisdiction (art. 156.1 CPC), but that this High Court also periodically controls the scientific knowledge of the registered experts through evaluations and re-evaluations carried out in relation to their professional training, their updated knowledge, and their professional experience.
>
> In some countries, such as Norway (NYLUND (Norway)), it is even permitted that "the judge may consult a colleague at another court to verify the competence of the expert."

Joan Picó

opinion must be rendered with the documents that support it and the documents that certify the suitability and experience of the expert. The opinion must be clear, precise, exhaustive and detailed. The opinion must explain the examinations, methods, experiments and investigations that have been carried out to adopt the decision, as well as the technical, scientific or artistic foundations of its conclusions. The expert opinion signed must contain, as a minimum, the following declarations and information:

1. The identification of the person who rendered the opinion and whoever participated in its preparation.
2. The address, telephone number, identification number and other data that facilitate the location of the expert.
3. The profession, art or special activity exercised by the person who rendered the opinion and who participated in its preparation. The appropriate documents that enable for its exercise must be attached, the academic qualifications and the documents that certify the respective professional, technical or artistic experience.
4. The list of publications related to the matter of expertise, from the last ten (10) years, if any.
5. The list of cases in which he has been designated as an expert or in which he has participated in the preparation of an expert opinion in the last four (4) years. Said list shall include the court or office where it was presented, the name of the parties, the attorneys of the parties and the matter on which the opinion was based.
6. Whether he has been designated in previous or ongoing proceedings by the same party or by the same attorney, indicating the purpose of the opinion.
7. Whether he has incurred in the causes specified in article 50.
8. Declare whether the examinations, methods, experiments and investigations carried out are different from those that have been rendered in previous processes that deal with the same matters, if different, the justification for the variation must be explained.
9. Declare whether the examinations, methods, experiments and investigations carried out are different from those used in the regular exercise of their profession. If different, the justification for the variation must be explained.
10. Relate and attach the documents and information used to prepare the opinion).[61]

4.3.2. The Reactive System

In other countries, the criteria for the admission of expert opinions are less strict, limiting themselves to factors such as relevance and necessity, leaving the substantive judicial control of their content for the final moment of the trial,

---

[61] Similarly, this restricted preventive system is found in Canada (PICHÉ and GAUTRAIS (Canada)).

The New Challenges of Evidence Law in the Fourth Industrial Revolution

when the judge assesses the entire evidence submitted, i.e., when issuing the judgment.[62] The fundamental right of the parties to evidence and the fact that what has been discussed in the civil proceedings has been delimited by the parties means that the content of the proceedings is, in principle, a matter for the parties and not for the court. This is the case, for example, in England and Spain:

(a) In England, as Sorabji points out, the judge must allow the parties' expert evidence if the subject matter of the dispute is of a specialized nature and they consider the expert's input to be relevant to the outcome of the case. Therefore, the judge must allow the expertise if it is "of such a nature that a person without instruction or experience in the area of knowledge or human experience would not be able to form a sound judgment on the matter without the assistance of a witness possessing special knowledge or experience in the area." As a consequence, the judge cannot control the nature of the substantive content of an expert's report because the content of evidence is a matter for witnesses and the parties who call those witnesses to give evidence, and not the court.

(b) And Article 347.1 Spanish Code of Civil Procedure (CCP) allows the parties to submit, together with their initial statements of claim, the expert opinion they consider necessary to prove scientific, artistic, or technical knowledge, and the court must admit it, provided that the contribution is relevant and useful (Article 283 CCP).[63]

Ultimately, this system trusts the judge's intellectual capacity to discern the "good" and the "bad" in the different expert opinions. Obviously, in order for this system to work well, the judge must have sufficient epistemological knowledge to be able to interpret expert opinions correctly,[64] especially when there is a contradiction between them. For this reason, when the judge is unable to interpret the content of expert opinions, the legal system usually allows him/her, *ex officio judicis*, to order the appointment of a new expert to enable the judge to resolve fairly the conflict before him/her.

---

[62] This is the case in most European countries (Germany, Belgium, Spain, England, Hungary, Italy, Poland, Portugal, etc.), and in Argentina and Mexico.

[63] Art. 283 CCP: "1. No evidence must be admitted which is considered to be irrelevant, as it has no relation to the subject matter of the proceedings. 2. Evidence which, according to reasonable and secure rules and criteria, can in no case contribute to clarifying controversial facts must not be admitted owing to its useless nature."

[64] Lösing (Germany), with regard to Germany, emphasizes that "thanks to the specialization of judges during their careers, they accumulate some experience in the analysis of opinions and the questioning of experts." However, this does not happen in all countries: for example, Giannini (Argentina) shows that in general in Argentina, judges lack the necessary tools to assess the scientific principles applied by the expert to reach their conclusions.

Intersentia

Joan Picó

This is the case, for example, in Germany and Spain. For Germany, Lösing points out that if, despite the expert's testimony in court, the judge still has doubts, he can appoint an additional expert. And with respect to Spain, after the freedom of the parties to provide the expert opinions they deem necessary (Article 336 CCP), the judge may order an *ex officio* expert opinion (Article 435.2 CCP) if the evidence submitted beforehand has not been conducive as a result of no-longer-existing circumstances, which were independent of the will and diligence of the parties, as long as there are solid reasons to believe that the new procedures will provide certainty regarding such facts.[65]

4.3.3. *Other Forms of Judicial Control of Expert Opinion*

Aside from the two systems described above, another mechanism that facilitates the judicial control of expert opinion is the challenge of its content by the parties. Undoubtedly, the challenges by the litigant adversely affected by the expert's opinion may shed light on weak aspects of an opinion that may have gone unnoticed by the judge. And this right of challenge is of course guaranteed in all legal systems[66] because, in short, it is part of the right of defense in all international legal texts on the protection of fundamental rights.[67] In some legal systems, this mechanism even reaches its maximum expression, permitting direct confrontation between the various experts with contradictory opinions.[68]

Also, to ensure maximum control of the parties' private expert opinions, there are legal systems that allow the judge to appoint technical assistants (or experts) to assist him in the task of assessing the technical or specialized content of the expert opinion.[69]

---

[65] Along the same lines, we find other European legal systems, such as those of Hungary (HARSÁGI (Hungary)) or Portugal (COSTA E SILVA and RUIVO (Portugal)), and American systems, such as those of Mexico (GÓMEZ FRÖDE (Mexico); art. 152 of the Federal Code of Civil Procedures of Mexico) or Colombia (BUSTAMANTE et al. (Colombia)).

[66] In this regard, with respect to Asia, see SHEN (Taiwan) (Taiwan: arts. 320 and 324 Taiwanese CCP); for North America, CAPRA (United States); for South America, PEREIRA and BARREIRO (Uruguay) (art. 181 Uruguayan CGP), or BUSTAMANTE et al. (Colombia) (art. 228 Colombian CGP); and for Europe, LÖSING (Germany), FLAGA-GIERUSZYŃSKA and KLICH (Poland), COSTA E SILVA and RUIVO (Portugal), and art. 347 Spanish CCP.

[67] Litigants' rights or procedural guarantee of defense of litigants is expressly recognized in art. 10 Universal Declaration of Human Rights; art. 14.3 e) International Covenant on Civil and Political Rights; art. 6.3 d) European Convention on Human Rights; and art. 8.2 f) American Convention on Human Rights.

[68] This is the case, for example, in England (rule 35.12 (1) of the Civil Procedure Rules) and Spain (art. 347.1.5° CCP).

[69] As is the case, for example, in Germany (see LÖSING (Germany)), China (see ZHIYUAN (China)), Hungary (HARSÁGI (Hungary)), and Peru (see PRIORI and PÉREZ-PRIETO (Peru)). The Norwegian regulation is very original, in respect of which NYLUND (Norway) stresses that "the court may appoint an expert judge to sit the case along the professional judge(s). The expert judge is an ad hoc judge appointed on a case-by-case basis. The expert judge will have an opportunity to control the scientific knowledge of the court-appointed expert."

The New Challenges of Evidence Law in the Fourth Industrial Revolution

Finally, it should be noted that whatever system of judicial control is carried out over the expert opinion, all the world's procedural systems expressly establish:

(a) that the judge may ask the expert questions directly;[70] and
(b) the non-binding nature of the expert opinion for the judge, who may reasonably give it greater or lesser probative effect.[71] However, I must point out that in some countries, private evidentiary contracts are gaining ground, some of which refer to the assessment of evidence and are binding on the judge. This is the case, for example, for contracts of arbitrational expert testimony, which in Taiwan have gained recognition both among scholars and in court practice. As Shen indicates, it is an evidentiary contract, with which the parties present fact-finding results yielded by "arbitrational expert testimony" in court and thereby precludes future disputes of the facts. In contrast to classic "expert testimony," which is used as a means of evidence-taking, the court shall respect the parties' disposition under the adversary system. In other words, the court is bound by arbitrational experts' opinions and makes judgments on that basis. The Taiwanese Supreme Court's 256/2008 ruling (the *Taishentzu* case) is very eloquent, according to which:

> If the parties reach an agreement of "arbitrational expert testimony," in which the parties commission a third entity to determine facts concerning cause of action and grant the results a binding and non-reviewable effect, this agreement is in essence an evidentiary contract (which falls under the broader category of litigation contracts). The effect of such an agreement is acknowledged since our civil procedure assumes the adversary system, which allows disposition of factual disputes and the procedural autonomy to resolve disputes.[72]

---

[70] Thus, with respect to South Africa, see BABOOLAL-FRANK (South Africa); for Asia, TEGA (Japan); for North America, GÓMEZ FRÖDE (Mexico) (art. 148 of the Federal Code of Civil Procedures of Mexico); for South America, GIANNINI (Argentina), or BUSTAMANTE et al. (art. 228.I Colombian CGP); and for Europe, TAELMAN and VANDENBUSSCHE (art. 984(1) of the Belgian Judicial Code), SORABJI (England and Wales) (England: rule 35.10(2) of the Civil Procedure Rules), LÖSING (Germany), DONDI and COMOGLIO (Italy), FLAGA-GIERUSZYŃSKA and KLICH (Poland), COSTA E SILVA and RUIVO (Portugal), and art. 347.2 Spanish CCP.

[71] In this regard, with reference to Asia, see TEGA (Japan) (art. 247 Japanese CCP); for North America, GÓMEZ FRÖDE (Mexico) (art. 211 of the Mexican Federal Code of Civil Procedures); for South America, PEREIRA and BARREIRO (Uruguay) (art. 184 Uruguayan CGP), and BUSTAMANTE et al. (Colombia) (art. 232 Colombian General Code of Procedure); and for Europe, TAELMAN and VANDENBUSSCHE (Belgium) (art. 962(4) Belgian Judicial Code), FLAGA-GIERUSZYŃSKA and KLICH (Poland), COSTA E SILVA and RUIVO (Portugal), and art. 348 Spanish CCP.

[72] Similarly, in England, such agreements are intended to be binding only on the parties in rule 35.12(5) of the Civil Procedure Rules, which establishes that: "Where experts reach agreement on an issue during their discussions, the agreement shall not bind the parties unless the parties expressly agree to be bound by the agreement." On the current expansion

Intersentia

509

5. PRIVATE COMMUNICATIONS BETWEEN LAWYERS AS EVIDENCE[73]

The rise of new technologies has also changed the way in which lawyers work: emails, conference calls, and Skype meetings have almost replaced face-to-face meetings, and have allowed lawyers to respond directly to their clients without the need to be physically at the office. Also, negotiations between lawyers have changed because they are able to negotiate through the mere exchange of emails, Skype meetings, etc.

Moreover, judicial proceedings and arbitration are nowadays not the only methods to solve a dispute between parties. The rise of, for example, mediation and collaborative proceedings has expanded the scope of dispute resolution, but has also highlighted the issue of confidentiality of the contents of such proceedings, as well as the communications between lawyers during them.

If we look at evidence issues, the above-mentioned facilities raise new questions that need to be answered from a global perspective. First of all, it is necessary to determine whether such communications between lawyers are protected under so-called "legal privilege" and therefore have to be kept confidential. Second, it is also necessary to determine whether a lawyer would be entitled to attach any communication between lawyers to a subsequent judicial proceeding. In the event that such an attachment is not allowed, it would also be necessary to highlight what consequences for the lawyer and for the evidence itself would result in the event that the lawyer tries to attach a communication between lawyers.

5.1. ARE SUCH COMMUNICATIONS COVERED OR PROTECTED BY LEGAL PRIVILEGE BETWEEN LAWYERS?

The first issue to be analyzed is the confidentiality of communications between lawyers themselves, or obtained via mediation proceedings, or during settlement negotiations that try to avoid a future judicial proceeding between their clients. According to the responses, they can be classified as follows:

5.1.1. Communications between Lawyers are Always Confidential

In several jurisdictions, communications between lawyers are always privileged and therefore confidential, including settlement negotiations and

---

that these "evidentiary procedural contracts" are having, I have been very critical, and for this I refer to the study by J. Picó Junoy, A vueltas con los pactos procesales probatorios ("Revisiting Procedural Pacts on Evidence Matters") in *La prueba en el proceso: Evidence in the Process*, editorial Atelier, Barcelona 2018, pp. 667–677.

[73] Professor Juan Antonio Andino helped with the writing of this section.

The New Challenges of Evidence Law in the Fourth Industrial Revolution

mediation proceedings.[74] This privilege would be applied to all communications between lawyers, irrespective of whether such communications are held within the framework of a settlement negotiation, mediation, and/or others, and the corresponding legal basis seeks a framework of confidentiality of such communications.[75]

5.1.2. *Communications between Lawyers are Confidential, but Only for Settlement Negotiations*

In this second group, several jurisdictions consider that communications between lawyers are confidential, but only when such communications are exchanged during settlement negotiations – i.e., they would be considered confidential in the event that they are used in a prior mediation or negotiation of an out-of-court settlement.[76]

Therefore, in some jurisdictions, there would be a "settlement privilege," which means that communications taking place during the settlement process are confidential. Its principles would be as follows: (a) settlement privilege extends beyond those documents and communications expressly designated as being "without prejudice" to any negotiations undertaken with the intention of settling; (b) settlement privilege covers settlement negotiations, whether or not settlement is successfully reached; and (c) a negotiated settlement amount is a "key component" of the "content of successful negotiations" protected by this privilege.[77]

---

[74] As stated in Argentina (GIANNINI (Argentina)), Belgium (TAELMAN and VANDENBUSSCHE (Belgium)) (except communications between lawyers during the judicial proceeding itself, for example, exchange of written pleadings and evidence during the judicial proceeding), France (BLÉRY (France)) (art. 66-5 Act n. 71-1130 of December 31, 1971), Spain (ANDINO (Spain)), Taiwan (SHEN (Taiwan)) and Uruguay (PEREIRA and BARREIRO (Uruguay)).

[75] A legal basis that protects legal professional privilege between lawyers is provided, for example, in Europe in art. 5.3 of the Code of Conduct for Lawyers in the European Union, in art. 113 of the Code of Conduct of the Flemish Bar Association (Belgium, TAELMAN and VANDENBUSSCHE (Belgium)); and art. 542.3 of the Organic Act on the Judiciary, as well as art. 34.e of the General Statute for Spanish Lawyers and art. 9 of Spanish Act 5/2012 of Mediation for Spain (ANDINO (Spain)). However, we will highlight the specific legal basis in the following footnotes.

[76] Such is the case of China (ZHIYUAN (China)) (art. 67 of Some Provisions of the Supreme People's Court on Evidence in Civil Proceeding) (but China will also be included in the next point, since confidentiality is protected in settlement negotiations *but also* in mediation proceedings), Portugal (COSTA E SILVA and RUIVO (Portugal)) (art. 92.1 of the Statute of the Portuguese Bar Association), and also of the United States (CAPRA (United States)), which protects statements used during settlement negotiations (Federal Rule of Evidence 408). (However, see also the comment concerning the United States regarding mediation proceedings.) See also England and Wales (SORABJI (England and Wales)) (Court of Appeal in *Director of the Serious Fraud Office v. Eurasian Natural Resources Corp. Ltd.* [2018] EWCA Civ. 2006).

[77] In Canada the "settlement privilege' is one of the legal privileges foreseen in the law, jointly with attorney-client privilege, litigation privilege, informer privilege and spousal privilege.

Intersentia

511

5.1.3. Communications between Lawyers are Protected, but Only for Mediation Proceedings

In this third group of jurisdictions, communications between lawyers are considered confidential, but only when they are handled within a mediation proceeding prior to a judicial proceeding, where the legislator aims to keep this information confidential and leave lawyers free to try to reach a solution under the umbrella of confidentiality, and where this confidentiality could be extended to any information generated by the parties during the mediation proceeding.[78]

The logic behind this is to guarantee the confidentiality of the mediation itself so as to allow the parties and their lawyers to obtain the best conditions for conducting the mediation and be free to try to solve any dispute issue,[79] and avoid the lawyer becoming a witness in a subsequent judicial proceeding.[80]

Finally, it is important to mention the United States here, since in some states there is a mediation privilege, but not under federal law.[81]

5.1.4. The Protection of Privilege Corresponds to Client–Attorney Communications

Regarding this issue, several countries referred to client–attorney privilege to stress the confidentiality of communications directly between the client and their lawyer.[82]

We highlight the settlement privilege at this stage since we understand that it fits the aim of the question raised, because litigation privilege is applied when the lawyer and the client have to build a litigation strategy or comment on issues regarding the judicial proceeding once it has begun (PICHÉ and GAUTRAIS (Canada)) (see also *R. v. Cunningham*, 2010 SCC 10, [2010]1 SCR 331).

[78] As stated in Brazil (GUIMARAES RIBEIRO (Brazil)) (art. 30 of the Negotiation for Dispute Resolution Act, 13.140 (2015)), China (ZHIYUAN (China)) (art. 67 of Some Provisions of the Supreme People's Court on Evidence in Civil Proceeding) (as mentioned above, China also states the settlement privilege), Croatia (UZELAC (Croatia)), Mexico (GÓMEZ FRÖDE (Mexico)) (art. 8 of the Alternative Justice Law of the Superior Court of Justice for the Federal District), and Norway (NYLUND (Norway)) (Dispute Act ss 8-6 and 7-3 subs. 6, which we can find at https://lovdata.no/dokument/NLE/lov/2005-06-17-90 (Retrieved March 11, 2021)), although client-attorney privilege also exists as well as the confidentiality of their communications (Dispute Act s. 22-5).

[79] For example, in Poland FLAGA-GIERUSZYŃSKA and KLICH (Poland)) (art. 183 §1 of the Polish Code of Civil Procedure).

[80] Hungary (HARSÁGI (Hungary)).

[81] The United States (CAPRA (United States)). However, in the United States, settlement privilege also exists, under Federal Rule of Evidence 408, as mentioned above.

[82] Colombia (BUSTAMANTE et al. (Colombia)) (art. 34 of the Disciplinary Code of the Lawyer), England and Wales (SORABJI (England and Wales)), Germany (LÖSING (Germany)) (communications between lawyers are not confidential), and South Africa (BABOOLAL-FRANK (South Africa)).

5.1.5. Communications between Lawyers are not Confidential, but the Lawyer has the Right to Refuse a Disclosure

In several countries, there is client–attorney privilege, and therefore communications between lawyers would not be considered confidential.

However, it could be understood in Japan that a lawyer would have the right to apply certain confidentiality because he is allowed to refuse to testify or to disclose a document with regard to any fact learned in the course of his duty that should remain confidential.[83]

Finally, and as a general rule, in Italy a lawyer can refuse to testify and to exhibit documents that affect client–attorney privilege, but could be obliged to speak and to reveal certain secrets in the event that it is necessary to pursue the client's case or to prevent a serious crime from being committed.[84]

5.1.6. Communications between Lawyers are not Confidential

Finally, in several countries, communications between lawyers are not confidential and therefore there is no legal protection and no confidentiality provided to protect them. The reasons behind this would be that in a particular judicial system, representation in court by an attorney is not compulsory, since self-representation is permitted. If someone who is not a lawyer is entitled to appear before a court and defend their client, communications between these professionals and lawyers, or between lawyers, are not confidential.[85]

Therefore, and as a conclusion, in most jurisdictions, the legal privilege of communications between lawyers is stated and such communications are confidential (in general terms limited to settlement negotiations or to mediation). A few jurisdictions (for example, Iran, Peru and South Korea) do not consider such communications to be confidential, but we could understand that even in these jurisdictions, client–attorney privilege would be in force.

---

[83] See Japan (TEGA (Japan)) (arts. 197.1.II and 220.4.c CCP).

[84] As occurs in Italy (DONDI and COMOGLIO (Italy)) (arts. 13 and 28 of the Italian Code of Professional Conduct).

[85] As is the case in Iran (MOHSENI and ELSAN (Iran)) (art. 186 of the Civil Procedure Code). Since there is no regulation regarding this issue in Peru (PRIORI and PÉREZ-PRIETO (Peru)), it is understood that the lawyer is free to attach said communications to a judicial proceeding. Finally, in South Korea (PARK (South Korea)) (art. 23 of the Judicial Conciliation of Civil Disputes Act states that the information within a mediation shall not be used as evidence in a civil proceeding, but the Supreme Court of South Korea states the possibility of using said evidence, including communications between lawyers, since the evidence will be admitted by the court).

5.2. REGARDING THE POSSIBILITY FOR A LAWYER TO ATTACH PRIVATE COMMUNICATIONS BETWEEN LAWYERS TO A JUDICIAL PROCEEDING

This matter tries to determine if a lawyer is allowed to attach any communication that has taken place between lawyers to a subsequent judicial proceeding. A response could be provided as follows because we will see differences between legal systems.

5.2.1. A Lawyer is Entitled to Attach Communications between Lawyers to a Judicial Proceeding at the Lawyer's or Client's Sole Discretion

The first group refers to the possibility granted to a lawyer to simply attach any communication between lawyers directly to a judicial proceeding, but only at the lawyer or client's sole decision, because only they are allowed by the law to do so or because the law does not provide for the confidentiality of communications between lawyers. As a matter of fact, the lawyer will be entitled under their sole criteria to attach these communications,[86] with the exception that, in the event of litigation by the lawyer directly against their client, these documents can never interfere with medical secrecy,[87] and the document will be assessed as evidence, but the lawyer may face disciplinary sanctions due to the breach of ethical rules.[88]

Regarding mediation proceedings, a comment will be made in section 5.2.3 below, since the disclosure of information in such proceedings would be forbidden in several countries.

5.2.2. Attachment is Allowed under Certain Conditions

As a general rule, the lawyer should keep communications confidential. However, in any of the following situations, and to the extent necessary, they may disclose them: (1) to avoid harm to any person's life, body, or health; (2) to avoid or mitigate the continuation of the person in question's criminal intent and plan when the committing of the criminal act may cause significant damage to the property of others; (3) when the lawyer and the client need to argue or defend against the dispute arising with regard to their relations, or when the lawyer becomes the defendant in a civil or criminal proceeding for their handling of

---

[86]   This is the case in Brazil (GUIMARAES RIBEIRO (Brazil)), Colombia (BUSTAMANTE et al. (Colombia)) (art. 164 of Act 1564 of 2012, which states that the limits to evidence would be when it has been obtained unlawfully or with violation of due process), Germany (LÖSING (Germany)), and Peru (PRIORI and PÉREZ-PRIETO (Peru)).

[87]   As regulated in France (BLÉRY (France)) (Cass. 1^{Re} Civ., June 28, 2012, N ° 11-14.486).

[88]   This is the case of Japan (TEGA (Japan)) (art. 23 of the Attorney Act), Italy (DONDI and COMOGLIO (Italy)) and Spain (ANDINO (Spain)), where communications between lawyers are confidential, but are accepted by courts as evidence, due to the right to evidence of art. 24 of the Spanish Constitution, leaving the consequences of the breach of confidentiality to ethical rules.

The New Challenges of Evidence Law in the Fourth Industrial Revolution

the matter, or is subject to disciplinary proceedings; and (4) in situations where disclosure is required by law.[89]

A lawyer would be able to attach correspondence between lawyers to a judicial proceeding unless such correspondence refers to a conciliatory proposal or is expressly defined as confidential by the sender,[90] or unless it refers to statements used during settlement negotiations (or under a "settlement privilege").[91]

In other countries, confidentiality of the communications between lawyers may be waived by the Bar Association[92] or by the court itself.[93]

Finally, another possibility would be that the lawyer is entitled to attach such communications if the client authorizes him/her to proceed and the attachment is necessary for the legal proceeding,[94] or the consent of the clients of both parties is necessary,[95] or with the prior consent of the other parties of the conversation.[96]

5.2.3. It is Forbidden for a Lawyer to Attach Communications between Lawyers to a Judicial Proceeding

In this category, it would be forbidden for a lawyer to attach a prior communication between lawyers to a judicial proceeding, even though it could provide an evidentiary advantage to the lawyer or to their client's defense.[97]

This also seems to be the situation when the exchange of private communication between lawyers is not typical during the evidence phase and

---

[89] As stated in Taiwan (SHEN (Taiwan)) (art. 33 of the Code of Ethics of Lawyers). However, in a mediation proceeding, mediators shall keep as confidential all information regarding another person's professional or business secrets or other matters (arts. 278 and 426 CCP) and the transcripts of mediation proceedings may not be used as evidence.

[90] As occurs in Italy (DONDI and COMOGLIO (Italy)) (art. 48 of the Italian Code of Professional Conduct).

[91] Canada (PICHÉ and GAUTRAIS (Canada)) states a real "settlement privilege" under the conditions stated in 5.1.2 above (also see *Sable Offshore Energy Inc. v. Ameron International Corp.* 2013 SCC 37), China (ZHIYUAN (China)) (a reference will be also made below regarding mediation proceedings), and the United States (CAPRA (United States)) (Federal Rule of Evidence 408).

[92] This is the case in Belgium (TAELMAN and VANDENBUSSCHE (Belgium)) (and in the event that the lawyer tries to attach a communication, the head of the Bar Association will then intervene in order to put pressure on the lawyers to respect and comply with ethical rules, warning them of disciplinary sanctions) and Portugal (COSTA E SILVA and RUIVO (Portugal)) (art. 92.4 of the Statute of the Bar Association and the Regulation of Professional Secrecy Waiver).

[93] As occurs in England and Wales (SORABJI (England and Wales)).

[94] As occurs in South Africa (BABOOLAL-FRANK (South Africa)), and it is a controversial issue regarding legal client-attorney privilege in Portugal, since there is no uniform case law (COSTA E SILVA and RUIVO (Portugal)).

[95] As stated in Norway (NYLUND (Norway)) (DA s. 22-5).

[96] Uruguay (PEREIRA and BARREIRO (Uruguay)) (art. 5.2.6 of the Code of Ethics of the Uruguayan Lawyer).

[97] This is stated in Argentina (GIANNINI (Argentina)), France (BLÉRY (France)) (except when the lawyer litigates against their client, as commented above) and Iran (MOHSENI and ELSAN (Iran)), as well as in Mexico (GÓMEZ FRÖDE (Mexico)).

Intersentia

515

Joan Picó

therefore the only way that a lawyer or a mediator could be put in the position of disclosing their knowledge would be via witness evidence, and in such a situation they could refuse to give testimony to the court. (Moreover, lawyers are obliged by their profession to keep confidentiality.)[98]

Finally, a lawyer would be entitled to attach communications between lawyers to a judicial proceeding in general, but with the exception of the mediation proceeding, which will be considered confidential.[99] In a mediation proceeding, the mediator, the parties, and other persons involved in the mediation proceeding are obliged to preserve the confidentiality of all the facts and arrangements made during the mediation meetings, and therefore it is forbidden to attach the content of these meetings to the court.[100]

5.3. CONSEQUENCES OF THE UNLAWFUL ATTACHMENT OF COMMUNICATIONS BETWEEN LAWYERS

In order to answer this question, we shall focus on the consequences that would result if a lawyer tries to attach communications between lawyers when such attachment is forbidden. Maybe the court will not have to deal with such a situation due to the fact that lawyers have a professional obligation of confidentiality, and giving testimony would breach that obligation, unless prior authorization has been given by the interested party.[101] Therefore, the only jurisdictions that will be quoted will be those that state a clear prohibition on attaching such communications to a judicial proceeding.

The procedural consequences in those jurisdictions would be as follows.

5.3.1. The Court may Exclude/not Admit Such Evidence

When there is a breach of confidentiality by the lawyer, it could be considered that such evidence would be materially prohibited and therefore it will not be able to be submitted as evidence in a trial.[102]

---

[98] This is the case in Hungary (HARSÁGI, (Hungary)).

[99] This is the case in China (ZHIYUAN (China)) (art. 67 of Some Provisions of the Supreme People's Court on Evidence in Civil Proceeding), Croatia (UZELAC (Croatia)) (art. 15 of the Croatian Conciliation Act), but also in certain states of the United States (CAPRA (United States)), although there is no federal law that establishes the confidentiality of mediation proceedings. However, in these countries, settlement privilege also exists, as mentioned above.

[100] Poland (FLAGA-GIERUSZYŃSKA and KLICH (Poland)) (art. 183.2 of the Polish Code of Civil Procedure).

[101] As occurs in Hungary (HARSÁGI, (Hungary)) (art. 290.1 of the Hungarian Code of Civil Procedure).

[102] Portugal (COSTA E SILVA and RUIVO (Portugal)) (art. 92.5 of the Statute of the Bar Association), and the same solution should apply for Spain (ANDINO (Spain)) (based on art. 24 of the Spanish Constitution and arts. 247 and 283.3 CCP), although ANDINO

516

Intersentia

When we refer to settlement privilege (extended for successful and unsuccessful negotiations), any evidence brought to the judicial proceeding that breaches said privilege will not be admitted by the court, subject to limited exceptions, since the purpose of the legislator and the courts is to try to promote settlement between the parties.[103]

With regard to a mediation proceeding, documentary evidence that refers to such proceeding will be *ex officio* excluded from the proceedings, and the court will be empowered to award damages if the obligation of confidentiality is breached by one of the parties.[104]

Finally, in the event that such evidence refers to a settlement privilege and/or mediation proceeding, and only if the other party challenges the attachment of the evidence, then it would be excluded by the court. Therefore, if the other party does not react to that attachment, it will be included as evidence in the proceeding.[105]

5.3.2. *The Court will not Assess Such Evidence*

Evidence is not excluded from the judicial proceeding, but the court will not assess it, and the obligations and waivers which the parties have granted will not be mandatory.[106]

5.3.3. *The Court will Accept Such Evidence, Even if it is Forbidden by Ethical Rules*

This category corresponds to jurisdictions where the confidentiality of correspondence between lawyers is established in ethical rules and therefore the court will not be bound by such rules, but the court is legally bound to procedural rules and the consequences of such attachment will be ethical and

---

highlights that the current judgments of courts and papers by the majority of the scholars lead to the conclusion that such evidence is accepted and they leave any further consequence to ethical rules, a current opinion which is challenged by ANDINO.

[103] This is the case in Canada (PICHÉ and GAUTRAIS (Canada)) (see *Sable Offshore Energy Inc. v. Ameron International Corp.* 2013 SCC 37) and the United States (CAPRA (United States)) (Federal Rule of Evidence 408).

[104] This is the case in Belgium (TAELMAN and VANDENBUSSCHE (Belgium)) (art. 1728, §4(2) and §4(2) of the Belgian Judicial Code), Germany (LÖSING (Germany)) and Poland (FLAGA-GIERUSZYŃSKA and KLICH (Poland)) (art. 183 §3 of the Polish CCP). In Norway, the court will intervene when a party attempts to present information on the mediation process (NYLUND (Norway)).

[105] As occurs in China (ZHIYUAN (China)) (art. 67 of Some Provisions of the Supreme People's Court on Evidence in Civil Proceeding, although this article only grants confidentiality protection to communications in a mediation or settlement process). Limited to mediation proceedings, see Croatia (UZELAC (Croatia)) (art. 15 of the Croatian Conciliation Act).

[106] Iran (MOHSENI and ELSAN (Iran)).

not procedural. Therefore, courts will tend to accept the evidence due to the right to evidence and due process and will lead any further consequence to the decision of the Bar Associations in the event that a sanction could be applied to the lawyer that breaches the ethical rules of the profession as lawyer.[107]

The breach of confidentiality by the lawyer could also be considered a criminal offense.[108]

Therefore, ethical, civil, and criminal liability could be applied to any lawyer who breaches the obligation of confidentiality.[109]

---

[107] Argentina (GIANNINI (Argentina)) (the validity and admissibility of the evidence should pass the "illegally obtained evidence" proportionality test, and ethical prosecution of the lawyer may take place), Belgium (TAELMAN and VANDENBUSSCHE (Belgium)), but see 5.3.1. above, since documentary evidence from a prior mediation proceeding will be excluded by the court, and Croatia (UZELAC (Croatia)). (However, this evidence will be inadmissible if it pertains to a mediation proceeding, as mentioned above.) The same would be the case in Spain, as this would be the conclusion of court cases and the majority of scholars (ANDINO (Spain)), although ANDINO states that the evidence should be excluded from the judicial proceeding, based on art. 24 of the Spanish Constitution and arts. 247 and 283.3 of the Spanish Civil Procedures Act. Reference is also made to South Korea (PARK)) (art. 23 of the Judicial Conciliation of Civil Disputes Act).

[108] As occurs in Mexico (GÓMEZ FRÖDE (Mexico)) (arts. 210, 211, and 211 *bis* of the Mexican Federal Penal Code).

[109] As occurs in Uruguay (PEREIRA and BARREIRO (Uruguay)).

ABOUT THE EDITOR

Koichi Miki is Professor of Law at Keio University, Tokyo, President of the Japan Association of the Law of Civil Procedure and Vice President of the International Association of Procedural Law. He has previously been a visiting scholar at the University of Melbourne, Yale University and UC Hastings Law, San Francisco. He was the representative of the Japanese Government at the UNCITRAL Working Group on Arbitration for 10 years and has long served on many advisory councils on the legislation of various procedural laws in Japan. He is interested in Civil Procedure Law, Arbitration Law and comparative legal systems on civil justice. His recent research focuses on access to information and evidence for civil litigation.

Ingram Content Group UK Ltd.
Milton Keynes UK
UKHW031136260423
420787UK00007B/85